The Routledge Handbook
of Multilingualism

The Routledge Handbook of Multilingualism provides a comprehensive survey of the field of multilingualism for a global readership, and an overview of the research which situates multilingualism in its social, cultural and political context. The *Handbook* includes an introduction and five sections with 32 chapters by leading international contributors.

The introduction charts the changing landscape of social and ethnographic research on multilingualism (theory, methods and research sites) and it foregrounds key contemporary debates. Chapters are structured around sub-headings such as early developments, key issues related to theory and method, and new research directions.

This *Handbook* offers an authoritative guide to shifts over time in thinking about multilingualism as well as providing an overview of the range of contemporary themes, debates and research sites. *The Routledge Handbook of Multilingualism* is the ideal resource for postgraduate students of multilingualism, as well as those studying education and anthropology.

Marilyn Martin-Jones is an Emeritus Professor based at the MOSAIC Centre for Research on Multilingualism, University of Birmingham, UK. She is the series editor of the *Routledge Critical Studies in Multilingualism* series.

Adrian Blackledge is Professor of Bilingualism, and Director of the MOSAIC Centre for Research on Multilingualism, University of Birmingham, UK. He is the author of several books including *Multilingualism: A Critical Perspective* (2010) with Angela Creese.

Angela Creese is Professor of Educational Linguistics at the MOSAIC Centre for Research on Multilingualism, University of Birmingham, UK. She is the author of a number of books and articles on multilingualism and linguistically diverse classrooms including *Multilingualism: A Critical Perspective* (2010) with Adrian Blackledge.

Routledge Handbooks in Applied Linguistics

Routledge Handbooks in Applied Linguistics provide comprehensive overviews of the key topics in applied linguistics. All entries for the handbooks are specially commissioned and written by leading scholars in the field. Clear, accessible, and carefully edited, *Routledge Handbooks in Applied Linguistics* are the ideal resource for both advanced undergraduates and postgraduate students.

The Routledge Handbook of Hispanic Applied Linguistics
Edited by Manel Lacorte

The Routledge Handbook of Educational Linguistics
Edited by Martha Bigelow and Johanna Ennser-Kananen

The Routledge Handbook of Forensic Linguistics
Edited by Malcolm Coulthard and Alison Johnson

The Routledge Handbook of Corpus Linguistics
Edited by Anne O'Keeffe and Mike McCarthy

The Routledge Handbook of World Englishes
Edited by Andy Kirkpatrick

The Routledge Handbook of Applied Linguistics
Edited by James Simpson

The Routledge Handbook of Discourse Analysis
Edited by James Paul Gee and Michael Handford

The Routledge Handbook of Second Language Acquisition
Edited by Susan Gass and Alison Mackey

The Routledge Handbook of Language and Intercultural Communication
Edited by Jane Jackson

The Routledge Handbook of Language Testing
Edited by Glenn Fulcher and Fred Davidson

The Routledge Handbook of Translation Studies
Edited by Carmen Millán-Varela and Francesca Bartrina

The Routledge Handbook of Language and Health Communication
Edited by Heidi E. Hamilton and Wen-ying Sylvia Chou

The Routledge Handbook of Language and Professional Communication
Edited by Stephen Bremner and Vijay Bhatia

The Routledge Handbook of Language and Digital Communication
Edited by Alexandra Georgakopoulou and Tereza Spilioti

The Routledge Handbook of Literacy Studies
Edited by Jennifer Rowsell and Kate Pahl

The Routledge Handbook of Interpreting
Edited by Holly Mikkelson and Renée Jourdenais

The Routledge Handbook of Multilingualism

Edited by
Marilyn Martin-Jones,
Adrian Blackledge
and Angela Creese

LONDON AND NEW YORK

First published in paperback 2015
First published 2012
by Routledge
2 Park Square, Milton Park, Abingdon, Oxon OX14 4RN

and by Routledge
711 Third Avenue, New York, NY 10017

Routledge is an imprint of the Taylor & Francis Group, an informa business

British Library Cataloguing in Publication Data
A catalogue record for this book is available from the British Library

Library of Congress Cataloging in Publication Data
The Routledge handbook of multilingualism / edited by Marilyn Martin-Jones,
Adrian Blackledge and Angela Creese.
    p. cm. – (Routledge handbooks in applied linguistics)
  Includes index.
  1. Multilingualism.   2. Language acquisition.   I. Jones, Marilyn Martin-.
  II.Blackledge, Adrian.   III. Creese, Angela.
  P115.R59 2012
  306.44′6–dc23
           2011022757

ISBN: 978-0-415-49647-6 (hbk)
ISBN: 978-1-138-93251-7 (pbk)
ISBN: 978-0-203-15442-7 (ebk)

Typeset in Times New Roman
by Taylor & Francis Books

Printed and bound in Great Britain by
TJ International Ltd, Padstow, Cornwall

This volume is dedicated to the memory of Peter Martin – an outstanding scholar of multilingualism and a cherished friend and colleague.

Contents

Contents

Contents

Illustrations

Acknowledgements

As this *Handbook of Multilingualism* finally goes to press, we would like to thank the contributors of all 32 chapters for their commitment to this project. Together, we have achieved much more than any one of us could have done in a single-authored monograph on this topic. We are especially grateful to those who sent their contributions on time and who showed such patience as we assembled the whole manuscript. The conversations that we have had with individual contributors along the way – both virtual and face-to-face – have been both enriching and challenging. The final manuscript presents a rich, multifaceted and multivoiced account. Thank you to you all!

We would also like to extend our thanks to Louisa Semlyen, Sophie Jaques, and Megan Graieg at Routledge for their support, encouragement and good guidance as we made this journey.

Here at the University of Birmingham, heartfelt thanks go to colleagues, doctoral researchers and visiting scholars at the MOSAIC Centre for Research on Multilingualism and the Department of Language, Discourse and Society for creating with us the kind of intellectual environment and inclusive research culture in which bold, innovative projects can be imagined and carried through.

We are also grateful to Lily Ilič and Sally Cliff, who gave us invaluable assistance with the management of the electronic version of the manuscript. Finally, we would like to acknowledge the crucial support we received from Jane Myhre, postgraduate student in the Department, as we went through the final stages of editing and formatting the manuscript. Her meticulous work was very much appreciated.

Marilyn Martin-Jones,
Adrian Blackledge and
Angela Creese

Contributors

Robert Adam is a postgraduate researcher at the ESRC Deafness Cognition and Language Research Centre (UK) and a native signer. He is a member of the World Federation of the Deaf Expert Group on Sign Language and is currently carrying out doctoral studies on language contact between dialects of Irish Sign Language and dialects of British Sign Language.

Benjamin Bailey received his PhD in Linguistic Anthropology from UCLA, USA. He is currently Associate Professor of Communication at the University of Massachusetts-Amherst, USA. His research focuses on issues of language, identity and meaning in interaction. He is the author of *Language, Race, and Negotiation of Identity: A Study of Dominican Americans*, as well as various articles and chapters on codeswitching, multilingualism, performance of race, immigrant acculturation and interethnic communication.

Adrian Blackledge is Professor of Bilingualism at the University of Birmingham, UK and Director of the MOSAIC Centre for Research on Multilingualism. His research interests include the politics of multilingualism, linguistic ethnography, education of linguistic minority students, negotiation of identities in multilingual contexts, and language testing, citizenship and immigration. His publications include *Multilingualism: A Critical Perspective* (with Angela Creese, Continuum, 2010), *Discourse and Power in a Multilingual World* (John Benjamins, 2006), *Negotiation of Identities in Multilingual Contexts* (with Aneta Pavlenko, Multilingual Matters, 2004), *Multilingualism, Second Language Learning and Gender* (Mouton de Gruyter, co-edited with Aneta Pavlenko, Ingrid Piller and Marya Teutsch-Dwyer, 2001) and *Literacy, Power and Social Justice* (Trentham Books, 2001).

Suresh Canagarajah is the Erle Sparks Professor and Director of the Migration Studies Project at Pennsylvania State University, USA. He teaches World Englishes, Second Language Writing and Postcolonial Studies in the departments of English and Applied Linguistics. He has taught before at the University of Jaffna, Sri Lanka, and the City University of New York (Baruch College and the Graduate Center). His book *Resisting Linguistic Imperialism in English Teaching* (Oxford University Press, 1999) won the Modern Language Association's Mina Shaughnessy Award for the best research publication on the teaching of language and literacy.

Jasone Cenoz is Professor of Research Methods in Education at the University of the Basque Country in Donostia-San Sebastián, Spain. She works on multilingualism and language acquisition in educational contexts. She is editor of the *International Journal of Multilingualism*. Her recent publications include a monograph on *Towards Multilingual Education* and an edited book on *The Multiple Realities of Multilingualism* (with Elka Todeva).

Constadina Charalambous is a Lecturer in Language Education & Literacy at the European University of Cyprus. Her main focus is on language learning in contexts of conflict and hostility, and has conducted research on Other-language classes in Cyprus. Her broader research interests include interactional sociolinguistics, linguistic ethnography, language education and intercultural communication. She has also been involved in peace education projects and teacher training.

Feliciano Chimbutane is Senior Lecturer in Linguistics at Universidade Eduardo Mondlane, Mozambique. His current research interests concern languages in education, with special reference to bilingual education. His focus is on policy, classroom practice and the relationship between classroom discourse, day-to-day talk and the wider social and political order. Recent publications include: *Rethinking Bilingual Education in Post-Colonial Contexts* (2011, Multilingual Matters).

Melanie Cooke is a researcher at the Centre for Language, Discourse and Communication at King's College London, UK. Her research interests include language and citizenship and the social and political contexts of ESOL in the UK. She is the co-author (with James Simpson) of *ESOL: A Critical Guide* (Oxford University Press, 2008).

Angela Creese is Professor of Educational Linguistics at the MOSAIC Centre for Research on Multilingualism, University of Birmingham, UK. She is the author of a number of books and articles on multilingualism and linguistically diverse classrooms. Her books include *Multilingualism: A Critical Perspective* (2010), *English as an Additional Language: Approaches to Teaching Linguistic Minority Students* (2010), *Encyclopedia of Language and Education, Volume 9: Ecology of Language* (2009); *Teacher Collaboration and Talk in Multilingual Classrooms* (2005), and *Multilingual Classroom Ecologies* (2003). Angela's research interests are situated in educational linguistics, linguistic ethnography, teacher collaboration and multilingual pedagogies in community learning contexts. She has held a number of ESRC-funded grants researching multilingualism in complementary schools.

Alexandre Duchêne is Professor of Sociology of Language and Multilingualism and Director of the Institute of Multilingualism of the University and HEP Fribourg, Switzerland. Recent publications include *Ideologies across Nations* (Mouton de Gruyter, 2008), *Discourses of Endangerment* (with Monica Heller, Continuum, 2007), *Language in Late Capitalism: Pride and Profit* (co-edited with Monica Heller, Routledge, 2012) and *Langage, Genre et Sexualité* (with Claudine Moïse, Nota Bene, forthcoming).

Nelson Flores is currently a doctoral student in Urban Education at the Graduate Center of the City University of New York, USA, where he is working towards a dissertation on language education policy and post-structuralism under the guidance of Professor Ofelia García. He also currently teaches Social Foundations in the Education Department at the College of Staten Island, USA. He is a former ESL teacher at a small high school in the Bronx.

Ofelia García is Professor in the PhD programme of Urban Education and of Hispanic and Luso-Brazilian Literatures and Languages at the Graduate Center of the City University of New York, USA. She has been Professor of Bilingual Education at Columbia University's Teachers College and Dean of the School of Education at the Brooklyn Campus of Long Island University, USA. Among her recent books are *Bilingual Education in the 21st Century: A Global Perspective* (2009), *Educating Emergent Bilinguals* (2010) (with J. Kleifgen), *Negotiating Language Policies in Schools: Educators as Policymakers* (2010) (with K. Menken),

Handbook of Language and Ethnic Identity (2010) (with J. A. Fishman) and *Imagining Multilingual Schools* (2006) (with T. Skutnabb-Kangas and M. Torres-Guzmán). She is a Fellow of the Stellenbosch Institute for Advanced Study (STIAS) in South Africa, and has been a Fulbright Scholar, and a Spencer Fellow of the US National Academy of Education.

Sheena Gardner is Head of Department of English and Languages at Coventry University, UK. She is an educational linguist with specific interests in multilingual classroom discourse and academic English. She has more than 70 publications, including two books in press for 2012: *Genres across Disciplines: Student Writing in Higher Education* (co-authored with Hilary Nesi, Cambridge Applied Linguistics Series, Cambridge University Press) and *Multilingualism, Discourse and Ethnography* (co-edited with Marilyn Martin-Jones, Critical Studies in Multilingualism Series, Routledge).

Durk Gorter is Ikerbasque Research Professor at the Faculty of Education of the University of the Basque Country in Donostia-San Sebastián, Spain, where he carries out work on multilingualism and minority languages in Europe. His two most recent edited books are *Linguistic Landscape: Expanding the Scenery* (with Elana Shohamy, 2009) and *Multilingual Europe: Facts and Policies* (with Guus Extra, 2008).

Monica Heller is Professor at the Ontario Institute for the Studies in Education of the University of Toronto, Canada. Her recent publications include *Bilingualism: A Social Approach* (Palgrave Macmillan, 2007), *Discourses of Endangerment* (with Alexandre Duchêne, Continuum, 2007), *Paths to Post-Nationalism: A Critical Ethnography of Language and Identity* (Oxford University Press, 2011) and *Language in Late Capitalism: Pride and Profit* (co-edited with Alexandre Duchêne, Routledge, 2012).

Christine Hélot is Professor of English at the University of Strasbourg, France in the teacher education department (IUFM d'Alsace). As a sociolinguist she has published extensively on bilingualism (family and school contexts), language policy in France and teacher education, language awareness and intercultural education.

Roger Hewitt is Emeritus Professor at Goldsmiths, University of London, UK and is currently Visiting Fellow at the Center for Social Policy, University of Massachusetts, Boston, USA. His research has been broadly concerned with issues of multiculturalism, particularly with regard to language.

Helen Kelly-Holmes is a lecturer in sociolinguistics and new media at the University of Limerick, Ireland. Her research interests focus on the sociolinguistics of market and media processes, particularly in relation to multilingualism. She has published widely in a range of international journals and is author of *Advertising as Multilingual Communication* (Palgrave Macmillan, 2005) and co-editor with Sue Wright of the Language and Globalization series published by Palgrave Macmillan.

Alexandra Jaffe is Professor of Linguistics and Anthropology at California State University, Long Beach, USA. Her research interests include bilingual education on Corsica, minority language revitalization and language ideologies, language in the media and orthography.

Sirpa Leppänen is Professor of English in the Department of Languages, University of Jyväskylä, Finland. Her research areas include discourse studies, multilingualism, new media studies and language and gender. She is currently working on multilingual YouTube, and has published widely on linguistic and discursive heterogeneity in various social media contexts. She directs a research project on the English in globalized Finnish society, which is part of the research programme of the Research Unit for Variation, Contacts and Change in English, a joint venture of the universities of Helsinki and Jyväskylä. The project directed by Leppänen investigates, with the help of both qualitative and quantitative methods, the forms, functions and meanings of English drawn on by Finns in a range of societal and cultural domains (for more information see www.jyu.fi/varieng).

David C. S. Li obtained his BA in English in Hong Kong, his MA in Applied Linguistics in Besançon, France, and his PhD in Linguistics in Cologne, Germany. His research interests are mainly related to the study of social aspects of language learning and use in multilingual settings. He has published in three main areas: World Englishes and perceptions of 'Hong Kong English', codeswitching in Hong Kong and Taiwan, and EFL learners' difficulties and error-correction strategies. His research was supported by various grants, including two government-funded Competitive Earmarked Research Grants (CERG). He speaks Cantonese, English and Putonghua/Mandarin fluently, and also some German and French.

Angel Y. M. Lin received her PhD from the Ontario Institute for Studies in Education, University of Toronto, Canada. She is currently an Associate Professor and Associate Dean in the Faculty of Education, the University of Hong Kong. She is well respected for her versatile, interdisciplinary intellectual scholarship in language and identity studies, bilingual education, classroom discourse analysis and youth cultural studies. She has published six research books and over 70 research articles and book chapters. She serves on the editorial boards of a number of international research journals including: *Applied Linguistics, British Educational Research Journal, International Journal of Bilingual Education and Bilingualism, Language and Education, Journal of Critical Discourse Studies, Pragmatics and Society, International Multilingual Research Journal* and *Pedagogies*.

Indika Liyanage is a senior lecturer in the School of Education, Griffith University, Australia where he conducts research, teaches and supervises graduate students in applied linguistics and TESOL. He also works as an international consultant on TESOL in the Pacific.

Bronwen Low is an Associate Professor in the Department of Integrated Studies in Education, McGill University, Quebec, Canada. She studies the implications of popular culture, and in particular hip-hop, slam poetry and spoken word, for curriculum, 'new' literacies, and adolescent identities and language practices. Her publications include: *Slam School: Learning through Conflict in the Hip-Hop and Spoken Word Classroom* (Stanford University Press, 2011) and *Reading Youth Writing: "New" Literacies, Cultural Studies and Education* (with Michael Hoechsmann, Lang, 2008).

Vally Lytra is Research Fellow at Goldsmiths/King's College London, UK. Her research interests are on multilingualism, multilingual literacies and identities in educational settings. Her book *Play Frames and Social Identities: Contact Encounters in a Greek Primary School* was published in 2007 by John Benjamins. She co-edited a special issue with Alexandra Georgakopoulou on *Language, Discourse and Identities. Snapshots from the Greek Context* (Pragmatics, 2008) and a book with the late Peter Martin entitled *Sites of Multilingualism: Complementary Schools in Britain Today* (Trentham, 2010). She is currently working on a research project on faith literacies (www.gold.ac.uk/clcl/belifs/).

Sinfree Makoni is a Pan Africanist. He has taught at a number of universities and currently teaches at Pennsylvania State University, USA. His main research interests are in colonial linguistics, urban multilingualism and communication and health. He is co-author of *Language and Aging in Multilingual Contexts* (2005), a monograph on colonial and post-colonial language policies in Zimbabwe, co-editor of *Disinventing and Reconstituting Languages* (2007), co-editor of *Black Linguistics: Language, Society, and Politics in Africa and the Americas* (2003), *Ageing in Africa: Sociolinguistics and Anthropological Approaches* (2002), *Freedom and Discipline: Essays in Applied Linguistics from Southern Africa* (2001) and *Language and Institutions in Africa* (1999).

Marilyn Martin-Jones is an Emeritus Professor based at the MOSAIC Centre for Research on Multilingualism, University of Birmingham, UK. Over the last 30 years she has been involved in ethnographic and discourse analytic research in bilingual and multilingual contexts in England and Wales. She is particularly interested in the ways in which multilingual discourse and literacy practices contribute to the construction of identities, in local lifeworlds and institutional contexts and the ways in which such practices are bound up with local and global relations of power. These themes are reflected in her recent publications, for example *Multilingual Literacy Practices: Reading and Writing Different Worlds* (with Kathryn Jones, John Benjamins, 2000); *Voices of Authority: Education and Linguistic Difference* (with Monica Heller, Ablex, 2001); *Discourse and Education* (vol. 3 of the *Encyclopedia of Language and Education*, with Anne-Marie de Mejía and Nancy Hornberger, 2008), a special issue of the journal *Compare* on 'Multilingual literacies in the Global South' (with Sjaak Kroon and Jeanne Kurvers, 2011) and *Multilingualism, Discourse and Ethnography* (with Sheena Gardner, Routledge, forthcoming). She also edits a book series for Routledge entitled *Critical Studies in Multilingualism.*

Katrijn Maryns works as an FWO postdoctoral researcher (Research Foundation-Flanders) in the Linguistics Department at Ghent University, Belgium. Her research examines discourse practices in legal-procedural contexts. She is the author of *The asylum speaker: language in the Belgian asylum procedure* (St Jerome Publishing, 2006).

Stephen May is Professor of Education in the School of Critical Studies in Education, Faculty of Education, University of Auckland, New Zealand. He is also a Senior Research Fellow at the Centre for the Study of Ethnicity and Citizenship, University of Bristol, UK. Stephen has written widely on language rights and language education. His key books include *Language and Minority Rights*, which was originally published by Longman in 2001 and reprinted by Routledge in 2008. The reprinted edition was recognized as one of the American Library Association Choice's Outstanding Academic titles. Stephen has edited, with Nancy Hornberger, *Language Policy and Political Issues in Education*, Volume 1 of the 10-volume *Encyclopedia of Language and Education* (2nd edn, Springer 2008). His most recent book, edited with Christine Sleeter, is *Critical Multiculturalism: Theory and Praxis* (2010). A fully revised second edition of *Language and Minority Rights* is to be published by Routledge in 2012. He is also Editor of the interdisciplinary journal, *Ethnicities* (Sage) and Associate Editor of *Language Policy* (Springer).

Teresa L. McCarty is the A.W. Snell Professor of Education Policy Studies and Applied Linguistics at Arizona State University, USA, where she also co-directs the Center for Indian Education. Trained as a sociocultural anthropologist, she has published widely on Indigenous/bilingual education, language planning and policy, critical literacy studies and ethnographic studies of schooling. She is the past President of the Council on Anthropology and Education, the former Editor of *Anthropology and Education Quarterly*, and Associate Editor of *Language Policy* and the *American Educational Research Journal*. Her recent books include *A Place To Be Navajo* (Lawrence Erlbaum, 2002), *Language, Literacy, and Power in Schooling* (Lawrence Erlbaum, 2005), '*To Remain an Indian*': *Lessons in Democracy from a Century of Native American Education* (with K. T. Lomawaima, Teachers College Press, 2006), and *Ethnography and Language Policy* (Routledge, 2011).

Anne-Marie de Mejía holds a PhD in Linguistics in the area of Bilingual Education from Lancaster University, UK. She currently works at the *Centro de Investigación y Formación en Educación* at Universidad de los Andes, Bogotá, Colombia. Her research interests include bilingual classroom interaction, processes of empowerment and bilingual teacher development.

Sheilah E. Nicholas is a member of the Hopi Tribe. She is an Assistant Professor in the Language, Reading and Culture Program, Department of Teaching, Learning, and Sociocultural Studies in the College of Education at the University of Arizona, USA. She provides consultant services for the Hopi Tribe's Hopi language revitalization initiatives as an instructor for the annual Hopilavayi (Hopi language) Summer Institute, which offers Hopi language teacher training and Hopi language literacy development services for local K-12 schools. Dr Nicholas is also a current member of the Hopi Education Endowment Fund General Board and Executive Committee.

Tope Omoniyi is Professor of Sociolinguistics at Roehampton University, London, UK. His area of research interest is language and identity, which he has explored in the context of language education, borderlands, popular culture and religion. He is Director of the Centre for Research in English Language and Linguistics and coordinator of the MPhil/PhD programmes. His publications include *The Sociolinguistics of Borderlands: Two Nations, One Community* (Africa World Press, 2004), and the co-edited volumes *Explorations in the Sociology of Language and Religion* (John Benjamins, 2006), *The Sociolinguistics of Identity* (Continuum, 2006) and *Contending with Globalization in World Englishes* (Multilingual Matters, 2010).

Donna Patrick is Professor at the School of Canadian Studies and the Department of Sociology and Anthropology at Carleton University, Ottawa, Canada. Her current research focuses on language and literacy practices among urban Inuit in Ottawa. Other interests include indigeneity, language rights and language endangerment discourse, with particular focus on Aboriginal languages in Canada, and the political, social and cultural aspects of language use among Inuit in the Canadian Arctic. Her book, *Language Politics and Social Interaction in an Inuit Community* (Mouton de Gruyter, 2003) examines these issues in Northern Quebec. Other publications include an edited volume with Jane Freeland, *Language Rights and Language Survival* (St Jerome Publishing, 2004), and a number of articles on Indigenous language endangerment and language rights discourse in Canada.

Aneta Pavlenko (PhD in Linguistics, Cornell University, USA, 1997) is Professor at the College of Education, Temple University, Philadelphia, USA. She is the author of *Emotions and Multilingualism* (Cambridge University Press, 2005, winner of the BAAL Book Prize), co-author (with Scott Jarvis) of *Crosslinguistic Influence in Language and Cognition* (Routledge, 2008), and editor of *Bilingual Minds* (Multilingual Matters, 2006), *The Bilingual Mental Lexicon*

(Multilingual Matters, 2009) and *Thinking and Speaking in Two Languages* (Multilingual Matters, 2011). Her research examines the relationship between language, emotions and cognition in multilingualism and second language acquisition.

Alastair Pennycook is Professor and Head of Language Studies at the University of Technology, Sydney, Australia. His best-known work is on the global spread of English (*The Cultural Politics of English as an International Language,* Longman, 1994), colonialism and language policy (*English and the Discourses of Colonialism,* Routledge, 1998), and critical applied linguistics (*Critical Applied Linguistics: A Critical Introduction,* Lawrence Erlbaum, 2001). His major recent research focus on language and popular culture has been published in his book *Global Englishes and Transcultural Flows* (Routledge, 2007), which won the British Association of Applied Linguistics book award in 2008, and the edited book (with Samy Alim and Awad Ibrahim) *Global Linguistic Flows: Hip Hop Cultures, Youth Identities, and the Politics of Language* (Routledge, 2009). Other work has focused on questions of how we understand language in relation to diversity (see his recent edited book, with Sinfree Makoni, *Disinventing and Reconstituting Languages,* Multilingual Matters, 2007). Together with Emi Otsuji these issues are currently being explored through the idea of *metrolingualism* (mixed language use in multilingual environments), early literacy in disadvantaged communities, and understanding language in relation to place and practice, which is the focus of his most recently published book, *Language as a Local Practice* (Routledge, 2010).

Isabelle Perez is a Professorial Fellow in the Department of Languages and Intercultural Studies at Heriot-Watt University in Edinburgh, UK, where she contributes to translation, conference and public service interpreting education. A practising interpreter, she has developed a research profile in liaison/public service interpreting, quality assessment in interpreting and interpreter-mediated interviews.

Saija Peuronen is a doctoral student in the Department of Languages, University of Jyväskylä, Finland and a member of a Research Unit for the Study of Variation, Contacts and Change in English (VARIENG). In her PhD research, she studies the ways in which members of one specific online community – Christians interested in extreme sports – use a variety of bilingual language resources for constructing a nexus of cultures, lifestyles and identities.

Ingrid Piller (PhD, Dresden 1995) is Professor of Applied Linguistics at Macquarie University, Sydney, Australia, where she directed the Adult Migrant English Program Research Centre (AMEP RC) from 2007 to 2008. Her research interests are in intercultural communication, language learning, multilingualism, and how they intersect with social inclusion and justice. Her most recent book, *Intercultural Communication* (Edinburgh University Press, 2011) provides a critical introduction to the field from a sociolinguistic and discourse-analytic perspective. Together with Kimie Takahashi she is the co-founder of the sociolinguistics portal *Language on the Move* at www.languageonthemove.org, where she also blogs about the sociolinguistics of multilingualism.

Vaidehi Ramanathan is a Professor of socio/applied linguistics and is interested primarily in the sociopolitical aspects of language learning and teaching, especially as they pertain to English, vernacular languages, globalization, language policies, teacher education, pedagogies and literacy practices. She is also interested in the languaging of 'bodies' and 'disabilities' (especially Alzheimer's disease and chronic ailments) and in the narrating and constructing of a 'self' both through speech and writing. Her publications include *Alzheimer's Discourse: Some Sociolinguistic Dimensions* (Lawrence Erlbaum, 1997), *The Politics of TESOL Education: Writing, Knowledge, Critical Pedagogy* (Routledge, 2002), *The English-Vernacular Divide: Postcolonial Language Politics and Practice* (Multilingual Matters, 2005) and *Bodies and Language: Health, Ailments, Disabilities* (Multilingual Matters, 2010). She has also edited a special issue of *Language Policy* with a focus on health, and has co-edited a special issue of *TESOL Quarterly* with a focus on language policy.

Ben Rampton is Professor of Applied and Sociolinguistics and Director of the Centre for Language Discourse and Communication at King's College London, UK. He does interactional sociolinguistics, and his interests cover urban multilingualism, ethnicity, class, youth and education. He is the author of *Crossing: Language and Ethnicity among Adolescents* (Longman, 1995; St Jerome Publishing, 2005) and *Language in Late Modernity: Interaction in an Urban School* (CUP, 2006) and a co-author of *Researching Language: Issues of Power and Method* (Routledge, 1992). He has also edited or co-edited *The Language, Ethnicity and Race Reader* (Routledge, 2003), *Working Papers in Urban Language and Literacy* (www.kcl.ac.uk/ldc), and special issues of the *Journal of Sociolinguistics* (3(4) 1999; 11(5) 2007), the *International Journal of Applied Linguistics* (7(1 and 2) 1997), *Critique of Anthropology* (21(1) 2001) and *Pragmatics* (13(1) 2003). He was founding convener of the UK Linguistic Ethnography Forum (www.uklef.net).

Mela Sarkar is an Associate Professor in the Department of Integrated Studies in Education, McGill University, Montreal, Quebec, Canada. She was raised in a multilingual environment in Canada and comes to the study of multilingualism in popular culture through Montreal hip-hop lyrics. Her work has also focused on majority-minority linguistic interaction and linguistically marginalized populations more generally. In recent years, she has published on the mixed languages of Montreal hip-hop and Indigenous Language revitalization initiatives in Canada.

Elana Shohamy is a Professor and Chair of the Language Education programme at the School of Education, Tel Aviv University, Israel where she researches a variety of topics related to language policy in the context of conflicts and coexistence in multilingual societies, mostly of Israel. Specific areas include language testing in the context of critical testing and the power of tests, including language tests for citizenship, an expanded and critical framework of language policy, language rights in the context of immigration and minority groups. In the past decade her work has focused on research on multiple dimensions of linguistic landscape, i.e. languages displayed in public spaces in context of multilingualism and language as a symbol of contestation in the public space. Her publications include *The Power of Tests* (Longman, 2001), *Language Policy: Hidden Agendas and New Approaches* (Routledge, 2006), *The Languages of Israel* (Sposky and Shohamy, Multilingual Matters, 1999), *Linguistic Landscape: Expanding the Scenery* (edited with D. Gurter, Routledge, 2009) and *Linguistic Landscape in the City* (edited with E. Ben Rafael and M. Barni, Multilingual Matters, 2010). Professor Shohamy is the Editor of the journal *Language Policy* and the winner of the 2010 Lifetime Achievement Award of ILTA (International Language Testing Association).

James Simpson is a Lecturer at the School of Education, University of Leeds, UK. His research interests include the teaching of English to Speakers of Other Languages, discourse analysis and literacy studies. He is the co-author (with Melanie Cooke) of *ESOL: A Critical Guide* (Oxford University Press), and the editor of *The Routledge Handbook of Applied Linguistics* (2011).

Kimie Takahashi (PhD, Sydney University, 2006) is a Lecturer at the Graduate School of English at Assumption University of Thailand. Prior to moving to Bangkok in early 2011, she was a Postdoctoral Fellow at Macquarie University, Australia, where she was involved in a multi-site ethnography of the role of multilingualism and language learning in tourism between Australia and Japan. Her research interests include the inter-relationship between bilingualism, second language learning and gender, particularly in the contexts of study overseas, migration and employment. Her work has appeared in edited volumes and her first book, *Language Desire: Gender, Sexuality and Second Language Learning*, will be published by Multilingual Matters in 2012. With Ingrid Piller, Kimie is a co-founder of *Language on the Move*, a non-profit website dedicated to research on multilingualism, language learning and social inclusion (www.languageonthemove.org). The website hosts some of their research projects including a multimedia collection of interviews with transnationals, *Japanese on the Move: Life Stories of Transmigration* (funded by the Australia-Japan Foundation, Australian Department of Foreign Affairs and Trading).

Graham H. Turner has been Chair of Interpreting and Translation Studies at Heriot-Watt University in Edinburgh, UK since October 2005. For 25 years, he has been researching social and applied areas of linguistics with special reference to sign languages. Co-author of *Interpreting Interpreting: Studies and Reflections on Sign Language Interpreting*, his research in translation and interpreting has included projects exploring domains including the law, the theatre, education, mental health and social care, and the workplace.

Doris S. Warriner is Assistant Professor of Language and Literacy in the Department of English at Arizona State University, USA. In her scholarship and teaching, she investigates the relationship between the social contexts of education, language learning and literacy, with a focus on the institutional, economic and historical processes that influence the lived experiences of immigrant and refugee families living in the USA. In a time of globalization, immigration and transnationalism, her work contributes to conversations about the intersections between language, literacy and learning across a range of settings. Recent publications have appeared in *Anthropology and Education Quarterly*, the *Journal of Language, Identity and Education, Linguistics and Education, Teaching and Teacher Education*, and *the Routledge Handbook of Applied Linguistics*.

Christine W. L. Wilson is a Lecturer (French) at Heriot-Watt University in Edinburgh, UK where she teaches interpreting and translation. Her research interests include public service and remote (telephone/video-conference) interpreting, interpreting in cross-cultural surveys and in sign language, lexicography and kinesics in interpreter-mediated events.

Bencie Woll is Director of the ESRC Deafness Cognition and Language Research Centre (DCAL), UK. Before coming to London, she was at Bristol University, where she first worked on language acquisition and then was a co-founder of the Centre for Deaf Studies, pioneering research on the linguistics of British Sign Language (BSL) and on Deaf Studies. Her research and teaching interests embrace a wide range of topics related to sign language, including the linguistics of BSL and other sign languages; the history of BSL and the deaf community; the development of BSL in young children; and sign language and the brain, including functional imaging research and studies of signers with developmental and acquired language impairments. She is co-author of *Sign Language: The Study of Deaf People and their Language* (CUP, 1985) and *The Linguistics of BSL: An Introduction* (CUP, 1999).

Introduction

A sociolinguistics of multilingualism for our times

Marilyn Martin-Jones, Adrian Blackledge and Angela Creese

Introduction

The last two decades have seen a rapidly growing interest, internationally, in multilingualism and multilingual literacy and in the ways in which multilingualism is represented in the media and in public discourse. This is largely due to the significant linguistic, cultural and demographic changes that have been ushered in by globalization, transnational population flows, the spread of new technology and the changing political and economic landscape of different regions of the world.

The last two decades have also seen the emergence of new strands of research on multi-lingualism, which have incorporated critical and post-structuralist perspectives from social theory and embraced new epistemologies and research methods. There has also been a shift of focus to empirical work, which is interpretive, ethnographic and multimodal in nature.

Research has been conducted in different cultural and historical contexts: in Indigenous and post-colonial contexts; in situations characterized by recent or long-established patterns of migration; and in contexts where there are or have been minority language movements. Research has also been conducted in different kinds of sociolinguistic spaces: in local neigh-bourhoods; across transnational diaspora; in multilingual workplaces; in complementary schools, community classes and in mainstream educational settings; in health care centres, religious gatherings, legal settings and in bureaucratic encounters; in the mass media and on the Internet.

These new strands of research on multilingualism have not only deepened our under-standing of the particularities of the multilingual practices emerging in specific research sites. They have also begun to provide new insights into the nature of the changes taking place within the wider communicative order. Research in multilingual settings is thus making a significant contribution to the forging of a new sociolinguistics, which is better attuned to the description and analysis of the profound cultural and societal changes taking place in the late modern era.

The aim of this *Handbook* is, therefore, to capture the range and depth of this contemporary research on multilingualism, focusing primarily on sociolinguistic and ethnographic research, which incorporates critical, post-structuralist perspectives. We begin by sketching the broad

1

historical and epistemological context for this research. First, we provide a brief genealogy of ideas about multilingualism, viewing these through the lens of research on language ideology and on the role of language in nation-building and the construction of citizenship. We then trace the broad shift in research on multilingualism, captured in this volume, from a 'linguistics of community' (Pratt 1987) to a critical and ethnographic sociolinguistics and we show how this shift has been linked to a broader turn, across the social sciences towards post-structuralist and post-modern perspectives. Finally, we touch on the new avenues of enquiry that have been opened up as sociolinguists working on multilingualism have turned their attention to globalization and to the political, economic, demographic and cultural processes at work in the post-global era. Along with the contributors to this volume, we emphasize the need for new approaches, of a critical, ethnographic and discourse analytic nature to the multilingual realities of the current global age, and to the investigation of the specific ways in which contemporary mobilities and shifting concepts of time and space have reshaped communicative practices in speech and in writing, in different media, in different genres, registers and styles and in different semiotic modes.

Multilingualism, nationalism and enduring monolingual ideologies

The nineteenth century saw an intense preoccupation with the standardization and codification of languages. Language academies were established in some European countries. Languages were constructed as distinct and bounded systems, of grammar and lexis, and monitored for their 'purity' of use and expression. As research in the field of language ideology has demonstrated over the last two decades (Joseph and Taylor 1990; Gal and Irvine 1995; Gal and Woolard 1995, 2001; Schieffelin *et al.* 1998; Blommaert 1999; Kroskrity 2000), drawing on archival and historical sources, the practices of standardizing, codifying and setting boundaries to languages were closely bound up with the development of discourses about states, nations and empires, and with the definition and discursive regulation of citizenship, during this period in Europe. Grammarians and lexicographers contributed in significant ways to the ideological processes involved in linking language to political authority and legitimacy in different national contexts.

With the expansion and consolidation of European colonial power in the late nineteenth and early twentieth centuries, the practices of mapping, codifying and labelling languages were exported to other regions of the world by missionaries, colonial administrators and anthropologists (Fabian 1986; Makoni and Pennycook 2007; Errington 2008; Omoniyi this volume). Orthographies were also devised for languages that had hitherto not been written. As part of a parallel process that has been called 'internal colonialism' (Hechter 1975), the linguistic repertoires of Indigenous people were also described, labelled and codified (e.g. Huss 1999; Patrick 2003, this volume; McCarty 2004, and McCarty and Nicholas this volume).

As Hobsbawm (1990) has shown, from the nineteenth century onwards, the nation-state came to be conceptualized in Western thought as an organic essence and as a linguistically and culturally homogeneous entity, linked to territory and to 'a people'. Multilingualism clearly posed a challenge to the discursive construction of nationhood and empire in these unitary terms and, as Heller has argued, it 'had to be explained and evaluated' (2007: 5) in the emerging social science disciplines of the time.

In the mid-twentieth century, in the period following the Second World War, with decolonization and with the emergence of new nations, the role of language in nation-building and in the organization of citizenship took on new salience in public and academic discourse. These discursive processes were played out differently across post-colonial contexts, such as

Indonesia (Anderson 1983; Errington 1998); Pakistan (Rahman 1997; Rasool and Mansoor 2007) and Mozambique (Stroud 1999, 2007; Chimbutane 2011, this volume). As Stroud has noted, drawing on his detailed analysis of developments in Mozambique:

> The transformation of societies from colonial to postcolonial states not only reconfigured the relationship of actors and agents to state, market and civil society, but was simultaneously regulated through practices and ideas about languages and their interrelationships.
>
> *(2007: 25)*

With the ethnic revival and language revitalization movements of the 1960s among linguistic minorities in Europe and North America, language was also taken up as a key symbol for group mobilization and solidarity. In fact, as Heller (1999) has pointed out, the notion of linguistic minority can only be understood within an ideological context where language is seen as central to nation-building. As she puts it: 'linguistic minorities are created by nationalism which excludes them' (1999: 7). Ironically, in challenging the monolingual order imposed by centralizing nation-states, some social actors within revitalization movements have also taken on a discourse of linguistic nationalism and have represented languages as clearly bounded systems in promoting their cause, albeit on a smaller scale (Urla 1993; Jaffe 1999, 2007, this volume; Heller 1999, 2011).

Although the ideological association of monolingualism and nationhood has now been widely critiqued across the social sciences, the belief that citizens of a nation-state should have just one shared language has proved to be particularly persistent, in public and political discourse and in some areas of linguistic enquiry. As Blackledge (2005) has shown, debates about multilingualism became increasingly prominent in political discourse and in media discourse in the UK, in the first decade of the twenty-first century, with the language repertoires of linguistic minority groups of migrant and refugee origin being cast in largely disparaging terms. In the USA, the English-only movements, in some states, have produced discourses that characterize the languages of minority groups in particularly disparaging terms. Commenting on the growing intolerance toward linguistic diversity in these contexts, Wiley has noted that 'monolingualism is the real linguistic deficiency' (2005: 600). Writing about the situation in Spain, Moyer and Martin Rojo (2007) show clearly how migrants speaking languages other than Spanish or Catalan are seen as a threat to the current sociolinguistic order. Drawing on ethnographic and discourse analytic research in schools and in health care centres, these researchers have revealed the specific local ways in which language ideologies and discourses about homogeneity are articulated in the routine interactions of daily life.

From a linguistics of community to a critical and ethnographic sociolinguistics

In an early critique of the legacy of the academic discipline of linguistics in the construction of languages as emblems of nations, peoples and social groups and in emphasizing uniformity and cohesion, Pratt wrote: 'Our modern linguistics of language, code and competence posits a unified and homogeneous social world in which language exists as a shared patrimony – as a device, precisely, for imagining community' (1987: 50). Her critique echoed Anderson's (1983) deconstruction of the origin and character of the modern nation-state, as an imagined community, while at the same time drawing our attention to the specific role of linguistics in the ideological processes involved in imagining national, regional and local communities. Pratt

(1987) called this trend within the study of language 'a linguistics of community' and traced its origins to the Saussurean linguistics of the early twentieth century.

Underpinning this approach to language was a concern with systems of signs, with the underlying rules of phonology, grammar and semantics, and a belief that such systems and rules are either the innate capacities of individuals or are acquired through 'apprenticeship' in families and local communities. The idealized object of study was the 'native speaker' (for a critique of this notion, see Rampton 1990, 1995). The term 'speech community' also became an essential part of the vocabulary of linguists (e.g. Bloomfield 1933; Lyons 1970) and was later taken up by variationist sociolinguists (e.g. Labov 1972: 158) and even in early work on the ethnography of communication (e.g. Gumperz 1962, 1972; Hymes 1974). Definitions varied across different areas of language enquiry, with descriptive linguistics (e.g. Lyons) drawing the closest parallels between language and speech community, making no allowance for multilingualism. Variationist linguistics made allowances for linguistic heterogeneity by defining a speech community as 'a group of speakers who all share the same norms in regard to language' (Labov 1972), that is, shared attitudes to the evaluation of linguistic forms. The early work on the ethnography of communication went a little further and focused on much smaller groups with 'common locality and primary interaction' (Hymes 1974: 51) and insisted on 'shared rules for the conduct and interpretation of speech' (ibid.). Reviewing these early attempts to accommodate linguistic diversity, Pratt (1987) concludes that, although challenging hegemonic accounts of the communicative resources and practices of groups other than the dominant group, the tendency towards a linguistics of community remained, with the focus shifting to 'subcommunities' linked to criteria for social categorization such as ethnicity, gender or class, in a manner equivalent to the shift of focus to 'subcultures' in the cognate fields of ethnography and sociology (e.g. Willis 1977; Hebdige 1979).

An alternative concept that has been introduced into sociolinguistics in the last two decades, and into the social sciences more generally, is that of 'communities of practice' (Lave and Wenger 1991; Wenger 1998). Some authors (e.g. Hanks 1996) argue that the concept has a number of advantages over the long-established notion of speech community. First, as in the early work in ethnography of communication, the focus is on quite small groups 'who come together around mutual engagement in an endeavour' (Eckert and McConnell-Ginet 1992: 464). This focus on mutual engagement shifts attention away from reified social categories of ethnicity, gender and class. Second, communities of practice are seen as collectivities that arise under different circumstances and last for different stretches of time, with some being quite short-lived. The concept is thus more open and dynamic than the bounded notion of speech community. Third, Lave and Wenger's (1991) conceptual framework allows for simultaneous or sequential participation in different communities of practice. Individuals are seen as engaging in multiple endeavours during the course of their lives.

Despite these conceptual affordances and their value as a heuristic for empirical work in specific local multilingual settings or in the study of multilingualism in Internet-based networking, the notion of communities of practice lacks a critical edge. As Barton and Tusting (2005) have noted, it does not allow us to address the relationship between day-to-day interaction within communities of practice and broader social and ideological processes or to investigate the role of interaction in the reproduction or contestation of asymmetries of power, within institutions or within the wider social order. Moreover, as others have pointed out, the conceptualization of discourse and interaction is relatively undeveloped (Creese 2005; Tusting 2005).

Over the last two decades, there has been a major shift away from a linguistics of community or 'subcommunities' in research on multilingualism and linguistic diversity. As Pratt (1987) pointed out, the main shortcoming of this approach is that it does not allow us to see dominant and dominated groups 'in their relations with each other' (1987: 56). She argued for a linguistics of contact, which she described as follows:

> Imagine ... a linguistics that decentred community, that placed at its centre the operation of language *across* lines of social differentiation, a linguistics that focused on modes and zones of contact between dominant and dominated groups, between persons of different and multiple identities, speakers of different languages, that focused on how such speakers constitute each other relationally and in difference, how they enact differences in language. Let us call this a *linguistics of contact.*
>
> *(1987: 60, emphasis in the original)*

In her own research, Mary Louise Pratt is immersed in different zones of contact: she is a scholar of literature and linguistics; she is a specialist in literature written in Spanish and in Latin American studies (e.g. Pratt 1991); and she teaches in English in a North American university. She has lived her intellectual life in and out of Spanish and English. This may well have enabled her to imagine new directions for research in sociolinguistics and to pose new kinds of questions in this seminal article in 1987.

Her article appeared at a time, in the latter half of the 1980s, when there was intense interest in linguistic anthropological circles in North America in the new epistemological spaces opened up by developments in social theory, notably the turn towards post-structuralism and critical theory. Within the field of multilingualism, three linguistic anthropologists, Gal (1989), Heller (1992, 1995a, 1995b) and Woolard (1985, 1989, 1998), were the first to lay theoretical foundations for a critical ethnographic sociolinguistics, one in which the focus of inquiry would, in Pratt's terms, be on 'the operation of language across lines of social differentiation' and on 'zones of contact between dominant and dominated groups'. Gal's research (1979) focused on the situation of Hungarian speakers in Austria who had become minority language speakers as a result of changes in political boundary marking in central Europe. Heller (1994, 1999) was doing extended ethnographic work in French-language minority schools in Ontario, Canada, while Woolard (1989) was engaged in fieldwork in Catalonia, focusing on different domains of social life. Like many of us working in multilingual settings over the last two decades, including many contributors to this volume, these scholars were seeking ways of linking their detailed accounts of language choices and interactional practices, in these different local sites, with their analyses of institutional and historical processes, with wider discourses about language and identity and with specific political and economic conditions.

The writing of the French anthropologist and social theorist, Pierre Bourdieu (1977, 1982, 1991), proved to be a particularly valuable resource in their project of linking the study of language in face-to-face interaction with the wider social and institutional order. Bourdieu foregrounded the role of culture in social reproduction and characterized the ways in which dominant groups come to exercise symbolic power. He represented language varieties or ways of speaking and writing as forms of symbolic capital that were unevenly distributed in society. The most valuable forms of symbolic capital were those that were legitimated by the social groups who dominated particular linguistic markets (a notion broadly equivalent to whole polities or nation-states). Such forms of symbolic capital could be exchanged for social or economic capital, in face-to-face encounters or in writing, such as when applying for or being interviewed for jobs. Bourdieu provided a detailed account of the social, political and ideological conditions he deemed to be necessary for a language to gain legitimacy within a linguistic market. For him, language legitimation took place through the institutions of the state and especially through education. He saw education as a key site for social and cultural reproduction and for the imposition of a particular symbolic order. A key dimension of his model was that symbolic domination is achieved when dominated groups come to see legitimized language varieties as inherently superior to their own linguistic resources.

Looking back at the ways in which a linguistics of community was gradually dislodged in a whole body of research on multilingualism from the mid-1980s onwards, we see that the most significant advances in theory-building were made at the interfaces (or contact zones) between disciplinary traditions: at the interface between sociolinguistics and literary studies (Pratt 1987); between anthropology and sociolinguistics (Woolard 1985; Gal 1989 and Heller 1992, 1995a, 1995b). Since the early 1990s, real advances have also been made in empirical work. A rich body of research has been conducted in different cultural and historical contexts and in different social spaces, taking account of face-to-face interaction and multilingual literacy practices (e.g. Sebba 1993; Rampton 1995; Arthur 1996; Lin 1996; Zentella 1997; Errington 1998; Heller 1999; Martin-Jones and Jones 2000; Pujolar 2001; Jones 2000; Heller and Martin-Jones 2001; Jørgensen 2003; Hinnenkamp 2003; Pavlenko and Blackledge and Baynham and da Fina 2005; Luk and Lin 2007; Kanno 2008; Budach 2009; Blackledge and Creese 2010; Cincotta-Segi 2011; Chimbutane 2011; Bonacina forthcoming). It is impossible to encompass the field as a whole here. Instead, we have listed studies in diverse cultural and historical contexts and social spaces. The chapters in this volume also open significant windows on research in other contexts and spaces.

In keeping with Heller's (1988: 268) original vision, the approach in this ethnographic tradition of research in multilingual settings has largely been a 'multilevel' one, with a tight focus on the lived texture and dynamics of everyday communicative life, on heteroglossic spoken language practices and/or multilingual literacies, while at the same time investigating ways in which everyday practices and literacies are embedded in wider social, cultural and historical processes. Much of the research has drawn on the robust conceptual frameworks and analytic approaches developed within the interlinked traditions of ethnography of communication and interactional sociolinguistics (Hymes 1968; Gumperz and Hymes 1972; Hymes 1974;Gumperz 1982): these include key concepts such as speech event, ways of speaking, indexicality, contextualization cues and emic perspectives. Some research has incorporated concepts and methodological premises from conversation analysis and from the ethnomethodological tradition, adapting them to the study of multilingualism (e.g. Auer 1984, 1998; Li 1994, 1998; Gafaranga 2001).

However, the bulk of the research has also been critical, in the sense of incorporating a critical reflexivity (Pennycook 2001) while aiming to reveal links between local practices (multilingual or monolingual) and wider social and ideological processes, either by tracking the ways in which language is bound up with social categorization and stratification (Heller 1999, 2011) or by researching the ways in which identities are constructed, negotiated or contested in different multilingual settings (Pavlenko and Blackledge 2004). In some cases, the focus has been on contexts where far-reaching political, economic and/or ideological changes are at work, in Indigenous contexts in Brazil (Cavalcanti 1996), in Jaffna (Canagarajah 2001), in Hong Kong (Luk and Lin 2007) or in French Canada (Heller 2011). The research has reflected different shades of thinking about ethnography (ethnography of communication, linguistic anthropology, linguistic ethnography or critical ethnographic sociolinguistics). However, all of the scholars listed above have paid close attention to interactional processes and the crucial role of agency in the local construction of social life while also tracking the circulation of wider discourses about language and the ways in which traces of these discourses are taken up in conversational encounters and in the exchange of texts that occur in real time.

Globalization and language in late modernity

As research in the field of multilingualism has changed, the world has been changing around us, giving rise to new epistemological and methodological challenges. Over the past two decades, globalization has altered the face of social, cultural and linguistic diversity in societies all over the world (Blommaert and Rampton forthcoming). Transnational migration and the new population flows of the end of the twentieth century and of the first decade of the twenty-first century have brought about major demographic changes. The populations of the nations of the global north and west, in particular, have become more diverse, as the number of migrants has increased and as their territorial origins have become more varied. This phenomenon has resulted in new patterns of migration and post-migration, termed 'superdiversity'. As Vertovec (2006, 2007a) has observed, with reference to recent patterns of migration to the UK, these movements are characterized by 'a dynamic interplay of variables among an increased number of new, small and scattered, multiple origin, transnationally connected, socio-economically differentiated and legally stratified immigrants who have arrived over the last decade' (Vertovec 2007a: 1024). The notion of 'superdiversity' has tended to attract the attention of scholars in migration studies, ethnic and racial studies, urban studies, and sociology, but has, until recently, been largely overlooked within sociolinguistics. The term 'superdiversity' was originally coined to refer to the meshing and interweaving of diversities, in which not only 'ethnicity', but also other variables intersect and influence the highly differential composition, social location and trajectories of various immigrant groups in the twenty-first century (Vertovec 2007b). Urban neighbourhoods are often organized as both local and translocal, real as well as virtual, and this has effects on the structure and development of language repertoires and patterns of language use. Investigation of these phenomena 'stretches the limits of existing frameworks for analysing and understanding multilingualism and the dynamics of language change' (Blommaert 2010: 8). The authors of this volume collectively engage with this need to extend our framework for the study of multilingualism.

A point that needs to be emphasized here is that superdiversity is characterized by the interplay of variables in the migrant and post-migrant experience. Certainly it is no longer (if it ever was) sufficient to view diversity simply in terms of 'ethnicity' or country of origin. Other factors that come into play include, *inter alia*, differential immigration statuses, gender, age, race, economic mobility, social class/caste, locality and sexuality. Blommaert (2010) points out that, in increasingly diverse neighbourhoods, linguistic diversity may generate complex linguistic repertoires in which elements of 'migrant' languages and lingua francas are combined. The notion of superdiversity further includes not only those who have been involved in migratory movements over the last decade, but also longer established and settled migrant communities comprising several age cohorts, as their experiences shift within and across generations. Of course there have been other periods in history when there has been a sudden and rapid increase in the movement of peoples across territories. So this phenomenon is not unique to late modernity. But superdiversity, however we characterize it, serves to remind us to set aside our assumptions about the national, regional, ethnic, cultural or linguistic characteristics of particular 'groups' (Blommaert 2010). Vertovec (2007a) calls for more and better qualitative studies of superdiversity, as neither social scientists nor policy makers currently have access to accounts of what meaningful interactions look like in superdiverse settings. The authors of this volume provide numerous accounts of everyday practice in which the intermeshing and interweaving of the above variables become clear.

Globalization has also ushered in major economic changes: one of these is the integration of global and regional markets into local ones through regimes of regulation based on economic cooperation, which rely on 'intensified and compressed circulation of people, goods, and information' (Heller 2011: 20). Globalization makes available new resources for local action, which include new discourses and practices, and it gives rise to new identities in which these discourses are internalized and operationalized (Fairclough 2006). In the globalized new economy, communication is central to the functioning of the market, and Heller identifies a shift from a discourse of rights to a discourse of profit, and from the state as protector to the state as facilitator of the producer. Those who seek to profit from globalization also want the protection of their status from the states of which they are citizens, and 'local identities actually gain meaning from being commodified on a global market' (Heller 2011: 20). These changing conditions often create a tension between language and culture as commodified skills or as markers of authenticity. Heller argues that the close investigation of such discursive shifts, in diverse local sites provides us with new and revealing insights into the impact of globalization. In order to conduct such investigations of language practices in globalized localities we need to 'rethink our conceptual and analytical apparatus' (Blommaert 2010: 1).

Blommaert points out that the world has become a complex web of villages, towns, neighbourhoods and settlements connected by material and symbolic ties in often unpredictable ways, and that complexity needs to be examined and understood. He argues that in order to understand the complexities of language in globalization, we need to think about phenomena as located in and distributed across scales, from the global to the local, and to examine the connections between levels, to develop a sociolinguistics of mobile resources, framed in terms of trans-contextual networks, flows and movements. Pennycook (2010) similarly argues that globalization needs to be understood not only in the sense of reactions to global movements from above, but also as local movements being made global. It is the mobility of these flows and networks that poses the greatest challenge to a sociolinguistics of multilingualism, as we interrogate language practices that are socially situated 'not purely in relation to temporal and spatial location, but in terms of temporal and spatial trajectories' (Blommaert 2010: 21). Pennycook points out that the local is always defined in relation to something else regional, national, global, universal, modern, new, from elsewhere. In an age of globalization and digital interconnectedness, we need to reflect on how and why we look at languages as separate, countable, describable entities, and to consider that 'language may be undergoing such forms of transition as to require new ways of conceptualisation in terms of local activities, resources, or practices' (Pennycook 2010: 86).

None of this is meaningful, though, without reference to the notion of *voice*. Blommaert (2010) notes that a notion of single 'languages' attached to single collections of attributes, values and effects is not sufficient as a framework for thinking about multilingual practice. We will always see complex blending, mixing and reallocation processes, in which the differences between 'languages' are just one factor. Blommaert argues that instead 'we need to develop an awareness that it is not necessarily the language you speak, but how you speak it, when you can speak it, and *to* whom that matters. It is a matter of voice, not of language' (2010: 196). In this respect, he echoes Hymes (1996), who argued for a focus on ways of speaking and on 'varieties and modalities, styles and genres, ways of using language as a resource' (1996: 70). If we are to understand the meanings of discourses in contexts where a wide range of diversities interweave and intermesh, we need to be alive to the idea that no 'voice' is single. This is not to say that every voice explicitly speaks from more than one point of view, but every voice bears the traces of other times and other spaces, of words uttered before. Even simple repetition is never simple repetition: 'repetition always entails difference, since no two moments, events, words can be the same' (Pennycook 2010: 43). Every utterance is therefore different, but bears the marks of repetition. As Bakhtin put it, every word is entangled, shot through with shared thoughts, points of view, alien value judgements and accents, weaves in and out of complex interrelationships, merges with some, recoils from others ... and having taken meaning and shape at a particular historical moment in a socially specific environment, cannot fail to brush up against thousands of living dialogic threads.

(1981: 276)

Here we move from a view of transnationalism as cultural 'bifocality' (Vertovec 2009) to a sociolinguistic view of superdiversity as 'multivocality'. It is by looking closely, putting language under the microscope but also in context, that we can identify at least some of Bakhtin's thousands of living dialogic threads. The authors of the wide-ranging studies represented in this volume collectively pay attention to the fine mesh and weave of multilingual practices, situating them in terms of their temporal and spatial trajectories, and in their global as well as their local contexts.

New multilingual realities

Heller (2007: 1) argues for an approach to researching multilingualism that moves away from a highly ideologized view of coexisting linguistic systems, to a more critical approach that situates language practices in social and political contexts, and 'privileges language as social practice, speakers as social actors and boundaries as products of social action'. Gal (2006) points out that in Europe a new elite of multilingual speakers (of, for example, French, German and English) sustains a breadth of linguistic repertoires that transcends national boundaries. For such groups, ethnolinguistic identity may be only an occasional issue. For multilingual speakers of languages with lower status, however, language issues may still be salient as people attempt to negotiate identities, often from relatively powerless positions. Language ideologies are neither simple nor monolithic, however. Notwithstanding the argument that minority language speakers are subject to the symbolic violence of the dominant language ideology, some speakers who (or whose families) may traditionally have been associated with minority 'ethnic' languages are using language and languages in new ways (Sebba 1993; Rampton 1995, 1999). Although some speakers are either unable to negotiate their identities from inextricably powerless positions, and others in powerful positions have no need to do so, some speakers in modern nation-states are using their linguistic skills to negotiate new subject positions (Blackledge and Pavlenko 2001; Pavlenko and Blackledge 2004). In what Gal (2006: 27) describes as 'self-conscious, anti-standardizing moves', such negotiations may include linguistic practices that reframe previous standard varieties, incorporating, *inter alia*, urban popular cultural forms, minority linguistic forms, hybridities and inventions. Here language practices associated with immigrant groups no longer (if ever they did) represent backward-looking traditions, but may be linked to global youth culture and urban sophistication. Languages and language practices are not necessarily equated to national identity (but may be so), and are not necessarily dominated by the standardized variety. Despite powerful ideologies of homogeneity, populations in many countries – especially countries with a history of recent immigration – continue to be heterogeneous in their practices. May (2005: 337) proposes that linguistic identities need not be oppositional, and asks 'what exactly is wrong with linguistic complementarity?' May calls for further ethnographic studies that articulate and exemplify broad linguistic principles of language ideological research in complex multilingual contexts. Heller and Duchêne (2007: 11) argue that rather than accepting ideological positions in which there is competition over languages, 'perhaps we should be asking instead who benefits and who loses from understanding languages the way we do, what is at stake for whom, and how and why language serves as a terrain for competition'.

Makoni and Pennycook point out that the notion of languages as separate, discrete entities, and 'countable institutions' (2007: 2) is a social construct. They argue for a critical historical account, which demonstrates that, through the process of classification and naming, languages were 'invented' (2007: 1). They add that, in direct relation with the invention of languages, 'an ideology of languages as separate and enumerable categories was also created' (2007: 2). Makoni and Pennycook point, in particular, to the naming of languages such as 'Bengali' and 'Assamese' as the construction of 'new objects' (2007: 10) and emphasize that languages cannot be viewed as discrete, bounded, impermeable, autonomous systems. Instead, they propose that 'local knowledge' is crucial to our understanding of language, and argue for research that enables us to develop an understanding of the relationships between what people believe about their language (or other people's languages), the situated forms of talk they deploy, and the material effects – social, economic, environmental – of such views and use.

If languages are invented, and languages and identities are socially constructed, we nevertheless need to account for the fact that at least some language users, at least some of the time, hold passionate beliefs about the importance and significance of a particular language to their sense of 'identity' (Blackledge and Creese 2010). It is now well established in contemporary socio-linguistics (Harris 2006; Rampton 2006) that one 'language' does not straightforwardly index one subject position, and that speakers use linguistic resources in complex ways to perform a range of subject positions, sometimes simultaneously. However, although accepting this, May (2001, 2005: 330) argues that 'historically associated languages continue often to hold considerable purchase for members of particular cultural or ethnic groups in their identity claims'. Although it is certainly an oversimplification to treat certain languages as 'symbols' or 'carriers' of 'identity', we are obliged to take account of what people believe about their languages, to listen to how they make use of their available linguistic resources and to consider the effects of their language use – even where we believe these 'languages' to be inventions. Makoni and Pennycook (2007) propose the 'disinvention' of languages, and a reinvention that acknowledges heterogeneity, arguing that languages are discursive constructions that perpetuate social inequities. Makoni and Mashiri (2007) suggest that rather than developing language policies that attempt at hermetically sealing languages, we should be describing the use of vernaculars that leak into one another to understand the social realities of their users. They argue that it is necessary to overcome existing ideas about language if we are to imagine alternative ways of conceptualizing the role and status of individuals in the world, and that 'a world in which plurality is preferred over singularity requires rethinking concepts founded on notions of uniformity over those predicated on diversity' (2007: 27). Stressing the speaker rather than the code or language is central to this argument.

García (2009: 45) proposes the term 'translanguaging' to refer to the multiple discursive practices in which multilingual speakers engage, as they draw on the resources within their communicative reportoires. In this view of the communicative practices of multilinguals, translanguaging is seen as incorporating phenomena such as codeswitching and crossing but also going beyond them. It includes but extends what others have called 'language use in multilingual settings'. García claims that, rather than focusing on language itself, translanguaging makes it apparent that there are no clear-cut boundaries between the 'languages' that people draw on as they communicate with one another. As we indicated earlier, Heller (2007) has also argued that we tend to understand the linguistic resources within our communicative repertoires as whole, bounded systems called 'languages' because nations and states have produced powerful discourses of national belonging, which construct 'languages' as emblems of nationhood. Applying this line of argument to the context of education, García

(2007: xiii) suggests that, if 'languages' are inventions, we must observe closely communication in action and base pedagogic practice on our observations. Although largely accepting these arguments, we also agree with another point made by Heller (2007: 342), which is that the terms, bilingualism and multilingualism, allow us a purchase on what count as relevant categories, and enable us to focus on how boundaries are created, how people and their communicative resources are included and excluded, and what happens to them as a result (Martin-Jones 2007; Blackledge and Creese 2010; Creese and Blackledge 2010).

New research lenses

The far-reaching social, cultural and linguistic changes that we have described above and the significant shifts in epistemologies that we have all witnessed over the last two decades necessitate new thinking about research methodology. Calls are increasingly being made for the development of new research lenses (e.g. Eisenhart 2001a, 2001b; Heller 2007). For instance, Eisenhart (2001a) notes the advances that have been made, in writing about the post-modern era, in reconceptualizing key constructs, such as 'culture', 'community', 'identity' and 'language', but she also expresses concern about the lack of parallel methodological advances in researching these features of contemporary life. She points to the difficulty of defining notions such as participant, community or site, and argues that we need to adjust our conceptual orientations and methodological priorities to take into account changing human experiences in the context of contemporary migration flows, diasporic connections and the use of new technologies. Eisenhart concludes that we must be ready to extend or go beyond ethnography's conventional methods to meet new challenges.

In this new era, we are challenged as researchers to respond to the complexities of the translocal worlds that Eisenhart describes (2001b: 21) or the globalized localities that Heller (2011) depicts. We need new ways of understanding context, which no longer paint normative, conventional and institutional pictures where coherent ethnographic realities are unproblematically presented. MacLure (2003) argues for opening up our ethnographies to reveal different configurations, interpretations and contradictions. Blackledge and Creese (2010) argue for bringing multiple voices into our multilingual ethnographic accounts. Demystifying the process of knowledge construction in ethnography, in these ways, echoes earlier work by Bauman and Briggs (1990: 71), who argued for boldness in deconstructing the notion of 'natural context' by confronting our own 'influence on what local sources offer us'.

Bauman and Briggs (1990: 68–9) describe inherent problems with the concept of context. One problem lies in the 'inclusiveness' of the concept. These elements might include context of meaning, institutional context, context of communicative system, social base, individual context and context of situation. They argue that: 'All such definitions of context are overly inclusive, there being no way to know when an adequate range of contextual factors has been encompassed' (1990: 68). This results in 'infinite regress' (ibid.), where more and more definitions of context are added to the list. Bauman and Briggs also touch on the problem of 'false objectivity' (ibid.). The criticism here is that most definitions of contexts are predicated on positivist models of social science, which view context as existing prior to and independently of social action itself. This leads to reified definitions of context, which fail to capture how the participants themselves determine the ongoing social interaction, shape the setting and transform social relations. Bauman and Briggs argue for an 'agent-centered view of performance' (1990: 69); one which shifts the balance from a focus on the product of context to the process of contextualization. They also warn against the limitations of a too tightly focused interactional analysis, which fails to make links to the wider historical, social and political ecology, asserting that 'performance provides a frame that invites critical reflection on communicative processes' (Bauman and Briggs 1990: 60–1).

An ethnographic approach is one that sees the analysis of small phenomena as set against an analysis of big phenomena, and in which 'both levels can only be understood in terms of one another' (Blommaert 2006: 16). McCarty (2005, 2011) reminds us that ethnography provides a particularly powerful 'way of seeing' both 'the fine-grained details of everyday discursive practices and their organization within larger cultural and historical frames' (2005: xxii). Erickson describes this movement between levels as an 'attempt to combine close analysis of fine details of behavior and meaning in everyday social interaction with analysis of the wider societal context' (1990: 80). Hornberger (1994) speaks of the value of ethnography in juxtaposing emic and holistic views so that we are introduced to the local and situated understandings and actions of members alongside the wider social scene. Hornberger reminds us that it is through this emic/holistic 'creative tension' that ethnographic research emerges and that each 'refines and reforms the other' (1994: 688).

Bauman and Briggs (1990: 78) propose that 'much of what we do as linguistic anthropologists amounts to the decontextualization and recontextualization of others' discourse, which means as well that we exercise power'. The studies in this volume pay close attention to aspects of signification in interactional processes while also tracking how these circulate in wider discourses. As researchers of multilingualism we are aware of how metadiscourses emanate from the discourses of the media and other social institutions as well as from daily discursive and interactional practices. These discourses become regimented and familiar (Silverstein 2003; Wortham 2001). Indeed, Erickson argues that ethnographic research is necessary because of the very invisibility of everyday life (1990).

Scholars working in the related and overlapping traditions of critical and ethnographic sociolinguistics, linguistic ethnography and linguistic anthropology all seek to make visible the connections between societal influences and the 'slippery phenomena of everyday interaction' (Erickson 1990: 80), and the ways in which participants make sense of these connections. The challenge of overcoming the macro/micro divide has, for some time, been a preoccupation in the field of sociolinguistics (e.g. Woolard 1985; Fairclough 1989; Heller 1999; Heller and Martin-Jones 2001). New proposals are now emerging, with scholars working with a range of concepts, such as scale (Blommaert 2010), flows and circulation (Heller 2011), and chains or trajectories (Agha and Wortham 2005). These researchers share an interest in the investigation of processes of signification in the current globalized world. However, Blommaert asserts that that it is unreasonable to 'make any a priori assumptions about the repertoires of people in globalization contexts' (Blommaert 2008: 439). These require empirical investigation.

Heller (2011: 41) points out that ethnography with a critical orientation, 'is no longer the ethnography focused on specific institutions or communities that has been the hallmark of linguistic anthropology for many years'. Heller's recent work argues for multi-site ethnography as a means of 'examining mobilities and linkages', which can help explain 'the nature of contemporary social, economic and political processes' (2011: 41). As we noted at the beginning of this section, these methodological challenges require new ways of describing and explaining these circulations, chains, trajectories and scale jumps. Eisenhart (2001a, 2001b) offers us some ways forward:

- Use of collaborative teams to broaden insights and perspectives.
- Development of models stressing mutual and shared relationship between researcher and researched.
- Experiments in writing that allow more perspectives or 'voices' to be revealed in final accounts.

- Use of research narratives that show divisions, struggles or inconsistencies in the data.
- Use of different media beyond 'textual writing' to represent the data; engaging audience through film, literature, television and computer.
- A movement away from focus on individual people and an emphasis on new technologies, to understand the translocal rather than only the local.

The chapters in this *Handbook* also provide rich and innovative examples of responses to these methodological challenges in different areas of research related to multilingualism.

Overall organization of the *Handbook* and individual contributions

We turn now to the wealth of contributions to this volume. They encompass a wide range of research related to multilingualism. As we indicated at the beginning of this chapter, our aim in compiling this *Handbook* has been to focus primarily on sociolinguistic and ethnographic research that incorporates critical post-structuralist perspectives. We also want to make visible the distance that researchers in this area have travelled in the last two decades, in terms of both theory and method. Yet, within this particular strand of research on multilingualism, we see considerable variation: we see a range of views and interpretive stances and we see different ways of addressing the theoretical and methodological challenges of research in these new times. We also see research being undertaken in very different cultural and historical contexts, in different sociolinguistic spaces, where different issues come to the fore.

The volume has been organized into five sections, which bring together researchers who are addressing similar research themes or locating their empirical work in similar kinds of research sites. Research related to the ideological processes involved in the association of monolingualism and nationhood, and the consequences of those processes, is presented in chapters included in the first section, entitled 'Discourses about multilingualism, across political and historical contexts'. These ideological processes and discourses are also illustrated with reference to different institutional contexts in several of the chapters in the second and third sections of the volume: 'Multilingualism in education' and 'Multilingualism in other institutional sites'. A recurring theme in these chapters is the contrast between dominant discourses about language and national unity, idealized representations of identity and the actual multilingual realities of contemporary social life. In section four, 'Multilingualism in social and cultural change', the focus shifts to the far-reaching processes of change at work in most societies in the global era and to their implications for our understanding of multilingualism. In the final section, 'Situated practices, lived realities', the research lens is narrowed to the details of the sociolinguistic texture of daily life, in spoken interaction and in local and globalized literacy practices. Here we have chosen not to use the term 'multilingualism' in the subheading, as a range of other terms are introduced by the authors. These terms include crossing, heteroglossia, literacies, metrolingualism, multilingual franca, polylingualism, multimodality and urbilingualism. They are employed to reveal some of the complex and nuanced ways in which people draw on the multiple, semiotic resources available with their communicative repertoires as they engage with others in different domains of their lives.

Discourses about multilingualism, across political and historical contexts

In Chapter 1, Donna Patrick approaches multilingualism in Indigenous contexts. She points out the crucial role of language in maintaining local identities and in accessing and participating in discourses of power, social transformation and resistance. Here multilingualism is viewed through an interdisciplinary lens, which interrogates language ideologies and practices in their historical, political and economic contexts. This chapter dispels the notion of static, socially bounded Indigenous groups located in a timeless past, looking instead to present and future directions in researching multilingualism in Indigenous settings.

Suresh Canagarajah and Indika Liyanage (Chapter 2) argue that, in order to understand multilingualism in late modernity, it is vital to understand language practices in pre-modern and pre-colonial times. In order to develop this understanding, they focus on the plurilingual tradition in pre-colonial South Asia, pointing to the spontaneous and uninhibited practice of plurilingualism in the period before constraining ideologies were introduced as a result of colonization. Canagarajah and Liyanage propose investigative approaches that treat language as an intersubjective social practice with a grammar that is emergent, hybrid and multimodal.

In Chapter 3, Vaidehi Ramanathan similarly focuses her contribution in a South Asian context. She discusses ideologies and practices related to 'vernacular' and English education in Gujarat, India. Ramanathan's detailed analysis demonstrates the need to move from reified conceptions of English as 'cosmopolitan' and the vernacular as 'parochial', and to open up spaces in which we can view meanings associated with language practices as in constant flux, forever modified and constantly transformed.

Alexandra Jaffe (Chapter 4) takes the Corsican case to investigate discourses about language and citizenship, and their implications for minority language speakers and minority language revitalization. She shows that these are shifting discourses, in which an idealized monolingual national citizen is being replaced by an idealized plurilingual European/global citizen, and where the emphasis is moving from bounded 'languages' to linguistic repertoires and their role in participatory frameworks of democratic practice. Jaffe shows how minority language citizenship is no longer conceptualized solely at a national scale, as European and global scales of reference have introduced concepts of linguistic citizenship based on plurilingual practices.

In Chapter 5, Bencie Woll and Robert Adam focus their discussion on the politics of deafhood. To be deaf, they argue, is to have a hearing loss; and, at the same time, to be deaf is to belong to a community with its own language and culture. Woll and Adam point out that deaf communities parallel other minority linguistic communities in terms of linguistic and cultural oppression by the majority culture. In the deaf community, as in the contexts discussed in the previous chapters, ideologies and practices of language are constantly on the move. The authors argue that studies of the deaf community, like studies of other groups, must be situated in their complex political contexts.

Melanie Cooke and James Simpson (Chapter 6) shift the debate to the domains of public and political discourses about multilingualism. Although linguistic diversity may be accepted and celebrated in some quarters, it is often a source of tension and debate in political discourse, where multilingualism is often constructed as a problem or threat to national unity. Cooke and Simpson provide examples from political discourse in the UK, where debates about language are invoked in arguments about immigration, national identity, citizenship, national security and social cohesion. This chapter argues, convincingly, that these powerful discourses about linguistic diversity are often at odds with the multilingual realities of contemporary practice.

In Chapter 7, Stephen May discusses multilingualism in relation to the development of language rights as an academic paradigm. He demonstrates that this development is rooted in the related traditions of language ecology, linguistic human rights, minority language rights, and a more overtly critical sociohistorical/sociopolitical analysis of language rights. May argues that the development of arguments in support of language rights has provided an impetus for challenging the conceptualization of processes of linguistic modernization as unproblematic. As we see in other contexts in earlier chapters, processes of linguistic change are often, if not always, the result of wider social and political processes. This recognition allows us to critique the otherwise apparently ineluctable link between majority language, mobility and progress, to argue for the rights of minority language speakers.

Multilingualism and education

Teresa McCarty and Sheilah Nicholas (Chapter 8) describe the interface of language, culture and self-determination in Indigenous education. Their chapter documents how grass-roots Indigenous movements have set their own agendas for reclaiming educational control, resulting in instructional models that serve Indigenous students and revitalize Indigenous language and cultures. They examine the heterogeneity of Indigenous knowledge systems and also the common process of silencing and suppressing them. The chapter illustrates how over many centuries, Indigenous mother tongues have successfully conveyed highly complex concepts in different sites of learning. The role that Indigenous protagonism has played in the rise of bilingual education is also described. The authors argue for more situated examinations of local processes of language shift, revitalization and maintenance, and suggest that one of the most powerful theoretical and methodological means of achieving this is ethnography. This position is also shared with many of the authors in this volume.

In Chapter 9, Feliciano Chimbutane discusses multilingualism in education in post-colonial contexts. Using sub-Saharan Africa as the particular focus, he explores how colonial language policies have influenced policy decisions taken in many countries since independence. He argues that language policy trends are often shaped by external forces including developments such as financial aid from former colonial powers. In his historical and theoretical review of language planning, he shows the failure of monolingual models of education and he documents ongoing work in many countries challenging the colonial language-in-education legacy through the use of local languages as media of instruction. Chimbutane argues for contextually based, pluralistic language policies, which include citizens' right to choose to be educated in the languages(s) they think will equip them with upward socio-economic mobility.

In Chapter 10, Durk Gorter and Jasone Cenoz provide an assessment of how regional minorities and local educational programmes, which are aimed at language maintenance and revitalization, have fared in Europe. The chapter also engages with European policy with regard to provision for regional minority languages and their speakers. Gorter and Cenoz describe a positive shift in Europe to a new climate, which has placed multilingualism higher on the political agenda. They argue for the importance of education in the revitalization of regional minority languages and illustrate two analytic frameworks that have been used in studies of attempts to reverse language shift. The chapter surveys the diversity among regional minority languages and shows the need for an understanding of historical and social processes in accounts of the contemporary sociolinguistic status of different languages across Europe.

Anne-Marie de Mejía (Chapter 11) considers immersion education as a route to multi-lingualism. She locates immersion education in the wider field of language teaching and learning while describing the importance of local circumstances for different models of immersion education. De Mejía shows how the different sociocultural-political circumstances of the communities concerned have given rise to considerable programmatic and pedagogical variation among such initiatives. The chapter also explores trilingual immersion, codeswitching and language separation in the classroom and questions some long held negative views about the use of the first language in immersion contexts. In addition, de Mejía draws attention to the need for robust teacher professional development programmes and she suggests that teachers working in immersion education should be knowledgeable about the principles and fundamentals of bilingual education. To conclude, she argues for a more detailed look at classroom interaction, pedagogy and contextual factors to better respond to the challenges of developing immersion education in our plurilingual and internationalized world.

In Chapter 12, Christine Hélot questions the monolingual habitus of our educational systems. Her chapter on linguistic diversity and education argues for a move from monoglossic to heteroglossic perspectives that stress the plurality of ways in which linguistic resources are drawn on in everyday communication. Despite the increased visibility of linguistic diversity in schools everywhere, Hélot shows how this is not reflected in classroom practices. She argues that education programmes for bilingual and minority language speakers need to provide support for learning in schools but, at the same time, they also need to develop second language teaching strategies and bi- and multilingual approaches to teaching and learning. She proposes a critical ecological model of language education, which seeks to reframe language education with reference to emancipatory educational practices.

Ofelia García's chapter, with Nelson Flores (Chapter 13), raises crucial questions regarding the nature of multilingual pedagogies for the twenty-first century. Arguing for a model that responds to the diversity of language and literacy practices that children and youth bring to school, García and Flores speak of going beyond acceptance or tolerance of children's languages, to 'cultivation' of languages through their use for teaching and learning. In their vision, the design and practices of multilingual pedagogies should aim to educate meaningfully and equitably and should seek to establish tolerance and appreciation of diversity. The chapter shows the pedagogic need for practices firmly rooted in the multilingual and multimodal language and literacy practices of children in schools of the twenty-first century. The chapter provides an overview of types of multilingual pedagogies embedded in different historical and socio-educational contexts and illustrates these with particular case study examples from around the world.

Sheena Gardner's chapter on global English and bilingual education (Chapter 14) describes the desire for participation in the global networks that English allows and the political and economic background to these developments. The chapter describes the impact on different bilingual education programmes around the world as English as a global language expands into different educational sectors. Three educational sectors are reviewed in detail: English for young learners; initiatives in upper primary and secondary schools to teach specific subjects or content areas in English; and university education in English. Gardner sets out the policy and practice implications of growth in these sectors of education and considers the importance of teacher education in these developments.

Multilingualism in other institutional sites

In Chapter 15, Roger Hewitt starts from a contextual historical note on Henry Ford's workplace language education programme in the USA and subsequent developments in the modern period. He then moves on to consider a global range of contexts in which multilingualism is evident in contemporary workplaces. This he does through an examination of the current research literature and an account of some of the popular debates over logistical and legal issues involved. Describing cases of both high- and low-status languages in workplace settings and drawing on a broad literature from sociolinguistics and the sociology of language, through economic sociology and migration studies, Hewitt provides a profile of multilingualism in a domain that occupies a critical social and economic position for both migrating and settled communities.

Chapter 16, by Ingrid Piller, examines the ways in which the root causes of social exclusion have been construed in research on multilingualism. Piller provides a genealogy of ideas about the relationship between language and social exclusion, noting the shifts in terminology from terms such as poverty, marginalization and disadvantage to social exclusion (and its opposite, social inclusion), from the 1990s onwards. She draws a broad distinction between the assimilationist ideas that developed from the time of the mass migrations of the late nineteenth and early twentieth century, and the pluralist thinking ushered in by the emancipatory movements of the 1960s, and notes that the pluralist discourses tended to foreground the discriminatory practices of institutions such as schools and social services. At the heart of the chapter, Piller then provides a trenchant critique of the assumptions about language, about multilingualism and about social structures that underpin research undertaken within both of these traditions. She emphasizes the need to take account of the highly situated nature of the relationship between multilingualism and social exclusion/inclusion as the outcomes of language policy interventions (e.g. adult language programmes or bilingual education) differ from one political and economic context to another. Like Hewitt, she focuses on the world of work and presents a case study from Australia, showing the constraints on social inclusion policies and language programmes aimed at increasing employment prospects for adults who are recent migrants.

Katrijn Maryns (Chapter 17) investigates the institutional management of multilingualism in legal-administrative settings. She demonstrates that multilingual repertoires are often not acknowledged as meaningful and functional resources in legal-institutional settings, as a deeply rooted nationalist ideology of language dominates. Maryns presents two legal cases from different contexts of legal decision making in Belgium: the asylum agencies in Brussels, and the Assize Court in Antwerp. Detailed ethnographic fieldwork reveals that in both settings a monolingual ideology is imposed on multilingual performance in the legal space, as homogeneity becomes a prerequisite for the production of bureaucratically manageable accounts. Maryns calls for a better understanding of the soliolionguistic realities of multilingual speakers in procedural contexts. Without such understanding linguistic minority speakers will remain persistently disadvantaged.

Chapter 18, by Christine Wilson, Graham Turner and Isabelle Perez, provides an overview of issues and developments in research and practice in the field of public service interpreting (PSI). The authors highlight the complexity of the interpreting process in this field, given its interactional and dialogic nature and they note that research on 'dialogic interpreting' in PSI contexts is currently less developed than research in the well-established area of 'conference interpreting' (involving long monologues and simultaneous translation). They then describe the particular challenges associated with interpreting in spoken and signed languages in different PSI contexts, such as education, healthcare, legal settings and workplaces. The authors' principal focus, in this chapter, is on research and practice with and for deaf people who are users of British Sign Language (BSL). However, they also show how research and practice within the field of sign language interpreting have served to raise awareness of issues and challenges in the wider field of PSI interpreting. They conclude the chapter with a detailed case study of one policy context – that of Scotland since political devolution in 1998. Here they illustrate the advantages that accrue from having a legislative framework and new policy drivers for the development of interpreting provision and for the professionalization of interpreting practice.

In Chapter 19, Helen Kelly-Holmes explores the media as a key site of multilingualism, arguing that media have a major role to play in maintaining or challenging existing language regimes, attitudes and ideologies. The analysis presented here finds that the evolution of language policy and planning in the media can be seen in terms of the distinct yet overlapping areas of modernity, the failure of modernity, and post-modernity. In the post-modern era, media production often involves multilingual and heteroglossic practices that challenge existing norms. Kelly-Holmes further argues that developments in multilingualism and media are inextricably linked to changing market ideologies and developments in technology. New media in particular challenge the distinction between consumption and production, opening up spaces for new types of multilingual practice.

Chapter 20, by Tope Omoniyi, considers the complex relationship between multilingualism and religion, taking account of a range of examples from different religions and different sociolinguistic settings around the world. Omoniyi identifies three broad macro-historical trends: first, the historical link between conquest, colonization and the spread of some religions (e.g. Catholicism and Protestantism); second, the significant population movements within colonial empires (e.g. the movement of indentured labourers), which gave rise to linguistic, cultural and religious diversity; third, the development of multilingualism in the wake of the spread of particular religions (e.g. Islam in sub-Saharan Africa, or Catholicism in South and Central America). Omoniyi also identifies two broad sociolingustic consequences of these macro-historical trends and argues that they are best viewed and researched from a micro-level perspective. The first consequence is that ritual practices in local sites of religious observance gradually have become more multilingual as the nature of religious groupings have become more diverse. The second, related consequence is that multilingual ritual practice is most often manifested in particular genres and in particular types of activity, such as the singing of sacred songs. Omoniyi concludes by calling for research of an interdisciplinary nature, with a view to drawing together both macro and micro perspectives and with a view to building a fuller understanding of the hybrid nature of language use in contemporary religious practices.

Multilingualism in social and cultural change

In Chapter 21, Alexandre Duchêne and Monica Heller examine how multilingualism has become an integral part of the new economy. In doing so they explore the impact of economic transformations on language and multilingual practices, and view multilingualism as both a product and process of economic activity. Analysis of the changing economic market reveals multiple forms of multilingual practices that are geared towards commercial goals. Duchêne and Heller propose that multilingual practices and ideologies must be understood in relation to the interests of the new economy. They contend that it is imperative to examine multilingualism and social change by questioning the underlying principles of institutional, historical and economic conditions in which language practices are embedded.

Sirpa Leppänen and Saija Peuronen (Chapter 22) review research on multilingualism on the Internet and describe two broad approaches in this area of study. The first approach describes the choice and diversity of languages as means of communication on the Internet, and analyses language visibility, accessibility and status. The second approach focuses on the study of multilingual Internet users and the ways in which they draw on and use multiple linguistic and semiotic resources in their computer-mediated communication. In this relatively new field, the landscape is rapidly changing and Leppänen and Peuronen chart how different studies draw on a range of different theoretical and methodological orientations to investigate multilingualism on the Internet. The chapter sets out the broad scope of existing research while also providing rich illustrations of how choices are made in multilingual practices on the Internet.

Chapter 23, by Mela Sarkar and Bronwen Low, focuses on multilingualism in hip-hop culture. Drawing on their own research on Montreal hip-hop, they illustrate how mixed-language is used in rap lyrics as a stylistic device that can be used to create new kinds of meaning with critical, analytical and sociopolitical purposes. Sarkar and Low ask why multilingualism as a field of study has been slow to focus on language use in popular culture and they make a compelling argument for increased research in this area precisely because of its ordinariness and pervasiveness. They also call for deconstruction of the exoticization of multilingualism and suggest that this will require a paradigm shift.

The chapter on multilingualism and gender by Kimie Takahashi (Chapter 24) offers insights into multilingualism and gender in two transnational contexts: the global politics of reproductive labour and cross-linguistic intimate relations. Reviewing the last four decades of research on the inter-relationships between multilingualism and gender, Takahashi refers us to the globalized present and its increased opportunities for contact. The chapter shows how the ever-expanding array of services and products offered in the global economy implicate women in gender inequalities, which perpetuate international labour market disparities. Drawing on a rich variety of ethnographic studies, Takahashi reveals how different discursive sites are used to perpetuate the reproduction of hegemonic notions of masculinity and femininity, which are also profoundly embedded in the hierarchy of other aspects of identity, particularly ethnicity and class.

Situated practices, lived realities

Sinfree Makoni and Alastair Pennycook (Chapter 25) argue that there is a need for models of language that question simplified notions of 'monolingualism' and 'multilingualism'. Rather than accepting the pre-existence of language as discrete, unified systems, Makoni and Pennycook demonstrate that languages are invented for political purposes, and call for their disinvention. For many people, the critical issue is not whether they are monolingual or multilingual but that they use language. The authors argue for a conception of practice that moves beyond the notion of multilingualism to a monolingualism of humanity, which is better captured by non-pluralized ideas such as urbilingualism, metrolingualism or a multilingua franca. The chapter calls for a move away from the enumeration of languages to open up the complexities of grass-roots metro- or urbilingualism.

In Chapter 26, Aneta Pavlenko reviews research to date related to multilingualism and emotions, taking account of the whole gamut of emotions from language attachment and desire to language anxiety and rejection. She concludes that this research reveals a two-way interaction between languages and emotions in multilingual speakers. On the one hand, emotions shape speakers' language choices, investments and learning trajectories. On the other hand, cross-linguistic differences in emotion lexicons and affective repertoires influence the ways in which multilingual speakers perceive themselves, the ways in which they relate to the world and the ways in which they use their linguistic resources in oral interaction and in writing.

Chapter 27, by Angel Lin and David Li, provides a genealogy of research on codeswitching, contrasting the subtle and nuanced ways in which bilingual speakers exchange meanings with popular and largely perjorative views of codeswitching. The opening sections of the chapter trace the development of different strands of sociolinguistic research on codeswitching and explain the thinking behind the use of particular terms, such as codemixing, situational and metaphorical codeswitching, marked and unmarked code choice and code alternation. In the main body of the chapter, the discussion focuses on research on codeswitching in classrooms and encompasses research carried out in two broad contexts: second language classrooms and bilingual programmes. Here Lin and Li give a detailed account of different phases of research on classroom codeswitching, illustrating different developments in theory and method with reference to their own work in Hong Kong and to studies conducted in other cultural and historical contexts. Their account spans three decades of research. They then conclude with reflections on the state of the art in classroom-based research and pose six different challenges for future research in this area.

Chapter 28, by Ben Rampton and Constadina Charalambous, addresses the significance of language crossing, a sociolinguistic practice in which social actors (re)negotiate ethnolinguistic (and sometimes other) boundaries. The authors situate the study of crossing within the 'linguistics of contact' and they distinguish crossing from related polylingual phenomena: multi-ethnic vernaculars, codeswitching, codemixing and stylization. They also review the literature on crossing and note that, so far, it has principally focused on young people in working-class urban contexts, on mediated popular culture, and on keyed interactional moments such as artful performance and interpersonal verbal rituals. Rampton and Charalambous then look at crossing in a different type of keyed activity: that of 'technical redoings'. In this part of their chapter, the focus is on Cyprus and on interethnic tensions. They describe and analyse instances of crossing from Greek into Turkish in educational settings and show that, for many Greek speakers, Turkish is so strongly associated with ethnic rivalry that it can only be used if it is represented as a neutral lexico-grammatical code, thereby ideologically erasing its social indexicality.

Chapter 29, by Benjamin Bailey, explores how Bakhtin's notion of heteroglossia can be used to approach language diversity, including multilingualism, as inherently social and political. For Bakhtin, language is not a neutral, abstract system of reference but a medium through which one participates in a historical flow of social relationships, struggles and meanings. The chapter contrasts this perspective with the more formal Saussurean perspective, centring on synchronic, referential meaning, against which Bakhtin was reacting when he conceptualized heteroglossia. A brief, multilingual transcript is analysed to suggest how the perspective of heteroglossia can be used to connect forms with multilingual, multivariety talk to social identities and history.

Chapter 30, by Doris Warriner, provides an overview of research on multilingual literacies, spanning three decades of developments in this field. Warriner takes account of both empirical work and theory-building with regard to literacy among children, youth and adults in a range of multilingual contexts. Her starting point is with some of the first studies to view literacy as a social and cultural practice in the 1980s. She then traces different lines of inquiry that were developed in the 1990s, and in the past decade, and she discusses some of the key notions underpinning this research on multilingual literacy – notions such as funds of knowledge, ecologies of language and literacy and language and literacy ideologies. She also explores the ways in which this research has contributed to debates about language-in-education policy and to teacher awareness of the wider context for the literacy learning of linguistic minority students. In her final section, Warriner charts some of the new ways in which research in this field has been re-oriented in the wake of globalization. Here she draws on her own recent research on transnational literacies – research that takes account of global population flows and the ways in which literacy and identity trajectories can be traced across time and space. She also outlines developments in the highly topical research on literacy in digitally mediated communication and on the specific, situated ways in which young people in multilingual settings are drawing on their language and literacy resources as they engage with new technologies in an increasingly interconnected world.

In Chapter 31, Vally Lytra presents key issues of theory and method at the intersection of multilingualism and multimodality and reviews some of the recent literature on multilingualism using a multimodal lens. In particular, she explores the different ways in which multimodal semiotics (Kress and van Leeuwen 2001; Kress et al. 2005), the New Literacy Studies (e.g. studies in Pahl and Rowsell 2008; and in Warriner 2007) and sociolinguistics and linguistic anthropology (e.g. Goodwin 2000) have theoretically informed research that has incorporated ethnographic perspectives. Lytra then goes on to discuss some data from her own work, focusing on young multilingual boys' engagement with new media through their mobile phones in a Turkish complementary (community) school class, where the focus was on literacy on paper. Finally, she suggests areas for future research. These include new media, new technologies and classroom interaction.

Chapter 32, the concluding chapter, by Elana Shohamy, takes stock of developments over the last decade in the relatively new strand of sociolinguistic research on linguistic landscapes; that is, research into language displayed in different kinds of 'texts' found in public spaces (e.g. billboards, public signage, graffiti) and into the ways in which these texts can be 'read' as traces of social and cultural processes and as indexical of power asymmetries. Shohamy argues that the study of language displayed in public spaces provides a unique lens on multilingualism, on language hierarchies (that are imposed and/or contested) and on the symbolic value of different languages within local linguistic markets. Her survey of studies conducted over the last decade, in different multilingual settings, clearly attests to this. The survey covers research focusing on particular cities or neighbourhoods and research involving comparisons of different urban settings, including those undergoing considerable social, cultural or political change. Shohamy also touches on research that captures the impact of globalization and the global spread of English, and, in addition, she shows how research into script choice in public signage can reveal the ways in which group, or even national identities are represented or contested. The policy dimensions of linguistic landscaping are also explored in the chapter, with the focus being on studies of the relationship between official language policies and the multilingual realities of signage in different settings. In addition, Shohamy provides us with a synthesis of developments in theory and method in research on linguistic landscapes and she illustrates the interdisciplinarity and bold eclecticism of studies in this field. Her chapter captures the broad scope of this new field of study and the nature of the debates taking place within it.

Bibliography

Agha, A. and Wortham, S. (eds) (2005) 'Discourse across speech-events: Intertextuality and interdiscursivity in social life', *Journal of Linguistic Anthropology* 15(1) (special issue): 1–5.

Anderson, B. (1983) *Imagined Communities: Reflections on the Origin and Spread of Nationalism*, London: Verso.

Arthur, J. (1996) 'Codeswitching and collusion: Classroom interaction in Botswana primary schools', *Linguistics and Education*, 8(1): 17–33.

Auer, P. (1984) *Bilingual Conversation*, Amsterdam: John Benjamins.

——(1998) 'Introduction: Bilingual conversation revisited', in P. Auer (ed.) *Codeswitching in Conversation: Language, Interaction and Identity*, London: Routledge.

Bakhtin, M. M. (1981) *The Dialogic Imagination: Four Essays*, Michael Holquist (ed.), C. Emerson and M. Holquist (trans.), Austin: University of Texas Press.

Barton, D. and Tusting, K. (2005) 'Introduction', in D. Barton and K. Tusting (eds) *Beyond Communities of Practice: Language, Power and Social Context*, Cambridge: Cambridge University Press.

Bauman, R. and Briggs, C. (1990) 'Poetics and performance as critical perspectives on language and social life'. *Annual Review of Anthropology*, 19: 59–88.

Baynham, M. and da Fina, A. (2005) *Dislocations/Relocations: Narratives of Displacement*, Manchester: St Jerome Publishing.

Blackledge, A. (2005) *Discourse and Power in a Multilingual World*, Amsterdam: John Benjamins.

Blackledge, A. and Creese, A. (2010) *Multilingualism: A Critical Perspective*, London: Continuum.

Blackledge, A. and Pavlenko, A. (2001) 'Negotiation of identities in multilingual contexts', *International Journal of Bilingualism*, 5(3): 243–59.

Blommaert, J. (ed.) (1999) *Language Ideological Debates*, Berlin: Mouton de Gruyter.

——(2006) *Ethnography Fieldwork: A Beginner's Guide*. Draft. Available online at www.jyu.fi/hum/laitokset/kielet/fidipro/en/courses/fieldwork-text

——(2008) 'Bernstein and poetics revisited: Voice, globalization and education', *Discourse & Society* 19: 425–51.

——(2010) *The Sociolinguistics of Globalization*, Cambridge, Cambridge University Press.

Blommaert, J. and Rampton, B. (forthcoming) 'Language and superdiversity', *Diversities,* www. unesco.org/diversities (online journal).

Bloomfield, L. (1933) *Language*, London: George, Allen and Unwin.

Bonacina, F. (forthcoming) 'Ideologies and the issue of access in multilingual school ethnography: a French example', in S. Gardner and M. Martin-Jones (eds) *Multilingualism, Discourse and Ethnography*, New York: Routledge.

Bourdieu, P. (1977) *Outline of a Theory of Practice*, Cambridge: Cambridge University Press.

——(1982) *Ce Que Parler Veut Dire*, Paris: Fayard.

——(1991) *Language and Symbolic Power*, Cambridge: Polity Press.

Budach, G. (2009) 'Multilingual education in Germany: Discourses, practices and experiences from a two-way immersion project', in M. E. Torres-Guzmán and J. Gomez (eds) *Imagining Multilingual Schools: Global Perspectives on Language in Education,* New York: Teachers College Press.

Canagarajah, A. S. (2001) 'Constructing hybrid colonial subjects: codeswitching in Jaffna classrooms', in M. Heller and M. Martin-Jones (eds) *Voices of Authority: Education and Linguistic Difference*, Westport, CT: Ablex,

Cavalcanti, M. (1996) 'Collusion, resistance and reflexivity: Indigenous teacher education in Brazil', *Linguistics and Education* 8(2): 175–88.

Chimbutane, F. S. (2011) *Rethinking Bilingual Education in Post-Colonial Contexts*, Clevedon: Multilingual Matters.

Cincotta-Segi, A. (2011) 'Signalling L2 centrality, maintaining L1 dominance: teacher language choice in an ethnic minority primary classroom in the Lao PDR', *Language and Education* 25(1): 19–31.

Creese, A. (2005) 'Mediating allegations of racism in a multiethnic London school: What speech communities and communities of practice can tell us about discourse and power', in D. Barton and K. Tusting (eds) *Beyond Communities of Practice: Language, Power and Social Context*, Cambridge: Cambridge University Press.

Creese, A. and Blackledge, A. (2010) 'Translanguaging in the bilingual classroom: A pedagogy for learning and teaching', *Modern Language Journal* 94(2): 103–15.

Eckert, P. and McConnell-Ginet, S. (1992) 'Think practically and look locally: Language and gender as community-based practice', *Annual Review of Anthropology* 21: 461–90.

Eisenhart, M. (2001a) 'Educational ethnography past, present and future: Ideas to think with', *Educational Researcher*, 30(8) 16–27.

Eisenhart, M. (2001b) 'Changing conceptions of culture and ethnographic methodology: Recent thematic shifts and their implications for research on teaching, in V. Richardson (ed.) *Handbook of Research on Teaching. 4th Edition*, Washington, DC: American Educational Research Association.

Erickson, F. (1990), 'Qualitative Methods', in R. L. Linn and F. Erickson (eds) *Research in Teaching and Learning*, vol. 2, New York: Macmillan.

Errington, J. J. (1998) *Shifting Languages: Interaction and Identity in Javanese Indonesia*, Cambridge: Cambridge University Press.

——(2008) *Linguistics in a Colonial World: A Story of Language, Meaning and Power*, Oxford: Blackwell.

Fabian, J. (1986) *Language and Colonial Power*, Berkeley, CA: University of California Press.

Fairclough, N. (1989) *Language and Power*, London: Longman.

——(2006) *Language and Globalization*, London: Routledge.

Gafaranga, J. (2001) 'Language identities in talk-in-interaction: Order in bilingual conversation', *Journal of Pragmatics* 33: 1901–25.

Gal, S. (1979) *Language Shift*, New York: Academic Press.

Gal, S. (1989) 'Language and political economy', *Annual Review of Anthropology* 18: 345–67.

Gal, S. (2006) 'Migration, minorities and multilingualism: Language ideologies in Europe', in C. Mar-Molinero and P. Stevenson (eds) *Language Ideologies, Policies and Practices: Language and the Future of Europe*, Basingstoke: Palgrave Macmillan.

Gal, S. and Irvine, J. (1995) 'The boundaries of languages and disciplines: How ideologies construct difference', *Social Research* 62: 967–1001.

Gal, S. and Woolard, K. A. (1995) 'Constructing languages and publics: Authority and representation', *Pragmatics* 5: 155–66.

Gal, S. and Woolard, K. A. (eds) (2001) *Languages and Publics: The Making of Authority*, Manchester: St Jerome Publishing.

García, O. (2007). 'Foreword', in S. Makoni and A. Pennycook (eds) *Disinventing and Reconstituting Languages,* Clevedon: Multilingual Matters.

García, O. (2009). *Bilingual Education in the 21st Century: A Global Perspective*, Oxford: Wiley-Blackwell.

Goodwin, C. (2000) 'Action and embodiment within situated human interaction', *Journal of Pragmatics* 32: 1621–49.

Gumperz, J. J. (1962) 'Types of linguistic communities', *Anthropological Linguistics* 4(1): 28–40.

Gumperz, J. J. (1982) *Discourse Strategies.* Cambridge, Cambridge University Press.

——(1972) 'Introduction', in J. J. Gumperz and D. Hymes (eds) *Directions in Sociolinguistics: The Ethnography of Communication*, New York: Holt, Rinehart and Winston.

Gumperz, J. J. and Hymes, D. (eds) (1972) *Directions in Sociolinguistics: The Ethnography of Communication*, New York: Holt, Rinehart and Winston.

Hanks, W. F. (1996) *Language and Communicative Practices*, Boulder, CO: Westview Press.

Harris, R. (2006) *New Ethnicities and Language Use*, Basingstoke: Palgrave Macmillan.

Hechter, M. (1975) *Internal Colonialism: The Celtic Fringe in British National Development*, London: Routledge and Kegan Paul.

Hebdige, D. (1979) *Sub-Culture: The Meaning of Style*, London: Methuen.

Heller, M. (ed.) (1988) *Codeswitching: Anthropological and Sociolinguistic Perspectives*, Berlin: Mouton de Gruyter.

——(1992) 'The politics of codeswitching and language choice', *Journal of Multilingual and Multicultural Development* 3: 1–13.

——(1994) *Crosswords: Language, Education and Ethnicity in French Ontario*, Berlin: Mouton de Gruyter.

——(1995a) 'Language choice, social institutions and symbolic domination', *Language in Society* 24(3): 373–405.

——(1995b) 'Codeswitching and the politics of language', in L. Milroy and P. Muysken (eds) *One Speaker, Two Languages: Cross Disciplinary Perspectives on Codeswitching*, Cambridge: Cambridge University Press.

——(1999) *Linguistic Minorities and Modernity*, London: Longman.

——(ed.) (2007) *Bilingualism: A Social Approach*, Basingstoke: Palgrave Macmillan.

——(2011) *Paths to Post-Nationalism: A Critical Ethnography of Language and Identity*, Oxford: Oxford University Press.

Heller, M. and Duchêne, A. (2007) 'Discourses of endangerment: Sociolinguistics, globalization, and social order', in A. Duchêne and M. Heller (eds) *Discourses of Endangerment: Ideology and Interests in the Defence of Languages*, London: Continuum.

Heller, M. and Martin-Jones, M. (2001) *Voices of Authority: Education and Linguistic Difference*, Westport, CT: Ablex.

Hornberger, N. (1994) 'Ethnography', in A. Cumming (ed.) 'Alternatives in TESOL research: Descriptive, interpretive and ideological orientation', *TESOL Quarterly* 28, (4): 688–90.

Hinnenkamp, V. (2003) 'Mixed language varieties of migrant adolescents and the discourse of hybridity', in J. N. Jørgensen (ed.) *Bilingualism and Social Change: Turkish Speakers in North Western Europe*, Clevedon: Multilingual Matters.

Hobsbawm, E. (1990) 'Introduction: inventing traditions', in E. Hobsbawm and T. Ranger (eds) *The Invention of Tradition*, Cambridge. Cambridge University Press.

Huss, L. (1999) *Reversing Language Shift in the Far North: Linguistic Revitalization in Northern Scandinavia and Finland*, Uppsala: Studia Uralica Upsaliensia.

Hymes, D. (1968) 'The ethnography of speaking', in J. Fishman (ed.) *Readings in the Sociology of Language*, The Hague: Mouton.

——(1974) *Foundations in Sociolinguistics: An Ethnographic Approach*, Philadelphia: University of Pennsylvania Press.

——(1996) *Ethnography, Linguistics, Narrative Inequality: Towards an Understanding of Voice.* London: Taylor & Francis.

Jaffe, A. (1999) *Ideologies in Action: Language Politics on Corsica*, Berlin: Mouton de Gruyter.

——(2007) 'Minority language movements', in M. Heller (ed.) *Bilingualism: A Social Approach*, Basingstoke: Palgrave Macmillan.

Jones, K. (2000) 'Becoming just another alphanumeric code: Farmers' encounters with the literacy and discourse practices of agricultural bureaucracy at the livestock auction', in D. Barton, M. Hamilton and R. Ivanič (eds) *Situated Literacies: Reading and Writing in Context*, London: Routledge.

Jørgensen, J. N. (2003) 'Linguistic construction and negotiation of relations among bilingual Turkish-speaking adolescents in north-western Europe', in J. N. Jørgensen (ed.) *Bilingualism and Social Change: Turkish Speakers in North Western Europe*, Clevedon: Multilingual Matters.

Joseph, J. E. and Taylor, T. J. (eds) (1990) *Ideologies of Language*, London: Routledge.

Kanno, Y. (2008) *Language and Education in Japan: Unequal Access to Bilingualism*, Basingstoke: Palgrave Macmillan.

Kress, G. and van Leeuwen, T. (2001) *Multimodal Discourse: The Modes and Media of Contemporary Communication*, London: Edward Arnold.

Kress, G., Jewitt, C., Bourne, J., Franks, A., Hardcastle, J., Jones, K. and Reid, E. (2005) *English in Urban Classrooms: Multimodal Perspectives on Teaching and Learning*, London: Routledge/Falmer.

Kroskrity, P. V. (ed.) (2000) *Regimes of Language: Ideologies, Polities, and Identities*, Santa Fe, NM: School of American Research Press.

Labov, W. (1972) *Sociolinguistic Patterns*, Oxford: Blackwell.

Lave, J. and Wenger, E. (1991) *Situated Learning: Legitimate Peripheral Participation*, Cambridge: Cambridge University Press.

Li W. (1994) *Three Generations, Two Languages, One Family*, Clevedon: Multilingual Matters.

——(1998) 'The 'why' and 'how' questions in the analysis of conversational codeswitching', in P. Auer (ed.) *Codeswitching in Conversation: Language, Interaction and Identity*, London: Routledge.

Lin, A. M. Y. (1996) 'Bilingualism or linguistic segregation? Symbolic domination, resistance and codeswitching in Hong Kong schools', *Linguistics and Education* 8(2): 49–84.

Luk, J. C. M. and Lin, A. M. Y. (2007) *Classroom Interactions as Cross-Cultural Encounters: Native Speakers in EFL Classroom*, Mahwah, NJ: Lawrence Erlbaum.

Lyons, J. (1970) *New Horizons in Linguistics*, Harmondsworth: Penguin.

McCarty, T. (2004) 'Dangerous difference: a critical-historical analysis of language education policies in the United States', in J. W. Tollefson and A. B. M. Tsui (eds) *Medium of Instruction Policies: Which Agenda? Whose Agenda?*, Mahwah, NJ: Lawrence Erlbaum.

——(ed.) (2005) (2005). *Language, Literacy, and Power in Schooling*, Mahwah, NJ: Lawrence Erbaum.

——(2011) 'Introducing ethnography and language policy', in T. McCarty (ed.) *Ethnography and Language Policy*, New York: Routledge.

Moyer, M. and Martin Rojo, L. (2007) 'Language, migration and citizenship: New challenges in the regulation of bilingualism', in M. Heller (ed.) *Bilingualism: A Social Approach*, Basingstoke: Palgrave.

MacLure, M. (2003) *Discourse in Educational and Social Research*, Buckingham: Open University Press.

Makoni, S. and Mashiri, P. (2007) 'Critical historiography: Does language planning in Africa need a construct of language as part of its theoretical apparatus?', in S. Makoni and A. Pennycook (eds) *Disinventing and Reconstituting Languages*, Clevedon: Multilingual Matters.

Makoni, S. and Pennycook, A. (eds) (2007) *Disinventing and Reconstituting Languages*, Clevedon: Multilingual Matters.

Martin-Jones, M. (2007) 'Bilingualism, education and the regulation of access to language resources' in M. Heller (ed.) *Bilingualism: A Social Approach*, Basingstoke: Palgrave Macmillan.

Martin-Jones, M. and Jones, K. (eds) (2000) *Multilingual Literacies: Reading and Writing Different Worlds*, Amsterdam: John Benjamins.

May, S. (2001) *Language and Minority Rights: Ethnicity, Nationalism and the Politics of Language*. London: Longman.

——(2005)'Language rights: Moving the debate forward', *Journal of Sociolinguistics* 9/(3): 319–47.

Pahl, K. and Rowsell, J. (eds) (2008) *Travel Notes from the New Literacy Studies*, Clevedon: Multilingual Matters.

Patrick, D. (2003) *Language, Politics, and Social Interaction in an Inuit Community*, Berlin: Mouton de Gruyter.

Pavlenko, A. and Blackledge, A. (2004) 'Introduction: New theoretical approaches to the study of negotiation of identities in multilingual contexts', in A. Pavlenko and A. Blackledge (eds) *Negotiation of Identities in Multilingual Contexts*, Clevedon: Multilingual Matters.

Pennycook, A. (2001) *Critical Applied Linguistics*, Mahwah, NJ: Lawrence Erlbaum.

——(2010) *Language as a Local Practice*, London: Routledge.

Pratt, M. L. (1987) 'Linguistic utopias', in N. Fabb, D. Attridge, A. Durant and C. MacCabe (eds) *The Linguistics of Writing: Arguments Between Language and Literature*, Manchester: Manchester University Press.

——(1991) 'Arts of the contact zone', *Profession* 91, New York: Modern Language Association.

Pujolar, J. (2001) *Gender, Heteroglossia and Power: A Sociolinguistic Study of Youth Culture*, Berlin: Mouton de Gruyter.

Rahman, T. (1997) *Language and Politics in Pakistan*, Oxford: Oxford University Press.

Rampton, B. (1990) 'Displacing the "native speaker": Expertise, affiliation and inheritance', *ELT Journal* 44(2): 97–101.

——(1995) *Crossing: Language and Ethnicity Among Adolescents*, London: Longman.

——(1999) 'Styling the Other: Introduction', *Journal of Sociolinguistics*, 3(4): 421–7.

——(2006) *Language in Late Modernity* Cambridge: Cambridge University Press.

Rasool, N. and Mansoor, S. (2007) 'Contemporary issues in language, education and development in Pakistan', in N. Rasool (ed.) *Global Issues in Language, Education and Development: Perspectives from Postcolonial Countries*, Clevedon: Multilingual Matters.

Schieffelin, B. B., Woolard, K. A. and Kroskrity, P. V. (eds) (1998) *Language Ideologies: Practice and Theory*, Oxford: Oxford University Press.

Sebba, M. (1993) *London Jamaican*, London: Longman.

Silverstein, M. (2003) 'Indexical order and the dialectics of sociolinguistic life', *Language and Communication* 23: 193–229.

Stroud, C. (1999) 'Portuguese as ideology and politics in Mozambique: semiotic (re)constructions of a post-colony', in J. Blommaert (ed.) (1999) *Language Ideological Debates*, Berlin: Mouton de Gruyter.

——(2007) 'Bilingualism: colonialism and postcolonialism', in M. Heller (ed.) *Bilingualism: A Social Approach*, Basingstoke: Palgrave Macmillan.

Tusting, K. (2005) 'Language and power in communities of practice', in D. Barton and K. Tusting (eds) *Beyond Communities of Practice: Language, Power and Social Context*, Cambridge: Cambridge University Press.

Urla, J. (1993) 'Cultural politics in an age of statistics: numbers, nations, and the making of a Basque identity', *American Ethnologist* 20(1): 818–43.

Vertovec, S. (2006) *The Emergence of Super-Diversity in Britain*, Centre on Migration, Policy and Society, Working Paper No. 25, Oxford, University of Oxford.

——(2007a) 'Super-diversity and its implications', *Ethnic and Racial Studies*, 30(6): 1024–54.

——(2007b) 'Introduction: New directions in the anthropology of migration and multiculturalism'. *Ethnic and Racial Studies* 30(6): 961–78.

——(2009) *Transnationalism*, London: Routledge.

Warriner, D. (ed.) (2007) 'Transnational literacies: immigration, language learning, and identity', *Linguistics and Education* 18 (special issue): 201–14.

Wenger, E. (1998) *Communities of Practice: Learning, Meaning and Identity*, Cambridge: Cambridge University Press.

Wiley, T. (2005) 'Discontinuities in heritage and community language education: Challenges for educational language policies', *International Journal of Bilingual Education and Bilingualism* 8(2&3): 222–9.

Willis, P. (1977) *Learning to Labour: How Working Class Kids Get Working Class Jobs*, Farnborough: Saxon House.

Woolard, K. A. (1985) 'Language variation and cultural hegemony: Towards an integration of sociolinguistics and social theory', *American Ethnologist* 12: 38–48.

——(1989) *Double Talk: Bilingualism and the Politics of Ethnicity in Catalonia*, Stanford: Stanford University Press.

——(1998) 'Language ideology as a field of inquiry', in B. B. Schieffelin, K. A. Woolard and P. V. Kroskrity (eds) *Language Ideologies: Practice and Theory*, Oxford: Oxford University Press.

Wortham, S. (2001) 'Ventriloquating Shakespeare: Ethical positioning in classroom literature discussions', *Working Papers in Educational Linguistics*, (Graduate School of Education, University of Pennsylvania) 17(1–2): 47–64.

Zentella, A. C. (1997) *Growing up Bilingual: Puerto Rican Children in New York*, Oxford: Blackwell.

Part I

Discourses about multilingualism, across political and historical contexts

1

Indigenous contexts

Donna Patrick

Introduction

Since the latter half of the twentieth century, we have come to take for granted a category of people called 'Indigenous', with distinctive collective rights and identities. Yet, Indigenous peoples themselves have, of course, been around for millennia, each group developing its own legal, cultural and economic systems. Central to maintaining this distinctiveness has been the use of languages in pursuing trade and maintaining relations between groups across time and space. Language has also been linked to changing cultural practices internal to Indigenous communities, as people have engaged with modernity in diverse ways, creating and reflecting religious, economic and other institutional transformations. As Indigenous identities develop on a global scale and Indigenous engagements with nation-states continue, the role of language in maintaining local identities and in accessing and participating in discourses of power, social transformation and resistance becomes crucial.

This chapter will approach the topic of multilingualism in Indigenous contexts by examining the ways in which Indigenous multilingualism has figured in the neighbouring disciplines of linguistics, anthropology, social psychology and education. This will involve examining the theoretical underpinnings and methodological practices of these disciplines and tracing the implications of research across these fields both for understanding Indigenous multilingualism and for applying this understanding to policy and other spheres. The perspective on Indigenous language contexts that will emerge is one that highlights the historical continuity of Indigenous multilingual practices as well as contemporary social and political realities of Indigenous communities and language use. In other words, this perspective will reveal the importance of studying language use among Indigenous groups before as well as after the onset of colonization, global capitalism, the intervention of the nation-state and other engagements of Indigenous groups with modernity.

The body of this chapter will begin by first addressing the complexity of the notion of 'Indigenous groups'. Of particular importance here are how this notion differs from that of 'linguistic minorities'; what contexts of language use and what language practices are uniquely Indigenous; and how historical, political and economic power relations have shaped these contexts and practices. The chapter will then turn to a review of early developments in the study of Indigenous languages. This will include discussion of the work of early linguists in developing language typologies and in tracing 'genetic' relations between Indigenous languages and groups, and the subsequent rise of the Boasian and structuralist traditions in North American linguistics and anthropology. The chapter will then offer a historical analysis of Indigenous multilingualism itself. Drawing primarily on examples from the North American context, it will consider how and why multilingualism developed among Indigenous groups in North America both before and after their contact with Europeans, and offer a critical perspective on descriptive approaches to Indigenous multilingualism. After addressing these questions, it will examine contemporary approaches to the study of multilingualism in Indigenous contexts, focusing on the role of quantifiable and descriptive survey methods, explanatory and ethnographic approaches to research, and critical and Indigenous-centred theoretical frameworks in the study of Indigenous multilingualism.

Finally, the chapter will take up the question of how Indigenous languages have recently gained prominence in Indigenous and other discourses of language rights and language survival and how and why Indigenous groups have mobilized around language in their struggles for political and cultural recognition. It will conclude with a brief discussion of potential policy implications of Indigenous multilingualism and directions for future research in the study of this area.

What is an 'Indigenous' group?

Indigenous groups and the term 'Indigenous'

In order to address multilingualism in Indigenous contexts, we first need to be clear about what we mean by an 'Indigenous' people or group. Significantly, 'Indigenous' is a transnational category created in the twentieth century, which has gained rapid currency in social, political, economic and legal domains. In this section, we shall examine this category and the rise of 'Indigeneity' as a global movement as well as the associated interest in Indigenous languages globally. We shall also examine the implications of this internationalization for Indigenous language speakers at both national and local levels. Crucially, Indigeneity has no 'unified trajectory': it is not 'a singular ideology, program, or movement, and its politics resist closure' (de la Cadena and Starn 2007: 4). Nor is Indigeneity isolated from other ideologies and movements – for political recognition, self-determination, socio-economic development, and cultural and linguistic 'survival'.

A basic observation that we can make is that Indigenous peoples are survivors of colonialism and resource exploitation on territories that they have occupied since 'time immemorial'. Their traditional subsistence-based communities and land-based economies have been threatened by states seeking political, economic and territorial control. In addition, their traditional cultural, linguistic, and spiritual practices and knowledge have at times been appropriated by others and otherwise demonized and threatened by proselytizing and cultural assimilation. They are groups that strive for recognition of their sovereignty, including the right to self-determination and to culturally and linguistically distinct forms of education, spirituality, justice, economic development and governance (Niezen 2003).

One way to understand Indigenous peoples as a group is in terms of the 'narrative elements' of Indigeneity described by Pratt (2007: 401), which include (1) 'unsolicited encounter', where Indigenous subjects are on the 'receiving end of an encounter [they] did not seek'; (2) 'dispossession', through conquest or settler colonialism, which involves losing control of one's land base and thus the need to sell one's labour; (3) 'perdurance', the continuation of a self-identifying collectivity through relations of exploitation, which is necessary to justify the 'distinct, nonequivalent group'; (4) 'proselytization', crucial to an ongoing 'asymmetrical engagement'; and (5) 'unpayable debt', which unfolds in the relationships embodied in Indigeneity.

Of course, the term 'Indigenous' itself is a non-Indigenous creation. Moreover, as Pratt explains,

> '[I]ndigenous' is rarely if ever the primary identity of [I]ndigenous people. One is first Maori, Cree, Hmong, Aymara, Dayak, Kung, Quiché or Adivasi and one claims [I]ndigeneity by virtue of that (temporally and socially) prior self-identification.
>
> *(2007: 399)*

The term, in fact, has its origins in the United Nations, where it figured largely in human rights initiatives and in the 1957 International Labour Organization (ILO) Convention No. 107, 'Concerning the Protection and Integration of Indigenous and Other Tribal and Semi-Tribal Populations in Independent Countries'. Yet, the development of this notion took place with little input from Indigenous populations themselves; and 'few, if any, had developed a self-referential "[I]ndigenous" identity' (Niezen 2003: 4). The idea of self-referential identity as 'Indigenous' did, however, soon become part of a working definition of 'Indigenous peoples' (ILO Convention 169; Hughes 2003: 19), a definition that included a sense of 'shared experiences' and global relatedness. This definition has served to unite Indigenous peoples and distinguish them from other ethnic minorities.

In addition to an expression of identity, 'Indigenous' has also become a legal and analytical category. According to the definition given in ILO Convention No. 169, people are considered to be Indigenous

> on account of their descent from the populations which inhabited the country, or a geographical region to which the country belongs, at the time of conquest or colonisation or the establishment of present State boundaries and who, irrespective of their legal status, retain some or all of their own social, economic, cultural and political institutions.
>
> *(ILO 1989)*

The notions of colonization, original descent, and geographical and social continuity that figure in this definition are often closely associated with those of collective rights, which have represented a remedy to collective oppression, vulnerability and marginalization. Claims to such rights have been basic to struggles of Indigenous groups to gain recognition and sovereignty (territorial authority, self-determination or autonomy) and to win control over land and waterways and the resources on, and under, these (Niezen 2003: 18).

What is also becoming recognized as a key element of definitions of 'Indigenous' is Indigenous language practices. But these practices must be seen to include not only those related to the traditional language of a particular group, but also multilingual practices. Such practices have arisen as dominant (often colonial) languages have entered into competition with Indigenous ones; or where migration, sometimes forced, has led to the interaction of Indigenous and other languages, creating new ways of speaking in new social contexts. During such interactions, Indigenous languages, like the cultures and peoples themselves, have been vulnerable to institutional and social processes of assimilation – although assimilation has, in many cases, not actually occurred – and to dispossession and state violence. State violence has included symbolic violence (Bourdieu and Passeron 1990: 4), whereby power has been legitimized in meanings institutionally produced and reproduced through everyday practices of negative stereotyping, derogatory labelling, and the devaluing of Indigenous languages and epistemologies.

These processes, along with disease and famine, drastically reduced Indigenous populations in the decades following contact, although Indigenous populations have been growing steadily in the twentieth and twenty-first centuries (Smith 2007). In fact, Indigenous languages and cultures have been remarkably resilient despite assimilation, dispossession and state violence. Although exact numbers are difficult to determine with any precision, the number of Indigenous societies is thought to be between 4,000 and 7,000, and, according to the UN, the world's Indigenous population is over 370 million. Aside from these numbers, many Indigenous groups have maintained their social and political institutions, and as just suggested, their cultural and linguistic practices have in many cases experienced a resurgence, even in the face of state and global pressures. Moreover, Indigenous linguistic practices turn out to be far richer than is often assumed, having long included various forms of multilingualism. It is these multilingual practices that are the focus of the rest of this chapter.

Some questions about Indigeneity and multilingual practices

The theoretical and methodological concern with multilingualism and multilingual practices raises some key research questions about the interaction of multilingualism and Indigeneity. These include such questions as how Indigenous languages and multilingualism became objects of study; how researchers of language and culture have approached Indigenous languages in multilingual contexts; and how contemporary research of Indigenous multilingualism can shed light on the engagement of Indigenous groups with global capitalism, neo-liberalism and modernity more generally. Such investigations also include the question of how such research impinges on Indigenous groups themselves, particularly given the concerns that Indigenous people have raised about the potential for both the research process and research results to have negative impacts on Indigenous political, economic and cultural well-being (see e.g. Smith 1999).

I shall be approaching these broad questions as follows. First, I shall be examining early developments in the field and how scholars approached Indigenous contexts in the development of linguistic and ethnographic study. These include late nineteenth-century and twentieth-century European investigations into language classification and twentieth-century American anthropological-linguistic approaches. I shall then consider historical perspectives on Indigenous multilingualism, with a focus on North America and Canada, in particular. All of these approaches and perspectives have set the stage for contemporary examinations and understandings of Indigenous groups' linguistic diversity, which I shall be discussing in the latter sections of the chapter.

Early developments in the field

Language typologies and comparative-historical linguistics

Indigenous languages, diverse and grammatically complex, have long been the objects of comparative-historical linguistic research, an approach to language study that blossomed in the nineteenth century. This approach focused on the 'phyletic' relations between languages (how languages are related to each other in terms of their 'evolutionary' development) and the 'proto-languages' (hypothesized original or ancestral languages) from which they were seen to derive. It involved documenting individual languages, as discrete objects of study, and placing them within language families, in order to determine how languages were related. This tradition of comparative-historical research has been seen as aiming 'to discover and maintain' the unity of humankind 'in the phenomena of language' by 'seek[ing] a unity of origin in the past' (Hymes 1974: 209). In the North American context, this approach was applied to Indigenous languages, which were carefully documented and analysed by the intellectual descendants of the European comparative-historical linguists, who were in fact continuing work initiated centuries before by missionaries. Most prominent among these linguists were Franz Boas (1858–1942), who brought the European tradition to North America and influenced a generation of North American linguists and anthropologists, and Boas's student Edward Sapir (1889–1939).

Boas and his students, in describing and documenting Indigenous languages, saw them as equal to European languages in complexity and cultural specificity and as worthy of study for their own sake. Such study led not only to the publication of grammars, including the four-volume *Handbook of American Indian Languages* (1911–41), but also to the pursuit of the more rarefied goal of understanding the general 'laws' of culture that united humankind. Anthropologists following in the footsteps of Boas collaborated with Indigenous informants and collected texts describing myths, legends and other narratives in addition to grammatical information. Although they made little space for understanding or documenting multi-lingualism, as I shall be explaining in the following section, their work did pave the way for more nuanced comparative work in linguistic and cultural systems. Such work included cognitive anthropology and linguistic research that embraced the idea of 'linguistic relativity', according to which language played a key role in shaping thought and structuring human cognition.

Language and ethnography

As just mentioned, the work of documenting and describing the Indigenous languages in North America was basic to the research of linguists and anthropologists starting in the late nineteenth century. As it happens, this work gave rise to the research programme of structural linguistics in the twentieth century – research that had a similar goal of seeking 'unity' within and across languages, but rather than hypothesize a 'proto'-language, the goals were to uncover the abstract linguistic structure hypothesized to exist in all of the world's languages. A key figure in this research programme was Leonard Bloomfield (1887–1949), who is generally credited with leading the development of this programme. Needless to say, the autonomous, abstract linguistic systems posited as 'languages' for study left little room for more messy, mixed multilingual practices of actual Indigenous speakers.

Structuralism, and its view of languages as autonomous systems worthy of study in themselves, dominated linguistic research in the early decades of the twentieth century. Yet, by mid-century, as noted below by Hymes, the limits of this research paradigm for the investigation of the linguistic practices of Indigenous communities were becoming clear, and the 1950s and 1960s saw the development of sociolinguistics and a return to ethnography in the study of Indigenous languages. This shift led to new kinds of research questions, related to the pragmatics of language use, language variation among speakers, language maintenance and shift, language and educational practice and policy, and the role of culture and political economic processes in these.

The limits of structuralism and the need for sociological and ethnographic methods to explain the linguistic practices were famously noted by Hymes (1974: 71). White Thunder, an Indigenous speaker of Menomini from Wisconsin, had been previously described by Bloomfield – in language that today is difficult not to be seen as arrogant, ignorant and offensive. White Thunder's language had been observed by Bloomfield, leading him to remark that he spoke less English than Menomini, and that is a strong indictment, for his Menomini is atrocious. His vocabulary is small; his inflections are often barbarous; he constructs sentences of a few threadbare models. He may be said to speak no language tolerably.

(cited in Hymes 1974: 71)

What Hymes recognized about this description of White Thunder's bilingual speech was that it was consistent with structuralism's analysis of language into discrete linguistic 'systems'. This left no room for the possibility of bilingual mixed-code speech or multiple contexts of language use or for the notion of a bilingual 'communicative competence'. The pragmatics of how the language was actually used in communication was not part of a structuralist view of language. In other words, Bloomfield had formed his opinion of White Thunder's speech only from attempting to elicit grammatical forms from him. Moreover, White Thunder was not the only member of this community who spoke 'no' language in its complete form: as Hymes points out, Bloomfield noted that other speakers spoke the same kind of 'threadbare language' as White Thunder did.

Yet, Bloomfield's assumptions about the nature of language had not allowed him to entertain the possibility that in other contexts of language use, White Thunder might have communicated effectively, using what linguistic resources he had at his disposal. Indeed, investigation of language use in a variety of social and cultural domains certainly reveals contexts in which full communication is effected through mixed language or morphologically or syntactically reduced forms. Although Hymes did not discuss this, it is also clear that, once we adopt a more nuanced, sociologically informed perspective on language, the particular forms of Menomini and English used by this speaker suddenly become worthy of investigation themselves. The questions that they pose for research then become how they reflect not an 'atrocious' semilingualism, but bi- and multilingual competence, and how the historical, social and cultural circumstances gave rise to them in the first place. Investigation of such circumstances, which include social, political and economic influences, all of which have had a great impact on Indigenous language use, can thus help us to understand the multiple forms of Indigenous multilingualism.

Hymes's ethnographically oriented work set the stage for the research programme in linguistic anthropology known as the 'ethnography of communication' or the 'ethnography of speaking'. The focus of such research, which encompasses work both within and across cultures, has been in the 'pragmatic' domain, specifying aspects of language use in broader and narrower communicative contexts. Research undertaken within this programme has addressed a range of questions related to Indigenous contexts, which will be discussed further in the section on ethnography in our discussion of contemporary theory and methods.

What our discussion has highlighted so far, is the usefulness found in contrasting ethnographically oriented research with more linguistically oriented research. The latter focuses on the often dramatic grammatical, phonological and morphological changes occurring in situations of language contact; whereas the former examines the cultural, economic and institutional domains in Indigenous communities in which more powerful languages encounter less powerful ones. I shall have more to say about these and other approaches to Indigenous language practices, including those coming from the disciplines of social psychology, education and policy studies, later in the chapter.

However, before embarking on further discussion of theoretical and methodological approaches, it might be worth returning to the discussion of Indigeneity that began this chapter. In this way, we can see how the insights about language practices that flow from that discussion can inform our understanding of the forms and continuity of multilingualism, within and between Indigenous groups and across time and space.

Historical perspectives

Indigenous language practices pre- and post-contact

Earlier, I noted that an understanding of Indigenous peoples must include an understanding of the term 'Indigenous' itself; and that a key part of the latter involved a recognition of the historical processes that have shaped their economic, cultural and linguistic practices. Given this chapter's focus on Indigenous language practices, it is worth exploring the historical dimension of these practices, and in particular examine the form that they took both before and after contact with encroaching states and with the European-dominant world economic system. These practices encompass phenomena such as mixed languages, bilingualism and multi-lingualism, which over the years have developed and been transformed in ways consistent with changing political and economic arrangements, and with socio-economic and cultural patterns of language use. The examples that I shall be drawing on to illustrate my discussion will be from North America, where colonial relationships were rooted in trade and the multilingualism necessary to achieve this. Similar patterns, however, may also be found on other continents and in other locales.

I shall begin this historical examination of Indigenous multilingualism in North America with the role of language in trade relationships. One place where this role is particularly easy to observe is the northwest coast of British Columbia. It was there that James Cook arrived in 1778, encountering the Mowachaht people on what has come to be known as Nootka Island. Cook wrote in his diary that the first word that these people uttered when he first met them was 'Makook', as he spelled it. This word meant 'let's trade', including in its meaning both 'buying' and 'selling' or 'exchange' (Lutz 2008: ix–x). From 1778 to the late 1790s, this coastal region in what is now British Columbia was the centre of European trade in the area. Every trading vessel stopped there – including ones from Spain, which led to the establishment of a Spanish settlement there (2008: ix). Trade shaped the encounters between the Europeans and the Indigenous peoples they met, as the Europeans sought wealth and resources for further exchange in Europe.

Although these encounters might have resulted in the first records of multilingual practices involving Indigenous peoples, such practices, and the vast networks of Indigenous trade that supported them, existed long before any Europeans arrived to write about them. Despite the lack of written records, other evidence exists that Indigenous multilingualism characterized social relations between various autonomous societies dependent on trade for survival. Although certain Western ideologies have taken languages and cultures to represent discrete systems and thus conjure up images of static and culturally and linguistically closed Indigenous groups, bi- and multilingualism appear to have flourished among Indigenous communities, indicating the dynamic nature of these communities and the relatively porous boundaries between them. The multilingual practices in which these communities engaged included the use of multilingual interpreters, lingua francas and trade jargons, and mixed languages, and the circumstances giving rise to these practices included exogamous marriage, trade and capture in conflicts. I shall discuss examples of each of these practices in the following section.

The role of interpreters as 'bilingual brokers'

One well-documented multilingual practice among Indigenous communities was the use of interpreters, who were needed to negotiate and interact with neighbouring groups. Of course, interpreters were also needed after European contact. Thus, in what is now British Columbia,

'wise chiefs' would send 'a son to learn a colonial or missionary language of the Europeans …
apparently following an [I]ndigenous pattern of training interpreters among political elites'
(Silverstein 1996: 121). This form of language education persisted in the region into the
twentieth century, although it came to involve educating a son or daughter in Western law,
politics and English, in order to advance Indigenous claims to sovereignty.

In many cases, Indigenous interpreters were women. However, these interpreters had not
been singled out for language learning to fulfil their roles as members of Indigenous elites.
Instead, they had often been taken prisoner or married off into another language group. It is
likely that these linguistic interpreters were as valuable before European contact as after it
(Miller 2004), although there is obviously more documentary evidence of their role in the latter
case. Throughout the eighteenth and nineteenth centuries, for example, women played a prominent role as interpreters in trade and as language teachers and diplomats for the Hudson's
Bay Company, a vast fur-trading enterprise founded in 1670, and other fur traders in Canada
(Van Kirk 1980: 65), their multilingual skills often advancing European trade.

The existence of some of these interpreters was documented by European traders and
explorers. One such interpreter was Thanadelthur, the most 'outstanding female diplomat in
fur-trade history' (Van Kirk 1980: 66). She was 'a young Chipewyan woman, who acted as guide,
interpreter, and, peace negotiator' for James Knight, a Hudson's Bay Company Governor at
York Factory, an early settlement in what is now northeastern Manitoba (ibid.). Thanadelthur
had been captured by the Cree and held prisoner, and in this way learned the Cree language.
The Cree had been aligned with the Hudson's Bay Company post, and good communication
between the English and the Cree became possible as multilingualism arose. The Chipewyans,
however, had not entered into trade and were fearful of doing so, as the Cree had firearms
obtained through their trading relationship with the Europeans. Thanadelthur escaped from
the Cree in 1714 and headed to the Hudson's Bay Company post, where she was hired by
Knight to help bring the Chipewyans into trade. They mounted an expedition into Chipewyan
territory to convince the Chipewyans that they could trade at the post in peace, without
retaliation from the Cree. When Thanadelthur returned to the expedition camp, after going
along for ten days to find her people, she had a hoarse voice from negotiating and was
accompanied by over 100 Chipewyans (Van Kirk 1980: 69). Thanadelthur's multilingualism
thus turned out to play a crucial role in the expansion of westward trade in this period.

Another Indigenous interpreter was described by William Clark, of the renowned Lewis
and Clark expedition of 1803–6 (cited in Silverstein 1996: 118). Clark recalled that a Shoshone
boy 'had been taken prisoner by … the Tushepaws [also known as Flatheads, a Salishan
group], whose language he had acquired'. Clark was able to communicate with him by
speaking English to a French-speaking Euro-American, who relayed the message in French to
Toussaint Charbonneau, another member of the Lewis and Clark expedition. Charbonneau
then relayed the message in Minnetarée (or Hidatsa), a Siouan language, to his wife, the
famous Sacagawea, a Shoshone who had learnt this language during the time that she had
been held prisoner by the Hidatsa. Sacagawea then spoke to the boy in Shoshone.

These examples show how interpreters were key to European expansion and how their
multilingualism had developed from patterns of multilingual language acquisition embedded
in long-standing cultural, economic and political practices. Those Indigenous people who had
close relations with the traders became language learners and language teachers themselves.
This multilingualism, aligned with European power, was coupled with the multilingual practices
of those who had been captured by or had married into other groups. As Miller (2004: 11) notes,
'in both the pre-contact period and after the Europeans established themselves', Indigenous
groups 'frequently incorporated members of other nations into their body, particularly to

replace individuals lost to disease or warfare'. For some Indigenous nations, such as the Iroquois, those adopted into another group 'found themselves accepted completely as members of their adoptive nation' (ibid.) – a status that involved being fluent in the adoptive language and thus a potential interpreter.

These individual cases of multilingualism, however, were not the only forms of trade or diplomatic communication. Various others also developed, as I shall discuss in the next section.

Lingua francas, trade languages and mixed languages

In other Indigenous contexts, multilingual practices arose through the use of gestures (a kind of sign language); lingua francas, languages used as a common language between speakers of different languages; trade languages, simplified language varieties that arise in a trade context when no common language exists between speakers; and 'mixed languages', which arise from the languages of fluently bilingual speakers. These new ways of speaking were encountered and documented by Europeans who, in their quest for mercantile trade and colonies, needed to communicate with Indigenous peoples.

According to Campbell (1997) and other authors, a number of Indigenous languages were used as lingua francas across broad regions of North America (Campbell 1997: 24). Several of them came into existence after contact with Europeans (Silverstein 1996: 118), although some would have been in use pre-contact (Campbell 1997: 24). The geographical expansion of these languages was assisted by the fur trade and by European expansion across the continent. By the eighteenth and nineteenth centuries, the Algonquian language (also called Chippewa, Ojibwa, Saulteaux or Ottawa) had become one such lingua franca, used in the Great Lakes region.

Trade languages were also used by various Indigenous groups for facilitating relationships between speakers of mutually unintelligible languages. Trade languages each had different historical trajectories and their use may have peaked at different times. Some of these languages, such as 'Eskimo trade jargon', were pidgins, grammatically and lexically reduced (second) languages. 'Eskimo trade jargon' had two distinct varieties: one, called 'ships' jargon', arose with the arrival of European whalers; the other may have been used solely by Indigenous peoples. These two varieties are described by Stefánsson:

> Among the Mackenzie River Eskimo there is, beside the ships' jargon, a more highly developed one used in dealing with Athabaska Indians around Fort Arctic, Red River, and Fort Macpherson. ... It has probably more than twice as extensive a vocabulary as the ships' variety and is so different from it that some white men who know the ships' jargon have employed as interpreters Loucheux Indians under the impression that the Indians spoke real Eskimo.
>
> *(Stefánsson 1909: 218–19, quoted in Campbell 1997: 18)*

Another trade language, Mobilian (also called 'Chikasaw trade jargon', as much of its lexicon was derived from the Muskogean languages Chickasaw and Choctaw), was used in Louisiana, where French settlers arrived in 1699. This language 'served as the general language of communication' in an extensive area, westward into Texas 'by the expansion and increase' of French and later American settlers (Crawford 1978: 7–8). It was spoken as far north as the Ohio River and east into Florida. And although, according to Drechsel (1984), it was in use prior to the arrival of the Europeans, the French 'likely contributed to its diffusion ... in the historic periods of greater Louisiana' (Drechsel 1984: 172, cited in Campbell 1997: 21).

A final example of a trade language is 'Chinook trade jargon', which developed on the northwest coast of British Columbia and persisted in more remote areas in Chilcotin territory into the 1930s. The language probably had its roots in Indigenous trade prior to the arrival of James Cook in 1778 at Nootka Island. As trade developed, however, so did this second language of communication. Thus, 'when trade shifted to the territory of the Chinook people at the mouth of the Columbia River after 1800, the traders took this simple jargon with them' (Lutz 2008: ix). From these origins, the language eventually developed 'from a trading language ... [into] the language of work, used in mills, canneries, and hop fields', where Indigenous people interacted with non-Indigenous immigrants and other Indigenous people who spoke no other common language (Lutz 2008: xi).

It is worth noting, however, that Chinook trade jargon and other trade languages had severe expressive limitations – although these could be both a blessing and a curse. Although these limitations 'led ... to misunderstandings', such misunderstandings 'had their uses. If the Nlaka'pamux of the Fraser River wanted to interpret the Chinook words used by the Anglican Bishop of Columbia to refer to the Christian God – Saghalie Tayee Papa (literally, 'the above chief father') – as the Sun and Creator, both sides could feel they had some common ground' (Lutz 2008: xi). Yet, as Lutz notes, other missionaries found it difficult to use Chinook jargon to convey their intended meanings. For example, one Methodist clergyman, writing in 1860, noted the difficulty of addressing the Indigenous people as 'children of the forest' with a language that rendered the phrase as 'little men among big stick' (ibid.).

Not all contact languages, however, had such expressive limitations. What also arose from contact between speakers of Indigenous languages and speakers of other languages were 'bilingual mixed languages' (Thomason 2001). Unlike pidgins, these languages did not begin as trade languages with reduced grammar and vocabulary, but were 'mixed' and complex from their inception, having developed from the languages of fluently bilingual speakers. In some cases, these new ways of speaking became the first language of speakers raised in bilingual and multilingual environments (cf. Media Lengua in Ecuador; Muysken 1997).

One mixed language in North America was Michif, used by the Métis people (Brown 2004), a group with mixed Indigenous and European heritage now recognized alongside First Nations and Inuit as having Aboriginal rights in the *Canadian Constitution Act*, 1982. Historically, Michif was used across the Canadian and northern American plains and north into the Northwest Territories by the descendants of the early fur traders in western Canada and their Indigenous wives and children. Michif was often spoken along with English, French or another Indigenous language, depending on a speaker's geographical location. The language itself is half Cree and half French, drawing its verbs from the former and its nouns from the latter (Bakker 1997: 1).

Interaction between the Métis, speaking Michif, and French- and Cree-speaking groups necessitated the use of Cree and French alongside Michif (Bakker and Papen 1997: 356). This multilingual situation changed during the twentieth century, however, leading to a situation in which 'few if any Michif speakers spoke Cree beside Michif, and only one in three spoke French beside Michif; most Métis had grown up as monolingual Michif speakers' (ibid.). By the latter half of the twentieth century, the number of Michif speakers had dropped from a few thousand to an estimated 1,000 speakers. As a result of urbanization and modernization, English has also entered the multilingual mix as another language that French, Cree and Michif speakers have had to contend with. Thus, multilingualism, which created the conditions for Michif to thrive in the first place, has been reduced to unilingualism over a few generations.

Even this decline of multilingual practices among the Métis reveals, just as the lingua francas, trade languages and other multilingual practices described in this section do, the dynamic linguistic practices of Indigenous groups. Far from being either static or unilingual, Indigenous groups often depended on interaction with other groups and found the linguistic means to do so. Thus, before state intervention and forced schooling in dominant languages intervened, multilingualism flourished in many trade contexts. If some of these multilingual practices had expressive limitations, others – in particular, the strategic learning of dominant languages – did not.

The contextualized descriptions given above provide a sense of how multilingualism was valued in a few specific cases. What, then, are still clearly needed to achieve a deeper understanding of multilingualism in contemporary Indigenous societies and its consequences for these societies are more explanatory approaches to multilingual practices and more extensive documentation of these practices. We saw earlier in the chapter that multilingualism in itself was not an important issue – whether for colonial powers or for those studying contact between Indigenous peoples and European traders – as long as European and Indigenous interlocutors remained partners in trade and the relation between these two groups was one of mutual dependence. Yet, as relations changed over time, and Europeans came to depend less on Indigenous traders, navigators and assistants to carry out the goals of colonization in the 'New World', Indigenous multilingualism did become an issue for state processes of nation-building. In other words, for European colonial ideologies, Indigenous multilingualism came to be seen as a hindrance to the assimilation of Indigenous peoples into the European or white settler social, economic and cultural order. According to these ideologies, then, assimilation meant unilingualism in the dominant state language.

This historical turn in the study of Indigenous language practices requires theoretical and methodological approaches rather different from those with which much of the research into Indigenous languages has been conducted. I consider some more recent approaches to this research and some of the issues that these approaches need to address in the next section.

Key issues of theory and methods

The previous section highlighted the role of historical processes in shaping linguistic interaction and creating new forms of multilingualism in Indigenous contexts. It also highlighted the linguistic ideologies associated with these historical processes. In this section, I shall be considering how these processes can best be documented, described and analysed, in order to help us to answer such general research questions as what forms Indigenous multilingual practices take; how and why they arose and have or have not persisted; and the implications of the answers for Indigenous language speakers. Of course, addressing these general questions forces us to confront a range of more specific ones.

Generally speaking, we adopt particular research methods in order to answer research questions like those just enumerated. These methods, operating within particular theoretical frameworks and epistemologies, are socially constructed systems of producing knowledge. Whichever methods we use can thus play a key role in how we interpret our findings. Moreover, although theories and methods often fall within particular disciplinary boundaries, what may turn out to be most productive for analysing Indigenous multilingualism, given its social, cultural and political complexity, is a multi- or interdisciplinary and community-based approach.

Doing research on Indigenous multilingualism

Research on Indigenous contexts of multilingualism can encompass a range of issues, including Indigenous language use and change, Indigenous language and culture, the politics of language and policy studies, literacy and education studies, and Indigenous language revitalization. Such research can likewise adopt one or more of a range of research orientations. These can be grouped into (1) general descriptive approaches (as used, for example, in census data research, sociolinguistics and social psychology) that draw on survey methods and interpret the data collected based on discrete factors, including sociological factors such as class and urbanization and psychological factors such as prestige and attitudes; (2) ethnographic explanatory approaches, which make observations of actual language use and draw on social theory as developed in sociology and anthropology to interpret data; (3) post-colonial and decolonization frameworks, which draw on studies in ethics, critical theory and Indigenous scholarship across a range of disciplines; (4) liberal rights and recognition-based approaches, which draw on legal studies, political science and political philosophy; and (5) policy studies, including education and language policy as these concern Indigenous languages and language revitalization. In that which follows, I shall briefly discuss each of these, drawing my examples from multilingual research in Canada and elsewhere. For ease of discussion, my examples will focus on contexts of Indigenous multilingualism related to the Inuit in Arctic Canada, but provide further clarification from other contexts. The question to be addressed is whether a language shift is under way among the Inuit in Arctic Canada, whereby these speakers of an Indigenous language, in this case Inuktitut, are using English in an increasing number of social contexts – with the implication that over the next generations members of this community will end up speaking only English.

Descriptive survey approaches

One productive way to address this research question would be to address general socio-linguistic questions such as what languages people use – speak, read and write – in various contexts and more generally, what forms Indigenous multilingualism takes in specific social settings. Thus, if one is interested in whether an Indigenous language is undergoing a language shift to a more dominant or powerful language, one can draw on empirical findings in order to assess the range of multilingualism in a community of speakers and the languages used in specific contexts. Here survey data can be particularly useful, as they can readily cover both a broad range and a large number of speakers. Surveys that make use of standardized written questionnaires – as used, for example, in censuses and in social psychological and sociolinguistic research on language use and attitudes – can provide useful contextual information about multilingualism. It is crucial to note, however, that the data collected in such surveys have distinct limitations, lacking the nuance and detail found in responses to discrete-answer questions. Of course, survey questions have other well-known drawbacks, such as the tendency of the particular wording of the question to elicit particular responses and, in the case of self-reported responses, the subjectivity inherent in such responses.

These and other difficulties with survey data emerge clearly from an examination of recent Aboriginal population surveys in Canada. As already noted, a key use of surveys is that of census-taking; in Canada, such surveys have asked about respondents' first language, their ability to understand and speak an Indigenous language, and their use of that language in the home (Statistics Canada 2003). Admittedly, these very large-scale surveys have offered a useful picture of various Indigenous languages. Moreover, statistics gathered over different census periods have provided snapshots of trends in language usage. As such, the picture of Inuktitut that emerges is one whereby the language has a large number of speakers and is relatively stable – the latter conclusion deriving from a comparison of Inuktitut language use across the seven-year span 1996–2001 and across the entire Canadian Arctic. These facts about the language are indicated in Table 1.1.

Table 1.1 Percentage of Canadian Inuit who learn and use Eskimo–Aleut languages

	All Inuit		Children under age 15	
	1996	*2001*	*1996*	*2001*
Have Inuktitut as their first language	78%	77%	74%	73%
Use Inuktitut at home	68%	64%	68%	64%
Can understand and/or speak Inuktitut	90%	90%	90%	90%
Can converse in Inuktitut	82%	82%	80%	80%

Source: Adapted from *Aboriginal Peoples Survey 2001—Initial Findings: Well-Being of the Non-Reserve Aboriginal Population* (pp. 29–30), by Statistics Canada, 2003, Ottawa. Copyright 2003 by Statistics Canada. Cited in Allen 2007.

Of course, a downside to these census data is that the picture of Indigenous language use that they provide is only a very general one. In particular, we are provided with no information about, for example, who is speaking what language to whom, how often speakers are speaking or what other languages they are speaking. Moreover, as these data are self-reported, we have no real idea of what counts as being able to understand or speak the language or what frequency of use is reflected in speakers indicating that they use the language at home.

Other survey data, collected by social psychologists and sociolinguists, have been more specific, highlighting the use of one language variety over another in a number of domains. Although the questions asked in these surveys are much narrower than those of the census surveys, the information that they provide is still rather limited. For instance, Taylor and Wright (1989) used a 10-point scale for self-reported language ability and language use in various domains, such as the workplace, home, and while hunting and fishing. Taylor and Wright's scale for language use started at 0–1, indicating that Inuktitut was 'never' used and went up to 9–10, indicating that Inuktitut was used 'all the time.' The one domain that displayed a 'significantly greater use of English' was the workplace (Taylor and Wright 1989: 99).

Of course, such a survey result does not tell us what kinds of workplaces were involved and who was speaking to whom there. The latter consideration is especially important. If Inuktitut was always being used between Inuit co-workers, with English or French used between Inuit and non-Inuit co-workers, then the result that there was more 'English usage' might really indicate only that Inuit more frequently appealed to multilingualism in these workplaces in dealing with non-Inuit interlocutors. In other words, the survey instrument cannot, without becoming too cumbersome, indicate which particular contexts in Arctic settings are the ones in which French or English might be used. Yet, without this information, it is difficult to assess the potential of Inuit communities to experience language shift.

A third type of survey of language practices in the Canadian Arctic, reported in Dorais and Sammons (2002), exploited more qualitative research methods. This survey involved interviewing almost 300 people, almost entirely in Inuktitut, and conducting focus groups in three Arctic communities about speakers' 'linguistic choices and opinions' (2002: 7). Also significant was that the study used oral rather than written elicitation methods, facilitating data collection in this Indigenous context; and that respondents were asked, among other questions, why particular languages were used with particular people, such as parents, a spouse or peers, and why a language might be used in particular settings. This type of survey could thus cover a wide range of speakers who were asked the same questions, yet still reveal a much more complex picture of bi- and multilingualism than the more discrete-point questions of the other survey types just described. For example, this survey reveals the importance of Inuktitut in maintaining Inuit identities in the Arctic regions. It also reveals the role of institutional factors such as education in shaping language choice, indicating that the use of English increases after around the age of eight, when the medium of instruction in schools switches to English. Nevertheless, this survey is still a survey, which by its nature cannot ask probing questions or foster detailed or exploratory discussion about language use.

Significantly, the survey data collected by Dorais and Sammons tend to support a key finding of the larger-scale census data: that Inuktitut is widely used in the communities where the surveys were conducted. But these data cannot support or explain the claim, advanced by many researchers and language activists, that bi- and multilingualism in Indigenous language contexts inevitably leads to language shift where one or more of the non-Indigenous languages used is associated with economic and social power and prestige. Even if the data suggested that a shift was under way, they could not explain why this was so; that is, the data could tell us little, if anything, about the mechanisms, social processes and language ideologies at play in language shift or maintenance. To address these sorts of questions, we need to adopt the ethnographic approaches to Indigenous multilingualism, as pursued by anthropologists and sociologists.

Ethnographic explanatory approaches

Perhaps the most salient aspect of ethnography is the way in which it documents social processes across time and space and examines ideologies and the political and social arrangements associated with these processes. Doing ethnography involves using a range of methods – participant observation, interviews, documentation of face-to-face interactions, visual and voice recordings, journal writing, text analysis – and engaging long term with a community of speakers. Language ethnographies, in particular, involve analysing a range of modes, including oral, written, gestural and visual, of languages and texts. Doing ethnography, moreover, involves understanding the power relations between the investigator and the individuals who are the subjects of this investigation. In Indigenous contexts, it also involves understanding the historical, political and material conditions of the Indigenous groups with whom one is working.

Ethnography can address a host of research questions related to Indigenous multilingual contexts. These include how modernity has affected the way that Indigenous languages are learned and children are socialized in and through language; what role language ideologies play in creating 'local modernities', specific social and cultural conditions for textual production arising from economic, social and other changes; how these changes shape multilingualism, language shift, social identities and literacy practices; and how language communities are 'converging', and becoming more 'modern', or 'diverging', and retaining local diversity (see e.g. Kulick 1992; Patrick 2001, 2003a, 2003b; Robbins 2001; Schieffelin 2000).

At various points in this section on theory and methods, we have discussed the phenomenon of language shift. As it happens, ethnographic work has offered illuminating answers to the 'how' and 'why' of this phenomenon. For example, Kulick's (1992) analysis of language shift in an Indigenous community in Papua New Guinea explains how speakers of an Indigenous language have come to use a dominant language when addressing each other and their children, even where this practice is at odds with what speakers say that they want to do. In this analysis, culturally situated language ideologies are examined – ideologies that shape multilingual language practice. This type of analysis thus requires not only an understanding of the Indigenous beliefs inherent in language socialization processes, but also an in-depth knowledge of the Indigenous language and how it is used.

What must also be recognized, however, is that ethnographic research, particularly in the current political and academic climate, generally requires the researcher to secure the approval of two distinct communities: the community that is the researcher's prospective host, and the academic community, in the form of ethics and granting committees, which must endorse the project's academic value and its treatment of the human subjects under investigation. Although obtaining the latter kind of approval can be difficult, obtaining the former kind of approval, given the current post-colonial political climate and the historically asymmetrical relations associated with Indigeneity, as discussed earlier in this chapter, is often even more so: the community may grant its permission only after long consideration of, for example, the ethical dimension of the research, its methodology, and its likely benefits to the community, and many details may need to be negotiated. One of the results of this shift in the politics of research has been the rise of more applied Indigenous language ethnographies, which are attuned to educational and language policy, pedagogy, literacy training and community development, among other areas.

In my own ethnographic study of multilingualism in Arctic Quebec, conducted in the early 1990s (Patrick 2001, 2003b), I investigated patterns of interaction involving Inuktitut, Cree, English and French in a variety of community settings in order to answer questions related to multilingualism, education and local economic participation. To undertake this research, I sought collaboration with the Inuit school board and the community. My analysis was both historical and sociological. Its historical analysis involved showing how Cree and Inuit in this region were bilingual and multilingual, indicating historical social and economic relationships between Cree and Inuit, and French and English, which were either not widely known or taken for granted. The study's sociological analysis highlighted the construction of social and ethnic boundaries through language use and the ways in which language is related to the social categorization of groups of people. But the ethnography itself was rooted largely in applied research about language learning and language use outside of the classroom, and examined language requirements and language practices in local workplaces in the community, adapting some of this information for use in schools and teacher training programmes. This kind of research, linked to local collaboration and applications, has increasingly become the norm for research in Indigenous contexts. I shall examine some of the reasons for this in the next section, which considers post-colonial and decolonizing contexts of Indigenous language research.

Post-colonial and decolonization frameworks

In the current global political context, shaped by post-colonial and decolonizing processes, power, colonization and intellectual property rights have become some of the many issues with which researchers must contend. These issues are often framed in terms of ethics in research and the need to acknowledge and deal with Eurocentric ontologies, or descriptions of 'what exists' and the categories into which the universe's entities can be placed, and epistemologies, or theories of knowledge and belief. On a practical level, this means that investigating Indigenous knowledge and beliefs as related to language requires collaboration with stakeholders in an Indigenous community who are committed to such investigation. Such partnering would aim to reduce the power imbalance between investigator and investigated. It would also be driven by the understanding that the study would be respectful of people and have some benefit to the community; would be sympathetic to Indigenous goals of self-determination, autonomy and social justice; and would lead to a renewed understanding of the inequitable relations between Indigenous peoples and the state or other colonizing forces and the consequences of these for Indigenous people.

Given these ethical constraints on research related to Indigenous speakers, what also seems to be required for meaningful research in this context is an understanding of the need for social transformation of Indigenous peoples to overcome the historical, social and economic deprivations of the colonial legacy (Smith 1999). Decolonization for Indigenous groups involves a process of establishing new relationships 'within and between peoples and the natural world' (Coulthard 2008: 201) and seeing what theoretical approaches and research methods can help to foster this. Linda Tuhiwai Smith, in her widely acclaimed book, *Decolonizing Methodologies*, urges Indigenous researchers to conduct Indigenous-based, respectful research. This shift in research is welcome for studies of Indigenous multilingualism and addresses to the need to encourage Indigenous scholars and scholarship. However, as Smith (1999: 39) notes, decolonization 'does not mean and has not meant a total rejection of all theory or research or Western knowledge'. Thus, although she advocates more Indigenous-centred research, which focuses on Indigenous 'concerns and world views' and 'understands theory and research' from Indigenous perspectives (ibid.), there is space for engagement with Western theories, methods and systems of knowledge. These engagements are necessary for cross-cultural understanding and the furthering of Indigenous perspectives regardless of the area of research.

Admittedly, the changes that have arisen in how Indigenous research is done and the ethical demands that such research imposes might now be so familiar to some, particularly in former European colonial contexts, as to go without saying. Yet, it is worth emphasizing that these demands have not come out of nowhere. Rather, they have emerged together with Indigenous mobilization and rights discourses associated with Indigeneity, as noted earlier. The rights-based approaches to understanding Indigenous multilingualism have also been prominent in the latter half of the twentieth century; we turn to a discussion of these now.

Liberal rights and recognition-based approaches

Although a great deal of research of Indigenous multilingualism has centred on the phenomenon of language shift, this phenomenon is certainly not the only one worthy of scholarly attention. This is particularly true in the post-colonial era, which has brought support for Indigenous languages, in the form of the recognition of language rights and programmes of language revitalization, and thus the promise that language shift may be slowed or even halted. Language rights have largely taken the form of official recognition of a particular language in institutional domains and the right of its speakers to be educated in that language. As noted earlier in the chapter, these rights are part of a larger rights discourse that has emanated from supranational organizations such as the United Nations (see Muehlmann and Duchêne 2007 and Patrick 2007: 120 for discussion of these).

Research into liberal rights discourses and state recognition of these rights involves critical text analysis and draws on legal studies, political science and political philosophy. Such investigation uses critical discourse analysis to critically assess laws, policies and rights documents, and to understand their limitations as well as their appeal.

In this context, one recent rights document worth noting is the *United Nations Declaration on the Rights of Indigenous Peoples*, adopted in 2007 after over 20 years of discussion and debate (although, tellingly, without the support of Canada, the USA, Australia and New Zealand, the four major 'settler states'). Articles 13, 14 and 16 of the Declaration pertain to language and ensure the right of Indigenous people 'to revitalize, use, develop and transmit' their languages; 'to establish and control their educational systems and institutions providing education in their own languages'; and 'to establish their own media in their own languages', respectively.

These articles governing language are part of a larger initiative to establish human rights standards for Indigenous peoples – an initiative welcomed by many language rights advocates.

In the 1990s the power of human rights discourses prompted many language scholars to support 'linguistic human rights' (LHR), a notion that drew support from language endangerment and language ecology and biodiversity movements (on the latter, see Muelhlmann 2007). However, even if we adopt a discourse of 'inalienable' human rights, it is nation-states that still decide whether or not to recognize them. Moreover, the granting of rights does not in itself make the 'language problems' or conflicts in nation-states disappear. Indeed, this might even serve to obscure other 'conflicts' between states and Indigenous people, as reflected in the endemic poverty and violence associated with many Indigenous communities and the loss of traditional territories and livelihoods. What is more, sociolinguistic critiques of the discursive treatment of 'language' have emphasized various dangers associated with this treatment. Among these are the dangers of (1) essentializing language and culture – that is, linking Indigenous language to reified ways of being Indigenous; (2) normalizing what counts as a language by unproblematically treating languages as fixed, bounded entities; and (3) devoting more attention to the languages as 'entities' than to the speakers of these languages themselves (on this, see e.g. Muelhlmann 2007; Freeland and Patrick 2004; Hornberger 2002). For further critique and discussion of rights discourses, see Freeland and Patrick 2004; Patrick 2007; and Chapter 7 of this book).

Notwithstanding these caveats, rights discourses have become extremely important symbolically, politically and legally in the recognition of Indigenous languages. Struggles for language rights have centred largely on creating a place for Indigenous language use in institutions such as schools, courts and governments. In addition, Indigenous language movements have often strategically drawn on discourses related to land, environmentalism, cultural heritage and traditional Indigenous epistemologies. Rights discourses have also been useful in garnering resources to maintain Indigenous languages and to promote Indigenous language revitalization. In short, the internationalization of Indigenous language discourses in turn creates a discursive space for Indigenous language researchers and activists to act. These initiatives are often driven by Indigenous communities themselves.

As already noted, investigating language rights and the recognition of them involves the analysis of texts used for justifying language rights and the critical assessment of the rights documents themselves. It also involves the question of how Indigenous groups have positioned themselves with respect to rights discourses and why have they done so. Language policies and language revitalization movements provide a large part of the answer: many Indigenous groups wish collectively to improve educational outcomes, regain Indigenous cultural practices and identities, and promote the Indigeneity of the group by regaining and strengthening Indigenous languages.

Policy issues: education, language policy and language revitalization

Given the attention currently devoted to language endangerment and language rights, language revitalization has become a major concern among Indigenous groups wishing to regain or stabilize the multilingualism undermined by decades of state intervention and economic transformations. Policy making and policy implementation play a large role in garnering the support and resources needed to undertake such initiatives.

Language revitalization involves a process of 're-establishing' a language that is no longer used for communication (Hinton 2001: 5); or teaching or promoting a language that may still be in use but is in need of formal support. The latter process may involve the creation of school and after-school or home-based programmes and materials and the development of curricula for these programs (2001: 7). More often than not, such initiatives involve academic partnerships. Partnering in this way can be part of an effort to obtain funding and technical and other know-how for curriculum development, in order better to promote multilingualism in Indigenous contexts. Crucial to these initiatives has been the focus on educational outcomes through the promotion of bi- and multilingual Indigenous language education.

Research in these contexts can take many forms. One such form is that of pedagogical studies of classroom interaction and cross-cultural contexts of learning, which have been largely qualitative and ethnographic in nature. One classic study of this kind is Philips (1983), which focuses on Indigenous classroom interaction, comparing two classrooms on the Warm Springs Reservation and the nearby off-reservation town in Oregon. Other forms include quantitative studies, which have involved the measurement of language proficiency in Indigenous and bilingual classrooms, such measurement being necessary to justify the continued funding and support of programs (see Allen 2007 for an overview of some of these cases in the Canadian Arctic). Such measurement of outcomes is, however, not unproblematic, given the questions that it raises about the utility of standardized testing in such contexts. Still other forms of research include studies that have focused on reading and writing pedagogy for bilingual Indigenous language classrooms, providing support for the view that learning in the medium of the first language assists second language acquisition (e.g. Francis and Reyhner 2002).

Language and educational policies are, of course, informed by research. Whether this research focuses on language acquisition inside or outside classrooms, on sociolinguistic interactions in different contexts or on cultural patterns of language use, it can all be valuable, as long it can benefit speakers and communities or be used to further our understanding of what is happening and why in particular sociolinguistic contexts. These are useful research directions for Indigenous multilingualism.

Conclusion

This chapter has examined multilingualism in Indigenous contexts through a study of research on language use both before and after colonization. The chapter's aim has been to show how the study of multilingualism has only relatively recently become an object of sociolinguistic concern, despite the long history of Indigenous multilingual practices. It has also aimed to dispel the myth of static, socially bounded groups located in a timeless past and to discuss current research directions in the study of Indigenous multilingualism.

We began by looking at the complexity of the concept of 'Indigenous' and how Indigeneity and Indigenous language groups differ from 'linguistic minorities'. We then examined how historical, political and economic power relations have shaped Indigenous contexts and practices, drawing on examples from North America. The language practices described have included ones based in trade and other more equitable power relations. When these relations gave way to assimilationist state policies and the incorporation of Indigenous peoples into broader social and economic processes, language practices also shifted. In this light, we examined early developments in the field, including the development of comparative-historical linguistic research, the rise of ethnographic approaches and the branching off of structural linguistics from this. Next, we examined different research approaches, doing so by addressing a research question relating to language shift. The research considered included that involving survey data collection and analysis; ethnographic research; Indigenous-based approaches; language, educational and legal rights-based approaches; language policy; and language revitalization. In sum, this chapter has provided an overview of the ways in which we can reflectively engage in questions surrounding Indigenous multilingualism.

Related topics

Lessons from pre-colonial multilingualism; language rights; Indigenous education; multilingualism in education in post-colonial contexts.

Further reading

de la Cadena, M. and Starn, O. (eds) (2007) *Indigenous Experience Today*, Oxford and New York: Berg. (An extensive overview of contemporary Indigenous issues.)

Grenoble, L. and Whaley, L. (1998) *Endangered Languages: Current Issues and Future Prospects.* New York: Cambridge University Press.
(A pioneering examination of indigenous languages and other minority languages, with a focus on language endangerment from various linguistic perspectives.)

Patrick, D. (2007) 'Language endangerment, language rights and indigeneity', in M. Heller (ed.) *Bilingualism: A Social Approach*, Basingstoke: Palgrave Macmillan.
(A useful overview of language issues related to Indigeneity.)

Smith, L. T. (1999) *Decolonizing Methodologies: Research and Indigenous Peoples*, London and New York: Zed Books.
(A key text about substantive and methodological issues related to Indigenous languages and peoples.)

Sturtevant, W. C. (ed.) (1978–2008) *Handbook of North American Indians*, Washington: Smithsonian Institution.
(A 20-volume set including classic ethnological and linguistic treatments of Indigenous peoples of North America; see especially vol. 17, *Languages*, Ives Goddard (ed.).)

Bibliography

Allen, S. (2007) 'Bilingualism or language shift in Inuktitut', *Applied Psycholinguistics* 28(3): 515–36.

Bakker, P. (1997) *'A Language of Our Own': The Genesis of Michif, the Mixed Cree-French Language of the Canadian Métis*, Oxford: Oxford University Press.

Bakker, P. and Papen, R. A. (1997) 'Michif: A mixed language based on Cree and French', in S. G. Thomason (ed.) *Contact Languages: A Wider Perspective*, Amsterdam and Philadelphia: John Benjamins.

Bourdieu, P. and Passeron, J. C. (1990) *Reproduction in Education, Society and Culture*, 2nd edn, London: Sage.

Brown, J. S. H. (2004) 'Michif', in G. Hallowell (ed.) *The Oxford Companion to Canadian History*, Don Mills, Ontario: Oxford University Press.

Campbell, L. (1997) *American Indian Languages: The Historical Linguistics of Native America*, New York and Oxford: Oxford University Press.

Crawford, J. M. (1978) *The Mobilian Trade Language.* Knoxville: University of Tennessee Press.

Coulthard, G. (2008) 'Beyond recognition: Indigenous self-determination as prefigurative practice', in L. Simpson *Lighting the Eighth Fire: The Liberation, Resurgence, and Protection of Indigenous Nations*, Winnipeg: Arbeiter Ring Publishing.

de la Cadena, M. and Starn, O. (eds) (2007) 'Introduction', in M. de la Cadena and O. Starn (eds) *Indigenous Experience Today*, Oxford and New York: Berg.

Dorais, L. J. and Sammons, S. (2002) *Language in Nunavut: Discourse and Identity in the Baffin Region*, Iqaluit: Nunavut Arctic College/GETIC, Université Laval.

Drechsel, E. O. (1984) 'Structure and Function in Mobilian Jargon: Indications for the pre-European existence of an American Indian pidgin', *Journal of Historical Linguistics and Philology* 1(2): 141–85.

Francis, N. and Reyhner, J. (2002) *Language and Literacy Teaching for Indigenous Education: A Bilingual Approach*, Clevedon: Multilingual Matters.

Freeland, J. and Patrick, D. (eds) (2004) *Language Rights and Language Survival*, Manchester: St Jerome Publishing.

Hinton, L. (2001) 'Language revitalization: an overview', in L. Hinton and K. Hale (eds) *The Green Book of Language Revitalization in Practice*, San Diego: Academic Press.

Hornberger, N. (2002) 'Multilingual language policies and the continua of biliteracy: An ecological approach', *Language Policy* 1: 27–51.

Hughes, L. (2003) *The No-Nonsense Guide to Indigenous Peoples*, Toronto: New Internationalist Publications and Between the Lines Press.

Hymes, D. (1974) *Foundations in Sociolinguistics: An Ethnographic Approach*, Philadelphia: University of Pennsylvania Press.

ILO Convention 169, available online at http://www.ilo.org/indigenous/Conventions/no169/lang–en/index.htm.

Kulick, D. (1992) *Language Shift and Cultural Reproduction: Socialization, Self, and Syncretism in a Papua New Guinean Village*, Cambridge and New York: Cambridge University Press.

Lutz, J. S. (2008) *Makúk: A New History of Aboriginal-White Relations*, Vancouver: UBC Press.

Miller, J. R. (2004) *Lethal Legacy: Current Native Controversies in Canada*, Toronto: McClelland & Stewart.

Muehlmann, S. (2007) 'Defending diversity: Staking out a common global interest?' in A. Duchêne and M. Heller (eds) *Discourses of Endangerment*, London: Continuum.

Muehlmann, S. and Duchêne, A. (2007) in M. Heller (ed.) *Bilingualism: A Social Approach*, Basingstoke: Palgrave Macmillan.

Muysken, P. (1997) 'Media Lengua', in S. G. Thomason (ed.) *Contact Languages: A Wider Perspective*, Amsterdam and Philadelphia: John Benjamins.

Niezen, R. (2003) *The Origins of Indigenism: Human Rights and the Politics of Identity*, Berkeley: University of California Press.

Patrick, D. (2001) 'Languages of state and social categorization in an Arctic Quebec community', in M. Heller and M. Martin-Jones (eds) *Voices of Authority: Education and Linguistic Difference*, Westport CT: Ablex.

——(2003a) *Language, Politics, and Social Interaction in an Inuit Community*, Berlin: Mouton de Gruyter.

——(2003b) 'Language, socialization and second language acquisition in a multilingual Arctic Quebec community', in R. Bayley and S. Schecter (eds) *Language Socialization in Bilingual and Multilingual Societies*, Clevedon: Multilingual Matters.

——(2007) 'Language endangerment, language rights and indigeneity', in M. Heller (ed.) *Bilingualism: A Social Approach*, Basingstoke: Palgrave Macmillan.

Philips, S. (1983) *The Invisible Culture: Communication in Classroom and Community on the Warm Springs Reservation*, New York: Longman.

Pratt, M. L. (2007) 'Afterword: Indigeneity today', in M. de la Cadena and O. Starn (eds) *Indigenous Experience Today*, Oxford and New York: Berg.

Robbins, J. (2001) 'God is nothing but talk: Modernity, language and prayer in a Papua New Guinea society', *American Anthropologist* 103(4): 901–12.

Schieffelin, B. (2000) 'Introducing Kaluli literacy: A chronology of influences', in P. Kroskrity (ed.) *Regimes of Language: Ideologies, Polities, and Identities*, Santa Fe: School of American Research Press.

Silverstein, M. (1996) 'Dynamics of Linguistic Contact', *Handbook of North American Indians*, vol. 17, Washington, DC: Smithsonian Institution.

Smith, L. T. (1999) *Decolonizing Methodologies: Research and Indigenous Peoples*, London and New York: Zed Books.

——(2007) 'The native and the neoliberal down under: Neoliberalism and "endangered authenticities"', in M. de la Cadena and O. Starn (eds) *Indigenous Experience Today*, Oxford and New York: Berg.

Statistics Canada (2003) *Aboriginal Peoples Survey 2001 – Initial Findings: Well-being of the Non-reserve Aboriginal Population*, Statistics Canada, Catalogue no. 89–589-XIE.

Stefánsson, V. (1909) 'The Eskimo trade jargon of Herschel Island', *American Anthropologist* 11: 217–32.

Taylor, D. and Wright, S. (1989) 'Language attitudes in a multilingual northern community', *The Canadian Journal of Native Studies* 9(1): 85–119.

Thomason, S. G. (2001) *Language Contact*, Washington, DC: Georgetown University Press.

Van Kirk, S. (1980) *'Many Tender Ties': Women in Fur-Trade Society in Western Canada, 1670–1870*, Winnipeg: Watson & Dwyer Publishing.

2

Lessons from pre-colonial multilingualism

Suresh Canagarajah and Indika Liyanage

Introduction

Multilingualism is often celebrated in the communicative context of late modernity, where languages come into contact in contexts of transnational affiliation, diaspora communities, digital communication, fluid social boundaries and the blurring of time/space distinctions (see Rampton 1997). However, this is not a new phenomenon. There is a small but growing body of scholarship on the types of multilingualism found in pre-modern and pre-colonial times. Scholars are using a different term for the type of multilingualism practised then: plurilingualism. Some believe that colonization and the influx of Western European language ideologies led to the suppression or distortion of the vibrant plurilingual practices in the pre-colonial southern hemisphere. An understanding of the pre-colonial language practices will help us to appreciate communicative practices in contemporary times.

It is important to distinguish multilingualism from plurilingualism. Plurilingulism has recently received some attention in the scholarly literature due to the promotion of plurilingual competence by the Language Policy Division of the Council of Europe (2000). According to the Council of Europe, plurilingualism is:

> The intrinsic capacity of all speakers to use and learn, alone or through teaching, more than one language. The ability to use several languages to varying degrees and for distinct purposes is defined in the Common European Framework of Reference for Languages as the ability 'to use languages for the purposes of communication and to take part in intercultural action, where a person, viewed as a social agent, has proficiency, of varying degrees, in several languages and experience of several cultures'. This ability is concretized in a repertoire of languages a speaker can use. The goal of teaching is to develop this competence (hence the expression: plurilingualism as a competence).
>
> *(2000: 168)*

Some aspects of this definition will sound unusual from the perspective of traditional orientations to multilingualism. In plurilingual competence:

- Equal or advanced proficiency is not expected in all the languages.
- Using different languages for distinct purposes qualifies as competence. One does not have to use all the languages involved as all-purpose languages.
- Proficiency in languages is not conceptualized individually, with separate competencies developed for each language. What is emphasized is the repertoire – the way the different languages constitute an integrated competence.
- Language competence is not treated in isolation from intercultural competence.
- There is a recognition that speakers may develop plurilingual competence by themselves (intuitively and through social practice) and not only through schools or formal means.

How is plurilingual competence different from multilingualism? Societal multilingualism refers to languages having their separate identities in (sometimes) separate areas of a geographical location. Individual multilingualism similarly refers to separate, whole and advanced competence in the different languages one speaks – almost as if it constitutes two or three separate monolingualisms. In both forms, the construct *multilingualism* keeps languages distinct. Plurilingualism allows for the interaction and mutual influence of the languages in a more dynamic way. For example, multilingual competence conceptualizes one language being added to another (in additive bilingualism), or supplanting another (in subtractive bilingualism). However, in plurilingual competence the directionality of influence is multilateral. Also, the languages may influence each other's development. More importantly, the competence in the languages is integrated, not separated. In plurilingual communication, diverse languages may find accommodation in a person's repertoire. The person may not have any advanced proficiency in all the languages, and yet mix words and grammatical structures of one language into syntax from other languages to form an integrated composite. In societal plurilingualism, speakers of language A and language B may speak to each other in a lingua franca mixed with their own first languages and marked by the influence of these languages. Without accommodating to a single uniform code, the speakers will be able to negotiate their different languages for intelligibility and effective communication. It is an intersubjective construct, in the manner similar to lingua franca English (LFE) as Canagarajah (2007) has defined it elsewhere.

The difference between multilingualism and plurilingualism is largely theoretical. These are not different practices. The terms connote different ways of perceiving the relationship between languages in society and individual repertoire. The dominance of monolingual assumptions in linguistics has prevented scholars from appreciating plurilingualism. For this reason, the understanding of multilingualism in the field is coloured by monolingual biases and fails to go far. Critical scholars have discussed the motivations in promoting values based on homogeneity, uniformity and autonomy in linguistic sciences. They have pointed out how there has been an ideological bias in European history toward unifying communities and identities around a single language (Singh 1998), treating multilingualism as a problem (Ruiz 1984) and establishing nation-states around the language of a dominant community (May 2001). These values are informed by the social conditions and ideologies gaining dominance since the rise of the nation-state, seventeenth-century enlightenment and the French Revolution in Europe (Dorian 2004; May 2001). As Dorian (2004: 438) reminds us, 'Monolingualism, now usually considered the unmarked condition by members of the dominant linguistic group in modern nation-states, was in all likelihood less prevalent before the rise of the nation-state gave special sanction to it'. Mary Louise Pratt (1987) interprets the imposition of homogeneity and uniformity in language and speech community as signifying the construction of *linguistic utopias* that serve partisan interests. Constructs based on monolingualism and homogeneity are well suited to communities that desire purity, exclusivity and domination. Acknowledging the heterogeneity of language and communication would force us to develop more democratic and egalitarian models of community and communication. Enabled by such historical processes as colonization and modernity, linguistics has reproduced its underlying enlightenment values elsewhere and hindered the development of plurilingual practices and knowledge.

Our theorization of plurilingualism is influenced by other well-known formulations of this practice in applied linguistics. The notion of *disinventing languages* (Makoni 2002) calls into question the separate labelling and study of languages, ignoring the ways that languages always come into contact and influence each other. If Makoni and Pennycook theorize the implications for the societal life of language and disciplinary discourses, Ofelia García's (2009) notion of *translanguaging* captures the implications of plurilingualism for one's own communicative repertoire and use. The term captures the ways multilinguals treat languages as a continuum and shuttle between them fluidly. There are other terms used by scholars to label what we theorize here as plurilingualism. Bakhtin's (1981) heteroglossia, Rampton's (1995) crossing, Jørgensen's (2008) polylingualism, Gutiérrez's (2008) third spaces, Blommaerts's (2008) heterography, and Young (2004) and Canagarajah's (2006) code-meshing share many things in common. Their terms arise from different domains and contexts of consideration. Rampton, Jørgensen and Gutiérrez develop their notion in relation to multicultural youth in urban contact situations. Blommaert, Young and Canagarajah develop their terms in the contexts of literacy. As we argue in a later section, there should be greater articulation between these constructs to tease out the differences and similarities to further theoretical and empirical exploration.

In this chapter, we wish to focus on the plurilingual tradition in pre-colonial South Asia, the region where we come from. However, plurilingualism has existed in other pre-colonial communities too. Although we do not have adequate scholarly descriptions of them in our field, these practices are not completely lost in these communities. We are beginning to see descriptions of such practices from Africa (Makoni 2002) and South America (de Souza 2002), among others (Dorian 2004). We are not arguing that plurilingual practices existed only in pre-colonial times. They are evident in today's society too. However, modernist linguistic constructs that value the separate identity of languages have resulted in a suppression of plurilingual practices. We focus on pre-colonial times, as plurilingual communication was practised more spontaneously and was uninhibited before the advent of modernist ideologies via colonization in this region. We are also not arguing that plurilingual communicative practices are not evident in communities in the northern hemisphere. Scholars are beginning to study such practices in Europe and the USA, as we noted earlier. In the past, these practices were overlooked or interpreted differently by scholars influenced by modernist ideologies. It is also possible that such practices have been suppressed to a greater degree in the West due to policies of linguistic purism and standardization. Plurilingualism is evident to a greater degree in non-Western communities, even in contemporary times, as the different language ideologies and values that still exist there sustain plurilingual practices. We need more research on plurilingual practices in both Western and non-Western communities to say if the differences are only in degree and not kind.

We do not discuss early developments in this chapter as this area of study does not have a long history. As is evident from our discussion above, the study of plurilingual practices is recent. Even scholars from non-Western communities are only now rediscovering the Indigenous communicative practices, having practised in the past modernist linguistics, which failed to encourage them in this study and worked actively to suppress such practices. We begin with the description of South Asia as a plurilingual region, analyse its plurilingual practices and explore the way they shaped language planning and education in this region. These plurilingual practices are striking in their differences from the dominant constructs in linguistics, and raise further questions that need exploration. We next explore the ways pre-colonial plurilingualism challenges the foundational constructs of linguistics. We go on to consider the implications of this communicative practice for language-in-education policies and outline areas of future research.

South Asia as a plurilingual region

Diversity, in all its multifaceted forms meshed in with thousands of years of sociopolitical history, is at the heart of the Indian subcontinent. Amidst all forms of diversity, linguistic diversity occupies a central place as it contributes to the rich complexity not just of India but also of its adjoining country, Sri Lanka. People who grew up in multilinguistic societies in this part of the world developed multiple memberships, both linguistic and otherwise, and their memberships overlapped and interlocked in amicable and productive ways to create fluid and hybrid identities (Canagarajah 2007). Not only the people but also the linguistic codes these people shared, grew amicably and in ways complementing each other; the complementarity was such that there is a strong and mutually identifiable lexico-grammatical affinity among these languages. For example, Khubchandani (1997) describes how many Indian languages belonging to different language families exhibit parallel trends of development over time.

In pre-colonial India and Sri Lanka, linguistic diversity and the resulting complexity of speech communities and societies have been so rich that researchers have not always appreciated this complexity. What the modernist scholars brought with them did not help them to understand the particular realization of multilingualism in this area. Even local historiographers were influenced to perceive the local plurilingualism through modernist interpretive spectacles. For example, Gunawardana (1990) believes that modern Sinhalese nationalism is a product of the British ideology introduced to the country during the late nineteenth century. On the other hand, others (Dharmadasa 1989; Rogers 1994) think that pre-colonial racial identities had to be rearticulated into models acceptable to scholars both during and after the British rule. These interpretations assume that multilingualism is a phenomenon within which different linguistic codes and communities who spoke them competed with one another for recognition and acceptance – a form of competitive multilingualism highlighting the differences and uniqueness of individual linguistics codes and communities who use them.

Even more damaging was the way modernist constructs helped Europe to establish its dominance over the communities it colonized in the nineteenth century. Local scholars point out that constructs like essentialist linguistic identity and homogeneous speech community were put to use in lands such as India to categorize people for purposes of taxation, administrative convenience and political control. In a very subtle way, these constructs have begun to shape social reality there with damaging results. Khubchandani observes:

> Until as recently as four or five decades ago, one's language group was not generally considered as a very important criterion for sharply distinguishing oneself from others. ... Following Independence, language consciousness has grown, and loyalties based on language-identity have acquired political salience.
>
> *(1997: 92)*

We can imagine how exclusive categories of identification can lead to ethnic and linguistic sectarianism. Furthermore, people have started to perceive themselves according to singular identities, lost their heterogeneity, and initiated conflicts and rivalries with members of what they perceive as alien language communities. Although we cannot blame colonialism for all the present-day evils in South Asia, we can understand how the ethnic and linguistic conflicts are partly attributable to the alien ways of perceiving group relationships introduced during colonial times.

Modernist scholarship has disregarded the fact that in the Indian subcontinent communities using different linguistic codes lived in harmony for hundreds, if not thousands, of years, before they witnessed forces of colonialism in modern history. What has also been forgotten in these discussions is the richly complex, constructive, amicable and complementary plurilingual ethos that existed during pre-colonial times (see Suseendirajah in Balasubramaniam *et al.* 1999: 272–80). The knowledge and ability to use languages other than one's mother tongue were considered to be resources that contributed to the amicable coexistence of speakers of different languages. They communicated with each other, perhaps in the most subtle ways, and established relationships in personal, social and administrative spheres (see Peiris 1969; Peter 1969; Rogers 1994, 2004 for examples of these in the context of Sri Lanka). The age-old folklore literacy traditions associated with different linguistic codes were enriched with religious ethics of people who practised them and, together, these bred mutual respect, uplifting the quality of life. People were not sharply distinguished from one another in terms of the linguistic codes they used (Khubchandani 1983; Wijesekera 1969) and, thus, 'a pluralistic world-view and the relativist approach in interpreting heritage and culture have been characterised as the essence of Oriental life' (Khubchandani 1998: 12).

Although plurilingualism is promoted by policy intervention or treated as an effect of atypical social conditions in present times (as in the European community), local scholars consider pluringualism as 'natural' to the ecology of South Asia. Bhatia and Ritchie (2004: 794) state: 'In qualitative and quantitative terms, Indian bilingualism was largely nourished naturally rather than by the forces of prescriptivism.' As evidence for this, scholars point to the status of the whole of South Asia as a *linguistic area* – 'that is, an area in which genetically distinct languages show a remarkable level of similarity and diffusion at the level of grammar' (Bhatia and Ritchie 2004: 795). This linguistic diffusion they consider inordinate in comparison with other regions of the world. Pattanayak (1984: 44) notes: 'If one draws a straight line between Kashmir and Kanyakumari and marks, say, every five or ten miles, then one will find that there is no break in communication between any two consecutive points.' Many scholars attribute this linguistic synergy to language attitudes in the region: that is, an 'accepting attitude, which has brought about the assimilation of features from Dravidian, Indo-Aryan, Islamic, and even Christian and European cultures into a single system, complex, but integrated' (Bright 1984: 19). Such features are a testament to the adaptive strategies of the local communities, which develop multilingualism when they come into contact with a new language, rather than rejecting or suppressing the language. The dominance of modernist constructs in linguistics has prevented scholars from understanding the communicative practices involved in plurilingualism. Despite the view of the aforementioned scholars that South Asia is a linguistic area that features a shared plurilingual tradition, we have to be wary of generalizing the communicative practices of diverse language and cultural groups in Nepal, Bangladesh, Pakistan and Afghanistan, let alone the diverse groups within India and Sri Lanka. More research is needed to tease out these differences.

Theorizing pre-colonial plurilingual practices

We will use Khubchandani's (1983, 1997) accounts to reconstruct the plurilingual tradition in South Asia. Although other scholars in the region apply plurilingualism to specific areas of interest (see Annamalai 2001; Bhatia and Ritchie 2004; Mohanty 2006; Pattanayak 1984), Khubchandani's is the most thorough and comprehensive theorization of this practice.

Khubchandani believes that plurilingualism (and cultural pluralism) comprises three salient features that in turn help define non-plurilingualism. These features are relativity, hierarchy and instrumentality. Relativity refers to the organization of verbal repertoire in relation to functional heterogeneity, a characteristic that is in contrast to the homogenized societies where promotion of a supreme benchmark for a linguistic code is sought through attitudes to usage. Hierarchy is a system of linguistic organization that uniformly promotes speech diversity in everyday use of language through aspects such as bilingualism, codeswitching, codemeshing and diglossia. This is in contrast to the selective promotion of certain linguistic codes at the expense of others. Instrumentality refers to the variation in speech in everyday settings by delineating interlocutor relationships as necessitated by speech contexts and purposes. In this process, the affiliation with a linguistic code is taken as assigned and the projection of its linguistic repertoire is flexible and adjustable to situational needs. In contrast, in non-pluralistic contexts, affiliation with a linguistic code is a 'defining' characteristic. The contribution of relativity, hierarchy and instrumentality in the use of language fortifies a plurilinguistic society as an organic whole. In such a society, affiliations with linguistic codes are not necessarily criteria for membership in select social groups; in such societies groups formed by linguistic affiliations are blurry and liquefied.

People in a plural society fit in with different identity factions that are formed around sociolinguistics and sociocultural characteristics such as cast, creed, religion, dialect and language. There is stupendous cultural and linguistic variation in everyday life and people who live in plural societies, according to Khubchandani (1998), develop common ways of thinking and interpreting life around them. The unity that develops out of this diversity and continuity of affiliations Khubchandani (1998: 84) calls a 'superconsensus'. Unlike other communities where individual differences have to be sacrificed for group identity, South Asian communities preserve their group differences while also developing an overarching community identity with other groups. Khubchandani (1983, 1997, 1998) uses a traditional Indian concept called *Kshestra* (approximate translation 'region') to encapsulate the wide sociocultural and sociolinguistic variation found in a plural society. According to him, this concept represents 'the feeling of oneness among diverse people in the region, creating in them "a sense of collective reality"' (1998: 9). He sees the concept of *Kshestra/region* as distinctly different from the modern Western model of *region,* which refers to an amalgamated area with diverse people yoked together by statutory policy.

Khubchandani (1983, 1997, 1998) further distinguishes between two types of pluralism: organic and structural. In organic pluralism, 'two identities are simply two sides of the same coin' (1983: 169). In an organically pluralistic society, individuals belonging to different ethnoreligious and ethnolinguistic backgrounds have an integral relationship that can be represented as 1 x 1 x 1 = 1. Structural pluralism as it exists in the Western world is based on the premise that different primary groups are separate in terms of their ethnolinguistic and ethnoreligious affiliations. This premise can be represented as 1 + 1 + 1 = 3, which is a combined relation (see Khubchandani 1997: 92 for a detailed discussion of organic and structural pluralism). Structural pluralism may be compared to the melting pot phenomenon in the West, characterized by ethnic enclaves. However, the pluralism in pre-colonial South Asia melded the different communities into a richer and integrated whole.

The above aspects of plurilingual ethos began to degenerate as 'language consciousness has grown and language loyalties have acquired political salience' (Khubchandani 1983: 9) after countries gained political independence. According to Khubchandani, the replacement of

Indigenous education systems with modern education systems and the introduction of compulsory bilingualism mandated by politically oriented language planning have expedited the substitution of grass-roots pluralism with modern bi- and multilingualism. He also believes that 'One of the most radical turnabouts in recent history transforming the concept of language pluralism on the subcontinent, has been the explicit recognition of language claims over "exclusive" territory' (Khubchandani 1983: 175). As he suggests, this is an attitude and practice alien to this region.

What are the implications of this plurilingualism for communication? Because of such intense social contact, languages themselves are influenced by each other, losing their 'purity' and separateness. Many local languages serve as contact languages, and develop features suitable for such purposes – that is, hybridity of grammar and variability of form. Khubchandani (1983: 80) says: 'Many Indian languages belonging to different families show parallel trends of development ... [They] exhibit many phonological, grammatical and lexical similarities and are greatly susceptible to borrowing from the languages of contact.' He goes on to say that differences 'between Punjabi and Hindi, Urdu and Hindi, Dogri and Punjabi, and Konkani and Marathi can be explained only through a pluralistic view of language' (1983: 91). Having been in close contact for many years, these languages have adopted many lexical and grammatical structures from each other, losing their respective family differences. Communities are so multilingual that in a specific speech situation one might see the mixing of diverse languages, literacies and discourses. It might be difficult to categorize the interaction as belonging to a single language. Khubchandani explains: 'The edifice of linguistic plurality in the Indian subcontinent is traditionally based upon the *complementary* use of more than one language and more than one writing system for the same language in one "space" (1983: 96, emphasis in the original).' If social spaces feature complementary – not exclusive – use of languages, mixing of languages and literacies in each situation is the norm, not the exception.

It is clear that this linguistic pluralism has to be actively negotiated to construct meaning. In these communities, meaning and intelligibility are intersubjective. The participants in an interaction produce meaning and accomplish their communicative objectives in relation to their purposes and interests. In this sense, meaning is socially constructed, not pre-given. Meaning does not reside in the language; it is produced in practice. As a result, 'Individuals in such societies acquire more *synergy* (i.e. putting forth one's own efforts) and serendipity (i.e. accepting the other on his/her own terms, being open to unexpectedness), and develop positive attitudes to variations in speech (to the extent of even appropriating deviations as the norm in the lingua franca), in the process of "coming out" from their own language-codes to a neutral ground (Khubchandani 1997: 94, emphasis in the original).' 'Synergy' captures the creative agency subjects must exert in order to work jointly with the other participant to accomplish intersubjective meaning. 'Serendipity' involves an attitudinal transformation. To accept 'deviations as the norm' one must display 'positive attitudes to variation' and be 'open to unexpectedness'. Subjects have to be radically other-centred. They have to be imaginative and alert to make on-the-spot decisions in relation to the forms and conventions employed by the other. It is clear that communication in multilingual communities involves a mindset and practices different from those in monolingual communities. We can also imagine the way the South Asian orientation to language departs from the tenets of modernist linguistics, which treats languages as pure and distinct products rather than fluid and hybrid social practices.

There is evidence that local communities began to appropriate and mix English with their other languages very early in the colonial period. This realization is sometimes missing in the World Englishes (WE) scholarship, and this omission makes it appear that the appropriation of English is a post-colonial development. The WE perspective is a natural outcome of the modernist focus on stabilized forms of language. However, there were occasions of very spontaneous borrowing and mixing much earlier than post-colonial development. Such practices occurred despite efforts by the British to keep the language from mixing and (from their perspective) impurity. We have records of English education in the region where students were kept in boarding schools so that their acquisition of English (and presumably British culture and knowledge) would be preserved from contact with their home culture and home language of the students (see Chelliah 1922). Students were also fined for each occasion of non-English language usage. However, we see references to some 'unruly' students who were dismissed from the boarding schools for escaping at night to attend Hindu temple festivals, maintaining secret miniature shrines for Hindu deities in their cupboards or desks, and surreptitiously practicing what are called 'heathen' songs and dances (ibid.). It is clear that students continued contact with the vernacular despite their isolation. That mixing of languages occurred and that students retained their vernacular and plurilingual competencies at that time is also evident from oral history and narratives (as Canagarajah 2000 recounts).

Manique Gunasekera (n.d.) notes that, soon afterwards, the British administration itself began to acknowledge this mixing of languages. It appears as if local people constructed texts that mixed English and Tamil or Sinhala in their official writing. The administration started to publish guidelines on the appropriate usage and spelling convention for local languages used in English texts. In 1869 the British administration published a *Glossary of Native and Foreign Words Occurring in Official Correspondence and Other Documents* (see Gunasekera 1893). Since then, there have been revised and updated glossaries to ensure a uniform policy on the spelling and meaning of Sinhalese and Tamil words in officialese in English. Through these glossaries, even the British administration implicitly recognized the fact that language mixing was an Indigenous phenomenon.

As has been discussed earlier, plurilingualism is a way of life and it finds expression in various social institutions such as administration, religion and education. In a truly plurilingual context, people with their different religious and linguistic identities mesh in while respecting and accommodating the differences between them. In other words, in such a context people enjoy differences found in social institutions in terms of language, religion and ethnicity, paving the way for an ideal of 'live and let live'. The powers that rule such communities facilitate and implement policies to protect such ideals. We are, however, cognisant that eccentricities existed within ethnic groups that led to the development of Sinhalese and Tamil group identities in Sri Lanka. In particular, claims of descent – that Sinhalese were from the Aryans and the Tamils were from the Dravidians – were ensconced in Sinhalese and Tamil consciousness (Samaraweera 1977). Samaraweera also believed that eccentricities existed within the two groups that led to the development of Sinhalese and Tamil group identities. However, they did not produce ongoing tensions or clashes in society. According to Samaraweera, beneath the occasional bickering was a strong ethnocultural and ethnolinguistic ambience that promoted firm social and economic relations between the two groups. The Moors also had harmonious relations with Sinhalese Buddhists who spoke Sinhala and with Tamil Hindus who spoke Tamil. The Moors were in fact protected against the atrocities committed by the Portuguese and the Dutch by the Sinhalese, who purposefully integrated them into the former Kandyan Kingdom where 'they retained their religious and cultural identity' (De Silva 1977: 392).

Furthermore, we cannot ignore the fact that there were power differences between language groups, despite plurilingualism. The biggest difference was between Sanskrit, the cosmopolitan literate language, and the regional vernaculars. The reason power is not accentuated in the

South Asian descriptions of conversational interaction is because vernaculars were only spoken, not written, for a long time. They all had relatively equal status in their own local domains. The written language, which enjoyed power in pre-colonial and pre-modern times, was Sanskrit. Pollock (2006) argues that the hegemony of Sanskrit was different from the power exerted by Latin or English. The latter imposed themselves on other communities through military might or political force. Sanskrit existed on a parallel plane to that of the vernaculars, but as the universally accepted written language. Other communities used Sanskrit if and when they wanted to write. As time went by, the vernaculars developed a written medium when they mixed with Sanskrit in their own literary, political or religious literature, around the sixth century. This unique form of writing, known as *manipralava* in South India (see Pollock 2006; Viswanathan 1993), is a linguistically hybrid form. This strategy of negotiation in literacy was not unlike the one discussed earlier for conversational interactions. Local communities merged their codes, made impure the dominant code and democratized the literate system.

Also, we must not ignore the fact that there are now heightened differences, even conflicts, between language groups in South Asia – such as between Hindus and Muslims in India, or Sinhalese and Tamils in Sri Lanka. How do we explain this inconsistency with the collaborative and accommodative practices of plurilingualism?

To answer this question we have to ponder the implications of Western European colonization since the sixteenth century. South Asian scholars have pointed out that colonization had dire implications for language and social life in the region. Mohan (1992) documents how unitary constructs of linguistic identity and speech community were put to use in colonies to categorize people for purposes of taxation, administrative convenience and political control. The stock question in the censuses about one's native or mother tongue was, and still is, confusing for local people when their mother speaks one language, father another and the family a third for domestic communication. In fact, the mother herself may have grown up with that level of multilingualism in her childhood, making 'mother-tongue' even more plural. For people who grow up with multiple languages in their everyday life, unitary notions of identity are reductive. Worse still, from the introduction of language censuses these notions of identity and community began to reproduce social life in the region.

Policy issues

What are the implications of pluralism for language planning and educational policy in present times? There is a general recognition in many communities nowadays that it is important for citizens of late modernity to shuttle between languages and develop plurilingual competence. However, some of the assumptions of traditional linguistics and education stifle efforts to develop this competence in language classrooms. In mainstream educational curricula and policy, models of subtractive or additive bilingualism are promoted. As we saw in the first section, these models develop language competence one at a time, in isolation from other languages and sometimes at the cost of the others. This is especially evident in Western communities, which treat multilingualism as a problem rather than a resource (see Hornberger 2003; Ruiz 1984). Other policies, such as treating the native speaker as the target for proficiency and treating additional languages as interference in developing proficiency (which Phillipson 1992 calls 'native speaker fallacy' and 'monolingual fallacy' respectively), also militate against plurilingual education.

Nor is this a problem only for countries in the northern hemisphere. South Asia itself finds it difficult to implement plurilingual policies in the aftermath of colonization and modernity. Ajit Mohanty (2006) feels that the modernist approach based on centralized languages and/or a hierarchy of difference (such as the three-language policy in India), are alien to the South Asian tradition. He argues that Indian pluralism works most effectively through functional distribution of languages, not hierarchies. What is conducive to the region is how individuals, families and communities assign different languages for different domains of communication without treating one as better than the other. He also argues that the imposition of English in colonial times and its glorified current status as the global language have also upset the plurilingual balance in South Asia. These issues have led to social and educational policies based on a hierarchical relationship of languages, resulting in the denigration of minority languages, language attrition and even language death. These post-colonial developments Mohanty finds damaging to the language ecology of South Asia. Drawing an analogy from his personal life to illustrate the complementary relationship between languages, Mohanty says: 'These languages fit in a mutually complementary and non-competing relationship in my life. Under such conditions of multilingual functioning individuals naturally need and use different languages because no language is sufficient or suitable for meeting all the communicative requirements across different situations and social activities (2006: 263).' Mohanty argues that such patterns of individual and community bilingualism at the local or regional level constitute 'the first incremental step towards concentric layers of societal multilingualism' (ibid.).

To some extent, certain non-Western communities (India, Singapore, Hong Kong, Brunei, and some countries in the Middle East and North Africa), have adopted forms of education that provide a complementary relationship to languages. García calls this *multiple multilingual education*. These programmes

> use more than two languages in education and often have moveable parts—that is, languages are weaved in and out of the curriculum as needed. Multilingualism is considered a resource for all children in the society. As a result of the inclusion of all children, there is considerable variation in bilingual proficiency; translanguaging is therefore a common feature of this education. Transculturalism is promoted, as not only languages, but also cultures, are blended.
>
> *(2009: 283)*

We can see how the practices promoted in this form of education go against dominant policies. Students may learn different subjects in different languages. The goal is not to develop parity of competence in all languages. Switching and mixing languages in classrooms is permitted. Language awareness is combined with intercultural competence.

We have to also consider the implications of plurilingualism for language teaching. Already communities in Europe are promoting plurilingual competence, as evident from our mention of the goal of the Council of Europe in the opening section. There are mixed reviews on the effectiveness of this pedagogy in Europe (for a critical review, see García 2009: 197–216). The problems include lack of training for teachers who have not transitioned from traditional pedagogical practices; lack of new teaching materials that promote plurilingualism; and the de facto dominance of certain languages and communities, which stifle the development of proficiency in less prestigious languages. The more pressing question is whether the type of spontaneous negotiation of languages that we see in face-to-face conversations can be taught in the somewhat constrained context of the classroom. What we need is a paradigm shift in language teaching. Pedagogy should be refashioned to accommodate the modes of communication and acquisition seen outside the classroom (see Canagarajah 2005a for a more elaborate pedagogical discussion). Rather than focusing on a single language or dialect as the target of learning, teachers have to develop in students a readiness to engage with a repertoire of codes in transnational contact situations. Whereas joining a new speech community was the objective of traditional pedagogy, now we have to train students to shuttle between communities by negotiating the relevant codes. To this end, we have to focus more on communicative strategies, rather than on form. Students would develop language awareness (to cope with the multiple languages and emergent grammars of contact situations), rather than focusing only on mastering the grammar rules of a single variety. In a context of plural forms and conventions, it is important for students to be sensitive to the relativity of norms. Therefore, students have to understand communication as performative, not just constitutive. That is, going beyond the notion of constructing prefabricated meanings through words, they will consider *shaping* meaning in actual interactions and even *reconstructing* the rules and conventions to represent their interests, values and identities. In other words, it is not what we know as much as the versatility with which we can do things with words that defines proficiency. Pedagogical movements such as learner strategy training and language awareness go some way toward facilitating such interactional strategies and repertoire development.

New directions in theoretical and disciplinary constructs

There is a need to theorize linguistics in more complex ways to accommodate the insights from plurilingual practices. The plurilingual view of language departs from many of the assumptions of modernist linguistics, posing questions such as the following: How do we classify and label languages when there is such mixing? How do we describe languages without treating them as self-contained systems? How do we define the system of a language without the autonomy, closure and tightness that would preclude openness to other languages? This perspective also challenges many dichotomies in modernist linguistics that need to be re-examined:

- Grammar versus pragmatics: is one more primary in communication, and are these in fact separable? Would pragmatic strategies enable one to communicate successfully irrespective of the level of grammatical proficiency? (House 2003).
- Determinism versus agency: are learners at the mercy of grammar and discourse forms for communication, or do they shape language to suit their purposes? (Canagarajah 2006).
- Individual versus community: are language learning and use orchestrated primarily by the individual even when they occur through interaction? Or do communication and acquisition take place in collaboration with others, through active negotiation, as an intersubjective practice? (Block 2003).
- Purity versus hybridity: are languages separated from each other, even at the most abstract level of grammatical form? And how do they associate with other symbol systems and modalities of communication? (Khubchandani 1997; Makoni 2002).
- Fixity versus fluidity: what is the place of deviation, variation, and alteration in language, and can a system lack boundedness? Similarly, is acquisition linear, cumulative, unidirectional and monodimensional? (Kramsch 2002; Larsen-Freeman 2002)
- Cognition versus context: do we formulate and store language norms detached from the situations and environment in which they are embedded? Is learning more effective when it takes place separately from the contexts where multiple languages, communicative modalities and environmental influences are richly at play? (Atkinson *et al.* 2007; Lantolf and Thorne 2006).
- Monolingual versus multilingual acquisition: how do we move beyond treating learning as taking place one language at a time, separately for each, in homogeneous environments (Cook 1999)? How do we explain the acquisition of multiple languages simultaneously?

It is now well recognized that the dominant constructs in linguistics are founded on monolingual norms and practices. We are also beginning to see a realization among mainstream scholars that their dichotomous constructs are misleading and distorting, especially for an understanding of plurilingual practices in non-Western communities (see Dorian 2004 for a discussion). McLaughlin recounts the belated recognition during her fieldwork in Senegal that a local collaborator whom she discounted as an informant of a language because he was associated with another language was in fact a proficient insider with authoritative knowledge (McLaughlin and Sall 2001). Her unitary assumption of 'native speaker' did not let her accept her informant as having native proficiency in more than one language. Similarly, Makoni (2002) has described how colonial practices of classifying and labelling languages distorted the hybrid reality of South African languages.

These limitations derive from the dominant assumptions of linguistics, informed by the modernist philosophical movement and intellectual culture in which they developed. To begin with, the field treats language as a thing in itself: an objective, identifiable product. The field also gives importance to form, treating language as a tightly knit structure, neglecting other processes and practices that always accompany communication. Scholars have traced this development to Saussurean linguistics and the structuralist movement (Lantolf and Thorne 2006). Other biases follow from this assumption. Khubchandani (1997) has pointed out the inordinate emphasis on the temporal life of language, motivating linguists to chart the linear stages by which imperfect forms develop to a stasis, at which point they become fully fledged forms. Inadequate attention is paid to the way in which various language forms and varieties are embedded in diverse environments, perfectly adequate in their own way for the functions at hand.

Therefore, Kubchandani (1997) calls for a spatial orientation. Such an approach would also rectify the lack of attention to the ecological factors of language. We have to understand how language is meshed with other symbolic systems and embedded in specific environments, both shaping and being shaped by these. Mainstream linguistics also fails to give importance to attitudinal, psychological and perceptual factors that mould the intersubjective processes of communication. This failing is partly due to the primacy of cognition and reason in communication. There is also a resultant lack of appreciation of the complexity of human communication, marked by indeterminacy, multimodality and heterogeneity. Mainstream linguistics prioritizes the homogeneity of community, competence and language structure, treating it as the basic requirement that facilitates communication. Even when diversity is addressed, it is treated as a variation deriving from a common form or shared norms.

However, in the context of post-modern globalization, as all communities become increasingly multilingual with the transnational flow of people, ideas and things, scholars are beginning to question the dominant constructs in the field. Even Western communities are beginning to acknowledge the diversity, hybridity and fluidity at the heart of language and identity. The struggle now is to find new metaphors and constructs that would capture plurilingual communication. How do we practise linguistics that treats human agency, diversity, indeterminacy and multimodality as the norm? As the constructs of modern linguistics are influenced by the modernist philosophical assumptions, some scholars are exploring alternate philosophical traditions to conceptualize the emerging realizations. Phenomenology (Kramsch 2002), ecological models (Hornberger 2003), chaos theory (Larsen-Freeman 2002) and Vygotskyan social cognitive theory (Lantolf and Thorne 2006) are some such attempts.

Scholars from post-colonial and non-Western communities are also beginning to represent their communicative practices in scholarly literature from the evidence they still find in their communities. This articulation is of course influenced by a world view and culture that differs from modernity. As we saw in the previous section, Khubchandani resorts to Indian spirituality and philosophy to represent what he perceives as Indigenous language practices. He uses metaphors like rainbow, symbiosis, osmosis, synergy and serendipity to describe a multilingual reality that lacks a suitable language in mainstream linguistics. Although these lesser known publications of periphery scholars are full of insight, they still lack elaborate theorization to produce sophisticated alternate models. There are other difficulties in working from untheorized local knowledge. One has to break the dominant hermeneutic moulds offered by modernism in order to interpret this knowledge. Modernism has denigrated local knowledge, and provided negative interpretations. Furthermore, local knowledge is not pure or whole, as dominant knowledge systems have appropriated it. At any rate, we must not glorify non-Western traditions. The local can contain chauvinistic tendencies, especially as the onslaught by modernity has been forcing the local to retreat further into more recalcitrant positions in a desperate attempt to maintain its independence. Also, although there are certain egalitarian practices at one level, inequalities in terms of caste, clan and gender have to be negotiated at other levels of communication.[1]

New research directions

What we know currently about pre-colonial forms of plurilingualism is derived from brief glimpses in archival records, incidental descriptions in literary works and theorization by informed scholars. We have to search for more in-depth descriptions of plurilingual communicative practices from archives. This is especially difficult because the knowledge of many colonized communities was suppressed or lacked the means for representation. However, without more evidence of plurilingual practices, discussions related to pre-colonial plurilingualism face the danger of being treated as figments of scholarly imagination.

A way to gain more empirical evidence of plurilingual communicative practices is by observing and recording vestiges of pre-colonial practices still found in many non-Western and traditional communities. We need more ethnographic research in these contexts to bring out the language practices and attitudes of people towards these practices from insider perspectives. Imposing mainstream linguistic perspectives on these practices has led to the distortion and suppression of local plurilingual practices in the scholarly literature.

Plurilingual practices are also found in contemporary youth and child communication in Western communities, especially motivated by digital and new media of communication. Not only do we need more studies of language negotiations in these contexts, we have to compare also how these practices are similar or different to pre-colonial plurilingual practices.

A particularly important area of study is plurilingual negotiation strategies. If speakers retain their own codes and depend on negotiation strategies to achieve intelligibility and meaning, we need a fuller description of the array of strategies used by multilinguals. This, again, requires more data-driven studies so that the negotiation strategies can be interpreted and explained for the functions they perform in context. The negotiation of English in transnational contact situations has generated some useful data for the study of plurilingualism (see House 2003; Meierkord 2004; Roberts and Canagarajah 2009).

As we gain more empirical data on these practices, we have to begin to compare how plurilingualism in different communities is similar or different. Although we generalize now to all communities because of a paucity of data, we should try to understand the community-specific nature of plurilingual practices and consider the strengths and limitations of these diverse traditions. Even within pre-colonial contexts, we know of plurilingual communication in Africa (Makoni 2002) and South America (de Souza 2002) in addition to those in South

Asia. There may be interesting differences between these traditions that will help us to develop a sharper understanding of plurilingualism in diverse communities.

In the same vein, we have to develop a better articulation between theorizations of plurilingual communicative practices by different theorists. There has been a proliferation of terms that need more clarity. We now have terms like code-meshing (Canagarajah 2006; Young 2004), third spaces (Gutiérrez 2008), crossing (Rampton 1995), polylingualism (Jørgensen 2008), translanguaging (García 2009) and heterography (Blommaert 2008). They need to be interrogated to examine their similarities and differences. We have to consider if these terms refer to plurilingualism in different contexts and domains of communication, or whether they mean the same thing in all contexts.

Conclusion

Plurilingual linguistic practices and the sociocultural values emanating from them existed long before countries such as India and Sri Lanka witnessed the forces of colonialism. The existing approaches that primarily interpret multilingual practices through modernist stances seem to be inadequate mainly because of their limited foundational assumptions. An understanding of the pre-colonial plurilingual ethos requires investigative approaches that treat language as an intersubjective social practice with a grammar that is emergent, hybrid and multimodal.

Plurilingual practices in pre-colonial societies have immense potential to inform postmodern multilingual practices. If unplanned language policies of the pre-colonial times bred social equality, intercultural contact and language maintenance among different linguistic communities, what led to the failure of planned policies that resulted in civil wars, social unrest and, in certain cases, the death of languages? Perhaps a comprehensive understanding of the differences between the multilingual practices during pre-colonial, colonial and post-colonial times may help to explain and perhaps inform us of their potential strengths, weaknesses and applications.

Related topics

Discourses about linguistic diversity; multilingualism and religion; rethinking discourses about the 'English-cosmopolitan' correlation; multilingualism in education in post-colonial contexts; codeswitching; heteroglossia; crossing.

Note

1 For a detailed discussion of the difficulties in rediscovering local knowledge of non-Western communities in our profession, see Canagarajah (2005b).

Further reading

Blommaert, J. (2008) *Grassroots Literacy: Writing, Identity and Voice in Central Africa*, London: Routledge.
(*Grassroots Literacy* addresses the relationship between globalization and the widening gap between 'grass-roots' literacies, or writings from ordinary people and local communities influenced by precolonial practices, and 'elite' literacies. The literacy practices of local communities involve multimodality and code-mixing, helping us to develop the notion of heterography. Jan Blommaert considers how 'grass-roots' literacy in the Third World develops outside the literacy-saturated environments of the developed world. In examining documents produced by socially and economically marginalized

writers, Blommaert demonstrates how the plurilingual practices of these writers are disqualified in contemporary institutions.)

Canagarajah, A. S. (2007) 'Lingua franca English, multilingual communities, and language acquisition', *The Modern Language Journal* 91(5): 923–39.

(This article brings out the unique features of language acquisition and communicative practices in multilingual communities. The article advances the ideas that language proficiency is adaptive and emergent and that language learning and use work through social negotiations in fluid communicative contexts via performance strategies.)

Pollock, S. (2006) *The Language of the Gods in the World of Men: Sanskrit, Culture, and Power in Premodern India*, Los Angeles: University of California Press.

(The book shows how Sanskrit as a cosmopolitan language in Asia had a relationship with diverse communities and languages that was markedly different from the relationship of other lingua francas like Latin or English. It also shows how local communities mixed their languages with Sanskrit to develop plurilingual communicative practices and literacies. The book helps us to understand the differences of pre-colonial plurilingualism from language practices in contemporary times.)

García, O. (2009) *Bilingual Education in the 21st Century: A Global Perspective*, Malden, MA: Wiley-Blackwell.

(This book critically challenges prevailing monolingual ideologies in bi- and multilingual education and advocates alternative pedagogical orientations. It acknowledges linguistic diversity as the norm and argues for a heteroglossically informed bilingual education.)

Bibliography

Annamalai, E. (2001) *Managing Multilingualism in India: Political and Linguistic Manifestations*, New Delhi: Sage.

Atkinson, D., Churchill, E., Nishino, T. and Okada, H. (2007) 'Alignment and interaction in a sociocognitive approach to second language acquisition', *Modern Language Journal* 91(2): 169.

Bakhtin, M. M. (1981) *The Dialogic Imagination*, Austin: University of Texas Press.

Balasubramaniam, A., Ratnamalar, K. and Subathini, R. (eds) (1999) *Studies in Sri Lankan Tamil Linguistics and Culture: Selected Papers of Professor Suseendirarajah*, Chennai: India Students' Offset Services.

Bhatia, T. K. and Ritchie, W. C. (2004) 'Bilingualism in South Asia' in T. K. Bhatia and W. C. Ritchie (eds) *The Handbook of Bilingualism*, pp. 780–807, Oxford: Blackwell.

Block, D. (2003) *The Social Turn in Second Language Acquisition*, Edinburgh: Edinburgh University Press.

Blommaert, J. (2008) *Grassroots Literacy: Writing, Identity and Voice in Central Africa*, London: Routledge.

Bright, W. (1984) *American Indian Linguistics and Literature*, The Hague: Mouton.

Canagarajah, A. S. (2000) 'Negotiating ideologies through English: Strategies from the periphery', in T. Ricento (ed.) *Ideology, Politics, and Language Policies: Focus on English*, Amsterdam and Philadelphia: John Benjamins.

——(2005a) 'Dilemmas in planning English/vernacular relations in post-colonial communities', *Journal of Sociolinguistics* 9(3): 418–47.

——(2005b) 'Reconstructing local knowledge, reconfiguring language studies' in A. S. Canagarajah (ed.) *Reclaiming the Local in Language Policy and Practice*, Mahwah, NJ: Lawrence Erlbaum.

——(2006) 'The place of world Englishes in composition: Pluralization continued', *College Composition and Communication* 57: 586–619.

——(2007) 'Lingua franca English, multilingual communities, and language acquisition', *The Modern Language Journal* 91(5): 923–39.

Chelliah, J. (1922) *A Century of English Education*, Vaddukoddai: Jaffna College.

Cook, V. (1999) 'Going beyond the native speaker in language teaching', *TESOL Quarterly* 33(2): 185–209.

Council of Europe (2000) *Common European Framework of Reference for Languages: Learning, Teaching, Assessment*, Language Policy Division: Strasbourg, available online at: www.coe.int/t/dg4/linguistic/CADRE_EN.asp

De Silva, K. M. (1977) 'The religions of the minorities', in K. M. De Silva (ed.) *Sri Lanka: A Survey*, Honolulu: University Press of Hawaii.

de Souza, L. M. (2002) 'A case among cases, a world among worlds: The ecology of writing among the Kashinawa in Brazil', *Journal of Language, Identity, and Education* 1(4): 261–78.

Dharmadasa, K. N. O. (1989) '"The people of the lion": Ethnic identity, ideology, and historical revisionism in contemporary Sri Lanka', *Sri Lanka Journal of the Humanities* 15: 1–35.

Dorian, N. (2004) 'Minority and endangered languages' in T. K. Bhatia and W. C. Ritchie (eds) *The Handbook of Bilingualism*, Oxford: Blackwell.

García, O. (2009) *Bilingual Education in the 21st Century: A Global Perspective*, Malden, MA: Wiley-Blackwell.

Gunasekera, B. (1893) *Glossary of Native and Foreign Words Occurring in Official Correspondence and Other Documents*, Colombo: The Government Printer.

Gunasekera, M. (n.d.) *The Postcolonial Identity of Sri Lankan English*, Colombo, Sri Lanka: Katha Publishers.

Gunawardana, R. A. L. H. (1990) 'The people of the lion: The Sinhala identity and ideology in history and historiography', in J. Spencer (ed.) *Sri Lanka: History and the Roots of Conflict*, London: Routledge.

Gutiérrez, K. (2008) 'Developing a sociocritical literacy in the Third Space', *Reading Research Quarterly* 43(2): 148–64.

Hornberger, N. H. (ed.) (2003) *Continua of Biliteracy: An Ecological Framework for Educational Policy, Research, and Practice*, Clevedon: Multilingual Matters.

House, J. (2003) 'English as a lingua franca: A threat to multilingualism?', *Journal of Sociolinguistics* 7(4): 556–78.

Jørgensen, J. N. (2008) 'Introduction: Poly-lingual languaging around and among children and adolescents', *International Journal of Multilingualism* 5(4): 161–76.

Khubchandani, L. M. (1983) *Plural Languages, Plural Cultures: Communication, Identity, and Sociopolitical Change in Contemporary India*, Honolulu: East-West Center by University of Hawaii Press.

——(1997) *Revisualizing Boundaries: A Plurilingual Ethos*, New Delhi: Sage.

——(1998) 'Plurilingual ethos: A peep into the sociology of language, *Indian Journal of Applied Linguistics* 24(1): 5–37.

Kramsch, C. (2002) 'Introduction: How can we tell the dancer from the dance?' in C. Kramsch (ed.) *Language Acquisition and Language Socialization: Ecological Perspectives*, London: Continuum.

Lantolf, J. P. and Thorne, S. F. (2006) *Sociocultural Theory and the Sociogenesis of Second Language Development*, New York: Oxford University Press.

Larsen-Freeman, D. (2002) 'Language acquisition and language use from a chaos/complexity theory perspective', in C. Kramsch (ed.) *Language Acquisition and Language Socialization: Ecological Perspectives*, London: Continuum.

McLaughlin, F. and Sall, T. S. (2001) 'The give and take of fieldwork: Noun classes and other concerns in Fatick, Senegal', in P. A. Newman and M. Ratiff (eds) *Linguistic Fieldwork*, Cambridge: Cambridge University Press.

Makoni, S. (2002) 'From misinvention to disinvention: An approach to multilingualism', in G. Smitherman, A. Spear and A. Ball (eds) *Black Linguistics: Language, Society and Politics in Africa and the Americas*, London: Routledge.

May, S. (2001) *Language and Minority Rights: Ethnicity, Nationalism and the Politics of Language*, London: Longman.

Meierkord, C. (2004) 'Syntactic variation in interactions across international Englishes', *English World-Wide* 25(1): 109–32.

Mohan, K. (1992) 'Constructing religion and caste: Manipulating Identities' *Social Science Research Journal*, 1: 1–12.

Mohanty, A. (2006) 'Multilingualism and predicaments of education in India: mother tongue or other tongue?' in O. García, T. Skutnabb-Kangas and M. E. Torres-Guzmán (eds) *Imagining Multilingual Schools: Languages in Education and Glocalization*, Clevedon: Multilingual Matters.

Pattanayak, D. P. (1984) 'Language policies in multilingual states', in A. Gonzalez (ed.) *Panagani: Language Planning, Implementation, and Evaluation*, Manila: Linguistic Society of the Philippines.

Peiris, E. (1969) 'Literary activity in Sinhala and Tamil during the Portuguese and the Dutch times', in U. D. I. Sirisena (ed.) *Education in Ceylon (from the Sixth Century B.C. to the Present Day) – A Centenary Volume, Volume 1*, Colombo: Ministry of Education and Cultural Affairs.

Peter, W. L. A. D. (1969) 'The Portuguese and the study of the national languages', in U. D. I. Sirisena (ed.) *Education in Ceylon (from the Sixth Century B.C. to the Present Day) – A Centenary Volume, Volume 1*, Colombo: Ministry of Education and Cultural Affairs.

Phillipson, R. (1992) 'ELT: The native speaker's burden?' *ELT Jounal*, 46(1): 12–18.

Pollock, S. (2006) *The Language of the Gods in the World of Men: Sanskrit, Culture, and Power in Premodern India*, Los Angeles: University of California Press.

Pratt, M. L. (1987) 'Linguistic Utopias', in N. Fabb, D. Attridge, A. Durant and C. MacCabe (eds) *The Linguistics of Writing: Arguments between Language and Literature*, Manchester: Manchester Universtiy Press.

Rampton, B. (1995) *Crossing: Language and Ethnicity among Adolescents*, London: Longman.

——(1997) 'Second language research in late modernity: A response to Firth and Wagner', *The Modern Language Journal* 81: 329–33.

Roberts, P. and Canagarajah, A. S. (2009) 'Broadening the ELF paradigm: Spoken English in an international encounter', in F. Sharifian (ed.) *English as an International Language: Perspectives and Pedagogical Issues*, Clevedon: Multilingial Matters.

Rogers, J. D. (1994) 'Post-orientalism and the interpretation of premodern and modern political identities: The case of Sri Lanka', *The Journal of Asian Studies* 53(1): 10–23.

——(2004) 'Early British rule and social classification in Lanka', *Modern Asian Studies* 38(03): 625–47.

Ruiz, R. (1984) 'Orientations to language planning', *NABE Journal* 8(2): 15–34.

Samaraweera, V. (1977) 'The evolution of a plural society', in K. M. De Silva (ed.) *Sri Lanka: A Survey*, Honolulu: University Press of Hawaii.

Singh, R. (ed.) (1998) *The Native Speaker: Multilingual Perspectives*, New Delhi: Sage.

Viswanathan, G. (1993) 'English in a literate society', in R. S. Rajan (ed.) *The Lie of the Land: English Literary Studies in India*, Oxford: Oxford University Press.

Wijesekera, O. H. de A. (1969) 'Language proficiency among scholars and literary activity in Pali and Sanskrit', in U. D. I. Sirisena (ed.) *Education in Ceylon (from the Sixth Century B.C. to the Present Day) – A Centenary Volume, Volume 1,* Colombo: Ministry of Education and Cultural Affairs.

Young, V. A. (2004) 'Your average nigga', *College Composition and Communication* 55(4): 693–715.

3

Rethinking discourses around the 'English-cosmopolitan' correlation

Scenes from formal and informal multilingual educational contexts

Vaidehi Ramanathan

Where do our disciplinary concepts come from? What are the processes by which they begin to garner particular associations and take root? In what ways do language policies enforce and thicken associations (and by extension inequities) and why is it important that we educators seek contexts whereby our default understandings of concepts and their terms are challenged? These questions form the backdrop against which the present localized discussion about the 'English-cosmopolitanism' and 'vernacular-parochialism' correlations are to be understood. Drawing on different kinds of ethnography data gathered in divergent contexts (in the same general multilingual geographic space in India), I shall argue that connections between these concepts and languages need to be constantly rethought and challenged, as they have crucial implications for all language educators and researchers. Doing so allows us to bring in grounded explorations around English and the vernaculars, and laminates existing scholarship in multilingualism by bringing in the political issues of equities, communities and civic engagement.

Within the research space of bi- and multilingualism, there has been, in recent years, some debate about English and its globalizing surges (especially in ESL) and its impact on local languages, with scholars writing about neo-liberalism (Phillipson 2008), changing national language policies that make social inequities more apparent (or at least apparent in different ways, see Ramanathan 2005a, 2006; Ramanathan and Morgan 2009) and ways in which educators effectively teach English while also creating contexts for home languages (cf. Blackledge 2001, 2005; Heller and Martin-Jones 2001; Martin-Jones and Jones 2000; McCarty 2002, 2005; Hornberger and Johnson 2007; Canagarajah 1997, 2002; Pavlenko and Blackledge 2004; Kramsch 2010). There appears to be, then, from some orientations at least, a split between other/home languages and English. The former is often associated with terms such as 'nativism', 'fundamentalism', 'chauvinism', 'homegrown-ness', 'parochialism', all of which connote to varying degrees, insularity and backwardness. English, on the other hand, given our globalizing surges, connotes 'Westernization', 'worldliness', 'liberalism', 'sophistication' and 'cosmopolitanism'. I draw on these connotations so as to counter and rethink them. When contextualized in grounded, multilingual realities, these concepts and their accompanying associations

(Delueze and Guattari 1994), find articulation in enactments around particular multilingual language policies that through reproduction perpetuate a host of inequities, thus adding to our accumulating sense of how particular concepts (and their realities) go together. As this chapter points out, we educators need to not only openly address the various associations that cluster around the concepts we use – the journeying these concepts and their associations do – but need constantly to find contexts whereby our collective assumptions about these terms are challenged, as it is only by doing so that we remain vigilant about not reproducing the very caveats we are also trying to counter (see Blackledge and Creese 2008 for an excellent discussion about contesting meanings around the term 'heritage').

Early developments in the field

Anchored as they are in various research domains in applied sociolinguistics, the key arguments in this essay seek to both contribute to domains of established scholarship while also pushing at their borders. Situated as the discussion is in a post-colonial space, namely, India, the essay builds on post-colonial scholarship that has addressed issues of the role of English and vernacular languages in formerly colonized, multilingual locales (Canagarajah 1997; Higgins 2009; Ramanathan 2005a), where English is the language of the elite, with tensions around the vernaculars emerging in a variety of contexts. This body of work, however, has thus far not adequately probed ways in which issues in non-formal, community domains laminate concerns in formal learning contexts. Addressing formal and non-formal learning concerns together allows us to also understand multilingualism in terms of local, vernacular, lived realities with sharp political edges. Such an orientation to multilingualism contributes to existing research on it, which has already alerted us to concerns around language removal (e.g. Pavlenko 2008), its impact in education-related contexts (e.g. Jessner 2006; Blackledge 2005; Creese et al. 2008; Creese and Martin 2003), and ways in which some languages get strategically used as lingua francas in domains in big cities (e.g. Block 2007). The essay also situates itself in the area of English and globalization (e.g. Blommaert and Omoniyi 2006; Seargeant 2009), which has focused on ideologies around English and internationalization, and ways in which an awareness of world Englishes is prodding us to rethink our language standards (Milroy and Milroy 1985), assessments (McNamara and Roever 2006) and tests (Shohamy 2006).

Issues of data and method

I will ground these terms – parochialism and cosmopolitanism – in relation to two points: (1) tracking issues in formal educational contexts, and (2) community issues in non-formal educational domains, with a view to probing the possibility that this breakdown – overscripted as it is becoming in several applied linguistics debates – is perhaps more bogus than we are willing to concede. My overall point here is a straightforward one: if we shift our gazes away from classrooms and tracking policies towards ways in which communities begin to heal themselves in the wake of traumatic events, this polarity more than falls apart; it actually gets turned on its head. And it is this reversal to which I intend to call our attention. Both domains of enquiry are based on my ongoing work, ethnographic research in India – indeed in the very city I was raised and schooled in (Ahmedabad in Gujarat), with Gujarati-medium (GM) and English-medium (EM) teachers in the city (Ramanathan 2006, 2005a, 2005b, 2004). Although my focus is localized, its implications, as I hope to point out, concern all scholars, regardless of discipline and our geographic positionings in the world.

My data – accumulated over a decade – comprise a range of materials gathered in Ahmedabad and with a variety of people in different institutions. Ahmedabad's population is approximately 4.5 million, and almost everybody speaks at least two languages. The official languages in the state and city are Gujarati, Hindi and English (although there are sizeable pockets of the population speaking a variety of other Indian languages), and all three languages are taught at the K-12 level (more on K-12 language policies presently). In the space of formal learning, my work has been based on three institutional sites: (1) a middle-class, EM Jesuit liberal arts institution (where I attended college) that has in the last decade been making changes to its institutional policies to accommodate vernacular-medium (VM) students of Dalit background, and where teachers freely intersperse the vernacular when teaching English in the language classes; (2) an upper-class, EM business college that encourages only English language use in its classes; and (3) a very poor, VM women's college where instruction is dominantly in Gujarati, including the teaching of English literature. Data from these institutions included extensive interviews with students, faculty and administrators, copies of pedagogic materials, texts, exams, student responses, and countless hours of classroom observations and field notes. Also part of this project are occasional individual and group meetings with both EM and VM teachers to discuss concerns about curriculum, especially the adapting of Western-based ELT materials partially made available by the British Council, and some of which I supply (when asked) in the Indian setting.

My data from the non-formal domain come from two sites, both of which embody Gandhian notions of 'non-cooperation': (1) an extracurricular programme run out of the women's college (mentioned above) that caters to addressing concerns of civic change; and (2) the Gandhi Ashram (which was historically Gandhi's home/office and continues to engage in Gandhian projects and be a source of Gandhianism in the state). Although my involvement with concerns in the women's college has been extensive, my involvement with the Gandhi Ashram is more recent. Whereas Gandhi's ideologies and ways in which they impact VM education in Gujarat are issues I have written about (see Ramanathan 2004, 2005a), it has only been in the last four years that I have begun to attend and participate in some of their workshops that are directly oriented to addressing community issues. Data from this space include three-hour interviews with key people running various civic projects in the city, field notes on workshops and a variety of historical materials written by and to Gandhi (letters, memos, bulletins) that are available in the Ashram and at the Rhodes House library in Oxford University (see Ramanathan 2009 for a discussion of some of this correspondence).

My seeking out of people at the Ashram has been intentional, and is propelled in part by the increasingly rabid Hindu nationalistic rhetoric emanating from the Gujarat state government (and until recently the central government as well).[1] My sustained engagement with one of the VM teachers (discussed here) prompted me to seek other pockets of practice that countered some of the dangerous political ideologies threatening secularism, and the workshops at the Gandhi Ashram seemed, in many ways, ideal. Not only do they have Gandhi's larger philosophy of non-cooperation against political hegemonies at their core (more on this presently) but they also opened up for me a way of understanding both how Gandhianism is situated and how particular dimensions of the identities of participants (Pavlenko and Blackledge 2004) get laminated. What I write about here, then, are skeins of Gandhianism that are echoed and enacted.

Policies around maintaining multilingualism: English and vernacular language learning in the formal K-12 domain

Most K-12 students in India get slotted into what are called VM (Gujarati in the present case) and EM tracks of schooling (see Ramanathan 2005a for a detailed discussion of inequities perpetuated by such tracking). Constitutionally, the Indian government promises the availability of an education in the mother tongue (in the 21 official languages) as well as an education in English (where English is the medium of instruction). In Gujarat, English is introduced as a foreign language in grade 5 in the GM classes, and Gujarati is introduced at the same grade level in EM classes. Hindi is introduced in grade 4 and Sanskrit in grade 7 in both mediums, and all EM and VM students learn these till grade 12. If policies existed in vacuums, this scene might be regarded as reasonably egalitarian; after all, students in both streams are becoming literate in several languages, with multilingualism being institutionally validated and legitimized.

But, as we know, educational policies and enactments of and around them, have rings of divisiveness and exclusionism around them (King 2001; Shohamy 2006; Hornberger 1988; McCarty 2005). Equity in this context, as indeed in many parts of the world, is directly tied to the selection of students for entry to college. Colleges in India, for the most part (except for a few liberal arts colleges), are in the EM, which of course means that students with VM backgrounds (where they have had access to a few hours of English instruction a week) have to compete with their EM counterparts (for whom English is almost a first language) in colleges and beyond. And given our globalizing world, inequities relating to who has access to English and how access to it opens other communal doors (jobs, interviews) play themselves out in differentiated ways, and fall directly into the 'parochiality-cosmopolitan' trap with which I began. In what follows, I show how English and the local vernacular (Gujarati) assume connotations and associations that contribute to cosmopolitanism and parochialism as composite singularities.

To underscore how the two tracks of education produce two very different 'literate in English' candidates, I offer Table 3.1 and Table 3.2, which lay out the 'minimal levels of learning' (MLL) (somewhat comparable to what in the California context is referred to as K-12 'standards') for English language learning in the two mediums. (I do need to note here that there has been a concerted effort to change state-wide educational policies so that English might now be introduced in the first grade instead of the fifth). For now, though, the present policies are still in place.

Two noticeable writing-related differences above are: (1) writing for VM students is presented as a discrete skill and is addressed separately from reading, a feature that contrasts with writing and reading being presented as conjoined entities for EM students; and (2) that writing for EM students is essayist in orientation from early on: 'writing paragraphs on given topics' (vs 'gaining the basic mechanics of English writing ... with proper spacing' for the VM student), or writing essays based on texts (vs learning to write words and sentences neatly for the VM student).

These unequal levels of literacy across the two mediums are evident in the very divergent kinds of English language readings for the two tracks for students. Table 3.2 offers a partial list of topics addressed in the English language textbooks used in each track.

Several interesting features emerge from a close comparison of the partial list of contents in the two sets of textbooks. VM texts with their general focus on survival English emphasize how language is used in particular Indian contexts (at the park, at the zoo or sending a telegram). The readings in EM texts, in contrast, are more cosmopolitan, drawing as they do from a variety of texts, including essays and short readings on Abraham Lincoln in grade 6, to those by Stephen Leacock and Tolstoy in grade 8, to those by Hemingway and Tagore in grade 10. Poetry, a genre that draws heavily on metaphorical use of language, is relegated to the 'optional' category in VM texts (indeed, prefaces to the textbooks say that poetry for VM students is to be regarded as 'supplementary reading'). Poetry is part of the mandated EM curriculum.

At a somewhat superficial level the two tables could be read as snippets of 'evidence'. However, it is their positioning in larger cultural and political interlocking chains (which include snobberies, pedagogies, ideologies) that contributes to sedimenting these inequities in

Table 3.1 Divergent MLLs for Gujarati-medium and English-medium students

	Excerpts from MLL from English textbooks used in the Gujarati medium	Excerpts from MLL from English textbooks used in the English medium
Grade 5	Writing: Gains control of the basic mechanics of writing in English like capital letters, small letters, punctuation, writing neatly on a line with proper spacing Transcribes words, phrases and sentences in English Produces words and spells them correctly Writes numbers up to 50, telephone numbers, road signs	Reading and writing: Reading textual material and writing answers to questions based on and related to the text Reading and interpreting and offering comments on maps and charts Reading children's literature and talking about it Writing paragraphs on given topics Reading and writing simple recipes
Grade 6	Reading: Reads aloud simple sentences, poems, dialogues and short passages with proper pauses Reads and follows given directions Reads numbers up to 100 Writing: Writes with proper punctuation marks Writes words and sentences neatly on a line with proper spacing, punctuation marks and capitalization Writes answers to questions based on text material	Reading and writing: Reading textual material and writing answers to questions based on the text Reading and interpreting simple abbreviations Reading narrative prose and adventure stories and talking about them Writing/building stories based on given questions/points Reading and using the telephone directory
Grade 7	Reading: Reads aloud simple sentences Finds key words and phrases from a text Writing: Writes words and sentences and paragraphs dictated with correct spellings, proper punctuation marks Learns to write words and sentences neatly on a line with proper spacing and punctuation Writes answers to questions based on the text	Reading and writing: Reading textual material and writing answers based on the text Writing essays based on the text Reading literary stories and prose lessons Reading simple passages of reflective prose Reading and interpreting common instructions such as railway timetables

Sources: Excerpts from MLL from English textbooks used in the Gujarati medium, Purani, Salat, Soni and Joshi 1998: 1–3 (for grades 5, 6 and 7, respectively). *Excerpts from MLL from English textbooks used in the English medium,* Purani, Nityanandan and Patel 1998: 2 (for grades 5, 6 and 7, respectively).

the formal realm. When reified in textbooks (crucial tools through which much of pedagogy takes shape, although by no means the only tool), it becomes quite obvious which set of students are becoming more 'cosmopolitan'. If, as Gunesch (2004) maintains, cosmopolitanism involves among other things, becoming a world citizen, becoming and viewing oneself as intercultural and breaking down national borders, then one could conceivably believe that the VM student is clearly not being given an adequate chance.

Shifting our gazes to non-formal domains

From a pedagogical standpoint, in a formal setting, we can see marked inequities contributing to a particular constellation of meanings summed up by the term 'cosmopolitan', a point that I, as researcher, reify when I openly say that the EM curriculum can be characterized in this way. It is precisely this extension of associations, though, that needs to be stopped in its tracks, both

Table 3.2 A partial list of contents for grades 6, 8 and 10

		VM list of contents	EM list of contents
Grade 6		Welcome, Friends	A Voyage to Lilliput
		A Fancy Dress Show	Farewell to the Farm
		A Seashore	The Changing World
		A Park	Abraham Lincoln (Parts 1 and 2)
		A Village Fair	Don Quixote Meets a Company of Actors
		In the School Compound	The Poet's House
		What Time is it Now?	Woodman, Spare that Tree!
		The Environment Day	City Streets and Country Roads
		(From: Nataraj *et al.* 1998: 3)	(From: Jadeja *et al.* 1999: 2)
Grade 8		GM (no authors provided)	Poetry: Under the Greenwood Tree: William Shakespeare
		Poetry: (optional)	She Dwelt among the Untrodden Ways: William Wordsworth
		Rhyme	To a Child Dancing in the Wind: W. B. Yeats
		Rhyme	The Listeners: Walter de la Mare
		Rhyme	Coming: Philip Larkin
		Only One Mother	A Blackbird Singing: R. S. Thomas
		The Picnic	Prose: Little Children Wiser than Men: Leo Tolstoy
		Two Birds	Do you know?: Clifford Parker
		Prose: Let's Begin	My Financial Career: Stephen Leacock
		Hello! I am Vipul	The Lady is an Engineer: Patricia Strauss
		A Railway Station	The Judgment Seat of Vikramaditya: Sister Nivedita
		At the Zoo	(From: Thaker 1999: 2)
		On the Farm	
		Good Manners	
		In the Kitchen	
		(From: Kotak *et al.* 1999)	
Grade 10		Poetry (optional)	Poetry:
		Laughing Song: Blake	Blow, Blow, Thou Winter Wind: Shakespeare
		In the Night: Naidu	London: Blake
		Wander Thirst: Gerald Gould	Upon Westminster Bridge: Wordsworth
		The Secret of the Machines: Rudyard Kipling	To–: Shelley
			La Belle Dame Sans Merci: Keats
			The Professor: Nissim Ezekeil
			The Fountain: Lowell
		Prose (no authors provided)	Prose:
		An Act of Service	Ramanujam: C. P. Snow
		Strange but True	On Saying Please: A. G. Gardener
		Have you Heard this One?	The Homecoming: Tagore
		Vaishali at the Police Station	Andrew Carnegie: E. H. Carter
		Prevention of Cruelty to Animals	A Day's Wait: Hemingway
		The Indian Village–Then and Now	After Twenty Years: O' Henry
		(From Kotak *et al.* 1998)	Vikram Sarabhai: M. G. K. Menon
			(From: Vamdatta *et al.* 2000: 44)

in our larger discipline and indeed, in my own thinking and texting. With a view towards reversing this polarity, I turn now to issues outside the four walls of the classroom. If we consider non-formal domains, then a completely different sense of the vernacular and cosmopolitanism arises. Although it may seem as if I am taking a major detour, I need to address some background in order to make the larger points about the concepts of English-cosmopolitanism and vernacular-parochialism, and their associations.

In 2001 and 2002 there were two devastating events that impacted the city of Ahmedabad in traumatic ways.[2] The first was an earthquake in 2001, the second, Hindu–Muslim riots in 2002. The earthquake of 2001 occurred around 9.00 am on 26 January (about the time that most educational institutions in the city were holding Republic Day celebrations) and measured 7.7 on the Richter scale, and although the epicentre of the quake was in the small town of Bhuj, about 200 miles from Ahmedabad, its tremors were felt for many miles around. An estimated 17,000 bodies were recovered, more than 30,000 people were reported dead or missing, 166,000 or more were injured and over a million homes were destroyed. The devastation in Ahmedabad, needless to say, was extensive, with school buildings crushing little children, flats and apartments coming down on families getting ready to start their day and businesses being decimated.

As if this were not enough, the following year, on 27 February 2002, the worst Hindu–Muslim riots in recent years broke out in the city. The events allegedly unfolded as follows (there is a lot of room for debate here about how planned or accidental the whole scenario was. Indeed, the case is still pending in the courts): 58 Hindu pilgrims returning from Ayodhya (a Hindu holy site) had their train cabin set ablaze outside Ahmedabad. The train had made a scheduled stop, during which a scuffle between some of the pilgrims and a tea vendor began, started to escalate and eventually culminated in the train compartment going up in flames and the pilgrims being burnt to death (allegedly by a group of Muslims). This led to a vicious collective anger on the part of hard-line Hindus that resulted in a horrendous week of rioting where Muslim homes were burnt, businesses looted, women raped and children killed. More than 1,000 Muslims died.

Although I cannot come close to accounting for the numerous local ways in which various groups in the city of Ahmedabad leapt into action, including the group of teachers I work with, I shall devote myself to explaining in some detail the work of two endeavours committed to communal and educational change in very different ways (see Ramanathan 2006 for a detailed discussion).[3] My point here is to underscore how vernacular resources – often seen as 'backward, rabid, fundamentalist, nativist', at least by the EM press in India – become a most valuable well of resources for the reconstruction of lives and communities. Learning and teaching in these contexts assume very different hues that complicate our collective notions of cosmopolitanism and of English.

A conceptual background for the two non-formal domains: Gandhian views on non-formal education, community service and non-cooperation

Because both providers of non-formal education echo Gandhian views in a variety of direct and indirect ways, I would like to provide in this section a brief and interconnected understanding of those aspects of non-cooperation that are most relevant to the issues at hand. Although world history documents non-cooperation in terms of civil disobedience, Satyagraha and non-violence, there are a host of details in this philosophy that are pertinent to the present discussion, including: (1) the value of harnessing the vernaculars (including those of promoting vernacular – medium education); (2) the importance of community service being an integral part of a basic education; and (3) promoting non-formal education that encourages a healthy development of civic citizenship.

Each of these ideals gets encased in the larger rhetorical strain of non-cooperation, which Gandhi advocated during his struggles for Indian Independence (see Ramanathan 2006 for a detailed discussion), and which people at the two institutions interpret and enact differently. The following are some excerpts from his writings on this topic.

Box 3.1 Gandhi's views on language and on non-formal and basic education

On vernacular (and English) education:

1 I hold it to be as necessary for the urban child as for the rural to have the foundation of his development laid on the solid work of the mother-tongue. It is only in unfortunate India that such an obvious proposition needs to be proved (Gandhi in *Harijan*, 9-9-'39, edited by Kumarappa 1954 (Gandhi 1954)).

2 The only education we receive is English education. Surely we must show something for it. But suppose we had been receiving during the past fifty years education through our vernaculars, what should we have today? We should have a free India, we should have our educated people, not as if they were foreigners in their own land, but speaking to the heart of the nation; they would be working amongst the poorest of the poor, and whatever they would have gained during the past fifty years would be a heritage for the nation (Gandhi, cited in Kumarappa 1954: 13) (Gandhi 1954).

On (non-)formal education:

3 But unless the development of the mind and body goes hand in hand with a corresponding awakening of the soul, the former alone would prove to be a poor lop-sided affair. By spiritual training I mean education of the heart. A proper and all-around development of the mind, therefore, can take place only when it proceeds *pari passu* with the education of the physical and spiritual faculties of the child. They constitute an indivisible whole. According to this theory, therefore, it would be a gross fallacy to suppose that they can be developed piecemeal or independently of one another (*Harijan*, 8-5-'37, in Prasad 1950).

4 By education I mean all-round drawing out of the best in children—body, mind, and spirit. [Formal] Literacy is not the end of education nor the beginning. It is only one of the means whereby men and women can be educated (Gandhi, *Harijan*, 31-7-'37, in Prasad 1950).

5 [Non-formal education] will check the progressive decay of our villages and lay the foundation for a juster social order in which there is no unnatural division between the 'haves' and the 'havenots' and everybody is assured a living wage and the rights to freedom...It will provide a healthy and a moral basis of relationship between the city and village and will go a long way towards eradicating some of the worst evils of the present social insecurity and poisoned relationship between the classes (*Harijan*, 9-10-'37, in Prasad 1950).

6 Fundamentals of basic education:

   1 All education to be true must be self-supporting, that is it will pay its expenses excepting the capital.

   2 In it the cunning of the hand will be utilized even up to the final stage, that is to say, hands of pupils will be skillfully working at some industry for some period during the day.

   3 All education must be imparted through the medium of the provincial language.

   4 In this there is no room for giving sectional religious training. Fundamental universal ethics will have full scope.

> 5 This education whether it is confined to children or adults, male or female, will find
> its way to the homes of the pupils.
> 6 Since millions of students receiving this education will consider themselves as of
> the whole of the India, they must learn an interprovincial language. This common
> inter-provincial speech can only be Hindustani written in Nagari or Urdu script.
> Therefore, pupils will have to master both scripts. (Harijan, 1-11-'47, in Prasad 1950).

Gandhi's views (see above) have to be interpreted in the political context in which they were made. From approximately 1920–47, Gandhi's views were decidedly nationalistic, as he and his allies were trying to rally the country towards destabilizing the Raj, and towards gaining Indian independence. Because his views on the above issues were directly anti-English – as he felt that the language divided the country – his championing of the vernaculars sits in a polarized position (somewhat simplistic by today's standards) vis-à-vis English. As I have pointed out in detail elsewhere, although the surge towards EM education is ever present, it is accompanied by pockets of deep ambiguities and tensions (Ramanathan 2005a), and one of my overall roles in this larger endeavour has been to actively carve out research and textual space – both in India and in the West – whereby these alternative voices are heard. Although Gandhi's message of non-violence seems to be ironically completely forgotten in Gujarat, given the horrific riots of 2002, the larger strain of non-cooperation still resonates. As we will see, non-cooperation in the two endeavours discussed presently is directed against perceived social forces that preserve inequities. The quiet way in which both projects work at bridging perceived gulfs is reminiscent of Gandhi's insistence on being 'civil' and of responding to tyranny by searching for non-violent, quiet alternatives. They also contest a host of associations around the vernacular and parochialism, thus permitting us to rethink the English-cosmopolitan set of relations.

The two endeavours: drawing on non-cooperation to expand 'education' and civic engagement

The National Social Service Scheme at the Women's College

Located in the inner-city, the Women's College is a low-income GM liberal arts college in downtown Ahmedabad where much of the rioting of 2002 occurred. In my previous writing (Ramanathan 2006) regarding this college, I have discussed ways in which the National Social Service (NSS) – a nation-wide, Gandhian, social service organization – a chapter of which is in this school, engages many of the institution's female students in extracurricular activities that directly target community needs. Begun in commemoration of Gandhi's centennial year in 1969, the organization encourages students to volunteer time towards social projects, including those relating to literacy, health, sanitation, women and children's welfare, AIDS awareness, drug addiction awareness, human rights and national integration.[4] Added to this list is the recent work by this school to address the needs of families most affected by the two events. Although I have addressed ways in which this extracurricular project harnesses vernacular resources in some detail elsewhere (Ramanathan 2006), I will for the purposes of the present discussion draw primarily on interview data with the key person that runs this project, namely Mr. P.

Although he teaches English literature, particularly nineteenth-century British literature, in Gujarati at the college, Mr. P. began this project more than 15 years ago with a commitment to translating the best of Gandhi's ideals – of service, self-respect, valuing the vernacular backgrounds of his students – to specific contexts of practice. Realizing that he operates in a space where speaking openly of sociopolitical issues is most incendiary – in downtown Ahmedabad where much of the rioting occurred, in a very poor, diverse college with students from both Hindu and Muslim (as well as other) backgrounds – this man works towards expanding his view of education by connecting it to issues of 'citizenship', taking pride in being 'Gujarati', and relying on what is currently within one's reach to ply instruments of change. When asked about why the classroom was not a viable sphere for his message, he said:

> The classroom is the most incendiary place to raise community issues. ... you see, the students come from such different backgrounds, with such divergent points of view, how can I bring up political and community issues, especially now when everyone, but everyone is reeling from the riots? Some of my students have lost their homes, some family members. *But I will say this: I know that I want to address these issues somehow; I want them to know that education is not only about what they learn and what we teach in classes about Dryden and Congreve, it is about participating in the community.* It is about taking the best of literary values – connecting to other humans – and living them. So rather than be overtly political about it, I channel their and my energy in my projects where the focus is on the community, regardless of who the members of the community are, and I have both Muslim and Hindu students working in these projects.
>
> *(FI: 2: 2, 2 June 2004)*[5]

When the earthquake hit, he organized his students into groups that went out and worked in the community: in communal kitchens for people who were left homeless, in contacting municipal authorities for clean drinking water, and in getting blankets and warm clothes because it was winter. Because the riots occurred around the time when many of the students were to take their final university exams, and because the exam centres were far away and there was a curfew in town, he organized buses that would take students from riot-affected areas to the exam centres.

As he explains in the excerpt above, 'education' for him is more about 'connecting to other humans' than it is about what is taught and learned in the classroom, and moving toward this end, without engaging in divisive political rhetoric, is instrumental in his mission, as his focus is on 'what needs to get done, what the reality in front of me is like' (FI 2: 5). One way in which he works toward this goal is by emphasizing in his workshops (for NSS volunteers) what being 'Gujarati' means: its diversity (that fact that it is a native language for a diverse set of people including Hindus, Muslims, Parsis and Jews) the fact that it is home to other migrant Indians (like my family who are originally Tamilian but who have settled in Gujarat); the fact that it is the birthplace of Gandhi who represented the last word on community service, non-formal education and above all Hindu–Muslim unity. As he says,

> My job is to create a space whereby such sentiments and values about community participation can flourish. The last 3 or 4 years have been so painful for so many people in this state. I want to be able to say that when my students graduate they do so with some pride and awareness of the ties that bind them to their fellow citizens. That the riots should have happened here in Gandhi's home state, when his life's actions centred around Hindu–Muslim unity – how do I not get my Gujarati students to see that irony? My problem is: how do I get them to realize this inductively? How can I make that realization happen quietly, without dogma, without saying too much?
>
> *(FI 2: 7)*

One way in which he communicates his message indirectly is by not speaking about NSS issues in the classroom, or in corridors where students abound, but by relying on his NSS student volunteers to 'spread the word' as indeed they do. As he explains:

> It is crucial that this work not become a dogma ... given my position, my speaking of it directly runs that risk. I speak of it in workshops, I organize their camps, I attend the training sessions with them; I want to do all that, but I will not seek students out by speaking of it directly. They have to want to do this work. The value of non-formal education is that it remain non-formal. You take it into the classroom and it is gone. Pfff ... like that! They have to hear of this community work from other involved students; they have to see their classmates being fulfilled by this.

> *(FI 2: 13)*

Echoes of Gandhi's views on non-formal education are obvious here, as indeed is the Gandhian insistence on proceeding with such work quietly and indirectly. Although non-formal education has traditionally been conceived of as an educational alternative operating outside the constraints of the classroom, the changes that such education seems to seek eventually make their way to classrooms.[6]

Education and community at the Gandhi Ashram

This theme of quietly working on community problems is most resonant in the Gandhi Ashram, as well, which houses a programme called *Manav Sadhna* (MS—*Human Improvement*). The Gandhi Ashram in Ahmedabad is the largest of Gandhi's ashrams, as this particular one served as his headquarters during the struggle for independence. On the banks of the river Sabarmati, the ashram is located on spacious grounds. One side holds his library and archival materials about him, and on the doorway to this section is a huge tribute to Martin Luther King. The other side of the ashram has what used to be his living quarters: his spinning wheel, his desk, rooms of his closest allies. The ashram, even today, is a place that welcomes the poorest of the poor and offers a haven and rehabilitation for those seeking it.

All work that goes on in the Gandhi Ashram seems to embody the quintessential 'Gandhian' ideals of self-reliance, cross-religious unities, non-formal and basic education, coupled with a thick strain of quiet non-cooperation. Begun by three people – Jayesh Patel, Anar Patel and Viren Joshi – in 1991, *Manav Sadhna* today runs more than 20 well-developed community-oriented programmes. Born and raised in the ashram because his father was a staunch Gandhian follower, the first of the three has Gandhi 'in his bones', so to speak and much of what follows in this section is drawn from my interviews with him, from participating in workshops he has led and from interviews with other people at the ashram with whom he has put me in touch.

Although there are several similarities between the NSS work of Mr. P. and the projects of *MS* – both have strong Gandhian strains, both enhance the vernaculars, both are community-oriented – there are interesting differences. Unlike the project run by Mr. P. where civic engagement is parallel to formal, classroom-based learning, the focus of the projects at the Gandhi Ashram is on interpreting all education as 'civic education' and on attending to the most basic of human needs (food, clothing, shelter) before addressing any issues related to formal learning. Also, unlike the NSS project, the children that the ashram caters to are the extremely poor. When I spent time at the ashram in May and June 2004, Jayesh recalled how the three of them began their programme with the explicit aim of working with the poorest persons they could find. Although he narrated this to me in Gujarati, I am presenting it below in translation. (I need to note here that I am deliberately choosing to present extensive, fuller quotes to mitigate the loss already encountered in translation, a process that necessitates the adding of more layers of 'distance' from the very first layer of the narrator's recounting and my interpreting in Gujarati, to my then presenting and interpreting this narrative in academic English.)

[T]he three of us had noticed that a lot of village people, because of a scarcity of resources in villages – equipment, money, water – migrate to the cities and they live in slums. And we found that mothers work as cleaners/maids in peoples' homes, fathers work in pulling handcarts and they send their children out to pick rags. The childhoods of these children are completely lost. Middle-class children have all they could possibly want but these others have no opportunities and we decided we wanted to work with these children. Think globally, act locally … so the three of us started our work. The three of us took along biscuits, chocolates, some clothes and we set out in a rickshaw and went to the Naranpura crossroads. I still remember this and there we saw two children working in a tea stall, making tea, and serving it to customers. We asked the tea-stall owner if we could sit with the children and chat with them. Hope you don't mind. We started talking to the children who were clearly suspicious of us. 'Who are these people who are asking me all these questions', they thought. We told the children, 'We came to be friends with you. Will you share a meal with us?' The children said yes. … and when we got to know them, we gave them clothes, cut their nails, shampooed their hair, got them shoes. We went again in a few days, and by then, these children had talked about what we had done for them with their friends and before long they would wait for us to come, calling 'Jayeshbhai Virenbhai' … We soon realized it was getting very difficult for us to cater to all the children there and so asked, 'Will you come to the Gandhi Ashram? We have a campus there and we can introduce you to people there. Can you come once a week?' Our very first programme was 'Back to childhood' in '91. While we had each done work with children before this, this was our first *Manav Sadhna* project. Soon thereafter, the children started coming, first 10, then 15 … they seemed to enjoy coming here. We used to give them baths, clothes and then began helping them with their homework. You'll see some of them today … they've grown but are still here. They were dirty, unbathed, with unwashed clothes … we showered them with care, told them stories, prayed with them, showed them films and sang songs with them. We did a lot through play and then would eat together with them.

(Jayesh Patel, Gandhi Ashram: 2, 3 June 2004)

As Jayesh explained to me: 'for us education is community work; if schooling does not teach you to connect with your fellow humans, then what good is it?' (3 June 2004).

Like the NSS-related work at the Women's College, MS is committed to working with and around social stratifications, including Hindu–Muslim tensions, some of which were exacerbated during the quake (and very definitely during the riots; indeed, there had been reports that particular groups of peoples, including Muslims, did not get the aid they needed, cf. Engineer 2003). Jayesh, Viren, Anar and the MS volunteers began working with some very poor destitute villages in a corner of Kutch (not far from the epicentre), where 80 per cent of the population are Muslim, and which have a high proportion of Hindu migrants. Almost all the homes had been decimated. As Jayesh explains:

There was almost nothing left there. We wanted to do something about this. *We did an initial analysis and educated ourselves of their needs*: broken down homes, no resources, no fodder or water for livestock, the general geographical conditions of the place (frequent cyclones and hurricanes). Over the last few years we have reached a point where it is self-sufficient, stopped migration, worked out Hindu–Muslim tensions to where during the recent riots, not one of these 47 villages reported anti-Hindu, anti-Muslim incidents.

(Jayesh Patel, Gandhi Ashram: 4, 3 June 2004)

This close attention to 'educating oneself', of figuring out and questioning one's own default assumptions has echoes of Gandhi's non-cooperation, and finds interesting articulation in the idea that we each need to 'not cooperate' with our default views but attempt to step outside them by 'educating ourselves' by learning from others. A point that illustrates this best has to do with MS's work in a set of villages after the massive earthquake and ways in which they went about rehabilitating the lives of the villagers after paying close attention to the needs of the local people, and by drawing extensively on their valued, vernacular ways of living. Robin Sukhadia with whom I have been in email contact, and who has worked with MS, in some of these villages, explains on his website the conflicts many of the villagers experienced between the modern kinds of houses that were being built for them after the quake and the 'traditional' homes they were used to and wanted:

There has been tremendous financial and infrastructural support pouring into Kutchh after the earthquake, and so many NGOs and international agencies and religious organizations have come here to build homes and rebuild this area ... new hospitals have been built, new roads, new homes, but sadly, it seems to me, that many of these projects (which are funded mainly from abroad) have very insensitively proceeded with building living 'communities' without much thought as to the traditional way of life here ... and it seems that many of the villagers and farmers who lost everything here, do not wish to live in homes that resemble city homes and pre-fabricated enclaves ... the villagers, who have lived off the land for generations, have nowhere to put their cattle, to grow their crops, or to stay connected to the land in these new homes ... sadly many of the homes are empty because the villagers have decided it is better to be homeless than succumb to these imposed forms of living which are being built in the name of service to the poor but ... MS's approach here, thankfully, has been very different. They have, instead of imposing designs and architects, rather empowered the local communities to design their own homes in their traditional methods ... they have built *Bhungas*, beautiful, mud-based round buildings that have been in use for hundreds of years here ... not surprisingly, these structures were the only ones that survived the earthquake ... they are very practical and make sense for this environment. So, *Manav Sadhna* provided the guidance for the reconstruction of their homes, and the community ... [look at] what happens in the name of service.

(Robin Sukhadia, www.bigcirclemedia.com/ahimsa/archives/000147.php)

The idea of drawing on, listening to and documenting what a community needs permeates all aspects of MS's projects and is a key issue in the orientation workshops for MS volunteers in which I participated. Not only are the volunteers – all of whom are Gujarati – reminded of and educated in Gandhi's ideals in the workshops, but they are encouraged to make connections between the work they do and the specific Gandhian ideals they are enacting. So, whether it is working in a very poor Urdu-medium Muslim school (that municipal authorities have largely ignored) or finding clothes and food supplies for a very poor farmer who is suffering the consequences of a bad crop and little rain, or organizing the celebrations of a key religious holiday (Hindu, Muslim, Christian, Jewish, Sikh, Parsi), among others, the volunteers are provided platforms and contexts whereby both their conceptual understanding of Gandhi and their practice are extended and looped into each other. As one of the volunteers tells me: 'these workshops are not just about educating ourselves about Gandhi, but about bringing our work back to Gandhi ... we go out and do Gandhi's work, but we each have to come back to Gandhi' (Volunteer 2: 2, 11 June 2004).

Interestingly, politically and community-oriented as all of this work by MS is, there is little or no reference to political events, and ways in which they have exacerbated social/religious stratifications in the city. When discussing the work done by MS volunteers after the riots, no overt mention was made of Gujarat's chief minister (who has been accused of not doing enough to protect the Muslims) or of the incendiary rhetoric of the ruling BJP state government. The ideas that 'there is a job to be done' and 'I have to do it' (Jayesh Patel: 5, 10 June 2004) seem to be a dominant theme, and non-cooperation during this time was and still is enacted in terms of quietly engaging in the opposite of all riot-related acts: of making shelter, finding lost relatives, distributing food and clothes, finding employment for the numerous widowed women and providing a haven for orphaned children. Although all of the volunteers at MS are engaged in various riot-related projects, it is with the children that they are most concerned. As Jayesh explains:

> If we wish to reach the parents, we have to start with children. It is only through our work that we pass on our message. We cannot formally teach anybody anything; we can only do. In the end, everything we learn goes back to the community. Why not start with the community in the first place? Why not start with children?
>
> *(Jayesh Patel, Gandhi Ashram: 6, 3 June 2004)*

Clearly, distinctions between 'civic engagement' and 'education' have blurred here; they are in this context almost synonymous.

Coming back to parochialism and cosmopolitanism

Leaving this local context of Ahmedabad aside now, I'd like to move back to the topic of parochialism and cosmopolitanism within multilingualism, with which I began. If cosmopolitanism is about extending oneself to the other, about bringing worldliness into the local, about reflecting the heterogeneity of the universe in the small spaces we occupy (teaching, learning, communal) then, how can the efforts of Mr. P. and of *Manav Sadhna* not be read as such? Steeped as they are in the vernacular – Gujarati in the present case – all their efforts are about engaging the other in the most humane and hospitable of terms. The boundaries we have to contend with in formal education in multilingual spaces (tracking, grading, judging students' language proficiencies and basing evaluations of 'intelligence' on them) breed the very insularity that I was talking about regarding VM education in Ahmedabad and that we can recognize in different forms in various parts of our planet. It is here, though, where we educators come in, where we seek spaces outside the formal realm of education, in non-formal spaces, so as to contest a chain of concepts and associations that emerge from our formal domains: where we hear in Mr. P.'s words that being identified as 'Gujarati' is not about being in the VM stream, as much as it is also about civic engagement in communities, and where we recognize in Jayesh Patel's endeavours the value of all education leading eventually to community developments and of drawing on the most local of resources to extend ourselves to others.

What these conceptual binarisms in multilingualism (parochialism/cosmopolitanism, vernacular/English, formal/non-formal) also open up are issues around the presumed staticity of these associations in discourses about multilingualism. A key issue here is that components of concepts and their associations are not constants or simple variations (that presume a core/ ideal), but clusters of ordinates that emerge at particular times in certain contexts that we then imbue with a set of meanings (through concepts). These 'meanings' move along particular paths, changing hues as they proceed and we researchers need to be ever mindful of our proclivities to see them as repeated enactments and iterabilities. Thus, it may not be a simple case of turning the English-cosmopolitan or vernacular-parochialism correlations on their head – the premise with which I began – but may be more that our concepts and the associations we garner around them are in constant flux, forever being modified and transformed (Blackledge and Creese 2008). From this point of view, English then is a vernacular, just as a language other than English is cosmopolitan.

Related topics

Multilingualism in education in post-colonial contexts; multilingualism and religion; discourses about linguistic diversity; global English and bilingual education.

Notes

1 There has been much discussion (in newspapers, among people, in schools and in the group of teachers I work with) about the state having 'forgotten Gandhi' and his teachings in the wake of the recent Hindu–Muslim violence in the city. Gandhi's views on Hindu–Muslim unity have generally been viewed as anathema by some factions of the right wing Hindu BJP party in the state, as he was seen as supporting Muslims too much, and for espousing a view of Hinduism that was generally deemed 'effeminate'.
2 Some of what follows has appeared in Ramanathan 2005a and 2006.
3 Some activist groups in Ahmedabad include:

   (a) Janvikas: an organization that focuses on the empowerment and development of NGOs in Gujarat;
   (b) Janpath Citizens Initiative: a coalition of over 200 local grass-roots NGOs coming together in the days following the Gujarat quake;
   (c) Navasarjan Trust: led by Martin Macwan: an organization representing Dalit rights in India;
   (d) Rishta: a Gujarat Jesuit writers' cell: engaged in a series of workshops for the development of vernacular media, especially for Christian and Muslim youth;
   (e) Manav Sadhna: run out of the Gandhi Ashram.

4 Yearly camps and training are offered for all volunteers for a minimal fee as well as extended camps for college-going youth. Themes of some camps in the last few years have been 'Youth for sustainable development', 'Youth for wasteland development' and Youth for greenery'.
5 FI refers to Faculty interview; GA to Gandhi Ashram.
6 This is certainly evident with the NSS-related work that student volunteers present. I was able to observe at least three or four such instances where NSS student volunteers would speak of their work before Mr. P. arrived in class. In several instances, students of their own accord also made connections between what they were learning in their classes with issues they were wrestling with in the field. In an Economics class, for instance, I heard several of these NSS student volunteers make valuable connections between how issues related to the state and national budget had direct connections to allowances for the farming women they worked with (*yeh j BJP ka budget hain na, usme to kheti-vaadi ke liye itna jagah nahin hain—the BJP's budget does not really have much room for farming-related issues*); how economic theories of rural development in Africa

resonated with issues in rural Gujarati (*Africa ki jo developmental economics ki baate ki, na, voh to hamaara Gujarat mein bahut relevant hain—the developmental economics of Africa that we have been studying is relevant to Gujarat*), how connections between the monsoon and agrarian economics percolated down to water purification projects they were involved in (*yeh agricultural economics aur baarish ka season hain, na, uska bahut sambandh hain hamaare water purification projects mein—there are many co-relations between the rainy season and agrarian economics on the one hand and the water purification projects we have been involved in, on the other*). Thus, although Mr. P. does not directly use the classroom as a site for promoting community change, his work eventually makes its way back to classrooms, a fact that seems to fill him with quiet pride.

Further reading

Auer, P. and Li, W. (2007) *Handbook of Multilingualism and Multilingual Communication*, Berlin: Mouton de Gruyter.

Blackledge, A. and Creese, A. (2010) *Multilingualism: A Critical Perspective*, London: Continuum.

Martin-Jones, M. and Jones, K. (2000) *Multilingual Literacies: Reading and Writing Different Worlds*, Philadelphia: John Benjamins.

Pavlenko, A. (2009) *Multilingualism in Post-Soviet Countries*, Clevedon: Multilingual Matters.

Pavlenko, A. and Blackledge, A. (eds) (2004) *Negotiation of Identities in Multilingual Contexts*, Clevedon: Multilingual Matters.

Bibliography

Blackledge, A. (2001) 'Language, literacy and ideology in a multilingual state', *The Curriculum Journal* 12(3): 291–312.

——(2005) *Discourse and Power in a Multilingual World*, Philadelphia: John Benjamins.

Blackledge, A. and Creese, A. (2008) 'Contesting "language" as 'heritage': Negotiation of identities in late modernity', *Applied Linguistics* 29(4): 533–54.

Block, D. (2007) 'Niche lingua francas: An ignored phenomenon', *TESOL Quarterly, Special Issue of Language Policy* 41(3): 561–6.

Blommaert, J. and Omoniyi, T. (2006) 'Email fraud: Language, technology, and the indexicals of globalization', *Social Semiotics* 16(4): 573–605.

Canagarajah, A. S. (1997) *Resisting Imperialism in English Teaching*, Oxford: Oxford University Press.

——(2002) *Critical Academic Writing and Multilingual Students*, Michigan: University of Michigan Press.

Creese, A. and Martin, P. (2003) *Multilingual Classroom Ecologies: Inter-Relationships, Interactions, and Ideologies*, Clevedon: Multilingual Matters.

Creese, A., Martin, P. and Hornberger, N. H. (2008) *Ecology of Language*, New York: Springer.

Delueze, G. and Guattari, F. (1994) *What is Philosophy?* H. Tomlinson and G. Burchell (trans.), New York: Colombia University Press.

Engineer, A. (2003) *The Gujarat Carnage*, New Delhi: Orient Longman.

Gandhi, M. K. (1954) *Medium of Instruction*. B. Kumarappa (trans.). Ahmedabad: Navjivan Publishing House.

Gunesch, K. (2004) 'Education for cosmopolitanism', *Journal of Research in International Education* 3(3): 251–75.

Heller, M. and Martin-Jones, M. (eds) (2001) *Voices of Authority: Education and Linguistic Difference*, Connecticut: Ablex.

Higgins, C. (2009) *English as a Local Language: Postcolonial Identities and Multilingual Practices*, Clevedon: Multilingual Matters.

Hornberger, N. H. (1988) *Bilingual Education and Language Maintenance: a Southern Peruvian Quechua Case*, Providence, Rhode Island: Foris Publications.

Hornberger, N. H. and Johnson, D. (2007) 'Slicing the onion ethnographically: Layers and spaces in multilingual language education policy and practice', *TESOL Quarterly* 41(3): 509–32.

Jadeja, R., Shrinivas, R. and Vansia, K. (1999) *English, Standard 5*, Gandhinagar: Gujarat State Board of Textbooks.

Jessner, U. (2006) *Linguistic Awareness in Multilinguals: English as a Third Language*, Clevedon: Multilingual Matters.

King, K. (2001) *Language Revitalization Processes and Prospects*, Clevedon: Multilingual Matters.

Kotak, G., Ghodiwala, A., Purani, T. and Pandya, N. (1996) *English, Standard 8*, Gandhinagar: Gujarat State Board of Textbooks.

McCarty, T. (ed.) (2002) *Rough Rock and the Struggle for Self-Determination Indigenous Schooling*, Mahwah, NJ: Lawrence Erlbaum, Inc.

McNamara, T. and Roever, C. (2006) 'Language testing: The social dimension', Boston, MA: Blackwell.

——(ed.) (2005) *Language, Literacy and Power in Schooling*, Mahwah, NJ: Lawrence Erlbaum.

Kramsch, C. (2010) *The Multilingual Subject*, Oxford: Oxford University Press.

Martin-Jones, M. and Jones, K. (2000) *Multilingual Literacies: Reading and Writing Different Worlds*, Philadelphia: John Benjamins.

Milroy, J. and Milroy, L. (1985) *Authority in Language: Investigating Language Prescription and Standardization*, Boston: Routledge and Kegan Paul.

Nataraj, S. and Joshi, P. (1999) *English, Standard 5*, Gandhinagar: Gujarat State Board of Textbooks.

Pavlenko, A. (2008) *Multilingualism in Post-Soviet Countries*, Clevedon: Multilingual Matters.

Pavlenko, A. and Blackledge, A. (2004) *Negotiation of Identities in Multilingual Contexts*, Clevedon: Multilingual Matters.

Phillipson, R. (2008) 'The linguistic imperialism of neoliberal empire', *Critical Inquiry in Language Studies* 5(1): 1–43.

Ramanathan, V. (2004) 'Ambiguities about English: Ideologies and critical practice in vernacular-medium settings in Gujarat, India', *Journal of Language, Identity, and Education* 4(1): 45–65.

——(2005a) *The English-Vernacular Divide: Post-Colonial Language Policies and Practice*, Clevedon: Multilingual Matters.

——(2005b) 'Situating the researcher in research texts: Dilemmas, questions, ethics, new directions', *Journal of Language, Identity, and Education* 4(4): 291–7.

——(2006) 'Gandhi, non-cooperation and socio-civic education: Harnessing the vernaculars', *Journal of Language, Identity, and Education* 5(3): 229–50.

——(2009) 'Silencing and languaging in the assembling of the Indian nation-state: British public citizens, the epistolary form, and historiography', *Journal of Language, Identity, and Education* 8(2–3): 203–19.

Ramanathan, V. and Morgan, B. (2009) 'Global warning: West-based TESOL, class-blindness and the challenge for critical pedagogies', in F. Sharifian (ed.) *English as an International Language: Perspectives and Pedagogical Issues*, Clevedon: Multilingual Matters.

Seargeant, P. (2009) *The Idea of English in Japan: Ideology and the Evolution of a Global Language*, Clevedon: Multilingual Matters.

Shohamy, E. (2006) *Language Policy: Hidden Agendas, New Approaches*, New York, Routledge.

Thaker, P. (ed.) (1999) *English, Standard 8*, Gandhinagar: Gujarat State Board of Textbooks.

Vamdatta, D., Joshi, P. and Patel, Y. (eds) (2000) *English, Standard 10*, Gandhinagar: Gujarat State Board of Textbooks.

4

Multilingual citizenship and minority languages

Alexandra Jaffe

Introduction

In this chapter, I use the Corsican case to examine shifting discourses about language and citizenship at supranational scales (European and "global") and their implications for minority language speakers and minority language revitalization. The shifts I am referring to involve the replacement of an idealized monolingual national citizen with an idealized plurilingual European/global citizen; a movement away from static/essentialist models of identity and language towards process-oriented models of identification and communicative practice; an emphasis on linguistic repertoires rather than languages as fixed and bounded codes and a focus on the role those repertoires play within participatory frameworks of democratic practice in the public sphere. Although the Corsican situation has its particularities, it also serves as a case study that illustrates how these kinds of discursive and ideological shifts constitute new resources for the articulation of minority language identity and for minority language policy, planning and educational practice. At the policy level, I show the way that these wider frameworks have been adopted in Corsican language planning documents that construe Corsican–French bilingualism as a privileged form of currency in new markets of linguistic exchange and new models of the ideal "plurilingual" citizen, defined by his or her intercultural competencies and dispositions of openness/tolerance for diversity. At the level of educational practice, I provide one extended example of how these general orientations are enacted on the ground in a trilingual (Corsican–French–Italian) theater project that took place in 2005.

Finally, I consider some of the limitations and challenges of the discursive shifts that I have described. That is, the progressive ideal of the plurilingual citizen coexists, in an often unresolved tension, with "older" discourses and their embedded ideologies. As Beacco and Byram put it, within the European context, both the linguistic ideology of the nation and the linguistic ideology of the economy continue to influence government language policies and practices (2003: 24–6). The former posits "linguistically homogenous political entities" (Beacco and Byram 2003: 20) and, as Gal (2006: 17) emphasizes, rely on the ideal of Herderian notions of linguistic authority and identity. The latter frames multilingualism as a "cost" for efficient communication and ranks codes in terms of market, rather than cultural value. Finally, the discourse of participatory citizenship begs the question of who defines what linguistic practices will "count" as adequate participation and leaves open the possibility of new forms of exclusion.

Globalization, repertoires and linguistic citizenship

Many scholars of language and globalization have pointed out how globalization results in changes in the number and nature of the "scales on which social activity and interaction take place" (Fairclough 2006: 21) and, hence, affects the composition of sociolinguistic repertoires and the value and legitimacy associated with the codes they include (Blommaert 2009: 561–62). One result of the mobility of persons, goods, services, capital and communication across national boundaries is an emphasis on the value of mobile, multilingual linguistic resources for translocal activities and exchanges (Blommaert 2009: 565; Stroud and Heugh 2004: 210). As Heller puts it, "speakers draw on linguistic resources in ways that make sense under specific social conditions" (2007: 2); conversely, when those social conditions change, the nature of those resources can also be reconceptualized (Stroud and Heugh 2004: 211). The significance of these global discourses about the exchange value of multilingualism for minority languages is complex and quite varied when viewed within a market logic, as market considerations can drive language hierarchies that can either benefit or disadvantage particular minority language groups (Block and Cameron 2000: 5; Heller 2001). Here, however, I want to focus on the significance of the notion of "exchange" within a political ideology and make the case that, to the extent that global citizenship is defined as the capacity for cultural and linguistic exchange and potential joint action, good citizens are those who cultivate the resources necessary to effect that exchange. Speaking more than one language thus becomes a resource for citizenship.

This is, in fact, the argument for "linguistic citizenship" made by Stroud and Heugh (2004). This post-liberal understanding of citizenship is founded on a "participatory" model of democracy and replaces definitions of the polity as requiring "a constituency of commonality" (2004: 205) in which cultural and linguistic homogeneity is "legitimately" imposed by the majority (Williams 2008: 56). Democratic/participatory citizenship emphasizes people's rights and obligations to participate in the economic, social and political life of the communities to which they belong, from the local to the supranational levels (Starkey 2002: 7) and to recognize the rights of culturally and linguistically diverse groups within those communities to participate. In this respect, it addresses unequal access to participation by different categories of social actors. As a set of fundamental human rights, citizenship in the participatory/democratic model is something that each person *has*; at the same time, it is conceived of as something that has to be actively accomplished. The basis of *belonging* is thus the exercise of choice/agency, rather than essential or primordial characteristics ("blood" or "mother tongue", for example). We can thus speak of *acts of citizenship*, like acts of identity, which produce and reproduce social memberships and relationships, and the moral and legal frameworks that govern community life. Within a participatory framework, we can productively view citizenship as a *stance* that individuals can take up through, among other things, linguistic choices and practices that include speaking a particular language, speaking it a particular way or engaging in particular modes of interaction with their attendant sociocultural implications for relationship and belonging (see Jaffe 2009). But stance is not simply a matter of individual adoption, it is also an interactional accomplishment: stances claimed by individuals can be ratified, ignored, modified or contested; stances can also be attributed to people without their full consent.

Acts of citizenship: the local and the supralocal intertwined

Viewing citizenship as stance thus underlines the importance of *recognition* of citizenship status and claims. That is, acts of citizenship have to be recognized by others; acts of recognition define both the status of the individual and the nature of the collectivity. Here, as Cerruti (2004) points out in her study of inheritance law and practice in the early French state, there is no "natural" space of belonging, nor is belonging simply "invented": it emerges out of interactions in which individuals position themselves as competent to fulfill the obligations of the social contract; that competence is a function of mobilizable social resources, language/communication being one of them. In a period where the letter of the law forbids foreigners from owning property, Cerruti shows that some foreigners became property owners. She attributes this to local level accommodations and interpretations of the law, relative to those individuals' social capital and networks. She concludes that a literal reading of the law (you can only inherit or transmit property if you are a French citizen) gets the causal relationships wrong: in fact, people became French because they managed to inherit or transmit property.

A process/practice approach to belonging also applies to the notion of the community itself, which is defined less in terms of the innate characteristics of its members but by the common vision enacted by collective acts of citizenship.

Language, plurilingualism and democratic citizenship: European frameworks

Within the European Union (EU), plurilingualism is defined as a set of competencies that are the precondition for social interaction among Europeans and the development of "the feeling of being European with all its cultural wealth and diversity" (Byram 2006). Beacco and Byram put it this way: democratic life in Europe requires the creation of a public space "in which everyone can play a part and be recognized as belonging to [a] community of citizens" (2003: 69). Because Europe is plurilingual, this space has to be too, especially if Europeans wish to deny the monopoly of English as a lingua franca. That is, developing lingua francas is an integral part of European Language Education policy (Breidbach 2003: 17). Thus, in the Council of Europe's *Guide for the Development of Language Education Policies in Europe*, we find the following statement: "Plurilingualism ... is above all crucial for social and political inclusion of all Europeans whatever their linguistic competences, and for the creation of a sense of European identity ... [it] ... allows participation in democratic processes not only in one's own country and language area but in concert with other Europeans" (Beacco and Byram 2003: 9). This perspective is realized in support for *education for plurilingualism* (2003: 16) and in the Council of Europe's 1999 Declaration and Programme of Action of the Committee of Ministers on *Education for Democratic Citizenship based on the Rights and Responsibilities of Citizens.* Plurilingualism for social interaction and cohesion and for participation in a shared public sphere is not conceived of solely in terms of elite, high-level, purely linguistic competencies. In fact, *The Common European Framework of Reference for Languages* distinguishes *multilingualism* (as individual knowledge of multiple languages or the presence of multiple languages in a given society) from *plurilingualism* (Council of Europe 2001), which is defined as a "complex or even composite" communicative competence based on "varying degrees of proficiency in several languages and experiences of several cultures." Plurilingualism is thus the ability to make flexible use of a linguistic repertoire in intercultural communication (2001: 4, 168).

In these European documents, plurilingual competencies are not just tools for the exercise of citizenship, becoming and being plurilingual are framed as fundamental ways of acquiring and exercising positive moral and social dispositions towards linguistic and cultural diversity (Beacco and Byram 2003). Plurilingualism is thus presented as a core act of citizenship. This translates into Council of Europe support for *education for pluricultural awareness*. This is aimed at forming a plurilingual citizen who is "able to recognize the wealth of linguistic repertoires [of others] and to identify collectively and affectively with that multiplicity" (Beacco and Byram 2003: 21); she recognizes language rights as cultural rights (particularly those of minorities) and is able to negotiate intercultural encounters. Recognition of language rights includes respect for languages and their historical associations with particular communities, but it also includes respect for individual and collective agency, for acts of identification through language (2005: 9). As such, plurilingualism is defined as an "essential component of democratic behavior" (Beacco and Byram 2003: 68). "Europe," writes Beacco, "should be identified not by the languages spoken within it, but by a common perspective on language diversity" (2005: 21). Education for plurilingual competence thus targets "existential competences": attitudes, motivations, values, beliefs, cognitive disposition; "*savoir être*" (knowing how to be) (Council of Europe 2001: 105).

Finally, plurilingual education is connected to the ideal of democratic citizenship as a model of practice, through its legitimation of multiple languages and in its recognition of differentiated strategies for the teaching of different languages to different speakers with uneven competencies (Council of Europe 2001: 134). That is, the practice of plurilingual education is linked with a commitment to *differential citizenship*, which pursues policies that create equity for weaker or threatened groups (Beacco 2003: 69).

The texts presented so far lend support for a plurilingualism that encompasses regional and minority languages without naming them explicitly. In addition, the 1992 *European Charter for Regional and Minority Languages* promotes

> the protection and promotion of regional or minority languages in the different countries and regions of Europe [because they] represent an important contribution to the building of a Europe based on the principles of democracy and cultural diversity within the framework of national sovereignty and territorial integrity.
>
> *(Council of Europe 1992: 1)*

Plurilingual citizenship in contemporary Corsican language planning

In this section, I examine the deployment of European notions of plurilingual citizenship in contemporary Corsican language policy and planning. I refer to the following motions and language planning documents:

- Deliberation 05/112 AC of the Corsican Assembly (1 July 2005) Approving Strategic Orientations for the Development and Dissemination of the Corsican Language;
- Deliberation 06/107 AC of the Corsican Assembly (29 March 2007) Authorizing the President of the Executive Council to Sign the Projects of Conventions between the State and the Corsican Territorial Collectivity Relative to the Plan for the Development of the Teaching of Corsican Language and Culture for the Period 2007–13;
- Council for Corsican Language and Culture (Cunsigliu di a Lingua è di a Cultura Corsa) "Lingua Corsa: un fiatu novu [The Corsican Language: A Second Wind] for the Corsican Language]" 2007; the final version of the 2005 report of the Scientific Committee to the Corsican Assembly on which the 2005 vote was based;
- PRDF: Strategic Plan for Language Development, Corsican Regional Assembly, 26 July 2006.

The timeline for the development of these documents can be explained thus: in 2004 the Corsican Territorial Collectivity convened a committee of experts (called the Scientific Committee) to report on the current state of the Corsican language and to make recommendations for strategic language planning policy for the next few decades. This committee was composed of linguists, language planners, bilingual educators and outside consultants, including Jean-Claude Beacco, who served in an expert advisory capacity at the EU level in the Language Policy Division in Strasbourg. It held both open/public forums on Corsican language in the media, education and economic life and drafted a report that served as a blueprint for the Strategic Plan that was voted in by the Assembly, as well as for a separate Language in Education Policy document approved by the Assembly the same year (29 June 2006). A final official version of this report was published in 2007 (see document 4, above).

Discourses of globalization: redefinitions of markets and linguistic value

In the Assembly's deliberation of 2005 (see document 1), the importance of the Corsican language is affirmed as "social bond, heritage, and resource for the development of Corsica" (Assemblée de Corse: 2005: 6). The discourse of heritage and of social bonds—that is, of Corsican as an essential characteristic of Corsican culture and identity—affirms the value of Corsican in terms that remain unchanged from the early days of the Corsican Regional Assembly, and the nineteenth-century Nationalist frame of reference for identity claims.

Under the heading "Openness," however, we find the following statement:

> European construction, the globalization of exchanges, tourism, population movements, urban mixing lead us to a view of language and identity that is no longer confined to intimate social circles and sites of ancestral allegiance, but as values of exchange, sharing and openness, be it with reference to the learning of the language by new residents, contact with other languages, consciousness of a Mediterranean and European identity, cultural exchanges or the economic valorization of [cultural] specificity (labels, "identity" products, tourism).
>
> *(Assemblée de Corse 2005: 5)*

The notion that the Corsican language is a resource for economic development is pursued in an executive summary document on Corsican language policy prepared by the head of the Corsican Language and Culture Office at the Corsican Territorial Collectivity, who writes that:

> through identity branding of [Corsican] products and of Corsica itself, [language] can be a source of differentiation (symbolizing the typicality of products; "Made in Corsica" for tourism) and of creativity that is not just cultural (popularity of polyphonic music, for example) but economic (the food industry but also all domains in which consumption is enhanced by a symbolic dimension: tourism, fashion, the craft industry.); markets which have been underdeveloped ... In a global context, [identity economies] make it possible to exploit "niches".
>
> *(Graziani 2008: 2)*

Of interest to us here is the marriage of a discourse of "openness" and cultural exchange with identity marketing in a global context. The Corsican language becomes a marker of a cultural authenticity and specificity that can be sold: it lets tourists know about the difference they can consume, and authenticates the cultural value of specific commodities. In this respect, the discourse of the Corsican Assembly draws on the potential of the global to give new value to the local, including local languages (Heller and Boutet 2006; Jaworski and Pritchard 2005).

There is a trace, in Graziani's text, of unease related to the fit between the "new market" value of Corsican as a display of cultural authenticity for commercial purposes and its historical value as a heritage language and between language as an instrument of communicative exchange versus a tool of economic exchange. It lies in the information structure of the phrase that alludes to creativity as "not just cultural ... but economic." That is, cultural creativity in this phrase is taken for granted/given; economic creativity is not. Readers are invited to view economic activity through the lens of the cultural forms (polyphonic music) they already view as legitimate.

Overall, however, market considerations are a very small part of the discourses about the value of Corsican in this corpus of deliberations and policy documents. The greatest emphasis is placed on harmonizing the historical legitimacy of Corsican as a language of local identity and heritage with progressive ideals of plurilingual European citizenship and a Mediterranean cultural identity. This goal is stated explicitly in all of the planning and policy documents above. For example, in its initial report to the Assembly before the 2005 vote, the Council for Corsican Language and Culture stated that it aimed to "articulate the collective identity aspirations [of Corsicans] with the plurilingual dynamic advocated by European authorities" (2007: 5). The Council Members and a subsequent policy document identify two key strategies towards this end: (1) strategies for "linguistic stimulation" targeted at Corsican; and (2) "openness" towards plurilingualism (Council for Corsican Language and Culture 2005: 3) within a European and Mediterranean geographical context (Collectivité Territoriale de la Corse 2007: 19).

Plurilingual repertoires and the reframing of language shift and revitalization

One of the ways in which the European discourse about plurilingual repertoires has been mobilized at the Corsican level has been to reframe the results of language domination and shift: that is, the mixed and uneven levels of competence many Corsicans have in the Corsican language. The Council for Corsican Language and Culture Final Report is careful to define plurilingualism as "the ability to use several languages in order to communicate, languages that one masters to varying degrees" (2007: 63) and to define the individual's plurilingual repertoire as being similarly made up of varied kinds and levels of competencies, in a variety of codes acquired at different stages of life (ibid.). The composition of that repertoire thus has the potential to shift across the lifespan (2007: 374). Council Members state explicitly that the repertoires approach as a tool of Corsican language revitalization is important because popular concern about the decline in spoken Corsican "tends to consider that understanding Corsican is not a competence." In contrast, they write that "adherents to a repertoires approach take the opposite position" (2007: 375) and go on to affirm that "every competence in a language, no matter how small, deserves recognition and can be officially certified, in contrast to dominant perspectives on language competence that only valorize high-level competencies and do not attribute any value to non-expert forms of language" (ibid.).

Let us unpack, for a moment, the following sociolinguistic phenomena being alluded to here: (1) hierarchies of value related to different forms of Corsican competence and practice; (2) linguistic insecurity among Corsican speakers with reference to a notion of expert knowledge or *bon usage* in the minority language; and (3) an idealized "balanced" bilingualism as a criterion for legitimate and authentic Corsican identity and minority language practice/skills. First, the text makes direct reference to the potential for a repertoires approach to repair social misrecognition of comprehension skills. But the over-valorization of active oral skills also indexes another form of misrecognition: the undervaluing of school competencies in Corsican, where children's levels of spoken practice tend to lag behind their abilities in comprehension, reading and writing. The repertoires approach thus helps to valorize the outcomes of language revitalization through schooling; outcomes that do not reproduce "traditional" forms of minority language linguistic knowledge. These new forms of competence are still subject to critique from the Corsican society at large, in a "resistance of separation" (Jaffe 1999) to academic definitions of a language that has historically been experienced and given value outside any formal contexts. But that society also exhibits a converse response to the ela-boration of a "high" form of Corsican in academic and literary circles: linguistic insecurity of both vernacular speakers and learners of Corsican who evaluate themselves negatively with reference to an academic norm. In short, in the current sociolinguistic context, there is competition between the value and authority of an "authentic" Corsican, defined almost exclusively as first-language oral skills practiced in informal domains and a "good" Corsican learned in school and practiced by "professionals": one or the other of these frames of evaluation has the potential to de-legitimize and disenfranchise many Corsicans' knowledge of the language. So too does the implicit, but powerful image of the "balanced bilingual" (Jaffe 2007), which is out of sync with the inherent "imbalance" (or differentiated practices, compe-tencies and values) of Corsican and French in both individual and societal repertoires that is the outcome of both language shift and language revitalization. Thus, the reference in the excerpt above to "non-expert" forms of language as "subject to certification." In short, the validation of multiple kinds and levels of competence in a plurilingual repertoire has significance in efforts to shape public opinion about what counts as Corsican, and what counts as being a Corsican–French bilingual in the current sociolinguistic context. The goal is to maximize the range of linguistic competencies and practices in Corsican that will "count" as gestures of solidarity, identification and belonging at the regional scale by tapping into discourses at a European/global scale.

Plurilingual repertoires in education

The concept of the plurilingual repertoire has also been widely adopted in Corsican bilingual education, where the phrase "bi-plurilingualism" has become the preferred term to describe its ultimate goals. The adoption of this phrase is important because it avoids a number of pitfalls associated with talking uniquely about Corsican–French bilingualism. First, the image of a plurilingual trajectory in the life of the learner reframes school bilingual practice as a stage along the way rather than as a final outcome. "Bilingualism," commented the Regional Inspector for Corsican Language and Culture, "is only a stage on the path towards plurilingualism" (Arrighi 2004: 1), going on to characterize monolingualism, and an associated monocultural view of the world as a deficit in the modern context (2004: 2). In another document, a member of a Corsican bilingual teachers' association marries a Whorfian take on language and thought with becoming a pluricultural person, rather than with becoming more authentically Corsican, writing that:

> Each language corresponds to a vision of the world, a way of thinking of it, creating it through the verb. The child quickly acquires a relativistic perspective on the world; he/she is capable of accepting the different visions of the world that other foreign languages will present to him. This makes him a pluricultural being.
>
> *(Sciolilingua 2004: 1)*

In a similar vein, Defendini and Pergola (Corsican Education Inspectors) write that "We have to meet the challenge of forming tomorrow's European citizens. Plurilingual citizens from a Mediterranean region integrated within Europe" (2007: 121). They evoke the linguist Claude Hagège and his advocacy of effective language education for plurilingualism, and go on to cite the following excerpt from the work of Gilbert Dalgaglian: "Plurilingual education consists of creating a symbiotic relationship between the small region and the larger geopolitical entity, cultural roots and openness, unity in respect for diversity" (ibid.).

The shift from a discourse of bilingualism to a discourse of "bi-plurilingualism" is significant for the promotion of minority language education in the Corsican context because it sidesteps competition with dominant languages (especially English, but also other romance languages like Spanish and Italian) for a place in a bilingual repertoire. This competition is very real and manifests itself in language choice practices in middle school (*collège*) and secondary school, where parents and students often opt for dominant foreign languages instead of Corsican whenever the curriculum permits or forces such a choice. Such competition is only intensified by widespread popular acceptance of the cognitive and academic advantages of early bilingualism, a point to which we will return. This allows Corsican–French bilingualism to be represented as a privileged point of departure—a springboard—for the development of additional linguistic competencies. The Collectivité Territoriale de la Corse thus asserts, supported by reference to the expert discourse of linguist Jean Duverger that "early bilingualism (acquired before the age of seven) prepares the child for the learning of other languages, and favors the acquisition of numerous other consequences. This is why it is important to privilege bilingualism even before school starts, in preschools and daycares" (2007: 19). Teaching Corsican is thus "not just about insuring the transmission of the language, but also about using it as a foundational resource for developing an aptitude for plurilingualism among schoolchildren" (ibid.). The unique value of Corsican as a language of intimacy, proximity and cultural value is then introduced into this discourse of cognitive and educational development: "Psycholinguists agree that bilingual education is most effective when the second language is present in the environment of the learner, and can be linked to his or her life history or personal experience" (ibid.). Because Corsican is "present in the environment of our students, close to Latin and other romance languages, [it] is the best language from which to promote schoolchildren's desire to learn other languages and plurilingual aptitudes. [Corsican] also helps them to better master the French language" (2006: 32). Learning the minority language is thus framed as a form of "extra" cognitive and pedagogical capital (that could not be obtained by the early learning of another dominant language) in a competitive linguistic marketplace that demands both French language proficiency and multilingualism. In this case, we could say that experience and opportunities for practice at the local scale (where there is a second language "present") are projected and valorized at an international one.

Second, the validation of multiple kinds and levels of competencies in different codes in the discourse of plurilingualism has obvious significance for the acts of teaching and learning Corsican. I have already alluded to its potential to legitimate school knowledge and to attenuate the conflict between school and "traditional" models of linguistic authenticity, practice and value. If school language is sometimes depreciated in popular "traditionalist" discourse, Corsican bilingual education is also sometimes evaluated with reference to excessively high expectations and judged a failure if it does not produce perfectly balanced 11-year-old bilinguals. Thus, the plurilingual repertoires approach makes it possible for schools (and the society at large) to "certify" levels and types of competence that fall short of that idealized balance, but which are in fact attainable in a bilingual elementary school curriculum. In this case, a European/international discourse is pressed into service to harmonize, at the regional level, images, expectations and models of the bilingual person with the potential of language planning through education in the current sociolinguistic context.

Bi-plurilingualism in educational practice: an example of the plurilingual repertoire in action

Chì si sbaglia, inventa! (Making mistakes is a form of invention!)

This is the title of a trilingual (Corsican–French–Italian) pedagogical resource book that resulted from a year-long, multi-school trilingual project based around the work of Gianni Rodari and conducted in two Corsican schools with a total of 28 bilingual classes in 2005 under the tutelage of the director Orlando Forioso, an Italian expatriate working in Corsica. Rodari was an innovative and award-winning Italian children's author of poetry, theater and prose who was famous for his writing and for his presentations and workshops for teachers and school-children on the "techniques of the fantastic" (Argilli 2007), which included improvisational prompts for acting and writing based around unexpected or "absurd" pairs of words and concepts. The second page of the book explains, in Italian, Corsican and French, that the title is an adaptation of an Italian proverb that says, "Sbagliando s'impara" (Mistakes are a path to learning). The promotional text on the back outside of the cover reads: "Here, we find errors at the very center of an active pedagogy, where making mistakes is no longer sanctioned, but is an integral part of the learning process ... this is an academic text where the pedagogical dynamic is propelled by dreams and humor." The message is twofold: creativity requires letting go of conventional notions of error and, as a pedagogical objective, can have equal status to "correctness." That correctness, furthermore, can be best achieved by the understanding that comes from accepting and analyzing error.

One of the short stories by Rodari included and translated into French and Corsican from the original Italian in Forioso's resource book illustrates the approach to linguistic correctness embedded in Rodari's work. Entitled "To be and to have," it features the character of a professor called Grammaticus who, while travelling by train, meets two Italian workers returning to Italy for elections after a long time abroad seeking work. "Io ho andato in Germania nel 1958" (I went to Germany in 1958), says the first, incorrectly using "to have" (*ho* andato) as the auxiliary verb instead of the verb "to be" (*sono* andato). His companion says "Io ho andato prima in Belgio nel miniere di carbone" (I went first to Belgium to work in the coal mines), making the very same error. Visibly distressed, the professor finally jumps up and berates the two of them: "'Io ho andato! Io ho andato!' Here's the classic error of Southern Italians, replacing the verb 'to be' with the verb 'to have' in the past participle. Didn't they teach you in school to say 'Io sono andato'? The verb 'to go' is intransitive, and requires the verb 'to be' as its auxiliary?" Taken aback, the workers respectfully agree that he must be right as he is so learned and they stopped their schooling at the age of 11. But one of them finally ventures the following commentary: "It's true, then, that 'to go' is an intransitive verb, something whose importance I couldn't possibly dispute. But in my view, it seems to me that it's a sad verb, very sad. Going to look for work among strangers ... leaving one's family, one's children." He continues: "I am, we are! Do you know where we are, with all the verb 'to be' and all our hearts? We are still in our country even if we went to Germany and France. We are always still there, and it's there that we would like to stay, to have nice factories to work in and beautiful houses to live in." In the end, the professor ends up declaring: "I am a fool, a fool. Here I am trying to look for errors in verb forms ... but the biggest mistakes are found in the state of the world" (Rodari 2007: 99–101).

In this story, the importance of grammatical correctness is subordinated to more pressing truths: the truth of the workers' attachment to their native soil, and the truth of the conditions that push them into economic exile; those truths are eloquently expressed in the workers' non-standard grammar. It is also a story in which identification (the verb "to be") is both subject to structural constraints and an active, individual, affective process. As such, it is a fable that has particular application to the contemporary Corsican context, where language shift (due to structural constraints) has made being Corsican through the use of the Corsican language a conscious and deliberate act of identification with complex repercussions rather than a simple condition of identity. It lends value to those acts of identification (the effort to learn and use Corsican) as acts of attachment to their culture, even if they are linguistically less than perfect. That is, in the context of language education, and Corsican language education in particular, the importance of "correct" speech is subordinated to communication, creativity and a collective project of identification.

Plurilingual practice has a significant role to play here. First, the introduction of a third language into the classroom that has neither the overwhelming historical authority of French nor the affective, symbolic, cultural value of Corsican provides students and teachers with the opportunity to enjoy playing with and making errors in a code with few to zero negative repercussions for identity or status. This shows us that the plurilingual repertoire is not just differentiated in terms of the nature and type of competencies an individual has in a set of codes, but also offers differentiated experiences of language. Second, the linguistic proximity of Italian and Corsican makes it possible for that linguistic play to take place at a relatively high level. That is, in these bilingual schools, most students' Corsican comprehension skills give them good to excellent comprehension of Italian. They thus experience the access that an "imperfect" or "unbalanced" bilingualism can give them to a satisfying plurilingual communicative practice and to metalinguistic experiences related to the subtleties of Corsican: Italian linguistic contrasts. In many cases, their Corsican teachers also model an adult plur-ilingualism made up of varied competencies in different codes. This is because many of them participate in the teaching of Italian and in trilingual projects such as the Forioso–Rodari one while openly acknowledging the gaps in their knowledge of Italian. They display a positive orientation to being learners of Italian and model the strategies they use to fill gaps in their knowledge of the language for specific communicative purposes. Finally, the linguistic proximity of Corsican and Italian also guarantees the possibility for learning through error, if error is defined as violating code boundaries. For both students and teachers in Corsica, speaking Italian inevitably results in "interferences" between the two languages. In the For-ioso–Rodini project, those interferences were simultaneously validated as part of the creative process and used as resources for contrastive analysis. These multiple goals are reflected in the assessment criteria elaborated by one team of teachers during the project (Muracciole *et al.* 2006).

Here we do find an attention to code boundaries and "correct" pronunciation and "error-free" performance, but this is accompanied by an emphasis on metalinguistic awareness of "errors" and a positive attitude towards correcting and learning from them. This frames metalinguistic know-how of two kinds as valuable: (1) knowing about and being able to police linguistic boundaries given the right resources and in specific circumstances; and (2) knowing how to disregard those boundaries for a variety of social, creative and communicative purposes. These understandings were developed through the learning sequence. In the improvisational stage of the students' dramatic work, language mixing and "errors" were accepted and encouraged. In a second stage, they revisited their improvisations and identified linguistic structures in all three languages for explicit instruction and review. The final products (dramatic performances)

Table 4.1 Assessment criteria for 'Chí si sbaglia inventa' theater project

Categories assessed	Skills/knowledge validated
A. Linguistic knowledge	
1. I understand what is asked of me in Corsican, Italian or French	*comprehension*
2. I am able to distinguish between Italian and Corsican	*code boundaries*
3. I express myself without interferences	*code boundaries*
4. I articulate and speak loudly	*expressive/performative skills*
5. I speak without pronunciation errors	*oral linguistic performance*
6. I am able to make appropriate word choices	*oral linguistic performance*
7. I know and use each language's unique characteristics (accents, gestures, forms of expression)	*code boundaries*
8. I am able to apply and demonstrate the lexical and syntactic knowledge I acquire	*active linguistic learning*
9. I can recite a text that I have learned from memory	*memorization*
B. Corsican language	
1. I have correct pronunciation	*oral linguistic skills*
2. I apply vocabulary and structures I have learned in new contexts	*active linguistic learning*
3. I am able to express myself spontaneously	*oral linguistic performance (high level)*
4. I demonstrate pleasure in playing with the language (errors, invented words, words with strong meanings)	*metalinguistic stance + creativity*
5. I coordinate words, gestures and attitudes in appropriate ways	*expressive/performative*
C. Dramatic performance	
1. I carry out directions	*attitude/comportment*
2. I use a discourse that is appropriate for my character	*expressive/performative*
3. I did not make any errors when I delivered my lines	*code boundaries + memorization + expressive/performative*
4. I recognize my errors	*code boundaries + metalinguistic awareness*
5. I am able to articulate the nature of my problems, be they lexical, syntactic or to do with dramatic expression	*metalinguistic awareness*
6. I self-correct my mistakes immediately	*metalinguistic stance/awareness + active linguistic learning*
7. I demonstrate through performance the lexical, syntactic and expressive competencies I have learned	*active linguistic learning + expressive/ performative*
8. My performance was smooth	*expressive/performative*
9. My level of physical movement and gesture was appropriate	*expressive/performative*
10 I demonstrated imagination	*creativity*
11. I ask to reimprovise in order to improve my performance	*active learning + attitude*

Source: (Forioso, 2007).

incorporated the results of that study, but did not exclude codeswitching and language mixing as creative choices. The evaluation grid also shows that linguistic skills and form were far from the unique focus of the project: there is a significant emphasis on creativity, expressive/performative skills, students' investment in memorization and their stance as active, cooperative learners.

The authors of the assessment grid reported that one of the "real, tangible benefits" of the project was the "pleasure and interest in being part of a bilingual program" exhibited by the children. They concluded with the following:

> We want to emphasize that the teaching of a minority language has a non-negligible affective dimension. This is a plus that gives bilingual education its power and its legitimacy. Children are conscious of learning a second language, a language of the region where they are growing up; for some a powerful link to family, for others a part of social life—these are the bases of their motivation to learn … If it is true that we must always try to make the link with the children's lives, it's also true that we need to make a connection with their imaginations, so that school can become a place where everyone who wants to can contribute a small piece of his or her history.
>
> *(Muracciole* et al. *2006)*

Defendini and Pergola, in their assessment of the project, note the same engagement and enthusiasm on the part of the students, and write that "the choice of activities, the work of comparison and reflection on practice lent meaning to the learning process, in the wider context of a plurilingual education" (2007: 121) that they define (see above) in terms of education for democratic European citizenship.

Taken together, these two assessments of the project suggest that creative plurilingual pedagogies make it possible for a local project of identity to be intimately coordinated with a wider plurilingual project. The former provides motivation for Corsican–French bilingualism, a precondition for being able to do advanced work in Italian, and the latter is a catalyst for the work of the imagination—identified as a crucial element in the individual student's personal investment in the bi-plurilingual enterprise.

Tensions in the plurilingual project: being vs becoming bi- and plurilingual

This coordination of the bilingual and plurilingual agenda is not a completely seamless one. One of the cornerstones of contemporary Corsican discourse about plurilingualism in language planning documents is the representation of Corsica as a bilingual society and of Corsicans as bilinguals. The 2005 Deliberation states that

> This plan is thus intended to make use of the still-widespread knowledge of the Corsican language. It aims, on the one hand, to develop and extend the domains in which Corsican-French bilingual competency is observed in use, and on the other hand, to make that competence the core of the linguistic repertoires of Corsican inhabitants.
>
> *(Collectivité Territoriale de la Corse 2007: 20)*

In a special annex to the Scientific Committee's Final Report entitled "Plurilingual and pluricultural education, definitions," the authors emphasize both Corsicans' diverse linguistic repertoires and their appreciation of that diversity as part of their aptitude for plurilingual citizenship:

> Plurilingual competence is one of the foundations of living together. If one recognizes the diversity of languages in one's own repertoire—their diverse functions and values—that consciousness of one's own personal diversity favors a positive appreciation of the languages of the Other … the role of education … is to lead learners/users to view the development

of their plurilingual competencies as a personal objective as well as the way that they can fully realize their responsibilities as democratic citizens.

(Thiers 2008: 395)

They state that "plurilingual competence is present in all individuals, who are potentially or effectively plurilingual, because this competence is the concrete outcome of the capacity for language that is the genetic heritage of all humans" (2008: 374).

I would argue that in speaking to Corsicans in general and to Corsican decision makers in particular, this text both describes and exhorts, characterizes and projects sociolinguistic identities and states of consciousness in an effort to simultaneously appeal to Corsicans to develop themselves as bilinguals and in doing so, to become better, plurilingual European citizens. The image of latent or incipient bilingualism and plurilingualism is what makes it possible for them to tell Corsicans they are both "already" good linguistic citizens while exhorting them to become better ones through greater use or knowledge of Corsican. This is captured in the description of the "central objective" of the Scientific Committee report: "to reinforce and develop bilingualism in Corsican society in order to better live European plurilingualism" (Thiers 2008: 326).

We find further evidence of this discursive strategy in the use of the term "linguistic *stimulation*" (*dynamisation* linguistique) as the target of policy in all of the Corsican documents referenced above. Compared to "development," or "revitalization," or "elaboration," the term "stimulation" casts Corsican as having an existing, albeit latent vitality that is susceptible to being boosted by a variety of interventions, identified as: (1) restoring Corsican's vitality in informal linguistic contexts; (2) consolidating Corsican's gains in formal contexts; (3) making the use of Corsican "normal" for the society in general and for its members; and (4) giving everyone a full linguistic competence in the Corsican language (understanding, speaking, reading and writing) (Thiers 2008: 332).

Corsicans are represented as having overwhelmingly positive attitudes towards Corsican: "For Corsica, knowing the traditional language is most often presented as one of the keys of the environment with respect to history, traditions and even geographic space via toponyms" (Thiers 2008: 328). These positive attitudes are not just "traditional" ones, they are also the outcome of successful language revitalization: "Corsican has significantly improved its symbolic status and has increased in its identity value and impact at the same time as it has lost ground in its traditional domains of use" (ibid.).

To return to the concept of the plurilingual European citizen as a disposition towards language, communication, equity and diversity, the picture that emerges in this foundational text is that a Corsican bilingualism in Corsican and French is the basis for the expression and development of plurilingual competencies (*savoir faire*) and dispositions/attitudes/values (*savoir être*, knowing how to be). The latent Corsican bilingual individual and society is represented as poised to assume this European plurilingualism, but not without *work* on both *savoir faire* and *savoir être*; work that language policy and planning measures are intended to facilitate.

It is here that we find a discursive and ideological tension between representations of Corsican bilingualism as being in place (based on "new" definitions of bilingualism as encompassing even passive competence) and being severely threatened and in need of vigorous political, social and economic investment.

For example, the Scientific Committee's Final Report notes that the positive valorization of Corsican as a result of revitalization efforts to date has some negative results at the level of identity: "The feelings associated with the loss of Corsican are of a loss of familial, social and cultural heritage; a loss of cultural bearings ... we can thus understand how the loss of Corsican competence can be interpreted as a deficit, even as a major handicap" (Thiers 2008: 328). In the Strategic Plan for Language Development, "deficits in intergenerational transmission of language and culture" are characterized as having negative psycho-linguistic and sociocultural repercussions, with "adolescents having a hard time situating themselves in insular space and time" (Collectivité Territoriale de la Corse 2007: 19) and having only "a fragmented vision of their immediate environment: their neighborhood, their school, in the best of cases their village, but no vision of the island as a whole because this space is not 'named' by the school as an institution and seldom evoked in its entirety in the society" (2007: 41). Bilingualism thus becomes a way to fix a cultural malaise, to "reconcile the Corsican community with its language and overcome once and for all the historical conflict with the language of the [French] State" (Thiers 2008: 333).

The stances taken by the authors of this policy document in response to these sentiments of cultural loss/handicap are multiple and complex. This complexity is in part because of the multiple scales within which the value of speaking Corsican is being located, and the multiple spheres of citizenship (local, European and global) in which speaking Corsican is being promoted. One of the tensions of "harmonization" of these multiple scales has to do with the status of the components of the plurilingual repertoire. In the European discourse, all plurilingualisms are potentially equal although practically tipped in favor of dominant languages as tools of wider exchange. European linguistic diversity, as we have seen earlier, is defined as resisting the hegemony of English as a lingua franca. At the regional scale, defending a culturally significant linguistic diversity that includes the minority language involves resisting not only English as the preferred language in a bilingual repertoire, but also resisting other national languages as potential priorities over Corsican language learning. European reference documents on language learning do provide some resources for one line of defense of minority over other languages in a bilingual agenda, on cognitive/pedagogical grounds (we have seen this in the Plan, in reference to the efficacy of bilingual instruction where the second language is "present" in the students' environment).

But the main line of defense for Corsican–French bilingualism as the baseline from which Corsicans build their repertoire by acquiring other European languages is that it is has intrinsic cultural value, that it is needed in order to make Corsicans "whole," balanced, and anchored in cultural space and time. This argument rests almost inevitably on nationalist rather than post-nationalist ideologies of fixed, bounded and homologous linguistic and cultural entities, of language as an essential marker of authentic cultural identity and comes into implicit conflict with the plurilingual citizenship framework. It also leads to a rather conventional view of language competencies and "good usage" (*bon usage*—language standards). Note, for example, the reference to giving everyone "full linguistic competence" in both oral and written usage as one of the key goals of Corsican language planning. This is a fairly clear allusion to balanced bilingualism defined as equal competencies in both languages, not to a plurilingual repertoire in which multiple levels of competence are validated. "Good usage" in Corsican is also identified indirectly as a target for language revitalization in the Scientific Committee's Final Report, where the authors comment on the linguistic effects of language shift:

> The linguistic erosion that [Corsican] has experienced in informal usage leads, in the long run, to processes of substitution: the language of everyday use [French] ends up infiltrating the vernacular [Corsican], creating linguistic hybrids and a progressive loss of awareness of linguistic standards [*bon usage* in Corsican].
>
> (*Thiers 2008: 335*)

These commentaries raise the question about how much, and what kind of linguistic and cultural capital "certifies" individuals as Corsican bilinguals at the regional level and, at a supranational scale, qualifies individuals or groups as good plurilingual citizens. The implication is that the individual needs to be culturally grounded, psychologically sound and should have relatively balanced linguistic competencies for their bilingualism to be a springboard for European plurilingual citizenship. From this perspective, the imperfections in Corsican bilingualism at the individual and societal level are handicaps and the glass of European plurilingualism half-empty rather than half-full.

In short, tears in the fabric of Corsican culture—linguistic, cultural and psychosocial rupture alluded to in the report—call for and benefit from the legitimation of practice, process and agency in the work of identification over fixed competencies, codes and identities. However, at this moment in Corsican history, the ideological conversion is not complete, and the model of the plurilingual citizen stands in a sometimes uneasy relationship with older, essentializing models of linguistic identity and legitimacy.

To return to a point made in the introduction, this ideological and discursive conflict at the local level is a refraction of the same phenomena at the European level, where the diversity in the European mantra of "unity in diversity" is still conceptualized in terms of bounded nations, regions, languages and cultures (Kraus 2008).

Conclusions

In the past, minority language citizenship was based primarily on nineteenth-century nationalist models in which minority cultural and linguistic authenticity was measured against an ideal of bounded and homologous codes and identities. Today, however, minority linguistic citizenship is no longer conceptualized solely at a national scale. In the Corsican case, European and global scales of reference have introduced new process and practice-based concepts of linguistic citizenship that are based on plurilingual practices and have the potential to validate forms of linguistic capital that minority language speakers have—even in a context of language shift— and to validate learning and using minority languages and other foreign languages as valuable acts of citizenship. Within a nationalist framework of identity, Corsican speakers with limited levels of Corsican competence risk being evaluated (by themselves or others) as culturally inauthentic. In contrast, we have seen how a plurilingual framework represents Corsican speakers with varied levels of minority language competence as privileged European citizens and promotes classroom practices that place the emphasis on student agency, engagement, imagination and communicative practice across languages rather than focusing solely on their formal knowledge within the boundaries of single codes. This "new" framework, however, has not fully replaced the "old" nationalist one either at the European or the local, Corsican level; this is reflected in the underlying struggle, in Corsican language planning documents, to validate both "being" and "becoming" through speaking Corsican.

Related topics

Regional minorities, education and language revitalization, language rights, discourses about linguistic diversity.

Further reading

Blommaert, J., Collins, J. and Slembrouck, S. (2005) 'Spaces of multilingualism', *Language & Communication* 25: 197–216.

(This article addresses how the notions of linguistic and communicative competence are tied to specifics of place and scale, and thus, how multilingualism has specific, differential value depending on the social and political environments in which it is evaluated.)

Coste, D., Moore, D. and Zarate, G. (1997) *Compétence Plurilingue et Pluriculturelle. Vers un Cadre Européen Commun de Référence pour l'Enseignement et l'Apprentissage des Langues Vivantes: Etudes Préparatoires*, Strasbourg: Conseil de l'Europe.
(This publication offers an introduction to the notion of plurilingual and pluricultural competence that has been widely adopted in subsequent Council of Europe publications.)

Heller, M. (ed.) (2007) *Bilingualism: A Social Approach*, New York: Palgrave Macmillan.
(This volume explores bilingualism from a social-theoretical perspective, taking a critical perspective on both bilingual practices and discourses about bilingualism.)

Stroud, C. and Heugh, K. (2004) 'Linguistic human rights and linguistic citizenship', in D. Patrick and J. Freeland (eds) *Language Rights and Language Survival: A Sociolinguistic Exploration*, Manchester: St Jerome Publishing.
(In this article, Stroud and Heugh propose a model of 'linguistic citizenship' that involves a critical look at the relationship between linguistic difference and social/political boundaries and hierarchies.)

Bibliography

Argilli, M. (2007) 'Gianni Rodari, biografia tratta dal libro onomimo', in O. Forioso (ed.) *Chi si Sbaglia, Inventa!* Bastia: Stamperia Sammarcelli.

Arrighi, J. (2004) *Discours de Clôture*, Presentation at Conference on Bilingualism, Corté, France, October.

Assemblée de Corse (2005) *Deliberation 05/112 AC (1 July 2005) Approving Strategic Orientations for the Development and Dissemination of the Corsican Language*, available online at www.corse.fr/documents/Assemblee/delib/53_878_DELIBERATION_N2007–64_AC.pdf

——(2007) *Deliberation 06/107 AC (29 March 2007) Authorizing the President of the Executive Council to Sign the Projects of Conventions between the State and the Corsican Territorial Collectivity Relative to the Plan for the Development of the Teaching of Corsican Language and Culture for the Period 2007–2013*, available online at www.corse.fr/documents/Assemblee/delib/53_878_DELIBERATION_N2007–64_AC.pdf

Beacco, J. (2005) *Languages and Language Repertoires: Plurilingualism as a Way of Life in Europe*, available online at www.coe.int/T/DG4/Linguistic/Source/Beacco_EN.pdf

Beacco, J. and Byram, M. (2003) *Guide for the Development of Language Education Policies in Europe, Main Version, draft 1 (revised) April 2003*, available online at www.coe.int/t/dg4/linguistic/Guide_niveau3_EN.asp

Block, D. and Cameron, D. (2001) 'Introduction', in D. Block and D. Cameron (eds) *Globalization and Language Teaching*, New York: Routledge.

Blommaert, J. (2009) 'A sociolinguistics of globalization', in N. Coupland and A. Jaworski (eds) *The New Sociolinguistics Reader*, New York: Palgrave Macmillan.

Breidbach, S. (2003) *Plurilingualism, Democratic Citizenship and the Role of English*, available online at www.coe.int/t/dg4/linguistic/Source/BreidbachEN.pdf

Byram, M. (2006) *Languages and Identities*. Council of Europe, Language Policy Division, Strasbourg.www.coe.int/t/.../Byram-Identities-final_EV.doc

Cerruti, S. (2004) 'Microhistory: social relations versus cultural models?' in A. M. Castrén, M. Lonkila and M. Peltonen (eds) *Between Sociology and History: Essays on Microhistory, Collective Action, and Nation-Building*, Helsinki: S.K.S. Press.

Collectivité Territoriale de la Corse (2007) *PRDF 2007–2013*, available online at www.corse.fr/documents/education/PRDF/cahier1.pdf

Council for Corsican Language and Culture (Cunsigliu di a Lingua è di a Cultura Corsa) (2007) 'Lingua Corsa: un fiatu novu [The Corsican language: a second wind for the Corsican language]' in J. Thiers (2008) *Papiers d'Identité*, Ajaccio: Editions Albiana.

Council of Europe (1992) *European Charter for Regional and Minority Languages*, available online at http://conventions.coe.int/Treaty/EN/Treaties/Html/148.htm

——(2001) *Common European Framework of Reference for Languages*, available online at www.coe.int/t/dg4/linguistic/Source/Framework_EN.pdf

Defendini, M. and Pergola, P. (2007) 'Arts, culture et langues romanes: La grammaire de l'imagination', in O. Forioso (ed.) *Chi si Sbaglia, Inventa!* Bastia: Stamperia Sammarcelli.

European Council of Ministers (1999) *Declaration and Programme of Action of the Committee of Ministers on Education for Democratic Citizenship based on the Rights and Responsibilities of Citizens*, available online at https://wcd.coe.int/ViewDoc.jsp?id=313139

Fairclough, N. (2006) *Language and Globalization*, New York: Routledge.

Forioso, O. (ed.) (2007) *Chi si Sbaglia, Inventa!* Bastia: Stamperia Sammarcelli.

Gal, S. (2006) 'Migration, language ideologies and multilingualism', in C. Mar-Molinero and P. Stevenson (eds) *Language Ideologies, Policies and Practices: Language and the Future of Europe*, New York: Palgrave Macmillan.

Graziani, F. (2008) *Structuration des politiques publiques en faveur de la langue corse*, available online at http://files.eke.org/pdf/topaketen_aktak/structuration_des_politiques_publiques/politique_linguistique_corse.pdf.

Heller, M. (2007) 'Bilingualism as ideology and practice', in M. Heller (ed.) *Bilingualism: A Social Approach*, New York: Palgrave Macmillan.

——(2001) 'Globalisation and the commodification of bilingualism in Canada', in D. Block and D. Cameron (eds) *Globalization and Language Teaching*, New York: Routledge.

Heller, M. and Boutet, J. (2006) 'Vers de nouvelles formes de pouvoir langagier? Langue(s) et économie dans la nouvelle économie', *Langage et Société* 118: 5–16.

Jaffe, A. (1999) *Ideologies in Action: Language Politics on Corsica*, Berlin: Mouton de Gruyter.

——(2007) 'Minority language movements', in M. Heller (ed.) *Bilingualism: A Social Approach*, New York: Palgrave Macmillan.

——(2009) 'Introduction: The sociolinguistics of stance', in A. Jaffe (ed.) *Stance: Sociolinguistic Perspectives*, New York: Oxford University Press.

Jaworski, A. and Pritchard, A. (eds) (2005) *Discourse, Communication and Tourism*, Clevedon: Channel View Publications.

Kraus, P. (2008) 'A one-dimensional diversity? European integration and the challenge of language policy', in J. Arzoz (ed.) *Respecting Linguistic Diversity in the European Union*, Philadelphia: John Benjamins.

Muracciole, A., Muracciole, F. and Pastinelli, M. (2006) *Presentation for Colloquium on Minority Language Education*, Corté, France, July.

Rodari, G. (2007) 'Essere e avere', in O. Forioso (ed.) *Chi si Sbaglia, Inventa!* Bastia: Stamperia Sammarcelli.

Sciolilingua, A. (2004) *Introduction à l'Atelier No. 1: Pédagogie du Projet et Enseignement Bilingue*, Presentation at Conference on Bilingualism, Corté, France, October.

Starkey, H. (2002) *Democratic Citizenship, Languages, Diversity and Human Rights: Guide for the Development of Language Education Policies in Europe from Linguistic Diversity to Plurilingual Education*, available online at www.coe.int/T/DG4/Linguistic/Source/StarkeyEN.pdf.

Stroud, C. and Heugh, K. (2004) 'Linguistic human rights and linguistic citizenship', in D. Patrick and J. Freeland (eds) *Language Rights and Language Survival: A Sociolinguistic Exploration*, Manchester: St Jerome Publishing.

Thiers, J. (2008) *Papiers d'Identité*, Ajaccio: Editions Albiana.

Williams, C. (2008) *Linguistic Minorities in Democratic Context*, New York: Palgrave Macmillan.

5

Sign language and the politics of deafness

Bencie Woll and Robert Adam

Introduction

In the context of Western society, the existence of the deaf community, deaf people's social identity, and the experience of deafhood (Ladd 2002) are the consequences of their experiences in the hearing world, not just as a result of exclusion but in equal part stemming from a desire to create structures alternative to those of hearing society. To be deaf is to have a hearing loss; to be deaf is to belong to a community with its own language and culture. Deaf communities parallel other minority linguistic communities in terms of linguistic and cultural oppression; by its very virtue of being a minority culture, the deaf community and its culture are oppressed by the majority culture (ibid.). In the deaf community the problems of communication and interaction with non-signing, hearing people are avoided. Through interaction with other deaf people, the individual is able to develop an awareness and acceptance of self. Through participation in the various organizations that make up the community, individuals are able to acquire a sense of self-esteem, which may be impossible to develop within the hearing world.

The deaf community in this sense represents a most complex response to the threat posed by a hearing and speaking majority society and the difficulties of communication that the deaf person experiences in the wider community. In this chapter we will discuss the different types of deaf communities that have emerged, their languages and culture. Deaf culture comprises a range of activities that are sufficiently powerful to nullify the negative experiences of daily life and enable deaf people to develop an acceptance and celebration of both the individual and collective deaf self. By sealing off those aspects of their lives that really matter, deaf people have made the existence of a positive deaf identity possible.

On a global level, the World Federation of the deaf released a survey report 'Deaf People and Human Rights' (Haualand and Allen 2009) that found that most deaf people did not have basic human rights; 19 countries do not recognize deaf people as equal citizens; and only 44 countries have legal recognition of sign language. Of equal concern is the very small number of countries (23) that provide bilingual education to deaf children in both sign language and spoken/written language. This chapter will illustrate the situation of sign language communities around the world in the light of political and linguistic policies.

The deaf community

Sign language

There are numerous studies that explore deaf identities and describe how deaf people create communities based on three factors: communication, deafness and mutual support (Higgins 1980; Lane 1984; Markowicz and Woodward 1978; Padden and Humphries 1988; Woll and Lawson 1982). All these concepts of deaf community conceive deaf social and cultural lives as being underpinned and driven by forms of communication that differ from those of the majority society. This differentiation primarily consists of the choice of a sign language as a preferred language. The centrality of these languages is reflected not only in the social and political organization of these communities, but in their strong cultural tradition of sign-play, jokes, story-telling and poetry. In the most practical sense, then, the central fact of deaf community membership is seen as linguistic membership.

Attitudinal identification

Membership of these deaf communities is also seen as determined, not by audiological measurement of hearing loss, but by self-identification as 'deaf', and reciprocal recognition of that identification – 'attitudinal deafness' (Baker and Cokely 1980). Individuals with minor hearing losses may be full members of the deaf community, whereas other individuals with profound hearing losses may not identify with deaf communities. When deaf people make the latter decision, deaf community members refer to them as preferring to try and live in the 'hearing world'. On a closer consideration of the boundaries or margins of these deaf communities, the issue is confused by different and in fact virtually opposing sets of terminology used by the two different communities. A good example is cited by Padden and Humphries (1988) who point out that to describe someone as acting as 'hard of hearing' in the American deaf community, is to comment that a deaf person has the behavioural and cultural characteristics of a hearing person. In English, such an expression would contrast with a hearing, rather than deaf norm.

Attitudinal deafness is seen by some writers as reflected in 'ethnic identity' as it applies to membership of a deaf community. In sociological and anthropological literature, ethnicity involves two features: 'paternity' defines members of a group in biological terms: in the case of the deaf community, this is a hearing impairment, and additionally for some community members, deaf family members. The other feature, 'patrimony', refers to customary patterns of behaviour and shared values: ' ... ethnicity is a social force, created from within the community, that both results from and [creates] interaction and identity with the group' (Johnson 1994: 103).

Solidarity

Both the linguistic and attitudinal differences, reinforced by restricted access to society, underpin a deaf solidarity and a sense of identification among deaf people who share similar experiences (Ladd 2002). In its highest forms of expression, this community is actually referred to as a nation, as in Berthier's proposal from the 1840s that 'la nation des sourds-muets' (the deaf–mute nation) should directly elect one representative to the French Parliament (Mottez 1993).

Conceptual solidarity is also perceived to exist across national boundaries, leading to the sense of belonging to an international deaf community. This was reported as long ago as 1815 in an account of Laurent Clerc's visit to the Braidwood school in London:

As soon as Clerc beheld this sight [the children at dinner] his face became animated; he was as agitated as a traveller of sensibility would be on meeting all of a sudden in distant regions, a colony of his countrymen ... Clerc approached them. He made signs and they answered him by signs. This unexpected communication caused a most delicious sensation in them and for us was a scene of expression and sensibility that gave us the most heartfelt satisfaction.

(Laffon de Ladébat 1815: 33)

Haualand (2007) discusses the transnational state of the deaf community in contemporary terms. To understand deaf culture, 'there is a need to go beyond national and territorial borders to grasp what deaf culture, society and identity are about. The deaf community is characterized by its scattered translocality; members may live at considerable geographical distance from one another' but still participate in a transnational ritual, which both reinforces and redefines deaf culture every time it takes place.

It is generally agreed that in Western societies, deaf residential schools and deaf clubs have formed the two cornerstones of the deaf community concept. In residential schools, deaf children came together, learned sign languages and began the process of accessing the wider deaf community. Despite continued attempts to suppress sign language throughout the twentieth century, schools maintained their role in ensuring the continuity of sign language use and the passing on of deaf culture and deaf historical traditions from one generation to another.

Similarly there is widespread agreement that deaf clubs provided a crucial central focus for deaf adult life, not merely creating and maintaining the language and culture of childhood, but extending the deaf experience into all the organizational forms required in adulthood – local, regional and national; social, cultural and political. Between them, these two cornerstones provide the context in which a sign language can be created and sustained, thus encompassing what is traditionally understood by the deaf community concept.

The minority status of the deaf community has led to the development of the concept of audism, which was first proposed by Humphries (1977) and re-introduced by Lane (1992), who moved the discourse to include social structures and institutions as well as systemic oppression of deaf people, as distinct from individual attitudes towards deaf people. In analyzing solidarity within the deaf community, deaf researchers have used this framework to analyze the threat and challenges posed by the majority hearing community, particularly Gertz (2008) who discusses how audism may manifest itself on a par with 'dyconscious racism' in which some of the values of the majority are internalized by individual members of a minority group.

International structures

The international deaf community is highly organized, with international political organizations (for example, the World Federation of the deaf[1]) as well as international sporting organizations representing deaf people (especially, the International Committee for Sports for the deaf (CISS)).[2] The WFD, the international non-government organization representing deaf people, was established in Rome in 1951. Today there are over 130 member bodies of the federation, which meets every four years at its General Assembly, usually taking place at the same time as the World Congress of the deaf. There are also six regional secretariats, and one regional cooperating member (the European Union of the Deaf). Each Ordinary Member is a deaf national organization representing deaf people, which must have a majority of deaf people with a governing board with a majority of deaf people. Often these national organizations are made up of branches that are either deaf clubs or regional associations of deaf people in the different countries.

The WFD also has B consultative status with the United Nations, which means that on all matters relating to deaf people the WFD is the first point of contact. A recent collaboration between the WFD and the United Nations was the proclamation of the Convention of the Rights of Persons with Disabilities, which has been signed and ratified by more than 20 countries around the world. This Convention among other things mentions the 'recognition of sign languages, recognition and respect for deaf culture and identity, the promotion of bilingual education in sign languages and the national languages as well as accessibility to all areas of society and life, including legislation to secure equal citizenship for all and prevent discrimination as well as the provision of sign language interpreting' (Haualand and Allen 2009). As previously mentioned, these rights are not a reality for most deaf people around the world.

Deaf sports are represented by the International Committee of Sports for the deaf, which was established in Paris in 1924 and holds the Deaflympics Games and the Winter Deaflympics Games every four years. The International Olympic Committee (IOC) in 1955 admitted the CISS as an International Federation with Olympic standing, and the Olympic flag has flown at all Games since 1985. Participation in all events is contingent on proving a hearing loss of more than 55 decibels in the better ear.

History of deaf communities

It is probable that people who communicate by gesture or sign have existed as part of humanity from its inception (indeed sign languages are now considered by some theorists of the evolution of language to represent the first form of human language (cf. Armstrong and Wilcox 2007), although this is highly contentious. In the West, the first written evidence of the existence of deaf individuals or groups communicating by gesture or signs can be found with the rise of the Mediterranean societies in the fifth century BC. From that time onwards, Greek philosophers like Herodotus, Socrates, Aristotle and Plato, and their equivalents in Jewish and Roman society, philosophized about the nature of deaf people's existence and their place in society (see Lang 2002) and discussed their situation in law: the Mishnah (the first-century compendium of Jewish law) discusses the legal status of signing, hints at the existence of a deaf community: 'A deaf-mute may communicate by signs and be communicated with by signs' (Danby, 1933: 4) and considers the situation of deaf individuals being married to other deaf individuals (ibid.).

Deaf 'emergence' from the Middle Ages to the eighteenth century

The clearest evidence for the existence of deaf communities before the creation of deaf education comes from the Ottoman Court from the fifteenth century onwards, where successive Sultans maintained as many as 200 deaf people charged with various responsibilities, including teaching sign language to the rest of the court (Miles 2000). Several were among the Sultans' closest companions. One reason for this is intriguing – speech was seen as an undignified method of communication in the presence of the Sultan, and sign language was felt to be more appropriate.

From the fifteenth century onwards, for a number of complex reasons, including the impact of the Renaissance with its revival of Greek philosophy, there was a considerable increase of interest in Europe in the education of deaf people. Two opposing perspectives can be seen. One focused on the development of deaf people's speech, discouraging contact with other deaf

people. The other saw the experience of deaf people as providing insight into larger philosophical questions, exploring deaf people's ability to make sense of the world through vision,
their ability to communicate in depth with each other and the communicative power found in
sign language itself (see Rée 1999). Little is known about the signing of deaf people in Britain
before the establishment of deaf education. It is likely that wherever deaf people were in contact with each other or where there were families with more than one deaf member, some form
of signing was found. The earliest British account of signing in a legal context is in the parish
record of a wedding in Leicestershire in 1575:

> Thomas Tillsye and Ursula Russel were married: and because the sayde Thomas was and
> is naturally deafe and also dumbe, so that the order of the forme of mariage used usually
> amongst others which can heare and speake could not for his parte be observed ... the
> sayde Thomas, for the expression of his minde instead of words, of his own accorde used
> these signs.
>
> *(St Martin's Parish Register 1575, quoted in Cockayne 2003: 493)*

An early account of deaf people's lives and communication is found in Richard Carew's
(1555–1620) description of a young deaf man, Edward Bone (cited in Jackson 2001). Bone was
the manservant of the Member of Parliament for Cornwall. Carew describes Bone's abilities in
lip-reading and signing with his employer and how he met regularly with a deaf friend, John
Kempe, who lived in a neighbouring village. There are sporadic references to signing
throughout the seventeenth century, one of which appears in the first book on sign language in
Britain, *Philocophus*, published in 1648 and dedicated to two deaf brothers: 'What though you
cannot express your minds in those verball contrivances of man's invention; yet you want not
speeche; who have your whole body for a tongue' (Bulwer 1648). Other contemporary writers
also noted that sign languages were unrelated to spoken languages: 'The deaf man has no
teacher at all and though necessity may put him upon ... using signs, yet those have no affinity
to the language by which they that are about him do converse among themselves' (Dalgarno
1661). The earliest record in the USA of a deaf person who communicated through sign
language is of Sarah Pratt, who was born in 1640 and is the subject of an essay published in
1684 (Carty *et al.* 2009). Her signed communication with her husband was 'Analogous to verbal
expressions', and they could 'communicate any matter much more speedily (and as full) as can
be by Speech'. She and her husband lived in New England and she was able to own land and
participate in community life, and quite significantly, in church fellowship.

How sign languages come into existence

All of the quotes in the section above describe what has been called 'home sign' – gestural
communication systems developed by deaf children who lack input from a language model in
the family. For such individuals, communication develops from gestural input from hearing
adults combined with the child's own creation of gestures. Frishberg (1987) set out a framework
for identifying and describing home-based sign systems. Unlike sign languages, home sign does
not have a consistent meaning-to-symbol relationship, does not pass from generation to generation, is not shared by one large group and is not the same over a community of signers.
However, home signs are the starting point for new sign languages that develop when deaf
people come together.

In the Old Bailey (Central London Criminal Court) records from 1725–1832, 31 references
to people as 'deaf and dumb' are found (Hitchcock and Shoemaker 2008). Deaf people not

only appear as prisoners but also as witnesses and complainants. Clearly, at this time the Court permitted deaf people to take part in criminal proceedings in all capacities, and hearing people, who were for the most part members of their family, work colleagues or employers, were brought in to interpret for them. For example, in a 1771 case, a person, 'with whom he had formerly lived as a servant was sworn interpreter' and 'explained to him the nature of his indictment by signs' (Stone and Woll 2008). Thus it is clear that some form of home signing existed and was recognized before the creation of education for deaf children.

By far the greatest amount of historical description and sociological research data, and consequently, theories about 'deaf communities' has been concentrated on European and North American society. There is widespread agreement that, although it may not be possible to define the boundaries of deaf communities, they are broadly understood to consist of those deaf people who use a sign language. In recent years, concern about the nature of these boundaries has grown, from both within and without those communities. In part this is due to the increasing headway made into the numbers of those formerly classified as 'deaf children' as a result of technological developments twinned with the educational ideology of oralism. These developments, and deaf children and adults' response to them, has resulted in community boundaries becoming cultural 'battlegrounds', where socializing patterns and contending cultural allegiances have become politicized.

Moreover, the socializing patterns of both middle-aged and young deaf people during the last 30 years have changed to the extent that deaf clubs, the traditional centres of deaf community and culture, perceive their continued existence to be threatened. These developments, which resemble similar patterns in wider Western societies, suggest that defining deaf communities will become increasingly problematic.

Extending research to other deaf communities

There have been recent attempts to extend theorizing about deaf communities to cover a wide variety of non-Western societies that have significant deaf membership, ranging from tribes to farming communities, to towns both small and large.

The most recent literature on deaf communities, notably Bahan and Nash (1996); Lane *et al.* (2000); Ladd (2002); and Woll and Ladd (2003), has begun the process of offering conceptual frameworks and models intended to include the various manifestations of deaf existence in different parts of the world. Woll and Ladd explore multidimensional models of deaf communities, based on attitudes, social choices and the size of the deaf population relative to the hearing population.

In Europe and North America, around 1 in 1,000 children is born deaf, and fewer than 1 in 20 deaf children is born to deaf parents. Such cultures, with few deaf people, exhibit negative attitudes to sign language. Different life opportunities for hearing and deaf people in these contexts can be described as an 'oppositional community' with bi-directional conflict between hearing and deaf members (Woll 2008). In such a community, hearing status defines access to society, with consequently lower socio-economic status and educational achievement of deaf people; the rate of marriage between deaf people is high; and the hearing community have little or no awareness of the deaf community and little knowledge of sign language. Most European and North American deaf communities in the past 200 years can be described as of this sort.

Communities in developing countries, where only one or a few deaf people live, partly resemble the oppositional community model, but life choices and experiences for deaf and hearing people in a non-industrialized community are similar in terms of literacy and occupation. In other societies, there are deaf communities that can be viewed as inseparable from the hearing community. In such communities, often small and isolated, with a high incidence of deafness, the socio-economic status and educational achievements of deaf members are largely equivalent to those of hearing members, and there exists considerable knowledge of sign language by the latter. In such communities there is a very low rate of marriage between deaf partners, and no apparent separate community of deaf people. Examples of such communities include those of Martha's Vineyard, Bali and the Yucatan (see below). In many of these societies, some might contest the existence of any deaf community, as there are limited cultural or social consequences of deafness and little sense of deafhood (Ladd 2002).

One possible model for Western society would be societies where the socio-economic status and educational achievement of deaf people is not highly differentiated from that of hearing people, but where deaf people would be empowered to gather together and where the hearing members would manifest an awareness of the existence of those deaf groupings, including various degrees of communication skills with deaf people and some knowledge of sign language.

Case studies

In recent years there have been a growing number of studies of deaf communities that differ from the Western model. These have often perceived by both deaf and non-deaf people as representing an idyllic opposite to the deaf communities of Europe and North America, with language, ethnic identity and solidarity thought to be common to hearing and deaf people.

These include Grand Cayman Island (Washabaugh 1981), Providence Island, off the coast of Colombia (Washabaugh *et al.* 1978), the Urubu of Amazonia (Ferreira-Brito 1984), the Yucatan Maya (Johnson 1994) the Enga of New Guinea (Kendon 1980), Martha's Vineyard (Groce 1985), etc. Discussion of all of these is beyond the scope of this chapter, but specific cases will be presented below.

Martha's Vineyard

The best-known account of a community where signing played a part in the lives of most people, hearing and deaf, is Groce's (1985) study of Martha's Vineyard, an island off the coast of Massachusetts, USA. Some areas of this island had a high incidence of genetic deafness throughout the nineteenth century. Groce (1985) and Bahan and Nash (1996) report that deafness was regarded as just normal variation among people, comparable to handedness. Most deaf people were married to hearing people and were well-respected and economically active. A sign language specific to the island formed an integral part of interaction, including prayer meetings, and in settings where distances were too great for spoken language conversation. However, town business was conducted using hearing family members as interpreters. Over time, as intermarriage with people from outside the community increased, the percentage of deaf people decreased and the multigenerational nature of the community changed. The last deaf members of the community died in the middle of the twentieth century, and the sign language and community are now extinct.

Yucatan

Johnson (1994) describes a Yucatan Mayan deaf community. Just over 3 per cent of the village population is deaf, and both deaf and hearing people are farmers. Hearing people appear to have a high degree of competence in the village's sign language. However, the deaf members are not fully integrated socially. Only three of the seven deaf men are married (all to hearing women), and none have deaf children. None of the deaf women is married, and they report that it is impossible for them to marry. Despite this limited integration with hearing villagers, they do not identify with deaf people from outside the village.

Bali

In the community of Desa Kolok on the island of Bali (Branson *et al.* 1996), 2 per cent of the 2,000 village residents are deaf, and marriage between hearing and deaf villagers is the norm. Deaf members of the community have equal status in decision-making at local community level, although few are reported to participate. Those who do, use family members to interpret, as not all village members are fluent in sign language. In earlier times, village deaf children received no formal education, although there has been a school for hearing children for over 50 years. Recent moves to offer specialist deaf education have resulted in the placing of deaf children in a school located outside the village and this has begun to alter the linguistic and social dynamics of the community.

In two of the examples above, the emergence of deaf schools, which did so much for deaf communities in general, appear to be destroying what are now seen as idyllic communities. It may be pertinent to ask what sort of community deaf people actually prefer, as it would appear that community changes have in the end taken place as a result of their own choices.

Al-Said Israeli Bedouin

Kisch (2008) has described a Bedouin tribe of around 2,000 people, of whom over 10 per cent are deaf. Deaf children are better educated than hearing children, as they attend a deaf school where Hebrew is taught, and hearing children often do not attend school at all. The deaf children therefore develop a degree of literacy in the majority language, which is a key to employability, and they are fully economically integrated. Although all hearing members of the community have some knowledge of the tribe's sign language, only hearing people in families with a high percentage of deaf members are fully fluent.

Nigeria

Schmaling (2000) provides a thorough and grounded description of a well-established deaf community within the Hausa tribe in Northern Nigeria. There is an oral tradition that deaf people have always had meeting points in towns and villages for sharing information and experiences. Their sign language is the main subject of Schmaling's study. The deaf community has its own leader, the Sarkin Bebaye ('Chief of the deaf') whose office is regarded as that of representative of the deaf, paralleling the system of chiefs that is one of the basic organizational principles of Hausa society.

Deaf people are well integrated into hearing Hausa society, and interaction and communication between deaf and hearing people is high. Many hearing people are able to converse with the deaf freely and effectively through signing, at least on a basic level. Hearing people do not feel ashamed of 'talking' with their hands; they generally try to use their hands as much as possible when communicating with deaf people and accept signing as an appropriate medium of communication. Schmaling discusses a number of features that may account for the high level of integration of deaf people in Hausa society, including life in extended families and a generally high incidence of deafness (and disability) in Hausa society.

Unlike the other communities described above, there is clear evidence of a level of what might be called 'deaf consciousness' among the deaf members. Schmaling does report that there is a danger that this state of integration may weaken, as individualization within Hausa society increases with a concomitant loss of traditional societal values.

Nicaragua

The apparently recent emergence of sign language in Nicaragua has been well documented (see Kegl *et al.* 1999), but the development of the community itself is less well known. Senghas and Kegl (1994) report on the social factors involved in the development of this community from an anthropological perspective. Unusually for reports of this kind, their focus is on the internal dynamics of the deaf community as well as on relations with the hearing community.

It is claimed that until the mid-1990s, there were no deaf children of deaf parents, that interaction between deaf people was limited, and there was a near total absence of a multi-generational deaf community structure. The modern deaf community began to form as schools were established, consisting primarily of teenagers and young adults, and is described as having an egalitarian, grass-roots quality. This community incorporated deaf, hard-of-hearing and dyslexic people (all educated together). As time has passed, the two latter groups have gradually separated from the deaf community and the deaf community itself has become more hierarchical and stratified. Because this is a community so clearly in a period of rapid change, Senghas and Kegl's observations highlight the importance of viewing all communities as dynamic entities.

Education and the deaf community

As deaf educational establishments began from the 1760s onwards to bring together large numbers of deaf children and adults, sign languages also began to flourish (cf. de l'Epée 1984 (original date 1776)). Although it can be argued that deaf people can maintain satisfactory lifestyles while existing outside education systems (cf. Desloges 1984 (o.d. 1779), especially where there are high enough numbers of deaf individuals within a community, there is no doubt that the concentration of deaf children and adults within a residential school system is important in maintaining a sizeable and healthy deaf community where the percentage of deaf people within a given population is small. Deaf education therefore was, and, continues to be, the battleground on which the communities' future existence and quality of life is contested.

Use of sign languages in schools varies greatly around the world and even within countries. Since as the beginning of general deaf education in the early nineteenth century, some schools have used a form of sign language for instruction and some have used the spoken language, relying on residual hearing, lip-reading and speaking (part of the philosophy of oralism). Whether taught manually (predominantly before the 1880s) or orally (predominantly from the 1880s to the 1980s), deaf children were usually educated in deaf schools with other deaf children and they usually managed to learn some sign language even though attitudes to signing in schools were often negative.

Since the 1980s sign languages have been more accepted in schools, but simultaneously there has been a very strong move towards mainstreaming deaf children. This has had serious social and linguistic consequences on sign language and the signing community. Some deaf children informally learn sign language once they arrive at primary schools but are neither formally taught the language, nor are exposed to it as a language of instruction. Their access to sign language may be via school staff (teachers, classroom aides and communication support workers) and other pupils, who all vary greatly in their competence. It is widely understood that deaf teachers are able to provide the best sign language role models to children but their numbers vary greatly around the world. For example, in the USA over 20 per cent of teachers of the deaf are deaf signers, while in England there are fewer than 5 per cent, and in Mexico there are none in the public sector. In Scandinavian countries, almost all deaf children, including those with cochlear implants, receive bilingual education.

The classroom has become an area of interest with respect to the cultural transmission patterns for deaf people. Ladd (2007) refers to colonialism and how the educational system has a strong colonizing influence on deaf children; children are not being taught to be deaf adults but because 'their languages and cultures are suppressed, colonised, in order to be "replaced" by the "hearing" languages and cultures' they are being taught to function as hearing people.

Studies consistently show superior sign language skills in deaf children from deaf families compared with deaf children from hearing families (Paul and Quigley 1994), as well as persistent inadequacies in the language environment provided by education systems that report using sign language (Ramsey 1997; Greenberg and Kusché 1987). Herman and Roy (2006) found that many deaf children do not achieve age-appropriate levels of British Sign Language (BSL).

Sign languages and sign language dialects

The main reason for dialect differences within many sign languages can generally be traced to schools, where signs have been developed spontaneously by children and then used for many years, and even by the teachers. BSL exhibits extensive regional variation despite the relatively small area of the country because Britain had 46 deaf schools that were independently set up and administered during the nineteenth century. Schermer (2004) describes five regional dialects of Sign Language of the Netherlands (SLN) based on the five deaf schools. Vanhecke and de Weerdt (2004) have described the regional variation of Flemish Sign Language (VGT) based on five main regions of Flanders, each with its own school. Significantly, Irish Sign Language (ISL) has very little regional variation because there were only two main deaf schools in Ireland, both in Dublin. American Sign Language (ASL) also has surprisingly little regional variation, given the size of the country and its deaf population, probably due to the centralizing effects of Gallaudet University and the original Hertford Asylum, where initially all teachers of the deaf were trained.

Education in many countries has also had a profound effect on national sign languages because educational systems are shared between nations. French Sign Language (LSF) has had the greatest impact on the world's sign languages and its influence can be seen clearly in ISL (Burns 1998), ASL (Lane 1984) and in some dialects of BSL (particularly where BSL has been influenced by ISL). In each case, educators were influenced by the French deaf education system and brought LSF back to their own countries. Other sign languages have also had this sort of influential role. For example, Swedish Sign Language (STS) has influenced Portuguese Sign Language (LGP) through its use of the manual alphabet, after a Swedish educator helped to found a deaf school in Portugal. ISL, originally heavily influenced by LSF, has also had considerable impact on sign languages around the world. Irish nuns and Christian Brothers have taught in Catholic schools for deaf children in countries including India, South Africa and Australia and the influence of ISL is noticeable in the sign languages in these countries (Aarons and Akach 1998).

ASL, itself originally influenced by LSF, now has a major impact on sign languages around the world through education. Gallaudet University attracts foreign deaf students who take

ASL back to their own countries. The USA has been especially generous in providing teacher training in many Third World countries. Andrew Foster, a deaf African American, led a movement for the establishment of schools in African countries where ASL was introduced as the language of tuition (Lane *et al.* 1996). In Nigeria today, ASL taught in schools is mixing with the indigenous sign languages (Schmaling 2003). Even when ASL is not deliberately taught in schools in other countries, the presence of fluent signers of ASL can exert an influence.

Diversity within deaf communities

In recent years researchers have begun to look at the existence of what are termed here as 'subcommunities' existing within the wider deaf communities, and there have been a number of studies of gay, Black, Jewish, Hispanic, Asian, Native American, etc. subcultures within those communities. Although it is beyond the scope of this chapter to discuss these in detail, it is possible to see that the same factors that influence the nature of deaf communities generally can also be applied to a consideration of these subcommunities. Some subcommunities have only recently developed. Gay and lesbian deaf people have only recently emerged from centuries of prejudice to declare themselves and develop their own groups (Lane *et al.* 1996). There is some evidence to show that a distinctive sign dialect exists in ASL, known as GSV (Gay Sign Variation) (Kleinfeld and Warner 1996).

In other examples, however, the majority of the deaf community can be viewed as acting as an oppositional community, and in its turn creating an oppositional minority deaf community. The earliest example in Britain is the Roman Catholic deaf community, who were educated in their own deaf schools (with their own very different sign languages, not dialects, which originated from ISL) and their own clubs. In some cities, such as Liverpool and Manchester, the degree of integration was greater than in others, such as Glasgow. In the last 20 years, most of the overt barriers of prejudice have come down.

The clearest example of an oppositional subcommunity can be found in the USA and South Africa, where Black and White deaf schools were strictly segregated and where there was very little interaction between the two races for the better part of two centuries (Anderson and Bowe 2001). In this example, it would seem fair to suggest that there were actually two separate communities, with their own distinct paths of origin and development (Hairston and Smith 1983). In the case of the USA, the fact that both use ASL, albeit distinctive dialects (Aramburo 1989), would appear to contradict the analysis of separation, but it is possible to construct such use of ASL as, in effect, a colonizing language brought from White deaf people to Black schools. However, the existence of a common language (as contrasted, say, with the situation in 'hearing' South Africa), has enabled an acceleration of Black and White deaf contact. Research is needed to ascertain the degree to which this acceleration has resulted in a unified community. In South Africa, where change has been more recent, where there are more languages to integrate, and where there is a relative absence of a deaf professional class to form a bridge, there is clearly some way to go (Aarons and Akach 1998). It is interesting, however, to note the extent to which new deaf television programmes in South Africa are being used as a medium to unify both the sign languages and the communities.

The British Black deaf community differs from those above in that this is a very new community, which began with the deaf children whose parents migrated to Britain from the Caribbean and Africa from the 1950s onwards, and which is only just beginning to develop a distinctive social network and dialect of BSL (James 2000; James and Woll 2002). A similar pattern can be found with Asian deaf people. In some areas the small number of Black/Asian deaf people has resulted in apparent integration with the White deaf community. In others, however, the extent of racism experienced by Black/Asian deaf people has caused them to withdraw from the White community altogether (Taylor and Meherali 1991), and this may have served as the impetus towards creating their own subcommunities.

Comparable American subcommunities formed by immigration, such as the Hispanic and East Asian deaf communities, have not yet been substantially researched. A pressing issue for these subcommunities is the extent to which they have access to their hearing equivalents. Gay deaf and lesbian groups report significant contact, and it has even been suggested that this contact is more extensive than for the rest of the deaf community. By contrast, however, other groups have found it difficult to access the languages and cultures of their originating communities. For example, Dively (2001) describes the experiences of Native American deaf people, and describes two important themes characteristic of other deaf subcommunities: limited participation within Native American culture, and difficulty in maintaining their Native American identity in the wider deaf community. This is paralleled by research in Britain on the experiences of deaf people of Asian backgrounds (Chamba et al. 1998).

The hearing community and sign language

It has been estimated that for every deaf person who uses BSL, there are nine hearing people who have some knowledge of the language. There has been national broadcasting of television programmes using BSL for over 20 years, and around 20,000 hearing people take basic-level examinations (equivalent to 120 hours of study) in BSL every year (Woll 2001). Furthermore, many more parents, siblings and friends of young deaf children have begun to sign, and many more professionals working with deaf people have done likewise. The creation of the profession of interpreting, deaf Studies and interpreting programmes at universities, and the numbers of deaf young people attending those universities has resulted in hearing and deaf students beginning to form friendships. This has had the effect of creating small 'subcommunities' of deaf and hearing signers in certain locations, ranging from Fremont in California and Rochester in New York to Wolverhampton and Preston in Britain. There is also a general shift in the siting of deaf community activity, especially among young deaf people, from deaf clubs to more public settings; this has served to make deaf communities and languages more visible, and contributed to the developments above.

Summary and Conclusions

The last 20 years has seen a surge in deaf confidence and pride, partly due to the revelation of the linguistic complexities of sign languages. In many places it has meant an improvement in the status of the community and its language. However, there has been limited consideration of social and cultural issues, and of the internal and external factors responsible for creating, maintaining, and changing deaf communities, compared to the amount of linguistic research that has been carried out. Until resources are available to study deaf communities in a consistent manner, progress will be slow.

If we are to assist in mitigating any negative developments that the future might bring, and in encouraging positive ones, we need to be able to take up positions and models that enable us to perceive deaf communities in ways as flexible as the ones they are themselves developing.

The deaf community in the twenty-first century

In the twenty-first century, deaf communities are not only becoming more complex, but may even be reinventing themselves in different ways. Indeed, the unique status of deaf communities may itself be a challenge. To define deaf people simply as disabled is to overlook the linguistic foundation of their collective life. To define them only as a linguistic group may possibly overlook the very real sensory characteristics of their existence, both positive (a unique visual apprehension of the world out of which sign languages have been constructed), and negative (communication barriers are not simply linguistic, but auditory too).

Any study of the deaf community, like other minority communities, cannot be separated from a study of its relationship with the majority language community which surrounds it, and its internal relationships, from the transnational level to the individual level. At the beginning of the twenty-first century, there are two contrasting futures. On the one hand, there are pressures, such as the decrease in opportunities for deaf children to use sign language with their peers as a result of the move to mainstream education, and a possible decrease in the deaf population as a result of medical intervention and advances in genetics. On the other hand, there is increased interest and demand from the hearing community for courses in sign languages, increased use of sign language in public contexts such as television, the potential for legislative recognition of the rights of deaf people to use their language, and increased pride of the deaf community in their distinctive language and culture. The future is finely balanced.

Acknowledgements

Bencie Woll and Robert Adam were supported by the ESRC Deafness Cognition and Language Research Centre (DCAL) Grant, Grant RES-620-28-6001 and Grant RES-620-28-0002. The support of the Economic and Social Research Council (ESRC) is gratefully acknowledged.

Related topics

Multilingualism and public service access: interpreting in spoken and signed languages; linguistic diversity and education; discourses about linguistic diversity.

Notes

1 www.wfdeaf.org
2 www.deaflympics.com/

Further reading

Bahan, B. (2008) 'Upon the formation of a visual variety of the human race', in H-D. Baumann (ed.) *Open Your Eyes: Deaf Studies Talking,* Minneapolis: University of Minnesota Press.
(This chapter reflects on the visual nature of the deaf community and invites the reader to rethink how deaf people are perceived: 'people of the eye' may be a more appropriate paradigm especially as the visual nature of the community manifests itself in its language and grammar, in how deaf people interact and in deaf arts and culture.)

Carty, B., Macready, S. and Sayers, E. E. (2009) '"A grave and gracious woman": Deaf people and signed language in colonial New England', *Sign Language Studies*, 9: 297–323.
(This journal article provides an historical insight to how sign language was used in America prior to the establishment of schools for the deaf, possibly challenging current thought on how sign language was brought to the USA.)

Haualand, H. (2007) 'The two-week village. The significance of sacred occasions for the Deaf Community', in B. Ingstad and S. Whyte (eds) *Disability in Local and Global World*, Berkeley: University of California Press.
(This chapter is an ethnographic study of the international or rather, transnational deaf community at the Rome Deaflympics Games where the various aspects of the multilingual and multicultural Deaf community manifests itself in a time and place, and its own space.)

Sutton-Spence, R. L. and Woll, B. (1999) *The Linguistics of British Sign Language: An Introduction*, Cambridge: Cambridge University Press.
(This book is an introduction for the non-specialist linguist and sign language learner.)

Bibliography

Aarons, D. and Akach, P. (1998) *South African Sign Language: One Language or Many?* Stellenbosch University: Stellenbosch Occasional Papers in Linguistics.

Anderson, G. B. and Bowe, F. G. (2001) 'Racism within the deaf community', in L. Bragg (ed.) *Deaf World: A Historical Reader and Primary Sourcebook*, New York: New York University Press.

Aramburo, A. (1989) 'Sociolinguistic aspects of the black deaf community', in C. Lucas (ed.) *The Sociolinguistics of the Deaf Community*, New York: Academic Press.

Armstrong, D. F. and Wilcox, S. E. (2007) *The Gestural Origin of Language*, Oxford: Oxford University Press.

Bahan, B. and Nash, J. (1996) 'The formation of signing communities', in *Deaf Studies IV: Visions of the Past, Visions of the Future*, Washington DC: Gallaudet University Press.

Baker, C. and Cokely, D. (1980) *American Sign Language*, Silver Spring, MD: TJ Publishers.

Branson, J., Miller, D., Marsaja, I. G. and Negara, I. W. (1996) 'Everyone here speaks sign language, too: A deaf village in Bali, Indonesia', in C. Lucas (ed.) *Multicultural Aspects of Sociolinguistics in Deaf Communities*, Washington, DC: Gallaudet University Press.

Bulwer, J. (1648) *Philocophus or the Deafe and Dumbe Man's Friend*, London: Humphrey Moseley.

Burns, S. E. (1998) 'Irish Sign Language: Ireland's second minority language', in C. Lucas (ed.) *Pinky Extension and Eye Gaze: Language Use in Deaf Communities: Sociolinguistics in Deaf Communities 4*, Washington, DC: Gallaudet University Press.

Carty, B., Macready, S. and Sayers, E. E. (2009) '"A grave and gracious woman": Deaf people and signed language in colonial New England', *Sign Language Studies* 9: 297–323.

Chamba, R., Ahmad, W. and Jones, L. (1998) *Improving Services for Asian Deaf Children: Parents' and Professionals' Perspectives*, Bristol: The Policy Press.

Cockayne, E. (2003) 'Experiences of Deaf in Early Modern England', *The Historical Journal* 4613, 493–510.

Dalgarno, G. (1661) *Ars signorum, vulgo character universalis philosophica et lingua* [Universal Character and Philosophical Language], London: Hayes.

Danby, H. (1933) (ed.) *The Mishnah*, Oxford: Oxford University Press.

de l'Epée, C. (1984) 'The true method of educating the deaf confirmed by much experience' (o.d. 1776), in H. Lane and F. Philip (eds) *The Deaf Experience* Cambridge, MA: Harvard University Press.

Desloges, P. (1984) 'A deaf person's observations about an elementary course of education for the deaf' (o.d. 1779), in H. Lane and F. Philip (eds) *The Deaf Experience*, Cambridge, MA: Harvard University Press.

Dively, V. L. (2001) 'Contemporary native deaf experience: Overdue smoke rising', in L. Bragg (ed.) *Deaf World: A Historical Reader and Primary Sourcebook*, New York: New York University Press.

Ferreira-Brito, L. (1984) 'Similarities and differences in two Brazilian Sign Languages', *Sign Language Studies* 13: 45–56.

Frishberg, N. (1987) 'Home sign', in J. V. Van Cleve (ed.) *Gallaudet Encyclopedia of Deaf People and Deafness*, New York: McGraw Hill.

Gertz, G. (2008) 'Dyconscious audism: A theoretical proposition', in H-D. Baumann (ed.) *Open Your Eyes: Deaf Studies Talking*, Minneapolis: University of Minnesota Press.

Greenberg, M. and Kusché, C. (1987) 'Cognitive, personal, and social development of deaf children and adolescents', in M. C. Wang, M. C. Reynolds and H. J. Walberg (eds) *Handbook of Special Education: Research and Practice*, vol. 3: *Low Incidence Conditions*, New York: Pergamon.

Groce, N. E. (1985) *Everyone Here Spoke Sign Language: Hereditary Deafness on Martha's Vineyard*, Cambridge, MA: Harvard University Press.

Hairston, E. and Smith, L. (1983) *Black and Deaf in America*, Silver Spring, MD: TJ Publishers.

Haualand, H. (2007) 'The two-week village: The significance of sacred occasions for the deaf community', in B. Ingstad and S. Whyte (eds) *Disability in Local and Global Worlds*, Berkeley: University of California Press.

Haualand, H. and Allen, C. (2009) 'Deaf people are not able to enjoy human rights', in *WFD News*, World Federation of the Deaf, February.

Herman, R. and Roy, P. (2006) 'Evidence from the wider use of the BSL receptive skills test', *Deafness and Education International* 8(1): 33–47.

Higgins, P. (1980) *Outsiders in a Hearing World*, Newbury Park, CA: Sage.

Hitchcock, T. and Shoemaker, R. (eds) *The Proceedings of the Old Bailey*, available online at www.oldbaileyonline.org

Humphries, T. (1977) *Communicating Across Cultures (Deaf-Hearing) and Language Learning*, doctoral dissertation, Cincinnati, OH: Union Institute and University.

Jackson, P. (2001) *A Pictorial History of Deaf Britain*, Winsford: Deafprint.

James, M. (2000) *Black Deaf or Deaf Black?*, PhD, City University London.

James, M. and Woll, B. (2002) 'Black deaf or deaf black?' in A. Blackledge and A. Pavlenko (eds) *Negotiation of Identities in Multilingual Contexts*, Clevedon: Multilingual Matters.

Johnson, R. E. (1994) 'Sign language and the concept of deafness in a traditional Yucatec Mayan village', in C. J. Erting, R. E. Johnson, D. L. Smith and B. D. Snider BD (eds) *The Deaf Way – Perspectives from the International Conference on Deaf Culture 1989*, Washington, DC: Gallaudet University Press.

Kegl, J. A., Senghas, A. and Coppola, M. (1999) 'Creation through contact: Sign language emergence and sign language change in Nicaragua', in M. DeGraff (ed.) *Comparative Grammatical Change: The Intersection of Language Acquisition, Creole Genesis, and Diachronic Syntax*, Cambridge, MA: MIT Press.

Kendon, A. (1980) 'A description of a deaf-mute sign language from the Engaprovince of Papua New Guinea with some comparative discussion: Parts I, II, III', *Semiotica* 32: 1–34, 81–117, 245–313.

Kisch, S. (2008) '"Deaf discourse": The social construction of deafness in a Bedouin community', *Medical Anthropology* 27(3): 283–313.

Kleinfeld, M. S. and Warner, N. (1996) 'Variation in the deaf community: Gay, lesbian and bisexual signs', in C. Lucas (ed.) *Multicultural Aspects of Sociolinguistics in Deaf Communities*, Washington, DC: Gallaudet University Press.

Ladd, P. (2002) *Understanding Deaf culture: In Search of Deafhood*, Clevedon: Multilingual Matters.

——(2007) 'Cultural rights and sign language peoples', paper given at the XV World Congress of the World Federation of the Deaf, Madrid, Spain.

Laffon de Ladébat, A. D. (1815) *Recueil des Définitions et Réponses les Plus Remarquables de Massieu et Clerc, Sourds-muets, aux Diverses Questions qui Leur Ont été Faites dans les Séances Publiques de M. l'abbé Sicard à Londres* [A Collection of the Most Remarkable Definitions and Answers of Massieu and Clerc], London: Cox and Baylis.

Lane, H. (1984) *When the Mind Hears*, New York: Random House.

——(1992) *The Mask of Benevolence: Disabling the Deaf Community*, New York: Alfred A. Knopf.

Lane, H., Hoffmeister, R. J. and Bahan, B. (1996) *A Journey into the Deaf World*, San Diego, CA: Dawn Sign Press.

Lane, H., Pillard, R. C. and French, M. (2000) 'Origins of the American deaf-world: Assimilating and differentiating societies and their relation to genetic patterning', in K. Emmorey and H. Lane (eds) *The Signs of Language Revisited*. Mahwah, NJ: Lawrence Erlbaum Associates.

Lang, H. G. (2002) 'Perspectives on the history of deaf education', in M. Marschark and P. Spencer (eds) *Oxford Handbook of Deaf Studies, Language, and Education*, Oxford: Oxford University Press.

Markowicz, H. and Woodward, J. (1978) 'Language and the maintenance of ethnic boundaries in the Deaf Community', *Communication and Cognition* 11: 29–37.

Miles, M. (2000) 'Signing at the Seraglio: Mutes, dwarves and jestures at the Ottoman Court 1500–1700', *Disability Handicap and Society* 15: 115–34.

Mottez, B. (1993) 'The Deaf Mute banquets and the birth of the Deaf movement', in R. Fischer and H. Lane (eds) *Looking Back*, Hamburg: Signum Verlag.

Padden, C. A. and Humphries, T. (1988) *Deaf in America*, Cambridge, MA: Harvard University Press.

Paul, P. V. and Quigley, S. P. (1994) *Language and Deafness* (updated and revised edition) San Diego, CA: Singular Publishing Group.

Ramsey, C. (1997) *Deaf Children in Public Schools*, Washington, DC: Gallaudet University Press.

Rée, J. (1999) *I See a Voice: A Philosophical History of Language, Deafness and the Senses*, London: Harper Collins.

Schermer, G. M. (2004) 'Lexical variations in Sign Language of the Netherlands', in M. van Herreweghe and M. Vermeerbergen (eds) *To the Lexicon and Beyond: Sociolinguistics in European Deaf Communities: Sociolinguistics in Deaf Communities 10*, Washington, DC: Gallaudet University Press.

Schmaling, C. (2000) *Maganar Hannu: Language of the hands. A descriptive analysis of Hausa Sign Language*. Hamburg: Signum.

Schmaling, C. (2003). 'A for apple: The impact of western education and ASL on the deaf community in Kano State, northern Nigeria', in: L. Monaghan, C. Schmaling, K. Nakamura and G. H. Turner (eds) *Many Ways to be Deaf: International Variation in Deaf Communities*. Washington, DC: Gallaudet University Press.

Senghas, R. J. and Kegl, J. A. (1994) 'Social considerations in the emergence of Idioma de Signos Nicaraguense (Nicaraguan Sign Language)', *Signpost* 7: 40–46.

Stone, C. and Woll, B. (2008) 'DUMB O JEMMY and others: Deaf people, interpreters and the London courts in the 18th and 19th centuries', *Sign Language Studies* 8(3): 226–40.

Taylor, G. and Meherali, T. (1991) 'The other deaf community?' *Issues in Deafness. Block 1, Unit 4*, Milton Keynes: The Open University.

Vanhecke, E. and de Weerdt, K. (2004) 'Regional variation in Flemish Sign Language', in M. van Herreweghe and M. Vermeerbergen (eds) *To the Lexicon and Beyond: Sociolinguistics in European Deaf Communities. Sociolinguistics in Deaf Communities 10*, Washington, DC: Gallaudet University Press.

Washabaugh, W. (1981) 'The deaf of Grand Cayman, British West Indies', *Sign Language Studies* 10: 117–34.

Washabaugh, W., Woodward, J. and DeSantis, S. (1978) 'Providence Island sign: A context-dependent language', *Anthropological Linguistics* 20: 95–109.

Woll, B. (2001) 'Language, culture, identity and the deaf community', *The Linguist* 40: 98–03.

——(2008) 'Opinion: Deaf in the 21st century', *Society Now*, Autumn, 17.

Woll, B. and Ladd, P. (2003) 'Deaf communities', in M. Marschark and P. Spencer (eds) *The Handbook of Deaf Studies, Language and Education*, Oxford: Oxford University Press.

Woll, B. and Lawson, L. (1982, revised edition 1990) 'British Sign Language', in E. Haugen, J. D. McClure and D. Thomson (eds) *Minority Languages Today*, Edinburgh: Edinburgh University Press.

6

Discourses about linguistic diversity

Melanie Cooke and James Simpson

Introduction

In many parts of the world, multilingualism is a fact of life, intensified in recent decades by processes of globalization characterized by an increase in the movement of people within and across borders, electronic mass media and online communication. Although in many quarters linguistic diversity is accepted, and indeed celebrated as an asset, at the same time it has become a source of tension and debate in public and political discourse, where multilingualism is often constructed as a problem or threat to national unity. Linguistic diversity is also a potential source of conflict in multilingual societies, particularly when choices have to be made about language use in domains such as government, broadcasting, education and public services. The work surveyed in this chapter explains how discourses about linguistic diversity produced in powerful domains such as the government and the media interact with other discourses and circulate through different levels of society, gain legitimacy and, importantly, impact on legislation. To illustrate our points we provide examples from debates in the UK where language is invoked in arguments about immigration, British identity, citizenship, multiculturalism, national security and social cohesion.

In the next section we define key terms underpinning the chapter: *discourse, ideology* and *power*, before sketching out some analytical approaches taken in the study of the area. We then turn to the discourses about linguistic diversity that dominate public and political debates, and illustrate these with examples from the UK. Finally, we emphasize that some of the dominant discourses about linguistic diversity are at odds with the multilingual realities of much contemporary life, examining ways in which they are contested.

Key concepts

Discourse

Discourses can be defined as ways of talking and writing that promote particular views of the world. This understanding of discourse is linked to the theoretical work of Foucault: discourses in the Foucauldian sense refer to what is 'say-able' or 'meaning-able' at a given time and in a given place, institution or society in regard to a given topic or theme; discourse constrains what it is possible for us to know (Foucault 1970). Discourses have a dual nature: they reflect the social order, i.e. they are constructed by it, and simultaneously they construct and shape it (Berger and Luckmann 1966; Burr 1996). Although language is central to discourse, some theorists view discourse as encompassing 'all forms of meaningful semiotic activity' (Blommaert 2005: 3; see also Gee 1996): visual images and representations, the body, architecture, symbols such as flags and so on. There are multiple discourses in any one society and any one individual draws on many discourses, sometimes simultaneously. Discourses are subject to contestation, hybridity and intertextuality, i.e. they interact with and inform each other. Discourses also compete with each other, some becoming more dominant than others at particular times. For analysts working in a critical tradition, the study of discourse is concerned with how sets of discourses work together to construct common sense knowledge (Fairclough 1992), which helps to bring powerful ideologies into being.

Ideology

Ideologies are made up of beliefs and assumptions that appear 'common sense' to members of a society and therefore often remain unquestioned. Blommaert and Verschueren (1998: 25) define ideology as 'any constellation of fundamental or commonsensical, and often normative, ideas and attitudes related to some aspect(s) of social "reality"'. They go on to point out that discourse is 'the most tangible manifestation of ideology' (1998: 26). An analysis of discourses and practices, therefore, can uncover the nature of the normally unexamined ideas, values and beliefs that underpin prevailing ideologies and, as we see later, the implementation of government legislation. The practices and discourses within which ideologies are constructed cut across social life. They may be, as Blackledge (2008: 51) notes, 'explicit and implicit, visible and invisible, official and unofficial, long-term and ephemeral, contested and uncontested, negotiable and non-negotiable'.

Power

The study of discourse and ideology matters because of power and its control by elites. Ideology, discourse and power are inextricably linked, and they intersect with the notion of *hegemony*. In Gramsci's account of hegemony (1971), power is retained by elites not through force but by their ability to project their own way of seeing the world onto those whom they subordinate. When they are able to match up their world view with those who are dominated, then the dominant perspective becomes the common sense one. Thus can generally accepted 'facts' – for example about culture or language – be aligned with the interests of elites. How hegemony is achieved – how and why particular ideologies about cultures and language can become dominant – is arbitrary, maintains Bourdieu (1977). He argues that for a particular view of culture and language to dominate, there must be a consensus, a shared false belief or *misrecognition*. Dominant and dominated alike need to accept, for example, that some languages have greater value than others.

Language ideologies

Pertinent to the analysis of powerful discourses about linguistic diversity is the study of language ideologies (Gal 1979; Heller 1999). Kroskrity (2001) traces the origins of this field of enquiry to Silverstein's (1979) paper 'Language Structure and Linguistic Ideology', in which it is

117

argued that speakers' awareness of a language and their rationalization of its structure and use are critical factors in shaping its evolution; linguistic ideology should therefore be recognized as a level of language, and an important one. Kroskrity (2001: 1) describes language ideologies as 'beliefs, feelings, and conceptions about language structure and use which often index the political interests of individual speakers, ethnic and other interest groups, and nation states'. Language ideologies are 'always socially situated and tied to questions of power in societies' (Blackledge 2008: 51). This being so, ideological debates about language are often actually about something else, 'language' serving as a proxy for more proscribed matters such as race, class and ethnicity. Language ideologies can be deeply entrenched: notions of a standard language or of 'one nation one language' are language ideologies that are often made manifest in public discourse: they themselves are interlaced with ideologies of national identity and the dogmas of homogeneism (Blommaert and Verschueren 1998) and monolingualism. We discuss these issues, along with others that are salient in contemporary language debates, later in the chapter.

The notion of common sense in the construction of ideology points to the crucial importance of encompassing the beliefs of speakers who are not language specialists in discussion of debates about linguistic diversity. This is despite them being 'wrong' or 'mistaken' in many of those beliefs, as many linguists have it (see for instance Pinker 1994 chapter 12). In her study of popular beliefs about language standards, Cameron identifies a 'gulf between linguists and lay language-users' (1995: xi), arguing the need to attend to everyday evaluative discourse about language. Kroskrity (2001) makes a similar point: ordinary beliefs are an important level of understanding language ideologies, and can certainly be more powerful than sociolinguistic descriptions in influencing the direction of legislation, for instance. Linguistic diversity may be celebrated by sociolinguists but popular opinion draws on and contributes to powerful discourses about linguistic diversity, for example that it is a problem that needs to be managed; hence we see the invocation of language in debates surrounding migration, of the type that we exemplify later.

Approaches

Critical Discourse Analysis

A field concerned with the study of language ideologies is Critical Discourse Analysis (CDA), a version of discourse analysis that brings together linguistic analysis (drawing principally on Hallidayan linguistics) with social theory (in particular Foucault). The aim of CDA is to 'disarticulate and to critique texts as a way of disrupting common sense' (Luke 1995: 20) and to focus on how 'language as a cultural tool mediates relationships of power and privilege in social interactions, institutions and bodies of knowledge' (Rogers 2008). Researchers who work in the tradition of CDA (Fairclough 2001; Wodak 2001; van Dijk 1991) are specifically concerned with the ideological nature of discourse; their attention is thus focused on spoken and written texts produced by powerful institutions such as the media, government, advertising, the law and the academy. Analysts seek to understand in particular the material interests that particular texts might serve and how that articulation works on listeners, readers and viewers. CDA has traditionally concentrated on how powerful ideologies such as racism and nationalism are produced and reproduced 'at the top' (Wodak and van Dijk 2000). Although not ignoring the fact that ideology circulates through discourses at all levels of society, critical discourse analysts believe that discourse produced by politicians and the media is more likely to influence public opinion than vice versa. In particular, they stress the need to understand the subtle, indirect and euphemized nature of modern political discourse in which discriminatory attitudes and illiberal policy might be constructed as liberal and egalitarian. This feature of modern political discourse, as it relates to debates about language in the UK, will be addressed later in this chapter, when we discuss the example of the British citizenship test.

Levels of discourse

Blommaert and Verschueren distinguish between two types of discourse data: data produced and controlled by powerful groups in society such as the media, government and academics, and 'grass-roots' data that reflect the way in which 'reigning ideologies have penetrated the commonsense theorising of those lower on the social ladder' (1998: 26). One central challenge for analysts is to show how discourses produced in different places by different speakers and writers are related to each other and work together to bring about hegemonic ideologies. Discourses and the ideologies underpinning them permeate and circulate through society at multiple levels and through historical time (Wodak 2001). This makes the issue of how different levels of discourse work together a knotty one: the same discourse is not uniformly produced throughout any given society. Individuals are unlikely to either completely accept dominant discourses or reject them outright, but rather, they develop 'complex configurations of thought in which some dominant ideological elements find expression in conjunction with individual and group-based understandings' (Augoustinos 1998: 165).

A key concept employed to address this question is *intertextuality*. The principle is that texts do not exist in isolation but connect with and refer to each other, sometimes deliberately and sometimes coincidentally, so that the same repeated and reiterated wordings, statements, themes and images appear across texts in different settings (Luke 1995). The result of this interconnectedness is the creation of a set of available discourses for readers of texts or hearers of spoken discourse (or indeed viewers of visual images). Related to intertextuality is the concept of *recontextualization*, that is, the process by which meanings shift across genres, domains and semiotic systems. When discourses move from text to text and genre to genre in different contexts they become transformed, either by the addition of new elements and voices or by the deletion of previous ones.

Here are three illustrations. In their study of debates about diversity in Belgium, Blommaert and Verschueren show how the discourses produced by politicians echo or respond to those of other 'ideology brokers' such as the media and social scientists and are then 'reproduced through an infinite series of echoes and references in secondary sources' (1998: 27) such as everyday talk and local sites where policy is enacted. Similarly, Milani's (2007: 169) study of the debates about language and citizenship in Sweden reveals a 'discursive network of voices ... engaged in the process of policy making' – not just politicians but academics, journalists and individual citizens as well. Blackledge (2004, 2006, 2007), analysing similar debates in the UK, describes the complex connections between different discourses and their movement along a 'discourse chain'. He analyses a series of texts that all appear to connect a lack of proficiency in English to a breakdown in law and order. The chain starts with a speech by a politician made in response to street disturbances between local Asian and white youth and the police in her local constituency. The speech makes some discursive links between a lack of competence in English among elders in the communities where some of the youth live. Blackledge traces how this discourse moves through subsequent commentaries in Parliament, debates in the media and ends finally enshrined in law. Blackledge shows how with each move along the chain and with each recontextualization the discourse becomes 'more powerful and authoritative as it is restated and transformed in increasingly authoritative contexts' (Blackledge 2006: 65).

Dominant discourses about linguistic diversity

In recent decades, public debates about linguistic diversity have intensified in many countries and regions. In this section we outline three of the most dominant discourses in these debates, giving examples from research from around the world. These inter-related discourses are about national identity, homogeneism and monolingualism and the process of 'othering'.

For Bakhtin (1981), heteroglossia, a multiplicity of different ways of speaking that are constantly intermingling with each other, is the normal condition of language. This view is in tension with the notion of a 'unitary language' that is created by centripetal forces of centralization and regimentation that are opposed by centrifugal processes of increasing differentiation. This opposition is a manifestation of the discrepancy between the increasingly well-documented reality of multilingualism, heteroglossia and diversity in language practice in the world's cities, towns and virtual spaces, and the monolingualist – and *monolingualizing* (Heller 1995: 374) – discourses of governments and policies.

One nation one language

Western governments tend to react to multilingualism within their borders as a 'problem', something that must be 'managed' (Hogan-Brun *et al.* 2009). This ideological stance is evident in debates ranging from, *inter alia*, the 'English only' question in the USA, the public funding of translation services, the issue of bi- and multilingual education, immigration policy – especially decisions regarding the country of origin of refugees seeking asylum (Maryns 2006) – and citizenship and language testing regimes. It is also clearly at play in multilingual countries undergoing 'nation building' (e.g. Singapore) and where there are regions with large numbers of speakers of minority languages (e.g. Canada, Spain).

Although the world is very obviously *not* divided up into monolingual states (Blommaert 2006), the modernist dogma of 'one nation one language' persists (see Joseph 2004, 2006; Wright 2004), underpinned by a belief that in order for societies to be strong, stable and 'cohesive' their populations must share a common language (or in some cases a set of official languages). The association of one language with the membership of one national community, sometimes known as *linguistic nationism*, is a relatively recent phenomenon in historical terms, intimately connected to the growth of nation-states and nationalism in the late eighteenth, nineteenth and early twentieth centuries (Hobsbawm 1990; Billig 1995). Theorists of nations and nationalism, such as Anderson (1983), regard nations as constructions, as 'imagined communities' that rely on language, in particular the mass media, for their construction. The imagined nation is seen as limited by finite boundaries, as a fraternal community of comrades ready to take up arms to defend their territorial integrity or economic interests (Kramsch 1998), linked together with a common culture and – fundamentally – language.

Homogeneism and monolingualism

The utopian nature of the 'nation' is similar to that of the view of language as shared patrimony, a self-contained linguistic system based on a homogeneous social world (Kramsch 1998). As Blommaert (2008b: 88) notes, 'language is one of the prime objects of the national order'. It follows that when nation-states perceive themselves to be under threat in some way, either from the outside or from within, nationalist and linguistic ideologies tend to become more dominant. Joseph (2006: 33) comments: 'multilingualism, language change and non-standard usage all feel like threats to the very foundation of a culture since the language itself is the principal text in which the culture's mental past and its present coherence are grounded'.

The ideology that underpins monolingualism is a theory of language and culture for which Blommaert and Verschueren (1998) have coined the term *homogeneism*. This they define as: '*the idea that the ideal society should be as uniform or homogeneous as possible*' [their italics]. They continue: 'Homogeneity is not only seen as desirable, but also as the norm, i.e. as the most *normal* manifestation of a human society' (1998: 117).

The dominant discourse of monolingualism is the linguistic dimension of the broad ideological stance of homogeneism. Homogeneism, explains Blommaert:

> holds monolingualism (and by extension monoculturalism) to be the norm or the desired ideal for a society, and which axiomatically projects this monolingualism-monoculturalism onto individuals, each individual being 'normally' monolingual and member of one culture.
>
> *(1999: 427)*

Monolingualist discourse is dominant in part because it is hegemonic: accepted as an unquestioned common sense 'given' by the majority of people in the areas where it is dominant. Hence the dominant position of the standard variety is *reproduced* (Bourdieu and Passeron 1990). Monolingualist policies appeal to, and resonate with, people's beliefs and everyday notions or ideologies about language and standards. For instance, the common sense understanding of the importance of a standard language as a unifying 'glue' for a nation (a case of *misrecognition* in Bourdieu's terms) works in the interests of the political elite whose interests national unity serves. In accepting ideologies about language that quite clearly work against them, they become subject to what Bourdieu terms *symbolic violence*: that is, the symbolic capital of the standard language is used against the dominated with the effect that they remain oppressed (see Simpson and Cooke 2010).

Monolingualist discourse dominates in the development and maintenance of a national identity. As such it is the preserve of the elites in whose interest such nation-building primarily takes place. Blommaert (2008a: 12) contends that 'the space in which languages are situated is invariably a *national* space, the space defined by states that have a name and that can be treated as a fixed unit of knowledge and information'. This is despite the notion of a stable distribution of languages following national boundaries running counter to the lived language experience and polyglot repertoire of people around the world. Mar-Molinero and Stevenson (2006: 1) point to the tension between 'the static framework of the national, with its fixed parameters, and the fluid forms of the transnational'. Yet in many parts of the world, monolingualism is promoted in the interests of nation-building and central power. As Joseph (2006: 45) says, monolingualism demands 'the marginalisation or outright ignoring of anyone who speaks something other than the majority language, or speaks the majority language in a way that diverges from the general norm, or both'.

State- and elite-driven discourses of homogeneism can be found around the world, and somewhat paradoxically are also prominent in many countries that have some sort of official status as bi- or multilingual. In those that are engaged in a process of nation-building, and in those that have strong regionalist nationalist movements the discourses are strongly evident, although debate itself might be more or less muted. In the case of Singapore, Bokhorst-Heng (1999) describes how the linguistic diversity characterizing the Chinese community has been homogenized through government decree and a series of 'Speak Mandarin' campaigns. As she notes, the Prime Minister's statements on language in relation to culture, ethnicity, history and society prove 'how easily certain linguistic ideologies can be transformed or absorbed into political ideologies, and how easily a rhetoric on language, culture, history and identity can become an instrument of societal streamlining and disciplining' (1999: 262). In Flanders

(Belgium), the Flemish language is promoted by elite political groups, and supported by public discourse in the media, as a dimension of Flemish nationalist movements (Blommaert and Verschueren 1998).

To maintain their hegemony, monolingualist discourses need *legitimization*. Political and media discourses of monolingualism and the privileging of a standard variety in the interests of unity tend to invoke an authoritative voice. This imbues legitimacy on the position of arguments that point out, for instance, the decline in standards in schools, the absolute necessity of a citizenship test, that multilingualism is a problem that must be 'managed', or the desirable position that a nation's inhabitants should be expert users of the authorized variety of the dominant language. Such discourses would also lack force if they were not able to make reference to the linguistic (and sociocultural) 'other', to which we now turn.

Othering

Concomitant with a homogenizing discourse, users of languages that are not the dominant language, or of non-standard varieties of the dominant language, are positioned as 'other'. *Othering*, or the creation in discourse of in-groups and out-groups ('we' and 'they'), is strongly evident in much homogenizing discourse in media and public debate, for instance in the campaigns of the English Only movement in the USA. The English Only movement encourages the use only of English in political and educational contexts, and presses for the establishment of English as the country's national language. From this perspective, the business of unifying (or homogenizing) the nation is equated with positioning English as the only acceptable language of the public sphere (Ricento 1996, 2003; Dicker *et al*. 1995). English Only debates are fuelled by a powerful discourse of monolingualism. To illustrate the discursive processes of othering, here is an example from a CDA perspective, which examines pronominalization on US-based electronic discussion forums. Lawton (2008: 93) quotes the following message-board post: 'If we keep on making it easy for people of another country to live here without even as much as learning our language then hell … we'll be over-run soon'. As Lawton points out: 'the poster refers collectively to monolingual and perhaps even Anglo-Americans as "we", while bilingual Spanish-speaking Latinos are collectively referred to as "people of another country"'. Lawton's example demonstrates the point made by those working in the tradition of CDA that 'the public' draws upon discourses that are also prevalent among elites: that is, discourses are produced and reproduced at different levels.

Othering is evident in language teaching, particularly English Language Teaching (ELT) (Pennycook 2001; Holliday 2005; see also Phillipson 1992; Hélot, this volume), echoing the othering in anti-diversity discourse more generally. Holliday discusses an essentialist view of non-Western culture that pervades ELT in his discussion of the 'unproblematic self' and the 'culturally problematic other' (2005: 19–20). In a 'native speakerist narrative', maintains Holliday, the 'non-native speaker' appears 'as a *generalized Other* in which we easily speak of *all* "East Asian students", "Arab teachers" and so on in very similar ways' (2005: 19).

Notably, the term 'speakers of other languages' (and its variants) is increasingly used to refer to migrants who are users of non-standard or non-dominant languages. Blommaert and Verschueren (1998: 131) talk about a 'rhetorical change': 'the gradual replacement of the term "migrants" as a problematized target group in educational policies with the notion of *anderstaligen* "speakers of other languages" or "linguistically other"'. Pennycook (2001: 122) wryly re-works the well-used acronym *ESOL* as: *English for speakers of othered languages*. In some sense then, the learning and teaching of English has – like language itself – become a proxy for other debates. Hence in the flow of public discourse associated with the English Only argument, things are said about the learning of English that would probably not be said about ethnicity and immigration. We take this point up again in the next section, where our examples are from the UK.

Linguistic diversity debates exemplified

In this section we illustrate some of the tensions between the reality of multilingualism on the one hand, and on the other, monolingualizing discourses. Our examples show how the tensions have manifested themselves in the UK since 2001. Several dominant discourses and ideologies from across different domains combine together in debates about linguistic diversity and the legislation introduced in this period: immigration, British identity, multiculturalism (and its purported failure), national security, 'social cohesion' and the distribution of resources – all of which draw on homogenizing nationalist and monolingual ideologies, 'othering' discourses and the problem-management notion of linguistic diversity.

The common sense ideologies underlying the UK debates, policies and legislation surrounding linguistic diversity are:

- that linguistic diversity and multilingualism (and by extension, immigration) are problems and they need to be managed; that some members of ethnic minority communities are unwilling to learn English; that they choose to live in enclaves; and that this is detrimental to social or 'community' cohesion.
- that Britain is a monolingual country, or at best tolerates a certain degree of regional bilingualism in Wales and parts of Scotland: that is, the ideology of one nation one language.
- that resources are scarce and that the costs incurred by linguistic diversity in public institutions such as health and education are very high and cannot be met from the public purse without jeopardizing other, more deserving public services.

Linguistic diversity as a problem

Since 2001, there has been a shift of emphasis in UK policy away from broad official support for multiculturalism to one which foregrounds 'social cohesion' and 'integration', which some regard as a return to an explicitly assimilationist approach to minority ethnic populations (van Avermaet 2009). Such an approach rests on the acceptance of the proposition that the policy of multiculturalism has failed and that 'too much diversity' (Goodhart 2004) is the main cause of a breakdown in cohesion. This is often played out in debates about culture and religion and what Vertovec and Wessendorf (2005: 15) call 'the iconic issues of diversity' – for example, about the wearing of the veil in schools and the vilification of undifferentiated Muslim 'communities' and practices (i.e. othering discourses) – and, increasingly, language. Indeed, media and government discourse since 2001 has been concerned with issues of language with an intensity and frequency previously unknown in British public life. However, as we noted earlier, studies in language ideology consistently point out that debates about linguistic diversity are rarely about language alone (Woolard and Scheiffelin 1994; Blackledge 2008): they are often proxies for other concerns such as race relations and immigration, and about how public resources should be prioritized.

The connection in public discourse between language and other, broader issues such as security, immigration, racial integration and 'social cohesion' gained prominence after certain events in 2001, both in England, namely the disturbances in the north of England involving Asian and White youths and the police in July that year, and on the world stage ('9/11'). High

123

profile inquiries after the July disturbances (e.g. Home Office 2001) proposed that communities were 'fractured' and segregated along religious, ethnic and linguistic lines and that people in those communities were living 'parallel lives'. This marked a shift in public discourse: previous analyses of urban disturbances (e.g. the Scarman Report into the Brixton riots in the 1980s) had traced the cause to the deprivation and marginalization of some ethnic minority youths, but not on their refusal to integrate (Young 2003). In 2001, however, the prevailing discourse was that separatism and people living apart is a choice, and that immigrants are *unwilling* to learn English and therefore to integrate. The notion of people living parallel lives arose frequently in political and media discourse, and the analyses of the events in northern England in 2001, although very specific to certain towns, were generalized to other populations.

Language and citizenship

At the same time, legislation was being prepared that would tighten controls on immigration and introduce for the first time a test of language and citizenship for those wishing to become British citizens. In addition to the English language and citizenship test, the White Paper, *Secure Borders, Safe Haven: Integration with Diversity in Modern Britain* (Home Office 2002) proposed changes in the law regarding war criminals, work permits, people trafficking, illegal entry, marriage visas and legislation covering refugees seeking asylum. Thus, competence in English became closely tied, in discourse and in law, to immigration, national identity and citizenship. Drawing on the experience of the 2001 disturbances, the White Paper and the subsequent 2002 Nationality, Immigration and Asylum Act stressed 'the need for us to foster and renew the social fabric of our communities and rebuild a sense of common citizenship, which embraces the different and diverse experiences of today's Britain'. The key to this would be English as a common language, which would enable all individuals 'to engage as active citizens in economic, social and political life' (2002: 30).

Some commentators have pointed out that there is little evidence to suggest either that ghettoization is more than a minor trend in Britain or that it is on the rise (Poulsen and Johnston 2006). Amin (2008) notes that the very specific problems affecting particular neighbourhoods or particular groups within some communities have been generalized across the board: 'the parallel lives led by elders, veiled women and very young children in a small number of neighbourhoods in Britain should not be read as the proxy for most minority ethnic communities' (2008: 1). There is a similar absence of research evidence confirming the notion that speaking languages other than English leads to a breakdown of social cohesion. Despite this, the links between the two have been made frequently in political discourse since 2001. The Member of Parliament for one of the troubled towns in northern England spoke of the need for minority families to use English in the home 'in addition to Panjabi and Bangla' (see Blackledge 2005: 97) in order to prevent educational disadvantage. This was closely followed by the now notorious comments of the former Home Secretary, David Blunkett, who wrote of the 'schizophrenia which bedevils generational relationships' in bilingual families (2002: 77).

In order to legitimize their discourses and to distance themselves from extreme right-wing ideologies, politicians who link English competence with citizenship and social cohesion usually couch their point in 'liberal' terms, that is, English is necessary for everyone to access their rights, to be able to fully participate in British society and to avoid being economically and socially marginalized. According to Blackledge (2005), masking illiberal proposals by embedding them in liberal discourse is one of the chief characteristics of British political debate. In Britain, though, as the first decade of the twenty-first century progressed, the discourse of politicians became less liberal and less apologetic about their views regarding

English, linguistic minorities and social cohesion. This might be because the public became more used to the terms of the debate. Perhaps also the debate aligned closer to right-leaning popular opinion on race and immigration from which governments had previously distanced themselves. This series of quotes from senior politicians demonstrates how their stance towards English learned by migrants had hardened.

Tony Blair, the former Prime Minister, in a speech given shortly after 7 July 2005, announcing a package of measures to combat Islamic extremism, stated: 'There are people who are isolated in their own communities who have been here for 20 years and still do not speak English. That worries me because there is a separateness that may be unhealthy'.

Margaret Hodge, the former Minister for Work and Pensions, said in October 2005: 'We have to make the learning of English an unavoidable must ... immigrants have to see language acquisition as an essential part of the contract they enter into when they settle in Britain. People should not opt out of their obligations on the back of multiculturalism'.

Gordon Brown, the former Chancellor of the Exchequer, said in June 2006: 'People who come into this country, who are part of our community, should play by the rules ... I think learning English is part of that. I think that understanding British history is part of that ... I would insist on large numbers of people who have refused to learn our language that they must do so. If someone is unemployed, who does not speak English, they should have to learn English to make themselves employable'.

The Britishness debate

A theme running through the language and citizenship agenda and surrounding public discourses is that of national identity and 'Britishness'. In the UK 'national identity' is complex and fraught: first, the UK is a multinational state characterized by struggle over the status of Wales, Scotland and Northern Ireland and by the common conflation of 'English' with 'British'; second, because the relationship of British 'subjects' to the Crown is historically problematic (Cohen 1994); and third because of the association of British nationalism with colonialism and construction along racial lines. British culture has been represented for much of its history as 'white' and English-speaking, a representation that has been contested by critics such as Gilroy (1987). Overt nationalism tends, therefore, to be associated with traditional conservatives and shunned by liberals or those on the left who wish to dissociate themselves from Britain's colonial past. The fact that nationalism is contested, and not embraced overtly by many, however, does not mean that it is not ever-present in day-to-day life: as Billig (1995: 6) points out, national identity is constantly flagged in the media through routine symbols and habits of language, and 'nationalism, far from being an intermittent mood in established nations, is the endemic condition'.

The report of the committee set up to develop the citizenship agenda, *The New and the Old* (Home Office 2003: 11), claimed that 'we neither need to define Britishness too precisely nor to redefine it', although this disavowal is less convincing given that much of the citizenship test is about British political, legal and cultural customs and traditions. The key to 'Britishness', said the report, is to be found in respect for 'the laws, elected parliamentary and democratic political structures, traditional values of mutual tolerance':

> To be British is to respect those over-arching specific institutions, values, beliefs and traditions that bind us all, the different nations and cultures, together in peace and in a legal order.

> *(ibid.)*

The other thing that 'binds' Britain together in this ideology is of course the English language. Although the British citizenship agenda stresses respect for difference and promotes the UK as a multicultural society, this does not stretch to an acceptance of the UK as a multi*lingual* society (apart from the concession that people can take the citizenship test in Welsh or Scottish Gaelic). The citizenship agenda does not permit the possibility that a person can be a 'citizen in the full sense' (Home Office 2003: 13) in any language other than English. According to the rhetoric of the handbook 'the English language itself' is the key to the participation of diverse communities in a common culture sharing common values – values that include respect for difference and diversity, but not, it would seem, linguistic difference and diversity. The ideological assumptions underpinning the belief that multilingualism is a problem are that only English (in its standard variety) can serve as an efficient means of communication, that migrants have no existing language tools that might be of use to them in the UK and that only if they learn English will they increase their opportunities for work, education and social mobility. This ideology, however, does not take into account the linguistic and cultural resources held by migrants – resources that in fact may well help, not hinder, their integration into many multicultural neighbourhoods (van Avermaet 2009; Vertovec 2006).

Contesting monolingualism

In many places, monolingual ideologies are strengthening and becoming enshrined in law. Some countries have seen legislation that imposes language and citizenship tests on prospective new citizens, for example. It is striking that these contexts are societies where the day-to-day reality is one of increasing linguistic diversity. Globalization, the attendant mass movements of people and dramatic developments in communications technologies have made multilingualism and hybridity in contemporary language use ever more prominent, and have given rise to explorations of notions such as cultural hybridity (Werbner and Madood 1997), new ethnicities (Hall 1992), 'third spaces' (Bhabha 1994; Kramsch 1993), liminality (Turner 1969; Rampton 1999; Baynham and Simpson 2010) and transnationalism (Stevenson 2006). These post-modern notions challenge modernist certainties of 'grand narratives', especially those of nationality, race and of cultures with fixed boundaries. There is a discrepancy, in fact, between post-modern realities and modernist responses to them (Blommaert 2008a: 2).

Sociolinguistic features of individuals' communicative repertoire such as codeswitching (Lin, this volume) and language crossing (Rampton and Charalambous, this volume) are foregrounded in areas of social life not previously noted for their linguistic variety. The emergence of new ethnicities and global cultures is accompanied by novel and transnational ways of using language (Harris 2006; Pennycook 2007; Block 2007). The dissociation of language from geographical space in online interaction also contributes to the destabilization of linguistic and cultural boundaries (Lam 2004; Leppänen and Peuronen, this volume). Moreover, some sociolinguists, pointing to the instability of language, the socially constructed idea of language as a concept, and the lack of correspondence between language varieties and national borders, increasingly question whether it is reasonable to talk in terms of discrete languages at all. Makoni and Pennycook (2007) take the position that language, conceptions of *languageness* and the metalanguage used to describe languages are inventions.

These multilingual realities challenge and potentially undermine monolingualist discourses. At a supranational level monolingualism is probably not the dominant force it is at the level of the nation-state. For example, in the European Union, multilingualism is promoted as the key to European citizenship and economic prosperity. And on a more individual level, multilingualism is valued as a personal asset, albeit unevenly: for people in the UK, for instance, the acquisition of 'modern foreign languages' – i.e. languages such as French and Japanese learned to be used 'abroad' – tends to be privileged over the learning of widely spoken 'community languages' – i.e. those spoken among migrant populations in the UK. Multilingualism remains most problematic at the national level: as we have seen in this chapter, discourses about multilingualism tend to treat it as a problem produced by migrant communities. In cases where diversity – including linguistic diversity and multilingualism – is not denied or ignored by elites at the centre, it might still be appropriated and commodified, as Heller (2003) records in her description of the emergence of state-sanctioned versions of heteroglossic practices. Diversity becomes a far more problematic notion – for elites and non-elites alike – when its contestation is overt; that is, when there is a demand to accommodate on equal grounds, for instance, different deep-seated cultural practices like religions.

It is not an entirely uneven world. Collins notes that people find agency even where the dominant structures may seem monolithic. He maintains that 'we need to allow for dilemmas and intractable oppositions; for divided consciousness, not just dominated minds; ... for creative, discursive agency in conditions prestructured, to be sure, but also fissured in unpredictable and dynamic ways' (1993: 134; see also Lin 2008). This agency can be witnessed in the emergence of new hybrid codes and practices such as 'crossing' among youth in multicultural towns and cities documented by Rampton (2005) and Harris (2006). And agency can be achieved even in contexts where power differentials are quite extreme – for example in asylum hearings. In these situations, as Shuman and Bohmer (2004) have shown, counter-discourses *can* get heard, when they are presented in ways that align with authorized practices (for example, by observing established patterns of courtroom interaction), when social actors engage in a kind of strategic compliance.

Related topics

Language rights; linguistic diversity and education; multilingualism and social exclusion; multilingualism and the media; heteroglossia.

Further reading

Blackledge, A. (2005) *Discourse and Power in a Multilingual World*, Amsterdam: John Benjamins.
(An in-depth critical analysis of the way a monolingual ideology is reproduced and achieves hegemony in a multilingual society, exemplified by the 2001 'race riots' in England.)

Blommaert, J. and Verschueren, J. (1998) *Debating Diversity: Analysing the Discourse of Tolerance*, London: Routledge.
(An extended analysis of public discourse surrounding policies concerning migration in Belgium.)

Johnson, S. and Milani, T. (eds) (2009) *Language Ideologies and Media Discourse: Texts, Practices, Policies*, London: Continuum.
(A collection of studies exploring the relationship between language ideologies and media discourse.)

Kroskrity, P. (ed.) (2000) *Regimes of Language: Ideologies, Polities and Identities*, School of American Research Press: Santa Fe.
(An edited collection examining the role of language ideologies and discursive practices in the formation of states and the creation of identities.)

Rings, G. and Ife, A. (eds) (2008) *Neo-Colonial Mentalities in Contemporary Europe? Language and Discourse in the Construction of Identities*, Newcastle: Cambridge Scholars Publishing.
(An interdisciplinary collection by linguists, literary critics, social geographers and discourse analysts, all exploring key issues in the negotiation of identities within the expanded EU.)

Bibliography

Amin, A. (2008) 'Thinking past integration and community cohesion', paper presented at Integration and Community Cohesion Seminar, Conflict Transformation Project, Belfast City Council.

Anderson, B. (1983) *Imagined Communities*, London: Verso.

Augoustinos, M. (1998) 'Social representations and ideology: Towards the study of ideological representations' in U. Flick (ed.) (1998) *The Psychology of the Social*, Cambridge: Cambridge University Press.

Bakhtin, M. M. (1981) *The Dialogic Imagination: Four Essays*, M. Holquist (ed.), C. Emerson and M. Holquist (trans.) Austin: University of Texas Press.

Baynham, M. and Simpson, J. (2010) 'Onwards and upwards: Space, placement and liminality in adult ESOL classes', *TESOL Quarterly* 44(3): 420–40.

Berger, P. and Luckmann, T. (1966) *The Social Construction of Reality: A Treatise in the Sociology of Knowledge*, London: Penguin.

Bhabha, H. (1994) *The Location of Culture*, London: Routledge.

Billig, M. (1995) *Banal Nationalism*, London: Sage.

Blackledge, A. (2004) 'Constructions of identity in political discourse in multilingual Britain', in A. Pavlenko and A. Blackledge (eds) *The Negotiation of Identities in Multilingual Contexts*, Clevedon: Multilingual Matters.

——(2005) *Discourse and Power in a Multilingual World*, Amsterdam: John Benjamins.

——(2006) 'The racialization of language in British political discourse', *Critical Discourse Studies* 3(1): 61–79.

——(2007) 'The men say "they don't need it". Gender and the extension of language testing for British citizenship', *Studies in Language and Capitalism* 1(1): 143–61.

——(2008) 'Liberalism, discrimination and the law: Language testing for citizenship in Britain', in G. Rings and A. Ife (eds) (2008) *Neo-Colonial Mentalities in Contemporary Europe? Language and Discourse in the Construction of Identities*, Newcastle: Cambridge Scholars Publishing.

Block, D. (2007) 'Niche lingua francas: An ignored phenomenon, *TESOL Quarterly* 41(3): 561–6.

Blommaert, J. (1999) 'The debate is closed', in J. Blommaert (ed.) *Language Ideological Debates*, Berlin and New York: Mouton de Gruyter.

——(2005) *Discourse*, Cambridge: Cambridge University Press.

——(2006) 'Language Policy and National Identity', in T. Ricento (ed.) *An Introduction to Language Policy*, Oxford: Blackwell.

——(2008a) 'Language, asylum, and the natural order', *Working Papers in Urban Language and Literacies* 50, London: King's College.

——(2008b) 'Commentary: Multi-everything London', *Journal of Language, Identity and Education*, 7(1): 81–9.

Blommaert, J. and Verschueren, J. (1998) *Debating Diversity: Analysing the Discourse of Tolerance*, London: Routledge.

Blunkett, D. (2002) 'Integration with diversity: Globalisation and the renewal of democracy and civil society', in P. Griffith and M. Leonard (eds) *Reclaiming Britishness*, London: The Foreign Policy Centre.

Bokhorst-Heng, W. (1999) 'Singapore's *speak Mandarin campaign*: Language ideological debates and the imagining of the nation', in J. Blommaert (ed.) *Language Ideological Debates*, Berlin and New York: Mouton de Gruyter.

Bourdieu, P. (1977) *Outline of a Theory of Practice*, R. Nice (trans.), Cambridge: Cambridge University Press.

Bourdieu, P. and Passeron, J-C. (1990) *Reproduction in Education, Society and Culture*, London: Sage.

Burr, V. (1996) *An Introduction to Social Constructionism*, London: Routledge.

Cameron, D. (1995) *Verbal Hygiene*, London: Routledge.

Cohen, R. (1994) *Frontiers of Identity: The British and the Others*, London: Longman.

Collins, J. (1993) 'Determination and contradiction: An appreciation and critique of the work of Pierre Bourdieu on language and education', in C. Calhoun, E. LiPuma and M. Postone (eds) *Bourdieu: Critical Perspectives*, Chicago: University of Chicago Press.

Dicker, S. J., Jackson, R. M., Ricento, T. and Romstedt, K. (1995) *Official English? No! TESOL's Recommendations for Countering the Official English-Only Movement in the US*, Alexandria, VA: TESOL.

Fairclough, N. (1992) *Discourse and Social Change*, Cambridge: Polity Press.

——(2001) *Language and Power*, 2nd edn, London: Longman.

Foucault, M. (1970) *The Order of Things: An Archaeology of the Human Sciences*, London: Tavistock.

Gal, S. (1979) *Language Shift: Social Determinants of Linguistic Change in Bilingual Austria*, New York: Academic Press.

Gee, J. P. (1996) *Social Linguistics and Literacies: Ideology in Discourse*, 2nd edn, London: Routledge Falmer.

Gilroy, P. (1987) *There Ain't No Black in the Union Jack*, London: Hutchinson.

Goodhart, D. (2004) 'Too diverse?' *Prospect Magazine* 95: 30–7.

Gramsci, A. (1971) *Selections from the Prison Notebooks*, London: Lawrence & Wishart.

Hall, S. (1992) 'New ethnicities', in J. Donald and A. Rattansi. (eds) *'Race', Culture, and Difference*, London: Sage.

Harris, R. (2006) *New Ethnicities and Language Use*, Basingstoke: Palgrave Macmillan.

Heller, M. (1995) 'Language choice, social institutions, and symbolic domination', *Language in Society* 24(3): 373–405.

——(1999) 'Heated language in a cold climate', in J. Blommaert (ed.) *Language Ideological Debates*, Berlin: Mouton de Gruyter.

——(2003) 'Globalization, the new economy, and the commodification of language and identity', *Journal of Sociolinguistics* 7(4): 473–92.

Hobsbawm, E. (1990) *Nations and Nationalism since 1780: Progress, Myth, Reality*, Cambridge: Cambridge University Press.

Hogan-Brun, G., Mar-Molinero, C. and Stevenson, P. (eds) (2009) *Discourses on Language and Integration: Critical Perspectives on Language Testing Regimes in Europe*, Amsterdam/Philadelphia: John Benjamins.

Holliday, A. (2005) *The Struggle to Teach English as an International Language*, Oxford: Oxford University Press.

Home Office (2001) *Community Cohesion: A Report of the Independent Review Team Chaired by Ted Cantle* (The 'Cantle Report'), London: Home Office.

——(2002) *Secure Borders, Safe Haven: Integration with Diversity in Modern Britain*, London: Home Office.

——(2003) *The New and the Old: The Report of the 'Life in the United Kingdom' Advisory Group*, London: Home Office.

Irvine, J. T. and Gal, S. (2000) 'Language ideology and linguistic differentiation', in P. Kroskrity (ed.) *Regimes of Language: Ideologies, Polities and Identities*, Santa Fe: School of American Research Press.

Joseph, J. E. (2004) *Language and Identity: National, Ethnic, Religious*, Basingstoke: Palgrave Macmillan.

——(2006) *Language and Politics*, Edinburgh: Edinburgh University Press.

Kramsch, C. (1993) *Context and Culture in Language Teaching*, Oxford: Oxford University Press.

——(1998) *Language and Culture*, Oxford: Oxford University Press.

Kroskrity, P. (2000) 'Regimenting languages: Language ideology perspectives', in P. Kroskrity (ed.) *Regimes of Language: Ideologies, Polities and Identities*, Santa Fe: School of American Research Press.

——(2001) 'Language Ideologies', in J. Verschueren, J.-O. Österman, J. Blommaert and C. Bulcaen (eds) *Handbook of Pragmatics*, Amsterdam: John Benjamins.

Lam, W. S. E. (2004) 'Second language socialization in a bilingual chat room: Global and local considerations', *Language Learning and Technology* 8(3): 44–65, available online at http://llt.msu.edu/vol8num3/default.html

Lawton, R. (2008) 'Language policy and ideology in the United States: A critical analysis of "English Only" discourse', in M. KhosraviNik and A. Polyzou (eds) *Papers from the Lancaster University Postgraduate Conference in Linguistics & Language Teaching*, vol. 2: *Papers from LAEL PG 2007*, Lancaster: University of Lancaster.

Lin, A. M. Y. (2008) 'Modernity, postmodernity, and the future of "identity": Implications for educators', in A. M. Y. Lin (ed.) *Problematizing Identity*, London: Routledge.

Luke, A. (1995) 'Text and discourse in education: An introduction to critical discourse analysis', *Review of Research in Education* 21: 3–48.

Makoni, S. and Pennycook, A. (2007) 'Disinventing and reconstituting languages', in S. Makoni and A. Pennycook (eds) *Disinventing and Reconstituting Languages*, Clevedon: Multilingual Matters.

Mar-Molinero, C. and Stevenson, P. (eds) (2006) *Language Ideologies, Policies and Practices*, Basingstoke: Palgrave Macmillan.

Maryns, K. (2006) *The Asylum Speaker: Language in the Belgian Asylum Procedure*, Manchester: St Jerome Publishing.

Milani, T. M. (2007) 'Voices of endangerment: A language ideological debate on the Swedish language', in A. Duchêne and M. Heller (eds) *Discourses of Endangerment: Ideology and Interest in the Defence of Languages*, London: Continuum.

Pennycook, A. (2001) *Critical Applied Linguistics: A Critical Introduction*, London: Routledge.

——(2007) *Global Englishes and Transcultural Flows*, London: Routledge.

Phillipson, R. (1992) *Linguistic Imperialism*, Oxford: Oxford University Press.

Pinker, S. (1994) *The Language Instinct*, London: Penguin Books.

Poulsen, M. and Johnston, R. (2006) 'Ethnic residential segregation in England: Getting the right message across', *Environment and Planning* A 38: 2195–9.

Rampton, B. (1999) 'Sociolinguistics and cultural studies: New ethnicities, liminality and interaction', *Social Semiotics* 9(3): 355–73.

——(2005) *Crossing: Language and Ethnicity Among Adolescents*, 2nd edn, Manchester: St Jerome Publishing.

Ricento, T. (1996) 'Language policy in the United States', in M. Herriman and B. Burnaby (eds) *Language Policies in English-Dominant Countries: Six Case Studies*, Clevedon: Multilingual Matters.

——(2003) 'The discursive construction of Americanism', *Discourse and Society*, 14: 611–37.

Rogers, R. (2008) 'Critical discourse analysis in education', in M. Martin-Jones, A. M. de Mejía. and N. H. Hornberger (eds) *Encyclopedia of Language and Education*, 2nd edn, vol. 3, *Discourse and Education*, New York: Springer.

Shuman, A. and Bohmer, C. (2004) 'Representing trauma: political asylum narrative', *Journal of American Folklore* 117: 394–414.

Silverstein, M. (1979) 'Language Structure and Linguistic Ideology', in P. Clyne, W. Hanks and C. Hofbauer (eds) *The Elements*, Chicago: Chicago Linguistics Society.

Simpson, J. and Cooke, M. (2010) 'Movement and loss: Progression in tertiary education for migrant students', *Language and Education* 24(1): 57–73.

Stevenson, P. (2006) '"National" languages in transnational contexts: Language, migration and citizenship in Europe', in C. Mar-Molinero and P. Stevenson (eds) *Language Ideologies, Policies and Practices: Language and the Future of Europe*, Basingstoke: Palgrave Macmillan.

Turner, V. (1969) *The Ritual Process: Structure and Anti-structure*, Chicago: Aldine Publishing Co.

van Avermaet, P. (2009) 'Fortress Europe? Language policy regimes for immigration and citizenship', in G. Hogan-Brun, C. Mar-Molinero and P. Stevenson (eds) *Discourses on Language and Integration: Critical Perspectives on Language Testing Regimes in Europe*, Amsterdam and Philadelphia: John Benjamins.

van Dijk, T. (1991) *Racism and the Press*, London: Routledge.

Vertovec, S. (2006) 'The emergence of super-diversity in Britain', *Working Paper No 25*, Oxford: Centre on Migration, Policy and Society, University of Oxford.

Vertovec, S. and Wessendorf, S. (2005) 'Migration and cultural, religious and linguistic diversity in Europe: An overview of issues and trends', *Working Paper No 18*, Oxford: Centre on Migration, Policy and Society, University of Oxford.

Werbner, P. and Madood, T. (eds) (1997) *Debating Cultural Hybridity: Multi-cultural Identities and the Politics of Anti-Racism*, London: Zed Books.

Wright, S. (2004) *Language Policy and Language Planning: From Nationalism to Globalisation*, Basingstoke: Palgrave Macmillan.

Wodak, R. (2001) 'The discourse-historical approach', in R. Wodak and M. Meyer (eds) *Methods of Critical Discourse Analysis*, London: Sage.

Wodak, R. and van Dijk, T. A. (eds) (2000) *Racism at the Top: Parliamentary Discourses on Ethnic Issues in Six European States*, Austria: Drava Verlag.

Woolard, K. and Scheiffelin, B. (1994) 'Language ideology', *Annual Review of Anthropology*, 23: 55–82.

Young, J. (2003) 'To these wet and windy shores: Recent immigration policy in the UK', *Punishment and Society* 5(4): 449–62.

7

Language rights

Promoting civic multilingualism[1]

Stephen May

This chapter explores the development of language rights (LR) as a nascent academic paradigm, along with its key theoretical and contextual concerns. The growing presence of LR in the disciplines of sociolinguistics, the sociology of language and language policy can be attributed to four distinct, albeit closely inter-related, academic movements. All these movements (discussed further below) adopt the usual distinction between so-called minority and majority languages – a distinction that is based not on numerical size but on clearly observable differences among language varieties in relation to power, status and entitlement – while also paying particular attention to the rights of minority language speakers.

The first of these is the Language Ecology (LE) movement, charting the links between linguistics and ecology, and situating the current exponential loss of many of the world's languages within a wider ecological framework (e.g. Mühlhäusler 1996; Nettle and Romaine 2000). A second is the linguistic human rights (LHR) movement that argues, often on the basis of LE premises, for the greater institutional protection and support of minority language within both national and supranational contexts (e.g. Kontra *et al.* 1999; Skutnabb-Kangas 2000). These arguments are also echoed in a third domain of academic legal discourse that has developed with respect to minority group rights generally, but with an increasing focus on the specific implementation of minority language rights (MLR) in national and international law (e.g. de Varennes 1996; Henrard 2000). A fourth, increasingly influential, position has seen a deliberate move away from the biological/ecological analysis of LE, and some LHR arguments, to a more overtly critical sociohistorical/sociopolitical analysis of language rights (e.g. Blommaert 1999; Patrick and Freeland 2004; May 2005a, 2008). This position continues to focus on the importance of minority language rights (MLR), while also addressing social constructionist and post-modernist understandings of language that highlight the constructedness of language(s) and the contingency of the language–identity link. The latter have too often been ignored in other MLR accounts, leading to an overly essentialized view of languages and those who speak them (see May 2005b for a useful overview).

Although these various positions are thus by no means uniform, there is sufficient overlap for them to constitute collectively an increasingly important field of academic enquiry and related advocacy about language rights – particularly, MLR – within sociolinguistics. In line with the particular emphases of the respective movements discussed above, five key concerns can be identified as underpinning much of this work.

Language shift and loss

The first concern has to do with the consequent exponential decline and loss of many of the world's languages. Indeed, of the estimated 6,800 languages spoken in the world today (Grimes 2000), it is predicted on present trends that between 20 per cent and 50 per cent will 'die' by the end of the twenty-first century (Krauss 1992). Language decline and loss occur most often in bilingual or multilingual contexts in which a majority language – that is, a language with greater political power, privilege and social prestige – comes to replace the range and functions of a minority language. The inevitable result is that speakers of the minority language 'shift' over time to speaking the majority language.

The process of language shift described here usually involves three broad stages. The first stage sees increasing pressure on minority language speakers to speak the majority language, particularly in formal language domains. This stage is often precipitated and facilitated by the introduction of education in the majority language. It leads to the eventual decrease in the functions of the minority language, with the public or official functions of that language being the first to be replaced by the majority language. The second stage sees a period of bilingualism, in which both languages continue to be spoken concurrently. However, this stage is usually characterized by a decreasing number of minority-language speakers, especially among the younger generation, along with a decrease in the fluency of speakers as the minority language is spoken less, and employed in fewer and fewer language domains. The third and final stage – which may occur over the course of two or three generations, and sometimes less – sees the replacement of the minority language with the majority language. The minority language may be 'remembered' by a residual group of language speakers, but it is no longer spoken as a wider language of communication.

Of course, such language loss and language shift have always occurred – languages have risen and fallen, become obsolete, died or adapted to changing circumstances in order to survive, throughout the course of human history. But never to this extent, and never before at such an exponential rate. Some sociolinguistic commentators have even described it as a form of 'linguistic genocide' (Skutnabb-Kangas 2000). Such claims may seem over-wrought and/or alarmist but they are supported by hard data. For example, a survey by the US-based Summer Institute of Linguistics, published in 1999, found that there were 51 languages with only one speaker left, 500 languages with fewer than 100 speakers, 1,500 languages with fewer than 1,000 speakers and more than 3,000 languages with fewer than 10,000 speakers. The survey went on to reveal that as many as 5,000 of the world's more than 6,000 languages were spoken by fewer than 100,000 speakers each. It concluded, even more starkly, that 96 per cent of the world's languages were spoken by only 4 per cent of its people (Crystal 1999).

These figures graphically reinforce an earlier suggestion made by Krauss (1992) that, in addition to the 50 per cent of languages that may die within the next century, a further 40 per cent of languages are 'threatened' or 'endangered'. Given the processes of language shift and decline just outlined, and the current parlous state of many minority languages, it is not hard to see why. Even some majority languages are no longer immune to such processes, not least because of the rise of English as a global language (Crystal 1997; Phillipson 2003). Thus, if Krauss is to be believed, as few as 600 languages (10 per cent) will survive in the longer term – perhaps, he suggests, even as few as 300.

The potential scale and rapidity of language loss predicted here also highlights the inevitable social, economic and political *consequences* for minority language speakers of such shift and loss. Language loss – or linguistic genocide, as Skutnabb-Kangas (2000) would have it – almost always forms part of a wider pattern of social, cultural and political displacement. We can see this clearly if we consider which groups are most affected by language loss – almost always minority groups, which are (already) socially and politically marginalized and/or subordinated. These groups have been variously estimated at between 5,000 and 8,000 and include within them the 250–300 million members of the world's Indigenous peoples (Tully 1995), perhaps the most marginalized of all people groups. As Crawford (1994) notes, language death seldom occurs in communities of wealth and privilege, but rather to the dispossessed and disempowered. Moreover, linguistic dislocation for a particular community of speakers seldom, if ever, occurs in isolation from sociocultural and socio-economic dislocation.

Nationalism, politics and the minoritization of languages

This brings us to the second principal concern that underlies the advocacy of MLR – why certain languages, and their speakers, have come to be 'minoritized' in the first place. Advocates of MLR argue that the establishment of majority/minority language hierarchies is neither a natural process nor primarily even a linguistic one. Rather, it is a historically, socially and politically *constructed* process (May 2005b, 2008), and one that is deeply imbued in wider (unequal) power relations. Following on from this, if languages, and the status attached to them, are the product of wider historical, social and political forces, there is, in turn, nothing 'natural' about the status and prestige attributed to particular majority languages and, conversely, the stigma that is often attached to minority languages, or to dialects.

There are two specific points at issue here. The first concerns what actually distinguishes a majority language from a minority language or a dialect. This distinction is not as straightforward as many assume. For example, the same language may be regarded as both a majority *and* a minority language, depending on the context. Thus Spanish is a majority language in Spain and many Latin American states, but a minority language in the USA. Even the term 'language' itself indicates this process of construction, as what actually constitutes a language, as opposed to a dialect for example, remains controversial (see Mühlhäusler 1996; Romaine 2000). Certainly, we cannot always distinguish easily between a language and a dialect on *linguistic* grounds, as some languages are mutually intelligible, whereas some dialects of the same language are not. The example often employed here is that of Norwegian, as it was regarded as a dialect of Danish until the end of Danish rule in 1814. However, it was only with the advent of Norwegian independence from Sweden in 1905 that Norwegian actually acquired the status of a separate language, albeit one that has since remained mutually intelligible with both Danish and Swedish. Contemporary examples can be seen in the former Czechoslovakia, with the (re)emergence in the early 1990s of distinct Czech and Slovak varieties in place of a previously common state language. And in the former Yugoslavia, we are currently seeing the (re)development of separate Serbian, Croatian and Bosnian language varieties in place of Serbo-Croat, itself the artificial language product of the post-Second World War Yugoslav Communist Federation under Tito.

What these latter examples clearly demonstrate is that languages are 'created' out of the politics of state-making, not – as we often assume – the other way around (Billig 1995). Independence for Norway and the break-up of the former Czechoslovakia and Yugoslavia have precipitated linguistic change, creating separate languages where previously none existed. The pivotal role of political context, particularly as it is outworked at the level of the nation-state, might also help to explain the scale of the projected language loss discussed earlier. One only has to look at the number of nation-states in the world today, at approximately 200, and the perhaps 300 or so languages that are projected to survive long term, to make the connection.

And this brings us to the second key point at issue here: the central and ongoing influence of nation-state organization, and the politics of nationalism, to processes of national (and international) language formation and validation, along with the linguistic hierarchies attendant upon them. In this respect, the model of the linguistically homogeneous nation-state – which has become the normative sociopolitical, as well as sociolinguistic model (c.f. Bourdieu 1982) – is actually only a relatively recent historical phenomenon, arising from the French Revolution of 1789 and the subsequent development of European nationalism. Previous forms of political organization had not required this degree of linguistic uniformity. For example, empires were quite happy for the most part to leave unmolested the plethora of cultures and languages subsumed within them – as long as taxes were paid, all was well. Nonetheless, in the subsequent politics of European nationalism – which, of course, was also to spread throughout the world – the idea of a single, common 'national' language (sometimes, albeit rarely, a number of national languages) quickly became the leitmotif of modern social and political organization.

How was this accomplished? Principally via the political machinery of these newly emergent European states, with mass education playing a central role (Anderson 1991; Gellner 1983). The process of selecting and establishing a common national language usually involved two key aspects: *legitimation* and *institutionalization* (Nelde *et al.* 1996; May 2012). Legitimation is understood to mean here the formal recognition accorded to the language by the nation-state – usually, via 'official' language status. Institutionalization, perhaps the more important dimension, refers to the process by which the language comes to be accepted, or 'taken for granted' in a wide range of social, cultural and linguistic domains or contexts, both formal and informal. Both elements, in combination, achieved not only the central requirement of nation-states – cultural and linguistic homogeneity – but also the allied and, seemingly, necessary banishment of 'minority' languages and dialects to the private domain.

If the establishment, often retrospectively, of chosen 'national' languages was therefore a deliberate, and deliberative political act, it follows that so too was the process by which other language varieties were subsequently 'minoritized' or 'dialectalized' by and within these same nation-states. These latter language varieties were, in effect, *positioned* by these newly formed states as languages of lesser political worth and value. Consequently, national languages came to be associated with modernity and progress, whereas their less fortunate counterparts were associated (conveniently) with tradition and obsolescence. More often than not, the latter were also specifically constructed as *obstacles* to the political project of nation-building – as threats to the 'unity' of the state – thus providing the *raison d'être* for the consistent derogation, diminution and proscription of minority languages that have characterized the last three centuries of nationalism (see May 2012 for a full overview). As Dorian summarizes it: 'it is the concept of the nation-state coupled with its official standard language … that has in modern times posed the keenest threat to both the identities and the languages of small [minority] communities' (1998: 18). Coulmas observes, even more succinctly, that 'the nation-state as it has evolved since the French Revolution is the natural enemy of minorities' (1998: 67).

Proponents of language rights for minority groups argue that the emphasis on cultural and linguistic homogeneity within nation-states, and the attendant hierarchizing of languages, are thus neither inevitable nor inviolate – particularly in light of the historical recency of nation-states, and the related, often arbitrary and contrived, processes by which particular languages have been accorded 'national' or 'minority' status, respectively. These arguments about the historical and geopolitical situatedness of national languages also apply at the supranational level. In particular, a number of prominent sociolinguistic commentators have argued that the burgeoning reach and influence of English as the current world language, or lingua mundi, is the result of equally constructed historical and political processes, most notably via the initial geopolitical influence of Britain and, subsequently, the USA (see e.g. Pennycook 1994; Phillipson 1992, 2003).

As with the construction of national languages, the current ascendancy of English is also invariably linked with modernity and modernization, and the associated benefits that accrue to those who speak it. The result, MLR proponents argue, is to position other languages as having less 'value' and 'use' and, by extension, and more problematically, to delimit and delegitimize the social, cultural and linguistic capital ascribed to 'non-English speakers' – the phrase itself reflecting the normative ascendancy of English. The usual corollary to this position is that the social mobility of the minority language speaker will be further enhanced if they *dispense* with any other (minority) languages.

Language replacement and social mobility

A third principal concern of proponents of language rights is to critique the principle of 'language replacement' that centrally underlies the social and political processes just outlined – that one should/must learn these languages *at the expense of* one's first language. Consequently, the promotion of cultural and linguistic homogeneity at the collective/public level has come to be associated with, and expressed by, individual monolingualism. This amounts to a form of linguistic social Darwinism and also helps to explain why language shift/loss/decline has become so prominent.

Central to these language replacement arguments is the idea that the individual social mobility of minority language speakers will be enhanced as a result. Relatedly, minority language advocates are consistently criticized for consigning, or ghettoizing minority language communities within the confines of a language that does not have a wider use, thus actively constraining their social mobility (see e.g. Barry 2000; Huntingdon 2005). Little wonder, such critics observe, that many within the linguistic minority itself choose to ignore the pleas of minority language activists and instead 'exit' the linguistic group by learning another (invariably, more dominant) language. It is one thing, after all, to proclaim the merits of retaining a particular language for identity purposes, quite another to have to live a life delimited by it – foreclosing the opportunity for mobility in the process. We can broadly summarize the logic of this argument as follows:

- Majority languages are lauded for their 'instrumental' value, whereas minority languages are accorded 'sentimental' value, but are broadly constructed as obstacles to social mobility and progress;
- Learning a majority language will thus provide individuals with greater economic and social mobility;
- Learning a minority language, although (possibly) important for reasons of cultural continuity, delimits an individual's mobility; in its strongest terms, this might amount to actual 'ghettoization';
- If minority language speakers are 'sensible' they will opt for mobility and modernity via the majority language
- Whatever decision is made, the choice between opting for a majority or minority language is constructed as oppositional, even mutually exclusive.

These arguments appear to be highly persuasive. In response, however, proponents of language rights argue that the presumptions and assumptions that equate linguistic mobility *solely* with majority languages are themselves extremely problematic. For a start, this position separates the instrumental and identity aspects of language. On this view, minority languages may be important for identity but have no instrumental value, whereas majority languages are construed as primarily instrumental with little or no identity value. We see this in the allied notions of majority languages as 'vehicles' of modernity, and minority languages as (merely) 'carriers' of identity. However, it is clear that *all* languages embody and accomplish both identity and instrumental functions for those who speak them. Where particular languages – especially majority/minority languages – differ is in the *degree* to which they can accomplish each of these functions, and this in turn is dependent on the social and political (not linguistic) constraints in which they operate (May 2003). Thus, in the case of minority languages, their instrumental value is often constrained by wider social and political processes that have resulted in the privileging of other language varieties in the public realm. Meanwhile, for majority languages, the identity characteristics of the language *are* clearly important for their speakers, but often become subsumed within and normalized by the instrumental functions that these languages fulfil. This is particularly apparent with respect to monolingual speakers of English, given the position of English as the current world language.

On this basis, advocates for MLR argue that the limited instrumentality of particular minority languages at any given time need not always remain so. Indeed, if the minority position of a language is the specific product of wider historical and contemporary social and political relationships, changing these wider relationships positively with respect to a minority language should bring about both enhanced instrumentality for the language in question and increased mobility for its speakers. We can see this occurring currently, for example, in Wales and Catalonia, with the emergence of these formerly subjugated languages into the public domain – particularly via, but by no means limited to, education.

Likewise, when majority language speakers are made to realize that their own languages fulfil important identity functions for them, both as individuals and as a group, they may be slightly more reluctant to require minority language speakers to dispense with theirs. Or to put it another way, if majority languages do provide their speakers with particular and often significant individual and collective forms of linguistic identity, as they clearly do, it seems unjust to deny these same benefits, out of court, to minority language speakers.

And this brings us to the fourth principal concern of proponents of language rights – the legal protections that can potentially be developed in order to enhance the mobility of minority language speakers while at the same time protecting their right to continue to speak a minority language, *if they so choose*. It is here that the influence of the LHR movement, championed by Tove Skutnabb-Kangas, is most prominent.

Linguistic human rights

The LHR research paradigm argues that minority languages, and their speakers, should be accorded at least some of the protections and institutional support that majority languages already enjoy (see e.g. Kontra *et al.* 1999; Skutnabb-Kangas and Phillipson 1995; Skutnabb-Kangas 2000). These arguments are also echoed in much of the academic legal discourse that has developed in recent years with respect to minority group rights more broadly, (see e.g. de Varennes 1996; Henrard 2000). A central distinction in both discourses is one made between national minority groups and indigenous peoples on the one hand, and ethnic minority groups on the other. The former may be regarded as groups that are historically associated with a particular territory (i.e. they have not migrated to the territory from elsewhere) but because of conquest, confederation or colonization are now regarded as minorities within that territory. The latter may be regarded as voluntary migrants and (involuntary) refugees living in a new national context (see Kymlicka 1995 for further discussion).

Three key tenets of international law can be applied to the further development of LHR in relation to these two broad minority groupings. The first principle, which is widely accepted, is that it is not unreasonable to expect from national members some knowledge of the common public language(s) of the state. This is, of course, the central tenet underpinning the current public linguistic homogeneity of modern nation-states. However, LHR advocates assert that it is also possible to argue, on this basis, for the legitimation and institutionalization of the languages of national minorities within nation-states, according to them at least some of the benefits that national languages currently enjoy. LHR proponents qualify this by making it clear that the advocacy of such minority-language rights is *not* the language replacement ideology in reverse – of replacing a majority language with a minority one. Rather, it is about questioning and contesting why the promotion of a majority (national) language should necessarily be *at the expense* of all others. By this, they argue, the linguistic exclusivity attendant on the nationalist principle of cultural and linguistic homogeneity can be effectively challenged and contested.

A second principle is that in order to avoid language discrimination, it is important that where there is a sufficient number of other language speakers, these speakers should be allowed to use that language as part of the exercise of their individual rights as citizens. That is, they should have the *opportunity* to use their first language if they so choose. As de Varennes argues, 'the respect of the language principles of individuals, *where appropriate and reasonable*, flows from a fundamental right and is not some special concession or privileged treatment. Simply put, it is the right to be treated equally without discrimination, to which everyone is entitled' (1996: 117, my emphasis). Again, this principle can clearly be applied to minority language speakers within particular nation-states.

The third principle arises directly from the previous one – how to determine exactly what is 'appropriate and reasonable' with regard to individual language preferences. Following the prominent political theorist, Will Kymlicka (1995), May (2012) has argued, for example, that only national minorities can demand *as of right* formal inclusion of their languages and cultures in the civic realm. However, this need not and should not preclude other ethnic minorities from being allowed *at the very least* to cultivate and pursue unhindered their own historic cultural and linguistic practices in the private domain. In other words, distinguishing between the rights of national and ethnic minorities still affords the latter far greater linguistic protection than many such groups currently enjoy – that is, *active* linguistic protection by the state for the *unhindered* maintenance of their first languages. This protection is applicable at the very least in the private domain and, 'where numbers warrant', a principle again drawn from international law, potentially in the public domain as well.

Extending greater ethnolinguistic *democracy* to minority language groups, via LHR, does not thus amount to an argument for ethnolinguistic *equality* for all such groups. Similarly, a call for greater ethnolinguistic democracy clearly does not amount to asserting linguistic equivalence, in all domains, with dominant, majority languages. Majority languages will continue to dominate in most if not all language domains, since, as should be clear by now, that is the nature of their privileged sociohistorical, sociopolitical position(ing). Conversely, arguing that only national minorities can claim minority language rights, as of right, is *not* an argument for simply ignoring the claims of other ethnic groups (see May 2003, 2012 for an extended discussion).

Avoiding essentialism

The final concern of the language rights paradigm – most prominent in more recent work in the area (see the collections by Patrick and Freeland 2004 and May 2005a) – addresses directly the question of how to recognize language rights, while at the same time avoiding essentializing the languages, and their speakers, to which these rights might apply. This difficult balancing act necessarily involves rejecting the 'essentialist tendency', closely allied with an often deterministic account of the links between language, identity and the wider ecological system, that is most evident in arguments for LE, as well as in those LHR arguments that are predicated on LE principles (e.g. in the work of Skutnabb-Kangas). Such arguments assume – in their less sophisticated manifestations, explicitly, and even in their most sophisticated forms, at least implicitly – an almost ineluctable connection between language and (ethnic) identity. And yet, this position stands in marked contrast to the widespread consensus in social and political theory, and increasingly in sociolinguistics and critical applied linguistics, that language is at most only a contingent factor of one's identity. In other words, language does not define us, and may not be an important feature, or indeed even a necessary one, in the construction of our identities, whether at the individual or collective levels (see e.g. Edwards 1994; Brutt-Griffler 2002). This critique on the detachability of language is complemented by a wider constructivist consensus within social theory of the merits of hybridity – that our social, political and linguistic identities are inevitably plural, complex and contingent (see e.g. Makoni and Pennycook 2007).

Clearly then, an acceptance of the contingent nature of the language-identity link, and the wider principle of hybridity, is a necessary prerequisite before language rights can continue to develop further theoretically. However, all is also not quite as it seems, because what constructionist accounts fail to address adequately is the central question of why, *despite* the clear presence of hybrid linguistic identities, historically associated languages continue often to hold considerable purchase for members of particular cultural or ethnic groups in their identity claims. As Canagarajah (2005: 439) observes of this: 'Hybridity of identity doesn't change the fact that ethnicity and mother tongue have always been a potent force in community relations … Change doesn't mean irrelevance or irreverence. Attachments to ethnicity and mother tongue are resilient, despite their limited value in pragmatic and material terms.'

To say that language is not an inevitable feature of identity is thus *not* the same as saying it is unimportant. Yet many constructivist commentators in (rightly) assuming the former position have also (wrongly) assumed the latter. In other words, they assume that because language is merely a contingent factor of identity it cannot therefore (ever) be a *significant* or *constitutive* factor of identity. As a result, contingency is elided with unimportance or peripheralism – an additional move that is neither necessary nor warranted.

Indeed, this position is extremely problematic, not least because of the considerable evidence that suggests that, although language may not be a *determining* feature of ethnic identity in many geo- and sociopolitical contexts in the world today, it remains nonetheless a *significant* one in many instances. Or to put it another way, it simply does not reflect adequately, let alone explain, the heightened saliency of language issues in many historical and contemporary political conflicts, particularly at the intrastate level (see e.g. Blommaert 1999; May 2012). In these conflicts, particular languages clearly *are* for many people an important and constitutive factor of their individual, and, at times, collective identities. This is so, *even* when holding onto such languages has specific negative social and political consequences for their speakers, most often via active discrimination and/or oppression.

In theory then, language may well be just one of many markers of identity. In practice, it is often much more than that. Indeed, this should not surprise us as the link between language and identity encompasses both significant cultural and political dimensions. The cultural dimension is demonstrated by the fact that one's individual and social identities, and their complex interconnections, are inevitably mediated in and through particular languages. The political dimension is significant to the extent that those languages come to be formally (and informally) associated with particular ethnic and national identities. These interconnections also help to explain why, as Fishman (1997) argues, a 'detached' scientific view of the link between language and identity may fail to capture the degree to which language is *experienced* as vital by those who speak it. It may also significantly understate the role that language plays in social organization and mobilization.

As for the ongoing concern over essentialism, this too can be addressed directly. Advocacy of MLR does not *necessarily* entail an essentialized, static view of the language–identity link, or a homogenous conception of the wider linguistic group. As Will Kymlicka has argued in relation to minority rights more generally, advocates of such rights are rarely seeking to preserve their 'authentic' culture if that means returning to cultural practices long past. If it were, it would soon meet widespread opposition from individual members. Rather, it is the right 'to maintain one's membership in a distinct culture, and to continue developing that culture in the same (impure) way that the members of majority cultures are able to develop theirs' (1995: 105). Cultural change, adaptation and interaction are entirely consistent with such a position. The crucial difference, however, is that members of the minority are themselves able to retain a significant degree of control over the process – something which until now has largely been the preserve of majority group members. The key issue for minority language speakers thus becomes one of cultural and linguistic *autonomy* rather than one of retrenchment, isolationism or stasis.

Conclusion

It should be clearly apparent from this brief overview that many challenges to the emergent paradigm of language rights still remain. Nonetheless, the development of arguments in support of language rights, particularly for minority groups, has provided a major impetus for rethinking processes of linguistic modernization, via the ascendancy of majority languages, as inevitable, apolitical and unproblematic. In contrast, arguments for minority language rights highlight centrally and critically the wider social and political conditions – and, crucially, their historical antecedents – that have *invariably* framed and shaped these processes of linguistic modernization, particularly with respect to the privileging and normalizing of majority languages within existing social and political contexts – often at the specific *expense* of minority languages. As Jan Blommaert argues, a sociolinguistic approach that fails to take cognisance of these wider sociopolitical and sociohistorical factors takes no account of human agency, political intervention, power and authority in the formation of particular (national) language ideologies. Nor, by definition, is it able to identify the establishment and maintenance of majority languages as a specific 'form of practice, historically contingent and socially embedded' (1999: 7). And yet, as advocates of language rights quite clearly highlight, it is exactly these contingent, socially embedded and often highly unequal practices, that have so disadvantaged minority languages, and their speakers, in the first place.

Moreover, if one can hold onto the fact that the language rights paradigm has so usefully highlighted – that processes of linguistic change are often, if not always the result of wider social and political processes – then this provides a useful basis from which to mount an effective political challenge on behalf of minority languages and their speakers. From this, one can also question and critique the apparently ineluctable link between majority languages, mobility and 'progress', and in turn look to ways in which minority languages may be reconstituted not simply as 'carriers' of identity but also as instrumentally useful. The issue of greater autonomy for minority language speakers that emerges from language rights arguments also highlights the need for greater reciprocity and accountability among majority language speakers – extending to minority language speakers the linguistic privileges that they themselves take for granted. After all, if members of dominant ethnolinguistic groups typically value their own cultural and linguistic membership(s), as they clearly do, it is demonstrably unfair to prevent minority groups from continuing to value theirs. That said, convincing majority language speakers of the merits of MLR – which I have elsewhere discussed, following Grin (1995), as the problem of tolerability (May 2000, 2002) – remains a formidable task.

Perhaps the greatest challenge, and opportunity, that the extension of minority language rights affords, however, is the promotion of a far more pluralistic, open-ended interpretation of language and identity, recognizing the potential for holding multiple, complementary cultural and linguistic identities at both individual and collective levels. On this view, maintaining one's minority ethnically affiliated language – or a dominant language, for that matter – avoids 'freezing' the development of particular languages in the roles they have historically, or perhaps still currently, occupy. Equally importantly, it questions and discards the requirement of a singular and/or replacement approach to the issue of other linguistic identities, which, as we have seen, has been the major historical legacy of nationalism and the nation-state system. And finally, such a view, of course, accords far more closely with the often complex linguistic repertoires of individual multilingual speakers themselves. This multilingualism has tended until now to be sanctioned (only) in the private, familial or community realm but, as MLR advocates, there is no reason why such multilingualism could not be extended to, and/or incorporated within, the public or civic realm as well.

Related topics

Discourses about linguistic diversity; regional minorities, education and language revitalization; global English and bilingual education; Indigenous education; Indigenous contexts; multilingual citizenship and minority languages.

Note

1 An earlier version of this chapter (May 2008) was published in *The New Sociolinguistics Reader*, edited by Nicolas Coupland and Adam Jaworski.

Further reading

Kymlicka, W. (1995) *Multicultural Citizenship: A Liberal Theory of Minority Rights*, Oxford: Clarendon Press.

May, S. (guest ed.) (2005) 'Debating language rights', *Journal of Sociolinguistics* (special issue) 9: 3.

——(2012) *Language and Minority Rights: Ethnicity, Nationalism and the Politics of Language*, 2nd edn., New York: Routledge.

Patrick, D. and Freeland, J. (eds) (2004) *Language Rights and Language 'Survival': A Sociolinguistic Exploration*, Manchester: St Jerome Publishing.

Skutnabb-Kangas, T. and Phillipson, R. (1995) 'Linguistic human rights, past and present', in T. Skutnabb-Kangas and R. Phillipson (eds) *Linguistic Human Rights: Overcoming Linguistic Discrimination*, Berlin: Mouton de Gruyter.

Bibliography

Anderson, B. (1991) *Imagined Communities: Reflections on the Origin and Spread of Nationalism*, revised edn, London: Verso.

Barry, B. (2000) *Culture and Equality: An Egalitarian Critique of Multiculturalism*, Cambridge, MA: Harvard University Press.

Billig, M. (1995) *Banal Nationalism*, London: Sage.

Blommaert, J. (ed.) (1999) *Language Ideological Debates*, Berlin: Mouton de Gruyter.

Bourdieu, P. (1982) *Ce Que Parler Veut Dire: L'économie des échanges Linguistiques*, Paris: Arthème Fayard.

Brutt-Griffler, J. (2002) 'Class, ethnicity and language rights: An analysis of British colonial policy in Lesotho and Sri Lanka and some implications for language policy', *Journal of Language, Identity and Education* 1(3): 207–34.

Canagarajah, A. S. (2005) 'Dilemmas in planning English/vernacular relations in post-colonial communities', *Journal of Sociolinguistics* 9(3): 418–47.

Coulmas, F. (1998) 'Language rights: interests of states, language groups and the individual', *Language Sciences* 20: 63–72.

Crawford, J. (1994) 'Endangered Native American languages: what is to be done and why?', *Journal of Navajo Education* 11(3): 3–11.

Crystal, D. (1997) *English as a Global Language*, Cambridge: Cambridge University Press.

——(1999) 'The death of language', *Prospect* (November 1999): 56–9.

de Varennes, F. (1996) *Language, Minorities and Human Rights*, The Hague: Kluwer Law International.

Dorian, N. (1998) 'Western language ideologies and small-language prospects', in L. Grenoble and L. Whaley (eds) *Endangered Languages: Language Loss and Community Response*, Cambridge: Cambridge University Press.

Edwards, J. (1994). *Multilingualism*. London: Routledge.

Fishman, J. (1997) 'Language and ethnicity: The view from within', in F. Coulmas (ed.) *The Handbook of Sociolinguistics*, London: Blackwell.

Gellner, E. (1983) *Nations and Nationalism: New Perspectives on the Past*, Oxford: Basil Blackwell.

Grimes, B. (ed.) (2000) *Ethnologue: Languages of the World*, 14th edn, Dallas, TX: SIL.

Grin, F. (1995) 'Combining immigrant and autochthonous language rights: A territorial approach to multilingualism' in T. Skutnabb-Kangas and R. Phillipson (eds) *Linguistic Human Rights: Overcoming Linguistic Discrimination*, Berlin: Mouton de Gruyter.

Henrard, K. (2000) *Devising an Adequate System of Minority Protection*, The Hague: Kluwer Law International.

Huntingdon, S. (2005) *Who Are We? America's Great Debate*, New York: Free Press.

Kontra, M., Skutnabb-Kangas, T., Phillipson, R. and Várady, T. (eds) (1999) *Language: A Right and a Resource. Approaches to Linguistic Human Rights*, Budapest: Central European University Press.

Krauss, M. (1992) 'The world's languages in crisis', *Language* 68: 4–10.

Kymlicka, W. (1995) *Multicultural Citizenship: A Liberal Theory of Minority Rights*, Oxford: Clarendon Press.

Makoni, S. and Pennycook A. (eds) (2007) *Disinventing and Reconstituting Language*, Clevedon: Multilingual Matters.

May, S. (2000) 'Uncommon languages: The challenges and possibilities of minority language rights', *Journal of Multilingual and Multicultural Development* 21(5): 366–85.

——(2002) 'Developing greater ethnolinguistic democracy in Europe: Minority language policies, nation-states, and the question of tolerability', *Sociolinguistica* 16: 1–13.

——(2003) 'Rearticulating the case for minority language rights', *Current Issues in Language Planning* 4(2): 95–125.

——(guest ed.) (2005a) 'Debating language rights', *Journal of Sociolinguistics* (special issue) 9(3).

——(2005b) 'Language rights: moving the debate forward', *Journal of Sociolinguistics* 9(3): 319–47.

——(2008) 'Language rights', in N. Coupland and A Jaworski (eds) *The New Sociolinguistic Reader*, London: Palgrave Macmillan.

——(2012) *Language and Minority Rights: Ethnicity, Nationalism and the Politics of Language*, 2nd edn., New York: Routledge.

Mühlhäusler, P. (1996) *Linguistic Ecology: Language Change and Linguistic Imperialism in the Pacific Region*, London: Routledge.

Nelde, P., Strubell, M. and Williams, G. (1996) *Euromosaic: The Production and Reproduction of the Minority Language Groups in the European Union*, Luxembourg: Office for Official Publications of the European Communities.

Nettle, D. and Romaine, S. (2000) *Vanishing Voices: The Extinction of the World's Languages*, Oxford: Oxford University Press.

Patrick, D. and Freeland, J. (eds) (2004) *Language Rights and Language 'Survival': A Sociolinguistic Exploration*, Manchester: St Jerome Publishing.

Pennycook, A. (1994) *The Cultural Politics of English as an International Language*, London: Longman.

Phillipson, R. (1992) *Linguistic Imperialism*, Oxford: Oxford University Press.

——(2003) *English-Only Europe: Challenging Language Policy*, London: Routledge.

Romaine, S. (2000) *Language in Society: An Introduction to Sociolinguistics*, 2nd edn, Oxford: Oxford University Press.

Skutnabb-Kangas, T. (2000) *Linguistic Genocide in Education – or Worldwide Diversity and Human Rights?* Mahwah, NJ: Lawrence Erlbaum.

Skutnabb-Kangas, T. and Phillipson, R. (1995) 'Linguistic human rights, past and present', in T. Skutnabb-Kangas and R. Phillipson (eds) *Linguistic Human Rights: Overcoming Linguistic Discrimination*, Berlin: Mouton de Gruyter.

Tully, J. (1995) *Strange Multiplicity: Constitutionalism in an Age of Diversity*, Cambridge: Cambridge University Press.

Part II
Multilingualism and education

8

Indigenous education

Local and global perspectives

Teresa L. McCarty and Sheilah E. Nicholas

Indigenous peoples have the right to establish and control their educational systems and institutions providing education in their own languages, in a manner appropriate to their cultural methods of teaching and learning.

(United Nations General Assembly 2007a: Article 14 [1])

At present, the most important issues are the right to self-determination in education and ... reviving the language and culture with the help of the school.

(Aikio-Puoskari 2009: 240, 241)

It is difficult to separate education and literacy from the struggle for rights and self-determination.

(López and Sichra 2008: 295)

Introduction

We begin with the statements above to highlight the interface of language, culture and self-determination in Indigenous education. Throughout the world, Indigenous languages and the knowledge they encode constitute the living heart of family- and community-based education. It is this living heart that colonial regimes have sought to still and destroy. State-sponsored schooling has been a primary instrument for linguistic and cultural genocide (Skutnabb-Kangas and Dunbar 2010). Yet, in recent years, grass-roots Indigenous movements have reclaimed education control over the content and medium of instruction in schools serving Indigenous students. Although still facing many challenges, these initiatives are having positive effects on Indigenous language and culture revitalization and student achievement (Hornberger 2008; May and Aikman 2003). In this chapter we examine these processes and the issues they raise for Indigenous self-determination and linguistic human rights. We preface our discussion with some background information and key terms.

There are 370 million Indigenous people in the world, residing in 90 countries and every continent on earth. Although there is no universally agreed definition of 'Indigenous', the United Nations Permanent Forum on Indigenous Issues (PFII) considers the term to reference people who (1) self-identify as Indigenous and are accepted as members of the community who so identifies; (2) have historical continuity with pre-invasion and pre-colonial societies in their territories; (3) possess distinct social, economic or political systems that are non-dominant within the larger society; and (4) are committed to protecting, maintaining, and developing their ecological and cultural systems as distinctive peoples (United United Nations Permanent Forum on Indigenous Issues [PFII] n.d.: 1). As the PFII notes, in some nation-states, other terms besides 'Indigenous' prevail, including tribes (India, New Zealand, the USA), First Nations peoples (Canada), Aboriginal peoples (Australia, Canada), national minorities (China) and ethnic minorities (parts of Asia and Africa). Here, we use the term Indigenous to represent original peoples and languages, marking it with a capital 'I' to signify a 'nationality parallel' (King and Benson 2008: 343). Ultimately, the names Indigenous peoples call themselves are the most precise identifiers. Among Native Americans, for instance, group names often translate as 'people', as with the Diné (Navajo), or with a place, as with the Akimel O'odham, the River People of present-day Arizona.

Indigenous peoples represent 4 per cent of the world's population, but they speak 60 to 75 per cent (4,000 to 5,000) of the world's languages (UNESCO 2005). The contexts in which these languages are spoken are highly varied, from situations such as Quechua, spoken by eight to 12 million people in six South American countries; to the Sámi of Scandinavia, where five of 10 original Sámi languages are used as mediums of instruction in three Nordic states; to the Indian subcontinent, with 84.3 million scheduled tribes who speak 159 Indigenous languages; to sub-Saharan Africa, where a proliferation of Indigenous mother tongues (400 in Nigeria alone) compete with a handful of powerful colonial languages for a place in school curricula (Aikio-Puoskari 2009; Mohanty *et al.* 2009a; Obondo 2008). We cannot do justice here to all of this diversity, and, indeed, a major point we will make is that Indigenous education must be locally defined. Our goal instead is to explore broad themes across diverse Indigenous contexts, illustrating those themes with case examples. To do this, we draw on our first-hand experience of Indigenous education and a growing international literature in the field.

Early developments

In her discussion of multilingual education in Africa, Heugh (2009: 103) critiques the colonialist 'loss of memory regarding the use of [Indigenous] languages in written form and as the primary mediums of education in pre-colonial times'. This loss of memory is linked to a false but persistent dichotomy between 'formal' education – often equated with Western schooling – and 'informal' education, equated with out-of-school learning and frequently marginalized in school. As Lomawaima and McCarty (2006: 28) explain the formal/informal binary:

> [It] developed to suit the circumstances of Western, industrial societies as institutionalized schooling grew to dominate notions of education. ... [O]ne by-product of the school = formal model is the expansion of 'informal' to subsume *all* non-Western modes of education. Indigenous modes of education have thus been suppressed or silenced.

We begin our analysis, then, by spotlighting what has been 'suppressed or silenced' in dominant narratives about Indigenous education systems: their planful, deliberate and systematic character, incorporating both 'formal' and 'informal' elements, as all education systems do (Lomawaima and McCarty 2006: 27). We emphasize again the heterogeneity of these systems, which are uniquely designed to prepare the young for productive citizenship in a distinctive ecological and social system, and for global citizenship as well. Nonetheless, certain shared patterns in these systems can be detected.

Indigenous knowledges and education systems

Indigenous education systems are designed with 'survival as the ultimate test' (Lomawaima and McCarty 2006: 30). In his description of Arakmbut education in the Peruvian Amazon, Sueyo (2003: 194) illustrates this with the lessons learned from his father during a trip down the Manu River on a balsa raft:

> During the trip [my father] taught me a lot about the forest and … its mysteries, how to respect it and care for it … for example how to hunt, fish, and track monkeys, birds and animals. … And he also taught me how to face life in the forest and on the river. This was education in the indigenous world.

In a parallel vein, Sarangapani describes the transmission of medicinal knowledge among the Baiga of central India, where, by the age of five or six, children 'can identify several of the more common medicinal plants around the village', and by the age of nine, are able to name 'over 60 plants with medicinal properties, and many more … that could be eaten or were useful' (2003: 203). Yupiaq scholar A. Oscar Kawagley (1995: 84) describes similar education processes among Alaska Natives: '[T]he Yupiaq people survived by learning to ask the right questions, use extensive observation … experiment, memorize useful data, apply data for explanation of natural phenomena, and use available resources to develop their technology'. The pedagogy for these lessons is 'carefully constructed around observing natural processes, adapting models of survival, obtaining sustenance from the plant and animal world, and using natural materials to make … tools and implements' (Barnhardt and Kawagley 2005: 10). Throughout the literature the values of relationships, responsibility and reciprocity recur (Brayboy and McCarty 2010).

In their study of family- and community-based education among the Mazahua of central Mexico, Paradise and de Haan note that, 'responsibility for the successful realization of the activity at hand is shared by all participants' (2009: 189). In learning to build a market stand, for instance, Mazahua 'parents did not exclusively assign the child a learner's role while assigning themselves a teacher's role', but instead, both parent and child participated 'with different levels of expertise and responsibility' (2009: 193). Mazahua pedagogy is informed by an 'underlying egalitarianism that emphasizes both individual responsibility and open reciprocity' in completing socially significant tasks (2009: 196).

Within Indigenous education systems, oral tradition – the stories, songs, prayers and other oral media that carry a people's repository of knowledge – is a primary conduit for producing and transmitting this knowledge. Ben Johnston, Ojibway from the USA, writes, '[I]t is [here] that the sum total of what people believe about life, being, existence, and relationships are symbolically expressed and articulated [and] that fundamental understandings, insight, and attitudes toward life and human conduct, character, and quality in their diverse forms are embodied and passed on' (1976: 7). Johnston's assertion encompasses Indigenous cosmology, epistemology and ontology – how Indigenous peoples founded societies premised on these knowledge systems – and the long-established customs, social institutions and oral traditions that have transported such knowledge systems across time. Indigenous education is predicated on an understanding of the concept of life, the relationship of humankind with the physical and metaphysical universe, the genesis narratives that provide the cultural map for physical and spiritual survival including the cultivation of a communal ethic or 'tribal consciousness' – that 'deep sense of solidarity … a tie between one and all others' from which stem rules governing conduct and the duties of individuals, families, and bands toward maintaining the cohesion of the group (Standing Bear 1978: 124). Indigenous education, *locally* understood, provides training in what is needed and valued by a particular society, a process by which youth are prepared to become competent, contributing members of their society and citizens of the world.

Among the Hopi, a historically oral society who reside in southwestern USA, the identity formation process is expressed as *Hopiqatsit ang nùutum hintsakme, Hopisinoniwtingwu* ('Participating along with others in the Hopi way of life, one becomes a Hopi'). This Hopi 'way of doing and being' derives from an ancestral event – the 'emergence' of humankind into the current Fourth World – encoded in their Emergence story and constituting Hopi 'identity, religious beliefs, ritual practices, and their daily engagements and concerns' today (Whiteley 1998: 191). This historical knowledge is transmitted to each succeeding generation through teachings manifest in ritual practices, cultural institutions, symbolism, song words and phrases, and prayer. The Hopi language is maintained in these traditional conventions, which serve to reinforce the Hopi way of life (Dongoske *et al.* 1993).

All of this is part of Indigenous symbolic literacies that, according to Mi'kmaq scholar Marie Battiste, interact with and depend on a collective oral tradition. In most Native American societies, symbolic literacies display an 'awareness of a highly concrete ideal implicit in the reality of nature. It knew no distinction between is and ought or between theory and practice' (1986: 27). An example from Hopi is the practice of growing corn by hand, embodying the principles of reciprocity, industry and humility as a way of life. This practice is both secular and religious. The secular activity emphasizes the skill of farming and becomes the metaphor for the work ethic of attaining the 'know-how' for making a living, *qatsitwi*, and survival in a harsh environment. The planting stick, *soya*, symbolizes a life of humility and becomes the instrument by which the Hopi farmer tests his faith. Planting is also a commitment to economic responsibility for one's nuclear family as husband and father, extending to the male role in the clan family, and to future generations of Hopi. In turn, female kin give reciprocal attention to the corn, harvesting and storing it, which encompasses the woman's role in the preparation of traditional food made from corn. Planting corn by hand allows each generation of Hopi men to participate in the ways of Hopi ancestors; to work the earth with a reverence for it as *itangu*, our mother, commanding proper thoughts and feelings toward a 'relative' (Loftin 1991: 9). The preparation of food by women, likened to Mother Earth, provides substance, *soona*, to all; we nurse from our mother, she is the provider of life, a mother to all. In turn, like Mother Earth, Hopi women are revered for their life-giving abilities. Symbolically, corn links Hopi intimately with their land and ancestors.

Indigenous texts such as winter counts, wampum, petroglyphs and pictographs use 'ideographic symbolization of concepts and ideas ... which helped to record and store valuable knowledge, information, and records on available natural materials such as birch bark, rocks and shells' (Battiste 1986: 25). Summarizing these hybrid literacies for Quechua communities in the Peruvian Andes, de la Piedra says, 'In other words, drawings, songs, and rituals together become a unity where people construct meaning' (2009: 111). These accounts suggest the ways in which Indigenous mother tongues have, for centuries, conveyed highly complex concepts through multiple modalities and across multiple fields of inquiry: agronomy, art, history, law, religion, philosophy, music, science, medicine, mathematics and commerce (Heugh 2009: 106).

Indigenous writing systems in learning and teaching

Although oral tradition is a primary carrier of this knowledge, written language has also been (and is) an important medium of Indigenous education. Indigenous writing systems have a long history, thriving 'independently of and prior to European writing systems' (King and Benson

2008: 342). Mayan scripts consisting of glyphs (pictures) and phonetic systems date from the second century BCE; Zapotec writing from present-day Mexico dates to the seventh century CE (Marcus 1980). Another example of Indigenous print literacy is the Popol Vuh, a corpus of historical narratives and creation stories written in the mid-1500s in Quiché using the Spanish alphabet. Along the Niger River in Timbuktu, the late twentieth-century discovery of educational documents from university mosques dating to the twelfth century 'provides extensive evidence of literacy and formal education across a wide range of fields in several [Indigenous African] languages' (Heugh 2009: 103–4; Makalela 2005). In present-day Liberia and Sierra Leone, the Vai script developed in 1820 by Memelu Duwalu Bukele is an early example of Indigenous syllabic writing. At the same time in North America, the Cherokee silversmith Sequoyah independently created the Cherokee syllabary. The extant historical record is replete with such examples of Indigenous print literacy and its educative role.

Colonial schooling and the 'vicious circle of language disadvantage'

Despite this rich legacy of oral and written literary traditions and the presence of contemporary autochthonous literacies and education systems, Indigenous languages and knowledges have been dismissed and denigrated in Western schooling. Contrasting his family- and community-based learning with what he encountered in school, Sueyo writes that the latter 'was a form of "Spanification" and the curriculum was not based in our reality at all. ... ' (2003: 194). In their account of schooling among the Karipuna and Mebengokré-Xikrin of Brazil, Tassinari and Cohn note that in addition to linguistic differences, Karipuna and Xikrin children face numerous obstacles on entering school, including being forced to work individually rather than collaboratively, as is the custom outside of school (collaborative work is 'considered cheating by the teachers'); being required to answer questions individually and aloud ('in the community no one would ask a child to stand out in a group and talk individually', as oratory is an adult male practice); having to comply within a specified time frame (e.g. for written exams); and being forced to respond to an older person – the teacher – by making direct eye contact (a practice widely reported as anathema to Indigenous students, for whom it is considered a sign of disrespect) (Tassinari and Cohn 2009: 160–1). In her study of the 'invisible culture' in community and classroom for Warm Springs American Indian children, Philips (1993: 127) maintains that different norms governing interpersonal interaction and talk, which she terms participant structures, 'contribute to the general uncertainty Indian children experience as they find they do not understand the teacher, and the teacher does not understand them'.

These processes create what Mohanty *et al.* (2009a: 284) call the 'vicious circle of language disadvantage' whereby Indigenous languages are 'considered inadequate, impoverished and under-developed and, hence, unfit for educational and scientific use'. According to Dorian, this is rooted in Eurocentric beliefs in the 'linguistic survival of the fittest' and the notion that European languages are 'exceptionally well suited to clear thinking and precise expression' (1998: 10). Heugh provides evidence of this ideology in sub-Saharan Africa, where African languages are dismissed by education officials as 'too primitive', 'without written traditions' and incapable of conveying mathematical or scientific thought (2009: 104). The net effect of these processes is to make Indigenous languages vulnerable to language shift, which weakens their functions and reduces their domains of use, justifying further exclusion as a medium of instruction (Mohanty *et al.* 2009a). This 'subtractive education', Skutnabb-Kangas and Dunbar assert, constitutes linguistic genocide, because 'children ... are effectively transferred to the dominant group linguistically and culturally ... [w]hen a whole group changes language, this also contributes to the disappearance of the world's linguistic diversity' (2010: 9).

149

Understanding contemporary Indigenous education requires an understanding of the sociohistorical contexts in which these practices arose. Throughout the world, physical and linguistic genocide, de-culturation and de-territorialization have been the combined goals of colonial regimes. In sub-Saharan Africa, this occurred as European missionaries constructed an 'artificial multilingualism' whereby closely related African varieties – akin to British and American English – were recorded as distinct tongues. These artificial linguistic boundaries became the template for dividing African peoples territorially and for 'de-Africanisation through the exclusive use of colonial languages in high-prestige domains' (Makalela 2005: 153). In North America, from the seventeenth through much of the twentieth century, Native children were forcibly removed from their families and compelled to attend distant residential schools where 'no Indian talk' was the cardinal rule (Spack 2002: 24; Reyhner and Eder 2004). During this same period, Australia's British colonial government implemented an infamous 'White Australia' policy designed 'to "breed out" [Aboriginal peoples'] black traits' and 'produce a homogeneous English-speaking Anglo-Saxon culture' (Romaine 1991: 3). Aboriginal and Torres Strait Islander children – known today as the 'stolen generation' – were forcibly taken from their homes, 'often in the absence of the parent but sometimes even by taking the child from the mother's arms', to distant schools where they were prevented from learning their heritage language and suffered physical and emotional abuse (Commonwealth of Australia 1997: 4). In the Nordic countries, beginning in the mid-nineteenth century, Sámi children 'were punished for using their language on school premises [and] teachers were … paid extra to keep a close eye on parents' language use' (McCarty et al. 2008: 300). In Latin America, 'a clear and often publicly conceded intention of eradicating Indigenous ethnocultural differences' underlay centuries of policies designed to configure a uniform 'national' society through segregated subtractive schooling; these policies can be characterized as apartheid (López 2008: 43).

Indigenous protagonism and the rise of bi-multilingual schooling

The past four decades have seen a significant repositioning of these power relations as a rising Indigenous activism has taken hold throughout the world. Borrowing from a theme in recent Brazilian education reforms (Tassinari and Cohn, 2009: 150, 164), we use the term 'Indigenous protagonism' to refer to political action for social justice and Indigenous linguistic, cultural and education rights. For instance, throughout Latin America, where 400 Indigenous languages are spoken, intercultural bilingual education (EIB) resulting from the 'active and … even belligerent demands by Indigenous leaders and organizations' (López 2008: 44) has become 'the common denominator' in schools serving Indigenous students (Rockwell and Gomes 2009a: 102). In Norway, the 1987 Sámi Language Act 'states that the Sámi and Norwegian languages are … of equal importance'; a Norwegian national curriculum initiative known as Reform 97 represents 'the first time in the educational history of … the Nordic countries [when] there was a separate Sámi curriculum' with equal status with the national curriculum (Hirvonen 2008: 21). In the USA, legislative victories by American Indian leaders and young people during the 1960s and 1970s ushered in the American Indian self-determination movement, a key component of which is Indigenous control over schools serving Indigenous students. In 1990 the Native American Languages Act (NALA) was passed, reversing two centuries of federal language policy and vowing to 'promote the rights … of Native Americans to use, practice, and develop Native American languages' (Native American Languages Act 1990 Sec. 104[1][5]). This legislation was augmented in 2006 by the Esther Martinez Native American Languages Preservation Act, which supports additional language recovery efforts. In Aotearoa/New Zealand, the Māori language was recognized as co-official with English in 1987; this was followed by the 'rapid (and highly successful) emergence of Māori-medium language education' (May 1999: 63). In post-apartheid South Africa, official language policy now includes nine Indigenous languages and the option for 'learners to be taught in *any* official language/s of their choice' (Makalela 2005: 147). Indigenous languages have been made official or co-official in many parts of the world.

At the international level, the establishment within the United Nations in 2000 of the 16-member PFII, whose mandate is to advise the UN Economic and Social Council on Indigenous issues 'relating to economic and social development, culture, the environment, education, health and human rights' (United Nations Permanent Forum on Indigenous Issues 2006, n.p.), has fostered the coordination of Indigenous initiatives within the UN system and its member regions. In 2007, after more than two decades of Indigenous struggle, the UN General Assembly approved the *Declaration on the Rights of Indigenous Peoples*, affirming the right to self-determination, freedom from forced assimilation, and 'to revitalize, use, develop and transmit to future generations their histories, languages, oral traditions, philosophies, writing systems and literatures' (United Nations General Assembly 2007a, Article 13 [1]).

This Indigenous 'conquest' of linguistic, cultural, and educational rights represents an historical turning point, as post-colonial governments now must provide 'an education that respects Indigenous languages and cultures' (Rockwell and Gomes 2009a: 106). And yet the conquest is not complete; voting against the 2007 UN Declaration were the USA, Canada, Australia and New Zealand – nations whose violations of Indigenous peoples' rights are among the most grievous in the world.[1] Moreover, the very fact that these transformations are being carried out within the historically alien institution of the school makes them problematic; schools are 'extremely contentious spaces' (Rockwell and Gomes 2009a: 105). At the same time, the models growing out of the new Indigenous protagonism carry important lessons for multilingual education theory, practice and policy – topics to which we now turn.

Key issues of theory and practice

> [A] firm grounding in the heritage language and culture indigenous to a particular place is ...
> fundamental ... for the development of culturally-healthy students and communities
> associated with that place.
>
> *(Assembly of Alaska Native Educators 1998: 2)*

We begin this section with the premise that pedagogies that build on the linguistic, cultural and sociocognitive resources children bring to school are basic to a quality education that serves local needs as well as the need for a critically conscious and skilled national and global citizenry. Such pedagogies go unquestioned for students from dominant language and culture back-grounds. Yet these approaches have only been implemented with Indigenous children in the past several decades and are still denied to millions of Indigenous children throughout the world. The consequences are both individual and societal. Compared with their White mainstream peers, American Indian and Alaska Native students are 73 per cent more likely to be placed in remedial education programmes and 117 per cent more likely to leave school without a high school degree (National Caucus of Native American State Legislators 2008). In Canada, subtractive education has resulted in a situation in which Indigenous students have 'impaired fluency' in both the mother tongue and the national language(s) (Skutnabb-Kangas and Dunbar 2010: 57). In India, where only 26 of 350 Indigenous languages are used as the medium of instruction in the primary grades, a quarter of young children 'face moderate to severe problems in the initial months and years of ... school because their home language differs from the school language' (Jhingran 2009: 263). In short, say Skutnabb-Kangas and Dunbar, Indigenous and minoritized children around the world 'are over-represented … on the negative side in studies and statistics amongst those children who never attend school and those who are pushed out early' (2010: 61). Moreover, as Indigenous mother tongues 'are weakened by marginalization and exclusion from education and other instrumentally significant domains' (Mohanty *et al.* 2009a: 291), linguistic and cultural diversity – the wellspring of human knowledge and planetary stewardship – is diminished. To reverse these negative effects, it 'is necessary to realize that [mother tongue] education is not a problem; it is the solution', Mohanty *et al.* insist (ibid.).

In the remainder of this section, we consider this solution in light of recent research on promising practices across a range of contexts, from multilingual states with large Indigenous populations to smaller, community- and school-based efforts. As we show, the research supports the implementation of academically, linguistically, and culturally 'strong' programmes (Skutnabb-Kangas and McCarty 2008: 4) designed to promote Indigenous language and culture maintenance alongside acquisition of the language(s) of wider communication (LWC) and mainstream content.

Promising practices when children's primary language is not the LWC

'Everywhere in the world', Heugh *et al.* write, 'students who study in their mother tongue are better able to learn to read and write efficiently, understand mathematical concepts, and develop higher levels of academic competence, than those who are not able to study in the mother tongue' (2007: 27). In a recent government-commissioned study to assess and make recommendations for medium of instruction (MOI) policies in Ethiopia, Heugh *et al.* provide comprehensive quantitative and qualitative documentation for this claim. The second most populous country in sub-Saharan Africa, Ethiopia, is home to 80 ethnolinguistic groups (Heugh *et al.* 2007: 44). From the advent of Western schooling in 1908 until the end of the century, Ethiopia had a monolingual education policy, with English and later Amharic (the lingua franca) as the MOI, despite government-sponsored studies documenting 'that educational quality was hampered by [their use] as languages of instruction at the primary and secondary levels' (Heugh *et al.* 2007: 49). Following the new (1994) Ethiopian constitution, the country has had a policy of mother tongue schooling at the primary level, followed by a transition to English (highly valued but spoken by only a fraction of the elite) in grades 5 through 9, with Amharic taught as a subject to non-Amharic speakers. However, throughout the country the policy has been differentially implemented due to pressures to introduce English as the MOI in earlier grades.

In an exhaustive review of policy and practice from several regions of the country, Heugh *et al.* show that students who have the benefit of mother tongue instruction for the full length of their primary schooling (8 years) perform as well as, or better than, their English MOI peers on assessments of English, science and mathematics. They attribute these outcomes to the fact that students 'who learn in their mother tongue can interact with the teacher, with each other, and with the curricular content in ways that promote effective and efficient learning' (2007: 6). 'The assumption, therefore, that English MOI leads to better achievement in English is *not* confirmed', Heugh *et al.* state (2007: 81, emphasis in the original). The Ethiopian data reinforce research from many parts of the world: for children from minoritized home language backgrounds, providing six to eight years of mother tongue schooling yields the greatest academic benefits.

Mohanty *et al.* report similar findings from India, where language barriers are accompanied by content barriers, 'as the daily life experiences and culture of tribal children are hardly present' in dominant-language schools (2009a: 289). Under the government's Education for All

Program, the states of Andhra Pradesh and Orissa have implemented mother tongue education in 1,495 schools for 18 Indigenous languages. In both state programmes, for the first three years of schooling the Indigenous mother tongue is the only MOI for all school subjects, followed by its use alongside the dominant state language (Telugu in Andhra Pradesh and Oriya in Orissa), English, then Hindi. Mother tongue-based multilingual education 'improved the basic competencies of literacy and numeracy among all children, increased their school attendance and ... resulted in greater parental satisfaction and community involvement' (Mohanty *et al.* 2009a: 295; for more on India see Jhingran 2009; Mohanty 2008; Panda and Mohanty 2009).

In Nepal, where one-half of the nation's 23 million people are non-Nepali speakers, the Multilingual Education Project for All Non-Nepali Speaking Students of Primary Schools is a grassroots effort being piloted in six Indigenous communities (Hough *et al.* 2009: 160). As part of the project, educators and community members work together to develop curricula around locally relevant knowledge: herbal medicines and traditional healing practices, traditional practices relating to agriculture and food, tribal oral histories, cultural values such as collectivism and sharing, life cycle rituals, and a highly endangered numerical system (Hough *et al.* 2009: 168–74). Although this 'is still very much a work in progress', data collected to date indicate that the project is having a positive impact on curricular reforms within local schools and teacher training programmes, and that it has become a bellwether for more systemic democratizing reforms (2009: 175).

Although the sociolinguistic and educational context differs greatly from the cases described above, the academic benefits of similar approaches are well documented in Native American communities. Within the Navajo Nation – geographically the largest Native American nation, with a land base the size of Ireland and a population of 300,000 – the community school at Rock Point, Arizona, has a long-standing bilingual–bicultural programme in which rigorous assessment of student learning has been an ongoing concern (Rosier and Farella 1976). Drawing on international research from well-implemented bi-multilingual education, Rock Point based its programme on the principle that children learn to read only once, most easily in their mother tongue. Using extant Navajo literacy materials and new ones developed locally, students at Rock Point learned to read first in Navajo, then English. They learned mathematics in both languages and studied science and social studies in Navajo, including Navajo clanship, history, social problems, government and economic development. Longitudinal data show that students not only outperformed comparable Navajo students in English-only programmes, they surpassed their own previous annual growth rates (Holm and Holm 1990, 1995; Rosier and Farella 1976). In a retrospective analysis of the Rock Point programme, programme co-founders Agnes Holm and Wayne Holm describe the 'four-fold empowerment' it has engendered: of the Navajo school board, teachers, parents and students who 'succeeded in school *through* Navajo' and, more importantly, 'came to *expect* to succeed in school' (Holm 2006: 33, emphasis in the original). These findings have been replicated at other schools with strong Native American language and culture programmes (for a review of this literature, see McCarty 2009, 2010).

Promising practices in Indigenous language and culture revitalization

The previous subsection has highlighted Indigenous education initiatives under way in settings in which children's primary language differs from the LWCs taught and used in school. But what about education for Indigenous children who enter school speaking the dominant language as a primary language, and for whom Indigenous language and culture revitalization is a prominent goal?

Among the most well-developed language revitalization programmes are those in Hawaii and New Zealand. Hawaiian and Māori are Eastern Polynesian languages within the Austronesia family, and their revitalization efforts have followed intertwined paths. In Hawaii, the Indigenous monarchy persisted until 1893, when the US military staged an illegal coup, annexing Hawaii as a US territory. At the time, Hawaiians had the highest literacy rate of any ethnic group in the Hawaiian islands (Wilson and Kamanā 2006). In 1959, Hawaii became the 50th US state. In New Zealand, although the Treaty of Waitangi, signed in 1840 between the British Crown and Māori leaders, guaranteed the Māori rights to their lands, homes and treasured possessions, it was quickly violated by White settlers in pursuit of Māori lands. In both cases, the Indigenous peoples experienced 'political disenfranchisement, misappropriation of land, population and health decline, educational disadvantage and socioeconomic marginalization' (May 2005: 366). By the mid-twentieth century, language death was imminent (May 2005: 367; Wilson *et al.* 2006: 42).

This situation was the impetus for parallel ethnolinguistic revitalization movements. In 1978, Hawaiian became co-official with English in Hawaii; in 1987, the Māori Language Act made Māori co-official with English (and more recently, also with New Zealand Sign Language). Full-immersion Māori 'language nest' preschools or *Te Kōhanga Reo* began in 1982; the first Hawaiian immersion preschools ('*Aha Pūnana Leo*) were established in 1983 (May 2005; Warner 1999; Wilson 1999). These family-run preschools facilitate interaction between young children and fluent speakers entirely in the Indigenous language, with the goal of nurturing knowledge of the Indigenous language and culture in 'much the same way that they were in the home in earlier generations' (Wilson and Kamanā 2001: 151). The preschools provided the basis for establishing Indigenous-language tracks and whole-school immersion programmes within their respective public school systems.

Hill and May (2011) examine factors that contribute to the educational effectiveness of Māori-medium schooling, looking specifically at Rakaumanga School on New Zealand's North Island. One of the largest and oldest Māori-medium schools, Rakaumanga provides Māori-medium schooling for students from year 1 (age 5) to year 13 (age 18). The school's philosophy embraces Māori culture as an essential factor in student achievement (ibid.). Entering students must have attended *Kōhanga Reo* for at least two years, laying the foundation for four years of full Māori immersion, after which English is introduced for three to four hours per week. To ensure integrity of the Māori language environment, Māori and English instruction are separated by time, place and teacher. The goal is full bilingualism and biliteracy to prepare students to be 'citizens of the world' (ibid.).

According to Hill and May, by year 8, students reach or are approaching age-appropriate literacy development in both languages and are 'well on their way to achieving the goal of bilingualism and biliteracy' (2011: 178). A recent study by Māori educator Cath Rau (2005) indicates that these findings extend to other Māori-medium schools; she reports a significant increase in student reading and writing scores from 1995 to 2002–3 as a result of increased support and resources for Māori curriculum development, reading materials and teachers' professional development.

Wilson and Kamanā (2001, 2006) describe similar outcomes at the Nāwahīokalani'ōpu'u (Nāwahī) Laboratory School in Hilo, Hawaii, a full-immersion, early childhood through high school programme affiliated with the University of Hawaii-Hilo's College of Hawaiian Language and the '*Aha Pūnana Leo*. The school offers a college preparatory curriculum, teaching all subjects through Hawaiian language and values; students also learn English and a third language (e.g. Japanese). Like Rakaumanga, the goal is for learners to achieve Hawaiian dominance alongside high levels of English fluency and literacy, and to produce students who 'psychologically identify Hawaiian as their dominant language and the one that they will speak with peers and their own children when they have them' (Wilson and Kawa'ae'a 2007: 39). Nāwahī students not only surpass their non-immersion peers on English standardized tests, they outperform the state average for all ethnic groups on high school graduation, college attendance and academic honours (Wilson *et al.* 2006: 42). Wilson and Kamanā, (2001: 153) cite two other outcomes of these efforts in Hawaii: the development of an interconnected group of young parents who are increasing their proficiency in Hawaiian, and the creation of a more general social climate of Indigenous language support.

Consistent with international research on second language acquisition, the most significant achievement gains for both Hawaiian and Māori students occur in whole-school settings that provide an overall additive language learning environment designed to produce high levels of bilingualism and biliteracy. Across a spectrum of outcomes, Māori and Hawaiian can rightfully be called Indigenous language revitalization 'success stories'.

Yet, the very fact that these Indigenous initiatives are carried out in the contentious space of schools infuses them with tensions. We conclude with a final example. The Sámi are the Indigenous people of the Nordic countries who live in what is now Norway, Sweden, Finland and western Russia – an Indigenous 'nation divided by four states' (Todal 2003: 185). Sámi is a Finno–Ugric language with three major branches and 11 subgroups. Of a total population of 100,000, about 40,000 live in Norway (Magga and Skutnabb-Kangas 2003). Well into the twentieth century, the Sámi were subjected to harsh assimilation policies carried out in schools. The 'turnaround' in Sámi schooling occurred as a result of Sámi activism. In 1997, the Norwegian government introduced a separate Sámi curriculum with equal status as the national curriculum; subsequently the Sámi Parliament assumed partial control over Sámi schooling (Todal 2003: 185–6). This reform not only guarantees Sámi language and culture instruction for Sámi children in high-density Sámi residential areas (the Sámi core), but also provides for teaching in and of the Sámi language outside the Sámi core area. The goal is for every student to learn about Sámi culture and for as many as possible to become bilingual (Hirvonen 2008).

In the core Sámi area these goals are being achieved with a high level of success. However, outside the core area, in mixed Sámi–Norwegian-speaking classrooms, Sámi children are typically instructed through Norwegian, with 'pull-out' instruction in Sámi language and culture. According to Hirvonen (2008: 33), these schools do not make it possible for children to become bilingual in their heritage language. Precisely *because* Sámi and other Indigenous languages are threatened and minoritized, they require additional support or 'positive discrimination', Hirvonen says (2008: 38), so that the Indigenous language and culture are integral rather than ancillary to the school curriculum.

Discussion

In this section we have explored a variety of Indigenous education initiatives, highlighting promising practices and ongoing challenges. The cases offer a glimpse of the work under way worldwide, but they differ in significant ways. In particular, it is important to recognize the different language education goals and needs among relatively 'large' Indigenous groups such as those in India and Africa and smaller communities such as those in the USA and Canada where there are many fewer Indigenous-language speakers. (For more on language education in the latter communities, see Hinton and Hale 2001.) Nevertheless, as a sample of the international literature, these cases foreground important theoretical and pedagogical insights. The first is that *context matters*; what is appropriate and effective in one setting may be ineffectual, even deleterious, in another. Each of the cases profiled here arose in response to local needs, epistemologies, resources and contingencies. A 'one-size-fits-all' approach is pedagogically and morally unsound.

The cases also reinforce findings from the wider international literature on the efficacy and equity of 'strong' Indigenous language and culture programmes. Table 8.1 provides a typology of such programmes. Strong programmes are characterized by the use of the Indigenous language as the MOI for at least the first five years of schooling and ideally (as in the Ethiopian, Hawaiian and Māori cases), for the first eight years. The Native American and Māori data show that the LWC will be learned 'even under circumstances where a strong academic program is provided through the "nationally weaker" language' (William H. Wilson, personal communication, 8 September 2008). A preponderance of evidence demonstrates that strong programmes produce salutary academic outcomes for children who enter school as primary speakers of the Indigenous language, as well as those who are learning it as a second language.

Finally, these data show that strong Indigenous education programmes rest on the ability of Indigenous peoples to exercise self-determination in the content and medium of their children's education. Indigenous communities 'need to be able to control curriculum content and its delivery as well as define achievement on their own terms', Rau insists (2005: 427). By definition, this requires the placement of education control in Indigenous hands – a policy issue we examine more closely in the next section.

Policy issues

Although the literature on language education policies for Indigenous peoples centres on colonial and post-colonial policies, we emphasize again that both formal and informal language policies have existed in Indigenous communities since pre-colonial times. '[T]he different ethnolinguistic groups … did not have a language of instruction problem', Brock-Utne and Hopson point out in their introduction to these issues for Africa, as 'each group used its own language to educate its children' (2005: 3). Today, core policy issues revolve around Indigenous efforts to reclaim this human right. Here, we provide examples of these efforts.

At the level of Indigenous tribes and nations, many groups have instituted policies that make the Indigenous language the official language of education, government and commerce. Tribal language policies in the USA provide one example. The official language policy of the Yaqui or Yoeme, a diasporic people who reside in northern Mexico and the southwestern USA, declares, '[A]ll aspects of the educational process shall reflect the beauty of our Yaqui language, culture and values. It shall be the policy of the Pascua Yaqui Tribe that no member of the Tribe shall be coerced by any outside non-Yaqui … authority or system to deny or debase the Yaqui language' (Zepeda 1990: 250). The language policy of the Tohono O'odham, who reside along the USA–Mexico border, calls on all education systems operating within the Tohono O'odham Nation to 'establish and operate educational programs using bilingual/bicultural practices' (1990: 253). The 2005 Navajo Sovereignty in Education Act (NSIEA) affirms the Navajo Nation's 'inherent right to exercise its responsibility to the Navajo people for their education by prescribing and implementing educational laws and policies applicable to all schools serving the Navajo Nation', including integrating Navajo language and cultural knowledge in school curricula (Navajo Sovereignty in Education Act 2005: Sect. 3.1).

A great deal of official policy activity is also under way at the state and provincial levels, as we have seen for Andhra Pradesh and Orissa, India, Ethiopia and Hawaii. In the Northwest Territories of Canada, an Official Languages Act recognizes English, French and all six Aboriginal languages of the province as co-official. In the Canadian territory of Nunavut, Bill 6, the Nunavut Official Languages Act, confers co-official status on Inuktitut, Inuinnaqtun, French and English; Bill 7, the Inuit Language Protection Act, promotes Inuit languages in public and private domains (Patrick 2010: 298). In Alaska, Indigenous cultural and linguistic standards parallel English-language standards in Alaskan schools. Guided by a network of partner school districts serving 20,000 Alaska Native students, this initiative fosters 'complementarity between the Indigenous knowledge systems ... and the formal education systems imported to serve the educational needs of rural Native communities' (Barnhardt and Kawagley 2005: 15). The network's *Standards for Culturally-Responsive Schools*, for example, help to ensure that Indigenous students achieve state standards 'in such a way that they become responsible, capable and whole human beings in the process' (Assembly of Alaska Native Educators 1998: 3). Alaska's *Guidelines for Strengthening Indigenous Languages* help schools provide 'appropriate [Indigenous] language immersion programs that strengthen the language in the community' (Assembly of Alaska Native Educators 2001: 2). These standards and guidelines 'encourage schools to nurture and build upon the rich and varied cultural traditions that continue to be practiced in communities throughout Alaska' (Assembly of Alaska Native Educators 1998: 3–4).

At the national level, Indigenous languages have been recognized as co-official in some nation states. Bi-multinational agreements also support some Indigenous language education initiatives, (e.g. Nepal's Multilingual Education Project). Perhaps the most comprehensive example of national policies for Indigenous bi-multilingual education comes from Latin America, where 'in almost every case, bilingual education ... is part of the national educational service' (López 2008: 44). As López writes of these policy developments, 'The fact that bilingual education has become part of government strategic plans ... is without doubt a noteworthy improvement for Latin American educational policy, which had always been based on the ethnocidal illusion of linguistic-cultural homogeneity' (2008: 45).

These political victories intersect with a growing language rights movement at the international level, which includes international conventions to promote Indigenous languages, regional charters for the use of Indigenous languages in education and declarations of linguistic, cultural and educational rights (Skutnabb-Kangas 2000; Skutnabb-Kangas and Dunbar 2010). Limiting these international conventions is their non-binding status and the hegemonic forces that continue to marginalize Indigenous peoples and violate their linguistic human rights. In the USA, tribal language policies and the federal Native American Languages Act notwithstanding, the implementation of 'strong' Indigenous education programmes faces challenges in the form of high-stakes English-only school accountability regimes enshrined in federal and state law. One consequence of these policies is the elimination of 'low-stakes' subject matter, including Indigenous language and culture instruction (McCarty 2009; Wyman *et al.* 2010). In addition to these challenges, as Bear Nicholas explains for Canadian First Nations peoples, are inequities in Indigenous education funding, declining numbers of Indigenous-language speakers, a 'desperate need for curriculum materials' and Indigenous community opposition to mother tongue schooling resulting from 'massive indoctrination of past decades that holds bilingualism to be useless and our languages to have no utility in the modern world' (Bear Nicholas 2009: 224, 234–5). López adds further the need for bi-multilingual-intercultural education to be reconceptualized as not only for Indigenous students but also for their mainstream counterparts to 'discover the richness of diversity and learn to appreciate the value of the Indigenous cultural legacy from an intercultural perspective' (2008: 61; see also Rockwell and Gomes 2009b).

Table 8.1 Types of Indigenous language and culture education programmes*

Programme type	STRONG (additive or full bi-/multilingualism/interculturalism)			WEAK (subtractive or limited bi-/multilingualism/interculturalism)		
	Child's language status	Language of classroom	Programme goals	Child's language status	Language of classroom	Programme goals
Indigenous language and culture immersion	Indigenous/minority	Indigenous language	Indigenous language maintenance/revitalization; full bi-multilingualism, interculturalism	N/A	N/A	N/A
Indigenous language and culture maintenance	Indigenous/minority	Bi-multilingual with emphasis on Indigenous language	Indigenous language maintenance/revitalization; bi-multilingualism, interculturalism	N/A	N/A	N/A
Two-way bilingual/dual language	Indigenous/minority and majority (50/50; 10%; 50%/50%, etc.)	Mixed Indigenous language/LWC (90%/10%; 50%/50%, etc.)	Indigenous language maintenance/revitalization; bi-multilingualism, interculturalism	N/A	N/A	N/A
Transitional	N/A	N/A	N/A	Indigenous/minority	Indigenous language used for first years of schooling, then replaced with LWC	Strong dominance in the LWC/monolingualism; may include some Indigenous language and culture enrichment

Table 8.1 (continued)

Programme type	STRONG (additive or full bi-/multilingualism/interculturalism)			WEAK (subtractive or limited bi-/multilingualism/interculturalism)		
	Child's language status	Language of classroom	Programme goals	Child's language status	Language of classroom	Programme goals
Mainstream with Indigenous language and culture pull-out classes	N/A	N/A	N/A	Indigenous/minority	Indigenous language and LWC	Strong dominance in the LWC/monolingualism, with some Indigenous language and culture enrichment
Mainstream with foreign language instruction	N/A	N/A	N/A	Indigenous/minority and majority	LWC with Indigenous language taught as a 'foreign' language	Strong dominance in the LWC; limited bilingualism; little or no cultural emphasis
Mainstream monolingual**	N/A	N/A	N/A	Indigenous/minority	LWC only	Monolingualism/monoculturalism in the LWC (assimilation)

* This typology is adapted from Baker (2006) and Skutnabb-Kangas and Dunbar (2010); a modified form of the table appears in McCarty (2010: 98–99).
** Mainstream monolingual programmes are 'non-forms' of bi-multilingual education, also known as 'submersion' or 'sink-or-swim' (see Skutnabb-Kangas and McCarty 2008: 4).

Summary and new directions

In this chapter we have sought to provide a sense of locally specific initiatives in Indigenous education as well as an understanding of broader issues connecting the local with the global. Across the contexts we have considered, the right to Indigenous linguistic, cultural and educational self-determination is an overriding theme. A multitude of promising practices and policies are being implemented to secure those rights. As this work unfolds, it opens up new possibilities for research, theory and the transformation of education inequities. We conclude with some of those possibilities.

Around the world, there is growing recognition of the complexity and importance of Indigenous knowledge systems. As Villegas *et al.* write, Indigenous knowledges offer 'a way to support our children and improve our communities by making central issues of power, place, and relationships' (2008: 1). Indigenous knowledge systems also offer a reservoir of intelligence about local and global stewardship from which all the world's citizens can benefit. A major area of emerging research, then, centres on documenting Indigenous knowledge systems and ways of knowing, including the complementarities and contrasts among Indigenous peoples and between Indigenous systems and those developed in Western contexts (Brayboy and Maughan 2009; McCarty *et al.* 2005; Romero-Little 2010; Villegas *et al.* 2008.)

Because knowledge is generated, transmitted and acquired through language, the role of Indigenous languages is central to this research. Hence, there remains a need for situated examinations of local processes of language socialization, use, shift, revitalization and maintenance. There are many facets to this research: how ideologies or taken-for-granted assumptions about language are formed and transformed into practice, and how this in turn strengthens or undermines intergenerational transmission (Kroskrity and Field 2009); the pathways and barriers to sustaining linguistic and cultural diversity (King *et al.* 2008; Skutnabb-Kangas 2000); the ways in which education can be (re)imagined in multilingual societies (García *et al.* 2008; Martin-Jones and Jones 2000) and the social justice ramifications of this work (Mohanty *et al.* 2009b); the role of Indigenous literacies in language revitalization and maintenance (Collins and Blot 2003; Francis and Reyhner 2002; Hornberger 1996; King and Benson 2008; McCarty and Zepeda 1995); and the place of schools in supporting Indigenous linguistic and cultural survivance (Hornberger 2008). One powerful theoretical and methodological tool for this work is ethnography, which provides situated, in-depth, systemic understandings of these sociolinguistic, socioeducational and sociopolitical processes (Canagarajah 2006; McCarty 2011). We also need an ethnological perspective that places local accounts gleaned from rigorous ethnographic investigation in the context of larger global shifts (Canagarajah 2005; Gilmore 2011), in particular the educational and sociolinguistic consequences of immigration, transmigration (King and Haboud 2011) and 'widening social and economic polarization' around the world (Collins 2011: 134).

Finally, an exciting new research direction centres on Indigenous youth negotiations of these local and global processes. As Szulc (2009: 144) notes in her ethnographic study of Mapuche language and culture instruction in Argentina, youth are not simply the object of identity struggles around language and ethnicity, 'they also act as agents, resignifying and articulating the different and conflicting messages' they receive from their learning experiences. In this regard, an emerging literature on 'Indigenous youth protagonism' is worthy of note (Lee 2007, 2009; McCarty *et al.* 2009; Messing 2009; Nicholas 2009; Tulloch 2004; Wyman 2009). Despite youth experiences with competing language ideologies (Lee 2009), much of this research indicates that youth are choosing to speak their heritage languages as 'an act of identity, or belonging to a particular group' (Nettle and Romaine 2000: 173). A key aspect of this research is its praxis potential, as nuanced understandings of youth language ideologies and practices gleaned from ethnographic accounts suggest new strategies for 'inviting youth into' language education planning (McCarty and Wyman 2009: 286–7).

All of this work centres on the right of choice of *what* language to use for *what* purposes, in *which* contexts and *with whom*. 'Children whose parents or schools deny them access to their language deprive the children of choice' (Holm 2006: 41–2). Language lies at the heart of choice and is the driver for sustaining distinctive local communities and cultural-linguistic pluralism. Language must be 'viewed as part of each group's rightful inheritance and part of our collective cultural human legacy' (Nettle and Romaine 2000: 177).

Finally, the sustainability of a language in its fullest sense entails the empowerment of the people who speak it. Indigenous researchers are critical to this endeavour. Indigenous protagonism in research, theory and praxis points the way out of the limiting binary of 'mother tongue versus other tongue' in Indigenous education. The challenge remains in continuing to imagine these possibilities and marshalling the collective will for their actualization.

Related topics

Indigenous contexts; discourses about linguistic diversity; language rights; multilingualism in education in post-colonial contexts; multilingual citizenship and language revitalization.

Note

1 According to the United Nations General Assembly (2007b), countries voting against the Declaration did so 'because of concerns over provisions on self-determination, land and resources rights and ... language giving indigenous peoples a right of veto over national legislation and State management of resources'. Australia, Canada, New Zealand and the USA have subsequently endorsed the document.

Further reading

Hinton, L. and Hale, K. (2001) *The Green Book of Language Revitalization in Practice*, San Diego, CA: Academic Press.
(The definitive resource on the revitalization of threatened tongues, including examples from Aotearoa/ New Zealand, Australia, Ireland, Native America and Wales.)

Lomawaima, K. T. (1994) *They Called It Prairie Light: The Story of Chilocco Indian School*, Lincoln: University of Nebraska Press.
(An award-winning account of the Native American boarding school experience as revealed through the memories of boarding school graduates who both accommodated and subverted the federal assimilationist agenda.)

Meyer, L. and Alvarado, B. M. (eds) (2010) *New World of Indigenous Resistance: Noam Chomsky and Voices from North, South, and Central America*, San Francisco: City Lights Books.
(An innovative exchange on Indigenous self-determination, modernity and cultural-linguistic sustainability between linguist Noam Chomsky and scholars, activists and educators from across the Americas.)

Skutnabb-Kangas, T., Phillipson, R., Mohanty, A. K. and Panda, M. (eds) (2009) *Social Justice through Multilingual Education*, Bristol: Multilingual Matters.
(Wide-ranging examples of multilingual education theory, research and praxis from the Americas, Africa, Asia and Scandinavia.)

Bibliography

Aikio-Puoskari, U. (2009) 'The ethnic revival, language and education of the Sámi, an indigenous people, in three Nordic countries (Finland, Norway and Sweden)', in T. Skutnabb-Kangas,

R. Phillipson, A. K. Mohanty and M. Panda (eds) *Social Justice through Multilingual Education*, Clevedon: Multilingual Matters.

Assembly of Alaska Native Educators (1998) *Alaska Standards for Culturally-Responsive Schools*, Anchorage: Alaska Native Knowledge Network.

——(2001) *Guidelines for Strengthening Indigenous Languages*, Anchorage: Alaska Native Knowledge Network.

Baker, C. (2006) *Foundations of Bilingual Education and Bilingualism*, 4th edn, Clevedon: Multilingual Matters.

Barnhardt, R. and Kawagley, A. O. (2005) 'Indigenous knowledge systems and Alaska Native ways of knowing', *Anthropology and Education Quarterly* 36(1): 8–23.

Battiste, M. (1986) 'Cognitive assimilation and Micmac literacy', in J. Barman, Y. Hébert and D. McCaskill (eds) *Indian Education in Canada: The Legacy, Volume 1*, Vancouver: University of British Columbia Press.

Bear Nicholas, A. (2009) 'Reversing language shift through a Native language immersion teacher training programme in Canada', in T. Skutnabb-Kangas, R. Phillipson, A. K. Mohanty and M. Panda (eds) *Social Justice through Multilingual Education*, Bristol: Multilingual Matters.

Brayboy, B. M. J. and McCarty, T. L. (2010) 'Indigenous knowledges and social justice pedagogy', in T. Chapman and N. Hobbel (eds) *Social Justice Pedagogy across the Curriculum: The Practice of Freedom*, New York: Teachers College Press.

Brayboy, B. M. J. and Maughan, E. (2009) 'Indigenous knowledges and the story of the bean', *Harvard Educational Review* 79(1): 1–21.

Brock-Utne, B. and Hopson, R. K. (2005) 'Educational language contexts and issues in postcolonial Africa', in B. Brock-Utne and R. K. Hopson (eds) *Languages of Instruction for African Emancipation: Focus on Postcolonial Contexts and Considerations*, Cape Town and Dar es Salaam: Centre for Advanced Studies of African Society (CASAS) and Mkuki na Nyota Publishers.

Canagarajah, A. S. (ed.) (2005) *Reclaiming the Local in Language Policy and Practice*, Mahwah, NJ: Lawrence Erlbaum.

——(2006) 'Ethnographic methods in language policy', in T. Ricento (ed.) *An Introduction to Language Policy: Theory and Method*, Malden, MA: Blackwell.

Collins, J. (2011) 'Language, globalization, and the state: Issues for the new policy studies', in T. L. McCarty (ed.) *Ethnography and Language Policy*, New York: Routledge.

Collins, J. and Blot, R. K. (2003) *Literacy and Literacies: Texts, Power, and Identity*, Cambridge: Cambridge University Press.

Commonwealth of Australia (1997) *Bringing Them Home: Report of the National Inquiry into the Separation of Aboriginal and Torres Strait Islander Children from Their Families*, Sydney: Human Rights and Equal Opportunity Commission.

de la Piedra, M. T. (2009) 'Hybrid literacies: the case of a Quechua community in the Andes', *Anthropology and Education Quarterly* 40(2): 110–28.

Dongoske, N. G., Jenkins, L. and Ferguson, T. J. (1993) 'Understanding the past through Hopi Oral Tradition', *Native Peoples* 6(2): 24–35.

Dorian, N. C. (1998) 'Western language ideologies and small-language prospects', in L. A. Grenoble and L. J. Whaley (eds) *Endangered Languages: Language Loss and Community Response*, Cambridge: Cambridge University Press.

Francis, N. and Reyhner, J. (2002) *Language and Literacy Teaching for Indigenous Education: A Bilingual Approach*, Clevedon: Multilingual Matters.

García, O., Skutnabb-Kangas, T. and Torres-Guzmán, M. E. (eds) (2008) *Imagining Multilingual Schools: Languages in Education and Glocalization*, Clevedon: Multilingual Matters.

Gilmore, P. (2011) 'Language ideologies, ethnography, and ethnology: new directions in anthropological approaches to language policy', in T. L. McCarty (ed.) *Ethnography and Language Policy*, New York, Routledge.

Heugh, K. (2009) 'Literacy and bi/multilingual education in Africa: Recovering collective memory and expertise', in T. Skutnabb-Kangas, R. Phillipson, A. K. Mohanty and M. Panda (eds) *Social Justice through Multilingual Education*, Bristol: Multilingual Matters.

Heugh, K., Benson, C., Bogale, B. and Yohannes, M. A. G. (2007) *Final Report: Study on Medium of Instruction in Primary Schools in Ethiopia*, Addis Ababa, Ethiopia: Ministry of Education, available online at www.hsrc.ac.za/research/output/outputDocuments/4379_Heugh_Studyonme diumofinstruction.pdf

Hill, R. and May, S. (2011) 'Exploring biliteracy in Māori-medium education: An ethnographic perspective', in T. L. McCarty (ed.) *Ethnography and Language Policy*, New York: Routledge.

Hinton, L. and Hale, K. (eds) (2001) *The Green Book of Language Revitalization in Practice*, San Diego, CA: Academic Press.

Hirvonen, V. (2008) '"Out on the fells, I feel like a Sámi": Is there linguistic and cultural equality in the Sámi school?' in N. H. Hornberger (ed.) *Can Schools Save Indigenous Languages? Policy and Practice on Four Continents*, New York: Palgrave Macmillan.

Holm, W. (2006) 'The "goodness" of bilingual education for Native American students', in T. L. McCarty and O. Zepeda (eds) *One Voice, Many Voices: Recreating Indigenous Language Communities*, Tempe: Arizona State University Center for Indian Education.

——(1995) 'Navajo language education: Retrospect and prospects', *Bilingual Research Journal* 19(1): 141–67.

Holm, A. and Holm, W. (1990) 'Rock Point, a Navajo way to go to school: A valediction', *Annals of the American Academy of Political and Social Science* 508: 170–84.

Hornberger, N. H. (ed.) (1996) *Indigenous Literacies in the Americas: Language Planning from the Bottom Up*, Berlin: Mouton de Gruyter.

——(ed.) (2008) *Can Schools Save Indigenous Languages? Policy and Practice on Four Continents*, New York: Palgrave Macmillan.

Hough, D. A., Magar, R. B. T. and Yonjan-Tamang, A. (2009) 'Privileging indigenous knowledges: Empowering multilingual education in Nepal', in T. Skutnabb-Kangas, R. Phillipson, A. K. Mohanty and M. Panda (eds) *Social Justice through Multilingual Education,* Bristol: Multilingual Matters.

Jhingran, D. (2009) 'Hundreds of home languages in the country and many in most classrooms: Coping with diversity in primary education in India', in T. Skutnabb-Kangas, R. Phillipson, A. K. Mohanty and M. Panda (eds) *Social Justice through Multilingual Education*, Clevedon: Multilingual Matters.

Johnston, B. H. (1976) *Ojibway Heritage*, Lincoln: McClelland and Stewart and University of Nebraska Press.

Kawagley, A. O. (1995) *A Yupiaq Worldview: A Pathway to Ecology and Spirit*, Prospect Heights, IL: Waveland Press.

King, K. A. and Benson, C. (2008) 'Vernacular and Indigenous literacies', in B. Spolsky and F. Hult (eds) *The Handbook of Educational Linguistics*, Malden, MA: Blackwell.

King, K. A. and Haboud, M. (2011). 'International migration and Quichua language shift in the Ecuadorian Andes', in T. L. McCarty (ed.) *Ethnography and Language Policy*, New York: Routledge.

King, K. A., Schilling-Estes, N., Fogle, L., Lou, J. J. and Souku, B. (eds) (2008) *Sustaining Linguistic Diversity: Endangered and Minority Languages and Language Varieties*, Washington, DC: Georgetown University Press.

Kroskrity, P. V. and Field, M. C. (eds) (2009) *Native American Language Ideologies: Beliefs, Practices, and Struggles in Indian Country*, Tucson: University of Arizona Press.

Lee, T. S. (2007) '"If they want Navajo to be learned, then they should require it in all schools": Navajo teenagers' experiences, choices, and demands regarding Navajo language', *Wicazo Sa Review* Spring, 7–33.

——(2009) 'Language, identity, and power: Navajo and Pueblo young adults' perspectives and experiences with competing language ideologies', *Journal of Language, Identity, and Education* 8(5). 307–20.

Loftin, J. D (1991) *Religion and Hopi Life in the Twentieth Century*, Bloomington and Indianapolis: Indiana University Press.

Lomawaima, K. T. and McCarty, T. L. (2006) *'To Remain an Indian': Lessons in Democracy from a Century of Native American Education*, New York: Teachers College Press.

López, L. E. (2008) 'Top-down and bottom-up: Counterpoised visions of bilingual intercultural education in Latin America', in N. H. Hornberger (ed.) *Can Schools Save Indigenous Languages? Policy and Practice on Four Continents*, New York: Palgrave Macmillan.

López, L. E. and Sichra, I. (2008) 'Intercultural bilingual education among indigenous peoples bilingual in Latin America', in J. Cummins and N. H. Hornberger (eds) *Encyclopedia of Language and Education*, vol. 5: *Bilingual Education*, New York: Springer.

McCarty, T. L. (2009) 'The impact of high-stakes accountability policies on Native American learners: evidence from research', *Teaching Education* 20(1): 7–29.

——(2010) 'Native American education in light of the Ethiopian case: Challenging the either-or paradigm', in K. Heugh and T. Skutnabb-Kangas (eds) *Multilingual Education Works: From the Periphery to the Centre*, New Delhi: Orient Blackswan.

——(ed.) (2011) *Ethnography and Language Policy*, New York: Routledge.

McCarty, T. L., Borgoiakova, T., Gilmore, P., Lomawaima, K. T. and Romero, M. E. (eds) (2005) 'Indigenous epistemologies and education: Self-determination, anthropology, and human rights', *Anthropology and Education Quarterly*, (special issue) 36(1).

McCarty, T. L., Romero-Little, M. E., Warhol, L. and Zepeda, O. (2009) 'Indigenous youth as language policy makers', *Journal of Language, Identity, and Education* 8(5): 291–306.

McCarty, T. L., Skutnabb-Kangas, T. and Magga, O. H. (2008) 'Education for speakers of endangered languages', in B. Spolsky and F. Hult (eds) *The Handbook of Educational Linguistics*, Malden, MA: Blackwell.

McCarty, T. L. and Wyman, L. T. (2009) 'Indigenous youth and bilingualism: Theory, research, praxis', *Journal of Language, Identity, and Education* 8(5): 279–90.

McCarty, T. L. and Zepeda, O. (guest eds) (1995) 'Indigenous language education and literacy', *Bilingual Research Journal*, (special issue) 19(1).

Magga, O. H. and Skutnabb-Kangas, T. (2003) 'Life or death for languages and human beings: Experiences from Saamiland', in L. Huss, A. C. Grima and K. A. King (eds) *Transcending Monolingualism: Linguistic Revitalization in Education*, Lisse: Swets and Zeitlinger.

Makalela, L. (2005) '"We speak eleven tongues": Reconstructing multilingualism in South Africa', in B. Brock-Utne and R. K. Hopson (eds) *Languages of Instruction for African Emancipation: Focus on Postcolonial Contexts and Considerations*, Cape Town, South Africa and Dar es Salaam, Tanzania: Centre for Advanced Studies of African Society (CASAS) and Mkuki n Nyota Publishers.

Marcus, J. (1980) 'Zapotec writing', *Scientific American* 242: 50–65.

Martin-Jones, M. and Jones, K. (eds) (2000) *Multilingual Literacies: Reading and Writing Different Worlds*, Amsterdam: John Benjamins.

May, S. (1999) 'Language and education rights for indigenous peoples', in S. May (ed.) *Indigenous Community-based Education*, Clevedon: Multilingual Matters.

——(2005) Introduction. 'Bilingual/immersion education in Aotearoa/New Zealand: Setting the context', *International Journal of Bilingual Education and Bilingualism* 8(5): 365–76.

May, S. and Aikman, S. (guest eds) (2003) 'Indigenous education: New possibilities, ongoing constraints' *Comparative Education*, (special issue) 39(2).

Messing, J. H. E. (2009) 'Ambivalence and ideology among Mexicano youth in Tlaxcala, Mexico', *Journal of Language, Identity and Education* 8(5): 350–64.

Mohanty, A. K. (2008) 'Multilingual education in India', in J. Cummins and N. H. Hornberger (eds) *Encyclopedia of Language and Education*, vol. 5: *Bilingual Education*, New York: Springer.

Mohanty, A. K., Mishra, M. K., Reddy, N. U. and Ramesh, G. (2009a) 'Overcoming the language barrier for tribal children: multilingual education in Andhra Pradesh and Orissa, India', in T. Skutnabb-Kangas, R. Phillipson, A. K. Mohanty and M. Panda (eds) *Social Justice through Multilingual Education*, Bristol: Multilingual Matters.

Mohanty, A. K., Panda, M., Phillipson, R. and Skutnabb-Kangas, T. (eds) (2009b) *Multilingual Education for Social Justice: Globalising the Local*, New Delhi: Orient Blackswan.

Navajo Sovereignty in Education Act (2005) *Navajo Sovereignty in Education Act of 2005*, Window Rock, Navajo Nation, AZ: Navajo Nation Tribal Council, available online at www.navajocourts.org/Resolutions/CJY-37–05.pdf

National Caucus of Native American State Legislators (2008) *Striving to Achieve: Helping Native American Students Succeed*, Denver, CO: National Conference of State Legislatures.

Native American Languages Act of 1990 (Public Law 101–477) (1990) *Native American Languages Act*, available online at www.nabe.org/files/NALanguagesActs.pdf

Nettle, D. and Romaine, S. (2000) *Vanishing Voices: The Extinction of the World's Languages*, Oxford: Oxford University Press.

Nicholas, S. E. (2009) '"I live Hopi, I just don't speak it": The critical intersection of language, culture, and identity in the lives of contemporary Hopi youth', *Journal of Language, Identity, and Education* 8(5): 321–34.

Obondo, M. A. (2008) 'Bilingual education in Africa: An overview', in J. Cummins and N. H. Hornberger (eds) *Encyclopedia of Language and Education*, vol. 5: *Bilingual Education*, New York: Springer.

Panda, M. and Mohanty, A. K. (2009) 'Language matters, so does culture: Beyond the rhetoric of culture in multilingual education', in T. Skutnabb-Kangas, R. Phillipson, A. K. Mohanty and M. Panda (eds) *Social Justice through Multilingual Education*, Bristol: Multilingual Matters.

Paradise, R. and de Haan, M. (2009) 'Responsibility and reciprocity: Social organization of Mazahua learning practices', *Anthropology and Education Quarterly* 40(2): 187–204.

Patrick, D. (2010) 'Canada', in J. A. Fishman and O. García (eds) *Language and Ethnic Identity*, vol. 1: *Disciplinary and Regional Perspectives*, Oxford: Oxford University Press.

Philips, S. U. (1993) *The Invisible Culture: Communication in Classroom and Community on the Warm Springs Indian Reservation*, Prospect Heights, IL: Waveland Press.

Rau, C. (2005) 'Literacy acquisition, assessment and achievement of year two students in total immersion in Māori programmes', *International Journal of Bilingual Education and Bilingualism* 8(5): 404–32.

Reyhner, J. and Eder, J. (2004) *American Indian Education: A History*, Norman: University of Oklahoma Press.

Rockwell, E. and Gomes, A. M. R. (2009a) 'Introduction to the special issue: Rethinking Indigenous education from a Latin American perspective', *Anthropology and Education Quarterly* 40(2): 97–109.

——(guest eds) (2009b) 'Rethinking Indigenous education from a Latin American perspective', *Anthropology and Education Quarterly* (special issue) 40(2).

Romaine, S. (1991) 'Introduction', in S. Romaine (ed.) *Language in Australia*, Cambridge: Cambridge University.

Romero-Little, M. E. (2010) 'How should young Indigenous children be prepared for learning? A vision of early childhood education for Indigenous children', *Journal of American Indian Education* 49 (1 & 2): 1–21.

Rosier, P. and Farella, M. (1976) 'Bilingual education at Rock Point: Some early results', *TESOL Quarterly* 10(4): 379–88.

Sarangapani, P. M. (2003) 'Indigenising curriculum: Questions posed by Baiga Vidya', *Comparative Education* 39(2): 199–209.

Skutnabb-Kangas, T. (2000) *Linguistic Genocide in Education: Or Worldwide Diversity and Human Rights?* Mahwah, NJ: Lawrence Erlbaum.

Skutnabb-Kangas, T. and McCarty, T. L. (2008) 'Key concepts in bilingual education: Ideological, historical, epistemological, and empirical foundations', in J. Cummins and N. H. Hornberger (eds) *Encyclopedia of Language and Education*, vol. 5: *Bilingual Education*, New York: Springer.

Skutnabb-Kangas, T. and Dunbar, R. (2010) *Indigenous Children's Education as Linguistic Genocide and a Crime Against Humanity? A Global View*, Guovdageaidnu/Kautokeino Gáldu, Resource Centre for the Rights of Indigenous Peoples, available online at www.e-pages.dk/grusweb/55/.

Spack, R. (2002) *America's Second Tongue: American Indian Education and the Ownership of English, 1860–1900*, Lincoln: University of Nebraska Press.

Standing Bear, L. (1978) *Land of the Spotted Eagle*, Lincoln: University of Nebraska Press.

Sueyo, H. (2003) 'Educational biography of an Arakmbut', *Comparative Education* 39(2): 193–7.

Szulc, A. (2009) 'Becoming *Neuquino* in Mapuzugum: Teaching Mapuche language and culture in the province of Neuqén, Argentina', *Anthropology and Education Quarterly* 40(2): 129–49.

Tassinari, A. I. and Cohn, C. (2009) '"Opening to the other": Schooling among the Karipuna and Mebengokré-Xikrin of Brazil', *Anthropology and Education Quarterly* 40(2): 150–69.

Todal, J. (2003) 'The Sámi school system in Norway and international cooperation', *Comparative Education* 39(2): 185–92.

Tulloch, S. (2004) *Inuktitut and Inuit Youth: Language Attitudes as a Basis for Language Planning*, PhD dissertation, Department of Languages, Linguistics, and Translation, Faculty of Letters, Université Laval, Québec.

UNESCO (2005) *Education for All Global Monitoring Report 2006. Literacy for Life*, Paris: UNESCO, available online at www.unesco.org/en/efareport/reports/2006-literacy/

United Nations General Assembly (2007a) *United Nations Declaration on the Rights of Indigenous Peoples*, New York: United Nations General Assembly, available online at www.un.org/esa/socdev/unpfii/documents/DRIPS_en.pdf/

——(2007b, September 13) 'General Assembly adopts declaration on rights of indigenous peoples: "major step forward" towards human rights for all, says President', New York: United Nations Department of Public Information, News and Media Division, available online at www.un.org/News/Press/docs/2007/ga10612.doc.htm

United Nations Permanent Forum on Indigenous Issues (PFII) (n.d.) *Who Are Indigenous Peoples?* Available online at www.un.org/esa/socdev/unpfii/documents/5session_factsheet1.pdf/

——(2006) *UNPFII: Structure within ECOSOC*, available online at www.un.org/esa/socdev/unpfii/en/structure.html

Villegas, M., Neugebauer, S. R. and Venegas, K. R. (2008) 'Editors' introduction', in M. Villegas, S. R. Neugebauer and K. R. Venegas (eds) *Indigenous Knowledge and Education: Sites of Struggle, Strength, and Survivance'*, Cambridge: President and Fellows of Harvard College.

Warner, S. L. N. (1999) 'The right, responsibility, and authority of Indigenous peoples to speak and make decisions for themselves in language and culture revitalization', *Anthropology and Education Quarterly* 30(1): 68–93.

Whiteley, P. (1998) *Rethinking Hopi Ethnography*, Washington, DC: Smithsonian Institution Press.

Wilson, W. H. (1999) 'The sociopolitical context of establishing Hawaiian-medium education', in S. May (ed.) *Indigenous Community-based Education*, Clevedon: Multilingual Matters.

Wilson, W. H. and Kamanā, K. (2001) '"*Mai loko mai o ka 'i'ini*: Proceeding through a dream": The 'Aha Pūnana Leo connection in Hawaiian language revitalization', in L. Hinton and K. Hale (eds) *The Green Book of Language Revitalization in Practice*, San Diego: Academic Press.

——(2006) '"For the interest of the Hawaiians themselves": Reclaiming the benefits of Hawaiian-medium education', *Hūlili: Multidisciplinary Research on Hawaiian Well-Being* 3(1): 153–81, available online at www.ahapunanaleo.org

Wilson, W. H., Kamanā, K. and Rawlins, N. (2006) 'Nāwahī Hawaiian laboratory school', *Journal of American Indian Education* 45(2): 42–4.

Wilson, W. H. and Kawa'ae'a, K. (2007) 'I kumu; i lālā: "Let there be sources; let there be branches": Teacher education in the College of Hawaiian Language', *Journal of American Indian Education* 46(3): 37–53.

Wyman, L. T. (2009) 'Youth, linguistic ecology, and language endangerment: A Yup'ik example', *Journal of Language, Identity, and Education* 8(5): 335–49.

Wyman, L. T., Marlow, P., Andrew, C. F., Miller, G., Nicholai, C. R. and Rearden, Y. N. (2010) 'Focusing on long-term language goals in challenging times: A Yup'ik example', *Journal of American Indian Education*, 49(1 & 2): 28–49.

Zepeda, O. (1990) 'American Indian language policy,' in K. L. Adams and D. T. Brink (eds) *Perspectives on Official English: The Campaign for English as the Official Language of the USA*, Berlin: Mouton de Gruyter.

Multilingualism in education in post-colonial contexts

A special focus on sub-Saharan Africa

Feliciano Chimbutane

Introduction

This chapter discusses some key features of language-in-education policies that have been adopted in post-colonial countries, with a special focus on sub-Saharan Africa. Although acknowledging the diversity of policies followed by different post-colonial countries and also policy fluctuations driven by particular sociopolitical forces operating in individual countries, this study underscores some of the main characteristics shared by most of these countries. With this perspective in mind, policy aspects salient in sub-Saharan Africa are compared with those attested in some Asian countries such as Hong Kong, India, Malaysia, Pakistan and Singapore.

To frame the analysis, the chapter starts with a sketch of the historical development of the field of language policy and planning (LPP), based on Ricento (2000). This is followed by an analysis of colonial language policies, which, as I will argue, have influenced the policy decisions that have been taken in many countries since independence. The main section considers two distinct phases of language policy and practice in the post-colonial period: the post-independence phase, characterized by the pervasiveness of monolingual and monocultural language-in-education policies; and the current new world order, a phase characterized by the promotion of multilingualism and multiculturalism in education but also by the concurrent advancement of English as the global language. The chapter ends with a discussion of three inter-related issues that permeate language-in-education policy and practice: the need to accommodate bottom-up initiatives, linguistic human rights (LHR) and the desire of citizens and states to invest in linguistic resources that allow them to compete in national and global markets.

Theory and method in the field of language policy and planning: changing perspectives

The historical evolution of the language policies adopted in post-colonial contexts is intimately linked with the development of the field of LPP: the multilingual landscape and associated sociolinguistic issues that characterize most of these contexts have played a key role in the constitution and theoretical development of LPP; at the same time, the management of multi-lingualism in these contexts has also been influenced by epistemological paradigms evolving within this research field. The fact that LPP was constituted as a research field in the early 1960s, the era when independence movements were burgeoning (especially in Africa), shows how its history is closely linked with decolonization and multilingualism in the new states that emerged out of these movements. In this context, a critical review of the evolution of LPP as a research field can help us to understand the contours of language policies that have been devised in post-colonial multilingual contexts. Ricento's (2000) analysis of the theoretical development of LPP provides an insightful framework for situating the history of language policies in post-colonial contexts.

Ricento (2000) identifies three historical phases in the development of LPP: (1) decoloniza-tion, structuralism and pragmatism (1960s); (2) the failure of modernization, critical socio-linguistics and access (early 1970s–1980s); and (3) the new world order, post-modernism and LHR (from the mid-1980s).

In the first phase, LPP was concerned with addressing linguistic 'problems' of newly inde-pendent nations. These included standardization and modernization of indigenous languages and lingua franca (through corpus planning) by linguists working with a broadly structuralist paradigm and definition of the domains and functions of the competing languages in these nations (status planning). According to Ricento (2000: 198), 'a widely held view among Wes-tern(nized) sociolinguists in this period was that linguistic diversity presented obstacles for national development, while linguistic homogeneity was associated with modernization and Westernization'. This view justified the adoption of former colonial languages (e.g. English, French or Portuguese) as official languages or the declaration of major local languages (such as Kiswahili in Tanzania or Urdu in Pakistan) as national (and official) languages. Ricento (ibid.) points out that language planning practitioners viewed this approach as ideologically neutral and as purely technical in nature and oriented towards problem-solving and as pragmatic in its goal.

The second phase was characterized by an acknowledgment of the failure and negative effects of these Western models of modernization and development. As Ricento (2000: 200) puts it, 'newly independent states found themselves in some way more dependent on their former colonial masters than they had been during the colonial era'. In response, practitioners, especially those situated within different paradigms derived from critical social theory, started to reconceptualize language and LPP. They began to see LPP as ideologically motivated, rather than neutral. Through their analyses of historical and economic contexts in which ear-lier policies were produced, analysts showed how the choice of languages of wider commu-nication (LWC) for high functions (e.g. government and formal education) and/or certain national languages for low functions (e.g. communication in informal and intra-ethnic domains) contributed to the production and reproduction of social stratification and to an increase in inequalities in post-colonial contexts. This approach is clearly expressed, for example, in Tollefson (1991) and Phillipson (1992). Tollefson (1991) argues that governments create conditions that ensure that large numbers of people are unable to acquire the language(s) or the linguistic competence they would need to succeed in school and efficiently participate in social and political life. Phillipson (1992) also notes that the promotion of LWC in former colonies involves a process of economic, political, social, cultural and educational domination and exploitation.

Ricento (2000: 202–3) concludes that the choice of European languages as resources for national development tended to serve the interests of metropolitan countries, whereas the privileging of certain national languages led to the marginalization of many other Indigenous languages and their speakers. This latter point can well be illustrated, among others, by the case of Botswana, in which the institutionalization of Setswana is threatening other local languages (see e.g. Nyati-Ramahobo 2000), and also by the case of Tanzania where the promotion of Kiswahili and its prestige status has been at the expense of other Indigenous languages of the country (see e.g. Abdulaziz 2003; Blommaert 2005).

A third and contemporary phase has been shaped by geopolitical transformations at a macro sociopolitical level. These include increased national and international mobility, the establishment of supranational coalitions and also the globalization of capitalism. From an epistemological point of view, this phase has been influenced by post-modernism, but with critical theory continuing to exert its influence. Among other things, the sociopolitical transformations that have taken place over the two decades or so have called into question the boundaries and power of nation-states. On one hand, LWC and associated cultures have been making their way into the domains of local and regional languages and cultural practices, and, on the other hand, the power of nation-states, especially the less powerful states, has weakened in the face of superpower regional coalitions and global capitalist forces. As a consequence, many low-status languages are being lost as, for integrative and socio-economic reasons, speakers of these languages have been 'forced' to shift into the languages of power and socio-economic mobility. This point is substantiated, for example, by the case of Singapore, where the majority of the population is shifting into English and speakers of other Chinese languages are shifting into Mandarin (Pakir 2008).

One response to these macro sociopolitical, economic and sociolinguistic transformations has been to articulate an 'ecology of language' paradigm. According to Phillipson and Skutnabb-Kangas (1996: 429), 'the ecology-of-language paradigm involves building on linguistic diversity worldwide, promoting multilingualism and foreign language learning, and granting LHR to speakers of all languages' (as cited in Ricento 2000: 206). In other words, there has been a discursive shift within the field of LPP from a language-as-problem to language-as-resource orientation (Ruíz 1984). The ecology of language paradigm has come to be widely regarded as a valid framework for addressing current multilingual policy demands (see Ricento 2000; Hornberger 2006). The plethora of language policy models using the ecological metaphor, such as the continua of biliteracy, illustrate this (see Hornberger 2003, 2008; Creese and Martin 2008). However, the use of the ecological metaphor has also been criticized 'given the potential for it to be misunderstood as suggesting that languages are involved in a natural evolutionary struggle, thereby downplaying the role of human agency and linguistic creativity' (Hornberger 2006: 34, responding to Pennycook 2003; see also criticism by Blommaert 2001; Blackledge 2008).

Ricento (2000) highlights human agency as the key element that distinguishes the current critical/post-modern approaches to LPP from the earlier positivistic/technicist approaches. In current approaches there is special consideration for the role that individuals and collectivities play in language use, in shaping attitudes and in policy making and implementation. This explains the importance accorded to bottom-up LPP initiatives (e.g. Ricento and Hornberger 1996; Freeman 1998; Stroud 2001; Omoniyi 2007).

In summary, from the macro sociopolitical point of view, LPP emerged from a context of decolonization and moved through a phase dominated by a preoccupation with modernization and into the new world order. The current phase has been characterized by efforts to devise approaches to LPP that can best respond to language-driven social inequalities, focusing on topics such as linguistic diversity, LHR, linguistic imperialism and language loss. In this context, LPP is intended to contribute to promote social change. Of course some discourses from the first and second phases are still articulated in some settings.

Early developments: colonial language-in-education policies

As various scholars have pointed out, in order to appreciate the current language and education issues in post-colonial Africa (and also in other post-colonial contexts), one needs to critically review the language policies that prevailed during colonial rule (Campbell-Makini 2000; Alidou 2004; Alidou and Jung 2001; Chimbutane 2011). This is because most current language policy decisions and commonly held views about former colonial and African languages and knowledge still reflect the colonial legacy (Bamgbose 1991). I would add that any historical overview needs to be taken further back, to the pre-colonial era, in order to contextualize some of the current influential ideological trends about the value of the African legacy in education and development, such as the ideology underpinning the 'African renaissance' movement (see Alexander 1999, 2003). A sociohistorical approach of this kind to language policy and practice is also applicable to other post-colonial contexts worldwide (see e.g. Ricento 2000, 2006; Rassool 2007).

It is now commonly understood that, in order to legitimate their colonial practices of domination and subordination, Europeans represented themselves as racially and culturally superior to colonized peoples. In their colonial discourse, they constructed the view that their superiority ascribed them the natural or celestial 'right to rule' and 'civilize' the allegedly inferior peoples they had subjugated (Campbell-Makini 2000; Rassool 2007; Errington 2008). Despite various cases of resistance across contexts, overall the colonized eventually assumed their constructed condition of inferiority vis-à-vis the superiority of their oppressors. Today, after more than half a century of independence for most of the former colonial countries, the symbolic domination of the West over these countries still prevails: more than ever, Western cultural values and languages, especially English, are still *the* sought-after symbolic commodities. How was this colonial discourse materialized by the different colonial powers in Africa, particularly with regards to language-in-education policies?

In the analysis of colonial language policies in sub-Saharan Africa, it is common to recognize two major groups of colonial powers, based on whether they tolerated/promoted or proscribed the use of African languages in official domains, including in education (e.g. Ansre 1978; Alidou 2004; Alidou and Jung 2001; Obondo 2008). Ansre (1978) uses the terms 'pro-users' and 'anti-users' to refer to these two groups. In the case of formal education, the 'pro-users', such as Belgium, Britain and Germany, tolerated or even promoted the use of African languages as media of instruction, particularly at the elementary level. The 'anti-users', like France and Portugal, imposed the use of colonial languages as media of instruction, at the same time that they proscribed the use of African languages.

The language policies adopted, including in education, reflected the general colonial philosophies entertained by each colonial power. For example, the British pro-user policy was compatible with its 'policy of indirect rule' (Alidou 2004: 199, and references therein): British colonial territories were indirectly administrated via local chiefs. Describing this policy, Obondo (2008: 152) notes that the British assumed that 'a colony's needs could well be served by training a rather small cadre of "natives" in English and allowing these to mediate between the colonial power and the local population'. In contrast, the anti-user policies of France and Portugal were consonant with their explicit assimilationist philosophies. For France and Portugal, one of their core missions in Africa was to 'civilize' the natives by spreading their languages and cultural values. Therefore, the use of African languages was, in both cases, viewed as an obstacle to the objectives of cultural assimilation in the colonial languages, namely French and Portuguese. Although the Portuguese followed the French assimilationist ideology, they are considered to have had a more intolerant policy towards African languages, which included measures to ensure that no African languages were promoted and the punishment of missionaries who used African languages in education (Abdulaziz 2003).

Despite the descriptive usefulness of the 'pro-user' versus 'anti-user' divide, I find it simplistic. For example, it gives the impression that the pro-users were altruistic and ideologically neutral; it may also lead to the interpretation that a given colonial power placed in a given category was consistent in its language policy throughout the time and across contexts, which was not the case.

Regarding cultural ideology, the distinction among colonial powers should not be understood as exempting the 'pro-users' from assimilationist pretension, as this was also part of their agenda. The difference was that, unlike France and Portugal, for example, who had overt and *de jure* assimilationist approaches, pro-user countries, such as Belgium and Britain, adopted what Bokamba (1991: 183) called 'an evolutionary or *laissez-faire*' policy of assimilation.

In addition, although, for example, Great Britain and Germany have both been deemed to be pro-users, in fact they differ in that while Britain usually only allowed the use of African languages at the elementary level (grades 1–3), the Germans generally promoted a policy of exclusive use of African languages in education, and, according to Rassool (2007: 43), they 'vehemently opposed the teaching of colonial languages'. Despite differences in terms of level of tolerance, in both cases the use of African languages in education was ideologically motivated. In both cases, literacy in African languages served the dissemination of the word of God, an important 'pacifying' colonial weapon. Moreover, whereas Britain wanted to facilitate the preparation of low-grade personnel who would better serve the interests of the colonial economy, by educating the locals exclusively through the medium of African languages, among other things, the Germans intended to avoid the emergence of an educated elite in European languages, who would threaten the colonial rule (Rassool 2007: 43, and references therein). The perception was that such educated natives would potentially place themselves on the same footing as the colonizers and contest exploitation and oppression (ibid.), as in fact happened across colonial contexts.

In terms of consistency of the policies adopted, there are indications that the same colonial power adopted different approaches in different colonies or even different approaches in the same colony in different historical periods. For example, although in most of its African colonies Great Britain tolerated the use of African languages in the first years of schooling, when the 'Mau Mau' Freedom Movement was perceived as a threat to the colonial establishment in Kenya, instruction in African languages was proscribed and English was mandated instead (Arnove and Arnove 1997, as cited in Rassool 2007: 44). That is, the British pro-user policy was reversed in order to respond to a political crisis. Fluctuations and ambiguities in the British language policy also occurred in colonial India (see Rassool 2007).

Among other consequences, the policies outlined above led to different scenarios in terms of language development and language attitudes in the countries concerned. In the countries where the use of African languages was tolerated and even promoted, they underwent relative development, here defined as the availability of standardized orthographic systems, glossaries, dictionaries, grammars, literature materials, etc. in such languages (e.g. Kiswahili in East Africa, see Rubagumya 1994; Campbell-Makini 2000; Abdulaziz 2003). Also in such cases, people have tended to be more positive regarding the use of African languages in formal arenas. This has been the case in former British and German colonies. In the countries where African languages were officially banned, they did not develop. They remained linked merely to informal domains, and were primarily used orally. In such cases, people have tended to be less tolerant about the use of these languages in official functions. This has been commonly the case in former French and Portuguese colonies.

Language in education policies in post-colonial contexts

The independence phase: nation-state building and the pragmatism of monolingualism

It has been a commonly held view that the choice of language(s) to be used in official domains, including for instructional purposes, is one of the most challenging questions facing decision-makers in multiethnic and multilingual societies (Field 2008). Among other reasons, this is 'because nobody wants the language of another ethnic group to be chosen, as this will give a special advantage to the native speakers of that language' (Abdulaziz 2003: 195).

Faced with this sensitive question as an integral part of the project of nation-state building at independence, the majority of African leaders opted for retaining the former colonial languages as official languages for government. In a highly multilingual sub-Saharan Africa, these were perceived as the neutral languages of integration and modernization (Bamgbose 1999).

Thus, with rare exceptions, the language-in-education policies that reigned in the colonial era were also maintained after independence: where African languages had been excluded, they remained excluded, and where they had been allowed in the lower primary school, they continued to be used but were limited to this level. The exceptions to this general trend included: (1) the abandonment of the use of African languages and adoption of the English-only monolingual model of education at all levels, a backwards move, as happened in Ghana, Kenya and Zambia; and (2) the extension of the use of African languages in education, as in Ethiopia, Eritrea, Somalia and Tanzania. The first trend was based on the perceived functionality of the societal use of a former colonial LWC, whereas the second trend was linked to the pursuit of nationalistic goals. Despite the differences in terms of goals, these two trends share the tendency to marginalize other languages in the society, as in both cases such other languages are not only excluded from the official domain of the school but also from other high status domains.

Indeed, even the case of Tanzania, which has been championed as a successful example of development and promotion of indigenous languages into high functions, it turns out that the promotion of Kiswahili, which is the first language of a tiny minority (mostly Zanzibari in origin), came at the price of exclusion of other local languages and their speakers. The same outcome applies to the privileging of Amharic in Ethiopia, Chichewa in Malawi and Setswana in Botswana (see Alidou *et al.* 2006; Heugh 2008; also Nyati-Ramahobo 2000, in relation to Botswana). As happens in contexts where a former colonial LWC is the sole medium of instruction, many children are forced to develop initial literacy and numeracy skills in a language different from the one that they speak at home or in their local communities. The same applies, for example, to India and Pakistan, where English and languages of local dominant groups (e.g. Hindi and Urdu) are superimposed in the educational field (see e.g. Rassool 2007; Rassool and Mansoor 2007; Mohanty 2008).

The failure of the monolingual model and attempts to change the colonial language-in-education legacy

Since the independence phase, but most notably following the successful Nigerian bilingual education project in the 1970s, there have been attempts to change the monolingual colonial legacy in Africa, although many attempts to introduce changes fail to go beyond the experimental phase.

Among the reasons that have been pushing African countries to experiment with alternative education programmes that involve the use of local languages as media of instruction is the growing consensus about the inefficiency of monolingual education systems in European languages, which are second and even foreign languages for most of the school children in Africa. The basic argument advanced has been that the high rates of academic failure attested in sub-Saharan Africa are to a large extent linked to the fact that a language foreign to the child (English, French or Portuguese) has been used since the first day of schooling (Bokamba 1991; Bamgbose 1999; Küper 2003; Alidou 2004) or the transition to a second language has been made too early, before the child has developed solid foundations in her/his own mother-tongue (Alidou *et al.* 2006; Heugh 2008).

Depending on their objectives, Bamgbose (2000: 51) groups the African bilingual education experiments into three types: the first type covers cases in which attempts are made to improve a previously existing bilingual programme, without changing the extent of use of African languages as media of instruction (e.g. the Primary Education Improvement Project in Northern Nigeria); the second type involves cases that try to extend the use of African languages as media of instruction from two to three years to all of primary education (e.g. the Six-Year Primary Project in Nigeria); and the third case covers cases where African languages are used for the first time as a medium of instruction (e.g. the PEBIMO project in Mozambique).

The very much quoted Nigerian Six-Year Primary Project in Yoruba, also known as the Ile-Ife Project, can be regarded as the overwhelming case of bilingual education success in post-colonial sub-Saharan Africa. In this project, which was conducted from 1970 to 1978, pupils were taught in Yoruba for the full six years of primary education while learning English as a subject, whereas a control group was first taught in Yoruba for three years and then switched into English medium. The evaluation of this project revealed that pupils in the experiment performed better than their peers in the control group not only in Yoruba but also in all other subjects, namely, English, mathematics, social studies and science (Fafunwa 1990; Bamgbose 2000). This project has been used as evidence of the superiority of an extended use of pupils' first languages as media of instruction coupled with a proper teaching of a second language.

Alidou (2004) and Alidou *et al.* (2006) also report on experimental bilingual schools initiated in the mid-1970s and early 1980s in Niger (*les écoles expérimentales*), Burkina Faso (*les écoles satellites*) and Mali (*les écoles de la pédagogie convergente*). In all these three countries, the use of Indigenous languages in formal education was proscribed during the colonial period, as was the case in all French colonies. According to Alidou, the objective of these schools was to promote the use of children's mother tongues as media of instruction in the first three years, with a switch to French at grade 4. Despite careful planning efforts, these projects posed the same problems identified in many other experimental bilingual programmes in Africa: the scarcity of trained practitioners, paucity of materials in local languages and corpus planning challenges, such as the codification of African languages.

Despite the attested success of some of the experimental projects in sub-Saharan Africa, a common trend is that, for various reasons, they are not expanded to wider contexts – they die at the experimental phase. Lack of funds, ideologically based misconceptions about education in African languages and lack of political will emerge as the key reasons why such successful initiatives have not been replicated and/or expanded. The lack of follow-up to successful African (and international) experiences has led some authors to conclude that language policy decisions in Africa are not guided by research findings but mainly by political pragmatism (see Alidou and Jung 2001; Küper 2003).

In addition to blaming domestic language planners and politicians for the perpetuation of the colonial language-in-education policies in sub-Saharan Africa, analysts have also pointed to former colonial masters and associated Western aid institutions, such as the World Bank and the International Monetary Fund (IMF), as equally responsible for this status quo. The perception by critics has been that, for political and economic reasons, the agenda of former colonial powers and some Western financial institutions is to perpetuate the hegemony of European languages in African high domains, including in education. In this context, they use all the means at their disposal, including 'economic blackmail', to impede the incursion of African languages into the domains 'traditionally' reserved to former colonial languages (e.g. Mazrui 2000; Alidou 2004).

Based on her experience as educational consultant in Africa, Alidou (2004) reports how France has used its power as the main supporter of African development programmes at the World Bank to lobby this institution for not supporting education in African languages in its former colonies. This is apparently because the use of local languages in education is contrary to the cultural and political agenda (a neo-colonial agenda) that France has set for its former colonies and also because it could hinder the chances of the French publishing companies competing in an eventual linguistic market dominated by local languages, instead of French. This issue is convincingly explored in Mazrui (2000).

Mazrui (2000) also shows how the World Bank follows double standards when it comes to the role of African languages in education: on the one hand, it adopts a discourse that appears to be favourable to the use of African languages in initial schooling and suggests that it is up to each African country to determine the language policy that best suits its specificities, while, on the other hand, it uses financial pressure to halt policy initiatives that favour African languages, thus ensuring that African states are not free to determine their language policies. Among others, Mazrui (ibid.) uses the case of Tanzania to illustrate how the World Bank and the IMF have been impeding African countries from implementing their stated language-in-education policies. According to Mazrui (2000: 51), when everything indicated that Tanzania would finally extend the use of Kiswahili as a medium of instruction to all levels of education, including the university level by 1992, the move 'was brought to an abrupt end after the country capitulated to the IMF and its draconian conditionalities, which forced it to reduce its subsidies in education and other social spheres'.

A conclusion that can be drawn from this historical outline is that, although local politicians have a stake in the perpetuation of the dominance of European languages in post-colonial contexts, it is also important to bear in mind the fact that language policy trends such as those I have outlined above are, to a large extent, influenced, if not determined, by external forces, including the influential power of metropolitan countries. Most post-colonial countries are still dependent on former colonial powers and international aid agencies for their financial support, which makes them also politically dependent. The financial power of former colonial masters and international aid agencies allows them to dictate economic, cultural and political decisions in post-colonial contexts. Indeed, as Mahamane pointed out in relation to sub-Saharan Africa, 'responsive language and education policies are possible only when governments are able to support the financial consequences of their decision' (as quoted in Alidou and Jung 2001: 68).

The new world order and the trend towards multilingual policies and practices

There are two competing tendencies taking place in the world today: on the one hand, we are witnessing a trend towards multilingual policies and practices, mainly aiming at promoting regional and local languages and their speakers; on the other hand, there is the advancement of English as a global language. In fact, many pluralist initiatives are, in one way or another, a response to the linguistic imperialism of English (Phillipson 1992) and other LWC. Both trends are having a huge impact on language-in-education policies and practices worldwide, including in post-colonial contexts.

As May (2000) has pointed out, contemporary phenomena such as increased national and international population mobility, the operation of supranational politico-economic structures and globalization are, at the same time, destabilizing the tenets of nation-state politics and reshaping linguistic and cultural pluralism. In the context of democratization and liberalization, the principle of 'political togetherness in difference' (Young 1993: 124) is gaining momentum worldwide, and, in tandem with other forms of political change, is being translated into multilingual language policies (Hornberger 2002). This has prompted the promotion of bilingual and multilingual education, even in the most conservative contexts. The current blossoming of multilingual education initiatives in the world illustrates this changing view of the relationship between multilingualism and national unity – multilingualism and multiculturalism are increasingly viewed not as problems but rather as resources that nations should capitalize on (Ruíz 1984).

This shift can be described not only as a response to the oppressiveness of monolingual and monocultural ideology but also to its limits. The oppressive nature of this ideology has to do with the fact that individuals and often minoritized linguistic groups are forced to conform to language entitlements defined at state-level, which invariably represent the interests of dominant linguistic groups. The limits of this ideological position can be illustrated by worldwide experiences showing that one common culture and one common language 'does not lead necessarily to a harmonious society' (Moses 2000: 343, citing Young 1990). In sub-Saharan Africa, the cases of Burundi, Rwanda and Somalia have been used to illustrate this same point (e.g. Campbell-Makini 2000; Küper 2003). All three countries are, in a sense, almost linguistically homogeneous, with at least 90 per cent of their populations sharing the same mother tongue. Despite that, however, these are (or were at some point) among the most unstable countries in Africa; the boundaries between social groups are not drawn along linguistic lines.

Additional evidence of the limits of a monolingual ideology in education comes from the fact that, despite being in place for centuries, it has failed to empower the majority of Africans and push the continent towards development. On the contrary, it has been argued that this ideology, along with educational policies promoting monolingualism, has a direct bearing on the under-development of sub-Saharan Africa (e.g. Fafunwa 1990; Küper 2003; Djité 2008) and has deepened inequalities among Africans, as an educated and socio-economically privileged minority and an uneducated and socio-economically marginalized majority are produced and reproduced across generations (e.g. Alexander 1999; Alidou and Jung 2001; Heugh 2008).

All these arguments are now being used to critique the monolingual and monocultural views embedded in institutional life in Africa and to forge an alternative vision of language policy and national identity based on the recognition and promotion of the different languages, cultural values and practices represented in the different polities. The underlying philosophy is that cohesion in difference is feasible and that African development can only be attained through the mediation of African languages.

Within this alternative ideological framework, there have been various initiatives within the African continent and elsewhere aiming at re-presenting African languages as legitimate tools for participation in the late modern world. Initiatives from outside or in partnership with Africa include UNESCO-sponsored activities such as the Regional Consultation on Education for All, held in November 1989 in Dakar (see UNESCO 1990) and the Jomtien Declaration, issued at the World Conference on Education for All in 1990 in Thailand (see Alidou 2004; Alidou and Jung 2001). In both cases, education specialists, practitioners and policy makers recognized the impact of school curricula and language of instruction on educational outcomes and, once again, recommended the provision of mother tongue-based bilingual education as a way to counteract the school wastage attested in developing countries, especially in Africa.

Internal continental initiatives include the Language Plan of Action for Africa, agreed in July 1986 in Addis Ababa, the work of the African Academy of Languages (ACALAN) and the Asmara Declaration. The Language Plan of Action for Africa is a political document that states the aims, objectives and principles of the language policy in Africa, including the promotion of African languages as media of instruction at all levels of education (see Alidou and Jung 2001; Küper 2003; Heugh 2008). Working under this same framework, one of the tasks of ACALAN is to steer the revalorization of African languages in the continent so that they can be increasingly used in official high status functions, including in tertiary education (Alexander 2003; Obondo 2008). The new African approach, conveyed through ACALAN, draws not only on international findings on the advantages of using familiar languages for education and development but also on a reclaimed, pre-colonial African legacy, from a historical period when some African languages (e.g. Ge'ez and Amharic) were already used as media of instruction at various levels, including at university level (see Campbell-Makini 2000; Hailemariam 2002; Rassool 2007; Heugh 2008; Asfaha 2009). This revalorization of African languages and history is one strand in the ongoing 'African renaissance' movement (see e.g. Alexander 1999, 2003).

The Asmara Declaration is a statement of linguistic rights with reference to African languages and their speakers, proposed by African scholars and writers in Asmara, Eritrea, in 2000. Drawing on the linguistic rights approach and the spirit of the African renaissance, the proponents called for the return of Africa to its languages and heritage as a way to counteract the colonial legacy, particularly the 'incongruity in colonial languages speaking for the continent' (see the Declaration as transcribed in Blommaert 2001: 132–3). Regarding education, the declaration states that 'All African children have the unalienable right to attend school and learn in their mother tongues' (2001: 132). In a critical analysis of this declaration, Blommaert (2001) casts doubts about the effectiveness of language policies based on the LHR paradigm, suggesting, among other things, that institutionalization of linguistic rights does not necessarily bring social justice, as claimed by LHR advocates. He warns that such policies could even deepen social inequalities.

The practical consequence of these continental and transcontinental efforts can be attested through a new trend of multilingual language policies in sub-Saharan Africa. The South African and Eritrean language policies are illustrative examples of constitutionally declared multilingual policies (see Hailemariam 2002; Obondo 2008). The blossoming of bilingual experimental schools can be illustrated by the cases of Burkina Faso, Mali, Niger (see Alidou and Jung 2001; Alidou 2004; Alidou et al. 2006), Angola and Mozambique (Benson 2000; Chimbutane 2009, 2011).

As mentioned earlier, concurrent with this trend towards multilingualism and multiculturalism, is the renewed advancement of English into the domains of local, national and regional languages. A salient feature here is the backward movement attested in some countries that, until recently, accorded a privileged space to some national languages. Some of these countries are now switching back towards English, especially for educational purposes. In all these cases, the advancement of English is associated with the globalization of the world economy: English is perceived as the language of science, technology, business and communication. That is, the language that allows individuals and states to compete in the global market. The cases of India (Mohanty 2008; Vaish 2008), Malaysia (Nunan 2003; Martin 2005) and Pakistan (Rassool and Mansoor 2007) are illustrative of this backward trend.

In the Indian Constitution of 1950, although Hindi was declared the national language, English was maintained as the official language of the country. The vision then was to develop Hindi for the following 15 years so that it could take over the role of the official language from English (Vaish 2008). However, protests from both Hindi and non-Hindi speakers, led to Constitution amendment in 1968, in which Hindi and English were declared co-official languages. Despite this institutionalized parity, as Vaish (2008: 23) notes, a few Indian scholars suggest that 'Hindi is losing a power struggle with English'. This is mainly because English emerges as the de facto language of administration, judiciary, business, science and technology. In addition, many parents, including those from lower social classes, are increasingly investing in their children's English medium education, as this language is perceived as a gateway to social mobility. However, Vaish (2008) minimizes this gloomy view by producing evidence of the strong vitality of Hindi in India and by defining knowledge of English as a workplace literacy skill that is added to the repertoire of a bi-multilingual individual. That is, unlike others, Vaish does not view English as a language that endangers Indian local languages and associated cultural values.

From independence until recently, Malaysia had abandoned English in favour of a national language policy. Malay was the exclusive language of instruction in state-run schools and Mandarin or Tamil were used in vernacular schools (Nunan 2003). English was taught as a subject from the age of seven, in Malay schools, and nine, in Mandarin and Tamil schools (ibid.). However, since a policy change in 2003, in addition to being taught as a subject, English has also been used as a medium of instruction for mathematics and science, a change reflecting the global importance attributed to this language in the world economy (Martin 2005).

Like Malaysia, Pakistan also adopted a national language policy at independence. Urdu was declared as the language of Pakistani nationhood, although English has been increasingly regarded as the de facto national official language (Rassool and Mansoor 2007). Although Urdu is still *de jure* language medium used in all government schools (grades 1–12), with English as a compulsory subject from grade 5 or 6, the number of private, English-medium schools serving children of local elites is on the rise (see indicative figures in Rassool and Mansoor 2007).

Similarly, the fact that Kiswahili is still not being used as the medium of instruction beyond primary level in Tanzania has in part also to do with the perception of English, and not Kiswahili, as the language that opens the prospects for national and international competitiveness (see Campbell-Makini 2000; Rubagumya 2003).

Universalism, linguistic human rights and socio-economic mobility

There are at least three issues associated with the promotion of national, regional or global multilingualism: these have to do with the need to find contextually situated language policies and the need to conciliate LHR and the demands of an increasingly globalized capitalist economy.

Supranational coalitions, such as the African Union and its African Academy of Languages, have the merit of allowing the coordination of efforts and statement of common visions/goals about common broad challenges, such as the promotion of local languages in education. Although I concur that this is a wise path to be followed, I shall also stress that the decisions taken at these supranational levels should be perceived as providing broad, sensitizing frameworks, needing to be adjusted to the particularities of each member state or social group. For example, as African countries are at different stages in terms of promoting and making effective use of African languages in official domains, including in education, we should not try to set uniform goals and find uniform solutions for all the cases, but rather try to respond to the historical, political, economic and linguistic specificities of each country or group of countries, which includes the consideration of their historical and sociopolitical backgrounds. For example, regarding the use of African languages in education, although for countries like Mozambique, which has never had such an experience before, it may be socially and culturally fulfilling, although not be technically 'correct', just to have an early-exit bilingual programme in place (Chimbutane 2009, 2011), for Tanzania the target may be to extend the use of Kiswahili medium to the secondary level and beyond. A critical analysis of the reasons why many countries failed to provide basic education for all by 2000, as declared in Dakar in 1990, or why many will fail to offer universal primary education by 2015, as declared in New York in 2000, should be instructive here.

Despite the recognized relevance of the LHR approach in affirming the rights of speakers of low-status languages, critics point to some practical and theoretical aspects that constrain the fulfilment of this ideal. In terms of practicalities, analysts have drawn attention to constraints such as poor development of many low-status languages (lack of a standardized orthographic system, paucity of printed materials, lack of a literacy tradition) and situations in which there are so few speakers of a certain language in a given setting that it is not economically viable to provide mother tongue-based bilingual education for such a group (e.g. Sridhar 1994, in relation to the Indian context).

In terms of theoretical approaches, advocates of LHR have mainly been criticized for not problematizing some of their key constructs (May 2000; Stroud 2001). May (2000: 371–2), for example, points out that the problem of advocates of LHR is that they 'assume the identity of linguistic minority groups as given, the collective aims of linguistic minority groups as uniform, and the notion of minority groups as unproblematic'.

The language rights debate revolves around the primacy that should be accorded to each of the following three levels of rights: individual, communitarian and societal rights. If all levels are taken into consideration, this suggests that there is a need to adopt a conciliatory approach to language rights in order to pursue the ideal of a cohesive society. This includes the consideration of the right of individuals and communities to choose not to be educated in their heritage language, but in a language they feel is appropriate, for example, for their socio-economic advancement.

Indeed, based on their social status and their expectations of material rewards in a particular historical context, people may favour, not prefer or even reject bilingual education for their children, or at least certain types of it. For example, the provision of bilingual education to speakers of low-status languages has led to mixed reactions, ranging from high demand to complete rejection. High demand is usually associated with cases in which bilingual education is highly valued, mainly based on the symbolic rewards it promises, whereas cases in which it is not preferred, or rejected outright, are usually associated with situations in which such assessment is based only on potential material rewards. Situations in which mother tongue-based bilingual education is not preferred (at least by some powerful social segments) have been attested in different post-colonial multilingual contexts, including Kenya (Bunyi 2008), South Africa (Martin 1997; Banda 2000; Makoe 2009), Tanzania (Rubagumya 2003), India (Sridhar 1994), Malaysia and Singapore (Gupta 1997) and Vietnam (Wright 2002). In all these contexts, parents' justifications for not preferring bilingual education gravitate around the idea that learning through a low-status language delays or even hampers access to the dominant language and culture, the perceived prerequisites for socio-economic mobility. In extreme cases, bilingual education can even be seen as denial of access to languages of privilege, as Gupta (1997) reports in relation to certain ethnic groups in Singapore and Malaysia and also Bamgbose (1999) in relation to reactions to Bantu education in Soweto, South Africa. These perceptions explain in part why many parents in multilingual contexts, especially middle-class parents, prefer to enrol their children in private or international schools using European languages (notably English) for instruction. This is increasingly seen as the quickest and most efficient way to assimilate the dominant language and associated culture (e.g. Hong Kong,

India, Kenya, Pakistan, South Africa, Tanzania and Vietnam). The erroneous rationale adopted is that a second or foreign language is better learnt when used as a medium of instruction, rather than when it is simply taught as a subject (see Rubagumya 2003; Brock-Utne 2005; Bunyi 2008).

As research and empirical evidence shows that good-quality initial education in one's first language leads to better proficiency and academic achievement in a L2 (Cummins 2000), parents' fears may be regarded as not justified. However, there are cases in which such concerns are real, not just a product of ideological discourses. Indeed, like in any form of education, if bilingual education is poorly designed and/or implemented, it cannot equip students with the necessary capital resources for social mobility. In fact, in various post-colonial contexts, including Kenya (Bunyi 2008) and Tanzania (Rubagumya 2003), in addition to the language medium, parents' preferences for private schools has also to do with the perception that public schools are failing to provide quality education for their children, although, as Rubagumya argues in relation to Tanzania, not all private schools are as good as parents think.

Despite the arguments about cognitive, cultural and psychological advantages that advocates of bilingual education have put forward to support instruction in children's first language, parental considerations about the socio-economic rewards associated with dominant languages and cultures pose a real challenge that needs to be addressed (Hornberger 2006). Adjudicating the right to mother tongue education is not enough, it must also lead to the acquisition of the resources equated with upward social mobility or at least lead to the re-valuing of a low-status language as a valid form of cultural capital in mainstream markets; otherwise, people may overlook their language rights. Therefore, in order to win the hearts of an increasing number of speakers of low-status languages, especially those of middle-class parents, who tend to give greater weight to socio-economic mobility than maintenance, bilingual programmes have to be designed and implemented in such a way that, in addition to the symbolic/heritage language, children achieve high levels of proficiency and academic attainment in the much sought-after language(s) of capital value.

In addition to being viewed as languages of national and international socio-economic mobility, we should also take into account the fact that, in many post-colonial contexts, European languages are also being 'nationalized': they are also nativized and adopted as symbolic languages of identity. *Nativization* is an acculturation process whereby a transplanted language acquires a localized linguistic identity (Kachru 1992). The nativization of European languages is celebrated as a way of taking ownership of them, instead of being sanctioned as is the case of English in schools and certain political circles in Hong Kong (Lin 2001) and Malaysia (Martin 2005), for example. Approaches favouring the nativization of European languages are being taken in certain circles in countries such as India (Mohanty 2008) and Singapore (Pakir 2008) in relation to English. Also freedom movements such as the Frente de Libertação de Moçambique (Frelimo) in Mozambique and the African National Congress (ANC) in South Africa adopted, respectively, Portuguese and English as languages of liberation. Thus, instead of being constructed as 'their languages', former colonial languages can also be adopted and adapted in the service of social change (Ricento 2006).

Therefore, in order to influence change in language ideology in post-colonial contexts, a 'soft' and situated approach that could conciliate the technical voice of experts and these of politicians and ordinary citizens (individually or organized in groups) may prove to be more productive than a confrontational and context-free one. Approaches that call for bottom-up agency in LPP are already being proposed across contexts. For example, using African experiences as illustrative cases, Stroud (2001) proposes the notion of 'linguistic citizenship', which is intended to capture the idea that speech communities should (and should be allowed to) exercise control over their languages and negotiate their political and socio-economic participation at the societal level. Among other things, this concept is meant to help mediate between universal and particular, between national and individual interests.

In a similar vein, and focusing on the sub-Saharan context, Omoniyi (2007) proposes a complementary relationship between micro- and macro-language planning. In his framework, macro-language planning comprises nation-state level planning and policy, whereas micro-level planning encompasses LPP, which focus on individual, group and community levels, including those involving non-governmental organizations. In order to operate effectively in different contexts, Omoniyi (ibid.) suggests that, rather than competing, micro- and macro-level agents ought to engage with and recognize each other's contribution.

The two models above are in tune with the view of LPP processes as interacting across different layers (Ricento and Hornberger 1996) and also underscore the importance of the post-modern paradigm, which highlights the role of human agency in social change.

In summary, what we need are contextually based, pluralistic language policies, ones that accommodate state, community and individual linguistic rights, including citizens' rights to choose to be educated in the language(s) they think will best equip them with the symbolic capital needed for their upward socio-economic mobility. Among other things, this approach accords greater significance to the role of citizens as social agents who are capable of negotiating the functions and ideologies associated with the languages in their repertoires (Canagarajah 2000).

Related topics

Lessons from pre-colonial multilingualism; discourses about linguistic diversity; rethinking discourses around the 'English-cosmopolitan' correlation; linguistic diversity and education; multilingual pedagogies; disinventing multilingualism.

Further reading

Djité, P. G. (2008) *The Sociolinguistics of Development in Africa*, London: Multilingual Matters.
(A study of the place and role of African languages in the development of the continent, with special focus on their place and role in education, health, economy and governance.)

Hornberger, N. H. (ed.) (2003) *Continua of Biliteracy: An Ecological Framework for Educational Policy, Research, and Practice in Multilingual Settings*, Clevedon: Multilingual Matters.
(A cross-contextual critical analysis of multilingual education practice, policy and research, based on an ecological framework.)

Rassool, N. (2007) *Global Issues in Language, Education and Development: Perspectives from Postcolonial Countries*, Clevedon: Multilingual Matters.
(A historical survey of the relationship between language-in-education policy and development prospects in sub-Saharan Africa and South Asian contexts.)

Ricento, T. (ed.) (2006) *An Introduction to Language Policy: Theory and Method*, Oxford: Blackwell.
(A historical take on theories and methods that have been used in language policy research and practice.)

Tollefson, J. W. (ed.) (2002) *Language Policies in Education: Critical Issues*, London: Lawrence Erlbaum.
(A critical analysis of language policies in education, with particular emphasis on their social and political implications in various multilingual contexts.)

Bibliography

Abdulaziz, M. H. (2003) 'The history of language policy in Africa with reference to language choice in education', in A. Ouane (ed.) *Towards a Multilingual Culture of Education*, Hamburg: UNESCO Institute of Education.

Alexander, N. (1999) 'An African renaissance without African languages', *Social Dynamics* 25(1): 1–12.
——(2003) *The African Renaissance and the Use of African Languages in Tertiary Education*, PRAESA occasional papers No. 13, Cape Town: Project for the Study of Alternative Education in South Africa (PRAESA).

Alidou, H. (2004) 'Medium of instruction in post-colonial Africa', in J. W. Tollefson and A. B. M. Tsui (eds) *Medium of Instruction Policies: Which Agenda? Whose Agenda?* London: Lawrence Erlbaum.

Alidou, H., Boly, A., Brock-Utne, B., Diallo, Y. S., Heugh, K. and Wolff, H. E. (2006) *Optimizing Learning and Education in Africa – The Language Factor: A Stock-taking Research on Mother Tongue and Bilingual Education in Sub-Saharan Africa*, available online at http://adeanet.org/biennial-2006/doc/document/B3_MTBLE_en.pdf

Alidou, H. and Jung, I. (2001) 'Education language policies in Francophone Africa: What have we learned from the field experiences?' in S. Baker (ed.) *Language Policy: Lessons from Global Models*, Monterey, CA: Institute of International Studies.

Ansre, G. (1978) 'The use of indigenous languages in education in sub-Saharan Africa: Presuppositions, lessons, and prospects', in J. Alatis (ed.) *Georgetown Round Table on Language and Linguistics*, Washington, DC: Georgetown University Press.

Arnove, A. K. and Arnove, R. F. (1997) 'A reassesment of education, language and cultural imperialism: British colonialism in India and Africa', in W. Cummings and N. McGinn (eds.) *International Handbook of Education and Development: Preparing Schools, Students and Nations for the Twenty-First Century*. Oxford: Elsevier Science Ltd, 87–101.

Asfaha, Y. M. (2009) 'Literacy acquisition in multilingual Eritrea: A comparative study of reading across languages and scripts', unpublished PhD thesis, Tilburg University.

Bamgbose, A. (1991) *Language and the Nation: The Language Question in Sub-Saharan Africa*, Edinburgh: Edinburgh University Press.
——(1999) 'African language development and language planning', *Social Dynamics* 25(1): 13–30.
——(2000) *Language and Exclusion: The Consequences of Language Policies in Africa*, Hamburg: Lit Verlag Munster.

Banda, F. (2000) 'The dilemma of mother tongue: Prospects for bilingual education in South Africa', *Language, Culture and Curriculum* 13(1): 51–66.

Benson, C. (2000) 'The primary bilingual education experiment in Mozambique, 1993 to 1997', *International Journal of Bilingual Education and Bilingualism* 3(3): 149–66.

Blackledge, A. (2008) 'Language ecology and language ideology', in A. Creese, P. Martin and N. H. Hornberger (eds) *Encyclopedia of Language and Education*, 2nd edn, vol. 9: *Ecology of Language*, New York: Springer Science+Business Media LLC.

Blommaert, J. (2001) 'The Asmara Declaration as a sociolinguistic problem: Reflections on scholarship and linguistic rights', *Journal of Sociolinguistics* 5(1): 131–55.
——(2005) 'Situating language rights: English and Swahili in Tanzania revisited', *Journal of Sociolinguistics* 9(3): 390–417.

Bokamba, E. G. (1991) 'French colonial language policies and their legacies', in D. F. Marshall (ed.) *Language Planning: Focusschrift in Honor of Joshua A. Fishman*, vol. 3, Amsterdam: John Benjamins.

Brock-Utne, B. (2005) 'Language-in-education policies and practices in Africa with a special focus on Tanzania and South Africa: Insights from research in progress', in A. M. Y. Lin and P. W. Martin (2005) *Decolonisation, Globalisation: Language in Education Policy and Practice*, Clevedon: New Perspectives on Language and Education.

Bunyi, G. (2008) 'Constructing elites in Kenya: Implications for classroom language practices in Africa', in M. Martin-Jones, A. M. de Mejia and N. H. Hornberger (eds) *Encyclopedia of Language and Education*, 2nd edn, vol. 3: *Discourse and Education*, New York: Springer Science +Business Media LLC.

Campbell-Makini, Z. M. R. (2000) 'The language of schooling: Deconstructing myths about African languages', in S. B. Makoni and N. Kamwangamalu (eds) *Language and Institutions in Africa*, Cape Town: Centre for Advanced Studies of African Society.

Canagarajah, A. S. (2000) 'Negotiating ideologies through English: Strategies from the periphery', in T. Ricento (ed.) *Ideology, Politics and Language Policies: Focus on English*, Amsterdam: John Benjamins.

Chimbutane, F. (2009) 'The purpose and value of bilingual education: A critical, linguistic ethnographic study of two rural primary schools in Mozambique', unpublished PhD thesis, University of Birmingham.

Chimbutane, F. (2011) *Rethinking Bilingual Education in Post-Colonial Contexts*. Clevedon: Multilingual Matters.

Creese, A. and Martin, P. (2008) 'Classroom ecologies: A case study from a Gujarati Complementary school in England', in A. Creese, P. Martin and N. H. Hornberger (eds) *Encyclopaedia of Language and Education*, 2nd edn, vol. 9: Ecology of Language, New York: Springer Science+Business Media LLC.

Creese, A., Martin, P. and Hornberger, N. H. (eds) (2008) 'Ecology of Language', in N. H. Hornberger (ed.) *Encyclopedia of Language and Education*, 2nd edn, New York: Springer Science +Business Media LLC.

Cummins, J. (2000) *Language, Power and Pedagogy: Bilingual Children in the Crossfire*, Clevedon: Multilingual Matters.

Djité, P. G. (2008) *The Sociolinguistics of Development in Africa*, London: Multilingual Matters.

Errington, J. (2008) *Linguistics in a Colonial World: A Story of Language, Meaning and Power*, Oxford: Blackwell Publishing.

Fafunwa, A. B. (1990) 'Using national languages in education: A challenge to African educators', in UNESCO/UNICEF (eds) *African Thoughts on the Prospects of Education for Al. Dakar, 27–30 November 1989*, Dakar: UNESCO Regional Office for Education in Africa.

Freeman, R. (1998) *Bilingual Education and Social Change*, Clevedon: Multilingual Matters.

Field, R. F. (2008) 'Identity, community and power in bilingual education', in J. Cummins and N. H. Hornberger (eds) *Encyclopedia of Language and Education*, 2nd edn, vol. 5: *Bilingual Education*, New York: Springer Science+Business Media LLC.

Gupta, A. F. (1997) 'When mother-tongue education is not preferred', *Journal of Multilingual and Multicultural Development* 18(6): 496–506.

Hailemariam, C. (2002) *Language and Education in Eritrea: A Case Study of Language Diversity, Policy and Practice*, Amsterdam: Aksant Academic Publishers.

Heugh, K. (2008) 'Language policy and education in Southern Africa', in S. May and N. H. Hornberger (eds) *Encyclopedia of Language and Education*, 2nd edn., vol. 1: *Language Policy and Political Issues in Education*, New York: Springer Science+Business Media LLC.

Hornberger, N. H. (2002) 'Multilingual language policies and the continua of biliteracy: An ecological approach', *Language Policy* 1: 27–51.

——(ed.) (2003) *Continua of Biliteracy: An Ecological Framework for Educational Policy, Research, and Practice in Multilingual Settings*, Clevedon: Multilingual Matters.

——(2006) 'Frameworks and models in language policy and planning', in T. Ricento (ed.) *An Introduction to Language Policy: Theory and Method*, Oxford: Blackwell.

——(2008) 'Continua of biliteracy', in A. Creese, P. W. Martin and N. H. Hornberger (eds) *Encyclopedia of Language and Education*, 2nd edn, vol. 9: *Ecology of Language*, New York: Springer Science+Business Media LLC.

Küper, W. (2003) 'The necessity of introducing mother tongues in education systems of developing countries', in A. Ouane (ed.) *Towards a Multilingual Culture of Education*, Paris: UNESCO Institute of Education.

Kachru, B. B. (1992) 'Models for non-native Englishes', in B. B. Kachru (ed.) *The Other Tongue: English across Cultures*, Urbana: University of Illinois Press.

Lin, A. M. Y. (2001) 'Symbolic domination and the bilingual classroom practices in Hong Kong', in M. Heller and M. Martin-Jones (eds) *Voices of Authority: Education and Linguistic Difference*, London: Ablex.

Makoe, P. B. (2009) '"Black children in a white school": Language ideology and identity in a desegregated South African primary school', unpublished PhD thesis, The Institute of Education, University of London.

Martin, D. (1997) 'Towards a new multilingual language policy in education in South Africa: Different approaches to meet different needs', *Educational Review* 49(2): 129–42.

Martin, P. (2005) '"Safe" language practices in two rural schools in Malaysia: Tensions between policy and practice', in A. M. Y. Lin and P. W. Martin (eds) *Decolonisation, Globalisation: Language-in-education Policy and Practice*, Clevedon: Multilingual Matters.

May, S. (2000) 'Uncommon languages: The challenges and possibilities of minority language rights', *Journal of Multilingual and Multicultural Development* 21(5): 366–85.

Mazrui, A. (2000) 'The World Bank, the language question and the future of African education', in S. Federici, G. Caffentzis and O. Alidou (eds) *A Thousand Flowers: Social Struggles Against Structural Adjustment in African Universities*, Trenton, NJ: Africa World Press, Inc.

Mohanty, A. (2008) 'Multilingual education in India', in J. Cummins and N. H. Hornberger (eds) *Encyclopedia of Language and Education,* 2nd edn, vol. 5: *Bilingual Education*, New York: Springer Science+Business Media LLC.

Moses, M. S. (2000) 'Why bilingual education policy is needed: A philosophical response to the critics', *Bilingual Research Journal* 24(4): 333–54.

Nunan, D. (2003) 'The impact of English as a global language on educational policies and practices in the Asia-Pacific region', *TESOL Quarterly* 37(4): 589–613.

Nyati-Ramahobo, L. (2000) 'Language situation in Botswana', *Current Issues in Language Planning* 1(2): 243–300.

Obondo, M. A. (2008) 'Bilingual education in Africa: An overview', in J. Cummins and N. H. Hornberger (eds) *Encyclopedia of Language and Education,* 2nd edn, vol. 5: *Bilingual Education*, New York: Springer Science+Business Media LLC.

Omoniyi, T. (2007) 'Alternative contexts of language policy and planning in sub-Saharan Africa', *TESOL Quarterly* 41(3): 533–49.

Pakir, A. (2008) 'Bilingual education in Singapore', in J. Cummins and N. H. Hornberger (eds) *Encyclopedia of Language and Education,* 2nd edn, vol. 5: *Bilingual Education*, New York: Springer Science+Business Media LLC.

Pennycook, A. (2003) 'The perils of language ecology.' Paper presented at the International Conference on Language, Education and Diverstiy (LED), Waikato University, New Zealand.

Phillipson, R. (1992) *Linguistic Imperialism*, Oxford: Oxford University Press.

Phillipson, R. and Skutnabb-Kangas, T. (1996) 'English-only worldwide or language ecology', *TESOL Quarterly*, 30: 429–452.

Rassool, N. (2007) *Global Issues in Language, Education and Development: Perspectives from Postcolonial Countries*, Clevedon: Multilingual Matters.

Rassool, N. and Mansoor, R. (2007) 'Contemporary issues in language, education and development in Pakistan', in N. Rassool *Global Issues in Language, Education and Development: Perspectives from Postcolonial Countries*, Clevedon: Multilingual Matters.

Ricento, T. (2000) 'Historical and theoretical perspectives in language policy and planning', *Journal of Sociolinguistics* 4(2): 196–213.

——(2006) 'Theoretical perspectives in language policy: An overview', in T. Ricento (ed.) *An Introduction to Language Policy: Theory and Method*, Oxford: Blackwell.

Ricento, T. and Hornberger, N. H. (1996) 'Unpeeling the onion: language planning and policy and the ELT professional', *TESOL Quarterly* 30(3): 401–26.

Rubagumya, C. M. (ed.) (1994) *Teaching and Researching Language in African Classrooms*, Clevedon: Multilingual Matters.

——(2003) 'English medium primary schools in Tanzania: A new "linguistic market" in education', in B. Brock-Utne, Z. Desai, and M. Qorro (eds) *The Language of Instruction in Tanzania and South Africa* (LOITASA), Dar es Salaam: E& D Publishers.

Ruíz, R. (1984) 'Orientations in language planning', *National Association for Bilingual Education (NABE) Journal* 8(2): 15–34.

Sridhar, K.K. (1994) 'Mother tongue maintenance and multiculturalism', *TESOL Quarterly* 28(3): 628–31.

Stroud, C. (2001) 'African mother-tongue programmes and the politics of language: Linguistic citizenship versus linguistic human rights', *Journal of Multilingual and Multicultural Development* 22(4): 339–55.

Tollefson, J. W. (1991) *Planning Language, Planning Inequality*, New York: Longman.

UNESCO (1990) *Education for All by Year 2000*, Paris: UNESCO.

Vaish, V. (2008) *Biliteracy and Globalization: English Language Education in India*, Clevedon: Multilingual Matters.

Wright, S. (2002) 'Language education and foreign relations in Vietnam', in J. W. Tollefson (ed.) *Language Policies in Education: Critical Issues*, London: Lawrence Erlbaum.

Young, I. M. (1990) *Justice and the Politics of Difference*. Princeton, N.J.: Princeton Universtiy Press.

——(1993) 'Together in difference: Transforming the logic of group political conflict', in J. Squires (ed.) *Principled Positions: Postmodernism and the Rediscovery of Value*, London: Lawrence and Wishart.

10

Regional minorities, education and language revitalization

Durk Gorter and Jasone Cenoz

Introduction

Speakers of regional minority languages in Europe are almost by definition bilingual and increasingly multilingual. From a young age onwards they learn a regional minority language, a majority state language and in many cases an international language, predominately English. During much of the nineteenth and twentieth century, many regional minority languages underwent serious decline and most of them are seriously endangered. More recently several minority groups have undertaken efforts to revitalize their language. Some languages have obtained an official status and a degree of legal protection. However, the support is often symbolic and solid language policies have only developed in a few cases.

Learning a language becomes a different issue when seen from the perspective of the speaker of a socially dominant language or for a speaker of a minority language. For the majority language speaker, it is taken for granted that the language of the home and the school are the same. Parents usually speak this language with their children and at school the language is a subject and the only medium of instruction. For a minority language speaker, however, there is frequently a mismatch between the language of the home and the school.

For a long time minority languages were neglected, or even forbidden to be used in educational contexts. Their speakers were distrusted and discriminated against. The focus was on teaching the dominant language and in making it a necessity for all the citizens. Over the last decades this has gradually changed and at the beginning of the twenty-first century the preservation and protection of linguistic and cultural diversity is more accepted. At the European level, there is a growing political consensus about the value of protection and promotion of regional minority languages, in which the European Parliament has played an important role (Strubell 2007: 169; Stolfo 2009). Nowadays, the official discourse in European documents contains expressions such as 'Multilingualism an asset for Europe', and 'the value and opportunities of the EU's linguistic diversity' (European Commission 2008). The promotion of multilingualism seems high on the political agenda of 'Europe'.

The changes in the climate can be illustrated with the case of the Irish language. In 2007 Irish was added to the list of official languages of the European Union (EU). When Ireland entered the forerunner of the EU (the European Communities) in 1973, the Irish language was not included as an official language, disregarding the fact that Irish had been the 'first national language' of Ireland since the foundation of an independent state in 1921. At that time Europe gave Irish only a special 'treaty-status'. That was a symbolic recognition, which meant that only a limited number of European documents (such as the treaties of Rome or Maastricht) were translated into Irish. For all practical purposes Irish was considered a minority language or a 'lesser used language'. Perhaps this was understandable because in Ireland itself the Irish language was also dealt with in much the same way. Education has been the main agency through which the Irish state tried, without much success, to revitalize Irish, after the language had lost the majority of its speakers in the eighteenth and nineteenth century. In the literature on language revitalization, the policy in Ireland has been put down as a case of failure (Spolsky 2004: 19; Mac Giolla Chríost 2005: 133; Ó Laoire 2008). That Irish became an official language of the EU alongside 22 other state languages indicates that an important change has taken place at the European level concerning the importance of recognizing and promoting linguistic diversity. At the same time, recent studies show that the provision for Irish in education has not equally improved (Harris 2008).

Various labels are in use to refer to language varieties spoken by minority groups. 'Minority language' does refer to a specific category of languages, for which sometimes also terms such as 'lesser used', 'heritage', 'stateless', 'indigenous', 'dominated', 'threatened', 'endangered' or 'ethnic' languages are used. Minority languages are distinguished from or in opposition to the category 'majority language'; languages that are also referred to as 'dominant', 'national' 'official' or 'state' languages (see also Grenoble and Whaley 2006: 14). In Europe, the term 'minority language' seems the common designation. Due to a number of factors, there is a major divide between Indigenous or regional language groups on the one hand and immigrant and refugee groups on the other hand (Extra and Gorter 2001: 2). In North America, the term 'heritage language' is more commonly used and refers to the languages of immigrants, refugees and Indigenous groups. In spite of the fact that many of the same or similar issues are involved in education and revitalization of minority languages in general, we will focus in this contribution on *regional* minority languages in Europe.

Although not undisputed, the definition given in the *Charter for Regional or Minority Languages* of the Council of Europe (1998) seems to have gained wide usage over the last ten years. The Charter refers to 'languages that are traditionally used within a given territory of a state by nationals of that state who form a group numerically smaller than the rest of the state's population and [are] different from the official language(s) of that state'. One of the contentious issues about the Charter is that it explicitly excludes dialects of the official state language(s) and the languages of migrants. The difficulty of arriving at an agreed definition is related to the different criteria that may be used to label a linguistic variety as a minority language (Capotorti 1979).

Early developments and current policy issues

Historically, minorities are related closely to the development of the modern system of nation states since the sixteenth century. In a process of state formation the usual aim is national homogeneity and uniformity. As nationalism developed, language was seen as essential to unify the state. The monolingualizing ideology of 'one nation, one state, one language' left no space for minority languages (Judge 2000). For a long time minority languages were stigmatized and disadvantaged. As a consequence most of those languages began to decline, in particular during the nineteenth and twentieth centuries. Important contributing factors were industrialization, the building of railroads, military conscription and generalized basic education. The school language in most cases became the dominant standardized language of the recently formed unitary states. The 'monolingual habitus' (Gogolin 2002) is a strong ideology that still persists today.

State formation is still going on in Europe as shown by the examples of the Baltic States, the splitting of Czechoslovakia and the new independent states belonging to the former Yugoslav Republic, most recently Kosovo. These developments have also led to the construction and definition of new minority groups.

Many language groups found themselves at a certain period of history inside the borders of a larger unitary state and became speakers of what we can call today 'unique minority languages', such as Corsican in France or Welsh in the UK. Other non-dominant groups were divided over more than one state and the language they speak may have a different status in the different states, but they are also 'unique minority languages' because they are a non-dominant language in any state. A clear example is Catalan, spoken by approximately 7.3 million people. The minority language has an official status in the regions of Catalonia, the Balearic Islands and Valencia in Spain. At the same time, it is the official language of the miniature state of Andorra, where Spanish and French are also widely spoken. However, Catalan has far less recognition and support in the town of Alghero on the island of Sardinia in Italy or in the south of France where it is also spoken by part of the population. Another example is Basque, which is spoken on both sides of the Spanish–French border but there are huge differences in the amount of support from the authorities (Cenoz 2008: 15–16).

The administrative borders inside a state can also have important consequences for a minority language. Examples are Sorbian in Germany that is divided between the *Länder* of Brandenburg and Saxony, and Ladin in Italy that is spread over five valleys in the Dolomites, which belong to three different provinces. Each *Land* or province has a different policy for the minority language on its territory.

During the last decades activities on behalf of minority languages have flourished, in part as a grass-roots reaction to processes of homogenization and globalization (Glaser 2007). A number of minority groups have obtained provisions for language learning, which could hardly be expected in 1970. In particular, the steps taken for Basque and Catalan in Spain or Welsh in the UK can be called remarkable. Their policies culminate in measures in high-prestige domains such as higher education, public administration and the mass media. The result of all these efforts is that the patterns of long-term language decline have at least slowed down and are seemingly reversed. It is clear that a strong, fully fledged policy for a minority language can be successful. However, there is no guarantee that the speakers will continue to learn and use their language and transmit it to the next generations because sustainable language relationships are hard to achieve. Unfortunately, those few language groups are the exception, and most other regional minority languages in Europe are less well off and many are severely endangered (Moseley 2009).

The outcome of historical processes is a multifaceted constellation of languages in Europe. The current 47 member states of the Council of Europe have 41 languages as official state languages. That figure includes the 27 member states of the EU, which share 23 official languages. As minorities are defined by their relation to the state, the number of regional minority languages on the territory of Europe is many times larger (Extra and Gorter 2008). Here we focus on regional minority languages. Among these regional minority groups there is a lot of variation. Some are extremely small and on the verge of extinction such as Livonian in Latvia or Ume Sámi in Sweden, where the youngest speakers are over 60 years of age. But other language groups are more vital because they have obtained political support and strong favourable attitudes by their speakers. Education can contribute to revitalizing those languages so that they have a sustainable future.

The way in which education can contribute to language revitalization for a minority language group is not uniform, but depends on several background factors and characteristics, such as demographic facts (size, location), and sociocultural, economic and political factors. The national state has a great deal of determining power. Over a long period of time states have built a national educational system, which is not going to be easily adapted to the needs of a minority language group.

In this chapter we focus on 'unique regional minority languages', such as Basque, Frisian or Welsh. We also include regional minority language groups with a kin state, such as German in Belgium or in Denmark because they may also be at risk in the region where they are spoken. Of course, these cross-border languages are not threatened languages as such; the same reasoning applies *mutatis mutandis* to most migrant languages.

Key issues: analytic frameworks

Many factors influence the social position and development of minority language groups. Some of these factors are language use in the family, protection by the government, provisions in the media, development of a written standard, attitudes towards the language and related identities, level of activism and, last but not least, education, that is, the schooling *in* and *through* the minority language.

The distinction between teaching 'in' a regional minority language (as the medium of instruction) and 'of' the minority language (as a subject on the curriculum) can be related to the distinction between 'weak' and 'strong' forms of bilingual education (Baker 2001, 2003). In the case of weak forms of bilingual education the aim is a shift of the home language of the child to the majority or dominant language of society (transitional bilingual education). In contrast, strong forms of bilingual education have bilingualism or multilingualism as their desired outcome. Language use inside the curriculum of the school is rather complex in practice. It can be summarized as a typology with four categories:

- No minority language teaching at all;
- Minority language as a subject, the dominant language as a medium of instruction;
- Both the minority language and the dominant language as a medium of instruction;
- The minority language as a medium of instruction, dominant language as a subject.

The fifth logical possibility, no teaching at all of the dominant language, does not occur.

The number of regional minorities where there is no teaching at all has decreased in recent decades, but the small amount of teaching available may be confined to primary education only. Most frequent is the pattern denoted in category (2), with the minority language only as a subject. Categories (3) and (4) contain fewer language groups, and in particular category (4) may, where it occurs, be limited to certain levels of the educational system, in particular pre-primary or primary education. This typology leaves aside the linguistic or philological study of languages in a language department at a university.

Even in a bilingual classroom where the aim is language maintenance, usage practices may reflect the position of the minority language and the dominant language in wider society. More subtle interactions may take place between teachers and students inside the classrooms. The teacher's discourse may let the student know that the minority language has less value, e.g. for economic advancement, or is less well developed linguistically, or cannot be used for all social domains (Gombos 2002; Heller 1994).

187

The teaching of the minority language is, of course, of greatest importance. Does this teaching lead to maintenance or does it encourage the transition to the dominant language? Especially in the latter case, a bit of mainly symbolic attention to the minority language in education (a few hours as a subject in primary schools, for example), works as a stimulus for assimilation to mainstream society, rather than as safeguard for the language. In the case of a stronger provision for minority education, the aim is often explicitly to contribute to revitalization. Learning the language is conceived of as enrichment. The outcome of such education is that pupils will become proficient bilinguals and biliterals. The issue of de facto language use outside the school remains a major challenge even in the strongest cases.

In order to determine the contribution education can make to revitalize a regional minority language, we have to look at the wider historical, political and socio-economic context. There are many studies that analyse the situation of minority languages in general. Those studies have led to the creation of typologies, models and scales, which may indicate degrees of risk or vitality of these languages. A well-known example is the model of Ethnolinguistic Vitality by Giles *et al.* (1977). But also others such as Anderson (1990), Churchill (1986) and Edwards (1991, 2007) have proposed typologies or lists of key variables that influence language shift and maintenance. These proposals diagnose language transmission in the family and the community, as well as language instruction in educational contexts as important factors that contribute to the survival and revival of European minority languages. The two models of Reversing Language Shift (Fishman 1991, 2001) and the Euromosaic study (2004; Williams 2005) will be discussed here as major approaches that have proven to be analytically strong.

Reversing language shift: GIDS

The debate on minority languages in general, and education in particular, got an important push by Fishman's 1991 book on '*Reversing Language Shift*' (RLS). His RLS perspective combines a more distanced academic study with a perspective of intervention and the choice of the most appropriate means of protecting minority languages (Fishman 2001: 450).

The fundamental assumptions of the RLS theory are summarized in the 'Graded Inter-generational Disruption Scale' (GIDS) (Fishman 1991: 335). The GIDS is similar to Richter's scale of earthquakes to indicate the degree to which a language is 'broken up' or 'at risk'. The GIDS is intended to be a diagnostic tool that offers a set of priorities. There are eight stages and those are 'nothing but a logical set of priorities or targets to guide RLS-efforts' (Fishman 2001: 465).

Fishman's scale is an effort to assess different forms of support for minority languages and their chances for survival. He draws attention to intergenerational mother tongue transmission as the most important element of language maintenance. It is the linkage of stages, i.e. language functions, that matters (Fishman 2001: 451). Stages 8 to 5 are on the 'weak side' and constitute the 'minimum program' of RLS (Fishman 1991: 400) for which speakers of the minority language do not need the cooperation and approval of those in power. In contrast, stages 4 to 1 are on the 'strong side', and they are related to the 'high power' stages (Fishman 2001: 473), which are less willingly relinquished by the dominant groups. Language learning in the home and the community are important according to Fishman, but he also emphasizes the importance of education in more than one stage. However, complete reliance on schools as an agent of language revitalization is an almost certain recipe for failure.

Table 10.1 Stages of the Graded Intergenerational Disruption Scale, with European regional minorities as examples

---

Stage 8: Reconstructing the language and adult acquisition of the language. Examples of this reconstruction work take place for Aroumanian, Cornish and Manx.

Stage 7: Cultural interaction in the language primarily involves the older generation of the community. Example: Sater Frisian in Germany (grandparents go to a playgroup to teach young children the fundamentals of Sater Frisian, a language their parents did not learn).

Stage 6: The intergenerational and demographically concentrated family–home–neighbourhood–community: the basis of mother tongue transmission. As Fishman (1991: 399) warns, 'If this stage is not satisfied, all else can amount to little more than biding time'. Examples: North Frisian, Occitan in France, Sardinian, Occitan in Italy, Catalan in Italy, Pomak in Greece, Berber in Spain.

Stage 5: Schools for literacy acquisition, for the old and for the young, and not in lieu of compulsory education. Many minority languages start promotional activities with adult classes and out-of-school lessons for children. Examples: Irish in Northern Ireland, Franco-Provençal in Italy, Mirandese, Breton, Catalan in Aragon.

Stage 4b: Public schools for minority children, offering some instruction via the minority language, but substantially under control of the dominant language group. For example, this is the case for Frisian in the Netherlands.

Stage 4a: Schools in lieu of compulsory education and substantially under curricular and staffing control of the minority. Examples: Diwan schools in Brittany, Friulian, Sorbian, Ladin, Asturian, Catalan and Basque in France.

Stage 3: The local/regional work sphere, both among minority and among majority speakers. Examples: Sámi in Sweden or Finland, Basque in Navarre, Irish, Occitan in Spain, Gaelic, Corsican.

Stage 2: Local/regional mass media and governmental services. Examples: Catalan in Valencia, Galician.

Stage 1: Education, work sphere, mass media and government operations at higher and nationwide levels. Examples: Catalan in Catalonia, Luxembourgish, Welsh, Basque in the Basque Autonomous Community.

Source: Adapted from Fishman 1991: 395; 2001: 466; examples for each stage from Grin and Moring 2002: 179.

Euromosaic

The Euromosaic study takes the economic restructuring of Europe as a major influence on the reproduction (learning as first language) and production (learning as second language) of minority language groups (Nelde *et al.* 1996). The Euromosaic study was carried out for the European Commission. Case study reports were drafted for 48 different language groups in the then-12 member states. It was updated twice after enlargement of the European Union (EU) with first three new member states (Austria, Finland and Sweden) and again with the 10 member states in 2004 (Euromosaic III 2004; Williams 2005).

The Euromosaic study develops a comparative perspective. The concepts of reproduction and production are related to three primary agencies of socialization: the family, education and the community. The media is a secondary agency of language and cultural socialization. Together these four agencies are responsible for the learning (or not) of a minority language. As far as language learning inside the family is concerned, the degree of language group endogamy is crucial. If members of different language groups intermarry a lot, the chances for language transmission to the next generation are smaller. Migration also can have an important influence.

Table 10.2 Euromosaic study: clustering of unique minority language groups in the EU

Cluster 1	Cluster 2	Cluster 3	Cluster 4
Luxembourgish	Irish (Irl)	Basque (F)	Mirandese (P)
Catalan (Cat, E)	Gaelic (UK)	Corsican (F)	North Frisian (G)
Galician (E)	Frisian (NL)	Catalan (I)	Irish (UK)
Catalan (Val, E)	Friulan (I)	Occitan (I)	Occitan (F)
Basque (CAV, E)	Sorbian (G)	Occitan (F)	Sardinian (I)
Ladin (I)	Basque (Nav, E)	Breton (F)	Sater Frisian (G)
Aranese (E)	Catalan (F)		Aroumanian (Gr)
Welsh (UK)			Cornish (UK)
Catalan (Bal, E)			

Source: Nelde, Strubell and Williams 1996: 35–42, 65.

The school can have a positive influence on production (language learning), but education is usually under control of the authorities, who may not be inclined to give the minority language a prominent place. In several cases education leads to non-reproduction because only the majority language is taught.

Apart from the family, education and the community, three other variables complete the Euromosaic framework. 'Language prestige' is defined as 'the value of a language for social mobility'; 'institutionalisation' refers to 'the extent to which language use … conforms to expected patterns of behaviour' and 'legitimation' refers to legislation and language policies (Nelde, Strubell and Williams 1996: 11–12). On the basis of the seven variables the regional minority groups are ranked according to overall strength. The main variables of the theoretical model are used to develop a scaling instrument, which makes a comparative approach possible. The scales give a good indication of the relative strength of the different groups. In the slightly adapted version the language groups are classified into four clusters (see Table 10.2). Although Euromosaic also includes cross-border minority language groups, here only unique minority language groups are included.

The table has 30 language groups distributed into four clusters. The first cluster contains the nine 'strongest' minority language communities in the EU and the fourth cluster has the eight 'weakest' groups. Grin and Moring (2002: 218) show that the GIDS and the Euromosaic scores are highly correlated. The GIDS and Euromosaic present an overall framework for analysis of revitalization efforts for minority languages, but there are also a number of other key issues that are of particular relevance for education.

Challenges of minority language education

Education is the institution of society where most of formal language learning takes place. The institution of education can be regarded as a crucial tool of language planning. The Euromosaic study (Nelde *et al.* 1996) emphasizes the relevance of education for 'producing' new speakers of a regional minority language group and when education succeeds to do that it will strengthen the language group. However, education can also be a weakening factor. It is clear that in many cases the majority language is dominant in the educational system. Therefore, children become proficient in the majority language and may thus learn to prefer that language over the minority language for many usage functions. In such cases, the schools may in the end contribute more to the endangerment than to the revival of a minority language.

One of the first measures undertaken to revitalize a minority language is most often the provision of some form of teaching. Many regional minority language groups have shown a similar pattern of action, starting with a few hours of extracurricular teaching at the primary level and gradually extending instruction inside the official curriculum, including preschool teaching and the stages of secondary and higher education. Some language groups, such as the Catalan, the Basque and the Welsh, have developed a rather elaborate system for the teaching of the minority language from the earliest stages of education until university and adult education. There, the target learner group has also expanded, from only home or first language (L1) speakers to include those students who do not speak the language with their parents, and learn the minority language as a second language (L2). At first, the aim may have been to stop the decline of the regional minority language, but over time it has become reversing language shift (Fishman 1991).

Most regional minority languages do not have a strong tradition of being used as languages of instruction in education. The introduction in the education system usually has been gradual and in many cases only in the last decades. Regional minority languages have a lot in common, but also differ regarding legal recognition, the curriculum, teaching materials, immigration, new technologies and the spread of English.

One of the most successful cases of the last 30 years is the teaching of the Basque language in the Basque Autonomous Community in Spain. The legal power rests with the regional government, which has led to a system where parents can choose between three models of education: Basque as the medium of instruction and Spanish as a subject; both languages more or less equally the medium of instruction and subject; and a Spanish-dominated model where Basque is a subject. Over the years the number of children who attend the Basque medium model has increased and the Spanish-dominated model is the choice of fewer and fewer parents. The advantages of bilingualism are generally acknowledged. English is introduced at an early age and the aim of the school system is multilingualism (Cenoz 2009). Still there are challenges when it comes to the training of sufficiently qualified teachers, the development of up-to-date materials and the use of new technologies in the classroom. In the last few years many immigrants have come to the Basque country, many from Spanish-speaking countries in Latin America, and a major challenge has been to integrate them into the existing system of three models (Etxeberria and Elosegi 2008). Furthermore, in the Spanish province of Navarre Basque as a minority language in education is not thriving, and in the Basque provinces in the south of France the situation is much worse.

An intermediate case is the Frisian language in the Netherlands. There is a degree of legal recognition, but the education system is still highly centralized at the state level. The minority language Frisian has been an obligatory school subject since 1980 for all primary school children, whether Frisian-speaking at home or not. However, the Inspectorate (2006) has concluded that over the last 30 years little has changed in teaching practices. Thus, the introduction of Frisian as a subject has not had a measurable effect on language promotion and protection. Dutch is very much the omnipresent majority language. In pre-primary education some recent developments point in the direction of a possible change because parents have the choice between a Frisian and Dutch medium stream, and more and more choose Frisian. Similarly, the popularity and the modest growth of the number of trilingual schools, where Frisian, Dutch and English are all taught as a subject and used as a medium of instruction, may lead to a better position for Frisian in education. It is part of a general trend in which trilingual schools are spreading across Europe (Cenoz and Gorter 2005).The problems of a sufficient number of qualified teachers for the three languages, the development of high-quality teaching materials, the demands of new technologies and also the influx of immigrants are also major challenges in the case of Frisian.

When we look at some of the weakest languages in Europe, in some cases the relatively small number of speakers may seem to make it difficult to establish educational provisions. For example, there are an estimated 8,000–10,000 speakers of North Frisian in Germany (Walker 2007). Developing learning materials, training teachers, introducing new technology, etc. may be difficult in such circumstances, in particular when a government neglects rather than supports the minority language. In this case an extra complication is to choose the variety of North Frisian to be used in schools because there are no fewer than eight different varieties. It is hard to imagine improvements for minority languages where the governments actively discourage their teaching, as is the case for Occitan in France or Aroumanian in Greece. Technology could be of help, although thus far the use of minority languages on the Internet is often more symbolic than functional, even when, in quantity, more texts may be published digitally in small minority languages than was possible with traditional printing technology (Wright 2004). Paradoxically, the value of knowing more languages is generally accepted. This opinion does not usually extend to minority languages. Multilingualism is generally seen as an asset when it concerns English as a second or third language (or other 'big' languages such as French, German or Spanish), but not when it concerns smaller state language or regional minority languages.

Policy issues

At the European level one can distinguish between preservationist and revivalist perspectives on minority language policy. In the preservation perspective, all languages have equal value and the loss of any language is the loss of a rich resource of knowledge. In the revivalist perspective, both the home and the school are important to support the transmission and the acquisition of the minority language (De Bot and Gorter 2005).

In recent years two important legal instruments have been established for the protection and promotion of minority languages in Europe: the *Framework Convention for the Protection of National Minorities* and the *Charter for Regional or Minority Languages* (Council of Europe 1995, 1998).

The drafting of the framework Convention is strongly related to the transition processes in Central and Eastern Europe in the early 1990s. The framework Convention was adopted in 1994 and entered into force in 1998. Today there are 39 states that have ratified the Convention and four have signed but did not follow up with ratification; four states are not party to the treaty, among them France and Turkey (as at July 2011).

The aims of the framework Convention are outlined in a rather general way. Education is limited to the encouragement 'to foster knowledge of the culture, language and history of the national minorities, also among the majority' (Article 12) and to 'the recognition of the right to learn the minority language' (Article 14). These articles imply that all citizens should be informed about minorities as part of the school curriculum. The second article confirms the fundamental right to obtain at least some minimal regional minority language teaching provision. Its impact has been greatest in Central Europe (Gal 2000).

The *Charter for Regional or Minority Languages* can be considered more important for language revitalization, in particular for education. The Charter was drafted over a long period of time, starting in 1981 (Ó Riagáin 2001; Woerhling 2006: 23–4). The political changes in Central and Eastern Europe in the early 1990s caused the process to speed up. The Charter was accepted in 1992 by the then-27 members of the Council of Europe. In 1998, the Charter came into operation. Today, there are 47 members, but after ten years only 25 states have ratified the Charter and another eight have signed but not ratified (as at July 2011). This implies that 14 states are not party to this treaty, among them, Belgium and Ireland, with a long tradition of elaborated language policies.

The framework Convention and the Charter may seem superficially more or less equivalent, but in legal terms they are rather different instruments. The aim of the framework Convention is to protect minorities (thus groups) and the Charter is concerned with languages as cultural assets (Woerhling 2006: 32–3).

The Charter wants to accommodate the variety of different languages in the member states of the Council of Europe (Woerhling 2006: 27–8). The degree of protection is not prescribed; thus, a state can choose loose or tight policies. The result is a wide range of provisions across EU member states (Grin 2003). The Charter has obtained increasing acceptance as an international instrument for the protection and promotion of minority languages and can be conceived of as a yardstick on how states ought to deal with the minority languages inside their borders (Craith 2003). Many publications on the Charter or its relevance in general or for one or the other minority language are available (Dunbar *et al.* 2008; Grin and Moring 2002; Grin 2003; Ó Riagáin 2001; Woerhling 2006).

The definition of minority languages in the Charter (quoted in the Introduction) seems to have found a favourable reception. However, it is not the minority language community itself, but the state that decides the degree of protection. Governments may have political reasons to accept or deny a language for inclusion in the Charter. The answer to the layman's question 'Is this variety a language or dialect?' may vary in different contexts. The answer lies not in beliefs about measuring linguistic distance (or mutual intelligibility) or in ideas about codification (in grammars or dictionaries), but it is political and depends on the authorities in power.

A state that ratifies the Charter is required to apply a minimum of 35 from a total of nearly 100 different measures. Most measures are presented as a sliding-scale, going from minimal to more extensive provisions or rights. The state has to choose among the measures 'according to the situation of each language'. This vague formulation gives ultimate discretionary powers to the state. The whole is akin to an *à la carte* menu, where some dishes are obligatory and where something has to be chosen from each course.

Education is seen as a crucial factor in the maintenance and preservation of regional or minority languages. Education is dealt with at all levels, going from preschool education through university and higher level education, including adult courses, teacher training and the teaching of history and culture in relation to minority languages. The Charter requires that regional or minority languages are present 'at all appropriate stages' of the education system. More, in particular as it is stated in the Charter, 'provision will need to be made for teaching "in" the regional or minority language and in others only for teaching "of" the language'. How much the minority languages are in fact used in the curriculum can vary widely.

Overall, most states have chosen a cautious approach. There is a trend to sign at the lowest level of obligation (which is 'to favour and/or encourage' or 'on request with sufficient numbers'). On average the level of protection is low. The optimistic conclusion is that countries now at least recognize the minority languages and provide some protection and promotion, which is a step forward compared to earlier neglect or discrimination. A more pessimistic vision points to the gap between the formal acceptance of soft legal arrangements and de facto implementation. In many cases there has been no improvement in the circumstances of the languages because legal procedures are impossible. Moreover, many factors are outside its scope. For instance, the crucial area of intergenerational transmission (Fishman 2001) is not dealt with at all, but also the private sector receives only scant attention. Apart from the framework Convention and the Charter there are other international instruments that support the principles of teaching minority languages, such as the Oslo and The Hague recommendations by the Organization for Security and Co-operation in Europe (OSCE), the declarations and reports by UNESCO, or the Universal Declaration of Linguistic Rights (Skutnabb-Kangas 2000; May 2001). However, all those instruments are mainly a moral appeal for linguistic human rights, and cannot be legally enforced.

New research directions

It has become clear that regional minority language education throughout Europe faces many complex teaching tasks and that there is a continuing need for further study. At the level of the Council of Europe or the EU there seems to be a rising consensus about the added value of multilingualism and the protection and revitalization of regional minority languages. Perhaps some regional minority languages have a somewhat better future in education, because nowadays they enjoy the support of regional or local governments. Still, most central state governments in Europe will only pay lip service to this ideology. Their dominant state language is perceived as being far more important. In an exceptional case where a minority language is successful in education, as for example Catalan, counter-reactions can be observed and then even Spanish can be construed as a threatened language.

Further work remains to be done on the general key issues (see the section on 'Challenges of Minority Language Education') but there is also considerable value in case studies of language revitalization. The consequences of learning a language at home, in a school context or through informal learning that goes on in all kinds of other out-of-school contexts have to be investigated further in order to learn more about the continuing existence of minority languages. The challenges faced by revitalization efforts of regional minority language groups in education in Europe are relevant all over the world. This type of education is hardly ever just bilingual; in most cases it will have more than two languages and thus be multilingual. A useful tool to compare different types of schools in which different languages are part of the curriculum is the 'Continua of Multilingual Education' (Cenoz 2009). This model, based on the idea of continua of biliteracy proposed by Hornberger (2003; 2007) considers multilingual education as a complex reality related to linguistic, sociolinguistic and educational variables, and highlights its dynamic character.

Research involving minority languages can be of interest not only to scholars and professionals working on language policy and the revitalization of 'small' languages, but also to many other researchers working in multilingualism. Some of the areas that are opening new directions are the following:

- The study of school achievement when the minority language is the language of instruction. This area is crucial for researchers, professionals and parents, and analyses the different areas in the curriculum (linguistic and non-linguistic) by comparing teaching through the minority language to teaching through the majority language (e.g. Joaristi *et al.* 2009; Cenoz 2009). This line of research shares some characteristics with research on CLIL, a teaching model that has recently attracted a lot of attention in Europe (Marsh 2007).
- The study of the linguistic landscape, understood as the language used in texts in the public space, has also developed in a short period. Studies involving minority languages have proved to be relevant to identity different patterns of multilingualism and to analyse the effect of language policy (Gorter 2006; Shohamy and Gorter 2009). The school context is a relevant field of further research into linguistic landscapes (Dagenais *et al.* 2009).
- Another area of study that has recently developed questions the relationships between multilingual identities, citizenship, the national state and processes of globalization. These

studies are also important for members of minority groups and have proliferated in recent years (Pavlenko and Blackledge 2004). Linked to classroom interaction and discourse in a wider context it opens up a whole range of interesting topics for further study (Blackledge and Creese 2010; Creese and Martin 2003; May 2008).

The ideal school where multilingualism is the ruling ideology can be imagined, but is far from reality (Shohamy 2006: 173). Minority language communities have to find new and different ways to teach their language to the next generation. In the late nineteenth and most of the twentieth centuries, language promotion consisted of having a Bible translation, a grammar book, a dictionary and sometimes a few hours teaching the minority language as a subject. They were the basic tools for language maintenance, as well as symbols of social prestige. Those elements have been replaced by a claim for language rights, schooling *through* the language and in the twenty-first century it is also essential to have a TV channel and presence on the Internet. However, few minority language groups thus far have reached the full range of digital media and culture and therfore they are in a weaker position for (informal) language learning. Schools can produce proficient multilinguals, but most minority language groups do not receive such multilingual education. It seems of utmost importance to convince dominant groups of the usefulness and benefits of multilingual education, which also includes minority languages.

Related topics

Regional minorities and language movements; language rights; linguistic diversity and education; multilingual pedagogies.

Further reading

Baker, C. (2006) *Foundations of Bilingual Education and Bilingualism*, 4th edn, Clevedon: Multilingual Matters.
(Basic reading on a wide range of educational issues.)
García, O. (2009) *Bilingual Education in the 21st Century: A Global Perspective*, Chichester: John Wiley.
(Groundbreaking work on bilingual education.)
Fishman, J. A. (ed.) (2001) *Can Threatened Languages be Saved?* Clevedon: Multilingual Matters.
(An update on his foundational work on reversing language shift.)
Grin, F. (2003) *Language Policy Evaluation and the European Charter for Regional or Minority Language*, London: Palgrave Macmillan.
(A language policy analysis of the European Charter.)
Skutnabb-Kangas, T. (2000) *Linguistic Genocide in Education, or Worldwide Diversity and Human Rights?* London: Lawrence Erlbaum.
(Major reference for minority language education.)

Bibliography

Anderson, A. B. (1990) 'Comparative analysis of language minorities: A sociopolitical framework', in D. Gorter, J. F. Hoekstra, L. G. Jansma and J. Ytsma (eds) *Fourth International Conference on Minority Languages,* vol. 1: *General Papers*, Clevedon: Multilingual Matters.
Baker, C. (2001) *Foundations of Bilingual Education and Bilingualism*, 3rd edn, Clevedon: Multilingual Matters.
——(2003) 'Education as a site of language contact', *Annual Review of Applied Linguistics* 23: 95–112.

Blackledge, A. and Creese, A. (2010) *Multilingualism: A Critical Perspective*, London: Continuum.

Capotorti, F. (1979) *Study of the Rights of Persons Belonging to Ethnic, Religious and Linguistic Minorities*, New York: United Nations (nr E.78.XIV.1).

Cenoz, J. (2008) 'Achievements and challenges in bilingual and multilingual education in the Basque Country', *AILA Review* 21: 13–30.

——(2009) *Towards Multilingual Education: Basque Educational Research in International Perspective*, Clevedon: Multilingual Matters.

Cenoz, J. and Gorter, D. (2005) 'Trilingualism and minority languages in Europe', *International Journal of the Sociology of Language* 171: 1–5.

Churchill, S. (1986) *The Education of Linguistic and Cultural Minorities in the OECD Countries*, Clevedon: Multilingual Matters.

Council of Europe (1995) 'Framework Convention for the Protection of National Minorities', Strasbourg: Council of Europe, ETS 157, available online at www.coe.int/minorities

——(1998) 'European Charter for Regional or Minority Languages', Strasbourg: Council of Europe. ETS 148, available online at www.coe.int/t/dg4/education/minlang/default_en.asp

Craith, M. (2003) 'Facilitating or generating linguistic diversity. The European charter for regional or minority languages', in G. Hogan-Brun and S. Wolff (eds) *Minority Languages in Europe. Frameworks, Status, Prospects*, Basingstoke: Palgrave Macmillan.

Creese, A. and Martin P. (eds) (2003) *Multilingual Classroom Ecologies*, Clevedon: Multilingual Matters.

Dagenais, D., Moore, D., Sabatier, C., Lamarre, P. and Armand, F. (2009) 'Linguistic landscape and language awareness', in E. Shohamy and D. Gorter (eds) *Linguistic Landscape: Expanding the Scenery*, New York and London: Routledge.

De Bot, K. and Gorter, D. (2005) 'A European perspective on heritage languages', *Modern Language Journal* 89(4): 612–16.

Dunbar, R., Parry, G. and Klinge, S. (eds) (2008) *The European Charter for Regional or Minority Languages: Legal Challenges and Opportunities*, Strasbourg: Council of Europe Publishing.

Edwards, J. (1991) 'Socio-educational issues concerning indigenous minority languages: Terminology, geography and status', in J. Sikma and D. Gorter (eds) *European Lesser Used Languages in Primary Education*, Leeuwarden: Mercator Education/Fryske Akademy.

——(2007) 'Societal multilingualism: Reality, recognition and response', in P. Auer and W. Li (eds) *Handbook of Multilingualism and Multilingual Communication*, Berlin and New York: Mouton de Gruyter.

Etxeberria, F and Elosegi, K. (2008) 'Basque, Spanish and immigrant minority languages in Basque schools', in J. Cenoz (ed.) *Teaching Through Basque: Achievements and Challenges*, Clevedon: Multilingual Matters.

Euromosaic III (2004) *Euromosaic III Presence of Regional and Minority Language Groups in the New Member States 2004*, European Commission: Education and Culture, Brussels: Publications Office.

European Commission (2008) 'Commission communication on multilingualism', 18 September, available online at http://eur-lex.europa.eu/LexUriServ/LexUriServ.do?uri=CELEX:52008DC0 566:EN:NOT

Extra, G. and Gorter, D. (eds) (2001) *The Other Languages of Europe*, Clevedon: Multilingual Matters.

Extra, G. and Gorter, D. (2008) 'The constellation of languages in Europe: an inclusive approach', in G. Extra and D. Gorter (eds) *Multilingual Europe: Facts and Policies*, Berlin: Mouton de Gruyter.

Fishman, J. A. (1991) *Reversing Language Shift. Theoretical and Empirical Assistance to Threatened Languages*, Clevedon: Multilingual Matters.

——(ed.) (2001) *Can Threatened Languages be Saved?* Clevedon: Multilingual Matters.

Gal, K. (2000) 'The Council of Europe framework convention for the protection of national minorities and its impact on central and eastern Europe', *JEMIE – Journal of Ethnopolitics and Minority Issues in Europe*, (winter): 1–17.

Giles, H., Bourhis, R. D. and Taylor, D. (1977) 'Towards a theory of language in ethnic group relations', in H. Giles (ed.) *Language, Ethnicity and Intergroup Relations*, London: Academic Press.

Glaser, K. (2007) *Minority Languages and Cultural Diversity in Europe: Gaelic and Sorbian Perspectives*, Clevedon: Multilingual Matters.

Gogolin, I. (2002) 'Linguistic and cultural diversity in Europe: A challenge for educational research and practice', *European Educational Research Journal* 1(1): 123–38.

Gombos, G. (2001) 'The message of code-switching. Trilingual kindergarten education in a minority context'. Paper presented at the 2nd International conference on third language acquisition and trilingualism, Leeuwarden: Fryske Akademy, The Netherlands, 13–15 September.

Gorter, D. (ed.) (2006) *Linguistic Landscape: A New Approach to Multilingualism*, Clevedon: Multilingual Matters.

Grenoble, L. A. and Whaley, L. J. (2006) *Saving Languages: An Introduction to Language Revitalization*, Cambridge: Cambridge University Press.

Grin, F. (2003) *Language Policy Evaluation and the European Charter for Regional or Minority Languages*, London: Palgrave Macmillan.

Grin, F. and Moring, T. (2002) 'Final report: Support for minority languages in Europe', Brussels: European Commission, available online at http://europa.eu.int/comm/education/policies/lang/languages/langmin/files/support.pdf

Harris, J. (2008) 'The declining role of primary schools in the revitalisation of Irish', *AILA Review* 21: 49–68.

Heller, M. (1994) *Crosswords: Language, Education and Ethnicity in French Ontario*, Berlin: Mouton de Gruyter.

Hornberger, N. H. (ed.) (2003) *Continua of Biliteracy: An Ecological Framework for Educational Policy, Research and Practice in Multilingual Settings*, Clevedon: Multilingual Matters.

——(2007) 'Continua of biliteracy', in A. Creese, P. Martin and N. H. Hornberger (eds) *Encyclopedia of Language and Education*, vol. 9: *Ecology of Language*, New York and Berlin: Springer.

Inspectorate (2006) *Inspectie Van Het Onderwijs – De Kwaliteit Van Het Vak Fries in Het Basisonderwijs en Het Voortgezet Onderwijs in de Provincie Fryslân*, Utrecht: Inspectie van het onderwijs.

Joaristi, L., Lizasoain, L., Lukas, J. F. and Santiago, K. (2009) 'Trilingualism (Spanish, English and Basque) in the educational system of the Basque country', *International Journal of Multilingualism* 6(1): 105–26.

Judge, A. (2000) 'France: One state, one nation, one language?' in S. Barbour and C. Carmichael (eds) *Language and Nationalism in Europe*, Oxford: Oxford University Press.

Mac Giolla Chríost, D. (2005) *The Irish language in Ireland: From Gíodel to Globalisation*, London: Routledge.

Marsh, D. (2007) 'Language awareness and CLIL', in J. Cenoz and N. H. Hornberger (eds) *Encyclopedia of Language and Education*, 2nd edn, vol. 6: *Knowledge about Language*, New York: Springer.

May, S. (2001) *Language and Minority Rights: Ethnicity, Nationalism and the Politics of Language*, London: Longman.

——(2008) 'Language education, pluralism and citizenship', in S. May and N. H. Hornberger (eds) *Encyclopedia of Language and Education*, 2nd edn, vol. 1: *Language Policy and Political Issues in Education*, New York: Springer.

Moseley, C. (ed.) (2009) *Unesco Interactive Atlas of the World's Languages in Danger*, available online at www.unesco.org/culture/ich/index.php?pg=00206

Nelde, P., Strubell, M. and Williams, G. (1996) *Euromosaic: The Production and Reproduction of the Minority Language Groups of the EU*, Luxembourg: Publications offices.

Ó Laoire, M. (2008) 'The language situation in Ireland', in R. B. Kaplan and R. B. Baldauf, Jr. (eds) *Language Planning and Policy in Europe: The Baltic States, Ireland and Italy*, Clevedon: Multilingual Matters.

Ó Riagáin, D. (2001) 'The European Union and lesser used languages', *JMS: International Journal on Multicultural Societies* 3(1): 33–43, available online at www.unesco.org/shs/ijms/vol3/issue1/art4

Pavlenko, A, and Blackledge, A. (eds) (2004) *Negotiation of Identities in Multilingual Contexts*, Clevedon: Multilingual Matters.

Shohamy, E. (2006) 'Imagined multilingual schools: How come we don't deliver?' in O. García, T. Skutnabb-Kangas and M. E. Torres-Guzmán (eds) *Imagining Multilingual Schools: Languages in Education and Glocalization*, Clevedon: Multilingual Matters.

Shohamy, E. and Gorter, D. (eds) (2009) *Linguistic Landscape: Expanding the Scenery*, New York and London: Routledge.

Skutnabb-Kangas, T. (2000) *Linguistic Genocide in Education, or Worldwide Diversity and Human Rights?* London: Lawrence Erlbaum.

Spolsky, B. (2004) *Language Policy*, Cambridge: Cambridge University Press.

Stolfo, M. (2009) 'Unity in diversity: The role of the European parliament in promoting minority languages in Europe', in S. Pertot, T. M. S. Priestly and C. H. Williams (eds) *Rights, Promotion and Integration Issues for Minority Languages in Europe*, Basingstoke: Palgrave Macmillan.

Strubell, M. (2007) 'The political discourse on multilingualism in the European Union', in D. Castiglione and C. Longman (eds) *The Language Question in Europe and Diverse Societies: Political, Legal and Social Perspectives*, Oxford: Hart Publishing.

Walker, A. (2007) *North Frisian: The North Frisian Language in Education in Germany*, 2nd edn, Ljouwert: Mercator European Research Centre on Multilingualism and Language Learning, available online at www1.fa.knaw.nl/mercator/regionale_dossiers/PDFs/northfrisian_in_germany2nd.pdf

Williams, G. (2005) *Sustaining Language Diversity in Europe: Evidence from the Euromosaic Project*, Basingstoke: Palgrave Macmillan.

Woerhling, J.-M. (2006) *The European Charter for Regional or Minority Languages. A Critical Commentary*, Strasbourg: Council of Europe.

Wright, S. (2004) 'Regional or minority languages on the www', *Journal of Language and Politics* 5(2): 189–216.

11

Immersion education

En route to multilingualism

Anne-Marie de Mejía

Introduction

It is interesting to notice that many of the publications referring to multilingual education use metaphors referring to movement. Thus, we have *Beyond Bilingualism* (1998), *Pathways to Multilingualism* (2008), *Forging Multilingual Spaces* (2008) and *Towards Multilingual Education* (2009), among others. These seem to indicate that although bilingualism and bilingual education are a well-established part of the field, emphasis on multilingualism is still evolving. This is ratified in Genesee's (2004: 570) discussion of key aspects of bilingual education for majority students where he observes, 'The evidence to date concerning trilingual education is encouraging; but we currently lack detailed understanding of the effectiveness of these programs.'

In this chapter I will briefly examine the development of bilingual (or single) immersion education from its beginnings in Canada and trace its progress in such different contexts as Ireland, Paraguay and Australia. Immersion education, in this sense, is a type of bilingual education programme in which majority language students (generally) are exposed to a second (or foreign) language in the classroom, which serves as a medium for subject-matter instruction (Swain and Johnson 1997). I will then go on to look in more detail at multilingual immersion in Canada, Finland, Catalonia and the Basque Country. In these cases, two or more languages are introduced in the school curriculum in addition to the student's first language, either as languages of content area teaching and learning, or as separate subjects. There will be a particular focus on three key aspects: pedagogical issues, the notion of codeswitching and professional development in relation to immersion programmes. I will end by suggesting ways forward and insights for the future.

Early developments in the field of immersion

Canadian (single) immersion

As is well known, the first experimental immersion programme was set up in St Lambert in 1965 to promote functional bilingualism by using French as a language of teaching and learning as well as English, in order to enable Anglophone children to acquire a high level of proficiency in

French while maintaining their proficiency in their first language. Furthermore, it was also hoped that the immersion programmes would lead to better relationships between members of the Anglo and Francophone communities.

Two types of provision were established. The first took into account the age at which students enter the programme: early immersion (four to five years old), middle or delayed immersion (nine to ten years old); and late immersion (secondary or high school level). The second indicated the amount of time spent studying in the immersion (second or foreign) language: total immersion (100 per cent immersion initially in the second language leading to 50 per cent contact at the end of primary school); and partial immersion (50 per cent immersion in the second language throughout the programme).

A separation or 'sheltered' approach was incorporated into the programmes from the beginning. The principle behind this is that learners of the target language are kept apart from native speakers, 'at least until their linguistic skills are sufficient to permit them to learn academic content on a par with native speakers' (Swain 1982: 84). In addition, Swain claimed that all children in programmes of this type should begin with the same zero level of target language skills. She recommended adopting three basic principles to achieve successful bilingual education. The first was the principle of 'First Things First', or ensuring a sound basis in the child's first language (L1) for second language (L2) learning. The second principle was 'Bilingualism through Monolingualism', by which she argued for the merits of a separation (rather than a concurrent) approach to classroom language use. She called her third principle 'Bilingualism as a Bonus', in which she advocated letting the students know the advantages of bilingualism for them, which would lead to a self-fulfilling prophecy (Swain 1983).

Overall, the results of assessments of the Canadian immersion programmes are positive in academic terms. Student proficiency in understanding and reading French has been evaluated as of native-speaker standard, first language development has not been affected and there are no negative reports on academic achievement levels. Student proficiency levels in speaking and writing French were below native-speaker level, yet higher than results from the regular Core French programme (Genesee 2004). There was, however, no noticeable effect of a change in attitude of the students towards the Francophone community in Canada.

Since 1965 there has been a steady spread of French immersion programmes throughout Canada. In 1977–8 there were 37,835 students enrolled in immersion, whereas in 1998–9 the number had jumped to 317, 351 students in around 2,000 schools. At primary school level the Quebec Department of Education maintains that 60 per cent of all students in the province are enrolled in immersion programmes (Rebuffot 2000).

We may well ask what the importance of this pedagogical innovation is in the future development of bilingual education. First of all, it is important to situate immersion education within the wider field of teaching and learning second or foreign languages. As Heller has noted,

> The basic idea underlying immersion, a notion borrowed from communicative language learning theory, is that by using the target language as a language of communication in authentic situations, such as subject-matter instruction or any other form of teacher-student or student-student communication outside strictly instructional contexts, students' acquisition of the target language will be improved.
>
> *(1990: 73)*

Thus, we can see that immersion with its emphasis on content instruction is an example of a wider approach, that of language as communication and use in authentic, contextualized situations, where the attention of the learner is focused on meaning rather than on form. This notion can be linked to concepts such as task-based learning and activity-based syllabuses characteristic of many foreign language teaching programmes, where the emphasis is not directly on language learning per se, but rather language learning results from carrying out tasks or doing activities related to other subjects in the curriculum.

Another important consideration to bear in mind in the rapid spread of immersion programmes is that they have been extensively funded by the Canadian Federal Government Administration as part of a highly publicized initiative designed to support official bilingualism within the country. They may, thus, be described as one of the most thoroughly investigated educational innovations (Stern 1984), being the first educational programme using the second language as a medium of instruction to be 'subjected to intensive long-term research evaluation' (Cummins 2000: 1).

Later developments

The success of immersion education is evidenced by the number of countries in different parts of the world that openly espouse this type of bilingual provision. In this section we will briefly look at some recent developments in Europe (Ireland), in South America (Paraguay) and in Australia.

Ireland

According to Ó Muircheartaigh and Hickey (2008), immersion education is available in the Republic of Ireland at preschool, primary and secondary levels. These programmes differ from the Canadian model in that all subjects are taught through Irish, and English, the L1 of the majority of the pupils, is a subject in primary. A foreign language is added in secondary school. In addition, another modality, denominated 'mixed' immersion, has its roots in the Two Way Immersion programmes popularised in the USA. This caters for both L1 and L2 learners of Irish, but in contrast to the majority of Dual Language programmes in the USA, in Ireland, first-language speakers of Irish are placed together with second-language speakers on grounds of practicality, due to the low density of Irish L1 speakers, particularly in rural areas, and also to avoid charges of discrimination. In research carried out on some of these early 'mixed' immersion groups at preschool level, Hickey (2001) found that their linguistic composition significantly affected the frequency of target language use by both L1 speakers of Irish and by Irish/English bilinguals, as classroom language use was predominately oriented towards English. The researcher recommended explicitly addressing the differing needs of all the children in this type of classroom 'in order to promote the mother tongue enrichment of the L1 children, as well as to encourage L2 acquisition by language learners' (Hickey 2001: 466).

More recently, Ó Muircheartaigh and Hickey (2008) conducted a comparative study into both the outcomes of early as opposed to late immersion students, and the levels of anxiety each group manifested. The results show that after only three years in immersion programmes, the late immersion students achieved similar levels of Irish-language proficiency to those of early immersion pupils. (The authors do, however, make some reservations about the parity of the two groups studied in the project). In this study, the authors urge us to go beyond scores on national examinations to look at the effect of non-linguistic factors, such as anxiety, in the development of proficiency. The researchers noted that in spite of their linguistic achievements, the late immersion students in the study experienced higher levels of anxiety than those in early immersion programmes. They hypothesize that this may be due to the fact that they had poorer communication skills initially in Irish than early immersion students, and this may lead to them feeling less comfortable in classroom interactions. Furthermore, late immersion students may also receive more correction, which could lead to higher anxiety levels. Ó Muircheartaigh and Hickey (2008: 574) argue that it is important to introduce and evaluate 'some transitional interventions, [such as] ... effective language learning strategies ... , for late immersion students so that they can make optimal progress in the target language'.

Paraguay

In Paraguay, Susan Spezzini (2005) carried out research into language learning variability in an elite immersion-type, bilingual programme in Asunción among predominately Spanish-speaking adolescents in twelfth grade. As a result of both qualitative and quantitative analysis, the researcher came to the conclusion that the students 'demonstrated a relatively high functional L2 proficiency, but not necessarily near native' (Spezzini 2005: 92). She also noted that variability in language learning, as well as comprehensibility and language use, may be directly influenced by the opportunities provided from within the specific language learning context as well as through individual investment. She maintains that, 'immersion classrooms are diglossic speech communities with each language reserved for certain communicative purposes' (2005: 93). English is mainly used for academic matters and Spanish for conversational interaction, and, thus, students' use of English is often restricted to a formal register, inhibiting the development of L2 productive skills.

Australia

In the 1970s there were two important developments in the traditional monolingual attitude of English-speaking Australia to the development of other languages. On the one hand, there was growing interest at government level in the Canadian immersion programmes, and, on the other, there was an evident determination on the part of the Australian Federal Government to offer all children a second language at primary school level, 'in order to reach out to the world' (de Courcy 2002: 3).

Consequently, the last three decades have seen the establishment of a number of immersion-type programmes, based on the Canadian model, in some of the major Australian cities. The most frequent foreign languages chosen were either French or German, but there is also evidence of initiatives involving Chinese, Japanese and Indonesian (de Courcy 2002). Most of the immersion programmes started in Australia were of the partial immersion-type, either early or late.

In 2002 de Courcy reported on a qualitative study into the experiences of a group of second-year students in a late Chinese immersion programme in Queensland. The researcher found that the students seemed to pass through four different stages in trying to make sense of classroom interaction in Chinese. Interestingly, the first of these was found to involve the use of translation as a receptive strategy, which seems to be at odds with the language separation approach advocated by Swain (1983).

Developments in the field of multilingual immersion

As Genesee (2004) has observed, multilingual forms of education have been implemented in contexts where more than two languages are used. The different socio-cultural-political circumstances of the communities concerned have given rise to considerable programmatic and pedagogical variation among such initiatives. In this section we will examine the genesis of some of these initiatives, beginning with Canada and then moving to a European context where we will look at aspects of multilingual immersion programmes in Finland, Catalonia and the Basque Country.

Canada

The earliest study that I have been able to find relating to multilingual immersion programmes is a piece of research carried out by Genesee and Lambert (1983) in multilingual (French–Hebrew–English) schools in Montreal. This study subsequently formed the basis of a chapter written about multilingual education in Canada (Genesee 1998). The interest of the two researchers was to determine the effectiveness of what they termed 'double immersion'. For purposes of the study, they selected two different types of school: early double immersion and delayed double immersion. The key difference between these two programmes was that in the former, the two second languages were introduced from preschool (kindergarten), whereas English, the students' first language, was only introduced in grades 3 or 4. However, in the second modality – delayed double immersion – so named because the amount of time allotted to the two second languages, French and Hebrew, gradually increased from kindergarten to grade 5, all three languages were taught right from the beginning of schooling.

The longitudinal study evaluated student progress in relation to four aspects, three of which have often been discussed in relation to immersion education: second language learning, the effect on the first language and the effect on academic achievement. The other issue considered was related to the effect of delaying and reducing L1 instruction in the programme. Although analysis of the data in the light of the first three questions led to similar results to those obtained in single immersion programmes in relation to second language learning, first language development and academic achievement, there were some interesting findings in relation to the comparative linguistic development of the students in the two different types of programme. According to Genesee (1998: 250), analysis of the results indicated that, 'there was a tendency for the *delayed* immersion students to score lower on the Hebrew language tests than the *early* immersion students despite the fact that both groups had had equivalent exposure to Hebrew'. The researchers hypothesized that the use of English (the L1) during the early years of double immersion might interfere with the learning of the other languages in the programme, due to it being such a powerful language of influence.

Finland

Scandinavian countries often teach three or more languages at school so that students are able to communicate in other Scandinavian languages and in a world language, such as German or English (Genesee 2004). It was within this general panorama that the first Swedish–Finnish immersion programme began in Vaasa in 1987. According to accounts by Laurén (1991, 1992) Vesterbacka (1991) and Björklund (1997), the immersion school movement in Finland has its origin in the Vaasa University bilingual education project led by Professor Crister Laurén. It was felt that the Canadian immersion programme would be a suitable model for this experimental project in the Finnish context. As Laurén explained,

> One advantage of following this model was that we did not experiment. The model is tested, we converted it for use in Finland, studied how our particular pair of languages, Finnish/Swedish, operates for immersion schools, and considered how the additional language taken in the programme should be treated.
>
> *(1992: 13)*

However, this time it was not parental pressure (as in Canada) or government policy (as in Australia) but the influence of a group of politically active women, in consultation with members of the Department of Nordic Languages of the University of Vaasa that led to the first Swedish immersion programme. Members of the Department of Nordic Languages gave information about the immersion model and explained why they thought immersion would be a suitable bilingual programme for Finland. Thus, from the beginning the Finnish–Swedish immersion programme enjoyed both political and academic credibility.

In line with early Canadian developments, the immersion modality adopted in the Vaasa project was early total immersion, where bilingual teachers and their assistants use Swedish consistently for the four hours per day that the children spend at preschool, although the children are allowed to reply in their first language if they wish. The pupils' first language, Finnish, is gradually introduced into the curriculum (around 10 per cent of teaching being carried out in Finnish during First Grade Primary) until there is an approximate language balance of 50 per cent Swedish, 5 per cent in a third language and 45 per cent Finnish) (Gustavsson and Mard 1992).

The third language used in the Finnish immersion programmes in Vaasa is English, but in other parts of the country, such as the South of Finland, German is often adopted. In the original design, English was taught as a subject area, rather than a medium of instruction. However, gradually the third language (and at times a fourth language) have become more integrated within the curriculum (Södergård 2008). In the present programmes, the third language is introduced in Grade 1 for one to two hours per week, and although still classed as 'language lessons', the teachers have introduced content-based teaching and learning and use the third language as a medium of instruction right from the outset (Björklund 2005, cited in Södergård 2008). Moreover, immersion principles have been applied to the teaching and learning of these languages in that L3 and L4 teachers only use this language with their students (Björklund and Suni 2000).

Although the results of the earlier introduction of the third and fourth language are still being evaluated, Björklund and Suni (2000) report that a small-scale study carried out among students in the Vaasa/Vasa Swedish immersion programme in 1997–8 has shown that students consider that they are active speakers of all four languages taught in the programme.

The enthusiastic reception given to the experimental project in Vaasa led to the creation of other immersion programmes in Espoo, Helsinki and in Kokkola and elsewhere, catering for different age ranges. By the end of the 1998–9 school year there were approximately 2,000 pupils involved in Swedish immersion programmes in Finland, and 2,500 in English immersion programmes. In 2006 data indicated that Swedish immersion programmes were offered in 30 schools and 30 kindergartens throughout the country (Södergård 2008).

It is interesting to note the role of the immersion model as developed in Canada in these developments. As Laurén (1992) recognizes, its tried and tested status provided a solid platform on which to construct the modifications necessary for the Finnish context. It is also instructive to see the gradual change from foreign language teaching to content-based teaching in line with immersion principles.

Catalonia

The Catalan immersion programme was a politically orientated development, considered by the regional government authorities as a means both to integrate a large non-Catalan-speaking immigrant population into Catalan life and to upgrade the status of Catalan in relation to Castilian (Spanish). An experimental total immersion programme was set up in 1983 in Santa Coloma de Gramat, an area where few people spoke Catalan and where an immersion programme was considered the most efficient means to achieve the autonomous government's aim of equal student proficiency in both Catalan and Spanish by the end of the compulsory education cycle (E.G.B.) at the age of 14 (Arenas i Sampera 1986).

The programmes were designed to include working groups of children in a classroom situation where more than 70 per cent were non-Catalan-speakers. The Spanish-speaking immigrant communities are primarily working class, but aspire to learn Catalan because Catalan is seen within Catalonia as a high-prestige minority language associated with social mobility (Mar-Molinero 1989).

Recently, however, a new demand for multilingual competence has arisen due to pressure on schools in Spain to raise their standards in the teaching and learning of international languages, particularly English. Thus, in 2004 the age for compulsory foreign language learning was lowered from sixth grade (12-year-olds) to first grade (six-year-olds). Moreover, in 2006, Decree 1630 officially recognized that a first contact with a foreign language in Spanish schools should begin at pre-primary level (Cenoz 2009). Furthermore, in line with European Union directives, there is evidence of a drive to encourage state schools to offer Content and Language Integrated Learning (CLIL) courses in their curricula (Escobar Urmeneta and Unamuno 2008).

In addition, a complex linguistic scenario has emerged as the result of increasing immigration to Catalonia and other regions of Spain, ensuring that Catalan schools are becoming ever more multilingual (Escobar Urmeneta and Unamuno 2008). As Huguet *et al.* (2008: 234) note, 'Immigrant students now make up 7.4% of the school population ... more than 10% in Madrid and Catalonia'. A reference document entitled 'The Languages and Social Cohesion Plan', or 'The LIC Plan', (according to the initials in Catalan), which guides the implementation of educational and linguistic measures to help to incorporate newly arrived pupils into the Catalan school system, promotes, on the one hand, the development of Catalan 'as the mainstay of a multilingual and intercultural education policy in order to achieve greater social cohesion' (LIC Plan: 4, cited in Escobar Urmeneta and Unamuno 2008: 234). On the other hand, the Plan requires that

> By the end of primary education pupils must be able to understand and express simple messages in a given context in one foreign language. By the end of secondary education they must be able to understand and produce oral and written messages in one foreign language ... In addition, ... have a basic level in understanding and speaking a second foreign language.
>
> *(LIC Plan, Appendix 2: 28 cited in Escobar Urmeneta and Unamuno 2008: 236–7)*

One of the interesting aspects of the development of the immersion programmes in Catalonia over the last few years is that they have moved from being considered a local means of promoting the status and use of the Catalan language by the Autonomous Catalan Government, after years of linguistic repression under General Franco (1939–75), to a vehicle to help Spain position itself within the growing demands for multilingualism in international languages in Europe. Simultaneously, in the LIC Plan there is recognition of the importance of developing the linguistic repertoires of newly arrived immigrants in the country to avoid the social exclusion of the immigrant population, although this is often seen by educational authorities as belonging to the optional after-school activity programme, rather than forming part of the mainstream school curriculum.

However, as Escobar Urmeneta and Unamuno (2008) have emphasized, there are tensions generated between these different visions of multilingualism in institutional practice. Thus, there are substantial differences noted between official plurilingualism for immigrants as set out in the LIC Plan, official plurilingualism for mainstream students (i.e. CLIL), and what may be termed 'backstage' plurilingualism, which the authors see as emerging 'from the social conditions, the tensions among opposing goals and the contradictions shown by the agents when they define institutional, educational and social aims [where] the learners' native languages/s ... occupy diverse contexts of learning and use' (Escobar Urmeneta and Unamuno 2008: 247). The researchers recognize the reputation of Catalonia as a pioneer in the establishment of an immersion modality where the minority language (Catalan) is used as the main working language. Now the challenge is that of integrating students from many different linguistic and cultural backgrounds, so that by the end of their compulsory education, all learners – regardless of their linguistic origin – should have developed a sound knowledge of at least a third language of international use (2008).

The Basque Country

Trilingual education in the Basque Country is seen as an important means of developing competence in three languages: two official languages, Basque and Spanish, and English, which has replaced French as the first foreign language taught in Basque schools, and which is now studied by more than 95 per cent of pupils (Cenoz 2009).

There have been a number of efforts undertaken by the Basque Government Department of Education, as well as other private organizations, to improve the teaching of English as part of a drive towards the development of multilingual competence, in line with the requirements of the European Commission for students to become 'proficient in at least three European languages' (Cenoz 2009: 86). Thus, in some cases, trilingual education consists of teaching academic subject areas through Basque and Spanish, whereas English is taught as a separate subject beginning in pre-primary, but is not used to teach academic subjects at primary school level. According to Huguet *et al.* (2008), in this type of programme, Spanish is usually the language used for teaching Maths, whereas Basque is the language of teaching and learning in the other areas of the curriculum. In other cases, such as the network of *Ikastolak* – or schools for pupils whose mother tongue is Basque – children start with Basque as the main language of schooling, but also study Spanish as a subject. They also start learning English as a subject at the age of four and at 14, they study Social Science through the medium of English for two years (Cenoz 2009).

There is an interesting development in this respect, reported by Elorza and Muñoa (2008) in relation to Cummins' (2000) notion of linguistic interdependence and transfer. Some trilingual schools have joined forces in order to develop an integrated curriculum to cover work done in the Basque, Spanish and English sections aimed at facilitating joint planning of language and content classes to 'ensure the adequate development of the different languages at the levels needed by Basque citizens of the 21st century' (Elorza and Muñoa 2008: 89). The model of curricular integration proposed first posits some common general competencies to develop between the different languages. These are then incorporated into a common framework for contents with complementary distribution, which, in turn, establishes the specific competences established for each of the languages in the curriculum with differential proficiency levels, based on the scales established in the Common European Framework of Reference for Languages (Council of Europe 2001). Thus, students need to achieve a B2+ level for Basque and for their contact language (either Spanish or French), a B1+ level for English and A2 level for a fourth language, which could be either French or Spanish. According to the results of evaluations carried out over a ten year period, the early introduction of English at the age of four had no negative effect on student linguistic competence in either Basque or Spanish, or on their cognitive abilities. It was also shown that students who started learning English in pre-primary did better than those who started at the age of eight (Elorza and Muñoa 2008).

As Genesee (2004) has recognized, trilingual immersion education raises a number of important issues in relation to programme effectiveness, the developmental relationship among the three languages and their sequencing. He also notes that there is little empirical evidence available to answer these questions and that which exists is highly variable in nature, perhaps because up until now multilingual immersion programmes are far less common than their bilingual counterparts. This can be seen by the three studies presented in this review. In the Hebrew schools in Montreal, English, the first language, is seen as having a possible negative effect on the development of Hebrew, whereas results in the Basque Country and in Finland on the early introduction of English (the third language) show a totally different scenario. Genesee (ibid.) also advises caution as there tends to be a bias to report successful programmes, rather than those that do not do so well. However, the pedagogical initiative in the *Ikastolak* schools is certainly instructive and brings to the fore the importance of pedagogical rather than linguistic issues in the effective development of multilingual immersion programmes, a theme to which we now turn.

Key issues of theory and method

Pedagogy: issues of language and content

Although for the first 25 to 30 years after St Lambert, Canadian researchers in the field of immersion education, such as Merrill Swain, seemed more concerned with linguistic rather than pedagogical matters, these have increasingly taken the floor in recent publications. In 1998 Genesee recognized that, 'the quality of the instruction and the nature of the pedagogy used to teach the language are important factors' (Genesee 1998: 252), and six years later, the same researcher emphasized that the 'nature and quality of classroom instruction are very important' (2004: 560) in accounting for the level of student L2 achievement. Nevertheless, if we look at developments in immersion programmes in other countries, we can see concern for immersion pedagogy has existed for many years.

In Finland, researchers at the University of Vaasa were interested in examining some of the methodological assumptions underlying the Swedish Immersion programmes, claiming that the adoption of immersion principles facilitated 'a pedagogic-didactic renewal' (Laurén 1992: 21). As a result of observation of teaching in the Swedish Immersion Programme, the researcher proposed, 'a two-phase-didactics for school' (Laurén 1992: 71) to create a basic level of linguistic fluency at an early stage of language learning when prerequisites are optimal, which can later be expanded on and extended.

Another member of the Vaasa Immersion research team, Vesterbacka (1991), was interested in the development of meaningful, ritualized routines in context-bound situations in immersion programmes. The researcher examined young children's language use in Swedish in relation to unchanging 'routines' and partially changing 'patterns'. She argued that these ritualized routines and patterns should be recognized as an important teaching and learning strategy at this level in immersion programmes. She saw them as a key means of providing confidence for young children to express themselves at an early stage in their bilingual development and to communicate with others in meaningful contexts in an effort to fulfil their basic needs as efficiently as possible.

In the USA, Elizabeth Bernhardt and her colleagues (1992) provided a much-needed focus on classroom practice claiming that it was important to recognize 'immersion teaching as a particular kind of teaching … not just language teaching' (Bernhardt 1992: 3). In their collection they provide detailed discussion of classroom routines and aspects of contextualized student–teacher interactions, allowing a fascinating glimpse of how teaching and learning is accomplished moment by moment in different immersion settings.

Later, Hoare (2001) continued this pedagogical focus by examining different teacher strategies used in the teaching of science in English by 'language aware' and 'non-language aware' teachers. Two Chinese teachers of science were studied teaching the same topic area, energy, to 12-year-old students in a Hong Kong secondary school. One of the teachers had received specific in-service training in the effective teaching of content and language in immersion, whereas the other teacher had not.

An interesting result of the study was that the 'language aware' science teacher provided evidence of enriched language use, using rich examples and fairly complex analogies in which he evoked his students' knowledge of the world, which helped to extend and challenge their knowledge and thinking. Thus, '[T]he language is not simplified so much that the concepts are diminished. Instead, it is enriched through a variety of means to provide multiple ways in which students can understand and learn' (Hoare 2001: 209).

Roy Lyster (2007) is one of the latest Canadian immersion scholars to have concentrated attention on processes of learning and teaching languages through content. He advocates a counterbalanced approach in relation to form-focused and content-based instruction in immersion pedagogy in order to frequently shift the focus between form and meaning. The idea of a 'counterbalanced' or integrated approach to the age-old question of the relationship between content and language teaching and learning is meant to avoid separationist stances, which either concentrate on content without paying attention to language development, or provide separate language instruction in language arts classes. These non-integrated approaches have been used to explain the lack of continued growth in students' proficiency in the immersion language (Harley et al. 1990, cited in Lyster 2008).

Recently the debate on the relationships between language and content teaching and learning enshrined within immersion pedagogy has been extended to include discussion about the importance of CLIL (Content and Language Integrated Learning) in mainland Europe. According to Gajo (2001, cited in Hélot 2007), CLIL (or EMILE in French, although Hélot maintains that these are not, in fact, synonyms) stems from the experience of the Canadian immersion programmes. In both types of programme there are bilingual teachers and there are different types of levels of contact possible between the two languages in the curriculum (Cenoz 2009). However, this researcher also emphasizes that a key difference between CLIL and immersion pedagogy is that CLIL has its origin in the teaching and learning of foreign languages rather than in bilingual education. Hélot (2007: 143) for her part considers that, 'reflection on the question of the integration between foreign languages and non-linguistic disciplines is still in its infancy' in France.

Codeswitching and language separation in the classroom

There is also a heightened awareness of the role of codeswitching and language choice as a communicative resource and as an indicator of identity among immersion researchers. In a recent review of immersion programmes, Genesee (2004: 574) stated that he considered bilingual classroom discourse a fruitful avenue for research in the future, asking, 'Is there a role for bilingual usage … in bilingual education? In other words, should the languages always be kept separate and if not, how can they be used co-extensively to promote language learning?' More recently, he has stated that, contrary to conventional wisdom, keeping languages completely separate in immersion may not be the best strategy and has argued that strategic use of L1 may facilitate L2 reading development, based on evidence of significant cross-linguistic transfer of skills related to reading, especially decoding (Genesee 2008).

Although this is a fairly new departure for Canadian immersion researchers, there has been work carried out on classroom codeswitching in immersion programmes in South America, among other places, which questions the strong separation view of languages that characterized the early work on immersion. This has now given way to a more integrated, 'bilingual' vision of classroom talk. Researchers have turned their attention to the recurrent bilingual routines and communicative practices evident in classroom participants' interaction. As examples of this, I will cite instances of recent work carried out in Colombia and in Paraguay.

The first study is based on qualitative study I carried out on storytelling events with young children in immersion classrooms in Colombia (de Mejía 2002, 2004). I came to the conclusion that far from being a deficit strategy used to supplement imperfect linguistic proficiency on the part of the teachers, the use of two languages in teaching and learning revealed a sophistication and complexity of language development often ignored by educationalists. Furthermore, Spezzini (2005) in Paraguay, has noted that some immersion students are conscious that their codeswitched discourse is significantly different from standard usage, and see this as a reflection of their unique identity as students of a particular bilingual school. The researcher shows that some students were conscious that their bilingual codeswitched school language use reflected a particular 'unique' social/group identity, as evidenced in the following observation,

> The students at the American School of Asunción (ASA) have their own language. When we speak English, we speak ASA English and when we speak Spanish, we speak ASA Spanish.
>
> *(Spezzini 2005: 87)*

The author speculates that this might be evidence of the creation of a non-native language variety based on covert prestige norms.

Teacher professional development

There have been various attempts to formulate guidelines for appropriate teacher education courses for practitioners working in immersion programmes. Hoare and Kong (2001) in Hong Kong maintain that there are six basic attributes required by immersion teachers: bilingual proficiency; immersion teaching strategies aimed at integrating language and content across the curriculum; knowledge of the target language system; understanding of the theories of second language learning and immersion education; commitment to immersion education; and knowledge of the target culture. Banfi and Rettaroli (2008) in Argentina, for their part, postulate a similar list involving knowledge of the languages and cultures used in particular bilingual programmes, as well as content knowledge, pedagogical knowledge and understanding of the principles of bilingualism and bilingual education.

In a recent research study (de Mejía *et al.* 2006: 97) carried out in six different regions of Colombia into the state of immersion-type schools in the country, one of the conclusions reached was that there was

> a lack of knowledge and attention paid to the principles and fundamentation of bilingual education, and unconcern on the part of some of the administrative staff of some of the schools visited of the importance of this for curricular development.

Valencia Giraldo (2007) has alluded to the type of pre-service preparation offered to foreign language teachers in universities in Colombia, which often does not prepare them to face classroom realities. In similar vein, Cárdenas has condemned 'the prescriptive practices for teaching and learning and the promotion of teacher qualification by the [National Bilingual Programme]' in contrast to 'the critical dimension of language education' (Cárdenas 2006: 5).

It is perhaps natural in such circumstances that teachers try to seek the latest 'method' to help deal with the situation, as the following comment by a teacher in a bilingual school in Bogotá reveals,

> At our school, we frequently talk about the needs of our [Second Language Learner] SLL students and how teachers can fulfil those needs. ... As educators, we must be proactive and try methods that help our students. As teachers we should be exposed to the latest methods successful teachers are utilizing in their classrooms ... this collaboration is discussed, but sadly, our training doesn't really include any methods. ... Teach us the methods!
>
> *(de Mejía* et al. *2008)*

However, it may be argued that this reliance on pre-established 'methods' ignores the current emphasis on post-method pedagogies (Kumaravadivelu 1994, 2003, 2006) and perpetuates the state of teacher dependency. The developing, through pre-service and in-service courses, of a critical, reflective capacity (Pennycook 2001) to evaluate current and new developments should help teachers value their own constructed pedagogical knowledge and insights in relation to the knowledge and insights gained from the study of those working in different settings, and aid them in helping their students to construct their own knowledge and meanings, without imposing a particular frame of reference (Gieve and Magalhaes 1994).

New research directions

As I suggested initially, there is much room for future research on multilingualism in immersion programmes. It is interesting to note, that the publications referenced in this chapter mainly stem from Canada and Europe, as there is little that I have been able to find about multilingual immersion in other parts of the world.

If we compare the collection on immersion education edited by Johnson and Swain in 1997 with a recent publication on the same topic edited by Williams Fortune and Tedick in 2008, there are some striking differences, which indicate changing perceptions in the field over the 11-year period. Whereas the earlier volume is concerned with present studies that exemplify the development of different categories of immersion programmes, such as immersion in foreign languages, immersion for language revival and immersion for language support, the emphasis in the later collection is on 'evolving perspectives' on immersion pedagogy, on language development in immersion classrooms and the influence of the social context on immersion programmes. This indicates, I would argue, a change from the justification of the merits of immersion per se and an interest in looking in more detail at classroom interaction, pedagogy and contextual factors. I would also agree with May (2008: 31) in his recognition that 'research on bilingual/immersion education could ... expand its base with more ethnographic studies of effective bilingual/immersion education – thus providing a basis of thick description for the more comparative and evaluative studies'.

In this chapter, I have discussed some important developments relating to the evolution of immersion education towards multilingualism. Although single immersion programmes have been very successful in responding to the challenges of helping students develop a high level of academic bilingualism, it remains to be seen whether multilingual immersion will help the transition from bilingualism to plurilingualism in an internationalized world.

Related topics

Linguistic diversity and education; regional minorities, education and language revitalization; multilingual pedagogies; codeswitching.

Further reading

Cenoz, J. (2009) *Towards Multilingual Education. Basque Educational Research in International Perspective*, Bristol: Multilingual Matters.
(Update on the development of multilingualism, CLIL and third language learning in Europe.)

de Courcy, M. (2002) *Learners Experiences of Immersion Education. Case Studies of French and Chinese*, Clevedon: Multilingual Matters.
(Research on classroom processes of language learning in two late immersion programmes in Australia.)

Genesee, F. (2004) 'What do we know about bilingual education for majority language students?' in T. K. Bhatia and W. C. Ritchie (eds) *Handbook of Bilingualism and Multiculturalism*, Malden, MA: Blackwell.
(Informative overview on key issues in immersion education.)

May, S. (2008) 'Bilingual/immersion education: What the research tells us,' in J. Cummins and N. H. Hornberger (eds) *Encyclopedia of Language and Education*, 2nd edn, vol. 5: 19–34.
(Overview of research developments in bilingual education, particularly in USA, and some reference to New Zealand.)

Williams Fortune, T. and Tedick, D. J. (eds) (2008) *Pathways to Multilingualism: Evolving Perspectives on Immersion Education* Clevedon: Multilingual Matters.
(Includes ethnographic studies on immersion classroom interaction and language learning.)

Bibliography

Arenas i Sampera, J. (1986) *La Immersio Linguistica Escrits de Divulgacio*, Barcelona: La Llar del Llibre.
Banfi, C. and Rettaroli, S. (2008) 'Staff profiles in minority and prestigious bilingual education contexts in Argentina', in C. Hélot and A.-M. de Mejía (eds) *Forging Multilingual Spaces. Integrated Perspectives on Bilingual Education in Majority and Minority Settings*, Clevedon: Multilingual Matters.
Bernhardt, E. (ed.) (1992) *Life in Language Immersion Classrooms*, Clevedon: Multilingual Matters.
Björklund, S. (1997) 'Immersion in the 1990s: A state of development and expansion', in R. K. Johnson and M. Swain (eds) *Immersion Education: International Perspectives*, Cambridge: Cambridge University Press.
——(2005) 'Toward trilingual education in Vaasa/Vasa, Finland.' *International Journal of the Sociology of Language*, 23–40.
Björklund, S. and Suni, I. (2000) 'The role of English as L3 in a Swedish immersion programme in Finland: impacts on language teaching and language relations', in J. Cenoz and U. Jessner (eds) *English in Europe. The Acquisition of a Third Language*, Clevedon: Multilingual Matters.
Cárdenas, M. L. (2006) 'Bilingual Colombia: Are we ready for it? What is needed?' Paper presented in 19th Annual EA Education Conference 2006, English Australia.
Cenoz, J. (2009) *Towards Multilingual Education. Basque Educational Research from an International Perspective*, Bristol: Multilingual Matters.
Council of Europe (2001) *Common European Framework of Reference for Languages: Learning, Teaching, Assessment*, Cambridge: Cambridge University Press.
Cummins, J. (2000) 'Immersion education for the millennium: What we have learned from 30 years of research on second language immersion', available online at www.iteachilearn.com/cummins/immersion2000.html

de Courcy, M. (2002) *Learners Experiences of Immersion Education. Case Studies of French and Chinese*, Clevedon: Multilingual Matters.

de Mejía, A.-M. (2002) *Power, Prestige and Bilingualism*, Clevedon: Multilingual Matters.

——(2004) 'The role of reformulation in bilingual storytelling', *The Welsh Journal of Education* 13(1): 30–43.

de Mejía, A.-M., Ordoñez, C. L. and Fonseca, L. (2006) 'Estudio Investigativo sobre el Estado Actual de la Educación Bilingüe (inglés-español) en Colombia', unpublished research report, Bogotá: Universidad de los Andes.

de Mejia, A.-M., López, A., Peña, B., Arciniegas, M. C. and Montiel, M. (2008) 'Bilingual education survey,' unpublished document, Bogotá: Universidad de los Andes.

Elorza, I. and Muñoa, I. (2008) 'Promoting the minority language through integrated plurilingual language planning: the case of the Ikastolas', in J. Cenoz (ed.) *Teaching Through Basque. Achievements and Challenges*, Clevedon: Multilingual Matters.

Escobar Urmeneta, C and Unamuno, V. (2008) 'Languages and language learning in Catalan schools: from the bilingual to the multilingual challenge', in C. Hélot and A.-M. de Mejía (eds) *Forging Multilingual Spaces*, Bristol: Multilingual Matters.

Gajo, L. (2001) *Immersion, Bilingualisme et Interaction en Classe*. Paris: Hatier.

Genesee, F. (1998) 'A case study of multilingual education in Canada', in J. Cenoz and F. Genesee (eds) *Beyond Bilingualism*, Clevedon: Multilingual Matters.

——(2004) 'What do we know about bilingual education for majority language students?' in T. K. Bhatia and W. C. Ritchie (eds) *Handbook of Bilingualism and Multiculturalism*, Malden, MA: Blackwell.

——(2008) 'Learning to read in a second language', paper presented at 'Immersion Education: Pathways to Bilingualism and Beyond', St Pauls, Minneapolis, 17 October.

Genesee, F. and Lambert, W. E. (1983) 'Trilingual education for majority language children', *Child Development* 54: 105–14.

Gieve, S. and Magalhaes, I. (1994) 'On empowerment', in *Centre for Research in Language Education, Occasional Report 6: Power, Ethics and Validity*, Lancaster: Lancaster University.

Gustavsson, R. and Mard, K. (1992) 'Language immersion in Finland', in *Code-switching Summer School, European Science Foundation Network on Code-switching and Language Contact*, European Science Foundation.

Harley, B., Cummins, J., Swain, M. and Allen, P. (1990) 'The nature of language proficiency.' In B. Harley, P. Allen, J. Cummins and M. Swain (eds.), *The Development of Second Language Proficiency*, Cambridge: Cambridge University Press.

Heller, M. (1990) 'French immersion in Canada: A model for Switzerland?' *Multilingua* 9(1): 67–86.

Hélot, C. (2007) *Du Bilinguisme en Famille au Plurilinguisme à l'École*, Paris: L'Harmattan.

Hickey, T. (2001) 'Mixing beginners and native speakers in minority language immersion: Who is immersing whom', *The Canadian Modern Language Review* 57(3): 443–74.

Hoare, P. (2001) 'A comparison of the effectiveness of a "language aware" and a "non language aware" late immersion teacher', in S. Björklund (ed.) *Language as a Tool*, Finland: University of Vaasa.

Hoare, P. and Kong, S. (2001) 'A framework of attributes for English immersion teachers in Hong Kong and implications for immersion teacher education', in S. Björklund (ed.) *Language as a Tool*, Finland: University of Vaasa.

Huguet, A., Lasagabaster, D. and Vila, I. (2008) 'Bilingual education in Spain: Present realities and future challenges', in J. Cummins and N. H. Hornberger (eds) *Encyclopedia of Language and Education*, 2nd edn, vol. 5: 225–38.

Johnson, R. K. and Swain, M. (1997) *Immersion Education: International Perspectives*, Cambridge: Cambridge University Press.

Kumaravadivelu, B. (1994) 'The postmethod condition: Emerging strategies for second/foreign language teaching', *TESOL Quarterly* 29: 27–48.

——(2003) *Beyond Methods: Macrostrategies for Language Teaching*, New Haven CT: Yale University Press.

——(2006) 'TESOL methods: Changing traces, challenging trends', *TESOL Quarterly* 40(1): 59–81.

Laurén, C. (1991) 'A two-phase-didactics for school', *Journal of Multilingual and Multicultural Development* 12(1&2): 67–72.

——(ed.) (1992) 'Introduktion', in *Language Acquisition at Kindergarten and School. Immersion Didactics in Canada, Catalonia and Finland*, Vaasa: University of Vaasa.

Lyster, R. (2007) *Learning and Teaching Languages through Content. A Counter-balanced Approach*, Amsterdam: John Benjamins.

——(2008) 'Counterbalancing form-focused and content-based instruction in immersion pedagogy', paper presented at 'Immersion Education: Pathways to Bilingualism and Beyond', St Paul, Minneapolis, 17 October.

Mar-Molinero, C. (1989) 'The teaching of Catalan in Catalonia', *The Journal of Multilingual and Multicultural Development* 10(4): 307–26.

May, S. (2008) 'Bilingual/immersion education: What the research tells us', in J. Cummins and N. H. Hornberger (eds) *Encyclopedia of Language and Education*, 2nd edn, vol. 5: 19–34.

Ó Muircheartaigh, J. and Hickey, T. (2008) 'Academic outcome, anxiety and attitudes in early and late immersion in Ireland', *International Journal of Bilingual Education and Bilingualism* 11(5): 558–76.

Pennycook, A. (2001) *Critical Applied Linguistics*, Mahwah, NJ: Lawrence Erlbaum.

Rebuffot, J. (2000) 'L'immersion au Canada: Politique, pedagogie et perspectives', paper presented at the 5th European Conference on Immersion Programmes, University of Vaasa/Vasa, Finland, 17–19 August.

Södergård, M. (2008) 'Teacher strategies for second language production in immersion kindergarten in Finland', in T. Williams Fortune and D. J. Tedick (eds) *Pathways to Multilingualism: Evolving Perspectives on Immersion Education*, Clevedon: Multilingual Matters.

Spezzini, S. (2005) 'English immersion in Paraguay: Individual and sociocultural dimensions of language learning and use', in A.-M. de Mejía (ed.) *Bilingual Education in South America*, Clevedon: Multilingual Matters.

Stern, H. (ed.) (1984) 'The immersion phenomenon' *Language and Society*, (special issue No. 12) 4–7, Ottawa: Commissioner of Official Languages.

Swain, M. (1982) 'Immersion education: Applicability for non-vernacular teaching to vernacular speakers', in B. Hartford, A. Valdman and C. Foster (eds) *Issues in International Bilingual Education: The Role of the Vernacular*, New York: Plenum Press.

——(1983) 'Bilingualism without tears', in M. Clarke and J. Handscombe (eds) *On TESOL '82: Pacific Perspectives on Language Learning and Teaching*, Washington, DC: Teachers of English to Speakers of Other Languages.

Swain, M. and Johnson, K. (1997) 'Immersion education: A category within bilingual education', in K. Johnson and M. Swain (eds) *Immersion Education: International Perspectives*, Cambridge: Cambridge University Press.

Valencia Giraldo, S. (2007) 'Empowerment and English language teaching (ELT) in public education in Colombia', paper presented in Language, Education and Diversity Conference, University of Waikato, Hamilton, New Zealand, 21–25 November.

Vesterbacka, S. (1991) 'Ritualised routines and L2 acquisition: Acquisition strategies in an immersion program', *Journal of Multilingual and Multicultural Development* 12(1&2): 35–43.

Williams Fortune, T. and Tedick, D. J. (eds) (2008) *Pathways to Multilingualism: Evolving Perspectives on Immersion Education*, Clevedon: Multilingual Matters.

12

Linguistic diversity and education

Christine Hélot

Introduction

With increased mobility and migration all over the world (Castles and Miller 2003), multilingualism has acquired a new visibility. Linguistic diversity is now a regular feature of our everyday experiences as can be witnessed in exchanges in public spaces, the workplace and in homes. Multilingualism is also visible in the linguistic landscape all around us, in films where it is no longer uncommon to hear actors speak in several languages, in various other media and on the World Wide Web where one is free to use any language in any form or shape.

Paradoxically, although schools everywhere and especially in urban centres have seen a growing change in their populations, the increased visibility of linguistic diversity is not reflected in classroom practices. Extra and Gorter (2001), for example, report 150 different languages spoken by pupils in schools in Hamburg and more than 350 in London, yet very few of these languages are supported by our education systems. Increased language contacts in the world and the growing need to communicate across language borders mean that educational language policies need to be reframed in order to take into account societal multilingualism. But although it is now accepted that multilingualism is the normal state of society as most people in the world speak more than one language, linguistic diversity remains a difficult challenge to address in education systems built on the ideology of linguistic uniformity, an ideology engrained in the formation of European nation-states. Conceived as linguistically and culturally homogenous spaces, our schools find it difficult to question their monolingual habitus, and to imagine that multilingual practices could become the norm in education as well.

Linguistic diversity in education raises many complex questions, which relate to language policy, language ideologies, educational history and language learning pedagogies. First, linguistic diversity challenges our traditional conceptualizations of language and language education. Second, it questions the assumption that teaching foreign or second languages is enough to protect linguistic diversity and, third, it points to the lack of recognition of migrant minority languages and different forms of bilingualism developed outside of the school context. What I would like to argue in this chapter is that the issue of linguistic diversity in education should not be approached only from the point of view of how to include as many languages as possible in the curriculum, or of how to answer the needs of students who do not speak the language of instruction. Although linguistic diversity in education obviously relates to areas of research such as foreign language teaching (FLT) or second language acquisition (SLA) and bilingual and multilingual education, it also has to do with developing new relationships to language and languages, new understandings of how language is used in society, an awareness of the rights of minority speakers to be educated in their home languages and a recognition that many languages in the world today are endangered.

These very wide issues concern society at large, politicians, employers, policy makers, the teaching community, parents and all learners. They should be a major concern for educationalists but it could also be considered paradoxical to ask schools to help sustain linguistic diversity when their main objective for over a century was to educate linguistically homogenous citizens through the eradication of differences. Indeed, over several centuries languages have been 'constructed' by states wanting to consolidate political power (Makoni and Pennycook 2007), and this has led to the division of language into different and discrete languages, to a belief that there is a privileged link between people and a territory and to languages functioning as autonomous entities in exclusionary relationships with each other. A long-held assumption was that knowledge of one language hindered the acquisition of another. Another common representation of languages is based on a hierarchy of values assigned to different languages and varieties, the national standard variety always being favoured, particularly by school systems, which reinforce and reproduce these attitudes.

Furthermore, language categorization and denomination as foreign or second, official or national, minority or majority, as well as speakers as native or non-native, have had a major influence on curriculum design and teaching approaches. On the one hand there is the 'mother tongue' and on the other 'foreign' languages, which have become separate university disciplines with distinct epistemologies. Even when foreign languages were introduced in the primary curriculum and taught by mainstream teachers they remained separate from the teaching of 'the' school language, in a somewhat similar manner to bilingual education models where the two languages of instruction are kept strictly separate. It is only more recently that the work of sociolinguists stressing the social dimension of language use and language learning has begun to have an influence on the way second languages are being taught, i.e. within a lifelong perspective that takes into account all the previous language experiences of the learner and recognizes both the cultural dimension and the process of identity negotiation involved in the learning of any new language.

The inclusion of foreign or second languages in school curricula is often believed to be a way of supporting linguistic diversity. For example, the European Commission Action Plan elaborated in Barcelona in 2002 decided that all Europeans should study at least two languages other than the school language during their obligatory schooling. Traditionally in Europe, many countries have had a long experience of offering several foreign languages in the curriculum but recent research (Cenoz 2009; Hélot 2008; Edwards 2010) has shown that it is not sufficient to ensure the sustainability of linguistic diversity: one of the reasons for this is that policy makers always favour dominant European languages at the expense of minority languages. Another reason is that many bilingual speakers of minority languages are not offered any support at schools to develop their home language, and often schools make them monolingual again. Furthermore, the wide choice of pedagogical approaches for the teaching of second languages are all aimed at improving linguistic competence – admittedly in more than one language – but teaching and learning strategies are designed with one specific language in mind. In other words, the monolingual perspective of foreign language learning, and up to a certain extent also of bilingual education (García 2009), has made it difficult to expand beyond the limited number of languages offered in schools and to include in classroom activities the diversity of languages spoken by today's students. Alongside focus on form and learning languages in isolation from one another, students should be made aware of the relationships between the multiplicity of languages spoken in the world today, of the extraordinary variety of writing systems, of the variety of speech forms within one single language and of the importance of valuing each language as part of an individual and societal form of cultural heritage or transmission (see, for example, the Ethnologue website, which offers an encyclopaedic reference work cataloguing all of the world's 6,909 known living languages at www.ethnologue.com/ and the Terralingua website at www.terralingua.org, which stresses the link between cultural and biological diversity).

One obvious way of opening our classrooms to linguistic diversity would be to include all the languages spoken by pupils at home in the pedagogical activities implemented in schools and to allow bilingual students to use their various languages to learn in class. I have previously pointed to the waste at work in our schools, which ignore the bilingualism of some students who end up becoming monolingual again in an education system where the aim is to educate future plurilingual citizens (Hélot 2006). The issue here concerns the linguistic support that should be given to bi- and multilingual learners irrespective of the status of the languages concerned. Bilingual education in Europe and elsewhere tends to be the preserve of elites who want to ensure a better future for their children; it is far less often offered as a model of language education to support immigrant minority language speakers. However, bilingual education in Europe has been a means to protect national or regional minority languages as in Ireland, Wales, the Basque Country and Catalonia for example, but immigrant minority languages on the whole have been left out of these programmes. Indeed, these languages are still being marginalized by most education systems reflecting immigration policies, which discriminate against immigrants from non-European countries. Yet in the same way that immigration brings wealth to a country, migrant languages are the very resource we need to sustain linguistic and cultural diversity and to foster intercultural understanding. For example, making space in a classroom for the languages spoken by some students whose parents or grandparents have migrated will give all students an opportunity to understand multilingualism, to become aware that some languages can become endangered when they are not passed on from parents to children and that they should be protected because they are part of our human heritage. Through the exploration of how different languages function, students can be brought to understand the relativity of differences at the linguistic and cultural level and that bi- or plurilingual speakers are the very ones who build bridges between people of different cultures (Hélot 2009).

In other words, understanding linguistic diversity in education means more than referring to a plurality of linguistic systems or to the coexistence of different languages in society, it means analysing the role of language(s) in education with a shift of perspective from the singular to the plural, or from a monoglossic to a heteroglossic perspective stressing the plurality of uses within each language and across different languages. And sustaining linguistic diversity in our schools is not the preserve of second or foreign language teachers, all teachers of all disciplines at all levels are concerned, including teachers working in bilingual programmes, because in a multilingual society we need citizens who can communicate in different languages and understand what it means to negotiate different languages and cultures in everyday exchanges. In terms of education this implies looking for a new conceptualization of language teaching as a whole, related not only to language use and needs in society, but also to the human and creative dimension of language central to our survival.

Early developments in the field: language awareness and knowledge about language

Following on from the remarks above, I consider that the area of research that has addressed the question of linguistic diversity in education is language awareness (LA) and/or knowledge about language (KAL) and, more recently, critical language awareness (CLA).

As distinct from aiming at linguistic competence in one or two languages other than the language of schooling, the objectives of LA as put forward by Hawkins (1999) were to develop a bridging subject that would

> stimulate curiosity about language as the defining characteristics of the 'articulate mammal' too easily taken for granted, to integrate the different kinds of language teaching met at school, and to help children to make an effective start in their foreign language learning.
>
> *(Hawkins 1999: 413)*

Hawkins was the first to point to the lack of coherence in language education and on the absence of any investigation into the phenomenon of language itself, in Britain in particular. He was critical of the lack of links between the teaching of the school language, of second languages (including classical languages) and of the languages of minority speakers. He saw the traditional borders within language education as preventing cooperation between teachers of English and teachers of other languages, and thought that the traditional approaches to foreign language teaching (FLT) developed excessive Eurocentrism. Hawkins was looking for a more integrated approach to language education to challenge the traditional atomistic curriculum. He believed that all languages at school – the language of instruction, the 'foreign' languages and the languages spoken by ethnic minorities – should serve the purpose of understanding the nature and the function of language in society. In other words, as made clearer by van Lier (1996) learners in school should make sense of their language learning experiences, they should be made aware of what language is, of its role at the individual as well as at the societal level, and of what language (and languages) does for us and for others.

In the context of TESOL, Bolitho and Tominson (1980) also used the term 'language awareness' to refer to three components in language teaching: knowledge of language, knowledge about language, and pedagogical practice. Knowledge about language (KAL) was further investigated by Carter (1990), who took a functional view of language and explained that in KAL emphasis is placed on the description of language in social contexts. According to van Hessen (2008), who gives a very incisive historical overview of LA going back to the nineteenth century, Carter's approach is more political than Hawkins', in that Carter argues for the empowerment of learners; he explains that the aims of KAL are to bring learners to see through language ideologies, to be informed about the sources of attitudes to language, to be aware of its social use and misuse and of the way language is used to manipulate. In other words, Carter believed that KAL should help learners to take ownership of their own language competence and understand the power of language to change their lives. Other authors such as James (1999) define KAL as knowledge aimed at bringing to the conscious attention of the learners particular aspects of how language functions as a system and how it can be used in society to exclude or discriminate speakers of minority languages, for example, or of non-dominant varieties.

LA and KAL have both been seen as important tools for learners but also for the education of language teachers in order to assist their understanding of language structure *and* function.

Both LA and KAL have been an issue of interest in the teaching of the language of instruction and in foreign language education, although with somewhat different perspectives and emphasis according to the linguistic and cultural background of researchers (see Kots 2008 for KAL). Van Lier (1996) considers that the range of interpretation of both terms makes it difficult to decide whether they are synonymous terms or whether one is a subset of the other. One notes the same ambiguity in the definition given on the website of the Association for Language awareness (www.languageawareness.org/), which states that LA is about 'explicit knowledge about language and conscious perception and sensitivity in language learning, language teaching and language use'.

In continental Europe, the work of Hawkins influenced researchers working in the field of 'language didactics' such as Dabène (1994) and later on Candelier (2003) and Hélot (2007) in France, Haenisch and Thürmann (1994) and Oomen-Welke (1998) in Germany. In Switzerland Perregaux (1998) and De Pietro (1995) were researching the domain of intercultural education and looking for ways to integrate minority languages and cultures in the mainstream primary curriculum. The expression 'language awareness' was translated, stressing different dimensions according to the various contexts of research: Candelier (2008) in France chose 'Awakening to Languages', whereas Perregaux et al. (2003) in Switzerland preferred 'Education and Opening to Languages and Cultures'.

However, what should be noted here is that the same objectives were present in these new approaches to language education: knowledge about language and linguistic diversity should be included in the mainstream curriculum alongside FLT, and learners speaking a minority language should see their linguistic competence in their first language (L1) acknowledged and valued in the school context. In other words, all learners should be given the opportunity to observe the differences between the language(s) of the classroom and the language(s) of real life, and should be educated to value linguistic and cultural diversity. Such aims were notably absent from FLT objectives, mainly because FLT implies that only one or two languages are taught, and the didactics of foreign languages (FL) are based on keeping each language separate, preventing learners from developing a more integrated or holistic approach to language learning. Such an approach would imply an engagement with language learning not only in the FL and mother tongue classrooms, but also across all subjects in the curriculum, and should eventually lead to multilingual education, i.e. the use of several different languages for instruction.

Furthermore, one needs to understand that starting FLT at an earlier stage in the curriculum might have some beneficial effect on linguistic competence, but it can also be counter-productive as far as supporting linguistic diversity is concerned: in most countries, because of the preferred choice for a dominant international language from the start of schooling, the hegemony of English has grown considerably, and affects all levels of education. For example, in the 1990s, when many European countries introduced the teaching of a foreign language into their primary curricula, English became the prevalent language taught in most schools across Europe, and such a choice means that it remains the main language learnt at university and in teacher education (see the Eurydice website for statistics: http://eacea.ec.europa.eu/education/eurydice/index_en.php).

Moreover, it soon became obvious that starting FLT earlier in the curriculum did not change attitudes nor approaches towards language learning: all learners were considered as beginners and as monolinguals who had no prior experience with language except with the language of schooling (Hélot 2007; Hélot and Young 2005). Not surprisingly, early FLT had no impact on attitudes towards students who came to school with a different home language. It did not help to dispel negative attitudes towards second language speakers of minority languages whose priority to acquire the school language should not be impeded by the learning of yet another language. This means that adding new languages in a curriculum does not necessarily work towards a better understanding of linguistic diversity and multilingualism.

Policy issues

Linguistic diversity in education has been at the core of all the language policy documents emanating from European institutions, as well as from some international organizations such as UNESCO or the Organisation for Economic Co-operation and Development (OECD). For example, UNESCO (available online at http://portal.unesco.org/education/en/ev.php-URL_ID=19635&URL_DO= DO_TOPIC&URL_SECTION=201.html), has reconsidered its position on linguistic diversity in education: whereas the declaration of 1953 insisted on the use of vernacular languages in education, the 2003 report entitled *Education Position Paper: Education in a Multilingual World* now stresses the role of languages and cultures – in the plural – as well as bi- and multilingual teaching at all levels of education. UNESCO still supports the rights of children to be educated in their first language, but the recent emphasis lies more with multilingual education as a key element of linguistically diverse societies and as a means to promote both social and gender equity. And safeguarding linguistic and cultural diversity is viewed as one of the most urgent challenges facing our world.

In the same way, European institutions such as the Language Policy division of the Council of Europe and the European Commission keep producing policy documents, recommendations and reports insisting that linguistic diversity must be protected because it is intrinsically linked to democratic citizenship. As the linguistic reality in Europe is of the utmost complexity and because everyone is aware that multilingual public spheres (Frazer 1994) will be a long-term phenomenon, the European Commission launched a new framework strategy for multilingualism in 2005. Part I.1 of this document refers to diversity in the following way:

> The European Union is founded on 'unity in diversity': diversity of cultures, customs and beliefs – and of languages. […] It is this diversity that makes the European Union what it is: not a 'melting pot' in which differences are rendered down, but a common home in which diversity is celebrated, and where our many mother tongues are a source of wealth and a bridge to greater solidarity and mutual understanding.
>
> *(European Commission 2005: 2)*

Further on in point 1.2. the main aims of the strategy are outlined in the following terms: 'to encourage language learning and to promote linguistic diversity in society'. Not surprisingly, the two dimensions refer to the distinction discussed above between knowledge of languages and knowledge about languages, the main problem remaining in the way both dimensions can be articulated in practice. But interestingly, the European Commission now sees multilingualism as a new field of policy in order 'to promote a climate that is conducive to the full expression of all languages, in which the teaching and learning of a variety of languages can flourish' (2005: 3).

The Council of Europe with its Language Policy Division created in 1994, has been particularly prolific in producing policies, reports, studies and frameworks all related to the promotion of language learning and to the protection of linguistic diversity in society and in education. At a conference organised in 1999 in Innsbruck entitled *Linguistic Diversity for Democratic Citizenship in Europe*, the various experts present recognized that learning one dominant language from the start of schooling did not necessarily lead to values such as openness to others, intercultural understanding and solidarity. As Byram (2000: 57–8) writes in the proceedings of the conference: 'We have to admit that the fact of teaching foreign languages is not enough to guarantee the development of a multilingual identity or other values such as tolerance, understanding of others and the desire for justice as is often proclaimed as a declaration of intent'.

The next year (2001), the *Council of Europe Common European Framework of Reference for Languages* was published with two main goals for language education in Europe: education for plurilingualism as a targeted competence with plurilingual awareness as a value. In this now well-known document among second language professionals, it is the notion of plurilingualism, which is seen as the form of education appropriate to European reality. Although everybody agrees with the necessity of learning several languages, or plurilingualism as a targeted competence, plurilingual awareness as a value has been more difficult to translate into pedagogical terms. As stated by Beacco and Byram (2003: 16), 'plurilingual awareness should be structured and assisted by schools since it is in no sense automatic'.

I would like to argue that this is where the various pedagogical approaches developed within language awareness (LA) find their *raison d'être* and there are several reasons for this: first, LA activities do not focus on just one language but include many languages that can be compared to one another and to the school language; second, they lend themselves particularly well to the inclusion of minority languages that can become integrated in pedagogical projects; and third, they are designed to foster an understanding of linguistic diversity and positive attitudes towards multilingualism. In other words, at the heart of LA approaches lies a new conceptualization of language education where the question of values – such as linguistic tolerance for example – is as important as the question of competence. Thus education for plurilingual awareness is seen as one of the requirements for the protection of linguistic diversity and through education for linguistic tolerance, it is linked to education for democratic citizenship.

What is noteworthy about the various policies promoted by the Council of Europe is that they are informed by the work of experts looking for a coherent and common approach as the basis for the development of language education policies and a global concept for languages. The best example of such work is Beacco and Byram's *Guide for the Development of Language Education Policies in Europe* (2003), which is available on the Council of Europe's website (www.coe.int/lang). This guide is not only highly readable, it is a model of the genre because the authors do not advocate any particular language education policy measures, rather they seek to clarify the issues involved and to define the goals at work in such policies. In their attempt to draw up common principles complying with the values of the Council of Europe, they see the concept of plurilingualism as central to a renewal in thinking on the language education policies that different member states have conducted (see the excellent report on Ireland for example, Council of Europe 2008). And plurilingualism, along with the notions of diversity, tolerance, and cohesion, is reorganized around two central concepts: plurilingual repertoire and plurilingual competence.

Plurilingual repertoire

A plurilingual repertoire encompasses all the language experiences of a person irrespective of the level of competence attained in the different languages. This means that all the languages (or varieties of languages) known by a person should be recognized and then supported so that her various linguistic competences find their legitimate place within her lifelong learning experiences. This is very important for languages acquired or learnt outside of formal schooling, such as minority languages for example, which should also be recognized as part of the linguistic repertoire of learners. Moreover, a plurilingual repertoire is by nature heterogeneous: it is a repertoire of communicative resources that speakers use according to their needs, and because it is dynamic it changes in time and in composition according to the person's experiences. Thus plurilingualism is seen as an unexceptional ability shared by all speakers and in terms of a competence that can be acquired and which is within everyone's grasp.

Plurilingual competence

Likewise the notion of plurilingual competence is interesting because it helps to reframe the notion of competence or mastery of several languages away from the benchmark of native-speaker ability. A plurilingual competence is not synonymous with mastering a great number of languages at high level but with acquiring the ability to use more than one linguistic variety to differing degrees and for different purposes. This has consequences for teaching as explained by Beacco and Byram (2003: 39):

> It is less a matter of deciding which and how many foreign languages should be taught in education systems than of directing the goals of language education towards the acquisition of a competence in fact unique, encompassing the mother tongue, the national language(s), regional and minority languages, European and non European languages, etc. This is a realistic goal if it is accepted that plurilingual repertoires developed through education can be diverse, that the languages that are components of plurilingual competence do not all have to be learnt at the same level and that language education takes place throughout life and not exclusively during school years.

To summarize, the language policies of the Council of Europe aim to promote multilingualism, to sustain linguistic diversity, to develop mutual understanding and democratic citizenship and they also consider access to language learning throughout life as a factor for social cohesion. However, one should not forget that such values are being promoted by European institutions working at a supranational level towards the development of a European identity, but that the policy documents are only recommendations, interpreted differently by each state in a Europe that has made sure education should remain a national prerogative. For example, the widely used *Common European Framework of Reference for Languages* (Council of Europe: 2001) claims to be an instrument to assist member-states to develop policies for plurilingualism, but its main focus is to propose a common basis for the elaboration of curricula, syllabuses and reference points to plan and evaluate foreign language learning and teaching. At no point does it question the use of the national official language as the main language of instruction and one is struck by the way the different competences described are also framed within a monolingual perspective. Although it is possible to use the language levels to evaluate one's competence in different languages, it remains based on an additive vision of plurilingualism, which does not take into account hybrid practices, translanguaging and the recursive and dynamic nature of bilingual practices (García 2009).

Key issues of theory and methods

Diversification vs diversity

One of the key issues relating to linguistic diversity in language education lies in the meaning ascribed to the term 'diversity' and to the way it is interpreted by policy makers and subsequently implemented in education systems. For example, it is quite common to think that linguistic diversity can be promoted through offering a wider range of languages in a curriculum, so that students have a large choice and do not all end up studying the same dominant European language. Although it seems obvious that a large choice of different languages should be offered to sustain linguistic diversity in our education systems, I agree with Beacco and Byram (2003: 36) who explain that 'Diversifying the supply of languages is a necessary, but insufficient condition for acting on motivation to undertake plurilingual education'.

I shall use France as an example to illustrate the limits of a policy of diversification. All children in France start studying a foreign language at the age of seven and have to learn a second one at the age of 12 and a third one is offered on an optional basis later on. When they take their final secondary examination (baccalaureate) they can choose from 56 'foreign' languages including eight 'regional' languages (BO 13 2008). The primary curriculum offers a choice of eight different languages: Arabic, English, German, Spanish, Italian, Russian, Portuguese and Chinese, and the Ministry of Education has published very useful pedagogical guidelines for teachers in each one of these languages. Detailed programmes for the teaching of regional languages and recently for French Sign Language have also been published (BO 33 2008), which means that FSL is now one of the many languages that can be taught in French schools. In reality, 86 per cent of primary students choose English and at secondary level 93 per cent choose English as a first FL (representing five million students) and 70 per cent Spanish as a second FL.

Clearly, it cannot be denied that at policy level, the Ministry of Education is putting into place all the necessary legal dispositions for a great variety of languages to be taught, as well as clear curricula for each language and pedagogical orientations based on the Council of Europe recommendations for language teaching. But the gap between support for linguistic diversity at the policy level and the restricted choice in practice at the school level is glaring. The reasons for this are numerous, no doubt relating to the cost of implementing such policies, as well as to social pressure for the teaching of English and a reluctance to give too much space to some languages of immigration like Arabic or Turkish. In other words, a policy of diversification does not mean that more languages are studied, or more space is given to language teaching or more importantly that the unequal status of languages is questioned. In fact, the way FLT is organized means that FLs are in competition with one another, as parents have to decide on one language at primary, and most minority languages stand little chance in the face of a dominant language like English. This means that top-down policies are far from sufficient to ensure that linguistic diversity is sustained in our education systems, and that linguistic diversity cannot be conceptualized solely on a quantitative basis.

Diversity as heritage

A different interpretation of the term diversity is proposed by Beacco and Byram (2003) who see linguistic diversity as heritage and thus distinct from the issue of foreign languages. They mention 220 Indigenous linguistic varieties in Europe, not including the languages of immigrants and refugees, and in the name of biodiversity this overall multiplicity of languages must be considered as an anthropological and cultural heritage worthy of protection. What is at stake here is the preservation of the living diversity of languages spoken in Europe and the multilingual nature of European societies. However, these authors do not use the term heritage to refer to the languages of minority speakers, as is the case in the USA for example (García 2005). Diversity as heritage is envisaged from a historical point of view, the linguistic and cultural diversity of the countries that make up the European Union being one of the core features of European identity, and language policy makers always assert the need to protect this diversity in the face of any threat of linguistic and cultural homogenization.

Many of these so-called regional, national minority or immigrant minority languages are spoken and transmitted in the family context before schooling. The question arising here is the extent to which schools acknowledge these minority languages, support their maintenance or prefer to ignore the linguistic and cultural competence acquired outside of the school context. Although many different answers to this question have been proposed throughout the world, the PISA evaluations (Programme for International Student Assessment 2009) have clearly shown that in all OECD countries most immigrant minority students achieve lower scores than their autochtonous peers. This is the very reason why many researchers have argued for more school support of the L1 of minority language speakers and for bilingual education (Cummins 2000, 2001; Baker 2001).

But today bilingual education is only available to very few students and, given the extent of linguistic diversity in some of our classrooms, it has become more difficult for teachers to envisage how to support the L1 of their pupils. Teachers often express their helplessness in terms of their limited competence in FLs as if the only answer was to be found in linguistic competence rather than in devising new pedagogical approaches that accommodate linguistic heterogeneity and support language transmission in the home. Several researchers have shown that teachers are inadequately prepared for dealing with linguistic diversity (Bourne 2003), which features remain on the margins of teacher education curricula. Young (2006) explains that it demands a lot of time for teachers' representations of multilingualism to evolve in a country like France, for example, but Hélot (2010) also shows that beginner teachers are able to negotiate their own language policies at the classroom level and become agents of change for their multilingual pupils.

Again, LA approaches are useful because they aim to normalize linguistic diversity in schools and to build knowledge about diversity from the language competence students bring to the classroom. Furthermore, as noted by Dabène (1994), LA approaches have a welcoming function in that the pedagogical activities make it possible to welcome as many languages as are present in a class. This welcoming function is particularly important for minority language speakers, who see some value put on their family culture as well as their bilingualism becoming an asset in traditionally monolingual classrooms. For example, in the Didenheim project researched by Hélot and Young (2006) and Hélot (2007) the teachers developed language awareness activities in collaboration with parents, which involved exploring 18 languages over three years. The project was inclusive of the languages spoken by the students and their families, and led to the formerly untapped resources of minority-language speakers becoming part of school knowledge. As a result, a new form of socialization developed in the classroom (and to a certain extent outside of the school) based on solidarity and reciprocity (Perregaux 1998) because students learnt from one another and teachers also learnt from their students and their parents. Without the collaboration of parents, the teachers could not have carried out their project; at the same time the project led to the empowerment of the minority language-speaking parents, because they were given real responsibilities in the new learning situation (see Feltin's 2008 film for more details).

From language awareness to multiliteracy pedagogies

However, one should not forget the danger of tokenism associated with LA approaches when they consist in superficial activities, which are not integrated into the mainstream curriculum. And rather than suggesting like Hawkins that LA should be integrated as a separate subject in the school curriculum, researchers have argued for a cross-curricular approach in which all school subjects can give rise to projects or activities in several different languages, bilingual learners can build on their knowledge of their L1 to acquire their second language (L2) and they can invest their identity to make sense of their learning experiences. One such example is given by Cummins (2006) who explains how educators can challenge the exclusion of students' linguistic and cultural capital from the school through the development of new forms of pedagogies for multiliteracy development.

These pedagogies are based on several principles: that students should be able to develop strong literacy skills in their home language as well as in the school language, that new technologies should be used to give a space to less dominant languages and that home language literacies should be supported. In other words, what Cummins (2006) is arguing for is the creation of interpersonal spaces within the mainstream classroom that support literacy in both the school language and the home language. The texts produced are called 'identity texts' because students invest their own identity in their creative work, which then holds a mirror up to them in which their identities are reflected back in a positive light. When these texts are shared with multiple audiences or posted on the web, they get an expanded exposure, they also have to be more accomplished and they can enhance the process of identity investment and affirmation.

Multiliteracy pedagogies go further than LA activities as conceived originally by Hawkins and European researchers who have developed materials for teachers to deal with the linguistic diversity of their pupils, because multiliteracy pedagogies allow bilingual students to learn at school through their two languages. Students not only learn about language diversity, but also use a diversity of languages to learn to read and write, for example, and are thus involved in a form of multilingual education.

Whereas in LA activities, the materials and the didactic approaches developed alongside make space for a diversity of languages to enter the mainstream classroom, and allow for the recognition of the cultural and linguistic capital that students bring to the classroom, multiliteracy pedagogies include a further dimension. As explained by Cummins (2006) in his analysis of a project in a school in Toronto, they challenge teachers in the mainstream class-room to rethink their approach to literacy teaching for all students, and at the same time they empower second language learners to build on their literacy skills in their L1 and the school language. In other words, multiliteracy pedagogies challenge further the exclusion of students' cultural and linguistic repertoires from instruction, rather than just sharing their knowledge about their L1 with their peers, they are allowed to learn through their L1, and build on it to learn through the language of instruction as well, thus developing bi- or multiliteracy. And because the languages of minority language speakers are more than just a subject of study but the means through which literacy is acquired alongside literacy in the school language, multi-lingualism is not merely valued, it becomes part of the learning experience of students who all experience the transformation of their classroom into a multilingual space.

Cummins is right to remind us that traditional pedagogical approaches based on transmission cannot accommodate the diversity of languages and cultures present in our classrooms because learning objectives are set to fit the whole class without taking into account the specificities of each learner and the social dimension of language. Social constructivist or transformative pedagogies, on the contrary, mean that students take ownership of their own languages by actively using their language for learning at school and out of school, they expand their linguistic and cultural capital and they have some control over their learning process. There-fore what must be implemented in our diverse classrooms today is not just a set of activities to include the numerous languages of students in a class but bi- and multilingual instructional strategies that make it possible for learners to transfer knowledge and cognitive strategies across languages, to compare language use and critically assess information; in other words to develop critical literacy.

From language awareness to multilingual language awareness in teacher education

Teacher education about linguistic and cultural diversity is a crucial domain to research if we expect our schools to prepare students to live and act in a complex world in which they will have to interact with various kinds of differences. But, as explained by Young (2006) who evaluated a new teacher education module in France, the journey can be very long for teachers who start with negative representations of their students' linguistic and cultural competence, or who frame the second languages spoken by their pupils as a problem for the acquisition of the school language and for learning in general. Compensatory approaches are so entrenched in educational practices aimed at supporting minority language speakers that it takes not only time, but also a complete shift of representations, for teachers to envisage their bilingual students' linguistic and cultural knowledge as central to the needs of contemporary society. Although most teachers are aware of the challenge posed by linguistic diversity, it is a rather complex matter to bring them to rethink pedagogical approaches to literacy within a multilingual framework.

As Hawkins (1999) noted, one of the principal challenges for the LA movement was to provide adequate preparation for teachers to guide their pupils in the kind of discovery-based learning that is required and at the same time to challenge their own linguistic prejudices towards bilingual learners (Hélot and Young 2006). Although we agree with García (2008) that today 'it behoves language teachers to put language difference at the centre of the educational enterprise', it entails a profound change of attitudes and beliefs in societies and education systems in which a very monoglossic ideology still prevails. And I would like to add that like Hawkins (1999) and Bourne (2003), I believe it is vital to design LA courses not just for language teachers but for all teachers, because all teachers of all disciplines are concerned by language and languages, issues of exclusion, discrimination, inequity, etc.

García (2008) is right to insist that what she calls 'Multilingual Language Awareness' (MLA) must be a thread that runs right through the entire teacher education curriculum, and for teachers working with multilingual populations as well as for bilingual teachers working in bilingual and multilingual schools. For example, Luxembourg is a country well known for its trilingual education system, yet the curriculum does not address the languages of all its learners (there are many Portuguese-speaking children, see Weber 2009) and teachers are left to find their own approaches to use the full repertoire of linguistic resources in the classroom. Again, this is not a question of merely adapting strategies, which have been used before with second language learners and bilingual children, rather it is about finding ways of using multilingual language awareness pedagogically.

'The key role played by teachers highlights the challenge for teacher education to address the continually changing needs of diverse multilingual populations', write Kenner and Hickey (2008: 186) who see teachers at the interface between policy and learners and who by necessity adapt their practices and their pedagogies to the needs of their students (Hélot 2010; Menken and García 2010). Nevertheless a lot of teachers feel ill-equipped to teach in multilingual classrooms and teacher education institutions are often slow to take on board the growing linguistic diversity of the school population because it means finding space in very crowded curricula for what is often perceived as an extra domain of knowledge rather than a cross-curricular issue. A noteworthy initiative has been developed at Goldsmiths, University of London where a teacher education course in five 'minority languages' is offered. As explained by Anderson (2008), the course builds on the experience of multilingualism that the student teachers bring with them, which means that the institution not only values minority languages as much as dominant European languages but that it also empowers bilingual students of minority background to join the teaching profession and to change general attitudes towards multilingualism in schools.

New research directions

Many reports highlight the urgent need for appropriate initial and in-service education for teachers and if linguistic diversity is to be sustained in and by our schools, educational institutions should be supported to prepare large numbers of bi- and multilingual teachers, not only for bilingual programmes but also for mainstream classrooms. As explained by Skilton-Sylvester (2003) and Menken and García (2010), teachers are at the epicentre of language policy in education and they can act as change agents of the various policies they must translate into practice. But in order to be able to act on their professional environment, they need an understanding of the reasons why models of language education as we know them have been dominated for years by concern for monolingual speakers.

The linguistic exclusion of bi- and multilingual students of immigrant background and of speakers from socially deprived backgrounds remains one of the main challenges for researchers and practitioners today. Despite all the discourses on inclusion and integration, very few bilingual students are given adequate support to develop their home languages fully alongside the language(s) of instruction and the variety of language use within one language is rarely given space in the teaching of the language of instruction. Apart from the serious issue of the linguistic rights of speakers, the result is loss of linguistic diversity and lower achievement at school.

There are various research directions in several domains that open up new doors for our understanding of the complex interactions between linguistic diversity in society and the necessary transformation of our education systems in the twenty-first century. We will mention particular studies that are based on an understanding of the social, political and economic struggles surrounding the use of language and languages.

Central to a new framing and a recontextualization of linguistic diversity is the work carried out by post-structuralist researchers focusing on language ideologies: rather than seeing linguistic diversity only in terms of a plurality or multiplicity of languages, they envisage it also as the expression of difference (see Le Nevez 2006 for a very clear review of theoretical approaches to linguistic diversity). The notion of difference adds an important dimension to the discussion because as Heller and Martin-Jones (2001) have shown, linguistic diversity also has to do with social differences bound up in language and these differences result in the reproduction of inequalities by our education systems. However, more importantly, Heller and Martin-Jones (ibid.) stressed the need to uncover the way ideologies pervade language choice and language policy in schools. The same concern for the deconstruction of ideologies is at the heart of the work of Creese and Martin (2003), Hornberger (2003) and García (2009).

The language ecology metaphor used by Creese and Martin and Hornberger is a further development to help rethink linguistic diversity in its relationship between the wider cultural and political environment and the classroom environment. Mühlhaüsler (1996) was one of the first researchers to argue for a radical reframing of language education within an ecological perspective. Because he was working in the Pacific region, he analysed the effects of education programmes on local linguistic ecologies, and questioned the impact of language learning at school on language maintenance outside the classroom. Creese and Martin studied specifically multilingual classrooms through an ecological perspective and explained how

> an ecological approach to language in society requires an exploration of the relationship of languages to each other and to the society in which these languages exist. This includes

the geographical, socio-economic and cultural conditions in which the speakers of a given language exist, as well as the wider linguistic environment.

(2003: 161)

Their excellent introduction and the subsequent chapters elaborating on the complex relationships at play between language use and interactions in the classroom and the wider environment, give a clear understanding of the dominant role of ideologies in language policies and practices and how the ecology of the classroom is influenced by the wider linguistic ecology.

As for Hornberger (2003), also working within the ecology of language approach, her 'continua of biliteracy' model not only makes transparent the ideologies that pervade language policies and language choice, but also helps to uncover the reasons for the unequal balance of power across languages and literacies, and why some languages and linguistic practices are supported by education systems and others are not. Through her model, educators can begin to understand how their language choices and practices in their own classrooms reproduce the relationships of power at play in society or challenge them to implement new learning spaces in which a diversity of linguistic practices can thrive.

García's recent volume (2009: 16) on *Bilingual Education for the Twenty-First Century* sees bilingual education as the only way to educate children as the world moves forward. She argues that, 'the challenge of bilingual schools is to prepare children to balance their own linguistic ecology, enabling them to go back and forth in their overlapping languages and literacies'. Most interesting is the way she analyses the notion of translanguaging as 'multiple discursive practices in which bilinguals engage in order to make sense of their bilingual worlds' (García 2009: 45). By focusing on discourse and the language practices of the bilinguals from the perspective of the users themselves and moving beyond the notions of language contact or codeswitching, as is so often the case in bilingual teaching, she points to a different epistemology of language. Like Pennycook (2004) she is interested in language as a productive effect of expression rather than as a prior defined system or code that exists independently of its speakers and she stresses the fact that the concept of translanguaging means that there are no clear-cut boundaries between the languages of bilinguals. Moreover, her proposal for new discursive and dynamic models of bilingual education based on a heteroglossic ideology in which the diversity of languaging practices and the linguistic heterogeneity of students is acknowledged, clearly shows that traditional bilingual education models are also challenged by the increased linguistic diversity of our globalized societies.

To conclude, I would like to quote Le Nevez's (2006: 77) remark that 'the question is not so much how can minority languages be promoted but rather how can linguistic diversity be rethought in ways that do not discursively disempower speakers whose language represents diversity and difference?' Exploring alternative ways of thinking about linguistic diversity in education is also about opening new spaces in which language activism can be situated. In my opinion, the most stimulating research to help rethink teacher education in terms of language activism comes from various critical approaches, such as critical pedagogies (Freire 1970; Giroux 1988), critical discourse analysis (Fairclough and Wodak 1996), critical literacies (Shor 1992; Street 1995) and critical applied linguistics (Pennycook 2001).

All these related critical approaches are involved in emancipatory educational practices, where difference is recognized within teaching as an oppositional practice in which all participants are working towards the prospects for empowerment, especially of students or structures that have been disempowered or excluded in the past. Critical language awareness (CLA) more specifically offers a new orientation to language education because it addresses teachers' awareness of the ideological and political nature of language functioning, it provides them with the linguistic tools to be socially committed and engaged, and it stresses their social responsibilities (Fairclough 1992). As argued by Pennycook (2001), not only do we need to focus on the politics of language (and text) and the politics of pedagogy, we need to understand *the politics of difference*, or the way the notion of otherness is framed in our methodologies and whether we conceive of learners as having multiple identities and drawing on their multiple linguistic resources or not. Because linguistic diversity and difference is about respect for the languages of people belonging to different linguistic communities, and we know that respect is essential to peaceful cohabitation. And because, as van Lier (2004) convincingly argues, diverse societies in terms of language, ethnicity, religion, etc., may in the long run be much healthier than homogeneous ones.

Related topics

Discourses about linguistic diversity; multilingualism in education in post-colonial contexts; regional minorities, education and language revitalization; immersion education; multilingual pedagogies; multilingualism and social exclusion; disinventing multilingualism; multilingual literacies; linguistic landscapes and multilingualism.

Further reading

Cenoz, J. and Hornberger, N. H. (eds) (2008) *Encyclopedia of Language and Education*, vol. 6, Knowledge about Language, New York: Springer.
(Twenty-nine review articles on language awareness and knowledge about language, language learning, bilingualism and multilingualism.)

Commins, N. L. and Miramontes, O. B. (2005) *Linguistic Diversity and Teaching*, NJ Mahwah, Lawrence: Erlbaum.
(An opportunity for teachers and educators to reflect on their teaching methods and principles through case studies of real classroom situations in the USA, classrooms with a very diverse student body.)

Conteh, J. (2003) *Succeeding in Diversity: Culture, Language and Learning in Primary Classrooms*, Trentham: Trentham Books.
(Interesting case study of ethnic minority students who became high achievers at primary school in Britain. For policy makers, teacher educators and teachers to understand the importance of linking home and school languages and cultures.)

Edwards, J. (2010) *Language Diversity in the Classroom*, Clevedon: Multilingual Matters.
(Provides a comprehensive coverage of language contact in classroom settings and an analysis of the sources and implications of social 'disadvantage' brought about by the use of non-standard dialects. Interesting volume for teacher educators.)

García, O. Skutnabb-Kangas, T. and Torres Guzman, M. E. (eds) (2006) *Imagining Multilingual Schools: Languages in Education and Glocalization*, Clevedon: Multilingual Matters.
(For teachers and researchers. Analyses pedagogical and policy efforts in different parts of the world to develop multilingualism in schools with different populations: immigrant students, Indigenous peoples, traditional minorities, majorities and multi-ethnic groups.)

Kenner, C. and Hickey, T. (eds) (2008) *Multilingual Europe: Diversity and Learning*, Trentham: Trentham Books.
(Analyses how to create multilingual learning communities and describes interesting case studies of innovative practice promoting language expertise, intercultural education and educational achievement in seven different countries in Europe and in Israel.)

Bibliography

Anderson, J. (2008) 'Initial teacher education for teachers of Arabic, Mandarin Chinese, Panjabi and Urdu', in C. Kenner and T. Hickey (eds) *Multilingual Europe: Diversity and Learning*, Trentham: Trentham Books.

Baker, C. (2001) *Foundations of Bilingual Education and Bilingualism*, Clevedon: Multilingual Matters.

Beacco, J. C. and Byram, M. (2003) *Guide for the Development of Language Education Policies in Europe: From Linguistic Diversity to Plurilingual Education*, Strasbourg: Council of Europe.

BO 13, *Bulletin Officiel de l'Éducation Nationale*, n°13 du 27 mars 2008, available online at www. education.gouv.fr/bo/2008/13/MENE0801840A.html

BO 33, *Bulletin Officiel de l' Éducation Nationale*, n°33 du 4 septembre 2008, available online at www.education.gouv.fr/cid22247/mene0817503a.html

Bolitho, R. and Tominson, B. (1980) *Discover English*, London: Allen and Unwin.

Bourne, J. (2003) 'Remedial or radical? Second language support for curriculum learning', in J. Bourne and E. Reid (eds) *Language Education, World Yearbook of Education, 2003*, London: Kogan.

Byram, M. (2000) 'Linguistic diversity and citizenship education', in Council of Europe (ed.) *Linguistic Diversity for Democratic Citizenship in Europe: Proceedings*, Strasbourg: Council of Europe.

Candelier, M. (2003) *L'éveil aux langues à l'école primaire. EVLANG: Bilan d'une innovation*, Bruxelles: De Boeck.

——(2008) 'Awakening to languages and educational language policy', in J. Cenoz and N. H. Hornberger (eds) *Encyclopedia of Language and Education*, 2nd edn, vol. 6, *Knowledge about Language*, New York: Springer.

Carter, R. (1990) *Knowledge about Language and the Curriculum: The LINC Reader*, London: Hodder and Stoughton.

Castles, S. and Miller, M. J. (2003) *The Age of Migration*, 3rd edn, Basingstoke and New York: Palgrave Macmillan

Cenoz, J. (2009) *Towards Multilingual Education. Basque Educational Research from an International Perspective*, Bristol: Multilingual Matters.

Council of Europe (2001) *Common European Framework of Reference for Languages*, Language Policy Division, Strasbourg: Council of Europe, available online at www.coe.int/T/DG4/Linguistic/ CADRE_EN.asp

——(2008) *Language Education Policy Profile*, Ireland, available online at www.coe.int/T/DG4/ Linguistic/Profils1_EN.asp

Creese, A. and Martin, P. (eds) (2003) *Multilingual Classroom Ecologies*, Clevedon: Multilingual Matters.

Cummins, J. (2000) *Language, Power and Pedagogy*, Clevedon: Multilingual Matters.

——(2001) *Negotiating Identities: Education for Empowerment in a Diverse Society*, Los Angeles: California Association for Bilingual Education.

——(2006) 'Identity texts: The imaginative construction of self through multiliteracies pedagogy', in O. García et al. (eds) *Imagining Multilingual Schools: Languages in Education and Glocalization*, Clevedon: Multilingual Matters.

Dabène, L. (1994) *Repères Sociolinguistiques pour l'enseignement des langues*, Paris: Hachette.

De Pietro, J. F. (1995) 'Vivre et apprendre les langues autrement à l'école – une expérience d'éveil au langage à l'école primaire', *Babylonia* (2): 2–36.

Edwards, J. (2010) *Language Diversity in the Classroom*, Clevedon: Multilingual Matters.

European Commission (2005) *Commission Communication. A New Framework Strategy for Multilingualism*, pdf file com596_en.pdf

Extra, G. and Gorter, D. (2001) *The Other Languages of Europe*, Clevedon: Multilingual Matters.

Fairclough, N. (1992) *Critical Language Awareness*, London: Longman

Fairclough, N. and Wodak, R. (1996) 'Critical discourse analysis', in T. van Dijk (ed.) *Discourse Analysis*, London: Sage.

Feltin, M. (2008) *Raconte Moi Ta Langue/Tell Me How You Talk*, 52' documentary film with English subtitles, Paris: La Curieuse, available online at www.racontemoitalangue.net

Frazer, N. (1994) 'Rethinking the public sphere: A contribution to the critique of actually existing democracy', in B. Robbins (ed.) *The Phantom Public Sphere*, Minnesota: University of Minnesota Press.

Freire, P. (1970) *Pedagogy of the Oppressed*, New York: Continuum.

García, O. (2005) 'Positioning heritage languages in the United States', *Modern Language Journal* 89(4): 601–5.

——(2008) 'Multilingual language awareness and teacher education', in J. Cenoz and N. H. Hornberger (eds) *Encyclopedia of Language and Education*, 2nd edn, vol. 6, *Knowledge about Language*, New York: Springer.

——(2009) *Bilingual Education in the 21st Century: A Global Perspective*, Chichester: Wiley-Blackwell.

García, O., Skutnabb-Kangas, T. and Torres Guzman, M. (eds) (2006) *Imagining Multilingual Schools: Languages in Education and Glocalization*, Clevedon: Multilingual Matters.

Giroux, H. (1988) *Schooling and the Struggle for Public Life: Critical Pedagogy in the Modern Age*, Minneapolis: Minneapolis University Press.

Haenisch, H. and Thürmann, E. (1994) *Begegnung mit Sprachen in der Grundschule. Eine empirische Untersuchung. Zum Entwicklungsstand, zur Akzeptanz und zu den Realisierungsformen von Begegnung mit Sprachen in den Grundschulen Nordrhein-Westfalens, Arbeitsberichte zur Curriculumentwicklung, Schul- und Unterrichtsforschung* n°30, Landesinstitut für Schule und Weiterbildung: Soest.

Hawkins, E. (1987) *Awareness of Language: An Introduction*, New York: Cambridge University Press.

——(1999) 'Language awareness', in B. Spolsky (ed.) *Concise Encyclopedia of Educational Linguistics*, Pergamon: Oxford.

Heller, M. and Martin-Jones, M. (eds) (2001) *Voices of Authority. Educational and Linguistic Difference*, Westport, CT: Ablex.

Hélot, C. (2006) 'De la notion d'écart à la notion de continuum. Comment analyser le caractère inégalitaire du bilinguisme en contexte scolaire', in C. Hélot, E. Hoffmann, M. Scheidhauser (eds) *Écarts de langue, écarts de culture. A l'école de l'autre*, Frankfurt: Peter Lang.

——(2007) *Du bilinguisme en famille au plurilinguisme à l'école*, Paris: L'Harmattan.

——(2008) 'Awareness raising and multilingualism in primary education', in J. Cenoz and N. H. Hornberger (eds) *Encyclopedia of Language and Education*, 2nd edn, vol. 6, *Knowledge about Language*, New York: Springer.

——(2009) 'La formation des enseignants en contexte plurilingue', in J. Vernaudon and V. Filliol (eds) *Vers une école plurilingue dans les Collectivités Françaises d'océanie et de Guyane*, Collection Cahiers du Pacifique Sud Contemporain, Hors Série n° 1. Paris: l'Harmattan.

——(2010) '"Tu sais bien parler maîtresse". Negotiating languages other than French in the primary classroom,' in K. Menken and O. García (eds) *Negotiating Language Policy in Schools: Educators as Policy Makers*, New York: Lawrence Erlbaum/Taylor & Francis/Routledge.

Hélot, C. and Young, A. (2005) 'Language education and diversity: Policy and practice at primary level in France', *Journal of Language, Culture and Curriculum* 242–57.

——(2006) 'Imagining multilingual education in France: A language and cultural awareness project at primary level', in O. García, T. Skutnabb-Kangas and M. E. Torres-Guzmán (eds) *Imagining Multilingual Schools: Languages in Education and Glocalization*, Clevedon: Multilingual Matters.

Hornberger, N. H. (ed.) (2003) *Continua of Biliteracy: An Ecological Framework for Educational Policy, Research, and Practice in Multilingual Settings*, Clevedon: Multilingual Matters.

James, C. (1999) 'Language awareness: implications for the language curriculum', *Language, Culture and Curriculum* 12: 94–115.

Kenner, C. and Hickey, T. (eds) (2008) *Multilingual Europe: Diversity and Learning*, Trentham: Trentham Books.

Kots, J. M. (2008) 'Knowledge about language in the mother tongue and foreign language curricula', in J. Cenoz and N. H. Hornberger (eds) *Encyclopedia of Language and Education*, 2nd edn, vol. 6, *Knowledge about Language*, New York: Springer.

Le Nevez, A. (2006) 'Language Diversity and Linguistic Identity in Brittany: A Critical Analysis of the Changing Practice of Breton', unpublished PhD dissertation, University of Technology, Sydney: Australia.

Makoni, S. and Pennycook, A. (eds) (2007) *Disinventing and Reconstituting Languages*, Clevedon: Multilingual Matters.

Menken, K. and García, O. (2010) *Negotiating Language Policy in Schools: Educators as Policy Makers*, New York: Lawrence Erlbaum/Taylor & Francis/Routledge.

Mühlhäusler, P. (1996) 'Linguistic Ecology: Language Change and Linguistic Imperialism in the Pacific Region', London: Routledge.

Oomen-Welke, I. (1998) 'Sprachen entdecken', in H. Giese and J. Ossner (eds) *Sprache Thematisieren – Fachdidaktische und Unterrichtswissenschatliche Aspekte*, Fribourg: Fillibach.

Pennycook, A. (2001) *Critical Applied Linguistics. A Critical Introduction*, Mahwah, NJ: Lawrence Erlbaum.

——(2004) 'Performativity and language studies', *Critical Enquiries in Language Studies* 1(1): 1–26.

Perregaux, C. (1998) 'Avec les approches d'éveil au langage l'interculturel est au centre de l'apprentissage scolaire', *Bulletin Suisse de Linguistique Appliquée* 67: 101–10.

Perregaux, C., De Goumoëns, C., Jeannot, D. and De Pietro, J. F. (2003) *Education et ouverture aux langues à l'école*, vol. 1 and 2, Neuchâtel: Conférence intercantonale de l'instruction publique de la Suisse et du Tessin.

Shor, I. (1992) *Empowering Education*, Chicago: University of Chicago Press.

Skilton-Sylvester, E. (2003) 'Legal discourse and decisions, teacher policymaking and the multilingual classroom: Constraining and supporting Kmer/English biliteracy in the United States', in A. Creese and P. Martin (eds) *Multilingual Classroom Ecologies: Inter-relationships, Interactions and Ideologies*, Clevedon: Multilingual Matters.

Street, B. (1995) *Social Literacies: Critical Approaches to Literacy in Development, Ethnography and Education*. London: Longman.

van Hessen, A. (2008) 'Language awareness and knowledge about language: A historical overview', in J. Cenoz and N. H. Hornberger (eds) *Encyclopedia of Language and Education*, 2nd edn, vol. 6, *Knowledge about Language*, New York: Springer.

van Lier, L. (1996) *Interaction in the Language Curriculum: Awareness, Autonomy and Authenticity*, London: Penguin.

——(2004) *The Ecology and Semiotics of Language Learning. A Sociocultural Perspective*, Norwell, MA: Kluwer Academic.

Weber, J. J. (2009) *Multilingualism, Education and Change*, Frankfurt: Peter Lang.

Young, A. (2006) 'How far along the road to providing effective SLA support can student teachers travel?' in A. Hancock, S. Hermeling, J. Landon and A. Young (eds) *Building on Language Diversity with Young Children. TESSLA*, Zürich: LIT Verlag.

13

Multilingual pedagogies[1]

Ofelia García, with Nelson Flores

Introduction

How can teachers enact ways of teaching and learning in the twenty-first century that support social justice and political participation of students around the globe? The answer to this question has much to do with the topic of this chapter, for unless teachers' pedagogies include the language practices of students, and unless all students are taught in ways that support and develop their diverse language practices, there cannot be any meaningful participation in education, and thus, in society. Multilingual pedagogies are thus at the center of all education that meaningfully includes learners; that is, education that is not simply done to students, but in which students do and participate.

In order for students to do and participate, education must include, in some ways, the language practices of children. Although it is easy to understand how monolingual education is simply not enough to fulfill this criterion, it is more difficult to envision how to build on the language practices of all students, as teachers and children with different characteristics work together in various geographical and socio-educational spaces. In fact, one of the difficulties in speaking about multilingual pedagogies is that it always has to be done in the plural. These multilingual pedagogies have to adapt to the different sociopolitical conditions of school systems, and to the shifting socio-educational spaces within schools, products of different communities' and educators' beliefs and values, varying students' experiences, and multiple socio-educational goals. Thus, this chapter not only reviews the development of multilingual pedagogies across time, but also across spaces.

Developments

Multilingual pedagogies have most often been viewed in the past as adjustments to monolingual pedagogies in order to teach and develop one additional separate language. But recently, multilingual pedagogies have started to acknowledge the hybrid language practices of bilingual people and their role in the development of more competent users of academic language practices in different standards.

Types of socio-educational contexts for multilingual pedagogies

Pedagogies do not develop on their own, but are products of different socio-educational contexts. We begin by identifying four different types of situations that have resulted in different pedagogical approaches:

- Foreign language instruction;
- Second language instruction;
- Bilingual/monoglossic instruction (native language pedagogies + second language/immersion pedagogies);
- Plurilingual/heteroglossic instruction (dynamic bi-plurilingual pedagogies).

Table 13.1 summarizes for the readers the differences in pedagogies, which we develop below.

Foreign language instruction

In *foreign language* instruction, the additional language is taught explicitly with the purpose of adding a language that is to be used in another different societal and national context. Foreign language instruction is most prevalent in secondary and tertiary education where sometimes more than one foreign language is taught to students. Foreign language pedagogies have a long history, although they have not been totally successful in developing bilingualism. Many times, the emphasis is on learning to read the foreign language, but not to communicate directly with speakers of that language. The predominant language in the nation-state is privileged over this "foreign" language. A specialized language teacher most often teaches the foreign language in different class periods and classroom space. Thus, foreign language pedagogies are based on a monoglossic ideology that assumes that legitimate linguistic practices are only those enacted by monolinguals and that foreign language acquisition is linear and always sequential. That is, a foreign language should be learned after the first one is developed.

Table 13.1 Type of multilingual pedagogies and language use, orientation, views, and arrangements

Type of pedagogies	Foreign language pedagogies	Second language pedagogies	Bilingual pedagogies (traditional)	Multilingual pedagogies (dynamic)
Language use	Explicit language instruction	Explicit language instruction	Languages used as media of instruction	Languages used as media of instruction
Language lens Language orientation	Monolingual Monoglossic	Monolingual Monoglossic	Bilingual Monoglossic	Multilingual Heteroglossic
Language views	Autonomous languages	Autonomous languages	Autonomous languages	Fluid language practices
Language arrangements	Diglossic	Diglossic	Diglossic	Transglossic
Bilingual orientation	Additive and linear (L1+L2=L1+L2)	Additive and linear (L1+L2=L1+L2)	Additive (L1+L2= L1+L2) or subtractive (L1+L2−L1=L2) and linear	Recursive or dynamic and complex (non-linear)

Second language instruction

At other times, the language being taught explicitly is to be used not across geographical space, but as a *second language* within the same space. This is the case of second language instruction. Second language pedagogies have been developed especially in the second half of the twentieth century, as people have begun to move steadily across educational spaces. Schools started paying attention to how to teach a second language, most often, the national language, to students whose language backgrounds were different. Successful second language acquisition requires that second language speakers behave in that language like a monolingual; and, as its name indicates, it also sees bilingual acquisition as linear and sequential. There are clearly first and second languages.

Most times, second language pedagogies pay little attention to the students' first language, focusing instead solely on the development of the second language. When the purpose is to educate while encouraging a shift to a majority language, it is *subtractive bilingualism* that is supported. That is, as the second language is added, the first begins to shrink, leading to language shift to the dominant language. *Subtractive bilingualism* can be rendered thus:

$$L1 + L2 - L1 = L2$$

Other times, however, the second language is added at no expense of the first language. Without effort, then, these programs aim to support what Lambert (1975) has called "additive bilingualism." That is, the second language is added to the students' repertoire and the expectation is that the student will become bilingual. *Additive bilingualism* can be rendered as follows:

$$L1 + L2 = L1 + L2$$

Bilingual/monoglossic instruction

Bilingual education came into its own during the second half of the twentieth century, as second language instructional programs were also being developed. Whereas second language education focuses on just teaching a second language, bilingual education often (although not always) attempts to equalize the power differential between minoritized and majority languages, by using the two languages as a medium of instruction. Because of the different sociopolitical situations in which bilingual education has been carried out, varying language pedagogies have been developed. But regardless of context, traditional bilingual pedagogies are also based on a diglossic arrangement that sees languages as autonomous skills that need to be separately and linearly developed. For example, bilingual education programs for the elite, what I have called elsewhere (García 2009) *prestigious bilingual education programs*, usually teach in one language during one part of the day, and the other language in the other part of the day. These programs aim to support additive bilingualism. Although additive bilingualism is encouraged and expected, it is a monolingual lens and a monoglossic ideology that is adopted. Students are expected to clearly separate languages and to move towards balanced bilingualism with equal competence in the two languages in all contexts and with all interlocutors.

In Canada, where bilingual education has been widely documented since the mid-twentieth century, it was the Anglophone majority in Quebec who clamored for educational programs in which their children could become bilingual in English and French, after the Québecois party won political power. This was the beginning of *immersion bilingual education.* As a type of bilingual instruction that aimed for additive bilingualism, immersion bilingual education used an immersion pedagogy that used the second language of the child for education, accompanied, later on, by instruction in the home language.

When the purpose of bilingual education is to ensure an education while encouraging a shift to a majority language, *subtractive bilingualism* is supported. This is the case of *transitional bilingual education* programs for immigrant language minorities in the United States. In the United States, bilingual education was initially seen as a way to teach English to Spanish speakers, while educating them, in the meantime, in the language they knew—Spanish (García and Kleifgen 2010). The pedagogy that these transitional bilingual education programs developed was not truly a bilingual pedagogy. Rather, Spanish was taught as a mother tongue, and English was taught as a second language.

Traditional bilingual pedagogies of either the immersion or prestigious type that consider the two languages to be autonomous skills and that build on diglossic classroom arrangements where the languages are carefully compartmentalized are being increasingly questioned. The greater awareness of the linguistic complexity in most countries in Africa and Asia, as well as the increased movements of people that are a result of globalization, have led to the development of bilingual/multilingual heteroglossic types of programs.

Plurilingual/heteroglossic instruction

Increasingly, all over the world, classrooms have children with different linguistic profiles and practices. It is clear that foreign language, second language, and even traditional bilingual education programs are no longer sufficient when classrooms are highly heterogeneous linguistically.

Bilingual education has become important not only as a way of equalizing power differentials between minoritized and majority languages, but also as a way of extending the plurilingual potential of students, and responding to the multilingualism of the world. At the same time, the potential of education to revitalize languages that had been oppressed has come to the forefront. In the case of language minority groups who have shifted almost totally to the language of power, students do not start out as monolinguals as when majority language speakers are taught a foreign language or are immersed in a second language, or as when minority language speakers are instructed through the medium of a dominant language or are taught a dominant language. In cases of language revitalization, the students have different degrees of bilingualism, bringing bits and pieces of their home languages as the basis from which to revitalize language practices. Thus, this bilingualism is not linear and cannot be considered purely additive. I speak of *recursive bilingualism* (García 2009) when referring to this bilingualism where ancestral language practices are reconstituted for new functions.

In Aotearoa/New Zealand, for example, where the Waitangi Tribunal declared Māori to be a *taonga* (treasured possession), *immersion revitalization bilingual education programs* built on traditional Māori cultural principles came into being to revitalize a language that had mostly been lost. These *Te Kōhanga Reo* for preschoolers, and later the *Kura Kaupapa Māori* (designed by Māoris for Māoris) adapted the Canadian immersion bilingual pedagogy, infusing it with cultural values. In this case, it was their own language (and not that of another group) that was now being developed and expanded beyond the use in traditional rituals, following an immersion pedagogy. English was taught separately, sometimes even in a different building. And yet, the socio-educational space is bilingual from the beginning, since the Māori children attending these programs could be placed at different points on the bilingual Māori–English continuum.

In Wales and other places where Welsh has suffered great oppression, but where the degree of language loss had not been as great as in New Zealand, *developmental bilingual education programs* have also come into being. These programs also use two languages in instruction, although separating them, and borrowing sometimes immersion pedagogy, other times second language pedagogy, to teach. But increasingly the children in these programs have different degrees of bilingualism, speaking more or less Welsh before starting the programs.

In some cases, educational programs have been set up precisely to build on the linguistic heterogeneity of different social contexts. This greater heterogeneity has to do with the presence in classrooms of students with different linguistic profiles (as in the case of poly-directional or two-way bilingual education programs described below), or of students who have to develop different language practices because of the multilingualism of their social context (as in Content and Language Integrated Learning (CLIL) bilingual education programs being promoted in Europe), or of students whose schooling includes the development of many languages (as in multiple multilingual education programs in Luxembourg, also described below). The bilingualism that these programs promote is more dynamic, in the sense that language practices are multiple and ever adjusting to the multilingual multimodal terrain of the communicative act in the twenty-first century. I have called this (García 2009) *dynamic bilingualism*, going beyond the ways in which the Council of Europe defines plurilingualism as "the ability to use languages for the purposes of communication and to take part in intercultural action, where a person, viewed as a social agent, has proficiency, of varying degrees, in several languages and experiences of several cultures" (Council of Europe 2000: 168).

In the United States, for example, in some schools language majority and language minority children are educated together in *two-way bilingual education programs* so that the language majority group develops the language of the minority and vice versa. Because of the silencing of the word "bilingual" in the United States, these two-way programs are usually referred to as "dual language programs" (Crawford 2004; García 2009; García and Kleifgen 2010). The European Schools for civil servants where children of different languages become at least trilingual are good examples of *poly-directional bilingual education programs,* with different groups being schooled, first separately in parallel sections, then increasingly together as they develop proficiency in second and third languages. But in both two-way and poly-directional bilingual education programs, the two or more languages are separated and carefully orchestrated as they are weaved in and out of the curriculum and traditional second language and immersion pedagogies are mostly used. Despite the structural separation guided by the teacher, students use their languages dynamically, as they make sense of instruction that builds mostly on collaborative learning.

The development of *CLIL bilingual education programs* in Europe also responds to the increased multilingualism of the world, and especially of the European Union. CLIL (Content and Language Integrated Learning) is a way of using students' second or third languages to deliver instruction. Unlike the bilingual education programs of the past that aimed to develop a balanced additive bilingualism by devoting equal or substantive time to the second language in the curriculum, CLIL usually takes up only one to two periods in the curriculum. It relies, in some ways, on what might be considered immersion pedagogy combined with second language pedagogy.

There are also societies that are built on a multilingual identity and thus they have developed *multiple multilingual education* types. One example is Luxembourg where schools first use the national language, Luxembourgish, then introduce literacy in German, and then French. By the time children are in secondary schools, they are being educated through the medium of either German or French. Although the schools' organization is linear and the languages are carefully introduced, the pedagogies in these classrooms are closer to what we are calling heteroglossic multilingual approaches, which are treated in the next section. Both teachers and students use the languages flexibly, as they make sense of lessons.

Because of the heterogeneity of languages found in most classrooms in the twenty-first century, a new type of bilingual education program is beginning to emerge, which García and Kleifgen (2010) have termed *dynamic bi/plurilingual* programs. In these programs the use of languages is not carefully controlled or planned in a top-down manner. Instead, emergent bilingual students, especially adolescents, are given the agency to negotiate their linguistic interactions, as the additional language is developed.

Multilingual pedagogical development

Grammatical approaches: foreign language pedagogies

Foreign language pedagogies have been developed over centuries, especially since Latin grammar started to be taught as an end itself. The *grammar-translation method* that was used in the past focused on translation of complex texts into the students' first language, as well as achieving grammatical accuracy. Reading and writing were emphasized, and there was no oral use of the foreign language. The grammar-translation method increasingly fell into disuse in the twentieth century, as foreign languages started to be heard over airwaves, and as air travel made contact among people speaking different languages more frequent.

Scholars such as Berlitz and de Sauze developed the *direct method* in the early twentieth century, as a reaction against the grammar-translation method. The direct method insisted that foreign language learning had to follow the same process as first language acquisition. Thus, emphasis was put on oral skills and printed language was kept away from learners. The use of the students' first language was avoided. The emphasis was on acquiring language structures from which rules were derived.

Based on a behaviorist theoretical framework that believed that language was acquired as a result of habit formation, the *audiolingual method* came into being in the 1950s. Students practiced language pattern drills and dialogues to develop particular language structures, and thus infer grammar structures.

Communicative approaches: second language and bilingual pedagogies

By the 1960s the behaviorist theoretical frameworks started to be abandoned for more constructivist approaches to teaching languages, supporting the belief that language learning occurs as students draw meaning from experience and interpersonal interaction. This shift from more grammatical approaches to more communicative approaches coincided with the growth and development of both second language and bilingual pedagogies, as language education turned from having the language explicitly taught to it being used in delivering content. Two language methodologies were developed during this time—*immersion methodology* and *integrated content-based methodology*. In both methods, language and content objectives are planned concurrently.

Immersion methodology uses language that is slow and simplified, with guarded vocabulary and short sentences, ample contextualization of language through the use of visuals and graphic organizers, and a modified grade level curriculum. Immersion methodology is used throughout the world in both immersion bilingual education programs (such as those in Canada) and immersion revitalization bilingual education programs (such as those in Aotearoa/New Zealand). It is also used in other types of bilingual education programs. Although developed as a way to teach content through a child's second language, that is, as a bilingual pedagogy, immersion methodology has been increasingly used as a strictly monolingual pedagogy. Especially in the United States, immersion methodology is being used to educate immigrant and refugee children where the goal is to make children monolingual in the dominant language of the country. This is the case, for example, in what is called "sheltered instruction" in the United States (see, for example, Sheltered Instruction Observation Protocol (SIOP) (Echevarria *et al.* 2004).

Integrated content-based instruction (ICB) is an adaptation of immersion methodology where the emphasis is more on the development of language and literacy in a second language, rather than the learning of content. During instruction, the key vocabulary is pre-taught and emphasis is placed on contextualizing the language of the lesson through visuals and building the background to a lesson. ICB started as a bilingual pedagogy and is most frequently used in all kinds of bilingual programs, but it has been increasingly adapted as a second language methodology in what is essentially monolingual instruction.

Cognitive approaches: second language and bilingual pedagogies

In the 1980s, language education also started to adopt the idea that children construct meanings not only by using language socially, but also by being in control over the cognitive processes that are used in learning; that is, by thinking and reasoning about language. Learning a language is seen as not only being social and interactive, but also cognitive. The focus is on developing declarative knowledge (what we know), procedural knowledge (what we know how to do), conditional knowledge (knowledge of when, why, or where to use information and skills), and in getting learners to actively control these processes as they work with academic texts and classroom discourse structures.

Cognitive Academic Language Learning (CALLA) is an example of such an approach. It develops academic language abilities, while combining teaching of content with language learning. To do so, there is explicit instruction of metacognitive learning strategies such as: learning to skim a text; attending to key words and linguistic markers; taking notes and summarizing; and asking clarifying questions. Students learn to manage their own language and content learning as they work with other students in cooperative groups to solve problems with the assistance of the teacher and peers (Chamot and O'Malley 1994).

Heteroglossic multilingual approaches: dynamic plurilingual pedagogies

Whereas both communicative and cognitive approaches and the pedagogies under both approaches are in essence monoglossic, keeping the two languages separate and observing a diglossic arrangement where language use is compartmentalized at all times, heteroglossic multilingual approaches are being developed today to respond to the more complex dynamic multilingualism found in classrooms (see, for example, Cummins 2008). These dynamic plurilingual pedagogies are being expanded as ways of going beyond traditional diglossic arrangements that compartmentalize languages and thus normalize the languages' power differentials without questioning them. Heteroglossic multilingual approaches question the notion of language itself, as "languaging" or what students do with language in multilingual spaces is taken up as the defining unit.

Dynamic plurilingual pedagogies do not separate languages as if they were autonomous skills, acknowledging the complex fluid language practices of children in schools. These plurilingual pedagogies can sometimes be seen in bilingual education programs that integrate different ethnolinguistic groups or different language practices and thus rely on fluid language practices or what I have called *translanguaging*[2] (García 2009). These dynamic plurilingual pedagogies should not be confused with the random codeswitching that is sometimes prevalent in bilingual classrooms. Unlike random codeswitching or what has been called concurrent translation (Jacobson and Faltis 1990) where language use is accidental and haphazard, plurilingual heteroglossic pedagogies are done with intent and are carefully planned. They represent a perspective on bilingualism that is not linear; that is, it is not simply about adding (additive bilingualism) or subtracting (subtractive bilingualism) a language, but rather about recognizing and building on the dynamic and complex language practices that are prevalent in all multilingual contexts. Thus, these dynamic plurilingual pedagogies build on a dynamic bilingualism that draws from the different interlocutors and contexts in which communication takes place. With languages no longer considered autonomous skills, but focusing on the heteroglossic language practices of the children themselves, dynamic plurilingual pedagogies support the bilingualism and plurilingualism of all children and the multilingual classroom contexts in which children come together. We consider these further under "Curricular arrangements: flexible multiplicity."

Key issues in multilingual pedagogies

Curricular arrangements

One of the key issues in thinking about multilingual pedagogies has to do with the curricular arrangements of the different language practices. Curricular arrangements are usually of three kinds:

- Strict separation;
- Flexible convergence;
- Flexible multiplicity.

Strict separation

As we have said before, because most of the methodologies that have been developed throughout the twentieth century have been developed following a monoglossic ideology, they rely on language separation of one kind or another. Most of the time, in both foreign language and second language classrooms, a teacher who is a language specialist is used. That teacher is often bilingual, but uses mostly the target language (the language which is being taught) in instruction. Sometimes, that teacher also has a different classroom, reflecting a territorial-based diglossia, where one classroom space is reserved for the specific target language.

Bilingual classrooms have more complex decisions to make regarding curricular arrangements. Most of the time, the languages are separated as in foreign language and second language pedagogies, but the ways in which this is done varies. Many times there is only one bilingual teacher in charge of the curriculum. That teacher then decides when one language or the other is used.

Most of the time, the arrangement that bilingual teachers make is *time-determined*, meaning that one language or the other is used at certain times. For example, some teachers teach in one language in the morning and another one in the afternoon. Other teachers teach in one language one day, and in another one the alternate day. Yet other teachers teach in one language one week, and in another language the following week.

Another way of separating the languages in bilingual instruction is by deciding which subject is going to be taught in which language. This is called a *subject-determined* arrangement. There is also *place-determined separation*, where a specific instructional space is dedicated to the use of only one language or the other.

Other times there are two teachers, each speaking a different language. This arrangement is called *teacher-determined.* Most of the time this means that there are two teachers in two different classrooms with what is often called a "side-by-side" model of instruction. But sometimes there are two teachers in one classroom. In this bilingual arrangement, languages are still separated, although they overlap, as different languages come in and out of the teacher's discourse.

Flexible convergence

Bilingual education pedagogies have been often used not to promote bilingualism, but to suppress it. When these pedagogies are used in subtractive bilingual programs with a goal of having the children shift to a dominant language, the curricular arrangement is always flexible with regards to language practices but without any intent of stabilizing practices. Without intent and consciousness, the *random codeswitching* that often characterizes the curricular language arrangements in these classrooms leads to language shift. Eventually, the teacher increasingly uses the more powerful language. The students get the message that this is the only valid language, as shift to the dominant language is supported.

Flexible multiplicity

When the intent is to build on the bits and pieces of language practices or the languaging in which children with different linguistic backgrounds engage, the curricular arrangement has to build on a flexible multiplicity. Flexible multiple bilingual arrangements in the classroom are not in themselves bad. Martin-Jones and Saxena (1996) have established that it is not necessarily codeswitching that is bad, but rather how language is used, and by whom, that shapes the students' perceived value of the two languages in a bilingual classroom. Views about the use of codeswitching in the classroom, which has traditionally been seen as always bad, are beginning to be questioned (Ferguson 2003; Gajo 2007; Heller and Martin-Jones 2001; Lewis 2008; Martin-Jones and Saxena 1996; Li and Wu 2009). Gutiérrez and her colleagues (1999: 289) have suggested that the "co-mingling of and contradictions among different linguistic codes and registers" offer significant resources for learning.

Bilingual education programs that have monolingualism as a goal encourage language mixing in ways that lead to language shift. But bilingual education programs that develop bilingualism not as the two balanced wheels of a bicycle but as an all-terrain vehicle adjusting to the ridges and craters of multilingual communication, build on translanguaging practices that ensure the functional inter-relationship of language practices (García 2009). Abilities such as translation, language switching, and designing information bilingually will be increasingly important in the twenty-first century, abilities that are supported by the community's translanguaging.

It is possible to alternate and blend language practices for effective learning to take place and to normalize bilingualism without functional separation. The ways in which this can be accomplished differ. Sometimes the many languages are presented together, sometimes one is used for one medium or function, the other for another; sometimes both languages are put alongside each other for comparisons.

Co-languaging refers to the strategy of presenting many languages side-by-side so students with different linguistic profiles can make meaning. Co-languaging is a prevalent methodology when there are many language groups in a single classroom. Sometimes, for example, PowerPoint presentations are presented in more than one language, whereas the instruction takes place in one or many. The students are free to choose the language through which they make sense of the lesson, and to compare and contrast the ways in which the languages are written and concepts are expressed. Many bilingual books offer examples of co-languaging, as students decide which language to read the text in, or to read in both, or to go from one to the other, making their own comparisons.

Cen Williams (as described by Baker 2001; Lewis 2008) has developed a kind of bilingual instructional strategy that he refers to as *trawsieithu (translanguaging)*. It involves the hearing, signing, or reading of lessons in one language, and the development of the work (the oral discussion, the writing of passages, the development of projects and experiments) in another language or vice versa. That is, the input and output are deliberately in different languages.

Another instructional strategy that responds to this flexible multiple arrangement is what is known as *preview–view–review*. Through this strategy, both languages are used sequentially, with different languages being given different functions, depending on the instructional needs of the teachers and the communicative needs of the students. Sometimes the language that students know best is used to build the background knowledge in a preview, whereas the lesson is taught in the students' second language. Other times, the opposite is done, with students hearing both a preview and a review in their second language, and the lesson in their home language.

It is imperative that education programs provide space for bringing the two or more languages together for contrastive analysis. In this way, vocabulary, structures and discourse patterns can be contrasted, while multilingual awareness is developed (Cummins 2008). At other times, there is instructional space for bilingual children to do cross-linguistic work, which allows them to translanguage, using both languages flexibly, in much the same way as experienced bilingual authors and bilingual communities often do.

Biliteracy models

In many ways, pedagogies of biliteracy, that is, "instances in which communication occurs in two or more languages in or around writing" (Hornberger 1990: 213), also reflect the types of programs and curricular arrangements described above. In foreign and second language programs, often the students' language and literacy abilities in their own home languages are used to make sense of the foreign language text.

Bilingual programs of different kinds use different models of biliteracy to develop different languaging abilities. Thus, subtractive bilingual education programs such as transitional ones often use a *convergent monoliterate model* where the two languages are used in oral communication to transact with a text written in only the dominant language. Other times, transitional bilingual education programs actually use the two languages in their literacy practices, but the literacy pedagogy in the minoritized language is often "calqued" on that of the dominant language. Thus, for example, in many Spanish/English transitional bilingual education programs in the United States, a phonics approach is used to teach initial Spanish reading, whereas when Spanish literacy is developed on its own right, a syllabic approach, much more sense-making for the Spanish language, is initially used. But the purpose of using a phonics approach in teaching initial decoding in Spanish has nothing to do with Spanish literacy development, and much to do with what many believe is the best way to teach initial English reading. The rationale is that students will be able to use the phonics skills learned in Spanish to decode English words. I refer to this kind of biliteracy model as *convergent biliterate*.

Bilingual programs that seek to develop an additive balanced bilingualism often use a *separation biliterate model*. As such, one language or the other is used to transact with a text written in one language or the other according to its own sociocultural and discourse norms.

The languages are kept separate and teachers and children match the language in which they are communicating around writing to the language of the written text. Students are encouraged to speak and think in the language in which they are reading and writing. Immersion bilingual education programs and many other prestigious bilingual education programs use this type of biliteracy model.

But as we said before, to develop the all-terrain vehicle that is needed for the linguistic complexity of the twenty-first century, a model of biliteracy has to allow for crossovers and to support translanguaging. Martin-Jones and Jones (2000) have proposed the term "multilingual literacies" to refer to the multiplicity of individual and group repertoires, and the varied communicative purposes for which groups use different spoken, signed and written languages, and the multiple ways in which people draw on, and combine codes. García *et al.* (2007) have argued for the concept of "pluriliteracy practices", which moves away from the traditional L1/L2 pairing, emphasizing instead that multiple language and literacy practices are inter-related and flexible and can be used in convergent ways to make meaning, positing that all literacy practices have equal value, and acknowledging the agency of speakers as they communicate around writing.

In the case of the *flexible multiple model of biliteracy*, multiple language practices and media are used in literacy practices. Teachers encourage children to use all linguistic practices and modes as resources in order to engage in pluriliteracy practices. The children use all their language practices to build background, to question the text, to think about strategies; and they draw not only from print to make sense of texts, but rely also on images, videos, music, and other technology-enriched signs.

Multilingual pedagogical principles and pedagogical core

Pedagogical principles

Two principles are important to keep in mind in developing multilingual pedagogies—(1) attention to social justice; and (2) attention to social practice. Because languages are spoken by groups of people who are situated differently socially, attention to social justice in developing multilingual pedagogies is paramount. That is, in some ways multilingual pedagogies should always be "critical" in the sense that they should aim to develop students' critical consciousness in order to transform the conditions that perpetuate human injustice and inequity (McLaren 1988). Attention to *social justice* involves the following:

- Providing *equity* for the students, their languages, their cultures and their communities by guaranteeing equal participation in a democratic classroom and school context. To do this, educators create democratic classrooms where everyone has an equal opportunity to participate;
- Building on the students' *linguistic and cultural strengths* and developing students' *multilingual awareness and tolerance*. To do this, educators plan carefully the ways in which all the students' home languages and their language practices are acknowledged, included and used in the classroom. Educators also focus on helping students understand the social, political, and economic struggles surrounding different language practices;
- Having *high expectations* and promoting *academic rigor*. Teachers encourage all students, regardless of abilities, to achieve by working hard and taking risks. They also focus on complex ideas that can generate future learning;
- Becoming *advocates of children* (Cummins 1986, 2000) and supporting *valid assessments*. Educators observe, engage students in conferencing, and construct equitable and valid formative assessments to improve students' learning. At the same time, they prepare students

for summative assessments, as they raise questions about the validity of assessments that have been standardized on a monolingual population.

Multilingual pedagogies also rely on *social practice*; that is, collaborative social practices in which students try out ideas and actions (Lave and Wenger 1991) and socially construct their learning (Vygotsky 1978). The *social practice* principle of multilingual pedagogies involves the following:

- Supporting *quality interactions*. To do this, educators support the sharing of ideas and focused dialogue that is generative and that encourages further understanding regardless of the language practices used;
- Focusing on the practice of *disciplinary and academic language*. Explicit language instruction in combination with language used in content has proven to be most effective in expanding bilingual competence (Baetens Beardsmore 1993). Educators should focus on syntactic structures, lexicon, vocabulary and types of discourses that promote the ways in which different disciplines use language to express key concepts and processes. Teachers engage students in discussion of how specific written and spoken texts are structured and how they work;
- Building *collaborative grouping and cooperative learning*. To do this, educators develop ways of using homogeneous groupings to practice particular language structures, and heterogeneous groupings for greater linguistic support. Collaborative grouping has been shown to increase students' opportunities to hear more language directed to them, as well as to participate and interact (Gibbon 2002). It also impacts positively on self-esteem;
- Focusing on *high relevance* of lessons and students' *maximum identity investment*. To do this, educators relate curriculum content to students' experiences as they analyze broader social issues relevant to their lives (Cummins 2001).

Pedagogical core

If the two principles of multilingual pedagogies can be reduced to that of social justice and social practices, the core of multilingual pedagogies is the strategy of *scaffolding*. Cummins (2000: 71) says that "language and content will be acquired most successfully when students are challenged cognitively but provided with the contextual and linguistic supports or scaffolds required for successful task completion."

Scaffolding is a combination of the constrain of structure with its release through the teacher's imagination and abilities as a result of innovation, exploration and improvization (van Lier 2006). A plurilingual scaffolding strategy adapts the five scaffolding structures so as to incorporate the dynamic languaging of plurilingual students and teachers:

- *Routines*, with the teacher establishing contextual and spatial instructional routines and language patterns. The languages of the routines can be varied and respond to students' interests and motivation, as well as the context of the lesson. Teachers' language use and children's language use in routines can be varied;
- *Contextualization* through the teacher's use of the students' home language practices, as well as other paralinguistic strategies such as: body language and gestures, visuals, manipulatives, realia, technologically enriched practices, graphic organizers, charts, diagrams and maps. Paralinguistic cues can also point to different language and cultural contexts;
- *Modeling* of all routines and language use, as well as verbalizing the actions and processes of the lesson through think-alouds. Again, these think-alouds can make use of all the language practices of the children;

- *Bridging and schema building* by having teachers build on prior knowledge by previewing the material to be taught. This can be done in a language other than that of the lesson, so as to build on the multilingualism of the classroom;
- *Multiple entry points,* with teachers allowing students to demonstrate their understanding in different ways and differentiating instruction, including different ways of languaging.

For scaffolding to be meaningful to bilingual children, the scaffolding strategies must build on the dynamic plurilingualism of the children in interaction with the teacher.

New research directions and summary

Multilingual pedagogies have been developed in the last fifty years, especially as bilingual education programs have grown throughout the world. In the twentieth century, the bilingual pedagogies that were developed matched the bilingual education programs that were often for just one linguistic group and which aimed at either subtractive bilingualism or additive bilingualism. Thus, these bilingual pedagogies kept the two languages separate—what Cummins (2008) calls "two solitudes"—and immersion methodology grew in importance.

In the last few decades, as the movement of people, ideas, and goods has increased as a result of globalization, the linguistic heterogeneity of classrooms has grown. The models of bilingualism developed for the twentieth century are no longer applicable in a more complex bilingual world. Bilingualism is now understood for its recursivity in the case of language revitalization situations and for its dynamism in the case of the plurilingual development needed for the twenty-first century. For these more complex situations in which we cannot recognize a first or a second language, but where complex and incomplete bits and pieces of diverse language practices make up the linguistic repertoire of most speakers, traditional foreign language, second language and bilingual pedagogies are no longer relevant.

Education and language pedagogy in the twenty-first century cannot solely be monolingual. But a traditional bilingual pedagogy no longer suffices either. We must experiment and innovate with dynamic plurilingual pedagogies that respond to the more complex bilingualism of students and to the more linguistically heterogeneous classrooms of the twenty-first century. New research must validate and expand these plurilingual pedagogies that are based on flexible multiplicity curricular arrangements, so as to build on the translanguaging of the multilingual students that populate our classrooms and that we must develop through educational programs to meet the language demands of the twenty-first century.

Related topics

Indigenous education; multilingualism in education in post-colonial contexts; discourses about linguistic diversity; rethinking discourses around the "English-cosmopolitan" correlation; language rights; multilingualism and social exclusion, codeswitching; heteroglossia; multilingual literacies.

Notes

1 We wish to acknowledge the help of Laura Ascenzi-Moreno in discussing these ideas.
2 We borrow this term from Cen Williams (Baker 2001) who used it to refer to a specific type of pedagogy that he called *trawsieithu*. Wr extend the definition of the term.

Further reading

Baker, C. (2001) *Foundations of Bilingual Education and Bilingualism*, Clevedon: Multilingual Matters. (A thorough treatment of bilingual education and bilingualism written in concise style.)

Blackledge, A. and Creese, A. (2010) *Multilingualism: A Critical Perspective*. London: Continuum. (A detailed ethnographic account of language ideologies, communicative practices and multilingual pedagogies in complementary schools in the UK.)

Cummins, J. (2000) *Language, Power and Pedagogy: Bilingual Children in the Crossfire*, Clevedon: Multilingual Matters. (A seminal work that provides an overview of Cummins' major theories in second language acquisition and bilingual pedagogy.)

Edwards, V. (2009) *Learning to be Literate: Multilingual Perspectives*, Clevedon: Multilingual Matters. (Brings research together on literacy and multilingualism from a variety of settings with a global perspective.)

García, O. (2009) *Bilingual Education in the 21st Century: A Global Perspective*, Malden, MA: Wiley-Blackwell. (Lays out in greater detail many of the points made in this chapter with regards to practices and policies in bilingual education.)

Martin-Jones, M. and Jones, K. (eds) (2000) *Multilingual Literacies: Reading and Writing Different Worlds*, Amsterdam: John Benjamins. (Integrates theoretical and methodological insights from the field of bilingualism and the field of literacy to reconceptualize literacy practices in multilingual environments.)

Bibliography

Baetens Beardsmore, H. (1993) 'European models of bilingual education: Practice, theory and development', in G. M. Jones and A. C. Ozog (eds) *Bilingualism and National Development*, Clevedon: Multilingual Matters.

Baker, C. (2001) *Foundations of Bilingual Education and Bilingualism*, Clevedon: Multilingual Matters.

Chamot, A. U. and O'Malley, J. M. (1994) *The CALLA Handbook: Implementing the Cognitive Academic Language Learning Approach*, Reading, MA: Addison-Wesley Publishing Company.

Council of Europe (2000) *Common European Framework of Reference for Languages: Learning, Teaching, Assessment. Language Policy Division*, Strasbourg, available online at www.coe.int/tdg4/linguistic/CADRE_EN.asp

Crawford, J. (2004) *Educating English Learners: Language Diversity in the Classroom*, 5th edn, (Formerly *Bilingual Education: History, Politics, Theory, and Practice*), Los Angeles, CA: Bilingual Educational Services.

Cummins, J. (1986) 'Empowering minority students: A framework for intervention', *Harvard Educational Review* 56: 18–36.

——(2000) *Language, Power and Pedagogy: Bilingual Children in the Crossfire*, Clevedon: Multilingual Matters.

——(2001) *Negotiating Identities: Education for Empowerment in a Diverse Society*, 2nd edn, Los Angeles: CABE.

——(2008) 'Teaching for transfer: Challenging the two solitudes assumption in bilingual education', in J. Cummins and N. H. Hornberger (eds) *Encyclopedia of Language and Education*, vol. 5, *Bilingual Education*, New York: Springer.

Echevarria, J., Vogt, M. E. and Short, D. J. (2004) *Making Content Comprehensible for English Learners: The SIOP Model*, Needham Heights, MA: Allyn and Bacon.

Ferguson, G. (2003) 'Classroom code-switching in post-colonial contexts: Functions, attitudes, and policies', *AILA Review* 16(1): 38–51.

Gajo, L. (2007) 'Linguistic knowledge and subject knowledge: How does bilingualism contribute to subject development?' *International Journal of Bilingual Education and Bilingualism* 10(5): 563–81.

García, O. (2009) *Bilingual Education in the 21st Century: A Global Perspective*, Malden, MA: Wiley-Blackwell.

García, O. and Kleifgen, J. (2010) *Educating Emergent Bilinguals: Policies, Programs and Practices for English Language Learners*, New York: Teachers College Press.

García, O., Bartlett, L. and Kleifgen, J. (2007) 'From biliteracy to pluriliteracies', in P. Auer and W. Li (eds) *Handbooks of Applied Linguistics*, vol. 5: *Multilingualism*, Berlin: Mouton de Gruyter.

Gibbons, P. (2002) *Scaffolding Language, Scaffolding Learning: Teaching Second Languages in the Mainstream Classroom*, Portsmouth, NH: Heinemann.

Gutiérrez, K., Baquedano-López, P. and Tejada, C. (1999) 'Rethinking diversity: Hybridity and hybrid language practices in the third space', *Mind, Culture, and Activity* 6(4): 286–303.

Heller, M. and Martin-Jones, M. (2001) *Voice of Authority: Education and Linguistic Differences*, Westport, CT: Ablex.

Hornberger, N. H. (1990) 'Creating successful learning contexts for bilingual literacy', *Teachers College Record* 9(2): 212–19.

Jacobson, R. and Faltis, C. (eds) (1990) *Language Distribution Issues in Bilingual Schooling*, Clevedon: Multilingual Matters.

Lambert, W. E. (1975) *Culture and Language as Factors in Learning and Education*, Toronto: OISE Press.

Lave, J. and Wenger, E. (1991) *Situated Learning: Legitimate Peripheral Participation*, Cambridge: Cambridge University Press.

Lewis, W. G. (2008) 'Current challenges in bilingual education in Wales', *AILA* 21: 69–86.

Li, W. and Wu, C. J. (2009) 'Polite Chinese children revisited: Creativity and the use of code-switching in the Chinese complementary schools', *International Journal of Bilingual Education and Bilingualism*, 12(2): 193–211.

Martin-Jones, M. and Jones, K. (eds) (2000) *Multilingual Literacies: Reading and Writing Different Worlds*, Amsterdam: John Benjamins.

Martin-Jones, M. and Saxena, M. (1996) 'Turn-taking, power asymmetries, and the positioning of bilingual participants in classroom discourse', *Linguistics and Education* 8(1): 105–23.

McLaren, P. (1988) 'Culture or canon? Critical pedagogy and the politics of literacy', *Harvard Education Review* 58(2): 213–34.

van Lier, L. (2006) 'Action-based teaching: autonomy and identity', lecture at the University of Groningen, 2 October 2006.

Vygotsky, L.S. (1978) *Mind and Society*, Cambridge, MA: Harvard University Press.

14

Global English and bilingual education

Sheena Gardner

This chapter focuses on the impact of English as a global language on bilingual education internationally.

In comparison with other World Languages, Graddol (1997: 13) positions English at the top of a hierarchy as *the* global lingua franca. What does this mean for English and which Englishes are implicated? Research in the world Englishes tradition (Kachru 1992) differentiates world Englishes, and established literature in the outer circle of Nigerian English or Singaporean English shows how 'the Western language can be used for communicating sociocultural nuances that are completely alien to Western culture' (Kumaravadivelu 2006: 19). In contrast, descriptions of English as an International Language (Strevens 1992) or a World Standard Spoken English (Crystal 2002: 185) assume a common core shared by 'standard' varieties such as British and American English, as codified in reference grammars informed by corpora of naturally occurring written and spoken language from the UK (Carter and McCarthy 2006) and the US (Biber *et al.* 1999), whereas research in English as a lingua franca (Seidlhofer 2004; Mauranen 2006; Jenkins 2006), and specifically the English used internationally among non-native speakers, sheds light on the English used for intercultural communication. Although corpus-informed grammars suggest a common core, as well as systematic variation across modes (e.g. spoken vs written), registers (e.g. academic vs conversational) and users (e.g. British vs American), others point to the boundaries of Englishes to show how English is 'fragmented, struggled over, resisted ... centrifugal and even incommensurable with itself' (Pennycook 1994: 28) in its mutually unintelligible varieties. In this vein, recent scholarship has explored how users draw on the resources of several languages in performances as diverse as hip-hop in Malaysia (Pennycook 2007) and complementary schooling in the UK (Blackledge and Creese 2010). Globalization processes mean that we have to look beyond national and international varieties. Indeed Pennycook (2007: 34) questions whether there is such an object of analysis as global English, and turns his attention instead to linguistic performance and transcultural flows:

> The notion of performativity can take us beyond views of language and identity that tie them to location and origins, and instead opens up possibilities for seeing how languages, identities and futures are constantly being refashioned. In both the claims that hip-hop is

a language itself, a language that transcends assumed divisions between languages, and the mixing of English with other languages, we can see the performative possibilities of a constantly shifting range of identifications.

(2007: 157)

Arguably, hip-hop English is as distinct from a core standard English as a highly specialized medical treatise replete with Latin borrowings would be. Could these simply be described as different albeit highly specialized registers of English, and if so, which would be the more global? Hip-hop in its response to the transcultural flows associated with globalization, or the medical treatise that perhaps responds in a similar way to transnational flows of scientific knowledge? Both registers are far from the basic or core English in most bilingual education programmes. In this chapter we focus not on the nature of English *per se* in education, but on the impact English as a world language, or global lingua franca, has had on bilingual education internationally.

English has been described as global since the mid-1990s (McArthur 1998: 86), reflecting the growing interest in globalization generally and its impact on English language teaching in particular (Block and Cameron 2002; Gnutzmann and Intemann 2005; Edge 2006; Ferguson 2006; Kirkpatrick 2007).

Definitions and interpretations of the processes of globalization differ. For instance Kumaravadivelu (2006: 5–7) points to (1) theories of [Western] cultural homogenization; (2) theories of nationalist and fundamentalist cultural heterogenization in response; and (3) to tensions between these where 'the global is localized and the local globalized' (2006: 7). Becher and Trowler bring together different perspectives:

> the development of global flows of information and resources along networks transcending nation-states' influence and disturbing nationally-organized systems and practices. Such networks intimately connect the local and the global and may have any combination of physical, social and economic characteristics. … The term is also used to refer to 'virtual' globalization: that sense of the global which comes to inform personal identities, perspectives and everyday practices.
>
> *(2001: 2)*

Both accounts are useful, and when applied here suggest that the globalization of English transcends American and British homogenizing practices; disturbs and increases heterogeneity in national education systems; and where global English interacts with local language use is significantly changing the identities, perspectives and everyday practices of children and teachers in schools around the world. We now turn to the globalization processes influencing English, before focusing in more detail on the second dimension, the disruption caused by the globalization of English to national education systems.

The spread of English internationally since the 1950s

As Crystal wrote in the preface to *English as a Global Language*, the role of English changed substantially in the second half of the last century:

> In 1950, any notion of English as a true world language was but a dim, shadowy, theoretical possibility, surrounded by the political uncertainties of the Cold War, and lacking

any clear definition or sense of direction. Fifty years on, and World English exists as a political and cultural reality.

(2002: xii)

In the 1950s English still functioned as a colonial language used to educate a select minority across Africa and Asia. The educated elite of subsequent generations became increasingly monolingual in English as the language of education, as reflected in the reach of English A-level exams from Delhi to Hong Kong to Nairobi. Likewise, immigrants to English-speaking countries such as Australia and Britain were expected to assimilate, and mainstream education for the majority was entirely in English.

Although the colonial heritage of English lays the foundation for the global use of English, its increasing use as an international lingua franca must be linked to the rise in power of the United States on the international economic, military, financial, political and cultural stage. Further indicators of American influence are that 'the scientific research output of the United States substantially exceeds that of any other single nation, while the country headquarters some of the world's best known, and iconic, multinational corporations (e.g. McDonald's, Microsoft, Time Warner, Disney, AT&T)' (Ferguson 2006: 111). Alongside the spread of popular culture were developments in information and communication technologies, with an estimated 80 per cent of the world's electronically stored information in English by the turn of the century (Crystal 2002: 115). The speed and reach of the Internet means that not only does information travel quickly, and international transactions can be easily conducted, but also information may be available in English before it is circulated in other languages. In all these arenas we are thus less bounded by physical location and more global networks are formed by people with shared interests.

Recently, technological innovation, the rise of global economic systems, transnational companies and increased global communication have all changed the forces from those linked to British or American imperialism to aspirations for participation in global communities populated by more non-native speakers of English than native speakers. In addition to its 'dominance ... in trade, commerce, banking, tourism, technology, and scientific research' the rise of English may be 'rightly justified on the basis of the numerical strength of its non-native speakers; the cross-cultural and localized functional range the language has developed in various domains; [and] the excellence of its literary traditions' (Kachru 1992: 355). Indeed, literature in world Englishes has been an important feature in decoupling the English language from its close connections with inner circle cultures. Importantly for many, perceptions of English have changed: 'Rather than a tool of linguicism, which it was during British coloni-alism, English in India today is an agent of decolonization that enables the urban poor to access the global economy' (Vaish 2005: 187).

Among languages, English is now 'at the apex of the complex political, economic and cultural hierarchy of languages in the world' (Graddol 2007: 251). Indeed, English has overtaken French as the language of the European Union (EU) (Truchot 2003 cited in Graddol 2007), and has become the language of regional organizations such as the Association of South-East Asian Nations (ASEAN) and corporations such as Siemens AG of Germany, the Dutch ABN AMRO Bank and the European Central Bank located in Frankfurt. Popular culture has a widespread impact, with some such as Dollerup arguing 'that the "present hegemony of English in Europe is primarily due to the entertainment industry, and only secondarily to war, technological lead, science and political domination"' (1996: 26) (cited in Kirkpatrick 2007: 164).

As English has become the leading world language of scientific communication, popular culture, international negotiation and business, it has gained its own momentum and its recent spread has been attributed to bottom-up factors related to individual, parental and community-based perceptions of economic and educational advantage. 'Such explanations accept ... the active agency of individuals in the "periphery", and ... give proper recognition to ... the tendency for language to gain in utility as new users join the communicative network' (Ferguson 2006: 144).

Graddol (2007: 243) describes the development of English as a most remarkable phenomenon in that 'For the first time in the history of human society, a single language has become so sufficiently universal that it can be used as a global lingua franca for communication among speakers of many languages.' There are of course other lingua francas, including Chinese, Arabic, Spanish and French, each with regional dominance, but English dominates globally.

English is prevalent not only in English-speaking countries, but also in countries where it has a special place alongside other languages. It is a national or official language alongside Hindi in India, alongside Kiswahili in Tanzania and alongside Malay in Malaysia. Identifying over 70 countries where English has a special place (2002: 4) and over 100 where it is the preferred foreign language (2002: 5), Crystal estimated that a quarter of the world's population was fluent or competent in English (2002: 6). With the growth in bilingual education, and the continuing expansion of users, that number has been steadily increasing. Where English has no special status, it is the foreign language of choice. English is the most widely studied foreign language at both secondary and primary school (Witt 2000 cited in Graddol 2007: 251). Indeed, Kubota points out that 'English' has become synonymous with 'foreign language' in Japan (2002: 19) and Görlach 2002 (cited in Kirkpatrick 2007) claims that it is taught in Europe more than all other European languages put together.

Although this is a phenomenal success story for English, its bounty is not equitably distributed. English-medium schools as a colonial or migrant community legacy persist in countries such as India, Pakistan, Hong Kong and Argentina and can be viewed as one source of increasing social division. English bilingual schools may be better resourced and access to English carries more than linguistic capital; it becomes synonymous with being educated and internationally mobile. Ninedan Nilekani calls it an aspirational language, and yet, he suggests, only 10 per cent of the population in India learn English at school. 'There is a need for all to learn it in the interests of greater democracy' (2009). For economic prosperity to be more widely spread, he argues, more people should have access to the English of call centres and the service industry; the English of international cricket; the English of technology and high-tech entrepreneurs; the English of Bollywood. Similar divisions are felt in countries as far afield as Taiwan, Brazil and Greece where private cram schools provide additional English instruction to those whose families can pay, and who are prepared to spend evenings and holidays investing in their children's futures.

Partly for such reasons, Graddol predicts that the future of global English lies in the hands of Asia, particularly China and India (2006: 15). He argues that as other languages are competing with English, the use of English on the Internet is now declining proportionally, and the economic advantage currently held by English will ebb away as it becomes a universal skill and other languages provide greater commercial advantage. He predicts that the number of learners of English will continue to increase for 10–15 years, then peak at around two billion users (2006: 14).

Linked to the demand for English is the rise of English in education internationally as governments introduce English in schools earlier and earlier, as content areas are increasingly being taught in English, as universities teach more courses through English, and as the demand for an education in a language with such valuable and portable global capital increases with migration and transnational lifestyles. This new wave of English-medium education has exploded across the world since the mid-1990s, disrupting national education systems. It is still largely experimental in nature, which means it is a rich site for research.

Key areas of expansion in global bilingual education

The growing recognition of English as a global language, with the desire for countries around the world to benefit economically, politically and culturally from the easier participation in global networks that English brings, has had an impact on English-language teaching in general and on bilingual education in particular (Block and Cameron 2002; Graddol 2006; Nunan 2003). This goes beyond established bilingual and international schools to providing bilingual education in mainstream education through 'the use of two (or more) languages of instruction at some point in a student's school career' (Cummins 2010: slide 3). There are three points where this is very evident: the introduction of English to increasingly young learners; the teaching of specific subjects or content areas in English at upper primary and secondary level; and international English-medium education programmes in higher education. In each of these sectors there are enormous challenges around teacher education and supply, teaching materials, curriculum development, assessment and evaluation, none of which are my main focus here. Instead, I aim to identify factors that link global processes around English to developments in bilingual education and to review research in the three areas.

Teaching English to/for Young Learners (TEYL)

Although the conditions for success in early bilingual education (Johnstone 2001) are often not well understood by policy makers (Johnstone 2009: 32), there are three forces that seem to prevail when English is introduced early. The first stems from the widespread popular beliefs that 'younger is better' and 'more is better', beliefs that persist almost as self-evident truths, despite the numerous caveats bilingual education researchers and TEYL specialists would place on them. The second arises from government hopes that a new generation will be able to compete in a globalized economy, to secure access to the latest scientific advancements and to negotiate internationally in English. The third relates to the global reach and spread of English not only through the number of speakers internationally but also through music and film, sports, advertising and other transnational discourses (e.g. Pennycook's 2007 account of hip-hop culture), which makes English increasingly familiar and available, and therefore more amenable to inclusion in the national education systems of countries around the world.

These forces have led to an unprecedented increase in young learners of and in English in mainstream school systems, alongside a flourishing industry of private kindergartens and private cram schools. In a British Council survey of 42 countries in 1999, Rixon found that 39 had compulsory English as part of the state education provision at primary school, with the majority starting at the age of six to eight and private English provision beginning for children at an even younger age than in the state schools.

Ten years later, the young learner trend continues with many new state-wide programmes. For example, English policies were introduced in Taiwan for Grade 5s in 2001 then for Grade 3s in 2005 (Chern 2009); in China for Grade 3s in 2001 (Wang 2009); and in Bahrain to Grade 1s in 2004 (Kneafsey 2009). In addition to such ambitious national programmes in Taiwan and China, the age of starting English has been lowered to Grade 1 in large cities where primary English had been established from the 1990s (Butler 2009; Wang 2009). Around the world private language schools flourish, for instance in Brazil (Gimenez 2009) and Greece, whereas in Hong Kong private kindergartens have moved into immersion education (Yee 2009).

Multilingual education at primary level is an ongoing concern from Argentina (Corradi 2009) to South Africa (Kgwadi 2009); from Malaysia (Gardner and Yaacob 2009) to India (Prabhu 2009). This global flood of early language learning has been hailed as 'possibly the world's biggest policy development in education' (Johnstone 2009: 39) and consequently 'an awesome challenge' (ibid.).

Of course, the early introduction of English is no guarantee of success, particularly where the number of hours devoted to English is limited, and the provision of primary teachers with appropriate expertise in primary teaching, bilingual or second language education, *and* English language proficiency is a serious concern in many contexts (Nunan 2003; Butler 2009; Enever and Moon 2009: 16; Graddol 2006: 89). The expansion has been rapid in many countries: Wang (2009) reports that in China primary English expanded from 7 per cent in 2000 to 62 per cent in 2006, with the number of primary English teachers increasing from 80,000 in 2000 to nearly 500,000 in 2006. Her research has shown that most of these teachers are young, female, with little teaching experience and that 40 per cent have degrees other than English. She found much good practice in the classroom, but in common with many countries where TEYL has expanded rapidly there are concerns about teachers' quality, both in terms of language proficiency and in TEYL pedagogy, and about teacher supply (Wang 2009).

Not all TEYL programmes aim to provide bilingual education in Cummins' sense of learning through two languages, but with the popularity of communicative approaches, much TEYL teaching occurs in English. Where this happens, the language of TEYL classrooms may be described as a distinct register. Teachers need to be able to manage classroom activities, to provide good models of English for input, to adjust their level of language to the children's, and to be able to encourage, reassure, engage and motivate the children through tasks with appropriate content. This kind of affective, interpersonal, supportive English for the young learner classroom is not the kind of English taught in most English language programmes at school or university.

To assuage the shortage of qualified TEYL teachers, some countries have brought in native speakers as teachers or assistants (Butler 2009). Although such schemes offer a solution, they also bring their own problems, one of which relates to the global nature of English. Particularly where preference is given to white North American and British native speakers as in Japan (Kubota 2002: 22), there is a risk that English is again seen as imposed from the outside, rather than being a language that can be used freely as appropriate in local contexts. Parental perceptions that local teachers are not as competent as native speakers undermine the confidence of local teachers and work against a view of English as a global language. Countries such as China, which have embarked on massive teacher education programmes (Wang 2009) and related research (Wang *et al.* 2009), seem best prepared to succeed in the TEYL enterprise (Johnstone 2009), and thus to reinforce the role of English as a global language rather than as a native-speaker privilege.

Research in TEYL tends to be fragmented, although there are a number of edited volumes (Rixon 1999; Moon and Nikolov 2000; Enever *et al.* 2009a), special issues (Language Testing vol. 17(2) 2000) and collections (Ellis and Morrow 2004). Nunan's 2003 paper compares TEYL in seven Asian countries through interviews with key stakeholders and highlights their different responses to the pressure to teach English younger. Butler's (2009) ethnographic study in Japan, Korea and Hong Kong makes similar arguments with more classroom data. In contrast, interestingly, Enever *et al.*'s (2009b) longitudinal study comparing primary EFL in six European countries has produced initial findings of significant similarities both in classroom learning environments and positive attitudes to foreign language learning, suggesting a common European approach to TEYL.

Whether English is introduced at the age of three, six, nine or 12, and whether it takes the shape of a communicative curriculum or of an immersion primary curriculum, it needs ultimately to provide a foundation for more specialized use of English. As Graddol (2006) argues, the role of TEYL is crucial in the transition to widespread bilingual education. Early English teaching is expected to provide the basics, and, he argues, English is becoming a key basic skill, rather like basic literacy and numeracy, on which learners can expect to build in their future studies and work lives.

This prospect of English as a basic skill may have liberating consequences:

> One of the avenues ... to create an environment in which multiple identities flourish is to move away from the prevailing notion of English as a cultural carrier to English as a communication tool. ... [for] common people who speak English as an additional language ... English is a language of communicational necessity, not of cultural identity.
>
> *(Kumaravadivelu 2006: 19)*

Such views of global English are radically different from those underlying existing foreign language curricula where learning the language is inextricably bound with greater appreciation of the literature and culture of its 'native' speakers.

The boom in TEYL in the 1990s has become an explosion in the last decade as English is taught more widely and at younger ages in kindergarten and primary schools around the world. If these programmes are sustained, they should provide learners with basic skills and prepare them for further study in English. Increasingly, content areas are being taught through English in primary and secondary schools, a phenomenon that is widely referred to as CLIL.

CLIL: English and the content areas in primary and secondary schooling

Whereas the aims of TEYL may be to develop positive attitudes to English and foreign language learning, to promote language awareness and to teach the basics of English vocabulary and structures through communicative activities and play (Enever and Moon 2009), the aims of CLIL (Content and Language Integrated Learning) and its sister EMILE (*Enseignement de matières par l'intégration d'une langue étrangère*) are to integrate foreign language teaching into the learning of other school subjects. For example, children in regular Spanish schools in Spain may learn history in English, and other subjects in Spanish. At this point, they have two different languages of instruction, and they are engaged in bilingual education.

As an approach to bilingual education, CLIL builds explicitly on Canadian immersion experience and instances of CLIL have many similarities to language and content approaches such as CALLA (Cognitive Academic Language Learning Approach), which are used in English as a Second Language (ESL) and English as an Additional Language (EAL) contexts in countries such as Australia, USA and Britain (Mohan *et al.* 2001). An important difference is that the current CLIL trend started in foreign language contexts, specifically in Finland in the early 1990s, and has been closely linked to EU language education and citizenship objectives and funding. Its blossoming in Europe has coincided with initiatives in Asia where, for instance, Malaysia initiated the teaching of mathematics and science in English in 2003 in Standard One (age six), Form One (age 11) and Lower Sixth (age 16). As a movement that has spread across Europe and beyond, CLIL is very broad, and all encompassing; it has therefore easily assumed a range of initiatives under its umbrella (see also García, this volume).

Three key factors related to global English encouraged the uptake of CLIL for English. First, there is a widespread hope that CLIL will be better placed than traditional and communicative foreign language programmes to produce fluent users of English, users who will readily become those educated citizens able to access the latest scientific advances and contribute to transnational business and politics through English. Second, whereas traditional approaches to teaching English involved developing an understanding of native-speaker cultures – from everyday social interactional practices through popular culture to literature and history – CLIL can be divorced from such cultural trappings to reflect the reality of global English and its use as an international lingua franca. Finally, as English becomes increasingly pervasive outside school, international mobility increases, and more children come to school with some English; the option of teaching content through English becomes attractive to learners and teachers.

The potential scope of CLIL has been mapped out in different ways (Coyle 2007: 545–56) to include how programmes vary according to context (monolingual, bilingual, multilingual); whether the CLIL language is a foreign, additional, minority or majority language; age of learners; class time available; whether teachers are usually language or content specialists; whether teachers are usually bilingual or monolingual; whether there is usually one teacher, two teachers or a teacher and assistant; relative emphasis on language and content; relative amount of transactional and interactional discourse in the target language; and expectation of translanguaging in class. The possibilities here are endless, and a growing body of literature exists that describes developments in particular contexts (see publications at www. clilconsortium.jyu.fi).

The implementation of CLIL programmes typically depends on the language proficiency and dedication of subject teachers, factors which have contributed to resources and networks becoming increasingly available online for teachers. CLIL programmes tend to involve opting in, with first language programmes running alongside them in the same school. Dalton-Puffer describes CLIL in Austria as a grass-roots movement in which

> the teachers who started the CLIL ball rolling were often mid-career, with plenty of professional experience, looking for a new challenge and new avenues for professional development. … subsequently, the impetus was taken up by many school heads, seeking to enhance their school's profile and customer appeal through advertising CLIL as part of their programme.
>
> *(2007: 46–7)*

Many such CLIL programmes have succeeded from the bottom up, whereas others have enjoyed support from national and international organizations such as the British Council. Programme levels adjust to the proficiency of the learners and subject teachers, the subject curricula, including the examination system, and the political will.

One of the most ambitious programmes is in Spain where a state-wide programme began with three to four-year-olds in 1996, increasing one grade each year through to 16-year-olds. Different states have implemented the programme in different ways, particularly in areas that were already bilingual (e.g. with Catalan). Where the project has been supported by the British Council, the education is explicitly bilingual and bicultural, drawing heavily on the English national curriculum and bringing in qualified British teachers:

> Initially, 44 UK primary teachers were engaged by the Spanish Government to teach in schools. This number has now increased to 230, and gradually more Spanish teachers of English (930) are being brought on board to teach a diverse curriculum in English which includes subject areas from both the Spanish and the English National Curriculum.
>
> *(www.britishcouncil.org/spain-education-bilingual-project)*

When the first students on these bilingual programmes turned 16, they became the first state school children in Spain to sit the International General Certificate of Secondary Education (Cambridge IGCSE), an international version of the exam pupils in Britain sit at the age of 16. This qualification was introduced in 1988 and its worldwide reach is perceived as evidence of its international value: 'pupils in about 120 countries sit the exam in some 60 subjects' (Morris 2009: 10). For example, Banfi and Day (2004: 406) report that around 150 schools offer IGCSE certification in Argentina, with around 35 offering the Advanced International Certificate of Education (AICE) and 45 offering the International Baccalaureate. They trace the development of private schools from Heritage Language schools for immigrant English speakers, through Dual Language schools as the Spanish-speaking population in the schools grew, to internationally oriented schools, which they describe as 'Global Language Schools' (2004: 405), 'meaning that many of the key features [such as international outlook] that characterise Argentine bilingual schools now may be connected with the processes of globalisation' (ibid.). Such international outlook reflects the aspirations of education systems and individuals for participation in further education and training internationally.

Not all CLIL programmes are bicultural, international or linked to the English national curriculum. Many have retained the national exams:

> If you go to a country like the Netherlands there are some 80 schools teaching 50% of all upper secondary through English. That's a lot. Fifty percent is a lot of CLIL over three years. They are assessing in Dutch. They are keeping their examinations in Dutch and separately assessing the English. ... that's the same thing we opted for in Finland. There we said there is an added value to CLIL through English but that we also need to keep the assessment procedure standard. But it is country by country, it is complicated and people are working on it.
>
> *(Marsh 2005)*

Such CLIL is therefore much more of a bilingual enterprise and much less a bicultural initiative than the British Council project in Spain or an international enterprise as in the private schools in Argentina.

The CLIL explosion has created many new transnational networks of teachers where ideas, experiences and materials are exchanged; it has brought changes to state and private teacher education programmes where TEFL programmes are being supplemented by programmes for teaching CLIL; it has generated an excitement around bilingual education, which has spilled back into English-speaking countries – for example CLIP, the Content and Languages Integrated Project sponsored by CILT in England involves integrating the teaching of French, German and Spanish with history, geography and PSE (Coyle n.d.). As with many CLIL programmes across Europe, there are strong links here to notions of European citizenship and mobility within the EU.

CLIL has generated its own research programmes (Coyle 2007) with many studies from around the world providing case studies of implementation (Dalton-Puffer and Smit 2007: 13). One productive strand of research focuses on classroom discourse (Dalton-Puffer 2007; Nikula 2007; Dalton-Puffer and Nikula 2006). For instance, research in Finnish biology and physics CLIL classrooms suggests that:

> CLIL students claim ownership of English by the way they confidently use it as a resource for the construction of classroom activities. Students' code switching practices are another indication that they ascribe to an identity as users rather than as learners of English.

> Instead of using Finnish when their skills in English fail them, students use the L1 for affective functions; and the way in which they slip in and out of English and Finnish indicates that they view the classroom as a bilingual space.
>
> *(Nikula 2007: 206)*

Dalton-Puffer (2007) also considers the learner vs user/EFL vs CLIL dimensions. She finds clear evidence of CLIL classes stretching learners' vocabulary development, as we might expect. This extends to identifying lexical gaps and making explicit attempts to fill them (2007: 281). She attributes the widely observed self-confident use of English in CLIL classes partly to the reassuringly familiar content classroom culture and learning discourses, but points out that this does restrict which aspects of communicative competence are acquired and practised by students (2007: 12). Such findings raise questions for teachers about, for instance, an appropriate balance of 'language vs content' discourse across programmes.

In Spain, a longitudinal study of students in a history CLIL class has found that students are developing skills in writing as historians through English (McCabe *et al.* 2009). Importantly, research is also being conducted to explore what the impacts of learning in English might be on Spanish academic language proficiency (Maxwell-Reid 2009).

Alongside such research agenda, the *International CLIL Research Journal* was established with the support of key international figures in the broader field of bilingual education (Baetens Beardsmore, de Bot, Cenoz, García, Genesee, Johnstone, Swain, Thürmann and Tsui). The first two volumes (2008 and 2009) report on CLIL research from Austria, the Czech Republic, Finland, Italy, Malaysia and Spain illustrating how CLIL has been taken up across Europe and Asia.

The impact of global English on bilingual education is therefore far from uniform. In some programmes English is bound inextricably with culture, with in this case a British-based organization exporting its native English-speaking teachers, curriculum and related assessment. In others, teachers are generally from the local contexts, where English is used for knowledge acquisition and negotiation in lessons and a mix of English and the majority language is used for more socio-affective functions. Research is characterized by a multiplicity of case studies (Dalton-Puffer and Smit 2007) which highlight numerous contextual differences. Among these, the studies of classroom discourse show particular promise in contributing to our better understanding of these developments in bilingual education, as these studies build a cumulative picture of classroom contexts and strategies for instructional, regulative and social discourses.

English-medium education at university

Since the days of the British Empire there have been English-medium universities internationally. With independence and heightened nationalism came an increase in national language medium universities, but the past decade has seen a shift to more English-medium education (EME) not only in post-colonial countries such as Malaysia and Sudan, but also in others such as Germany and China. Examples from these latter two countries are discussed below, illustrating a continuum from programmes where English functions as a lingua franca for international applicants, which may be more or less bilingual according to the use of the language of the host institution and/or of the students, to those where English is used in explicitly bilingual programmes designed for nationals.

Three key factors in the rise in EME at university are, first, English has become the language of scientific publication:

In 1950, all contributions to the 'oldest specialist journal in the field of behavioural science' *Zeitschrift fur Tierpsychologie,* were in German. By 1984 95% were written in English (Viereck 1996: 20). The European Science Foundation's working language is English and its journal *Communication* is exclusively in English (Ammon 1996). The dramatic shift to English in the academic domain means that European languages are not developing appropriate scientific terms (Hoffmann 2000: 10).

(Kirkpatrick 2007: 164)

Students therefore need to be able to read in English, and faculty need to be able to write and publish in English. In this respect many non-English-medium programmes are increasingly bilingual. De Swaan (2001) very clearly explains how English is being perpetuated as the language of science and social science. 'Practically the entire scholarly community of the natural sciences reads English, and the vast majority publishes in that language' (de Swaan 2001: 73), which leads to the need to translate the science for those with less English, often into a local variety of English. For social sciences he explains the difficulties of translating social science into English (first language of informants is translated into an academic register, then this is translated into English). Much is lost in translation, but without translation, comparative social science is not possible and social theory becomes too specific to particular instances; then because social comparison is done in English, it has become the best language to pursue social theory in. Again and again we see this spread of English; the more English enters an area, the more the logic of the situation demands it pervade further.

The second factor is that education in English permits greater international mobility for staff and students. Student mobility continues to rise encouraged by schemes such as the ERASMUS student exchange programme in Europe, and the Bologna agreement, which intends to enable students to move easily across Europe for different parts of their degree. Ammon (2001: 357) reports that 'International programmes' taught in English at German universities were initiated to increase the number of international students in Germany to benefit the country's economic and political future. From the initial 18 universities that participated in 1997/8, there were 42 in 1999/2000, a third of all universities (2001: 358). A Brussels study reported by Spencer (2008) found that the number of university programmes offered in English in continental Europe increased threefold in the five years to 2008; of the 2,400 programmes, the Netherlands leads with 774 programmes, Germany offers 415, Finland, 235, and Sweden, 123; most programmes are in engineering, business and management, and more than two-thirds of the students are not from the host country. English is the natural lingua franca for most international programmes worldwide.

Third, students coming up to university through bilingual and English medium school programmes expect to be able to continue their education in English. With this last point in particular we again see the self-perpetuating nature of global English. The more (school) bilingual programmes there are, the greater the demand for more (university) bilingual programmes. This means increased demand for English-medium and bilingual education in certain subjects at university level.

Nunan explains how this works in China:

The Degree Committee of the State Council has approved 45 Sino-foreign joint programs, which can grant degrees from foreign universities in China. All programs are taught bilingually (English and Chinese). Also in September 2001, all colleges and universities under the control of the Ministry of Education were instructed to use English as the main teaching language in the following courses: information technology, biotechnology, new-material technology, finance, foreign trade, economics, and law. Other courses would be added as resources became available. Criteria for selecting courses were that they facilitate entry to the WTO [World Trade Organization], and that they not be 'politically sensitive.' (Politically sensitive courses have to be taught using textbooks written in China. Courses that are not politically sensitive can use foreign textbooks.) The main obstacle to implementing this policy was obtaining suitably qualified teachers (Chan 2001).

(2003: 595–6)

Here again we see the trend of divorcing English-medium education from the cultural trappings more likely to be found in the arts and social sciences.

Research in university EME is wide-ranging, as illustrated by the presentations at a recent international conference in Hong Kong (www.hku.hk/clear/conference08/) and a special issue of the *Nordic Journal of English Studies* in 2008, which describes programmes in Sweden, Denmark and Norway. Of particular interest in both collections is the research on spoken English as a lingua franca (ELF), or English used predominantly in communication among non-native speakers. As a register of English, it is found in ELF contexts internationally, and differences can be identified, for instance, between ELF in ASEAN and European contexts (Kirkpatrick 2007). ELF research is producing detailed empirical accounts of ELF use, although it has proved controversial, particularly in its implications for teaching (Jenkins 2006; Seidlhofer 2004). For instance,

> ELF is conceptualized and accepted as a distinct manifestation of English not tied to its native speakers, this perspective opens up entirely new options for the way the world's majority of English teachers can perceive and define themselves: instead of being non-native speakers and perennial, error-prone learners of ENL, they can be competent and authoritative users of ELF.
>
> *(Seidlhofer 2004: 229)*

Although some teachers oppose this as an undesirable situation, others see how the inherent logic matches their lived experience, and are encouraged to participate in EME.

The ELFA corpus (ELF in Academic Settings, Maurenen 2006) consists of seminar, lecture, conference presentation and thesis defence speech events where not all speakers share a first language, from universities in Finland that offer programmes in English. Research on phraseological units (Maurenen 2006: 155) suggests that learners use English creatively in ways that are more similar to native speakers than had been thought from studies of learner data. In other words, speakers in the ELFA corpus who are learning in English create phraseological units in English in ways that suggest they are learning through English.

Although most of the ELF research focuses on descriptions of spoken interaction, applications to writing are the focus of a related project SELF (Studying in English as a Lingua Franca), in which essays, term papers and reports will also be examined. The research may be written in ELFA. For example, the *Nordic Journal of English Studies* 2006 volume, which includes different perspectives on the existence of a European ELF register or variety and papers on the ELFA corpus, is 'written in ELFA':

> Although native speakers have not been excluded from the volume, they have not acted as the ultimate authorities of linguistic correctness or comprehensibility. Thus, the papers have not been 'checked by a native speaker', as the saying goes. As ELF-speaking editors,

we have not imposed our idiolects on the papers with a heavy hand either. The writers are all expert users of English despite their varying status of nativeness.

(Maurenen and Metsä-Ketelä 2006: 6)

The ELF research recognizes that studying in English at university builds on an education in another language; its contribution is to naturalize ELF varieties of English in the context of such consecutive bilingual education experiences.

University education is going global in many ways. In Britain a recent move towards internationalization of universities includes not only trying to attract larger numbers of international students, but also aiming to ensure an internationalized experience for all students by including international curricular content, encouraging student and staff exchanges, and generally by making universities welcoming for all. Universities are setting up campuses in Asia; mega universities offer distance education globally; consortia of universities are forming to offer global education. All of this global networking and programming increases the use of English. This in turn spreads the use of English, as universities in non-English majority countries offer international programmes. Increasingly such countries are also offering pre-university English language training. For instance, English foundation courses are being offered by Malaysian universities to students from around Asia. In these ways the teaching of English, the ELT industry itself, is feeling the effects of globalization (Edge 2006).

Researching the future?

The role of English has gained in significance over the last ten years such that it is now indisputably a world language; it is the major language of scientific and technological advances; it is the major language of negotiation for international politics, for business, for popular culture; and it is widely decoupled from its links with native-speaker varieties such as British or American English. Its position in the world has made it attractive to the key stakeholders in education – governments, ministries, parents, employers and students themselves – such that the demand for more teaching of English, in English and through English has led to the introduction of new bilingual programmes of all sorts, many of them experimental, all with teacher supply issues, some imposed and planned for nationally, others much more dependent on the availability of teachers and students prepared to take up the challenge of working in English.

Research suggests that moving too far or too quickly towards education in English for all is not a sensible strategy, as examples from Hong Kong and Malaysia suggest.

Although the textbooks, written work, and examinations were in English in many EMI [English medium of instruction] schools, oral and aural communication was conducted in Cantonese, and students only encountered English in its written form. This resulted in students who were functionally illiterate in Chinese on the one hand and unable to communicate effectively in spoken English on the other.

(Nunan 2003: 598)

Indeed, Hong Kong is now moving back to more Chinese-medium education, supported by research (Tsui 2005) that shows how students in English medium were two years behind those in Chinese medium; how the self-perception, self-esteem and motivation of English-medium students was significantly lower than that of Chinese-medium students; and that where schools switched to Chinese medium, overall exam performance was greatly enhanced.

English-medium schools existed in Hong Kong for decades, whereas the introduction of science and maths teaching in English in Malaysia is relatively new. Nevertheless, influenced by disappointing exam results, and political concerns about widening divisions between the performance of Malay students in urban and rural areas, it was announced in July 2009 that teaching of science and maths would revert to Malay in 2012. Such evidence highlights not only the vital need for research on the implementation and ongoing development of existing programmes, but also points to a future turning point in the rapid expansion of bilingual education, which echoes Graddol's predictions for a turning point in the role of English as a world language.

Just as global English has led to a remarkable expansion of bilingual programmes, so too will the expansion of bilingual programmes have an influence on the future of English internationally. More research is needed to track changes in the nature of English and in the nature of the other language(s) of education. As these languages converge, as we might expect them to, the English in one context will naturally become increasingly different from that in other contexts. Paradoxically, as explained by Grey (2002), the ease of global communication means that textbooks and other materials can be circulated internationally and customized to local contexts for delivery. These factors increase both the global reach of ideas and local identification with English. Paradoxically, they increase both the diversity of registers and varieties of English and lead to more widespread use of a common core.

Research in the next decades is needed to link changes in English to longitudinal studies of how partial, opt-in, additive bilingual and other programmes flourish or fade. Of particular interest will be a focus on age, on the role of English and other languages in content instruction, and on how transitions not only across sectors from primary to secondary to tertiary education, but also across domains from school to leisure and travel, and across locations as few corners of the world remain untouched by bilingual speakers. If English does become part of a basic education, as computer literacy has become an integral part of education today – something that some older teachers are slower to accommodate, but young learners and teachers adapt to very readily – how recognizable universally will that global English be?

Summary

This chapter has considered the processes of globalization as they relate to the spread of English and its rise as a global lingua franca. It has identified specific factors that have led in the past decade to the widespread introduction of teaching in English around the world in each of three areas of bilingual education programming: the teaching of English in school at an increasingly young age (TEYL); the teaching of content areas such as history or science in English at school (CLIL); and the international marketing of university courses in English by non-English-medium universities (EME).

Research in all three areas includes individual case studies of programme implementation, with comparative studies across national contexts in TEYL and CLIL. Research is beginning to show the impact of global English on participants in bilingual programmes: on relationships between English-speaking and local teachers or assistants, particularly in TEYL; on learner identities in classroom discourse particularly in CLIL vs 'regular' programmes; and on the nature of English as a lingua franca, particularly in EME contexts.

If the demand for English continues to rise as predicted, we need to better understand not only the disruptions to national education systems caused by globalization, but also its impact on the identities, perspectives and everyday practices of those caught in its wake.

Related topics

Immersion education; multilingual pedagogies; multilingualism and popular culture; multi-lingualism on the Internet.

Further reading

Dalton-Puffer, C. (2007) *Discourse in Content and Language Integrated Learning (CLIL) Classrooms*, Amsterdam: John Benjamins.
(A lucid, multilayered study of CLIL classrooms in Austria.)
Davison, C. and Bruce, N. (eds) (forthcoming) *Language Issues in English Medium Universities across Asia*, Hong Kong: Hong Kong University Press.
Graddol, D. (2006) *English Next*, British Council.
(With the *Future of English* (1997) Graddol presents a compelling, detailed and comprehensive analysis and forecast of global English including its impact on education.)
Enever, J., Moon, J. and Raman, U. (eds) (2009) *Young Learner English Language Policy and Implementation: International Perspectives*. Reading: Garnet Press.
(The 28 papers here include 12 national case studies and reports on research in TEYL.)
Kumaravadivelu, B. (2006) 'Dangerous liaison: Globalization, empire and TESOL', in J. Edge (ed.) *(Re) Locating TESOL in an Age of Empire,* Basingstoke: Palgrave/Macmillan.
(Clear account of major theories of globalization and their impact on ELT.)

Bibliography

Ammon, U. (ed.) (2001) *The Dominance of English as a Language of Science: Effects on Other Languages and Language Communities*, Berlin: Mouton de Gruyter.
——(2001) 'English as a future language of teaching at German universities? A question of difficult consequences, posed by the decline of German as a language of science', in U. Ammon (ed.) *The Dominance of English as a Language of Science: Effects on Other Languages and Language Communities,* Mouton de Gruyter.
Banfi, C. and Day, R. (2004) 'The evolution of bilingual schools in Argentina', *Bilingual Education and Bilingualism* 7(5): 398–411.
Becher, T. and Trowler, P. R. (2001) *Academic Tribes and Territories: Intellectual Enquiry and the Culture of Disciplines*, 2nd edn, Buckingham: Open University Press.
Biber, D., Johansson, S., Leech, G., Conrad, S. and Finegan, E. (1999) *Longman Grammar of Spoken and Written English*, Harlow: Pearson Education.
Blackledge, A. and Creese, A. (2010) *Multilingualism: A Critical Perspective,* London: Continuum.
Block, D. and Cameron, D. (eds) (2002) *English and Globalization*, London: Routledge.
Butler, Y. (2009) 'Teaching English to young learners: The influence of global and local factors', in J. Enever, J. Moon and U. Raman (eds) *Young Learner English Language Policy and Implementation: International Perspectives*, Reading: Garnet Press.
Carter, R. and McCarthy, M. (2006) *Cambridge Grammar of English: Spoken and Written English Grammar and Usage*, Cambridge: Cambridge University Press.
Chern, C.-L. (2009) 'Trainer training innovation in Taiwan', in J. Enever, J. Moon and U. Raman (eds) *Young Learner English Language Policy and Implementation: International Perspectives*, Reading: Garnet Press.
Corradi, L. (2009) 'Beyond English: Primary plurilingual schools in Buenos Aires', in J. Enever, J. Moon and U. Raman (eds) *Young Learner English Language Policy and Implementation: International Perspectives*, Reading: Garnet Press.
Coyle, D. (n.d.) 'CLIL in Europe and the UK'.
——(2007) 'Content and language integrated learning: Towards a connected research agenda for CLIL pedagogies', *International Journal of Bilingual Education and Bilingualism* 10(5): 543–62.

Crystal, D. (2002) *English as a Global Language*, 2nd edn, Cambridge: Cambridge University Press.

Cummins, J. (2010) 'Promoting academic success in CLIL programs: A synthesis of the research and what it means for classroom practice.' Presentation at the 3rd CLIL Symposium, Universidad de la Solana, Chia, Colombia, September 2010. www.clilsymposium.org/archivos/cummins_Colombia_CLIL_Sert_2010.pdf

Dalton-Puffer, C. (2007) *Discourse in Content and Language Integrated Learning (CLIL) Classrooms*, Amsterdam: John Benjamins.

Dalton-Puffer, C. and Smit, U. (2007) 'Introduction', in C. Dalton-Puffer and U. Smit (eds) *Empirical Perspectives on CLIL Classroom Discourse*, Frankfurt am Main: Peter Lang.

Dalton-Puffer, C. and Nikula, T. (2006) 'Pragmatics of content-based instruction: teacher and student directives in Finnish and Austrian classrooms', *Applied Linguistics* 27(2): 241–67.

de Swaan, A. (2001) 'English in the social sciences', in U. Ammon (ed.) (2001) *The Dominance of English as a Language of Science: Effects on Other Languages and Language Communities*, Berlin: Mouton de Gruyter.

Dollerup, C. (1996) 'English in the European Union,' in R. Hartmann (ed.) *The English Language in Europe*. Exeter: Intellect Books.

Edge, J. (ed.) (2006) *(Re)Locating TESOL in an Age of Empire*, London: Palgrave Macmillan.

Ellis, G. and Morrow, K. (2004) *ELT Journal Year of the Young Learner Special*, Oxford University Press.

Enever, J. and Moon, J. (2009) 'New global contexts for teaching primary ELT: Change and challenge', in J. Enever, J. Moon and U. Raman (eds) *Young Learner English Language Policy and Implementation: International Perspectives*, Reading: Garnet Press.

Enever, J., Moon, J. and Raman, U. (eds) (2009a) *Young Learner English Language Policy and Implementation: International Perspectives*, Reading: Garnet Press.

Enever, J., Mihaljevic Djigunovic, J. and Szpotowicz, M. (2009b) 'Early language learning in Europe: A multilingual longitudinal study', in J. Enever, J. Moon and U. Raman (eds) *Young Learner English Language Policy and Implementation: International Perspectives*, Reading: Garnet Press.

Ferguson, G. (2006) *Language Planning and Education*, Edinburgh: Edinburgh University Press.

Gardner, S. and Yaacob, A. (2009) 'CD-ROM multimodal affordances: Classroom interaction perspectives in the Malaysian English literacy hour', *Language and Education* 23(5): 409–24.

Gimenez, T. (2009) 'English at primary school level in Brazil: Challenges and perspectives', in J. Enever, J. Moon and U. Raman (eds) *Young Learner English Language Policy and Implementation: International Perspectives*, Reading: Garnet Press.

Gnutzmann, C. and Intemann, F. (2005) (eds) *The Globalisation of English and the English Language Classroom*, Tübingen: Gunter Narr Verlag.

Görlach, M. (2002) *Still More Englishes*. Amsterdam: John Benjamins.

Graddol, D. (1997) *The Future of English*, London: British Council.

——(2006) *English Next*, British Council.

——(2007) 'Global English, global culture?' in S. Goodman, D. Graddol and T. Lillis (eds) *Redesigning English*, Abingdon: Routledge.

Grey, J. (2002) 'The global coursebook in English language teaching', in D. Block and D. Cameron (eds) *English and Globalization*, London: Routledge.

Jenkins, J. (2006) 'Current perspectives on teaching World Englishes and English as a lingua franca', in *Tesol Quarterly* 40(1):157–81.

Johnstone, R. (2001) 'Immersion in a second or additional language at school: Evidence from international research', Report for the Scottish Executive Education Department, University of Stirling: Scottish CILT.

——(2009) 'An early start: What are the key conditions for generalized success?' in J. Enever, J. Moon and U. Raman (eds) *Young Learner English Language Policy and Implementation: International Perspectives*, Reading: Garnet Press.

Kachru, B. (ed.) (1992) *The Other Tongue: English across Cultures*, Chicago: Illinois University Press.

Kgwadi, T. (2009) 'Teaching of English to young learners in South African schools: Subject and policy implementation', in J. Enever, J. Moon and U. Raman (eds) *Young Learner English Language Policy and Implementation: International Perspectives*, Reading: Garnet Press.

Kirkpatrick, A. (2007) *World Englishes: Implications for International Communication and English Language Teaching*, Cambridge: Cambridge University Press.

Kneafsey, C. (2009) 'OUP teacher-training in Bahrain', in J. Enever, J. Moon and U. Raman (eds) *Young Learner English Language Policy and Implementation: International Perspectives*, Reading: Garnet Press.

Kubota, R. (2002) 'The impact of Globalization on language teaching in Japan', in D. Block, and D. Cameron (eds) *English and Globalization*, London: Routledge.

Kumaravadivelu, B. (2006) 'Dangerous liaison: Globalization, empire and TESOL', in J. Edge (ed.) *(Re) Locating TESOL in an Age of Empire*, London: Palgrave Macmillan.

McArthur, T. (1998) *The English Languages*, Cambridge: Cambridge University Press.

McCabe, A., Whittaker, R. and Llinares, A. (2009) 'Development of participant identification and tracking in Spanish learner discourse in a CLIL context', paper presented at the 21st ESFLCW, Cardiff, July.

Marsh, D. (2005) 'Learning English or learning in English: Will we have a choice?' CLIL Debate, IATEFL Conference, 8 April, Cardiff.

Maurenen, A. (2006) 'A rich domain of ELF: The ELFA corpus of academic discourse', *Nordic Journal of English Studies* 5(2): 145–59.

Maurenen, A. and Metsä-Ketelä, M. (2006) 'Introduction', in A. Mauranen and M. Metsä-Ketelä (eds) *Nordic Journal of English Studies* (special issue) *English as a Lingua Franca*, 5(2): 1–8.

Maxwell-Reid, C. (2009) 'Learning (through) language: The effect of studying through English on the choices Spanish students make in their written Spanish', paper presented at the 21st European Systematic Functional Lingustics Conference and Workshop, Cardiff, July.

Mohan, B. Leung, C. and C. Davison (eds) (2001) *English as a Second Language in the Mainstream: Teaching, Learning and Identity*, London: Longman.

Moon, J and Nikolov, M (2000) 'Research into teaching English to young learners', University of Pécs Press.

Morris, S. (2009) 'Class act', in *Hand in Hand: The Bilingual Project*, 8: 10–11, British Council and Ministry of Education, Spring, Spain.

Nikula, T. (2007) 'Speaking English in Finnish content-based classrooms', *World Englishes* 26(2): 206–23.

Nilekani, N. (2009) *Imagining India: The Idea of a Renewed Nation*, Allen Lane: Penguin Press.

Nunan, D. (2003) 'The impact of English as a global language on educational policies and practices in the Asia-Pacific region', *TESOL Quarterly* 37(4): 589–613.

Pennycook, A. (1994) *The Cultural Politics of English as an International Language*, London: Pearson.

——(2007) *Global Englishes and Transcultural Flows*, London: Routledge.

Prabhu, N. S. (2009) 'Teaching English to young learners: the promise and the threat', in J. Enever, J. Moon and U. Raman (eds) *Young Learner English Language Policy and Implementation: International Perspectives*, Reading: Garnet Press.

Rixon, S. (ed.) (1999) *Young Learners of English: Some Research Perspectives'*, Harlow: Longman.

Seidlhofer, B. (2004) 'Research perspectives on teaching English as a lingua franca', *Annual Review of Applied Linguistics* 24: 209–42.

Spencer, D. (2008) 'Europe: Huge increase in English-medium courses', *University World News*, Issue 0022, 6 April 2008.

Strevens, P. (1992) 'English as an international language: Directions in the 1990s', in B. Kachru (ed.) *The Other Tongue: English across Cultures*, Chicago: Illinois University Press.

Truchot, C. (2003) 'Language and supranationality in Europe: The linguistic influence of the European Union,' in J. Maurais (ed.) *Language in a Globalising World*. Cambridge: Cambridge University Press.

Tsui, A. (2005) 'Learning English or learning in English: Will we have a choice?' CLIL Debate, IATEFL Conference, 8 April, Cardiff.

Vaish, V. (2005) 'A peripherist view of English as a language of decolonization in post-colonial India', *Language Policy* 4(2): 187–206.

Wang, Q. (2009) 'Primary EFL in China: From policy to classroom practice', in J. Enever, J. Moon and U. Raman (eds) *Young Learner English Language Policy and Implementation: International Perspectives*, Reading: Garnet Press.

Wang, Q., Sun, L. and Ma, X. (2009) 'An impact study of a TEYL innovation in Beijing, China', in J. Enever, J. Moon and U. Raman (eds) *Young Learner English Language Policy and Implementation: International Perspectives*, Reading: Garnet Press.

Witt, J. (2000) 'English as a global language: The case of the European Union.' http://webdoc.gwdg.de/edoc/ia/eese/artic20/witte/6_2000.html

Yee, K. W. (2009) 'Second language in HK kindergartens: The missing link', in J. Enever, J. Moon and U. Raman (eds) *Young Learner English Language Policy and Implementation: International Perspectives*, Reading: Garnet Press.

Part III

Multilingualism in other institutional sites

15

Multilingualism in the workplace

Roger Hewitt

Language, literacy and the multilingual workplace

Soon after Henry Ford opened his Ford Motor Company on the outskirts of Detroit in 1909 his aim was to create a modern workforce of maximum productivity along the lines suggested by Frederick Taylor's influential book *The Principles of Scientific Management* (1911), and to do so in a way that included a cultural strategy of 'Americanization'. Within a very few years, his workforce grew to 41,000 of which 18,000 were American- or Canadian-born English first-language speakers. The remaining 23,000 were foreign-born, many with little or no English. To maximize the kind of resource his workforce constituted, Ford initiated two unusual departments within his management system. One was called the 'Sociological Department', which between 1914 and 1916 sent out investigators, together with interpreters where necessary, to the homes of almost all of its employees and collected data on their families, age, religion, nationality, languages spoken and prospects of citizenship, as well as other questions on their financial standing, debts, insurance, health, recreational activities and much more (Nevins 1954: vol. 1: 554). The other was the 'Ford English School', which was to address the needs of the 5,000 workers who were without English, plus others whose English was weak. The pupils were grouped into classes with 25 to a class, meeting twice a week for an hour and a half. One manager of the English school explained: 'If a man declines to go to school, the advantages of training are carefully explained to him. If he still hesitates, he is laid off and given a chance for uninterrupted meditation and reconsideration. He seldom fails to change his mind' (Schwartz 1989: 60).

Successful graduation from the school was ritualized in a ceremony held on a stage on which was represented an immigrant ship in front of which was a huge melting pot. As a manager explained: 'Down the gangplank came the members of the class dressed in their national garb ... Down they poured into the Ford melting pot and disappeared into the pot. The teachers then began to stir the contents of the pot with long ladles. Presently the pot began to boil over and out came the men dressed in their best American clothes and waving American flags' (Schwartz 1989: 61–2). The reality behind the pageant, however, was rather more discordant. After a thousand Ford workers from Eastern Europe took the day off to celebrate the Orthodox Church Christmas in January 1914, the *Detroit Times* reported: 'When they returned to work on Thursday, they were escorted in one door of the plant, their [employee] numbers taken away and they were then escorted out of the door onto the street' (Schwartz 1989: 57).

Time and 'the new capitalism' has transformed the management practices described here (Gee *et al.* 1996; Gerber and Lankshear 2000.) Ford itself cooperated in the launch of a unique workplace learning scheme in 1982 after negotiations with the United Automobile Workers (UAW) following the forced lay-off of a large section of its workforce. In this 'Employee Development and Training Program' management and union had an equal role in the sourcing of a range of learning activities for its workers, from basic language and literacy to Masters degrees. The model was replicated in Ford's UK factory again in 1987 following negotiations with the trade unions and has been much copied by companies within and beyond the motor industry. The new models of management and worker participation lying behind such schemes have, of course, the same ultimate goals as earlier management styles – workplace efficiency, a flexible workforce and capacity for growth. This can lead to contradictions in the ways such provision can serve the workforce, and particularly where migrant workers are concerned. This eventuality was already foreseen in the innovative approach of the UK's National Centre for Industrial Language Training (NCILT), which started in 1974 when government funds were made available to local authorities to help the 100,000 largely South Asian migrant workers develop their skills and abilities through English language training and thereby improve communication and standards of safety at work and enable migrants to participate more fully in the life of the community. The NCILT was concerned to situate English-language training for workers within training for trade union representatives and company managers, as well as service providers of many kinds. This placed particular emphasis on potential blockages to job appointments, career advancement and the accessing of social and other services that might constitute institutional racism.

This important intervention, which continued into the late 1980s, was seen as part of a context that included the maintenance and development of minority languages and the provision of trained interpreters, although the work of the Industrial Language Training service was not directly concerned with those issues. Its concern was with socially situated English language training for a multi-*ethnic* workforce and specifically not with a multi*lingual* work*place* per se (Roberts *et al.* 1992: 2–3). Its work is more broadly relevant in putting flesh on the concept of institutional racism in demonstrating how organizational procedures regarding language issues in a multi-ethnic workforce can themselves constitute socially exclusionary action. This notion of institutional racism was embedded in UK legislation in the Race Relations Act 1976 (and enlarged further in the Race Relations Amendment Act, 2001), drawing on a code of practice that cited as an example of racism any employer who 'requires higher language standards than are needed for safe and effective performance of the job'. These matters continue to intrude into debates over the multilingual workplace in many different national settings. The work of Celia Roberts, drawing on the work of John Gumperz (1982) and Frederick Erickson (Erickson and Schultz 1982) constitutes an important thread in research concerning the CILT and subsequent developments (see Roberts *et al.* 1992; Sarangi and Roberts 1999).

Other trajectories relating to training have sometimes lacked this kind of clarity over the social dimensions of workplace language, thus 'skills training' and 'diversity awareness' can be found side by side with 'the English-only workplace', even within the multilingual workforce. The early Ford example of multilingualism in an industrial setting described above displays many issues that remain of concern including workplace language education, integration/assimilation and national productivity – however transformed by modern technology and contemporary migration flows. Taylorist managerial paradigms are still in evidence and the cultural hegemony of dominant groups remains the site of some of the most contested issues in workplace relations. In the USA, legal cases where employers have insisted on English-only workplaces – for casual as well as work-related communication and sometimes following pressure from native English-speaking workers – have risen steeply in recent years (Dicker 1998; Shim 2000; NAPALC 2003; Rodriguez 2006). At the same time, workplace English for Speakers of Other Languages (ESOL/ESL), literacy provision and translation services have risen internationally to constitute three new industries in themselves, serving new managerial approaches seeking to improve the efficiency of a substantially migrant workforce. Here political and ideological frames have often influenced public perceptions, which in turn have influenced/legitimated managerial policy and practice.

Hull (1997: 3–39) makes a powerful case against the wave of popular opinion in the 1980s and 90s, that a lack of literacy and other basic skills among the US workforce was to blame for the poor economic performance of US industry. These assumptions, she argues, fuelled a proliferation of workplace-learning schemes that paid little or no attention to the appropriateness of what was being delivered nor to its reception. Mawer (1999) questioned the scale of significance of (English) language skills in the workplace, pointing out that, even overlooking all the inconsistencies in language assessment tests, attempts to draw links between individual general linguistic ability and the ability to perform in the workplace have been notably unsuccessful. She further argues that, despite low proficiency in English, workers have often shown themselves to acquire successfully the specialized registers of their technical field or 'shopfloor language' (an issue discussed further below) and that workers also often use compensatory strategies like relying on bilingual workmates or taking 'shortcuts' in acquiring necessary skills (Mawer 1999: 42–8),

The road to research into workplace multilingualism

Such discussions as the above are properly part of the context relating to the multilingual workplace. For a more directly relevant literature we need to turn elsewhere. Workplace multilingualism (mostly without the inclusion of a European language) has long been a common feature of rural and urban life in places such as India, China and most African countries, where large numbers of languages and dialects commonly generate overlaps in work contexts (Badejo 1989; Mesthrie 2002; Clingingsmith 2006). Similarly, in countries such as Belgium, Canada, Luxembourg and Switzerland, multilingualism has been a long-standing fact of life, which has also had its impact on the workplace. However, international migration within and towards Western Europe and to countries like the USA, Canada and Australia that have been economically dependent on immigration, has created diversely multilingual workplaces with increasing frequency over the past 50 years. Issues such as cross-cultural communication, social and economic exclusion, workplace learning and workplace efficiency have all been addressed in academic research, forming, if unevenly, the basis of the study of workplace multilingualism. With the greatly increased volume of global migratory processes at the end of the twentieth and start of the twenty-first centuries, the relevance of some of these core areas has shifted and created new research possibilities, theoretical needs and paradigms for academic work. Furthermore, political transformations in places like the former Soviet Union or South Africa – where 11 official languages and many unofficial ones create a truly complex set of social, economic and political issues that are quite unanticipated by the existing state of research into multilingualism in the workplace – provide new and challenging empirical sites.

The academic literature on workplace multilingualism has been historically driven by a fairly narrow range of disciplinary interests, with Education – specifically concerned with ESOL and workplace literacy – being one of the most active (Belfiore et al. 2004). From this base, other areas of concern such as social exclusion, power relations and inequality in the workplace, based on ethnicity or gender, resulting from managerial policies and practices have also developed (Gumperz 1982; Roberts *et al.* 1992; Holmes 2006; Holmes and Stubbe 2003). Beyond these domains the other strands of academic interest in workplace language – in particular those whose disciplinary base lies in linguistics, pragmatics, conversational analysis (CA) and discourse analysis of various kinds (Firth 1995; Drew and Heritage 1992), have paid almost no attention to workplace multilingualism. Clyne's (1994) study of multi-ethnic communication in a number of workplaces in Melbourne, Australia is an exception to the trend. It examined workplace discourse taking place between workers from a wide variety of ethnic backgrounds in sites including motor manufacturers, a textile factory, an electronics factory and a caterers. Audio recordings were made of 39 workers who agreed to wear lapel radio-microphones for periods of up to 90 minutes in their normal work situations. The resulting recordings were transcribed and analysed at the level of discourse – i.e. stretches of talk larger than the sentence. The study placed considerable emphasis on cultural differences between the different ethnic groups and their expression through discursive practices. In this sense it was a study of multi-ethnic workplace discourse. However, its data were exclusively stretches of English language used as a lingua franca. These were approached through a combination of discourse analysis, conversational analysis and speech act theory. This was a rigorously conducted piece of research and to some extent a model of workplace research, which seeks naturally occurring speech as its primary data. Nevertheless, it did not constitute a study of multilingualism in the workplace in any strict sense. Studies that involve the making of the audio/video recordings on which the detailed transcriptions of naturally occurring talk depends are relatively few, although they may now increase. Access to relevant research sites has been hampered in part by the intrusive nature of recording equipment, by the simple pressure of workplace rhythms and processes and by the confidentiality or secretiveness necessary for competitive workplace settings. Although recording technologies have now overcome one set of problems, many of the other issues remain.

The sociology of language constitutes another avenue to language in the workplace and one that has been explored by a number of authors. Hywel Coleman edited two volumes of papers exploring language at work from a sociological perspective: *Language and Work 1: Law, Industry and Education* (1984), and *Language and Work 2: The Health Professions* (1985), although by the time of his third edited collection *Working with Language: A Multidisciplinary Consideration of Language Use in Work Contexts* (1989), the limited range of these and similar studies was already troubling him. He notes that 'investigations of language use in non-professional contexts are scarce'. He also adds the following comment: 'adopting society's own classification system and then restricting research to the most prestigious – though numerically smallest – group within that system inevitably means that the resulting picture is seriously incomplete'. A quarter of a century later this imbalance is still very evident in workplace-language studies, although there are a number of important exceptions to this generalization. Distinctive 'sociology of language' accounts concerned with multilingualism would certainly include McAll's theorization and overview of research conducted into workplace language in Montreal. In particular he draws attention to 'the history of language groups in their attempts to occupy and control different sectors of the labour market and different territories or niches within the workplace' (McAll 2003: 246). He distinguishes work where language is itself the 'principle raw material' that is subject to transformation – in the production of various kinds of texts, written instructions, plans, etc. – and those where some other raw material is being transformed. These may form different phases of a single production process that can be described as 'language centred' and 'language marginal' phases. As competence levels with the language of use are of fundamental significance in 'language centred' work, this may become a site of competition/conflict where – as with French and English in the Montreal workplace – parity of status between languages is approximately established. McAll draws on a cluster of important studies conducted in the 1990s by the *Equipe de recherche en sociologie du langage* (Sociology of Language research team) of the Department of Sociology at the University of Montreal. Workplaces investigated included the garment industry, a pharmaceutical company, and companies involved in aerospace, and health and social services.

Another Canadian study of workplace multilingualism, in this case focusing on a single factory in Ontario, presents itself in a series entitled *Contributions to the Sociology of Language*, edited by Joshua Fishman (for Mouton de Gruyter), and methodologically sits on the uneasy borderline between sociolinguistics and the sociology of language. Tara Goldstein's *Two Languages at Work: Bi-lingual Life on the Production Floor* (1997) is an important contribution in the tradition of sociolinguistic ethnography. Its starting point lies in the educational world of workplace ESL (English as a Second Language) teaching, of which she was a part, but it opens up onto an unusually frank discussion of the value of such teaching to the Portuguese-speaking workers in a section of an English–Canadian-owned factory manufacturing novelty goods. She found that although the assumption behind the ESL classes to the staff had been that the workplace language used by the staff was English, albeit of a deficient kind, in fact Portuguese was the main language used between the line-workers, both for their work-relevant exchanges and in their social and casual interactions at work. She also found that not all of the workers in need of better English chose to attend the classes and for those that did: 'even after successful attempts at learning English our students do not often get promoted into better-paying positions. Nor do they frequently leave their present job to find better-paying work elsewhere' (Goldstein 1997: 4). In other words, one of the main claims made for the benefits of learning English – and particularly in the workplace – was found to be in this case largely untrue.

In this part of the factory a simple three-tier structure existed with an English-speaking senior management, a Portuguese-speaking workforce and a mediating tier of bilingual supervisors brokering the two. The naïve assumption of the ESL teaching design that a workforce of Portuguese co-linguals would, unremarkably, communicate mainly in Portuguese, was not the focus of interest but rather the catalyst for an extended exploration of the role of Portuguese in individual identity work, in collective belonging, in friendship and in seeking help and advice from others on the assembly line. These activities were all enabled by the fact of a shared, but non-English, language, and, it is argued, contributed both to workplace efficiency and, complexly, to loyalty to the company. Although fully aware of the problems experienced by those with little or no English in this setting, Goldstein argues for the essential rationality of their linguistic choices. In moving on to consider the implications of this for ESL workplace provision, she questions the notion that students are empowered by a process that implicitly re-enforces both the dominance of English (as against any minority language) and the power-relations within the workforce as expressions of the wider capitalist order. In her words: 'A vision that links empowerment with participation in dominant language networks is at odds with a vision that links empowerment with effort to re-define and change existing unequal linguistic relations of power.' That latter vision, Goldstein asserts, is to be found within a 'critical pedagogy of ESL', rather than the well-established vision of ESL embedded within the contemporary 'empowerment' practices of new capitalist managerialism.

Some challenges to workplace English

In the case study pursued by Goldstein we can see the emergence of an implicit challenge to the hegemony of workplace English in the de facto practices of the Portuguese immigrant workers.

This case is related to the similar situation obtaining in many US worksites with respect to Spanish and takes us back to the debates alluded to earlier concerning the 'English-only workplace'. The US 2000 census showed that 47 million people (18 per cent of the population) did not speak English in the home – an increase of 14 per cent since the previous census. The census also showed that 46 per cent of foreign-born workers have limited English, and of those 73 per cent speak Spanish. Inevitably, in many US workplaces, Spanish is spoken alongside English and in many others it is spoken to the exclusion of English. Workplace ESL schemes have been promoted and utilized often on the basis of the argument that both safety at work and workforce efficiency depend on workers understanding instructions, and as a result, ESL provision satisfies both legal requirements and economic sense. More recently, however, economic need has suggested another scenario: safety and job training delivered in workers' home languages. As ESL training has failed to keep pace with needs, the logic of delivering training in the employee population's native tongue becomes inescapable. Against the grain of the English-only workplace, some Human Resources consultants are recommending this course unambiguously. One online Human Resources magazine argued:

> Employers who offer job training to ESL employees in their native language can expect various types of payback. Chief among them ... is employees' greater understanding of aspects of their jobs, from benefits to workplace procedures. Improved compliance with workplace laws and regulations is particularly important, experts say, and it may help to shield against litigation.

(Tyler 2005)

It also argued that productivity can improve. Quoting one HR consultant concerning the improvement in work quality reported by a coating manufacturer after it moved to training in Spanish:

> 'The workforce was entirely Latino', he says 'but the supervisors could not speak Spanish. The instructions – spray to one millimeter thickness and bake for so long at a certain temperature – were all in English and they couldn't read it.' After the language change productivity went up 14 per cent and customer returns went down 90 per cent.

(ibid.)

Indications other than size of ESL workforce that moving to native tongue training would be wise were offered by another HR consultant. These included 'labor unrest, productivity slippage and complaints about product or service quality' (ibid.), thus seeming to scotch any simple equation between shifts in linguistic power relations and emergent 'critical' perspectives.

Economic sociologist Alejandro Portes describes as 'occupational niches' situations where a certain ethnic group come to numerically dominate within a company owned by a non-group member, which:

> consists of the activities initiated by already employed individuals to bring others of the same national origin to work with them and the gradual transformation of the workplace into an ethnic 'enterprise', even if formal ownership lies elsewhere. Use of the immigrants' language for communication at work and the implementation of distinct cultural practices in the performance of tasks are indicators of this transformation, which simultaneously reduces the power of formal managers and owners.

(1995: 28)

Such processes of colonization of selected occupational niches would seem to constitute another site of the kind of linguistic territoriality analysed by McAll (2003).

This kind of non-English-speaking workforce may perhaps more commonly be created by more explicit forms of ethnic entrepreneurialism. Elsewhere Portes describes the impressively speedy progress of non-English-speaking Cubans in Miami in establishing businesses based on trust between would-be entrepreneurs and Cuban banks, which made 'character loans' on the basis only of close community ties and knowledge. According to Portes and Stepick, such character loans 'allowed numerous exiles who spoke little English and had no standing in the American banking world to get a foothold in the local economy' (Portes and Stepick 1993: 132–3). Thus 'six years after arrival and despite low average levels of education and knowledge of English 21.2 percent of [our research project's] Cuban sample in Miami had become self-employed'. Such entrepreneurs would then hire co-ethnic workers with similarly low levels of education and little or no English. For these workers, 'low wages were accepted in exchange for preferential access to employment even in the absence of English or formal certification' (1993: 145).

In these ways, as shown by other similar studies, social ties frequently compensate for the human capital deficiencies of migrant workers. What the Cuban example demonstrates is how the collective progress of a group can become established through the fluid interaction of entrepreneurs and their co-ethnic, co-lingual workers, where opportunities for both categories of participants become activated, positions can become exchanged and collective group identity becomes established within the wider society. Whether the low pay accepted by workers for 'preferential access' to jobs creates an exploitative static stratification or a fluid one in regard to economic opportunity structures may depend on many variables. However, the situation of co-ethnic, co-lingual workplaces within a dominant English-speaking (or other major European-language-speaking) setting does present a considerably different situation to that based on the familiar model.

What Hewitt (2008) found in a study of Polish, Chinese and Kurdish entrepreneurs in London was how such companies develop their interaction with mainstream institutions and agencies – banks, health and safety inspectors, tax offices, etc. – through bilingual agents placed at nodes within the predominantly minority language company, sometimes external to it, such as accountants or lawyers. Thus the multilingualism of the workplace is characterized by the use of one or more non-English language, for most work-task and social purposes, and the use of English only at certain strategically important nodes, e.g. interaction with customers, where these are not also co-linguals (as they often are), with suppliers (ditto) and with banks, e.g. the in-house accountants.

In terms of efficiency these kinds of companies frequently prefer co-ethnic employees both for their cultural knowledge of, say a specific range of market goods or for interactions with clients, and for the general efficient running of the company. This is a fairly universal preference. One Canadian study reported:

> Mr. Yin from Taiwan finds that English-speaking employees reduce the efficiency of communication within the firm: 'We still look for people from our own culture to work for us. I tried to use Caucasian people too but when we set up a meeting, if we speak in English it is very difficult to present our ideas'.
>
> *(Froschener 2001: 232).*

This kind of basis for preferences was also found in Hewitt's study. Another aspect of non-English-speaking workplaces in London was the variety of minority languages found in some small companies – particularly where ability to complete specific tasks and to maintain high output was more important than command of any particular language. For quick workers with previous experience the simple, wordless demonstration of a task was all that was needed. One Kurdish textile factory owner in north London had a small workforce of 32 workers. Half of those workers were Kurds from Turkey, and spoke no English. The other half were Chinese, none of whom spoke English or Kurdish. The owner of the company spoke almost no English and was interviewed through an interpreter, and only the manager spoke a little English. He would accompany the owner to the bank for any meeting and to other necessary encounters with the wider system. The owner explained that the Chinese workers had appeared at his door one day with a piece of paper explaining in English that they needed work and could cut and sew fabric. He took them on and set them up in more or less wordless exchanges. They proved themselves to be already very skilled. Now they were a significant part of his workforce.

Even more varied multilingualisms were also encountered in this research. One pastry factory owned by a Chinese bilingual (Cantonese/English) woman employed four staff who were Cantonese-speaking plus one Sri Lankan machine operator who spoke no Chinese and very little English; a Polish driver who had no Chinese and very little English but understood instructions well and could handle the paperwork; another Pole with no Chinese and no English who had worked for the company for nine years as a baker; and a Portuguese worker who also had no Chinese and no English. The business-owner explained: 'I show them what to do. They learn rolling, cutting, filling. They just learn. No language' (Hewitt 2008). Companies that conduct their business primarily through a single language other than English are far from unusual internationally and, Hewitt argues, whatever their role in the survival strategies of *individuals*, they often contribute to the civic and political profile of the ethnic *groups* in significant ways.

Work of this kind in the sociology of language reminds us that although workplace multilingualism is an internationally recognized phenomenon, it is increasingly evident that for a number of reasons reference to a broad-based literature is necessary to capture much of what is and has been happening in the workplace in response to the scale and variety of global migration. So broad are the social ramifications of much of this new surge in workplace-language variety – including technical and information-related domains of work – that the disciplinary bases cannot be restricted to familiar areas. Now of necessity they include economic sociology, political science, economics and the sociology of language. From these disciplines we gain descriptions of languages in particular work situations, how language choice relates to opportunity structures within local economies and how these relate to wider institutional structures that influence the prosperity of groups and individuals. We learn about waves of migration and their relationship to the economies in which they occur and to the development of cultural organizations where language resources exist and community language support takes place (e.g. Portes and Bach 1985; Portes and Rumbout 1996; Min 1996; Grin 1999; Grin and Sfreddo 2009). There are also legal and policy-related literatures that have bearing on the subject. In many cases these represent significant dimensions that need to be given serious attention as sources of both knowledge and theoretical development even when working at the level of spoken discourse.

Thus a number of recent research programmes investigating contemporary workplace communication involve multidisciplinary teams, for example the EC-funded DYLAN programme with 20 partner research institutions in 12 countries and many different disciplines, spread over 5 years. This project seeks to identify the conditions under which Europe's linguistic diversity can be an asset rather than a liability. The empirical work is taking place in three domains of relevance to the management of multilingualism in Europe: private companies, EU institutions and educational systems. One strand of this project is based in Basle, Switzerland under the direction of Professor George Lüdi and is called: 'Plurilingualism at the workplace: the gap between the planning of "internal communication" and real world language behaviour'. This project combines the recording and transcription of actual communication in the professional workplace with interview, documentary and other evidence, and compares practices with companies' declared language-practice profiles. A Swiss-based project LEAP (see below) also employs interdisciplinary methods to examine the macro-economic impact of multilingual communication on Swiss businesses.

These kinds of studies are particularly concerned with high-end technical, and business workplace contexts for multilingualism. Here multilingual workplaces are increasingly mediated by the use of English as a lingua franca. As sociologist Ivan Light put it when discussing class-cultural endowments:

> In non-English-speaking countries, bourgeoisies learn English because English is now the lingua franca of international business. Whether in Taiwan or Finland, bourgeoisies learn English and their knowledge of it represents a class resource precisely because and insofar as all business owners share this knowledge.
>
> *(Light and Gold 2000: 84)*

However, there are some indications that this does not create a uniform pattern of resource utilization everywhere that English is in play. Contra Light and Gold, a recent study of the language needs of university graduates in the contemporary Finnish workplace showed that language skills were highly valued by employers but that it was *not sufficient to use only English* alongside Finnish. As today's workplaces are 'plurilingual' and successful communication is of utmost importance, this places heavy demands on graduates' language skills across the board (Lehtonen and Karjalainen 2008). In a similar vein, the Swiss research mentioned above drew on a number of major databases and 200 companies in the industrial sector in French- and German-speaking Switzerland were also surveyed. LEAP researchers in Geneva calculate that the multilingual nature of many businesses in Switzerland (principally French, German and English) contributes 9 per cent (46 billion Swiss francs) to Switzerland's gross domestic product. Nevertheless, to some extent because of its increasing usage, English in itself is again not a key to individuals' and individual companies' commercial success. François Grin, director of the LEAP project has argued that, in Switzerland, knowledge of French or German plays a more important role in terms of business competition. 'Competence in English is becoming usual, even banal, so you need to set yourself apart from your competitors by knowing other things, such as the national languages of Switzerland, which play a major role' (Alan 2008).

Getting the work done

A final example of high-end multilingualism shares some features in common with examples above but adds the dimension of multilingual workplaces where English functions as an indispensible technical language. Research by Hill and van Zyl (2002) into the South African engineering workplace was concerned with the relative use and value of languages in play in a number of engineering companies in the Witwatersrand. Following the transition from apartheid, the democratically elected new South African government extended the number of official languages from two – English and Afrikaans – to 11 and committed the state to 'elevate and advance the use' of those indigenous African languages previously disadvantaged. However, perhaps reminiscent of Lüdi's research described above on the gap between policy and practice, some have argued that whereas the power of Afrikaans appears to have decreased, the status of the Indigenous languages is little changed and the dominance of English has been further entrenched.

Given the global dominance of English, it is unsurprising that most South African companies have followed a predominantly 'English-only' policy, whereas companies 'allow' local languages for everyday workplace spoken interactions, all have a policy of English as the basic language of business, as do the major mining houses. As Hill and van Zyl report:

> The engineering workplace ... uses English as more than just a business language. The technical knowledge upon which engineering practice is based, and the global interests of many South African engineering companies ensure that both theory and practice are discussed in an international standard language which possesses the necessary technical terms. In addition many engineers receive their professional training in an international language which connects them to a world wide 'community of experts' ... who use the same language and its specialized resources. In South Africa that language is English.
>
> *(2002: 24)*

For young black engineers, whose primary language is commonly one of the African languages, being professionally fully functional makes demands of a high order on English-language competency but at the same time can also involve important strategic use of African languages. The engineering profession necessarily involves regular and critical interactions with a multilingual workforce. Here the black engineers are at an advantage, particularly as many bring to their work a fluency in several African languages and familiarity with a range of cultures.

Hill and van Zyl's research was designed to investigate the linguistic context of engineering in South Africa and particularly the practices and attitudes of young black engineers. A sample of 58 engineering students with varying amounts of site work experience and newly qualified engineers participated in this research. Methods included focus groups, interviews, survey questionnaire and observational work. Engineering fields covered included electrical, chemical, mining and aeronautical. Respondents were asked to specify the languages used predominantly at work, whether there was a company policy prescribing language use and, crucially, to indicate any other language used 'to get the work done'.

As well as the anticipated finding that English was important across a range of interactions and was also used for documentation and that Afrikaans was suffering from an erosion of its use in some areas of work, a more complex picture emerged of workplace language than was stated in policy documents. During the site observations, English and Afrikaans were found to be mixed by the engineers for practical purposes at foreman level. For example, mixed language and codeswitching was used to discuss planned and unplanned work hours and problems with a boilermaker, and with a planner to discuss seals and temperature probes. The researchers report: 'The ground handling planner on the diamond mine was busy processing his month-end report in English while speaking Afrikaans to his (African) clerk.' From the survey the researchers found that very few of the respondents were aware of an English-only policy and 58 per cent of respondents' perceived languages other than English to be used predominantly in the workplace. The researchers, leaving behind the 'workplace', perhaps as a rhetorical abstraction, turned their attention more precisely on the 'workface' as the place where things get done. There Afrikaans was seen as one of the main languages:

> A whole stratum of workpeople including foremen and planners, artisans, fitters and technicians, engineers, mine captains and other technical operatives who accomplish the

day-to-day work of big companies have Afrikaans as their primary language, and some speak nothing else. Their operatives speak Afrikaans to black clerks or semi-skilled workers, although they might speak Fanakalo [the informal, mixed language of the mines] to labourers.

(Hill and van Zyl 2002: 29)

Focus groups and interviewees reported better cooperation from operatives when they spoke Afrikaans: 'If you speak Afrikaans to them, they will show you short cuts and tell you tips. But if you only come to them in English – oh well, they just answer the question and that's it' (ibid.). Thus 'despite the historical antagonism of black people towards Afrikaans, most of those surveyed accepted the predominance of Afrikaans as natural' (2002: 30).

With regard to Indigenous African languages, these were primary languages spoken by a large cross-section of black workers from unskilled labourers to increasing numbers of better educated personnel including engineers. African languages were therefore used on posters in the mines, in reception areas for job-seekers and, in the diamond mine, they were used for safety meetings. As with the question above concerning the informational pay-off for using Afrikaans, the use of an African language between engineers and machine operators was also seen to promote understanding and cooperation. Eighty-three per cent of the questionnaire respondents understood more than five South African languages other than English, and 51 per cent could speak five or more.

These skills are clearly a fluid resource for young black engineers. They also contribute on a broad front to the better running of the companies where they work. Engineers frequently translate for workers. One would translate briefs issued by management and was asked by management to address a meeting of local farm workers about the mine's expansion using Sesotho and isiZulu. Another translated a hearing health-and-safety brochure into isiZulu and yet another had written a teaching manual in Sesotho and isiZulu to upgrade skills and give workers accreditation.

The researchers concluded that:

> During the period when management was still totally monolingual, or at best bi-lingual in English and Afrikaans, Fanakalo was a solution imposed by management on communication problems between foremen and workers in mines and parastatals. As more educated multilinguals are recruited to foreman and management positions, and as the workforce itself has better access to English, it could be that multilingual accommodation will emerge as a natural and organic facilitator of communication in the workplace as well as at the workface.

(Hill and van Zyl 2002: 33)

Although multilingualism as a intermediary function between sections of a workforce remains one dimension of workplace multilingualism (as we have seen in several of the other cases discussed above), as with any other workplace function it remains a matter of significance whether that role functions to the benefit of one section more than another, or how far it is fairly rewarded. In the South African situation we see some very big companies involved in the recognition of the importance of multilingualism to their smooth running. It will be for the South African government to judge how far that achieves their aim to 'elevate the status and advance the use' of Indigenous languages, and for the workforce itself to judge how far it functions to enhance the social dynamics of work*place* relations.

What applies to this South African case study also applies in different ways to all of the instances of workplace multilingualism discussed in this chapter. How indelible was the trade-off between low wages and access to the labour market in the relationship between Cuban would-be entrepreneurs and the Spanish-speaking workers that they recruited? How exploitative or empowering are the relationships between the non-English-speaking workers in a small London multilingual factory? These are questions that throw up similar issues. Generalized answers will certainly be too glib. Similarly, in the case of pan-European interest in the benefits of multilingualism to industry and commerce, questions concerning what kinds of multilingualism have to be asked. Whose multilingualism is in and whose is out in the game of 'European economic growth'? How far and in what ways are the minority languages of Europe, spoken largely by its relatively new migrant populations as well of some of its oldest communities, included – other than rhetorically – in the consideration of the multilingual workplace? Will multilingualism, as Hill and van Zyl hope for South Africa, be allowed to become a 'natural and organic facilitator of communication in the workplace', or is the default mode of the workplace still ultimately left with the contradictory paradigm of the Ford Motor Company circa 1916?

Inevitably, multilingualism in the workplace, possibly more than in any other location, raises economic and social questions of a particular kind. For this reason, it is important that any research approaching it is vigilant of the breadth of its disciplinary interest. It is in all respects a very under-researched and under-theorized area and one that offers rich possibilities for future work.

Related topics

Multilingual literacies; multilingualism and social exclusion; multilingualism and gender; multilingualism and the new economy.

Further reading

Belfiore, M. E., Defoe, T. A., Folinsbee, S., Hunter, J. and Jackson, N. S. (2004) *Reading Work: Literacies in the New Work Order*, Mahwah, NJ: Lawrence Erlbaum.
(Although primarily about workplace literacy practices, this volume touches on wider issues important to multilingualism research in workplace contexts.)

Goldstein, T. (1997) *Two Languages at Work: Bilingual Life on the Production Floor*, Berlin, Mouton de Gruyter.
(Detailed ethnographic account of how English and Portuguese function together in one Canadian factory.)

Heller, M. (2003) 'Globalization, the new economy and the commodification of language and identity', *Journal of Sociolinguistics* 7(4): 43–492.
(Presents new directions in thinking about the commodification of language in the context of globalization and the emergence of the new economy; new theory-building that is grounded in sociolinguistic ethnographic research in Canada.)

Hill, P. and van Zyl, S. (2002) 'English and multilingualism in the South African engineering workplace', *World Englishes* 21(1): 23–35.
(Reports on study of complex multilingual relations in the new South Africa.)

McAll, C. (2003) 'Language dynamics in the bi- and multicultural workplace', in R. Bayley and S. R. Schecter (eds) *Language Socialization in Bilingual and Multilingual Societies*, Clevedon: Multilingual Matters.
(An interesting theorization of workplace language plus a good overview of research into multilingualism in Quebec.)

McElhinny, B. (ed.) (2007) *Words, Worlds and Material Girls*, Berlin: Mouton de Gruyter.
(This collection has several chapters that relate to language and gender in the new economy.)

Bibliography

Alan, J. (2008) 'Multilingual workplace adds 46 billion francs to economy', available online at www.
unige.ch/eti/recherches/groupes/elf/medias/Swisster.pdf

Badejo, B. R. (1989) 'Multilingualism in Sub-Saharan Africa', *Africa Media Review*, African
Council on Communication Education, 40–53.

Belfiore, M. E., Defoe, T. A., Folinsbee, S., Hunter, J. and Jackson, N. S. (2004) *Reading Work:
Literacies in the New Work Order*, Mahwah, NJ: Lawrence Erlbaum.

Clingingsmith, D. (2006) *Bilingualism, Language Shift, and Economic Development in India*, 1931–61,
available online at http://isites.harvard.edu/fs/docs/icb.topic466116.files/Clingingsmith_061031.pdf

Clyne, M. (1994) *Inter-Cultural Communication at Work: Cultural Values in Discourse*, Cambridge:
Cambridge University Press.

Coleman, H. (1984) *Language and Work 1: Law, Industry and Education*, Berlin: Mouton de
Gruyter.

——(1985) *Language and Work 2: The Health Professions*, Berlin: Mouton de Gruyter.

——(1989) *Working with Language: A Multidisciplinary Consideration of Language Use in Work
Contexts*, Berlin: Mouton de Gruyter.

Dicker, S. (1998) 'Adaptation and assimilation: US business responses to linguistic diversity in the
workplace', *Journal of Multilingual and Multicultural Development* (19)4: 281–302.

Drew, P. and Heritage, J. (eds) (1992) *Talk at Work: Interaction and Institutional Settings*, Cambridge:
Cambridge University Press.

Erickson, F. and Schultz, J. (1982) *The Counselor as Gatekeeper*, New York: Academic Press.

Firth, A. (ed.) (1995) *The Discourse of Negotiation: Studies of Language in the Workplace*, Oxford:
Pergamon.

Froschener, K. (2001) 'Early Asian and European migrants in British Columbia, Canada: Post
migration conduct and pre-migration context', *Journal of Ethnic and Migration Studies* 27(2):
225–40.

Gee, J., Hull, G. and Lankshear, C. (1996) *The New Work Order: Behind the Language of the
New Capitalism*, Boulder, CO: Westview Press.

Gerber, R. and Lankshear, C. (2000) *Training for a Smart Workforce*, London: Routledge.

Goldstein, T. (1997) *Two Languages at Work: Bilingual Life on the Production Floor*, Berlin:
Mouton de Gruyter.

Grin, F. (1999) 'Economics', in J. Fishman (ed.) *Handbook of Language and Ethnic Identity*, Oxford:
Oxford University Press.

Grin, F. and Sfreddo, C. (2009) *The Economics of the Multilingual Workplace*, London: Routledge.

Gumperz, J. (1982) *Discourse Strategies*, Cambridge: Cambridge University Press.

Hewitt, R. (2008) 'The capital's "language shortfall" and migrants' economic survival', Economic
and Social Research Council, UK Research Report: R000 22 1846.

Hill, P. and van Zyl, S. (2002) 'English and multilingualism in the South African engineering
workplace', *World Englishes* 21(1): 23–35.

Holmes, J. (2006) *Gendered Talk at Work: Constructing Gender Identity through Workplace Discourse*,
Oxford: Blackwell.

Holmes, J. and Stubbe, M. (2003) *Power and Politeness in the Workplace: A Sociolinguistic Analysis
of Talk at Work*, London: Longman.

Hull, G. (ed.) (1997) *Changing Work, Changing Workers: Critical Perspectives on Language,
Literacy, and Skills*, Albany: State University of New York Press.

Lehtonen, T. and Karjalainen, S. (2008) 'University graduates' workplace language needs as
perceived by employers', *System* 36(3) (September): 492–503.

Light, I. and Gold, S. J. (2000) *Ethnic Economies*, San Diego: Academic Press.

McAll, C. (2003) 'Language dynamics in the bi- and multicultural workplace', in R. Bayley and
S. R. Schecter (eds) *Language Socialization in Bilingual and Multilingual Societies*, Clevedon:
Multilingual Matters.

Mawer, G. (1999) *Language and Literacy in Workplace Education*, London: Longman.

Mesthrie, R. (ed.) (2002) *Language in South Africa*, Cambridge: Cambridge University Press.

Min, P. G. (1996) *Caught in the Middle: Korean Merchants in America's Multiethnic Cities*, Berkeley: University of California Press.

NAPALC (2003) (National Asian Pacific American Legal Consortium) *The Politics of Language. Your Handbook to English-Only Laws and Policies*, 2nd edn, Washington, DC: NAPALC.

Nevins, A. (1954) *Ford: The Man, the Times, the Company*, 3 volumes, New York: Scribners.

Portes, A. (1995) 'Economic sociology and the sociology of immigration: A conceptual overview', in A. Portes (ed.) *The Economic Sociology of Immigration*, New York: Russell Sage Foundation.

Portes, A. and Bach, R. (1985) *Latin Journey: Cuban and Mexican Immigrants in the United States*, Berkeley: University of California Press.

Portes, A. and Rumbout, R. (1996) *Immigrant America: A Portrait*, Berkeley: University of California Press, (chapter 6: Case for bi-lingualism).

Portes, A. and Stepick, A. (1993) *City on the Edge: The Transformation of Miami*, Berkeley: University of California Press.

Rodriguez, C. (2006) 'Language diversity in the workplace', *Northwestern University Law Review* 100(4): 1689–1773.

Roberts, C., Davies, E. and Jupp, T. (1992) *Language and Discrimination: A Study of Communication in Multi-Ethnic Workplaces*, London: Longman.

Sarangi, S. and Roberts, C. (eds) (1999) *Talk, Work and Institutional Order: Discourse in Medical, Management and Mediation Settings*, Berlin: Mouton de Gruyter.

Schwartz, J. M. (1989) *In Defense of Homesickness: Nine Essays on Identity and Locality*, Kutursociologiske Skrifter, 26, Academisk Forlag, Institute for Cultural Sociology, Copenhagen University, Copenhagen.

Shim, M. (2000) 'English-only workplace suits continue to rise', *American Lawyer Media*, October 18th, available online at http://englishfirst.org/workplace/workplaceacluprop63.htm

Taylor, F. ([1911]1967) *The Principles of Scientific Management*, New York: Norton and Harper and Row.

Tyler, K. (2005) 'Clear language/claro lenguaje: By delivering workplace training in the language employees understand best, you can improve their productivity, compliance and morale', *HR Magazine*, 1 December.

16

Multilingualism and social exclusion

Ingrid Piller

Introduction

It is the aim of this chapter to provide an overview of research into the ways in which social exclusion and multilingualism articulate. 'Social exclusion' and its inverse, 'social inclusion', are relatively new terms, which first started to be used in Europe in the 1990s in reference to those excluded from the Social Contract, particularly through lack of paid work. The term has since gained prominence due to its use in the European Union's Lisbon Strategy of 2000, which aims 'to strengthen employment, economic reform and social cohesion as part of a knowledge-based economy' (European Parliament 2000). Social exclusion is sometimes used to refer narrowly to the absence of economic well-being, particularly unemployment and underemployment, and sometimes it is used more broadly to include the absence of civil and social rights, particularly to health care and education (Birchardt *et al.* 2002). The usefulness of the term 'social exclusion' over older terms such as 'poverty' or 'deprivation' (Welshman 2007) or over its North American equivalents 'marginalization' or 'underclass' (Hills *et al.* 2002), lies precisely in this broad conceptualization and in the recognition that identities are a major source of exclusion from material well-being. Key aspects of identity that are widely recognized as being bound up with access to material resources include gender, ethnicity/race, class and citizenship status and the myriad ways in which these intersect (see e.g. Browne and Misra 2005; Burman 2003; Valentine 2007; Westwood 2005; Yuval-Davis 2007). Although the intersection between social exclusion and these ascribed identities is well researched – if not necessarily well understood – there is a relative lack of attention to the ways in which linguistic identities, linguistic proficiencies and language ideologies mediate social inclusion.

In this chapter I use 'social exclusion' primarily to refer to the absence of material well-being, the importance of which is enshrined in Paragraph 23 of the *Universal Declaration of Human Rights* (1948) as the human right to work. Social inclusion is necessarily a multifaceted and complex phenomenon, but the *Human Development Indices* (2008) provide useful indicators of development on the national level, which can also serve as indicators of social inclusion on the group level within a nation: the three indices identified by the United Nations Development Programme, which publishes the *Human Development Indices*, are (1) 'a long and healthy life' as measured by life expectancy; (2) 'access to knowledge' as measured by the adult literacy rate and gross enrolment ratio in primary, secondary and tertiary education; and (3) 'a decent standard of living' as measured by gross domestic product (GDP).

Social inclusion is usually conceptualized with reference to the state – the Social Contract is between the state and its citizens – or with reference to international bodies that have taken on some functions of the nation-state, particularly the European Union. However, although the state remains the almost exclusive reference point for research into and discussions of social inclusion, economic globalization has partly eroded the capacity of the nation-state to be an effective agent of economic development (Reinert 2008), and, hence, social inclusion. Some states in the Global South never developed the capacity to be an effective agent of social inclusion in the first place (Carr and Chen 2004). In order to understand the articulation between multilingualism and social inclusion, we therefore need to write two additional factors into the account: transnational migration and development, as the *Human Development Report* (2009) does.

Transnational migration needs to be considered because on the national level, language regimes serve to exclude particularly transnational migrants in ever-increasing numbers. I will thus focus on the social exclusion of transnational migrants in this chapter (for a discussion of the social exclusion of Indigenous minority groups, refer to Chapters 1 and 8). Of course, segments of the native-born population face exclusion, too – youths, the elderly, people with disabilities, etc. However, multilingualism usually only plays a minor part, if any at all, in the exclusion of native-born populations other than Indigenous minorities. Some groups are always in a more privileged position vis-à-vis the state than others – as far as language is concerned, speakers of the standard of the official language of a nation are in the most privileged position. So, the key question is around the social inclusion of speakers of migrant languages in a given context.

Language as a factor in social exclusion thus arises in the context of transnational migration. However, it is also enabled by global inequality. 'Development' and 'social inclusion' are usually treated in two separate baskets: 'social inclusion' is an intranational issue for the countries of the Global North and 'development' is an international issue for the countries of the Global South. I am bringing them together here for a range of reasons: to begin with, the majority of the world's 'excluded' live in the Global South and there might be some value in trying to understand the articulation of multilingualism and exclusion in general terms, rather than by reference to only a relatively small group, i.e. those excluded internally in the countries of the Global North. Second, the exclusion of communities, nations and even a whole continent (i.e. Africa) from economic well-being, education and health care is a key factor in international migration and often a precondition for the internal exclusion of migrants, often without citizenship rights, in the cities of the Global North (Ehrenreich and Hochschild 2002; Sassen 2001). Finally, the countries of the Global North achieved their relatively high levels of social inclusion internally in large part through maximizing external inequality and exclusion through colonialism and neo-colonialism (Djité 2008). The articulation between social inclusion and multilingualism is therefore best understood within a global system of the (de)valorization of certain speakers and certain languages.

In the following, I will begin by reviewing early developments in thinking about the interrelationship between poverty and language. Two broad viewpoints can be distinguished: one that sees poverty as inherently connected with non-standard speech and predicts that linguistic assimilation will result in greater social inclusion; and another one that sees the monolingual bias of institutions as agents in the exclusion of linguistically diverse populations and argues for linguistic recognition and multilingual provision as ways to promote social inclusion.

I will then move on to review key issues of theory and method by considering two different approaches to understanding the articulation of language and social exclusion: one that starts with a consideration of language and another that treats social exclusion as the core problem. I will argue that the role of language in social exclusion can only be meaningfully understood from a social rather than a linguistic perspective. I will make that argument on the basis of an Australian case study of the employment of contemporary transnational migrants from non-English-speaking backgrounds (NESB). In the final sections on policy issues and future directions in research, I will suggest that there might be a need to shed those professional blinkers that view language and culture as core factors in social phenomena. In the case of social exclusion, they often make us blind to socio-economic structures.

Early developments in the field

As I pointed out above, 'social exclusion' and 'social inclusion' are relatively new terms. However, concerns with the relationship between language and (economic) disadvantage have a long tradition. It is useful to distinguish two broad developments: one that grew out of the mass migrations of the nineteenth century to the New World and which came to associate bilingualism with poverty. This tradition with its assumption that linguistic assimilation will enhance economic well-being and social inclusion continues to be influential today. The second tradition grew out of the various emancipatory movements of the 1960s with their call for the recognition of diversity. In this tradition, individual bilingualism came to be celebrated and the monolingual bias of institutions tended to be blamed for the disadvantages experienced by speakers of minority languages and non-standard varieties. These two strands broadly coincide with two opposing assumptions about the root cause of social exclusion (Birchardt et al. 2002): although one school of thought blames poverty squarely on the individuals mired in poverty (e.g. their delinquency, drug addiction, promiscuity, weak character, low IQ or, increasingly, their genes), an opposing school of thought sees disadvantage as built into institutions and 'the system' (e.g. racial discrimination, capitalism, class exploitation, colonialism, sexism, etc.). If bilingualism has been incorporated into these analyses of social exclusion, it has been done within this overall dichotomy: bilingualism is either seen as a 'fault' of the individual, which prevents their social inclusion, or social exclusion is traced to the monolingual bias of the state and its institutions. I will now discuss each of these two strands.

Bilingualism as an obstacle to social inclusion

The 50 years around the turn of the nineteenth to the twentieth century are known in American history as the 'Great Transatlantic Migration'. This period saw unprecedented numbers of non-English-speaking migrants, particularly from Eastern and Southern Europe enter the USA and the percentage of the foreign-born population hovered around 35 per cent during the period levels never seen before nor since (*Foreign-Born Population and Foreign Born as Percentage of the Total US Population, 1850 to 2007*, 2007). Many of these new arrivals joined the urban and rural poor, particularly the working poor, and it did not take long before their relative lack of proficiency in English was singled out as a cause of their relative disadvantage vis-à-vis the native-born population. Sometimes this link was seen to be indirect, as was the case when bilinguals were determined to have lower IQ levels than monolinguals, and a conclusion was drawn that their lower IQ levels prevented their full participation in American society. Hakuta (1986) explores the flawed reasoning behind such tests, which were administered in English to non-English-speakers, who were then – rather unsurprisingly – found to be 'feeble-minded'.

   Those authors who saw a direct link between lack of English proficiency and social exclusion have had a much more lasting influence. Beginning with the English instruction of the Americanization campaign (Pavlenko 2005), the argument that migrants need to learn English – or whatever the national language of a particular destination country may be – in order be included into the mainstream has been with us ever since. The policy results of this conviction have often been coercive with their attempts to force migrants into English, as is the case with anti-bilingualism or 'English Only' legislation in some US states (Gunderson 2006) or language testing for citizenship (McNamara and Shohamy 2008). Rather more rarely has there been a consistent state response to the perceived link between lack of proficiency in the national language and social exclusion through a national language teaching program. An exceptional example is the Australian Adult Migrant English Program (AMEP), which I will review below.

The perceived conflict between linguistic pluralism and social inclusion, can be observed not only at the national level where the inclusion of Indigenous and migrant speakers is at stake but also in global development discussions. During the period of political decolonization in the middle of the twentieth century, development policies typically associated development with linguistic assimilation towards national monolingualism, mostly the language of the former colonial master but sometimes also a regional language (e.g. Bahasa Indonesia). Taylor and Hudson's (1972) data on 'ethno-linguistic fractionalization' have often been used to demonstrate a correlation between linguistic diversity and underdevelopment: correlating linguistic diversity in a country and gross domestic product, these authors found a negative correlation between the number of sizable language groups in a country and the size of the country's GDP; in other words, the greater a country's linguistic diversity, the greater its poverty. Data such as these were then used to argue for the promotion of linguistic assimilation as a way to grow the national economy.

Pool (1990) offers an incisive analysis of the flawed reasoning behind the assumption that linguistic assimilation will further development and social inclusion. The reasoning in all these cases goes something like this: members of a nations' dominant group are better educated, find jobs more easily, have a longer life expectancy, etc., than members of Indigenous and migrant groups. Similarly, an observation can be made that monolingual countries are more often economically and technically advanced and less likely to experience civil unrest or even war than multilingual countries. On the basis of these facts, many observers have concluded that promoting the linguistic assimilation of minority members in a national unit, will be beneficial for the individuals concerned (i.e. enhance their access to education, employment, health care, etc.) and the nation as a whole (i.e. enhance national unity and national development resulting from better education, employment, health care, etc.). The problem with this kind of reasoning – as Pool (1990) shows for linguistic assimilation and Reinert (2008) shows for a raft of other development policies that the rich force upon the poor – is that they are a correlational fallacy based on static data. The fact that multilingualism and social exclusion co-occur does not mean that there is a causal relationship between the two, nor does it mean that changing the language variable towards linguistic assimilation will necessarily have the desired development outcomes.

Social exclusion as a result of the monolingual bias

Indeed, by the 1960s, the fact that linguistic assimilation did not necessarily lead to social inclusion had become all too apparent – in the USA, for instance, large-scale language shift to English had produced little if any inclusion benefits for African Americans or Native Americans. At the same time, the ways in which language intersects with power and inequality became a key concern of both some of the emancipatory movements of the time, particularly the Civil Rights Movement and the Second Wave Feminist Movement, as well as the emerging discipline of sociolinguistics (see Philips (2005) for an overview). In particular, it was new investigations into the role of 'Black English' (the term in use at the time) in sustaining the continued disadvantage of African Americans that helped to shift thinking around language and social inclusion away from a focus on the individual speaker and orient it towards the institutions in which these speakers have to interact. One foundational study (Labov 1972) showed how schools made it difficult for African American children to succeed by devaluing the language they spoke and forcing them to interact in Standard English, a variety with which they were not familiar. Labov's (ibid.) work was critical in creating a paradigm shift: rather than blaming the linguistic repertoire of the speaker – and trying to intervene at the level of the individual in order to achieve social inclusion outcomes – the focus shifted to institutions and how they set up certain speakers with certain repertoires for success and others for failure. Labov's (ibid.) work, with its focus on Black English, was not framed as bilingualism research, but it sparked a wide variety of research into the ways in which disadvantage and inequality were sustained in institutions, both in contexts that are typically seen as monolingual (i.e. involving more than one variety of 'the same language') and as multilingual.

The valorization of a particular linguistic practice in a particular institution or social space pertinent to social inclusion – such as employment, welfare, the police and the courts, health care or education – automatically enhances or restricts access to those spaces on the basis of having the right sort of linguistic proficiency. As Bourdieu (1991: 55) puts it: '[S]peakers lacking the legitimate competence are de facto excluded from the social domains in which this competence is required, or are condemned to silence'.

Below, I will specifically review work on the role of language in access to employment in contemporary Australia. The policy outcomes of recognizing the monolingual bias of institutions centre around enhancing access to key institutions through multilingual provision.

Summary: what is better: linguistic assimilation or linguistic diversity?

For the sake of clarity, I have presented the two main assumptions about the relationship between social inclusion and linguistic diversity as diametrically opposed. I now have to hasten to add that they are not, of course. However, oftentimes, their proponents do present them as diametrically opposed and set the other camp up as a kind of bogeyman. Linguistic assimilationists sometimes like to deride the naivety of multiculturalists, and the fans of multilingualism sometimes like to present the arguments of assimilationists as somewhere on the slippery slope to fascism. None of this is helpful and it is itself based on a fallacy that both viewpoints sometimes share, namely that multilingualism exists as a unitary phenomenon. However, socially, it does not. Multilingualism is always mediated by context, particularly language status and speaker status (Heller 2007). Speaker status refers to the fact that the same bilingual proficiency, for instance in English and Spanish, will be of different value to an illegal Mexican immigrant in the USA than to a middle-class Anglo-American citizen. Language status refers to the fact that multilingualism in small languages in many contexts is relatively less useful than monolingualism in English (see de Swaan (2001) for a good overview of the global language system). A pertinent example of the differential value of the same linguistic skill to different speakers is offered in Grin's (2001) study of the economic value of English in Switzerland. When this researcher correlated proficiency levels in English in a sample of 2,000 Swiss wage earners, he found that the economic reward of high-level proficiency in English was higher for men than it was for women, and it was higher for residents in the German-speaking area of Switzerland than it was for residents in the French-speaking area.

In sum, the early framing of the relationship between social inclusion and multilingualism as a problematic one where the problem is either the bilingual speaker or the monolingual institution has been replaced with a view of the relationship between social inclusion and multilingualism as intersecting in different ways in different contexts. Policies that work in one context may be counterproductive in another. There are examples where linguistic assimilation has indeed promoted social inclusion: a number of studies of the labour market integration of immigrants have documented that proficiency in the language of the destination country is the most important predictor of immigrant earning potential (Chiswick 1978; Chiswick and Miller 1995, 1998; Chiswick and Taengnoi 2007; Kossoudji 1988). However, there are also examples where linguistic assimilation has retarded social inclusion, as is for example the case with Native Americans and Indigenous Australians, as well as a number of immigrant communities in various European countries (Martin-Jones and Romaine 1986). Pool (1990: 251) cites Lenin as speculating that 'voluntary linguistic assimilation promotes political development but coerced (or apparently coerced) linguistic assimilation damages political development'. In the same way that monolingual policies have differential social inclusion outcomes in different contexts, multilingual policies and practices are not automatically more inclusive than monolingual ones. In the following, I will explore the theoretical issues underpinning differential outcomes.

Key issues of theory and method

Sociolinguistics as a discipline has a long-standing problem with its own interdisciplinary status and how, or even if, to avoid privileging one of its component disciplinary perspectives over the other. Analyses of the role of language in social inclusion tend to be no exception. A recent volume on *Language and Poverty* (Harbert *et al.* 2008: 1), for instance, is concerned with these two central research questions: 'On the one hand, it addresses the question of how poverty affects language survival. [...] On the other hand it examines the role of languages in determining the economic status of speakers.' Both these questions start with 'language' as the end from which they try to unravel the Gordian Knot of poverty. The effort to focus on language as a principal cause of social exclusion is most prominently displayed by proponents of so-called linguistic human rights, but can also be found in the less influential 'language and economics' paradigm (e.g. Grin and Vaillancourt 1997; Vaillancourt 1985). As their principal focus on the role of language in social inclusion and their theoretical positions on what a language is are similar, I will review only the linguistic human rights approach before moving on to present a case study to argue for an alternative position, which starts with the domains that are known to be crucial to achieve social inclusion, namely employment, citizenship, education, health and governance. I will then go on to explore how multilingualism – which, in this perspective, is usually framed as 'communication' rather than 'language' – intersects with access to and capacity building in these domains.

Putting language first

The view of language that underlies the research questions about the articulation between language and poverty quoted above (How does poverty affect language survival? How does language determine the economic status of speakers?) is characterized by two problematic assumptions. The first is that for linguists the central issue of concern is language survival, and poverty is one of the variables that affect language survival. Even though language is obviously at the core of linguistic enquiry, I feel that it is a moral duty to take a perspective that puts poverty alleviation – more broadly, social inclusion – first and then ask how language issues, including language survival, contribute to social inclusion. Social inclusion is quite obviously more important for the Common Good than language survival – which may or may not further social inclusion. The second problematic assumption is that a language is a static unit that can be labelled and counted and that is best understood through anthropomorphic metaphors as a living being that can 'die' or 'survive'. As this assumption underlies the movement for linguistic human rights, which has in recent years come to occupy a key position in discussions of language and social inclusion, I will explore it in greater detail (see also Piller and Takahashi 2011).

The concept of 'linguistic human rights' originates in the work of Tove Skutnabb-Kangas (e.g. Skutnabb-Kangas 2000, 2003; Skutnabb-Kangas and Phillipson 1994, 1998) and finds its most comprehensive expression in the *Universal Declaration of Linguistic Rights* (Follow-up Committee 1998). The concept of linguistic human rights is characterized by an understanding that sees the right to use a particular language as a human right and thus places language itself at the core of social exclusion. The imposition of a language other than the mother tongue, particularly through schooling, is seen as a human rights violation and thus a key manifestation of social exclusion. Linguistic human rights are conceptualized as both a collective and an individual right, or, conversely, the violation of linguistic human rights results in the exclusion of both groups and individuals. Minority groups are seen as having a right to their ancestral tongue and individuals are seen as having a right to their mother tongue. Although the concept of linguistic human rights has been enthusiastically embraced by some non-governmental organizations and international organizations such as UNESCO, it has been controversial within sociolinguistics. One key criticism of the concept of linguistic human rights has been that the understanding of 'language' it is based upon – a bounded entity that is associated with a particular ethnic or national group – is in itself the product of a particular language ideology that brought the modern nation-state and its colonial relationship with internal (and sometimes external) minorities into being (Blommaert 2001; Duchêne and Heller 2007). As Blommaert (2001: 136) explains:

> [W]hat counts is not the existence and distribution of languages, but the availability, accessibility and distribution of specific linguistic-communicative skills such as competence in standard and literate varieties of the language. Granting a member of a minority group the right to speak his or her mother tongue in the public arena does not in itself empower him or her. People can be 'majority' members (e.g. they can speak the language of the ruling groups in society) yet they can be thoroughly disenfranchised because of a lack of access to status varieties of the so-called 'power language'.

Putting social exclusion first: an Australian case study

Although linguists tend to start with language as the most important variable, policy makers and practitioners usually need information that starts from social exclusion or inclusion. What is it that helps or hinders the social inclusion of a particular group? It is useful to ask negative questions and learn from mistakes. The key negative question is how language serves to exclude transnational migrants from the Social Contract, and specifically how language mediates access to employment. It is also useful to ask positive questions in order to learn from successful social inclusion practices. The key positive question is how does language serve to promote social inclusion, and specifically enhance access to employment? These questions, which are based on an understanding of the intersection between language and social inclusion as context-specific, suggest a case study approach. I will therefore present in the following an Australian case study of the labour market experiences of contemporary migrants from NESB. There are two reasons why I focus on language and social inclusion in contemporary Australia. First, in contrast to European and Asian nations that have seen significant immigration in recent history but have failed to include migrants in their national narratives, immigration has been a cornerstone of Australian nation building since the 1940s and consecutive governments have been committed to the social inclusion of migrants (Castles and Vasta 2004; Jupp 2007). Furthermore, in comparison to the USA, another country where immigration is part of the national imagery, Australia has consciously adopted and experimented with state intervention to facilitate social inclusion, including language programs (Martin 1998).

The search for employment and economic opportunity has always held first place among the many reasons why humans choose to migrate and many migrants measure the success of their migration in economic terms (see e.g. Ong 1998). Likewise, receiving societies tend to measure successful settlement largely in economic terms. Indeed, employment can be considered key to social inclusion as economic well-being powerfully impacts all other dimensions of human life. As I will show in this section, although limited proficiency in English dramatically limits access to employment, increased proficiency does not automatically lead to access to careers commensurate with qualifications and experience; as such access is mediated by a range of factors including accent, race and social networks.

The experience of unemployment and underemployment tends to be more common for transnational migrants than for the native born. In Australia, for instance, even during the period of low unemployment and labour and skills shortages that characterized much of the first decade of the twenty-first century, the unemployment rate of recent migrants (5.5 per cent) was considerably higher than that of the Australian-born population (4.1 per cent) (Australian Bureau of Statistics 2008). Furthermore, these statistics only reflect unemployment not underemployment.

A report on the labour force status of recent migrants (Australian Bureau of Statistics 2008) provides evidence for the role of proficiency in English in finding employment. Table 16.1 lists the unemployment rate for four levels of self-reported English proficiency. As can be seen, as proficiency in English goes down, the unemployment rate goes up.

Another indicator of the role of proficiency in English can be gleaned from the fact that of recent migrants those born in an English-speaking country were more likely to be employed (88 per cent) than those from non-English-speaking countries (76 per cent) (Australian Bureau of Statistics 2008). Finally, 35 per cent of recent migrants reported that language difficulties were the main obstacle they experienced to finding work. A recent report to the Victorian Equal Opportunity and Human Rights Commission (Berman 2008: 21f) notes that 'those from non-English speaking backgrounds struggle to find gainful employment within Australia and are often underemployed, even when they have relative proficiency in the language'. Even when they find work, employees with English as an additional language experience salary discrimination,

Table 16.1 Self-reported English proficiency and unemployment rate

Self-reported level of proficiency in English	Unemployment rate (%)
English spoken very well	7.0
English spoken well	8.7
English not spoken well	4.9
English not spoken	23.1

Source: (adapted from Australian Bureau of Statistics 2008).

as the same report notes: 'NESB (non-English speaking background) employees with degrees and post-graduate qualifications also receive 8% and 14% lower pay respectively than similarly qualified Australian-born employees' (Berman 2008: 29). Colic-Peisker (2005: 632) sums up the exclusion of people with limited proficiency in English from the Australian labour market as follows: 'The language barrier seems to be the single most important reason: the "original obstacle" that hampers all aspects of social inclusion'.

Indeed, the fact that limited proficiency in English would make it difficult to gain employment in Australia seems like a common-sense proposition and the Australian state has for more than six decades been committed to reducing the language barrier for new arrivals through the provision of a national language training service, the Adult Migrant English Program (AMEP). This is open to all new arrivals, who have less than 'functional English' and fulfil certain visa requirements (i.e. they must have a permanent visa as humanitarian entrants, family reunion migrants, or skilled and business migrants and their dependants) (for detailed overviews of the AMEP see Lo Bianco (2008) and Martin (1998)).

There can be no doubt that by international standards the AMEP is an exemplary language programme for the social inclusion of new migrants (Piller 2009). At the same time, the question remains: why do NESB migrants face significantly higher rates of unemployment and underemployment and lower salary rates than the native born given that, overall, the levels of English proficiency of Australia's new migrants are high? Those entering as skilled migrants need to meet high standards of English before being admitted, many of those who gain permanent residency are former overseas students with degrees from Australian universities and the AMEP is catering to all those entering with low levels of English. Media debates on the issue often blame Australian universities for graduating overseas students with insufficient language skills to meet the communication needs of professional employment or the AMEP for not teaching 'good English' fast enough. There is the obvious reality that not everyone is a good language learner but the following story allows us to approach the question of the relationship between employment and language proficiency from another angle.

Masterman-Smith and Pocock (2008: 29) in their exploration of low-wage work in Australia quote an unemployed migrant fitter and turner with 20 years' overseas experience in the trade as follows:

> I have tried to apply for many jobs in that field of fitter and turner but the requirements are with the English. They have to be like high standard of English … and this is the difficulty I have had in the past. I've been to (over 20) interviews with different companies regarding a job but I haven't been successful and I think the main problem would have been the English.

To this point this is a familiar story: the fact that this person's English is not good enough for the demands of work in Australia makes sense. However, on second thoughts, we might ask what level of English is actually required for the fitter and turner trade? According to an Australian job website, the job specification for a fitter and turner is as follows:

Duties: A mechanical engineering tradesperson may perform the following tasks:

examine detailed drawings or specifications to find out job, material and equipment
  requirements
set up and adjust metalworking machines and equipment

operate machines to produce parts or tools by turning, boring, milling, planing, shaping,
   slotting, grinding or drilling metal stock or components
fit and assemble metal parts, tools or sub-assemblies, including welding or brazing parts
cut, thread, bend and install hydraulic and pneumatic pipes and lines
dismantle faulty tools and assemblies and repair or replace defective parts
set up and/or operate hand and machine tools, welding equipment or computer numerically
   controlled (CNC) machines
check accuracy and quality of finished parts, tools or sub-assemblies.

Personal requirements:

enjoy technical work
physically fit
good hand–eye coordination
able to work as part of a team
able to work independently
practical ability
attention to detail
normal hearing
no skin allergies.

(www.youthcentral.vic.gov.au/)

It is obvious from this description that the linguistic and communicative demands on a fitter and turner are not very high – certainly not high enough to warrant specific mention in the job description. We can only speculate whether the English proficiency of Masterman-Smith and Pocock's (2008) interviewee would suffice to meet the linguistic and communicative demands of the job for which he has qualifications. However, the story raises the possibility that 'lack of English proficiency' is actually not the reason for exclusion but a pretext. Further evidence that this might be the case comes from a recent field experiment in which almost 5,000 fictional CVs were sent in response to job ads for entry-level jobs in waitstaff, data entry, customer service and sales (Booth *et al.* 2009). The CVs differed only in the names of the applicants, which were names typical of five distinct ethnic groups, namely Anglo-Saxon, Indigenous, Chinese, Italian and Middle Eastern. The CVs made it clear that the fictional applicant's high school education had been in Australia, so the assumption that their English was not good enough was unlikely to arise and the response rates can be seen as employers' indicators of their attitudes towards these ethnic groups. The researchers found

clear evidence of discrimination, with Chinese and Middle Easterners both having to submit at least 50% more applications in order to receive the same number of callbacks as Anglo candidates. Indigenous applicants also suffer a statistically significant level of discrimination, though the effects are smaller [...]. We observe virtually no discrimination against Italian applicants.

(Booth et al. *2009: 20)*

In another study, Colic-Peisker and Tilbury (2006) compared the unemployment and underemployment rates (as measured by working below one's skill level) of three groups of recent refugees and found that those of refugees from Europe (Bosnia) were substantially lower than those from Africa (Eritrea, Ethiopia, Somalia, Sudan) and the Middle East (Iraq). If we combine evidence such as this of discrimination in employment against non-European job seekers with the evidence cited above that the charge of lack of English proficiency is levelled against more migrant job-seekers than is to be expected on the basis of existing proficiency levels relative to the language requirements of a given job, we must conclude that 'lack of English proficiency' is not only a factor in the social exclusion of transnational migrants but also a pretext for their exclusion. In a context where employers are bound by equal opportunities legislation and can be assumed to be genuinely committed to upholding the values of equal opportunities and human rights, 'lack of linguistic proficiency' becomes a substitute for racial and ethnic discrimination (see Hill (2008) for a detailed version of this argument in the US context). In contrast to ethnic and racial discrimination, linguistic discrimination is largely invisible, including to those discriminated against themselves. After all, most users of English as an additional language themselves recognize that their English is 'far from perfect' and believe in the ability of 'native speakers' to judge the quality of the English of non-native speakers – forgetting that the question is not whether their English is perfect (no one's ever is) but whether their communicative competence is such that they can do the job.

So far, I have argued that some transnational migrants in Australia are excluded from the employment sector because their English proficiency is factually insufficient to do a particular job. At the same time, employers and the general public extend this argument to a much larger group of transnational migrants whose English levels factually meet the requirements of a particular position. However, why would employers actually want to discriminate against appropriately qualified workers? Is it not in their economic self-interest to select the best person for a job whatever their background? Well, no, actually not. Colic-Peisker and Tilbury (2006) argue that discrimination is a perfectly rational – and highly exclusionary – response to the specific circumstances of the contemporary Australian labour market where – in contrast to other advanced economies – only a relatively small pool of cheap labour (e.g. illegal aliens) exists to fill vacancies in low-wage, rural, seasonal or otherwise undesirable work (e.g. abattoirs, cleaning, aged care).

> In this context, racism is not simply an irrational prejudice, but a basis for rational, economically advantageous behaviour of employers: it keeps certain 'marked' groups out of the mainstream labour market and good jobs and thus ensures that undesirable job vacancies are filled.
>
> *(2006: 221)*

In sum, the unemployment and underemployment of NESB migrants is not only a function of their English proficiency but of existing labour market segmentation. Multilingualism and employment thus articulate in at least two different ways in the Australian context: on an individual level, the English competence of a person may not match their skill level and thus exclude them from employment at their skill level. On a systemic level, the exclusion of migrants on the basis of their real or perceived lack of proficiency in English creates a pool of people with a lack of employment options at their level and thus forces them into low-paid work. In the following section, I will address the policy issues that result from this dual nexus.

Policy issues

The case study presented above suggests two distinct policy issues, one relative to language policy and one relative to labour policy. In cases where linguistic competence limits access a language policy response is called for, which ideally should take a two-pronged approach as is the case in Australia through the AMEP and multilingual provision, i.e. transnational migrants need access to language learning opportunities and at the same time there needs to be multilingual provision of services, particularly in areas directly controlled by the state, such as citizenship, education, health and the justice system.

Furthermore, language policy that aims at raising the status of languages other than English also can serve to increase employment opportunities for transnational migrants, as is evident from the 'Productive Diversity' policy, which was launched in 1992 with the dual objective of increasing Australian business access to diverse domestic and export markets as well as taking advantage of Australia's multilingual and multicultural workforce (Pyke 2005). The policy has indeed resulted in the creation of 'cultural mediator' roles, particularly in the service industry and thus created employment opportunities for migrants (Bertone 2004; Bertone and Esposto 2000).

At the same time, language policy can only be effective in the context of industrial policies that address the conditions under which 'undesirable', i.e. undervalued work is performed, specifically minimum wages at community standards, working conditions and job security, a social wage, and the dignity of work (Masterman-Smith and Pocock 2008). Language policies for social inclusion can only be effective if they are undergirded by industrial policies that indeed allow for work to be the foundation of social inclusion and justice. According to a recent report by the International Labour Office, *Global Employment Trends Update*:

> It is estimated that in 2007, 624 million workers – 21 per cent of all workers in the world – lived with their families in extreme poverty on less than USD 1.25 per person per day. This share is down sharply from the early part of this decade, when the global working poverty rate exceeded 30 per cent. [...] An estimated 1.2 billion workers lived with their families on less than USD 2 per person per day in 2007, representing more than 40 per cent of all workers in the world.
>
> *(2009: 16f)*

If a society does not face the true cost of work and reward it justly, language proficiency can emerge as a 'natural' criterion to force migrants into low-paid work and thus exclude them even from a country that is overall as prosperous and inclusive as Australia is.

Summary and new research directions

The key focus of social inclusion policies is on economic capacity building and I have therefore concentrated on language and work as the central issue for the articulation of language and social inclusion in this chapter. I have described the inter-relationship between language and employment as a three-layered one: (1) the economic value of a particular language or variety; (2) language competence as a criterion for access to employment; and (3) language ideologies as a criterion for exclusion from decent work. It will be an important direction for future research to explore those articulations in a wider range of contexts and also for other aspects of social inclusion, namely education, health care and citizenship.

I have also argued that linguistic and cultural ways of seeing diversity are marred by two shortcomings when it comes to understanding the intersection between multilingualism and social inclusion: first, they render people and their differential linguistic capital invisible, and, second, they render inequalities, discrimination and socio-economic exclusion invisible. It follows that future research would do well to start from actual instances of social exclusion and actual social justice issues and explore what, if any, role is played by language.

Methodologically, I have argued for a case study approach and suggested that an important function of research would be to provide evidence of the situated ways in which language can play a role in social exclusion. This ties in with the final research direction, which I ultimately see as the key challenge for research in the field. The central challenge for multilingualism and social inclusion research will be to write language into the social inclusion agenda and to contribute to the cause of social justice in ways that are meaningful outside of the academy.

Related topics

Multilingual workplaces; multilingualism in legal settings; multilingualism in institutional contexts; multilingualism and the new economy.

Further reading

Hills, J., Le Grand, J. and Piachaud, D. (eds) (2002) *Understanding Social Exclusion*, Oxford: Oxford University Press.
(Important edited collection on various aspects of social exclusion without attention to language.)
http://hdr.undp.org [n.d.]
(The website of the United Nations Development Programme offers a wide variety of reports on global development.)
www.ilo.org [n.d.]
(The website of the International Labour Office is another important resource.)
Piller, I. and Takahashi, K. (eds) (2011) 'Linguistic Diversity and Social Inclusion', *The International Journal of Bilingual Education and Bilingualism* (special issue) 14(4).
(A collection of recent international case studies of the intersection between multilingualism, second language learning and social inclusion.)

Bibliography

Australian Bureau of Statistics (2007) 'Labour force status and other characteristics of recent migrants', Canberra, available online at www.ausstats.abs.gov.au/ausstats/subscriber.nsf/0/7A12E CFE4A0E12D5CA2574560014CD36/$File/62500_nov%202007.pdf
Berman, G. (2008) 'Harnessing diversity: Addressing racial and religious discrimination in employment', Melbourne: Victorian Multicultural Commission Victorian Equal Opportunity & Human Rights Commission, available online at www.humanrightscommission.vic.gov.au/pdf/ Harnessing%20Diversity%20report.pdf
Bertone, S. (2004) 'From Factory Fodder to Multicultural Mediators: A Typology of NESB Immigrant Work Experience in Australia', Unpublished PhD thesis, Sydney: University of Sydney.
Bertone, S. and Esposto, A. (2000) 'Reaping the "Diversity Dividend": Productive diversity in Australian business and industry', in S. Bertone and H. Casey (eds) *Migrants in the New Economy: Problems, Perspective and Policy*, Melbourne: Workplace Studies Centre, Victoria University.
Birchardt, T., Le Grand, J. and Plachaud, D. (2002) 'Introduction', in J. Hills, J. Le Grand and D. Piachaud (eds) *Understanding Social Exclusion*, Oxford: Oxford University Press.
Blommaert, J. (2001) 'The Asmara Declaration as a sociolinguistic problem: Reflections on scholarship and linguistic rights', *Journal of Sociolinguistics* 5: 131–55.
Booth, A., Leigh, A. and Varganova, E. (2009) 'Does racial and ethnic discrimination vary across minority groups? Evidence from three experiments', *Australian Policy Online*, available online at http://apo.org.au/node/17347
Bourdieu, P. (1991) *Language and Symbolic Power*, Cambridge: Polity Press.
Browne, I. and Misra, J. (2005) 'Labor-market inequality: intersections of gender, race, and class', in M. Romero and E. Margolis (eds) *The Blackwell Companion to Social Inequalities*, Oxford: Blackwell.

Burman, E. (2003) 'From difference to intersectionality: Challenges and resources', *European Journal of Psychotherapy & Counselling* 6: 293–308.

Carr, M. and Chen, M. (2004) 'Globalization, social exclusion and work: With special reference to informal employment and gender', *Working Paper No. 20*, Geneva: Policy Integration Department: World Commission on the Social Dimension of Globalization, International Labour Office, available online at www.ilo.org/dyn/dwresources/docs/625/F1146925582/gender%20and%20globalisation.pdf

Castles, S. and Vasta, E. (2004) 'Australia: New conflicts around old dilemmas', in W. Cornelius, T. Tsuda, P. Martin and J. Hollifield (eds) *Controlling Immigration: A Global Perspective*, Stanford: Stanford University Press.

Chiswick, B. R. (1978) 'The effect of Americanization on the earnings of foreign-born men', *Journal of Political Economy* 86: 827–921.

Chiswick, B. R. and Miller, P. W. (1995) 'The endogeneity between language and earnings: international analysis', *Journal of Labour Economics* 13: 246–88.

—— (1998) 'English language fluency among immigrants in the United States', *Research in Labour Economics* 17: 151–200.

Chiswick, B. R. and Taengnoi, S. (2007) 'Occupational choice of high skilled immigrants in the United States', *International Migration* 45: 3–34.

Colic-Peisker, V. (2005) '"At least you're the right colour": Identity and social inclusion of Bosnian refugees in Australia', *Journal of Ethnic and Migration Studies* 31: 615–38.

Colic-Peisker, V. and Tilbury, F. (2006) 'Employment niches for recent refugees: Segmented labour market of the 21st century Australia', *Journal of Refugee Studies* 19: 203–29.

de Swaan, A. (2001) *Words of the World: The Global Language System*, Cambridge: Polity press.

Djité, P. G. (2008) *The Sociolinguistics of Development in Africa*, Clevedon: Multilingual Matters.

Duchêne, A. and Heller, M. (eds) (2007) *Discourses of Endangerment: Ideology and Interest in the Defence of Languages*, London: Continuum.

Ehrenreich, B. and Hochschild, A. R. (eds) (2002) *Global Woman: Nannies, Maids, and Sex Workers in the New Economy*, New York: Metropolitan Press.

European Parliament (2000) Lisbon European Council 23 and 24 March 2000 *Presidency Conclusions*, available online at www.europarl.europa.eu/summits/lis1_en.htm

Follow-up Committee (1998) *Universal Declaration of Linguistic Rights*, Barcelona: Institut d'Edicions de la Diputació de Barcelona, available online at www.linguistic-declaration.org/versions/angles.pdf

Foreign-Born Population and Foreign Born as Percentage of the Total US Population, 1850 to 2007 (2007), Washington, DC: Migration Policy Institute, available online at www.migrationinformation.org/DataHub/charts/final.fb.shtml

Global Employment Trends Update, May 2009 (2009), Geneva: International Labour Office, available online at www.ilo.org/wcmsp5/groups/public/-dgreports/-dcomm/documents/publication/wcms_106504.pdf

Grin, F. (2001) 'English as economic value: facts and fallacies', *World Englishes* 20: 65–78.

Grin, F. and Vaillancourt, F. (1997) 'The economics of multilingualism: Overview and analytical framework', *Annual Review of Applied Linguistics* 17: 43–65.

Gunderson, L. (2006) *English-Only Instruction and Immigrant Students in Secondary Schools: A Critical Examination*, Mahwah, NJ: Lawrence Erlbaum.

Hakuta, K. (1986) *The Mirror of Language: The Debate on Bilingualism*, New York: Basic Books.

Harbert, W., McConnell-Ginet, S., Miller, A. and Whitman, J. (eds) (2008) *Language and Poverty*, Clevedon: Multilingual Matters.

Heller, M. (2007) 'Bilingualism as ideology and practice', in M. Heller, (ed.) *Bilingualism: A Social Approach*, London: Palgrave Macmillan.

Hill, J. H. (2008) *The Everyday Language of White Racism*, Malden, MA: Wiley-Blackwell.

Hills, J., Le Grand, J. and Piachaud, D. (eds) (2002) *Understanding Social Exclusion*, Oxford: Oxford University Press.

Human Development Indices: A Statistical Update 2008 (2008) New York: United Nations Development Programme (UNDP), available online at http://hdr.undp.org/en/media/HDI_2008_EN_Complete.pdf

Human Development Report 2009: Overcoming Barriers: Human Mobility and Development (2009) New York: United Nations Development Programme (UNDP), available online at http://hdr.undp.org/en/

Jupp, J. (2007) *From White Australia to Woomera: The Story of Australian Immigration*, Melbourne: Cambridge University Press.

Kossoudji, S. (1988) 'English language ability and the labour market opportunities of Hispanic and East Asian immigrant men', *Journal of Labour Economics* 6: 205–28.

Labov, W. (1972) *Language in the Inner City: Studies in the Black English Vernacular*, Philadelphia: University of Pennsylvania Press.

Lo Bianco, J. (2008) 'Language policy and education in Australia', in S. May, and N. H. Hornberger (eds) *Encyclopedia of Language and Education*, New York: Springer.

McNamara, T. and Shohamy, E. (2008) 'Language tests and human rights', *International Journal of Applied Linguistics* 18: 89–95.

Martin-Jones, M. and Romaine, S. (1986) 'Semilingualism: A half-baked theory of communicative competence', *Applied Linguistics* 7: 26–38.

Martin, S. (1998) *New Life, New Language: The History of the Adult Migrant English Program*, Sydney: NCELTR Publications.

Masterman-Smith, H. and Pocock, B. (2008) *Living Low Paid: The Dark Side of Prosperous Australia*, Sydney: Allen & Unwin.

Ong, A. (1998) *Flexible Citizenship: The Cultural Logics of Transnationality*, Durham and London: Duke University Press.

Pavlenko, A. (2005) '"Ask each pupil about her methods of cleaning": Ideologies of language and gender in Americanization instruction (1900–1924)', *International Journal of Bilingual Education and Bilingualism* 8: 275–97.

Philips, S. U. (2005) 'Language and social inequality', in A. Duranti (ed.) *A Companion to Linguistic Anthropology*, Oxford: Blackwell.

Piller, I. (2009) 'Eigo wo tooshita shakaitekihousetsu: Gengoseisaku to iminkeikaku [The Adult Migrant English Program: Language Learning, settlement and social inclusion in Australia]', in C. Kawamura, A. Kondoh and H. Nakamoto (eds) *Minseisaku eno approach: Raifusaikuru to tabunkakyousei [Living Together in a Multicultural Society: Approaches to Immigration Policy]*, Tokyo: Akashi Shoten.

Piller, I. and Takahashi, K. (2011). Language, migration and human rights, in R. Wodak, B. Johnstone and P. Kerswill (eds) *Handbook of Sociolinguistics*, London: Sage.

Pool, J. (1990) 'Language regimes and political regimes', in B. Weinstein (ed.) *Language Policy and Political Development*, Westport, CT and London: Greenwood Press.

Pyke, J. (2005) 'Productive diversity: Which companies are active and why', Paper delivered at the Australian Social Policy Conference, Sydney: University of New South Wales, available online at www.sprc.unsw.edu.au/ASPC2005/papers/Paper205.doc

Reinert, E. S. (2008) *How Rich Countries Got Rich ... And Why Poor Countries Stay Poor*, London: Constable.

Sassen, S. (2001) *The Global City: New York, London, Tokyo*, Princeton and Oxford: Princeton University Press.

Skutnabb-Kangas, T. (2000) *Linguistic Genocide in Education or Worldwide Diversity and Human Rights?* Mahwah, NJ: Lawrence Erlbaum.

——(2003) 'Linguistic diversity and biodiversity: The threat from killer languages', in C. Mair (ed.) *The Politics of English as a World Language: New Horizons in Postcolonial Cultural Studies*, Amsterdam: Rodopi.

Skutnabb-Kangas, T. and Phillipson, R. (eds) (1994) *Linguistic Human Rights: Overcoming Linguistic Discrimination*, Berlin and New York: Mouton de Gruyter.

Skutnabb-Kangas, T. and Phillipson, R. (1998) 'Language in human rights', *The International Communication Gazette* 60: 27–46.

Taylor, C. L. and Hudson, M. C. (1972) *World Handbook of Political and Social Indicators*, New Haven, CT: Yale University Press.

Universal Declaration of Human Rights (1948) United Nations, available online at www.un.org/Overview/rights.html [n.a.]

Vaillancourt, F. (ed.) (1985) *Économie et Langue [Economy and Language]*, Québec: Conseil de la langue française.

Valentine, G. (2007) 'Theorizing and researching intersectionality: A challenge for feminist geography', *The Professional Geographer* 59: 10–21.

Welshman, J. (2007) *From Transmitted Deprivation to Social Exclusion: Policy, Poverty and Parenting*, Bristol: The Policy Press.

Westwood, S. (2005) 'Unequal nations: Race, citizen, and the politics of recognition', in M. Romero and E. Margolis (eds) *The Blackwell Companion to Social Inequalities* Oxford: Blackwell.

Yuval-Davis, N. (2007) 'Intersectionality, citizenship and contemporary politics of belonging', *Critical Review of International Social and Political Philosophy* 10: 561–74.

17

Multilingualism in legal settings

Katrijn Maryns

Introduction

This chapter investigates the institutional management of multilingualism in legal-administrative contexts. Research in the field of language and the law has topicalized the critical role of language in shaping sociolegal realities. Language has been considered a powerful tool in the transformation of social conduct into legal categorizations and a majority of studies in this field have analysed the legal space as a site of linguistic inequality. Whereas much has been written about the linguistic asymmetries between legal and lay participants in courtroom interaction (Conley and O' Barr 1990, 1998; Drew and Heritage 1992; Mertz 1994; Matoesian 1999; Cotterill 2004), a searching examination of the language-based discrimination of linguistic minority participants in legal contexts has developed only recently. The primary focus of analysis in these studies has been the institutional hegemony of monolingual ideologies that persistently disadvantage speakers of minority languages in procedural contexts. The observed clash between monolingual ideologies and multilingual realities has become prominent in the fields of discourse analysis and interpreting studies alike. Discourse analysts in the area of sociolinguists and linguistic anthropology have investigated the way that monolingual ideologies inform legal institutions and affect the evaluation of multilingual competences in legal-bureaucratic settings (Eades 2003; Haviland 2003; Maryns 2006). Critical scholars in the field of legal interpreting and translation have been similarly concerned about the ideological underpinnings of what counts as legitimate language use in legal encounters. their analysis of interpreting as a 'monologizing' practice that reinforces a one-sided treatment of multilingualism in the courtroom, has challenged the more canonical views of interpreting in terms of bilingual mediation between two neatly separated monolingual codes (Inghilleri 2003; Wadensjö 2004; Angermeyer 2008). Drawing on and elaborating the language ideological topics raised in these writings, I investigate how the legal institution manages and controls the multilingual performance of its clients.

My analysis starts from the observation that multilingual speakers draw on a broad range of communicative resources to position themselves and others in the social activity in which they are engaged (Pavlenko and Blackledge 2004). Their multilingualism can be conceived of as a fused repertoire of socially, regionally and situationally defined varieties and it is the interplay between these varieties that causes each of them to be conditioned by the entire repertoire to which it belongs (Auer 1998; Matras 1998; Maryns and Blommaert 2001; Maryns 2005). In our ever more global society, the multilingual legal space is increasingly the norm. Still, no matter how valuable for speakers to constitute their identity, their multilingual repertoires are generally not acknowledged as meaningful and functional resources in legal-institutional settings. Procedural language ideologies, notwithstanding the fact that they apply to increasingly multi-ethnic and multilingual contexts, entail highly culture-specific interpretations of the relationship between language and identity. A deeply rooted nationalist idea of language – an ideology that prob- ably endures for longer in the legal sphere than in other, less hegemonically structured facets of society – causes the multilingual performance of litigants to be measured against hegemoni- cally organized regimes of language that impose a 'monoglot standard' – preferably a national standard – that serves as a functionally differentiated norm against which all language use is measured (Silverstein 1996; Blommaert et al. 2005). Put into practice, these ideologies imply that multilingual clients are compelled to distil one single variety from their total set of lin- guistic resources, all of which seriously diminishes their chances to express themselves and motivate their claim.

In order to substantiate these arguments, I present two legal cases from two strikingly different contexts of legal decision making in Belgium. The first is the case of an African asylum-seeker who had to motivate his claim at the Belgian asylum agencies in Brussels. The second is a murder case that came before the Assize Court in Antwerp. The assize court is the highest criminal court in Belgium that is composed of professional judges and citizens who act as jurors. Both cases were collected through ethnographic fieldwork: during my first fieldwork period (2001), I collected a corpus of 39 files and audio-recordings of asylum cases; my second corpus (2007–8) comprises seven audio and (partially) video-recorded assize trials. Notwith- standing the fact that application procedures are essentially different from criminal procedures in many respects, legal argumentation and decision making are, in both procedures, premised on discursive (re)constructions of what counts as evidence in the legal space and in both cases – although in different degrees – linguistic diversity and multilingualism are deeply implicated in the process. In fact, two legal procedures that could be considered complete opposites from a juridical perspective, actually display some remarkable similarities when it comes to the assessment of multilingual performances and identities. Not only do they equally impose a monolingual ideology on the multilingual performances encountered in the legal space, they also equally underestimate the filtering effects of translation on the discursive production of evidence. In the following sections, I analyse how linguistic diversity and mul- tilingualism are treated in the data. I subsequently argue that the displacement of the linguistic minority speakers in both cases constrains the functionality of their multilingual resources in the legal space. I discuss some possible avenues of further research at the end of the chapter.

Multilingualism in asylum cases

The Belgian asylum procedure is an interview-based procedure in which the applicants have to explain their motivation for seeking asylum in Belgium. It is the task of the asylum authorities to determine whether or not, on the basis of the related narrative, applicants produce a credible account and fulfil the required criteria of refugee status. As the main input in the asylum procedure is language-based, each case can be approached as a textuality complex in which the narrative of displacement occupies a central place. Nonetheless, no matter how crucial for the further development of the case, the discourses produced on occasions of direct interaction between the individual applicant and the institution are the first to disappear from the bureaucratic processing of information: asylum hearings are not recorded and thus no more than the written report of the spoken interaction survives the procedure. Utterances that are locally produced in dialogic interview settings become the input of a sequence of entextualizations – now turned into a 'case' – that move through various stages of bureaucratic treatment (Silverstein and Urban 1996; Maryns 2006).

The data for this section are taken from a two-hour interview between an African asylum-seeker and a Flemish official at the asylum agencies in Brussels. It is the asylum-seeker's second interview. It was at the first stage of investigation that both the procedural language and the language of interrogation were established: Dutch was selected and formalized as the asylum-seeker's procedural language, whereas English was established as the language of interrogation. Strictly speaking, in cases such as this one, the interaction between the asylum-seeker and the official requires the mediation of an interpreter in English–Dutch. In practice, however, the role of English is ambiguous here: although English has no official status, given the fact that it is used as a third language in Belgium, the agencies responsible for the asylum interviews provide no further translation into the official languages, Dutch or French. In this way, English is often used as a lingua franca, either for direct interaction between asylum-seeker and official, or as a target language in the case of translation. In the end, it is up to the interviewing official to further translate the English declarations of the asylum-seeker (or the interpreted version of these declarations) into the procedural language. English, in other words, is considered a neutral medium of information exchange in the investigation.

In the data below, however, it soon becomes clear that although initially English had been formalized as language of interrogation, it turns out to display so much variation that it cannot properly serve its functions as lingua franca for the purpose of this interview. The official clearly experiences a lot of difficulty understanding the English of the asylum-seeker and therefore he considers abandoning the standard procedure according to which the inter-locutors stick to the applicant's initial language choice in the subsequent hearings. What actually makes him reconsider the formalized language situation is the presence of a Krio interpreter who had been asked for one of the interviews scheduled later that day. Given that Krio is a West African creole language that is widely spoken in Sierra Leone, the asylum-seeker is expected to express himself better in Krio than in English. Therefore, before proceeding with the hearing, the interviewer checks with the asylum-seeker whether Krio is his mother-tongue indeed. The asylum-seeker, however, has difficulty understanding the term 'mother tongue' and the official reformulates his question. Regarding the home as indicative of native language usage, he asks the applicant whether Krio is the language that he speaks with his parents. The asylum-seeker confirms and this prompts the official to offer the asylum-seeker the opportunity to express himself through the Krio interpreter, as he takes it for granted that the asylum-seeker's rights are best served if he can use his native language. But as the data extract will illustrate, nothing is further from the truth, for the interpreter's deplorable decision to interpret from Krio into French, instead of English, is just one of the many things the official had not reckoned with. Given that Sierra Leone is a former British colony, the interpreter's choice of French as a target is a very unusual one. Afterwards, he told me that his main motivation to do so was to practise his French in order to improve his proficiency in one of Belgium's official languages as a crucial move towards societal integration. What he apparently failed to realize, however, was that this linguistic choice works against the asylum-seeker. After all, the use of French causes the asylum-seeker to be entirely excluded from the translation process and a translation into English not only would have involved him more closely in the interaction between the other participants in the interview – the official, the interpreter and the lawyer – it would also have offered him the oppor-tunity to exercise control over the quality of the translation. The official's decision to go for

K. Maryns

interpreter-mediated interaction, no matter how well intended, turns out to be counterproductive in that it unnecessarily complicates the situation for the asylum-seeker, a situation that is already very demanding in itself. This explains why such a complex network of codes is used in the extract:

> The interviewing official (O) uses Dutch (L1) to address the lawyer and to eventually write up his report, a mixture of French (L2) and English (L3) to address the interpreter and a mixture of English and Krio to address the asylum seeker.
>   The asylum seeker (AS) expresses himself in a fused repertoire of Njala (endogenous West African language), English and Krio to address the interpreter and the official. He also uses non-verbal signs which at some points even precedes verbal language (first the sign, then sustained by the word).
>   The interpreter (I) uses a mixture of English and Krio to address the asylum seeker, and a non-native speaker variety of French when he talks to the official and the lawyer.
>   The lawyer (L) speaks Dutch (L1) with the official, addresses his client in English (L3) and uses French (L2) when he talks to the interpreter.

The extract consists of two main passages: in the first passage, the interviewer asks the asylum-seeker to situate the chiefdom he was born in; in the second passage, the asylum-seeker has to explain why he left his home country.

Transcription key:

...	pauses
==	latching, overlaps
CAPITALS	increased pitch
( )	my English translation of Dutch phrases
(( ))	my meta-comments
(*italics*)	my reconstruction of Krio utteraances

Extract 1

(1) O: my question was.Njala. in what chiefdom is that ...
(2) AS: we de we de under Kabala. ... we we de under Kabala. ... we de under Kabala.
(3) O: Kabala Chiefdom ...
(4) AS: Ka hen.no
(5) I: c'est ça oui (*that's it yes*)
(6) AS: Wara Wara.di Wara Wara.
(7) O: Wara Wara
(8) AS: di Wa di di Wara Wara.
(9) O: yes ...
(10) AS: xxxxx Wara is xxx. so. we de under.
(11) O: ((directing I)) do you exp = do you understand him
(12) I: I understand him
(13) O: yeah.what is he saying ...
(14) I: he deee this. this this urm ... place xxx où là on a des Mende là (*the place where the Mende are*)
(15) AS: uhum
(16) O: c' est dans quel (*it is in what*).chiefdom.so this is down Kabala. chiefdom uhum
(17) I: c'est tout les ... (*it is all*)

300

(18) O: try. I'm not sure. if I understand you well.

(19) AS: Mansara

(20) O: Mansara

(21) AS: hen in Mansara.

(22) O: uhum.

(23) AS: we have Mansara we have Marra ... Mansara people.

(24) O: uhum

(25) AS: Mansara people ... xx di Wara Wara ... and then the chiefdom CHIEFdom of Wara Wara. ... Mansara ...

(26) L: est-ce qu'il ne sait pas expliquer ça dans la langue.maternelle à vous. le Creole = (*can't he explain this in your mother tongue. creole*)

(27) I: c'est Creole = (*it is creole*)

(28) O: mais oui mais (*but yes but*)

(29) I: il ne sait pas le Krio même (*he doesn't know proper Krio*)

(30) O: il ne parle pas xxx (*he doesn't speak*)

(31) I: xxx il ne parle pas bien. je ne comprends pas (*he doesn't speak well. I don't under- stand*). because what they aks you what they aks you.you said you said urm Mara uurm

(32) O: no no no no Njala

(33) I: ah Njala c' est dans quel chiefdom ... (*Njala in what chiefdom is it*)

(34) AS: Njala no chiefdom

(35) I: no no xxxxx

(36) O: ok. my question is again. in what chiefdom you were born. and you lived

(37) AS: Njala.

(38) O: ok. ok tell me. urm. why you left your country. because. this is Sierra Leone hen

(39) AS: I lef. I lef my country because of the war. ...

(40) O: yes ... ok.take your time. explain me. ... what happened. in your country. what the problems were. thee the problems from which you left your country

(41) AS: the RUF.

(42) O: yeah ...

(43) AS: RU RUF this xxxx

(44) O: I would prefer you to speak in your mother language Krio ok. ...

(45) AS: we lef we lef the village.

(46) I: tok Krio ... tok Krio to him beco xxx

(47) AS: we lef we lef the village.Kaba urm we left to flee to Kabala

(48) O: uhum ...

(49) AS: Ka Kabala Kaba urm.RUF the RUF.

(50) I: ((Krio)) us language you do speak

(51) AS: I speak. Krio little. I speak.because we. ... we speak. urm. a little bit little words

(52) I: ((Krio)) what I want to aks you. us language do you speak.xx language do you speak with

(53) AS: ((Krio)) we speak di Njala language ...

(54) I: ((Krio)) xxx language

(55) AS: ((Krio)) xxx.

(56) O: hold on please. yeah y you are not really speaking Krio hen ...

(57) AS: w because people.

(58) O: only a few words I heard but. otherwise you don't speak Krio. tell me what it is NJALA language. ...

(59) AS: uhum. we speak the language =

(60) o: what is that.it's a language

(61) AS: urm.Njala people speak Njala ...

(62) o: NJALA.

(63) AS: in Njala people speak Njala. language

(64) o: ok.

(65) AS: we come. but to do to do something with. urm to do something.urm.for people. we speak Krio.to = to talk to people. say business.we do Krio.

(66) o: are you explaining me that Krio is the language that YOU use =

(67) AS: we we use

(68) o: for business =

(69) AS: we use =

(70) o: with other people =

(71) AS: xx to sell we want to sell we =

(72) o: = but. in reality you're speaking Njala.Njala Language. ... now. who is speaking Njala language. only in Njala. or in other parts

(73) AS: some some people speak ...

(74) o: Njala language. but you told me.that your parents. they speak Krio ...

(75) AS: they speak because we speak we speak together. ...

(76) o: yes

(77) AS: we speak together.

(78) o: uhum

(79) AS: so when when we sell market. speak.

(80) o: when we?

(81) AS: when we sss sell ma

(82) o: when you SELL on the market

(83) AS: aha

(84) o: you speak.Krio

(85) I: you speak Krio xxxx ...

(86) AS: (to sell).

(87) o: but I asked you what is.the language of your father and your mother and you told me. the language of my father and my mother

(88) AS: nono

(89) o: is Krio

(90) AS: no no we speak with people. we =

(91) o: so I'm gonna going to ask you the question again ... what is the language of your father and your mother

(92) AS: we speak Njala ...

(93) o: ((makes gesture that he does not understand))

(94) AS: NJALA

(95) o: Njala

(96) AS: yeah but we speak creole to people. ((O expresses lack of understanding, but leaves it for what it is and moves on to the next question))

In this extract, it can be seen how the interlocutors get stuck in a situation where every attempted exchange of information emanates in difficult meta-linguistic negotiations. These discussions between the official, the interpreter and the lawyer, discussions which are often held on behalf of and even beyond the control of the asylum-seeker, give evidence of a very static conception of language that ignores some fundamental sociolinguistic realities:

- Languages are dynamic constructs that display regionally, socially and situationally defined variation.
- Multilingual users draw on functionally organized repertoires of speech.
- Given the variability that characterizes languages and their users, one should be very cautious about establishing a link between language, nation and identity.

First, it is taken for granted that Krio is a language that displays very little variation. The interaction between the asylum-seeker and the interpreter is supposed to take place in a homogeneous standard variety of Krio. Arguably, the asylum seeker fails to meet the expected level of Krio competence and this prompts the interpreter to suspend his translation activity and interrogate the asylum-seeker about his true linguistic identity (turn 50). In other words, it is the interpreter who gives himself the capacity to assess the asylum-seeker's linguistic proficiency, showing not the slightest notion of the geographical distribution of Krio, its internal variation and its social use. In his evaluation of the asylum-seeker's speech, the interpreter apparently confines himself to a broadly generalized and ideologically marked distinction between 'proper Krio' – the Krio spoken by the native Krio settlers in the capital Freetown – and 'broad Krio' – the Krio spoken up-country (Hancock 1986; Maryns 2000). This binary opposition between Freetown Krio and countrified Krio, however, is a misrepresentation of what is in fact a sociolinguistically much more complex reality. The massive spread of Krio in Sierra Leone and the fact that people from various ethnic groups have acquired the language, accounts for the emergence of several subvarieties of Krio such as Temne Krio, Mende Krio, Fula Krio and Limba Krio. In other words, what the institutional participants fail to acknowledge, is that the variability that problematized English as a lingua franca, just as well characterizes the Krio used for the communication between the applicant and the interpreter. It is therefore not inconceivable that part of the troubled communication relates to this internal variation and the use of different subvarieties of Krio.

Second, the interlocutors presuppose a native monolingualism on the part of the asylum-seeker, that is, full proficiency in at least one of the languages spoken in Sierra Leone. Despite the participants' insistent urgings to speak Krio (the lawyer in turn 26, the official in turns 44, and the interpreter in turn 46), however, the asylum-seeker sticks to what could be identified as a fused repertoire of Njala, Krio and English. His speech is restricted to short stretches of nouns, interrupted by pauses and hesitations with hardly any causal relations between them. As the transaction of even the most basic information is not getting anywhere, the official starts an inquiry into the 'true' native language of his interviewee. In fact, what the official expects is a plain answer to what appears to be a plain question to him, viz. 'What is your native language?'. Whereas previously, the applicant stated that he uses Krio to communicate with his parents, he now introduces Njala as a home language. The reported *and/and* situation (turn 92–96 'we speak Njala ... but we speak creole to people'), no matter how natural for the asylum-seeker, is considered a very unnatural and contradictory situation by the official. What is at stake here is the relevance of the term 'native language' to the applicant's multilingual repertoire: the official expects the asylum-seeker to speak *either* Njala *or* Krio to address his parents but this requirement clashes with the topically and situationally organized multilingualism of the asylum seeker. No matter how hard the asylum-seeker tries to explain the functional segmentation of his linguistic repertoire (turns 65, 71, 79), he is eventually forced to isolate one language variety from his total range of resources.

In the literature on bilingualism and multilingualism, however, it has been amply documented that bilingual and multilingual competence does not necessarily imply full competence in the different language varieties making up the repertoire of the speaker (Rampton 1995; Harris 1997; Woolard 1999; Maryns and Blommaert 2001). A multilingual speaker like the asylum-seeker, may therefore not be expected to single out one 'native' code from his repertoire for this may seriously curtail his functional repertoire of socially, regionally and situationally defined resources needed to give a contextually dense account. After all, what is required from the asylum-seeker is a factual, detailed and consistently organized account of the events that made him leave his home country. Paradoxically enough, the imposed monolingualism seriously restricts the asylum-seeker in his ability to qualify his argument and provide a detailed account of his experiences, an argumentative vagueness due to which he fails to meet procedural-textualist criteria of facticity.

What is more, these formal genre characteristics serve as a guiding principle for the assessment of the credibility of the speaker. According to the guidelines for interviewers formulated by the UNHCR, a reliable account is expected to comply with a set of very specific textualist criteria (UN High Commissioner for Refugees 2005: 124):

> The decision maker must assess the reliability of any evidence and the credibility of the applicant's statements. Credibility is established if the applicant has presented a claim that is coherent, plausible, consistent with generally known facts and therefore, on balance, capable of being believed.

Also in my data corpus, the idea that there exists a standard norm that indexes objectivity, neutrality and veracity is an ideological construct that guides the evaluation of many asylum applications. In line 56 of the extract for instance, a turning point in the official's understanding of the language situation of the asylum-seeker, it could already be seen how the official developed his own sociolinguistic inquiry from a question suggesting insincerity on the part of the asylum-seeker (turn 56: 'you are *not really* speaking Krio hen?'). More importantly, the official's written report of the hearing also involves a strikingly explicit evaluation of the applicant's linguistic behaviour as reflected in his footnotes and asides:

> Tolk stelt dat KV geen Krio spreekt: KV spreekt geen Krio, verstaat wel enkele basisvragen in Krio, maar nu hij verhaal moet vertellen spreekt hij Engels met haar op en veel gebaren. Zoekt naar woorden. Stottert. (...) Gaandeweg blijkt KV gewoon Engels te spreken en alleszins alle vragen in Engels perfect te begrijpen en meteen erop te antwoorden zonder tolk.
>
> Interpreter states that the AS does not speak Krio: AS speaks no Krio, understands some basic questions in Krio, but now that he has to tell story, he speaks broken English and many gestures. Can't find the right words. Stutters. (...) Gradually, AS happens to speak normal English and in all respects perfectly understands all the questions in English and immediately answers them without an interpreter.

On the basis of the interpreter's remarks and his own evaluation of the interview, the official expresses his doubts about the applicant's true linguistic identity. He even identifies the applicant's linguistic behaviour as 'a pose':

> Noot: KV gaf indruk Engelse taal goed te begrijpen, beter dan hij voordeed tijdens zijn verklaringen.
>
> Note: AS gave the impression of understanding the English language well, better than he pretended in his declarations.

The official's comments clearly suggest a suspicion of pretence and insincerity on the part of the applicant. Linguistic diversity, and the divergence between actual and expected competence in particular, comes to be made indexical of speaker identity, the inference being that shattered linguistic competence raises conjectures about the true (linguistic) identity of the asylum-seeker. The question is to what extent this perceived indexicality between language and identity is sociolinguistically justified. Communicative behaviour reflects speaker identity indeed: the asylum-seeker's fused repertoire indexes his language socialization in a community where linguistic multiplicity is the norm rather than the exception. Moreover, far from being an indicator of fragmentation and unreliability, the applicants' struggle to perform 'adequately' in the locally defined regimes of language, reflects the specific conditions of his displacement in time and space (Maryns and Blommaert 2001). In other words, the asylum-seeker's account lacks fluency and consistency, not because he is insufficiently competent to express himself, but rather, because he is restricted in his communicative abilities to function adequately in the locally defined spaces of multilingualism. His communicative repertoire undergoes a reallocation of its functional potential and in this way, no matter how valuable elsewhere, loses a great deal of its functionality in the legal-bureaucratic environment in which it has to operate (Blommaert 2003; Blommaert et al. 2005). The bottom line: in bureaucratic encounters such as the asylum application interview, in which individuals of different social, cultural and linguistic backgrounds have nothing but their 'voice' to motivate their claim, sticking to a one-sided, Eurocentric assessment of this indexicality between language and identity may lead to dangerous conclusions with far-reaching consequences for the asylum-seeker.

Multilingualism in criminal cases

Multilingualism is deeply involved in asylum settings and asymmetries between local and translocal competences are perhaps more pertinent here than in many other legal-procedural contexts. On the other hand, in a society that is becoming ever more globalized, increased minority participation amounts to higher visibility of linguistic inequalities in civil and criminal cases as well. The data in this section illustrate the implications of multilingualism in a criminal case. The transcript represents a short extract from the audio recordings I made in a murder trial that came before the Belgian Assize Court (Antwerp 2007). The extract is taken from the witness hearing of the mother of one of the defendants charged as accomplice to murder. Both mother and son are of Serbian origin and acquired Belgian nationality through regularization. The mother states that her son had been taken in by the other defendants in the case. Her distrust of the legal system made her submit a false document to the police in which it was stated that her son was not able to attend his trial in Belgium as he had been called up for military service in Serbia. The extract represents the hearing of the witness (W) by the presiding judge (J), which is mediated by a court interpreter (I) who translates from Serbian (SSS) into Dutch.

Extract 2 (original)

(1) J: ik citeer nu letterlijk, ze heeft gezegd over hem "mijn zoon is alles voor mij.hij is het enige wat ik nog heb. mijn zoon is voor mij als god. hij is geen slechte jongen en met de zaak waarvoor hij nu is opgesloten heeft hij niets te zien. hij is daarin meegesleurd door de andere.ik weet dat hij zoiets nooit zou doen.dat is niet de opvoeding die ik hem gegeven heb".dat hebt u gezegd?

(2) W: ja dat is wat heb ik daar gezegd.daar blijf ik bij

(3) I: ik blijf erbij

(4) J: zegt u duidelijk dat het de twee anderen zijn die hem derin meegesleurd hebben.

(5) I: SSSSSSSSSS

(6) w: SSSSSSSSS

(7) I: xxx ongewapend. dus op het slechte moment. en urm ... xxxxx verkeerde plaats

(8) J: en der is dan nog de geschiedenis, we gaan daar nu nie te uitvoerig op terug komen maar we moeten *der* toch iets van zeggen, op *nen* bepaalde moment *hebt* u naar de politie gegaan met een attest dat 'm bij het leger was he.

(9) I: SSSSSSSSS

(10) w: SSSSSSSSSSS

(11) DEF: SSSSSSS ((opgewonden))

(12) DEF COUNSELS': sssssssssssttttt

(13) I: alle drie, de laatste vijf jaar hebben in een in een soort angst geleefd, moesten wij verwachten een assisenzaak ... wij dan wisten we xxxx. ...

(14) J: ja mijnheer Andrija

(15) w: = = = NEE MAAR MIJN ZOON DIE HEEFT TEGEN MIJ ALLEEN GEZEGD "mama, praat alstublieft Nederlands".en urm ik heb alleen die taal urm. alleen tegen hem. urm verstaat u wat ik wil zeggen

(16) J: is dat wat u.

(17) DEF: mijnheer de vertaler, de vertaler vertaalt nie nie goe he xxx

(18) J: = = = mijnheer Andrija mijnheer MIJNHEER ANDRIJA. he

(19) w: ik urm

(20) J: he

(21) DEF: maar de vertaler die vertaalde nie goed

(22) J: die vertaalde niet goed ok

(23) w: ok xxxxxx

(24) J: = = als het niet goed vertaald is

(25) w: = = = = IK GA IK GA ook (een poging) doen

(26) J: wel ok zegt u het dan

(27) w: in het Nederlands maar ik kan niet. kan ik da nie dan zal ik mij op de. vertaler x jaren geleden ik heb zo zorgen van die zoon, mijn zoon is nie meer dezelfde persoon als van die dag als alles xxx, verstaat u wat ik zeg

(28) J: ik ik versta u

(29) w: toen die feiten begon daarna is dat gekommen de die brief die ontvangen in januari da schreiben die assisen kommen

(30) J: ja

(31) w: en dan die brief die draait in mijn kopf. sorry dat ik het heb gedaan. echt sorry maar ik denk heel veel moeders zouden dat doen voor voor zijn eigen kind.

Extract 2 (my translation)

(1) J: Now I quote literally, she said about him 'my son is everything to me.he is the only thing I have left. my son is as a god for me.he is not a bad boy and he has nothing to do with the case for which he is detained now. he has been taken in by the others ... I know that he would never do such a thing.that's not the upbringing I gave him'. that's what you said (isn't it)?

(2) w: Yes that is what have I there said. I still think that

(3) I: I still think that

(4) J: do you say explicitly that he was taken in by the two others?

(5) I: SSSSSSSS

(6) w: SSSSSSS

(7) I: xxx weaponless. so at the bad moment. and urm … xxxxxxx wrong place

(8) J: and then also there is the history [of this case], we will not elaborate too much on that now but we do have to say something about it, at a certain moment, you went to the police with a certificate that he was in the army, right?

(9) I: SSSSSSSSSSSSSSS

(10) W: SSSSSSSSSSSSSSSSSSSSSS

(11) DEF: SSSSSSS ((agitated))

(12) DEF COUNSELS: sssssst ssssssst

(13) I: all three, the last five years we have lived in some sort of a fear, did we have to expect an assize case … we then knew we xxx.

(14) J: yes mister Andrija. = =

(15) W: = = NO BUT MY SON HE JUST SAID TO ME 'mommy, please speak Dutch'. and urm I just have that language urm. just to him. urm do you understand what I want to say?

(16) J: ((addressing the DEF)) is that what you = =

(17) DEF: = = SIR, THE TRANSLATOR, THE TRANSLATOR DOES NOT TRANSLATE WELL YOU KNOW xxx

(18) J: mister Andrija. MISTER ANDRIJA. hey (come on)!

(19) DEF: I urm

(20) J: hen?

(21) DEF: but the translator he didn't translate well

(22) J: he didn't translate well, ok.

(23) DEF: ok xxx = =

(24) J: = = but if it is not well translated

(25) W: I WILL I WILL ALSO make (a try)

(26) J: well right you say it then (go ahead)

(27) W: in Dutch but I cannot. (if) I cannot do that then I will [count] on the translator. years ago I have so many worries about that son, my son is not the same person any more as from that day when everything xxx, you understand what I say?

(28) J: I = I understand you

(29) W: when that events happened then that is gekommen (came) the = that letter that received in January that schreiben (writing) that assize kommen (come)

(30) J: yes

(31) W: and then that letter that turns in my kopf (head). sorry that I did it. really sorry but I think many mothers would do that for = for *her* own child

The judge starts the hearing by asking the witness for a confirmation of her declaration as it was taken down in the case file. It is striking that she begins answering in Dutch without waiting for the interpreter to translate the question (turn 2). Although she is not explicitly instructed by the chair to answer only through the interpreter, she observes the protocol in the turns to follow (turns 5–10). The interpreter, however, cannot express himself clearly in Dutch and this is why the defendant eventually gets worked up (turn 12) and addresses his mother directly from the dock, in Serbian. His lawyers try vainly to soothe him until the judge intervenes and gives him the opportunity to express his grievance. At this point, however, it is the mother who takes the floor to openly explain to the court that her son got so excited over the bad quality of translation and therefore begged her to speak Dutch instead of Serbian (turn 15). Even before the judge comes up with an answer to the problem, the mother spontaneously proposes to try and express herself in Dutch. Her argument, however, is over-shadowed by the medium in which she has to address the court: a variety of colloquial and informally acquired Dutch that is interspersed with words from German and in which syntactic and lexical errors are frequent when measured against normative standard Dutch.

The participants in the two data cases, the asylum application interview and the assize court hearing, find themselves in very similar multilingual situations. Just like the asylum-seeker in the first extract, the witness in the assize trial is compelled to express herself in a mixed code that makes up for only a small part of her total linguistic repertoire. The circum-stances under which she is persuaded to do so are different though. Whereas in the first extract, a particular linguistic identity is assumed and imposed on the asylum-seeker, the wit-ness in the second extract is free, albeit at the insistence of her son, to address the court in Dutch. In both cases, multilingualism is perceived as a problem that calls for immediate remedial action. Subsequently, both interactions involve a shift in focus from content (what is conveyed) to form (how it is conveyed). It is striking that the linguistic minority speakers, the asylum-seeker and the witness, end up in a situation that compels them to account for their multilingual behaviour and, in doing so, they both reflect on the functional segmentation of their communicative repertoire: in the asylum case, it is the official, in his quest for his interviewee's native language, who explicitly asks the asylum-seeker to explain his language situation. In the assize case, on the other hand, it is the defendant's procedurally incorrect behaviour – his state of agitation combined with the fact that he interferes in the hearing of his mother in a language that is not understandable to the majority of the court – that arouses his mother's metalinguistic comment. She elucidates her multilingual behaviour, the fact that she always speaks Serbian with her son, to make clear that her son used Serbian, not to exclude the court from their interaction, but just because this is how his multi-lingual repertoire works. In both cases, there is ambivalence about interactional uptake, but the participants develop different reactions to it: in the asylum case, it is the public official who expresses his uncertainty in understanding what the asylum-seeker says. In the assize case, on the other hand, it is the witness who displays linguistic insecurity. However, con-ditions for interactional uptake are clearly much more favourable in the latter case: not only is the witness given permission by the judge to express herself in the language she feels most comfortable with, also her suggestion to have the interpreter on 'stand-by' – assisting her if she has difficulty expressing herself or understanding particular terms – is accepted by the judge. Soon it becomes clear, though, that this 'stand-by' mode is not put into practice for the judge's backchannelling and his confirming feedback encourage the witness to stick to Dutch.

Discussion: multiple monolingualism in legal procedures

Multilingualism is absolutely prevalent in the observed translocal contexts of legal-institutional interaction, but there is clearly no consistency in what this multilingualism actually means to its participants. For the linguistic minority participants, it serves as a repertoire of func-tionally differentiated resources and linguistic competences that cut across traditional 'language' borders' and are deployed for specific domains or activities. This form of 'translanguaging' (García 2009) is essential to their polycentric identity and functions as the most natural and necessary resource for them to manage the complex translocal situation in which they have to operate. Their flexible multilingualism (Creese and Blackledge 2010), as a set of com-plementary partial competences, runs up against an essentially different type of multi-lingualism that assumes full proficiency in the separate languages making up the individual repertoire of the speaker. The institutionally acknowledged multilingualism, in other words, is in fact a very specific multilingualism that assumes multiple monolingual competence (Heller 2007). Multiple monolingualism is manifestly articulated in the statutorily based imposition of monolingual standard usage for procedural interaction, and it is particularly pertinent to the use of interpreters in these encounters, which is just as well premised on the coexistence of neatly separated monolingual standard codes. This persistent inconsistency between mono-lingual ideologies and multilingual realities clearly constrains what can be said and done in the legal space.

In the data discussed in this chapter, it can be seen how the multilingual behaviour of the minority participants is measured against hegemonic language ideologies that are premised on the assumption that by nature all language users have a native monolingual language – preferably a national standard language – that covers their whole range of resources needed to express themselves to the best of their ability. This ideological assumption underlies the generally held belief among institutional representatives that the interests of linguistic minority speakers are best served if they express themselves in their native language through an interpreter. However, an unquestioned reliance on interpreter-mediated interaction as the most effective and efficient answer to the perceived multilingual complexities, overlooks two important issues: first, the fact that consistent monolingual usage cannot be taken for granted in translocal spaces of communication and, second, the fact that interpreting, like any other form of discourse representation, is a subjective activity that inevitably testifies to the conditions under which it is produced.

First, the use of an interpreter in the observed institutional settings assumes full monolingual competence on the part of the speakers. That this imposed monolingual 'choice' is not an obvious choice for the linguistic minority participants is particularly evident in the data. In both cases, the linguistic minority speakers are restricted in their abilities to express them-selves and subsequently, they feel the need to elucidate their functionally calibrated repertoire. Nevertheless, they are both urged to distil one code from their total range of resources. This institutional efficiency measure urges them to recalibrate their scale of communicative functions, all of which considerably cuts down on their total set of linguistic resources and all of which disables them to deploy their actual communicative skills.

Second, some important social and ideological implications of the interpretation process threaten to be overlooked in the observed settings of institutional practice. In the extended literature on interpreting as a social activity, the practice of interpreting is understood in relation to the sociocultural context in which it operates (Toury 1995; Wadensjö 1998; Pym 2006; Wolf 2007). This approach emphasizes the constitutive effects of interpreting in the construction of social identities and challenges the interpreter's prescribed role as a neutral, objective and non-participating actor in the mediation process. Interpreting, it is argued, is intimately involved with interpretive choices (what is translated?) as well as representational ones (how is it translated?) and interpreters should therefore be considered as social agents who are actively involved in the interaction. No matter how salient these arguments are in interpreting studies, however, issues of social agency and variability tend to be obscured in settings of legal-institutional practice. Although professional community interpreters aim at observing the deontological standards of objectivity and comprehensiveness, that is, a faithful and complete rendering of what the participants say, the judicial authorities – and the asylum agencies in particular – still contend with an acute shortage of sworn interpreters. Nevertheless, despite the frequent mobilization of lay interpreters in asylum and other legal settings, interpreter-mediated interaction in the observed legal contexts is based on an unquestioned belief in the interpreter being a neutral mediator between two neatly separated monolingual standard codes. It is clear from the data, however, that far from maintaining a neutral stance, the interpreters are themselves deeply implicated in the production of discursive evidence. In the asylum case, the interpreter's behaviour strikingly flies in the face of this alleged neutrality. Clearly in many respects, the interpreter violates professional deontology standards of professional community interpreters in the asylum procedure. In fact, labelling the observed practices as 'interpreting' could rightly be considered an insult to the profession and hence the term 'multilingual bystander' would probably be in order here. Deontological violations range from his ill-considered selection of the target language to a lack of proficiency in this target and even a persistent negligence in interpreting what the asylum-seeker and the official actually say. Moreover, the interpreter also ignores neutrality and confidentiality requirements in the way he explicitly ventilates his opinion on the linguistic identity of the asylum-seeker.

From the second data example it also seems clear that as a standard of practice for interpreters in the legal system, neutrality is not an easily accepted stance. Unlike the asylum-seeker, who has no control whatsoever over the interpreting process, the linguistic minority speakers in the second extract are the only ones who stay in control of the representation of their utterances in translation and it is the defendant who takes advantage of this monopoly, rightly or not, to judge the quality of the translation. In other words, whereas the interpreter's alleged neutrality remains undeservedly unaddressed in the asylum case, it is explicitly used as an argument against translation in the assize court hearing.

Considering the constraining conditions of communicating through an interpreter in legal practice – the imposition of a monolingual standard and the unquestioned neutrality of the interpreter – it is understandable that in both cases, the linguistic minority speakers prefer to express themselves in the same language as their interlocutors, despite the observed restrictions in their ability to do so. However, they are not equally given the opportunity to express themselves in their language of choice. Although the asylum-seeker wants to speak English rather than being interpreted, the institutional participants insist on interpreter use during the interview. The presiding judge in the assize trial, on the other hand, is much more flexible in that he allows the witness to testify in Dutch, despite the presence of a Serbian interpreter. But still, although language variation is to a certain extent negotiable in the assize court, due to the institutionalized dominance of Dutch in Flemish courtrooms, the linguistic minority speakers remain persistently disadvantaged. For just like the asylum-seeker, the witness in the assize court is compelled to make choices, neither of which enables her to express herself naturally. On the one hand, if she opts for interpreter-mediated interaction, her performance and perception as a witness are inevitably affected by the interpreter's way of speaking, irrespective of the quality of translation (Berk-Seligson 1990). On the other hand, in case she decides to address the court directly in Dutch, which she eventually does, she is considerably restricted in her ability to use the full range of her linguistic resources.

Concluding remarks and further research directions

This chapter has shown that the exchange of densely contextualized information in the observed legal-bureaucratic contexts – and in fact in most instances of translocal institutional interaction – is thwarted by a curtailing ideology of language that assumes choice where linguistic minority participants face constraints. What generally passes as the multilingual space par excellence, a legal-administrative space where the right to an interpreter is statutorily based, actually privileges a very specific type of multilingualism that imposes a set of either/or options on the linguistic minority speaker. Arguably, it is the legal-bureaucratic system itself – the dominance of one language being institutionally formalized – which structurally disadvantages linguistic minority participants, for this ultimate orientation towards the institutionalized standard forces them to make choices that, in any case, keep them from using the full range of their semiotic potential. Linguistic minority speakers are encouraged to express themselves *either* in their 'own' language through an interpreter (Krio, Serbian) *or* directly in the institutionalized standard (English, Dutch). In either case, they are compelled to isolate one language from their linguistic repertoire – *either* Krio *or* English, *either* Serbian *or* Dutch – while the other resources in their repertoire, no matter how valuable for them to constitute their identity, are disqualified and suppressed.

The question is whether this insistence on consistent monolingual performance is the only manageable way of dealing with the multilingual realities encountered in the legal space. Given the increasing complexities of modern bureaucracies in an ever more globalized society where multilingualism is the rule rather than the exception, it is no longer tenable to value the multilingual competences of minority speakers against homogeneous language ideologies. If the legal system is to render justice to its linguistic minority participants, then a better understanding of the sociolinguistic realities of multilingual speakers in procedural contexts is urgently called for. The data discussed in this chapter demonstrate that equal treatment of linguistic minorities in the legal system would require a revaluation of their entire set of linguistic resources needed to actively participate in the proceedings. In Blommaert's terms, what is needed in globalized contexts of institutional practice, is a sociolinguistics of mobility, that is, an understanding of language use in terms of mobile resources instead of fixed linguistic profiles (Blommaert 2003). Important developments in this direction are under way in the field of sociolinguistics and linguistic anthropology (Blommaert 2005; Jacquemet 2005; Rampton 2006). Similarly in the field of court interpreting, recent developments (Cooke 1996; Angermeyer 2009) suggest alternative forms of communication with linguistic minorities that move beyond more canonical conceptions of interpreting, anticipating the grey area between mediated and non-mediated interaction. This includes proposals that encourage the use of stand-by interpreting as a means to combine the advantages of direct communication with the assistance of an interpreter. Raising awareness among legal practitioners of the sociolinguistic intricacies encountered in the legal space will continue to be one of the greatest challenges faced by legal scholars and linguists today, for as long as imposed homogeneity is considered an inevitable prerequisite for the production of bureaucratically manageable accounts, linguistic minority speakers will remain persistently disadvantaged.

Related topics

Discourses about linguistic diversity; multilingual workplaces; multilingualism and public service access: interpreting in spoken and signed languages; codeswitching; heteroglossia.

Further reading

Jacquemet, M. (2001) 'The making of a witness. On the beheading of rabbits', in A. Di Luzio, S. Günthner and F. Orletti (eds) *Culture in Communication*, Amsterdam and Philadelphia: John Benjamins.
(An analysis of narrative performances in a cross-cultural legal-institutional setting.)

Eades, D. (2003) 'Participation of second language and second dialect speakers in the legal system', *Annual Review of Applied Linguistics* 23: 113–33.
(An overview of theory and research on the provision of language services to second language speakers in the legal system.)

Haviland, J. (2003) 'Ideologies of language: Reflections on language and US law', *American Anthropologist* 105: 764–74.

(A linguistic-anthropological analysis of the clash between theoretical and judicial perspectives on language in court.)

Angermeyer, P. S. (2009) 'Creating monolingualism in the multilingual courtroom', *Sociolinguistic Studies* 2(3): 385–403.

(An ethnographic study of monolingualism in the courtroom and the way it affects the interaction between minority speakers and legal professionals.)

Bibliography

Angermeyer, P. S. (2008) 'Translation style and participant roles in court interpreting', *Journal of Sociolinguistics* 13(1): 3–28.

——(2009) 'Creating monolingualism in the multilingual courtroom', *Sociolinguistic Studies* 2(3): 385–403.

Auer, P. (ed.) (1998) *Code-switching in Conversation: Language, Interaction and Identity*, London: Routledge.

Berk-Seligson, S. (1990) *The Bilingual Courtroom: Court Interpreters in the Judicial Process*, Chicago, IL: University of Chicago Press.

Blommaert, J. (2003) 'Commentary: A sociolinguistics of globalization', *Journal of Sociolinguistics* 7: 607–23.

——(2005) *Discourse: A Critical Introduction*, Cambridge: Cambridge University Press.

Blommaert, J., Collins, J. and Slembrouck, S. (2005) 'Spaces of multilingualism', *Language & Communication* 25: 197–216.

Conley, J. and O' Barr, W. (1990) *Rules Versus Relationships: The Ethnography of Legal Discourse*, Chicago: University of Chicago Press.

——(1998) *Just Words: Law, Language and Power*, Chicago: University of Chicago Press.

Cooke, M. (1996) 'A different story: Narrative versus "question and answer" in Aboriginal evidence', *Forensic Linguistics* 3: 273–88.

Cotterill, J. (2004) 'Collocation, connotation, and courtroom semantics: Lawyers' control of witness testimony through lexical negotiation', *Applied Linguistics* 25(4): 513–37.

Creese, A. and Blackledge, A. (2010) 'Translanguaging in the bilingual classroom: A pedagogy for learning and teaching', *The Modern Language Journal* (forthcoming).

Drew, P. and Heritage, J. (eds) (1992) *Talk at Work: Interaction in Institutional Settings*, Cambridge: Cambridge University Press.

Eades, D. (2003) 'Participation of second language and second dialect speakers in the legal system', *Annual Review of Applied Linguistics* 23: 113–33.

García, O. (2009) 'Education, multilingualism and translanguaging in the 21st century', in A. Mohanty, M. Panda, R. Phillipson and T. Skutnabb-Kangas (eds) *Multilingual Education for Social Justice: Globalising the Local*, New Delhi: Orient Blackswan.

Hancock, I. (1986) 'The domestic hypothesis, diffusion and componentiality: An account of Atlantic Anglophone creole origins', in P. Muysken and N. Smith (eds) *Substrata Versus Universals in Creole Genesis*, Amsterdam and Philadelphia: John Benjamins.

Harris, R. (1997) 'Romantic bilingualism: Time for a change?' in C. Leung and C. Cable (eds) *English as an Additional Language: Changing Perspectives*, London: Naldic.

Haviland J. (2003) 'Ideologies of language: reflections on language and US law', *American Anthropologist* 105: 764–74.

Heller, M. (2007) 'Multilingualism and transnationalism', in P. Auer and W. Li (eds) *Handbook of Multilingualism and Multilingual Communication*, Berlin: Walter de Gruyter.

Inghilleri, M. (2003) 'Habitus, field and discourse: Interpreting as a socially situated activity', *Target* 15: 243–68.

Jacquemet, M. (2005) 'Transidiomatic practices: Language and power in the age of globalization', *Language and Communication* 25(3): 257–77.

Maryns, K. (2000) *English in Sierra Leone: A Sociolinguistic Investigation*, Ghent: Ghent University.

——(2005) 'Monolingual language ideologies and code choice in the Belgian asylum procedure', *Language & Communication* 25: 299–314.

——(2006) *The Asylum Speaker: Language in the Belgian Asylum Procedure*, Manchester: St Jerome Publishing.

Maryns, K and Blommaert, J. (2001) 'Stylistic and thematic shifting as a narrative resource: Assessing asylum seekers' repertoires', *Multilingua* 20(1): 61–84.

Matoesian, G. (1999) 'Intertextuality, affect, and ideology in legal discourse', *Text* 19(1): 73–109.

Matras, Y. (1998) 'Utterance modifiers and universals of grammatical borrowing', *Linguistics* 36(2): 281–331.

Mertz, E. (1994) 'Legal language: pragmatics, poetics, and social power', *Annual Review of Anthropology* 23: 435–55.

Pavlenko, A. and Blackledge, A. (2004) *Negotiation of Identities in Multilingual Contexts*, Clevedon: Multilingual Matters.

Pym, A. (2006) 'Introduction: On the social and the cultural in translation studies', in A. Pym, M. Shlesinger and Z. Jettmarova (eds) *Sociocultural Aspects of Translating and Interpreting*, Amsterdam: John Benjamins.

Rampton, B. (1995) *Crossing: Language and Ethnicity Among Adolescents'*, London: Longman Group Limited.

——(2006) *Language in Late Modernity*, Cambridge: Cambridge University Press.

Silverstein, M. (1996) 'Monoglot "standard" in America: Standardization and metaphors of linguistic hegemony', in D. Brenneis and R. K. S. Macaulay (eds) *The Matrix of Language: Contemporary Linguistic Anthropology*, Boulder, CO: Westview Press.

Silverstein, M. and Urban, G. (eds) (1996) *Natural Histories of Discourse*, Chicago, IL: University of Chicago Press.

Toury, G. (1995). *Descriptive Translation Studies and Beyond*, Amsterdam and Philadelphia: John Benjamins.

UN High Commissioner for Refugees (2005) *Refugee Status Determination: Identifying who is a Refugee. Self-study Model*, Geneva: UNHCR Training Service.

Wadensjö, C. (1998) *Interpreting as Interaction*, London and New York: Longman.

——(2004) 'Dialogue interpreting: A monologising practice in a dialogically organised world', *Target* 16: 105–23.

Wolf, M. (2007) 'Introduction: The emergence of a sociology of translation', in M. Wolf and A. Fukari (eds) *Constructing a Sociology of Translation*, Amsterdam and Philadelphia: John Benjamins.

Woolard, K. (1999) 'Simultaneity and bivalency as strategies in bilingualism', *Journal of Linguistic Anthropology* 8(1): 3–29.

18

Multilingualism and public service access

Interpreting in spoken and signed languages

Christine W. L. Wilson, Graham H. Turner and Isabelle Perez

Introduction

'Home', the adage declares, 'is not where you *live* but where they *understand* you'. In the twenty-first century, as people make and move their homes within globalized communities, new demands arise for those concerned to ensure social understanding. One consequence of societal multi-lingualism is the growing demand for translation and interpreting services. Such services may be offered for exchanges involving a migrant language or when both of the relevant languages are indigenous. Here, we focus on face-to-face interaction in multilingual settings where individuals encounter the state, and therefore on the work of public service interpreters as facilitators of communication between would-be interlocutors who do not share common linguistic ground.

Public perceptions of the role of interpreters tend to assume that linguistic structures are readily, indeed more or less automatically, transferable between languages and therefore that interpreting is a very straightforward, non-technical task. A significant body of research and scholarship now attests to the opposite view: interpreting is actually highly complex and can impose an extremely demanding cognitive and emotional load. The impact of such misperception can be seen at all levels of policy and practice. This account describes and reflects on the current picture before exemplifying the resulting 'state of play' in one increasingly multilingual country, Scotland. We suggest that, although management of multilingualism via translation and inter-preting remains very much 'work in progress', some aspects of appropriately enhanced provision already exist here in respect of users of one of Scotland's indigenous languages, British Sign Language (BSL). Drawing together aspects of research and policy described in the literature, we show how both sign language (SL) interpreting and wider public service interpreting have progressed, and yet leave many unresolved issues pressing for attention as those who wish to be 'at home' in a multilingual society seek ways to ensure that they understand and are understood.

Interpreting studies

Translation and interpreting are often defined by professional organizations of practitioners as distinct and contrasting activities requiring different skills, as the former usually involves written

314

target texts that can be revised, whereas the latter deals with fleeting messages, conveyed orally or signed by the interpreter under time constraints and, therefore, with little room for error-repair or stylistic improvement. Whereas translation has a long history as a profession and has been extensively studied by scholars – albeit only since the second half of the twentieth century as a fully developed academic discipline (see Munday 2008 for an overview) – interpreting in some settings is still far from achieving professional status. Equally, interpreting research remained a little-explored subset of translation studies prior to the last two decades. However, in spite of clear differences in terms of the process used to transfer and deliver the message from the source to the target language, both activities involve careful analysis and understanding of meaning in context, as well as attention to extra-linguistic aspects of communication.

Some researchers have argued that it might be more useful to focus on what activities involving linguistic transfer have in common rather than on the traditional divisions within translation studies. Translating is then defined as a communicative process taking place within a social context (Hatim and Mason 1990) and, furthermore, as an act of communication that attempts to relay across cultural and linguistic boundaries another act of communication (Hatim and Mason 1997). Users of translation and interpreting services are often unaware of the distinctions and often expect the same practitioner to be able to perform both tasks. It is true that many professionals do offer a whole range of services, but those who are full-time employees of public organizations (from city councils to the United Nations or European Union institutions) tend to be specialists in one activity.

The field of interpreting studies tends to divide its territory into two primary subsets: conference interpreting, which often revolves around the simultaneous interpretation of longer stretches of monologue, and dialogue interpreting, where 'bilateral' interaction is more typical. Dialogue interpreting (DI) is not so extensively reported in research, nor is it perhaps so readily recognized by the general public. Its status is confused further by the fact that it may also be called community, *ad hoc*, cultural or liaison interpreting: Roberts (1997: 7–26) reviews these terms. Yet DI is probably the most common form of interpreting activity today. The interpreter is usually physically present, visible to all participants (unlike the conference interpreter who is often in an enclosed, soundproof booth) and mediates between two or more individuals who do not use each other's language. (It is appropriate to mention two variants: telephone interpreting – increasingly used, for example, by the emergency services – and whispered interpreting or *chuchotage*, used in settings where full simultaneous interpreting is impracticable.) DI is used in environments such as business and diplomatic meetings, sight-seeing tours and educational or cultural contacts, as well as many situations in which people who are not fluent speakers of the official language(s) have to communicate with the providers of public services, such as in legal, health, education, government and social service settings. Interpreting in the latter contexts is specifically referred to as Community Interpreting or, as it is commonly known in the UK, Public Service Interpreting (PSI).

Dialogue interpreting studies

Interpreting studies emerged as an analytical enterprise in the 1970s and 1980s after a few early, speculative studies based on personal intuition with scholars such as Gile (1990) advocating a more scientific, less subjective approach. Recent times have seen the consolidation of key approaches, particularly those that adopt the insights of pragmatics and discourse analysis (e.g. Berk-Seligson 1990; Wadensjö 1998). A shift has been made towards a more analytical perspective on mediated communication as a whole, which advocates looking at the interpreter's output as text and discourse with a specific purpose and within a specific sociocultural context (Pöchhacker 2004).

To date, DI as a separate activity has generally not been associated with high professional status, except when performed in settings deemed prestigious such as those involving high level international business negotiations or court hearings. However, there are differences by region and country, as well as between language groups. For instance, dialogue interpreters are afforded higher professional status in Australia and Scandinavia than in other parts of the world. Likewise, with more stable client populations, those working with a SL may be more organized professionally than interpreters working with other minority languages. Serving state employees and members of linguistic minorities at local levels, and facilitating unglamorous exchanges that rarely occur before a wider audience, PSI tends to remain particularly low on any professional scale of reference. However, the more systematic and scientific research of recent decades is beginning to feed back into training courses for students and for interpreter trainers as well as into policy. PSI research is gaining momentum against a background of political interest, in the UK and elsewhere, across the whole range of issues relating to social inclusion and equality of access to public services, in particular in connection with the movement of immigrants, economic migrants and asylum seekers.

Face-to-face settings are de facto a major difference between DI and conference interpreting. Authors such as Roy (2000), Wadensjö (1998) and Roberts (1997) have pointed to the implications of this in terms of the interpreter's role, which they see as going far beyond being a mere 'conduit' allowing interlingual mediation, and extending to being an active, third participant in the communication event, with the potential to influence the path, manner and outcome of the talk-event. Debates surrounding the dialogue interpreter's role, including questions relating to footing and positioning (see Mason 2009 for a recent example), foreground issues of interpersonal and intercultural power relations between the participants in the interpreter-mediated triad, and thereby animate a key theme of multilingualism research, including the nuanced issues highlighted at the interface between the individual, representatives of the state and its institutions, and those – including the interpreter – seeking to find a position of equilibrium between the two (see Inghilleri 2004). The focus in DI studies on interaction (and therefore on interpreting as an inherently sociobilingual activity), as opposed to cognition (which inevitably foregrounded the personal bilingualism of the practitioner) led scholars in the field to draw on areas of sociolinguistics including conversational analysis and ethnography. PSI is often characterized by significant power differentials between the interpreter's canonical 'two clients' (one who accesses the service and one who provides it), for example, between the police officer and the interviewee or between doctor and patient. In this context, issues surrounding the ethical behaviour of all or any of the participants in the exchange, as well as the social psychological analysis of professional versus client attitudes, personal versus professional identities and impact on practice (e.g. advocacy) feature prominently on the current research agenda.

PSI in the UK and beyond

As in many other parts of the world, PSI emerged as a field in the UK in less 'glamorous' settings than conference interpreting and usually in connection with immigration (Gentile et al. 1996). This was highlighted by a number of speakers at the first conference organized by the European Babelea Association for Community Interpreting (November 1999, Vienna) where the PSI situation in a number of countries was reviewed. Corsellis (2005, 2009) confirms that the needs created through the increased mobility of people coming to the UK led to the emergence of public service interpreters involved primarily in legal, health, education, housing, environmental health and social services. Interpreting in these settings can be characterized as 'high impact', as the interpreter-mediated exchanges may aim at making significant decisions related to individuals' health, life, freedom and future prospects.

Public service interpreting is often carried out in circumstances that are far from ideal. Provision is not always professionalized and examples of *ad hoc* situations involving untrained interpreters (also referred to as 'lay', 'natural' or 'informal' interpreters who are frequently family members of the minority language user at the heart of the interaction) abound, particularly when rarer languages are used. Raising the profile of practitioners working in the public services so that they may reach equivalent professional status to the doctors, police officers and lawyers they work alongside is therefore a priority. This, in turn, requires consistent, accountable and transparent professional structures for selection, training and accreditation (Corsellis 2005). To date, progress has been made in this respect, albeit at a very different pace in different parts of the world, and as a function of the position in social and legal terms accorded to linguistic minority groups in the country in question. Initial steps towards the professionalization of public service interpreters were taken in countries such as Sweden and Australia in the 1960s and 1970s, whereas the UK began the process in the 1980s.

The two main UK-wide professional organizations for translators and interpreters are the Chartered Institute of Linguists and the Institute of Translation and Interpreting. Whereas the former administers one of the few existing vocational qualifications in PSI and is linked to a national register of practitioners, the latter provides industry and public services with a directory of its members. Both organizations now have SL interpreters (SLIs) as well as spoken language interpreters among their members. Efforts towards enhanced professionalization call for systematic, in-depth academic training. The publication of agreed *National Occupational Standards in Interpreting* (latest revision CILT 2006), which set out the knowledge and skills required to be a competent professional interpreter, may provide a way forward in this respect. The standards are designed to promote understanding of what constitutes the most professional and advanced level of interpreting performance (the equivalent of postgraduate outcomes in higher education) in a range of contexts. Such developments steadily cement an appreciation that PSI is not to be casually undertaken and that responding appropriately to multilingualism demands serious engagement.

Although new questions about PSI provision are being faced, they also naturally bring into focus the need to facilitate communication with Indigenous minority language groups. In many cases, the deepest-rooted and yet most overlooked among these groups may be SL users, to whom our attention now turns.

Sign language interpreting, focusing on BSL

It is now widely recognized that SLs are identifiable as complete, real languages amenable to linguistic description (Sutton-Spence and Woll 1999) in parallel with spoken languages. Contrary to common assumptions, SLs are neither universal nor unusually restricted in expression. Furthermore, they are not mere reformulations of spoken or written language: although such artificial tools as 'Signing Exact English' do exist, natural SLs are neither artificial nor do they replicate the structures of speech or writing, but exploit the inherent potential of their own visual-gestural medium. SL interpreting therefore aligns analytically, professionally and pedagogically with other forms of interpreting. As we shall see, SL interpreting is often practised in public service contexts, although its use is by no means confined to these situations.

When a hearing non-signer meets a deaf signer in the UK, the latter will typically be a user of British Sign Language (BSL). Although the deaf person almost certainly has some understanding of English, this will predominantly be in the written mode: BSL has no common orthographic form and – despite the poverty of educational opportunity available to them, and the resulting difficulty in attaining fluency in English (Conrad 1979) arising especially from the historic rejection of BSL as a language of educational transmission – deaf people are expected to contend with the social world through written English in its many everyday forms. Face-to-face communication between deaf and hearing people in such circumstances can therefore best be effected via the intercession of a BSL/English interpreter. As such interpreters need to be able to hear the utterances of the speaking participant, they must themselves have functionally adequate levels of hearing.

SL interpreting differs in several key ways, however, from other forms. As we have noted, SL interpreting is exceptional in requiring the transfer of meaning between linguistic *modalities* (visual-gestural and oral-aural) as well as languages. SLs have undoubtedly occupied the position of minority languages (in socio-economic and geopolitical terms): BSL was not recognized as a language even by linguists until the mid-1970s (Brennan 1975), and no governmental acknowledgment of this status was forthcoming until 2003 (Turner 2003). Issues of relative power and status – of the interpreters and of their clients, expressed through their languages – have therefore been prominent in the development of the field. The work of SLIs is most commonly bilateral: but the biological inaccessibility of spoken utterances to deaf people results, as implied above, in a profession staffed almost exclusively by people whose dominant language is spoken, producing a highly imbalanced workforce and an intensity of focus on issues of cultural allegiance (Mindess 2006).

Historical background

Historically, SL interpreting of some description has doubtless existed wherever communication has been mediated between signing and non-signing people. The hearing children of deaf, signing parents, becoming fluent bilinguals through natural language transmission, were most likely to act as interpreters (Preston 1994). This task began to receive formal recognition in the 1960s: the first recorded attempt at institutionalization took place in 1964 with the formation of the Registry of Interpreters for the Deaf in the USA (Frishberg 1990). In recent decades, SL interpreting has developed as an independent profession in many countries (for details, see www.wasli.org), with increasingly structured and extensive education leading to professional status and practitioner associations providing collective representation and strategic development. BSL/English interpreters have been increasingly prominent in PSI contexts since the early 1980s when two professional associations of SLIs were formed covering Scotland and England, Wales and Northern Ireland. Thus, an independent occupation arose, marking its distinction from its historical antecedents within the community (social work, teaching, the clergy) by the development of codes of professional practice and ethics.

As reflected in the presentation of such codes, the role of the BSL/English interpreter has, for over 20 years, been construed in terms that recognize the 'visibility' of interpreting within the communication process. The natural disparities between modalities and languages, and the non-linear, multilayered structure of naturally occurring dialogue require practitioners actively to reach decisions about how to convey meanings and maximize communicative equivalence (Roy 2000). Nevertheless, although the normative image of the SLI within the profession may acknowledge the co-participant status of the interpreter (Metzger 1999; Harrington and Turner 2001), the strong but misguided expectation of the general public – that interpreters are communicatively neutral, do not change the course of dialogue and make no self-generated contribution to interaction – remains largely in place, making the education of consumers a continuing priority (Marschark, *et al.* 2005). Practitioners are also expected to deliver consistent provision across a wide range of circumstances: there is little opportunity to be trained in depth for work with the police, for example, or in health care settings. Equally, the SL-using client-group is heterogeneous, and includes growing numbers of users of SLs other than BSL, as well as signers whose output is disordered or atypical for reasons of mental health, education and other aspects of personal life-history. To meet the needs of such clients, 'relay' interpreting – in which two practitioners collaborate to transfer source output into the target language using a third language between themselves as a 'pivot' – has become more widespread in the last decade, bringing more deaf practitioners into the field (Turner 2007a).

Despite the fact that the existence of SLs per se has simply not been understood until relatively recently, the status of SL interpreting in the UK is now, in key respects, significantly more secure than that of other PSI provision. Two factors lie behind this situation. First, deaf populations are largely stable and demand for services is correspondingly constant, with fewer than 1,000 registered practitioners UK-wide working frequently with a relatively small number (well under 100,000) of minority language clients and therefore developing a certain mutuality of purpose and greater occupational cohesion. Second, deaf people are identified within public policy as disabled persons, and their right to interpreting services is seen to arise from the nature of their disability. In contrast, members of other Indigenous language minorities seem – reasonably or otherwise – to have been expected to use English and therefore manage with unmediated communication: for them, PSI has historically been seen as a temporary measure, an ad hoc response requiring only *ad hoc* social arrangements.

BSL and PSI

The provision of professional interpreting services inevitably comes at a price and one that has, historically, been beyond the means of the individual service user in the UK. In the case of BSL users, the challenges thrown up by being deaf in a world where most are hearing have, across the years, largely been seen as matters for the individual or the deaf community to address (Ladd 2003). As deaf people could not afford to pay professional wages, interpreting was a matter of voluntary effort, often made by hearing family or church members. Since 1945, however, the state has increasingly accepted responsibility to ensure that people recognized as disabled are supported by the public purse in accessing civic society and enacting their citizenship. Initially, this responsibility was devolved to specialist welfare officers and then to social workers as part of their wider remit. Such arrangements came to be seen as inappropriate, as the interventionist aspects of the social work role were perceived to conflict with the defined neutrality of the interpreter (Scott Gibson 1991; Harrington 2000a), and the result has been the emergence of independent, professional interpreting services, funded largely by the state and made available in public service contexts – including education, health care, legal settings and the workplace – at taxpayers' expense.

Education

Although the issue of multilingualism in the classroom has become increasingly pressing in the UK in the course of the last decade – with the percentage of primary school pupils whose first language is known or believed to be other than English reported to be 15.2 per cent and rising at almost 1 per cent per annum (DCSF 2009) – access to education always has been and remains a problem for deaf people. Although signing deaf children have been schooled for much longer, it was not until the *Lewis Report* (DES 1968) that any formal concession was made to the use of manual communication in their education. The influential *Warnock Report* (DES 1978) paved the way for specialist support, which acknowledged the linguistic difference between deaf and hearing children, recasting deaf education as the complex communicative context which is widely recognized today (Swanwick and Gregory 2007).

As it is not a requirement anywhere in the UK that teachers of deaf people can use BSL fluently, the law requires 'adjustment' to occur in order to take into account the learning needs of the individual. In the case of deaf children, provision may be made in the shape of a classroom assistant: although such assistants are rarely qualified as SLIs, their wide-ranging role may include interpretation between pupil and teacher. This pattern of educational experience – indirect communication with the primary educator mediated by a 'communication facilitator' who is most unlikely to be fully equipped with the skills for the job – is now commonplace for many deaf people of all ages across the developed world (Marschark and Spencer 2003; Monaghan *et al.* 2003). It is reported that 'more interpreters work in education than in any other specialized setting' (Janzen 2005: 16). All too frequently, such 'adjustments' are made with good intentions but inadequate resources and the quality of the educational outcome for the learner is not investigated (Winston 2004). As a setting for public service interpreting, the classroom can be seen as a high-stakes and highly demanding context. As the majority of learners have traditionally been expected to align themselves with a monolingual education system, however, it has only recently been more widely appreciated that greater support of classroom-based BSL/English interpreting is required if the approach is to succeed (Harrington 2000b).

Health care

As a site of potentially critical interaction, the health care interface is one of the most significant public service contexts for BSL/English interpreters. It is also, however, one of the sites least accessible to research (particularly where this would require video-recording, as much SL research inevitably does), owing to the sensitivity of the situation and the closely guarded confidentiality of the doctor–patient relationship. Nevertheless, it is clear nationally and internationally that deaf people report fear, mistrust and frustration as typical characteristics of health care encounters (Kyle *et al.* 2004; Steinberg *et al.* 2006). In terms of service provision, the key issue for SL interpreting in hospitals is clear: how to ensure that, for a relatively small population of consumers, there will be effective communication services regardless of place and time. The response to this challenge has, since the first such service in the UK was launched in 2006 (Guy's and St Thomas' NHS), increasingly been to turn to digital technologies to provide remote interpreting services via a video-link. As yet, the efficacy of such services has not been robustly established, and significant questions have been raised (Wilson 2007) about the quality of provision arising from remote delivery.

The role of the interpreter in health interactions is an intense one. Whereas other public service dialogue often takes place in multiparticipant situations – classrooms, courtrooms, committee meetings – doctor–patient dialogue is up close and personal in the extreme. This has led to considerable general exploration of the optimal approach for the interpreter to adopt in these situations (Davidson 1998; Metzger 1999; Angelelli 2004): as an advocate for the patient's interests when addressing an institutionally empowered gatekeeper, as a co-diagnostician, jointly managing the encounter with the health practitioner, as a strictly non-aligned conduit who takes no responsibility for brokering in instances of communication breakdown, and so on. Functioning as public servants, SLIs may be conscious of an obligation to the institution paying their wages, which can lead to a sense of responsibility 'to work with the provider to jointly manage the communication process to ensure that both our expectations mesh (which) might suggest being more a part of the healthcare team' (Mapson and Schofield 2010: 11). This balance will remain delicate.

Legal settings

A glance at any daily newspaper in the UK reminds the reader of the extensive public awareness of prominent legal cases, and it is no surprise in this context to find attention also turning to cases where multilingualism is a feature of the proceedings. A significant catalyst for changes in the approach to these issues was the Nuffield Interpreter Project (Nuffield Interpreter Project 1993), which reviewed practices and offered recommendations for tightening up the system. At the time, one survey found that there was no universally accepted formal process for checking any aspect of a court interpreter's competence and that no more than half of courts using interpreters took steps to ensure such competence (Butler and Noaks 1992). Very little attention had been paid to deaf participants involved in legal cases prior to the *Access to Justice for Deaf People in the Bilingual, Bimodal Courtroom* study (Brennan and Brown 1997), which centred on ethnographic analysis of recorded trials in Scottish courtrooms and cast new light on the experiences of BSL users and the interpreters working with them in these public service contexts, making 45 recommendations for principles and practices to address the reported shortcomings.

Even if time were allowed for the BSL/English interpreter to consider at length the interpretation of each utterance in legal interaction, there would remain inherent dilemmas in working between two language systems and additional problems – especially salient in legal contexts (Brennan 1999) – in juggling two quite different modalities (visual-gestural and oral-aural). The dynamics of the interaction – the flow of turn-taking, the cut and thrust of cross-questioning, and so forth – are inevitably affected by the interpreting process (Turner and Brown 2000). Nevertheless, few if any members of such proceedings are aware of the linguistic and interactional challenges that must be faced, all of which are frequently exacerbated by the participating authorities' inappropriate attitudes to deafness and fundamental misunderstandings of the nature of signed language (Reed et al. 2000). All of these issues are intensified when the nature of the proceedings relates to immigration or to deaf refugees and asylum seekers: although interpreting studies in general has begun to address matters of political migration and multilingualism (e.g. Inghilleri 2005), and legal practitioners have started to raise concerns about the ill-prepared response when deaf people arrive in the UK from overseas (see, for example, Deaf Blawg 2005) very little attention has, as yet, been paid to the highly complex character of such cross-linguistic signed interaction.

Workplace

Multilingualism in the workplace is a feature of the modern economy. Deaf people have become more visible in the workplace since the industrialization of employment, when they moved from agriculture into manufacturing trades where they were often seen as good workers 'undistracted by sound' (Kyle and Pullen 1988: 51). In situations where there is little or no understanding of deaf culture or accommodation of communication differences, the potential for conflict and misunderstanding is immense. Harris and Bamford (2001) report lack of awareness and flexibility in employers regarding expectations for deaf workers; employee reluctance to seek workplace support; inaccessible application procedures for requesting support; problems with knowledge about and the provision of work-related equipment; and an overall sense that provision remains service-led rather than needs-led. Deaf people thus find their work practices constrained by norms designed for or evolved in hearing workplaces: informal knowledge within the workplace is particularly hard to access (Trowler and Turner 2002). Hearing staff feel that they are expected to make considerable adjustments to their communicative behaviour (Young *et al.* 2000): it is easy to see how the communication needs of deaf employees can be seen as a low priority.

The impact of the Disability Discrimination Act 1995 and changing attitudes to disability mean that the modern workplace is more accessible to disabled people (Goldstone 2002) and that ensuring fair access to work is regarded as a public duty. In Britain, the Government-funded Access to Work scheme currently enables deaf and disabled people to apply for support in the form of technical or human resources, and most profoundly deaf applicants are allocated funding to pay for interpreting provision at work. Employed on both a staff and freelance basis, BSL/English interpreters can be contracted to support deaf people in a wide variety of settings, ranging from offices, social services and schools to factory floors. They can interpret across a wide spectrum of interactions – team meetings, formal and informal discussions, training events, supervisions, everyday social workplace interaction and formal events such as professional conferences (Turner 2007b). Nevertheless, Dickinson and Turner (2008) report that practitioners' experiences are routinely of interlingual tension as they seek to make the impossible – perfect multilingual harmony – possible. With interpreters frequently expected to switch between confidant, co-worker, interpreter, assistant and advocate within a single interpreted interaction, it is no wonder that confusion and inconsistency are widely reported along with a sense of guilt, anxiety and frustration.

PSI in Scotland: a case study of spoken and signed language provision

Scotland is a multilingual country with a monolingual bias where the main language is a dominant world language, namely English. Nevertheless, Scotland (population marginally above five million) has a number of Indigenous languages: two heritage spoken languages – Gaelic (the country's second official language since the introduction of the Gaelic Language Act 2005) and Scots – plus the language of the Scottish Deaf Community, BSL. There are also a number of long-established minority language communities: primarily speakers of Bengali, Chinese (Cantonese), Punjabi and Urdu, but also Italian and Polish. Since the late 1990s, the number of languages spoken by individuals or communities who have come to reside in Scotland exceeds 150 (O'Rourke and Castillo 2009: 36). Moreover, as the country identifies tourism as one of its leading industries, and welcomes international visitors for business or educational purposes, any of the world's languages is liable to be spoken on Scottish soil. The Scottish context highlights the challenges of how to respond to societal multilingualism in the face of a varied and shifting pattern of demand for interpreting in the public sector; how to ensure quality of provision where there is no critical mass in demand (for example, in rural areas or where demand is concentrated across a very wide spectrum of languages and dialects); how to cope with changing trends in demand (for example, as geopolitical circumstances bring users of new languages to the country, or as the need for support in certain languages or dialects shifts when social groups relocate).

Legislative and policy framework

The Scottish Parliament (re-established under political devolution in 1998) focused on placing the mainstreaming of social inclusion at the core of its policies and required those delivering services to the public to embed an equality perspective into their work, including equality of access to information and services. Coupled with legislation, this acted as a motivational force driving forward interest in language issues. In 2000–1, the Scottish Executive established two consultative committees, the Translating, Interpreting and Communication Support Group and the BSL and Linguistic Access Working Group. These groups commissioned a number of pieces of research focusing on translation, interpreting and communication support in the public sector in Scotland, including a literature review (McPake *et al.* 2002) and a study specific to BSL (Kyle *et al.* 2004). In addition, an extensive review (Perez and Wilson 2006a, 2006b) of PSI provision was undertaken. Although this study focused on Scotland, many findings have resonance for other locations.

During the same time frame, organizations at grass-roots level were striving to drive forward improvements in interpreting provision. These included groups representing both the users (e.g. Scottish Association of Sign Language Interpreters 2002, Scottish Refugee Integration Forum 2003, Scottish Consumer Council 2005) and the providers of interpreting services (the Scottish Translation, Interpreting and Communication Forum 2004). In addition, the Happy to Translate scheme (Equality Scotland) was launched in 2005 (with government support) to indicate the availability of translation/interpreting support within an organization and monitor the quality of support provided.

The combination of action at governmental and grass-roots levels helped to create a climate of cooperation among interested parties: everyone has a right to information and interpreting provision should therefore be built into systems from the start (O'Rourke and Castillo 2009: 48) and provided by public bodies without cost to the individual. Moreover, Perez and Wilson (2006a: 149) found that, although bodies have a budget for interpreting, none would refuse interpreting support even when this budget was spent. Commitment is crucial: the Association of Chief Police Officers in Scotland, for example, has underlined that translation services are a fact of life in modern policing and that, from their point of view, this is money well spent (Gray 2006). Legislation remains a key motivating factor, and indeed many interpreting agencies in Scotland were established in parallel with the introduction of legislation in the 1990s (Perez and Wilson 2006a: 37).

Positive developments in the PSI domain

A number of positive developments have been observed in Scotland's progress towards the use of interpreting as a resource for managing multilingualism. In particular, within the course of a generation, we have seen growing awareness on the part of public sector bodies of the need for *professional* interpreting provision. Public sector bodies have rank-ordered four types of interpreting (Perez and Wilson 2006a, 2006b): face-to-face provision by professional interpreters is the preferred option, followed by telephone interpreting, provision by an in-house public service staff member (not trained as an interpreter) or *ad hoc* interpreting by a family member, friend or member of the local community. The research also significantly showed that some respondents were aware that the interpreting service is not only required for the non-English-language speaker, but that they, as public sector staff, also require professional interpreting support to ensure that they can do their job properly (Perez and Wilson 2006a: 165). Since 2004, further action has also been taken in some sectors to address earlier criticisms, such as the failure of institutional policy makers to ensure that staff understand the organization's policies and procedures regarding interpreting provision, and the lack of joined-up thinking within sectors (e.g. failure to pass information 'downstream' from the family doctor to the hospital).

In the criminal justice sector, to take a specific example, very positive steps have been taken following allegations of institutional racism made in connection with the handling of the case investigating the murder of Surjit Singh Chhokar in 1998 (Her Majesty's Inspectorate of

Constabulary for Scotland 2000; Jandoo 2001). For example, in 2002, guidelines were published by the Lord Advocate (chief law officer in Scotland) for the information of the Chief Constables of the Scottish police forces, which contained recommendations relating to interpreting provision, including for the families of victims (The Lord Advocate 2002). Extensive internal guidelines have been supplied to staff in the court system since March 2003 (Crown Office and Pro-curator Fiscal Service 2003). Interpreting guidelines for all levels within the criminal justice system have been publicly available since 2008 (The Working Group on Translation and Interpreting 2008). Some effort has also been concentrated on training provision; for example, a series of courses on working with interpreters, offered regularly throughout the year, has been provided to police officers. In addition, the Crown Office and Procurator Fiscal Service/ Scottish Court Service and the police contribute to training developments, organizing simulated trials in courtrooms for training purposes.

Challenges in the PSI sector

Despite clear progress, weaknesses still exist. For example, cases have collapsed due to the quality of interpreting (see Howie 2007a, 2007b, 2009; McLaughlin 2009). As a general rule, there is a disparity in the availability of competent, trained interpreters across Scotland. There are shortages in certain languages, in certain regions and in certain settings. There are several reasons for these shortages, fundamentally the lack of specific training in certain languages and the lack of funding to support the provision of such training. Moreover, the general working conditions, low status and lack of career path do not attract potential interpreters into the profession. Spoken language interpreters, in particular, are paid very poorly considering the rigorous standards expected of them and are unlikely to be able to make a living from inter-preting. Therefore, this work may be carried out as an 'extra' activity supplementing their main job, which further reduces their availability.

The move towards the procurement of interpreting provision by awarding contracts to commercial agencies may also have a negative effect. Although this strategy allows public sector bodies to devolve responsibility for provision and quality, interpreters may find that their income falls and that they may be subject to inappropriate pressures. Indeed, some public sector informants express concern about the possibility of being 'held to ransom', especially if a monopoly situation emerged (Perez and Wilson 2006a: 213). Currently, there is no body functioning as impartial ombudsman for any concerns relating to interpreting. Quality control remains a concern, not only regarding interpreters' qualifications and skills and the monitoring of their performance while working, but also regarding issues such as whether interpreters have been cleared by police checks. Once again, the verification of such issues tends to be devolved to agencies. However, no national system exists for registering or monitoring agencies. Fur-thermore, there is no central collation of information concerning the demand for and supply of particular services, nor any accurate data regarding unmet demand. The picture regarding the demand for interpreting may be further blurred by the fact that a number of potential users are still not fully aware of their right to support. Systematic and complete collection of data centrally is seen as key to informing policy and planning (Perez and Wilson 2006b), and should extend to capturing information regarding the full spectrum of communication preferences.

Managing multilingualism

Overall, the situation in Scotland seems to illustrate the observations made about the field of interpreting worldwide (see Pöchhacker 2004: 195–204). For example, a growth in the use and availability of telephone interpreting has been noted: whereas the 2004 research found that only companies based outside Scotland provided telephone interpreting services, in 2009 local agencies are providing such support. Other forms of remote interpreting using videophones or videoconferencing are also emerging (especially for BSL). The example of the SL interpreting profession in Scotland has been highlighted (Perez and Wilson 2006a: 234) as a model of good practice (possessing a Scottish professional body with a recognized register of interpreters, encouraging Continuing Professional Development (CPD), creating a system for the monitoring of registered members, promoting a recommended pay scale). The overarching recommendation that has emerged from stakeholders is for a single, Scotland-wide body, which could act as a unified resource for information and data collection regarding all languages and interpreting services – and possibly as a registration or accreditation body (Perez and Wilson 2009: 25) – thus creating a more coherent framework. The existing arrangements show that the need to respond proactively to the increasing multilingualism of the polity has been recognized, but that the management of such organic responses needs to be structured to maximize efficiency and effectiveness.

Priorities for further development

The last years have seen a shifting of the landscape of the interpreting world at local and international levels. This is manifest in the convergence of the fields of conference interpreting, PSI and SL interpreting. Whereas previously the boundaries delimiting these fields were distinct and the focus was often on defining activities to underline differences, now the boundaries are blurred or have completely vanished. Increasingly, the focus recognizes the overarching similarities. A first shift led to the blurring of boundaries between signed and spoken languages in PSI. A more recent shift is seeing boundaries blurring between PSI and conference interpreting. This is evident in the interest in PSI on the part of professional bodies representing conference interpreters and conference interpreting practitioners, trainers and researchers. These shifts have, no doubt, emerged from increased mutual awareness and understanding, but are also driven by economic and market forces. Consequently, at and around the junction between BSL, spoken language interpreting and PSI, a number of priorities for future development are emerging in relation to policy, research and theory, and training.

Policy

The overriding priority in the area of policy remains the ongoing professionalization of the interpreting world. It is essential to defend the professional status of interpreters working in the public sector. On the one hand, this means giving due recognition to the specific skills required of interpreters working in this sector (i.e. that PSI is not a lower or less demanding type of work). On the other hand, there are issues to be addressed regarding the professional framework: for example, remuneration and working conditions; establishing professional bodies; career structure and training needs; implementing standards; creating mechanisms for quality control and monitoring (with an independent ombudsman to handle complaints or questions of ethics).

Professionalization implies recognition of the role of the interpreter as a fellow professional and awareness of the cost-effectiveness of quality interpreting. But it is also vital to highlight the role and impact of the public service professionals as members of the interpreting triad on the successful outcome of the interpreter-mediated communicative event and their need for training. This should lead to the embedding or mainstreaming of appropriate, quality interpreting support within the public services. Quality support may require new solutions to be considered to respond to gaps in provision, to improve the overall quality of service provision or to cope with new challenges (e.g. ecological and fiscal constraints). These new solutions may include variations in working patterns, taking advantage of globalization and the use of new technologies. Indeed, rather than threatening existing provision, technology has the potential to extend and increase the availability of provision – many clients dream of the 'interpreter in their pocket' through mobile phone technology.

Research and theory

As the professional level of PSI evolves, research activity and related theories move onto new ground. Initially, when the field was emerging as a profession, thinking was very prescriptive, in order to make the break with untrained interpreting provision. As the field has matured, there is the confidence to return to empirical observation and analysis highlighting good practice and problem areas alike. Research is further facilitated by advances in technology (which make the capture of data less intrusive and the analysis simpler). However, efforts are no longer focused on achieving basic, minimum standards and approaches, but on exploring more complex issues, at deeper levels. Moreover, exploration is increasingly rounded, e.g. approached from the perspective of all of the participants in the interpreting triad, rather than solely from that of the interpreter-practitioners.

This aggregation of perspectives must be a priority for future research activity. As PSI practice is a triadic activity, multifaceted research is needed, involving academics, clients, interpreter-practitioners and other professionals. For example, development of models or theories that only consider the perspective of the interpreter, without taking account of the 'fit' with any models or theories developed by the public sector domains, will be incomplete. However, interdisciplinarity also needs to continue to build on already established links with other fields of social science and to extend into less-charted fields for PSI research such as jurisprudence, ethics in the professions, computer and information science, psychology, and so on. Moreover, in this new converged era of interpreting, basic research questions relating to the definition of the profession and impact of the professional activity on society are still to be fully answered.

Training

It is also important that interdisciplinarity should feed into an interlinked approach to training. A basic premise must be that theory and practice are interconnected. The PSI world is a dynamic and evolving one and practitioners cannot be prepared for every working scenario they will encounter in training. Therefore, the PSI world needs to be staffed by reflective practitioners and practice must be grounded in theory and research so that practitioners can make informed decisions in the field. Training needs to offer a balance of these two, which entails positioning education at higher education levels. In training institutions and programmes, there should also be an interlinked approach as regards the worlds of interpreting and translation, for example between modes and styles of interpreting, as well as between languages. In addition, connections rather than divisions should be made between SL and spoken language provision, between majority and minority spoken languages. No activity or language combination should be regarded as superior and each should be prepared to learn from the other. A growing number of institutions offer courses integrating signed and spoken languages and make PSI available to students studying conference interpreting, but there is scope for development. Ultimately, there may be three main priorities for future training. First, to adopt a holistic, interlinked approach to training: both through involving the three parties in the interpreting triad and also exploiting the overlapping and shared needs between different contexts and languages of interpreting. Second, to embrace the potential of technology as a vehicle for delivering and aiding training, and as a medium through which interpreters must be trained to interpret. Finally, we can further exploit the potential of globalization, working with colleagues across national borders to develop training and resources.

Society, technology, the geopolitical circumstances affecting the migration of people and governmental strategies are in constant flux. Interpreters working in the public sector function in varied, evolving worlds with real people, living real lives. Their working circumstances may therefore not always conform to any ideal model. The challenge is to offer quality training, to an appropriate level, in a flexible manner that can accommodate new language pairs or skills, given the resource constraints. It is essential to integrate all stakeholders into the training process and that this integration is not cosmetic, but rather is handled in an interlinked manner that creates a positive spiral. This relates to both the training of student interpreters and to the training of public sector staff to work with interpreters. As the parties work together, there is the potential for them to learn from each other. Mutual respect as fellow professionals can be established and awareness raised of the role of the public sector professional as part of the solution in the interpreter-mediated event: in short, the interpreter cannot do it alone (Turner 2007c). Such an approach has the potential to facilitate the mutual development of responses to challenging questions (e.g. ethical dilemmas) through negotiation. Effective management of multilingualism is thus made a cooperative issue.

Conclusion

BSL/English interpreting acts as an excellent vehicle for illustrating the nature of the field of interpreting, as it encapsulates all the possible variations and demonstrates how barriers can be broken down. As an interpreting activity, at its most fundamental level, BSL/English interpreting spans not only two distinct languages, but also two different media. Its practitioners demonstrate how conference interpreting and PSI overlap as areas of activity, at both local and international levels. Moreover, it encompasses all modes of interpreting and styles of interpreting and involves both a dominant, majority language and a minority and indigenous language. Its interpreters come both from within the community (growing up bilingual) and outside (learning the language later in life); and they may be employed as salaried staff, subcontracted through voluntary organizations or private agencies or be self-employed as freelancers. As a rule, the field of BSL/English interpreting is better organized and structured than that of interpreters with other language combinations working in the public sector in the UK. There is also less of a differential in status, where BSL is concerned, between public service and conference interpreters than is the case for other spoken language combinations (e.g. PSI training is better structured and often positioned at a higher level, and there are better rates of remuneration defended by professional bodies).

In some ways, this idea of BSL interpreting as an example of good practice is the mirror image of the dynamic between conference interpreting and SL interpreting. When SLs gained recognition as languages, they first turned to conference interpreting between spoken languages to inform their professional development and to establish theoretical models. However, interpreting in the public sector (from the perspective of professionalization, research and development, and training) is now being informed by SL interpreting. These shifting tides of influence between types of interpreting highlight the similarities, rather than the differences and emphasize the need to advance together in addressing this aspect of the modern multilingual world.

Related topics

Sign language and the politics of deafness; multilingual citizenship and minority languages; language rights; linguistic diversity and education; multilingualism in legal settings; multilingualism in the workplace.

Further reading

de Pedro Ricoy, R., Perez, I. and Wilson, C. (eds) (2009) *Interpreting and Translating in Public Service Settings: Policy, Practice, Pedagogy*, Manchester: St Jerome Publishing.
(International snapshot of public service interpreting policy in practice.)
Hale, S. (2008) *Community Interpreting*, London: Palgrave Macmillan.
(Up-to-date introduction to interpreting in public service contexts.)
Harrington, F. J. and Turner, G. H. (eds) (2001) *Interpreting Interpreting: Studies and Reflections on Sign Language Interpreting*, Coleford: Douglas McLean.
(Collection of essays reflecting on sign language interpreting in the UK, with special reference to legal, medical and educational contexts.)
Pöchhacker, F. (2004) *Introducing Interpreting Studies*, London and New York: Routledge.
(The most comprehensive overview of scholarship on the interpreting field.)
Wadensjö, C. (1998) *Interpreting as Interaction*, London and New York: Longman.
(The canonical empirical study of dialogue interpreting.)

Bibliography

Angelelli, C. V. (2004) *Medical Interpreting and Cross-cultural Communication*, Cambridge: Cambridge University Press.
Berk-Seligson, S. (1990) *The Bilingual Courtroom*, Chicago: Chicago University Press.
Brennan, M. (1975) 'Can deaf children acquire language? An evaluation of linguistic principles in deaf education', *American Annals of the Deaf*, October.
——(1999) 'Signs of injustice', *The Translator* 5(2): 221–46.
Brennan, M. and Brown, R. (1997) *Equality Before the Law? Deaf People's Access to Justice*, Durham: Deaf Studies Research Unit.
Butler, I. and Noaks, L. (1992) *Silence in Court? A Study of Interpreting in the Courts of England and Wales*, School of Social and Administrative Studies, University of Wales College of Cardiff and London: Nuffield Interpreter Project.
CILT National Centre for Languages (2006) *The National Occupational Standards in Interpreting (revised 2006)*, London: CILT National Centre for Languages, available online at www.cilt.org. uk/home/standards_and_qualifications/uk_occupational_standards/interpreting.aspx
Conrad, R. (1979) *The Deaf School Child*, Oxford: Oxford University Press.
Corsellis, A. (2005) 'Training interpreters to work in the public services', in M. Tennent (ed.) *Training for the New Millennium*, Amsterdam and Philadelphia: John Benjamins.
——(2009) *Public Service Interpreting*, London: Palgrave Macmillan.
Crown Office and Procurator Fiscal Service (2003) *Interpreting and Translation Handbook: Guidance on Policy and Best Practice*, Edinburgh: Crown Office and Procurator Fiscal Service.
Davidson, B. (1998) *Interpreting Medical Discourse: A Study of Cross-linguistic Communication in the Hospital Clinic*, unpublished doctoral dissertation, Stanford, CA: Stanford University.
DCSF (Department for Children, Schools and Families) (2009) *Statistical First Release: Schools, Pupils and Their Characteristics, January 2009 (Provisional)*, London: SFR 08/2009.

Deaf Blawg (2005) *Deaf People from Overseas Conference*, available online at www.deaflawyers.org. uk/blawg/category/immigration

DES (Department of Education and Science) (1968) *The Education of Deaf Children: The Possible Place of Finger Spelling and Signing (The Lewis Report)*, London: HMSO.

——(1978) *Special Educational Needs: Report of the Committee of Enquiry into the Education of Handicapped Children and Young People (The Warnock Report)*, London: HMSO.

Dickinson, J. and Turner, G. H. (2008) 'Sign language interpreters and role conflict in the workplace', in C. Valero-Garcés and A. Martin (eds) *Crossing Borders in Community Interpreting: Definitions and Dilemmas*, Amsterdam: John Benjamins.

Disability Discrimination Act 1995 (1995) London: OPSI, available online at www.legislation.gov. uk/ukpga/1995/7/contents

Equality Scotland (2005) *Happy to Translate*, available online at www.equalityscotland.com/happy totranslate/happytotranslate.php

Frishberg, N. (1990) *Interpreting: An Introduction*, revised edn, Silver Spring, MD: RID Publications.

Gaelic Language (Scotland) Act 2005 (2005) Edinburgh: OPSI, available online at www.legislation. gov.uk/asp/2005/7/contents

Gentile, A., Ozolins, U. and Vasilakakos, M. (1996) *Liaison Interpreting: A Handbook*, Melbourne: Melbourne University Press.

Gile, D. (1990) 'Scientific research vs. personal theories in the investigation of interpretation', in L. Gran and C. Taylor (eds) *Aspects of Applied and Experimental Research on Conference Interpretation*, Udine: Campanotto.

Goldstone, C. (2002) *Barriers to Employment for Disabled People*, Department of Work and Pensions In-house Report 95.

Gray, L. (2006) 'Immigrants push up translation bill', *The Scotsman*, 24 November, available online at http://news.scotsman.com/immigrationandrefugees/Immigrants-push-up-translation-bill.2829612.jp

Guy's and St Thomas' NHS Foundation Trust (2006) *First British Sign Language Video Interpreting Service in the Country*, available online at www.guysandstthomas.nhs.uk/news/newsarchive/ archive06/signvideo.aspx

Harrington, F. J. (2000a) 'Interpreting in Social Services: Setting the boundaries of good practice?' in F. J. Harrington and G. H. Turner (eds) *Interpreting Interpreting: Studies and Reflections on Sign Language Interpreting*, Coleford: Douglas McLean.

——(2000b) 'The rise, fall and re-invention of the communicator: Re-defining roles and responsibilities in educational interpreting', in F. J. Harrington and G. H. Turner (eds) *Interpreting Interpreting: Studies and Reflections on Sign Language Interpreting*, Coleford: Douglas McLean.

Harrington, F. J. and Turner, G. H. (eds) (2001) *Interpreting Interpreting: Studies and Reflections on Sign Language Interpreting*, Coleford: Douglas McLean.

Harris, J. and Bamford, C. (2001) 'The uphill struggle: Services for Deaf and hard of hearing people: issues of equality, participation and access', *Disability and Society* 16: 969–79.

Hatim, B. and Mason, I. (1990) *Discourse and the Translator*, London: Longman.

——(1997) *The Translator as Communicator*, London: Routledge.

Her Majesty's Inspectorate of Constabulary for Scotland (2000) *Without Prejudice?: A Thematic Inspection of Police Race Relations in Scotland*, Edinburgh: Scottish Executive, available online at www.scotland.gov.uk/hmic/docs/wprr.pdf

Howie, M. (2007a) 'Immigrants jailed for "cannabis factory" work', *The Scotsman*, 16 October, available online at http://news.scotsman.com/drugspolicy/Immigrants-jailed-for-cannabis-factory.347 1164.jp

——(2007b) 'Translation errors may see criminals escape', *The Scotsman*, 30 October, available online at http://thescotsman.scotsman.com/immigrationandrefugees/Translation-errors-may-see-criminals.3 475462.jp?CommentPage=1&CommentPageLength=1000

——(2009) 'Courts to hire interpreters in £6m bid to safeguard justice', *The Scotsman*, 14 May available online at http://news.scotsman.com/scotland/Courts-to-hire-interpreters-in.5265049.jp

Inghilleri, M. (2004) 'Habitus, field and discourse: Interpreting as a socially-situated activity', *Target: International Journal of Translation Studies* 15(2): 243–68.

——(2005) 'Mediating zones of uncertainty: Interpreter agency, the interpreting habitus and political asylum adjudication', *The Translator* 11(1): 69–85.

Jandoo, R. (2001) *Report of the Inquiry into the Liaison Arrangements between the Police, the Procurator Fiscal Service and the Crown Office and the Family of the Deceased Surjit Singh Chhokar in Connection with the Murder of Surjit Singh Chhokar and the Related Prosecutions*, vol. 1, October, Edinburgh: Scottish Parliament, available online at www.scottish.parliament.uk/business/committees/historic/equal/reports-01/chhokar-vol01–00.htm

Janzen, T. (2005) 'Introduction to the theory and practice of signed language interpreting', in T. Janzen (ed.) *Topics in Signed Language Interpreting*, Amsterdam and Philadelphia: John Benjamins.

Kyle, J., Reilly, A. M., Allsop, L., Clark, M. and Dury, A. (2004) *Investigation of Access to Public Services in Scotland Using British Sign Language*, Edinburgh: Scottish Executive, available online at www.scotland.gov.uk/Resource/Doc/930/0012107.pdf

Kyle, J. G. and Pullen, G. (1988) 'Cultures in contact: Deaf and hearing people', *Disability, Handicap and Society* 3(1): 49–61.

Ladd, P. (2003) *Understanding Deaf Culture*, Clevedon: Multilingual Matters.

McLaughlin, M. (2009) 'Battle of words threatens chaos in the courts', *Scotland on Sunday*, 1 November 2009, available online at http://news.scotsman.com/scotland/Battle–of.5784353.jp

McPake, J. and Johnson, R. (2002) *Translating, Interpreting and Communication Support Services across the Public Sector in Scotland: A Literature Review*, Edinburgh: Scottish Executive, available online at www.scotland.gov.uk/Resource/Doc/156792/0042162.pdf

Mapson, R. and Schofield, M. (2010) 'More harm than good? Just how involved should an interpreter be when working in a medical setting?' *Newsli: the magazine for the Association of Sign Language Interpreters for England, Wales and Northern Ireland*, 71: 6–12.

Marschark, M., Peterson, R. and Winston, E. (eds) (2005) *Sign Language Interpreting and Interpreter Education: Directions for Research and Practice*, Oxford: Oxford University Press.

Marschark, M. and Spencer, P. E. (eds) (2003) *Oxford Handbook of Deaf Studies, Language, and Education*, New York: Oxford University Press.

Mason, I. (2009) 'Role, positioning and discourse in face-to-face interpreting', R. de Pedro Ricoy, I. Perez and C. Wilson (eds) *Interpreting and Translating in Public Service Settings: Policy, Practice, Pedagogy*, Manchester: St Jerome Publishing.

Metzger, M. (1999) *Sign Language Interpreting: Deconstructing the Myth of Neutrality*, Washington, DC: Gallaudet University Press.

Mindess, A. (2006) *Reading Between the Signs: Intercultural Communication for Sign Language Interpreters*, 2nd edn, Boston, MA: Intercultural Press.

Monaghan, L., Schmaling, C., Nakamura, K. and Turner, G. H. (eds) (2003) *Many Ways to BeDeaf: International Variation in Deaf Communities*, Washington, DC: Gallaudet University Press.

Munday, J. (2008) *Translation Studies: Theories and Applications*, 2nd edn, London: Routledge.

Nuffield Interpreter Project (1993) *Access to Justice: Non-English Speakers in the Legal System*, London: The Nuffield Foundation.

O'Rourke, B. and Castillo, P. (2009) '"Top-down" or "Bottom-up"? Language policies in public service interpreting in the Republic of Ireland, Scotland and Spain', in R. de Pedro Ricoy, I. Perez and C. Wilson (eds) *Interpreting and Translating in Public Service Settings: Policy, Practice, Pedagogy*, Manchester: St Jerome Publishing.

Perez, I. A. and Wilson, C. W. L. (2009) 'A TICS Model from Scotland: A profile of translation, interpreting and communication support in the public services in Scotland', in R. de Pedro Ricoy, I. Perez and C. Wilson (eds) *Interpreting and Translating in Public Service Settings: Policy, Practice, Pedagogy*, Manchester: St Jerome Publishing.

Perez, I. A., Wilson, C. W. L., King, C. and Pagnier, C. (2006a) *Translating, Interpreting and Communication Support: A Review of Provision in the Public Services in Scotland*, Edinburgh: Scottish Executive Social Research, available online at www.scotland.gov.uk/Resource/Doc/90506/0021781.pdf

——(2006b) *Translating, Interpreting and Communication Support: A Review of Provision in the Public Services in Scotland (Research Findings)*, Edinburgh: Scottish Executive Social Research, available online at www.scotland.gov.uk/Resource/Doc/90537/0021782.pdf

Pöchhacker, F. (2004) *Introducing Interpreting Studies*, London and New York: Routledge.

Preston, P. (1994) *Mother Father Deaf: Living between Sound and Silence*, Cambridge, MA: Harvard University Press.

Reed, M., Turner, G. H. and Taylor, C. (2000) 'Working paper on access to justice for Deaf people', in F. J. Harrington and G. H. Turner (eds) *Interpreting Interpreting: Studies and Reflections on Sign Language Interpreting*, Coleford: Douglas McLean.

Roberts, R. (1997) 'Community interpreting today and tomorrow', in S. E. Carr, R. Roberts, A. Dufour and D. Steyn (eds) *The Critical Link: Interpreters in the Community*, Papers from the First International Conference on Interpreting in Legal, Health, and Social Service Settings (Geneva Park, Canada, June 1–4, 1995), Amsterdam and Philadelphia: John Benjamins.

Roy, C. (2000) *Interpreting as a Discourse Process*, Oxford: Oxford University Press.

Scott Gibson, L. (1991) 'Sign language interpreting: An emerging profession', in S. Gregory and G. Hartley (eds) *Constructing Deafness*, London and Milton Keynes: Pinter Publishers in association with the Open University.

Scottish Association of Sign Language Interpreters (2002) *Creating Linguistic Access for Deaf and Deafblind People: A Strategy for Scotland*, Edinburgh: Scottish Association of Sign Language Interpreters.

Scottish Consumer Council (2005) *Is Anybody Listening? The User Perspective on Interpretation and Translation Services for Minority Ethnic Communities*, Glasgow: Scottish Consumer Council.

Scottish Refugee Integration Forum (2003) *Scottish Refugee Integration Forum. Action Plan*, Edinburgh: HMSO, available online at www.scotland.gov.uk/Resource/Doc/47032/0027032.pdf

Steinberg, A. G., Barnett, S., Meador, H. E., Wiggins, E. A. and Zazove, P. (2006) 'Health care system accessibility: Experiences and perceptions of deaf people', *Journal of General Internal Medicine* 21(3): 260–6.

Sutton-Spence, R. and Woll, B. (1999) *The Linguistics of British Sign Language: An Introduction*, Cambridge: Cambridge University Press.

Swanwick, R. and Gregory, S. (2007) *Sign Bilingual Education: Policy and Practice*, Coleford: Douglas McLean.

The Lord Advocate (2002) 'Assessment of language needs and cultural sensitivities', *The Lord Advocate's Guidelines to Chief Constables*, Edinburgh: Crown Office, available online at www.copfs.gov.uk/Resource/Doc/9/0000075.pdf

The Scottish Translation, Interpreting and Communication Forum (2004) *Good Practice Guidelines*, Edinburgh: Scottish Executive, available online at www.scotland.gov.uk/Resource/Doc/47210/0025542.pdf

The Working Group on Translation and Interpreting (2008) *Code of Practice for Working with Interpreters in the Scottish Criminal Justice System*, Edinburgh: Crown Office and Procurator Fiscal Service, available online at www.copfs.gov.uk/Resource/Doc/13928/0000467.pdf

Trowler, P. and Turner, G. H. (2002) 'Exploring the hermeneutic foundations of university life: Deaf academics in a hybrid "community of practice"', *Higher Education* 43: 227–56.

Turner, G. H. (2003) 'Government recognition and £1m boost for British Sign Language', *Deaf Worlds: International Journal of Deaf Studies* 19(1): S74–S78.

——(2007a) 'Re-thinking the sociology of sign language interpreting and translation: Some challenges posed by deaf practitioners', in M. Wolf (ed.) *Übersetzen – Translating – Traduire: Towards a "Social Turn"?* Münster: LIT Publishers.

——(2007b) 'Exploring inter-subdisciplinary alignment in interpreting studies: sign language interpreting at conferences', in F. Pöchhacker, A. L. Jakobsen and I. M. Mees (eds) *Interpreting Studies and Beyond. Copenhagen Studies in Language*, 35, Frederiksberg: Samfundslitteratur Press.

——(2007c) 'Professionalisation of interpreting *with* the community: Refining the model', in C. Wadensjö, B. Englund Dimitrova and A-L. Nilsson (eds) *The Critical Link 4: Professionalisation of Interpreting in the Community*, Selected papers from the 4th International Conference on Interpreting in Legal, Health and Social Service Settings, Stockholm, Sweden, 20–23 May 2004, Amsterdam and Philadelphia: John Benjamins.

Turner, G. H. and Brown, R. K. (2000) 'Interaction and the role of the interpreter in court', in F. J. Harrington and G. H. Turner (eds) *Interpreting Interpreting: Studies and Reflections on Sign Language Interpreting*, Coleford: Douglas McLean.

Wadensjö, C. (1998) *Interpreting as Interaction*, London: Longman.

Wilson, C. W. L. (2007) 'Working through technology: A study of interpreter mediated encounters when interpreting is provided by video-conferencing link', paper presented at *Critical Link 5: Interpreting in the Community*, Parramatta, Sydney, Australia, 11–15 April.

Winston, E. A. (ed.) (2004) *Educational Interpreting: How it Can Succeed*, Washington, DC: Gallaudet University Press.

Young, A. M., Ackerman, J. and Kyle, J. G. (2000) 'On creating a workable signing environment: Deaf and hearing perspectives', *Journal of Deaf Studies and Deaf Education* 5(2): 186–95.

19

Multilingualism and the media

Helen Kelly-Holmes

Introduction

In this chapter, I explore the media as a key site of multilingualism. Given the role that media play in contemporary societies in many parts of the world, they are one of the main means by which individuals may engage with and be exposed to discourses about multilingualism and multilingual practices. As such, media have a major role to play in maintaining or challenging existing language regimes, attitudes and ideologies. I begin by looking at early developments in the field, particularly the evolution of parallel monolingualisms as a type of multilingual practice in the media, with a focus on multilingual media. I then go on to look at some key issues of theory and method, particularly in terms of media texts and mediatized texts and issues of policy and how these have evolved and impacted on multilingualism in the media, especially, although not exclusively, in relation to minority language media. I then go on to look at new research directions in the area of new media practices, which can be seen to have fundamentally altered the relationship between multilingualism and the media. Finally, I look at two contemporary multilingual media texts to illustrate how practices are constantly evolving and to show the extent of possibilities in the new media age.

Early developments in the field

The early development of media can be seen in many ways as a negative development from the point of view of multilingualism. Giving language written form that is to be widely distributed inevitably involves choices about that particular language, which both includes some and excludes others. Also, in practical terms and for reasons of cost as well as ideology (national media being an important vehicle for standardizing language in newly developing nations), those who produce media have tended to think of targeting geographic areas with standard media in a standard language.

For example, in its conditions for membership, the European Broadcasting Union (EBU) automatically links national media with national language, and territory with speakers, invoking the territoriality principle in contrast to the individuality principle. For example, a multilingual country is conceived of by the EBU as a country with separate linguistic territories, as exemplified by the statement: 'Where in a country there are two or more linguistic areas, this criterion refers individually to each such area' (European Broadcasting Union 2007). Because of its nature, in terms of the demarcation of media space, again highlighted in the EBU statement, media communication forces people into national and regional groups; they are categorized according to territory first, then language (which are assumed to be co-terminous). This conception is also based on the Herderian assumption that one national culture equals one language equals one people. This issue is not confined to broadcast media. When an attempt was made to launch a Turkish-German magazine, one of the first obstacles the producers came up against was the distribution of the magazine: newsagents were unsure of where to place it in their outlets – in the German section or in the Turkish section (cf. Kelly-Holmes 2005). As we shall see below, newer media challenge this categorization by having the capacity to address speech communities without regard to territory.

One result of this era of media and language policy and planning has been the codification of monolingualism as a normal state of affairs in the media through a variety of explicit and implicit policies and practices, with multilingualism being conceived as parallel monolingualisms (Heller 1999). This clearly differs from the everyday lived experiences of many people, which involve much more hybrid and blurred practices.

The developments in media outlined above are also crucially linked to technological and ideological developments. For example, representing variation in the media speech community became much more feasible with the development of multichannel broadcasting and the dismantling of state monopolies in broadcasting. Similarly, digital technology has led to exponential fragmentation as well as heteroglossic media practices. However, much of the implementation of linguistic human rights in the sphere of media (linked to the fragmentation of media speech communities) has actually reinforced the demarcating and monolingual ideology of one language = one people. This has in many instances led to multiple, parallel crops, rather than cross-fertilization to borrow the biodiversity metaphor. Also, the challenge to minority language media communities is to overcome their delineation by language and a resulting lack of what Moring (2007) describes as functional and institutional completeness. In other words, they are required to be all things to all speakers of a particular minority language, all of whom may have very diverse interests (for an overview of these issues, cf. Cormack and Hourigan 2007). Equally, even though media are now more easily and readily available to speakers of languages other than the dominant media language in a particular society, and bottom-up, heteroglossic and ideolectal practices are possible in new media formats (cf. Danet and Herring 2007; Androutsopoulos 2007, 2006b; Wright 2006), the representation of multilingualism is still a complex process (regardless of who is doing the representing), as the work of Jaffe (2007, 2008) and Johnson and Turner (2008) and others has shown.

Key issues of theory and method

In many ways, multilingualism in the media could be treated in the same way as multilingualism in any other domain, private or public, in everyday life. Indeed, the distinction between 'mediated' and 'real' multilingualism has been criticized, particularly in terms of the valuing of the former as more authentic by sociolinguists (cf. Androutsopoulos 2007 for a discussion). What makes multilingualism in the media different from 'everyday' or 'person-to-person' or other occasions of multilingualism is the presence – seen or unseen, human or technical – of some intermediary or facilitator or controller. This mediation (or facilitation or control) links to policy, in the sense that decisions have to be made at a whole range of levels not just about what multilingual practices to adopt, but also about how to depict and value multilingualism in a particular media context or channel.

Media can be seen to constitute speech communities, in terms of 'location(s) in which the patterned variations in selection from the available repertoire takes place' (Spolsky 2004: 27). The speech community constituted by media could be large, for example, an entire nation, as in the case of the target audience of a national broadcaster or national newspaper (cf. Billig 1995). It could also be much smaller, for example, a blog or discussion group on the Internet (cf. Baron 2008; Androutsopoulos 2006b, 2007; Thurlow et al. 2003). There is no limit on size or location, as a mediated speech community (like any speech community) is 'defined by its sharing a set of language varieties (its repertoire) and a set of norms for using them' (Spolsky 2004: 25). We can see, particularly in relation to new media, that size and location have become far less relevant factors in constituting bi- and multilingual, heteroglossic and minority language media speech communities (cf. for example Androutsopoulos 2006a, 2006b; Menezes 2006; Cunliffe and Herring 2005a; Danet and Herring 2003).

In practical terms, media constitute and demarcate homogenous or monolingual speech communities in a number of both explicit and implicit ways. First of all, by the provision of space and the demarcation or delineation of that space (e.g. printed paper, channels, etc.). Second, as pointed out above, by the use and dissemination of a common code, which involves not just the choice of one particular language or variety of a language over another, but also the dissemination of knowledge about language. The constitution and demarcation are further reinforced by some element of gatekeeping, which controls access or membership. This may involve material means (e.g. a licence fee, cost of newspaper) or it may involve having access to particular technology (e.g. having a television, computer, etc.), or it may simply involve registration of individual details. A further dimension to the demarcation and constitution of a homogenous speech community is the dissemination, through a shared code and nomen-clature, of shared knowledge, cultural references, etc. (cf. Billig 1995). Finally, and particularly relevant to Ricento's first era of language policy and language planning (see below) are the explicit policies enacted by media actors to constitute and demarcate speech communities.

In terms of looking at the relationship between multilingual practice and its connection to policy, it might be useful to think in terms of a continuum of texts and speech acts, ranging from *media* texts and speech acts to *mediatized* texts and speech acts. Text here is of course understood as encompassing not just written, but all kinds of media texts – audio, visual, hyper, multimodal, etc. Media texts and speech acts can be understood as being specifically related to and in fact inseparable from a medium, and would not be possible or would be radically altered without mediation (e.g. news reporting, advertising, television drama, editor-ials, radio show, etc.). They tend to be monologic (cf. Bakhtin 1981) in nature in terms of the relationship between audience and media text – even though they may contain dialogic speech acts (e.g. soap operas, radio dramas). They are also generally rehearsed, scripted, edited, planned, researched, staged in some way, with attention being given in advance to language choices. Finally, they lack the 'noise' (Shannon and Weaver 1949), mistakes, interventions, etc. that characterize 'normal', face-to-face communication.

One good example of a media text is advertising, which, as Piller (2003) points out, is a key site of language contact, with brand names, slogans and marketing texts such as advertisements frequently featuring multilingual and heteroglossic play (cf. for example Martin 2006; Bishop et al. 2005; Ustinova and Bhatia 2005; Piller 2003). This process is perhaps best described by Haarmann's (1989) term 'impersonal bilingualism', by which he means the practice of a type of multilingualism in advertising and marketing that has practically nothing to do with everyday lived multilingualism on the ground and everything to do with symbolic associations and a type of safely packaged and contained otherness. Global brands use languages to divide up the market into speakers of different languages and create glocalized marketing and advertising materials for these language groups. For instance, the provision by a global brand of advertising and product information in a central or peripheral language (de Swaan 2001) may be motivated less by a desire to communicate a message that would not otherwise be understood, as speakers of peripheral languages tend by definition to be multilingual, than by a desire to be seen as sympathetic to speakers of the group, to be supporting diversity or simply to stand out as being different from other brands, particularly dominant national brands. For example, two airlines, which specifically position themselves as 'European' (rather than national) and 'budget', Ryanair and EasyJet, have offered options in Catalan on their global websites, whereas the Spanish national carrier, Iberia, has offered only Castilian/ Spanish and English.

The term *mediatized* speech acts, on the other hand, can be used to refer to 'spontaneous' or 'real world' speech acts that become mediated (e.g. texting, email, blogging, Internet chat, phone-in, reality TV). They tend to be dialogic in nature in terms of the relationship between media actor and audience and are generally linked to new media. A further feature is that they are characterized by the participation of non-professionals (Sky News, for instance, urges watchers to send in their news stories and images, which may then be broadcast, using the slogan 'You make the news') or a mix of professional and non-professional, and they are generally subject to (or at least appear to be subject to) less editing and preparation. These seem more obviously like 'real' sociolinguistic data about multilingualism and linguistic diversity; however, there is still some degree of mediation, gatekeeping or editing. As the next section highlights, new media in particular have facilitated the growth of mediatized texts featuring multilingualism.

The distinction between media speech acts and mediatized speech acts can be seen as more of a continuum than a dichotomy. In terms of multilingualism, top-down media speech acts would be situated at the start of the continuum. In general, these are conceived in terms of monolingualism as the norm – and even where such texts and speech acts are multilingual, the multilingualism is in fact parallel monolingualisms, with strict borders being maintained between languages. At the other end of the continuum, we have bottom-up mediatized speech acts, which feature heteroglossic and mixed forms (cf. Androutsopoulos 2007, 2006b; Mahootian 2005; Pietikäinen 2008a). Linking back to policy, it seems clear that media speech acts are much more a product of top-down policies (identified by Ricento (2006) as the first and second eras of language policy – see below) and which correspond loosely to Wenham's (1982) first and second ages of broadcasting, whereas mediatized speech acts are bound up with the later era of fragmentation, what Wenham has termed the third age of broadcasting. At the end of this chapter, we will look at an example of a media speech act and a mediatized speech act.

Policy issues

Media can be seen as key agents in the process of 'political interventions into collective patterns of language use' (Coulmas 2005: 185). For example, media institutions may have explicit (Shohamy 2006) language policies, which are part of larger, macro-level policies concerned with maintaining or changing a particular language regime; or, in the absence of specific policies relating to them, media actors may interpret and disseminate directly or indirectly national or regional language policies or de facto language policies, or mediate what is perceived as the sociolinguistic status quo. For instance, in the USA, where there is no national official language, the majority or national media still broadcast predominantly in English, thus replicating and reinforcing the dominant language status quo, with bilingual media being left generally to regional and local levels. There may be a mix of both explicit (official or overt) policies and implicit (covert, unofficial) policies, which are constituted by practice. Language practices, as Shohamy (2006) points out, are a key aspect of policy and may in fact constitute policy in the absence of explicit policy statements. So, in a media context, we can see that discourses about multilingualism (cf. Johnson and Ensslin 2007a, 2007b for an overview of thematizing of language in the media) as well as actual practice and indeed any decision about language that is practised in a habitual way, becomes a type of policy. For example, linguistic decisions about the target audience, decisions about what is appropriate style, language, etc. for communicating with this particular speech community (cf. Bell 1984), and the assumptions underpinning these decisions about what the norm is (e.g. whether the 'normal' or 'average' listener is multilingual or not), all combine to constitute policy.

Media can therefore be seen to carry out all of the key functions of language policy and planning for the regulation of linguistic variation and multilingualism in speech communities. They act as agents of corpus planning, by using official terminology and disseminating new terminology, a particularly strong feature of minority language media (cf. O'Connell 2001). They also act as agents of status planning, for example, by allocating space, prominence, etc. to particular language(s) and variety(ies) (cf. Cormack and Hourigan 2007; Kelly-Holmes 2001), and as agents of standardization, spreading a standard language and notions about norms (implicitly through use and explicitly through prescriptive comment and advice). Furthermore, they act as agents of language diffusion, by encouraging people to learn a particular language (e.g. BBC, Deutsche Welle), by decisions taken about dubbing versus subtitling, and as agents of language learning (e.g. by scheduling foreign language learning programmes or showing television programmes in other languages). Finally, media act as agents of language ideology – they constitute their speech community, both explicitly (through policies) and implicitly (through practice in terms of actual language choices and discourse about language) as mono-, bi- or multilingual, and through discourse about language(s) they inform perceptions by members about their particular speech community as mono-, bi- or multilingual (cf. Horner 2007; Johnson and Ensslin 2007a; Milani 2007; Blackledge 2006).

As pointed out by Anderson (1983) and others (e.g. Wright 2000; Billig 1995), media play a major role in constituting this 'virtual' or 'imagined' speech community. In his historical overview of language policy and language planning (LPP), Ricento identifies the 'decolonization, structuralism and pragmatism' era as one characterized by 'the pervasive belief at least in the West that language problems could be solved through planning, especially within the public sector' (2000: 197). Linguistic diversity was seen as problematic for the modernization project and for the provision of national media. Therefore, one result of this era is that a diglossic situation emerged in media contexts with the 'first age' of broadcasting Wenham (1982) characterized by a great distance between how people speak in 'normal conversations' and how people in the media speak (cf. Smith 1998).

In the next era of language policy and planning, Ricento identifies a move away from this, and a recognition that this modernizing project, distinguished by the attempt to create homogeneous speech communities, had failed. The privileging of some languages (or varieties) over others was no longer seen as acceptable (Ricento 2000). In terms of media, this was reflected in a move away from prescription towards greater recognition and representation of variation within the speech community in national media and the development of some subnational (primarily regional) media, and greater diversity in terms of the range of accents and varieties represented in these media. This also corresponded with Wenham's (1982) second age of broadcasting, when the monopoly of state control of broadcast media was broken down gradually, due to a combination of ideological and technical factors, and multiple media channels emerged (cf. Smith 1998).

The next development in LPP identified by Ricento, which corresponds roughly to the contemporary era (the third age of broadcasting (Wenham 1982) and what is now the digital age), is characterized by '[a] new world order, postmodernism and linguistic human rights' (Ricento 2000: 203). The features of this era include the penetration of English-language media and cultural products throughout the globe, as well as an emphasis on individual agency rather than explicit ideologies. The issue of language loss is a key focus of this era with the employment of notions of biolinguistic diversity and linguistic imperialism. This has been reflected in media contexts by the fragmentation of media and traditional media speech communities (cf. Morley and Robins 1995; Richardson and Meinhof 1999), the activation and implementation of language rights through media (cf. Pietikäinen 2008a, 2008b; Hourigan 2003) and the realization that media could be a tool in 'saving' endangered languages (cf. Cotter 2001). Furthermore, digital technology in particular can be seen to have taken control of media production away from institutions more closely associated with macro-level LPP objectives. Thus, the crucial difference between the second and third eras is that in the second era, the speech community was dependent on media institutions to represent their multilingualism and linguistic diversity in a particular way, whereas in the third era, speech communities have the possibility, with obvious limitations, to represent themselves.

New research directions

As Cunliffe and Herring (2005b) point out, 'the relationship between minority languages and communications technology in the broadest sense has always been complex and problematic. On the one hand communication technology can be a powerful force for propagating a majority language and its cultural values; on the other hand it can provide vital new opportunities for media production and consumption in minority languages' (Cunliffe and Herring 2005b: 131). Despite initial fears that English would become the normal or default language of the Web and yet another tool of English language imperialism (cf. Crystal 2001), studies have shown increasing rather than decreasing linguistic diversity on the World Wide Web (cf. Danet and Herring 2007, 2003; Androutsopoulos 2007, 2006a, 2006b; Menezes 2006; Cunliffe and Herring 2005a, 2005b; Wright 2004), also seen in commercial contexts (cf. Kelly-Holmes 2006a); particularly as technical improvements have made it possible to provide content not just in different languages but also in an increasing number of alphabets other than Roman that require non-ASCII characters (cf. Wong et al. 2006; Gee 2005). Such technical improvements can clearly be seen to have had an impact on normalizing language relations in a number of diglossic or contested contexts. Technical improvements have meant that minority language communities have not had to compromise in terms of omitting special characters, which would fundamentally change and homogenize their alphabets, bringing them visually closer to majority languages and consequently reducing their visibility and the ability to perform meaningful searches in them (cf. Kelly-Holmes 2006b).

The technical possibilities afforded by digital technologies also mean that content can now be made available in an economically viable way, not only in any number of languages, but also in 'small' languages that do not have large numbers of speakers to support correspondingly large print runs. Such availability inevitably challenges existing hierarchies and the status quo, whereby common-sense assumptions about language are disseminated and reinforced by the ideologies and norms of the publishing and traditional media industries. Seeing content equally available in multiple languages, as, for example, in situations where parallel monolingual versions are made available, in commercial and other 'real world' domains, removed from official domains that are frequently subject to language policy regulations (e.g. European budget airlines' Ryanair and EasyJet use of Catalan on their websites as mentioned earlier) can be argued to have a strong effect in normalizing a minoritized language. The Dingle Skelligs Hotel on the Dingle Penninsula in Ireland, an Irish-speaking or *Gaeltacht* area, offers eight language options on its website that lead to synopses of the main site, which is in English. The language selection includes a predicable set of supercentral languages (de Swaan 2001) French, German Russian, Spanish, Chinese and Japanese, as well as Italian, a large central (ibid.) language and Irish. Furthermore, what were previously covert policies and decisions in terms of which language communities to provide with localized content are now made overt in new multimedia environments, thus highlighting language norms and ideologies, which in turn can be utilized for claiming linguistic rights. The use and indexing of minority languages in Web environments can have multiple outcomes and effects: what is used by the tourist provider to differentiate or authenticate their product can be a feel-good factor and attractive package for the tourist or consumer and may potentially be empowering for minority language speakers, leading either to an up-scaling of their linguistic resources or conversely a feeling of disenfranchisement. It may be all of these things at one and the same time. In Figure 19.1 we can see the example of the Dingle Skelligs Hotel, situated in the *Gaeltacht* area of Kerry in the West of Ireland. An Irish-language version of the site is offered alongside French, German, Italian, Russian, Spanish, Japanese and Chinese versions.

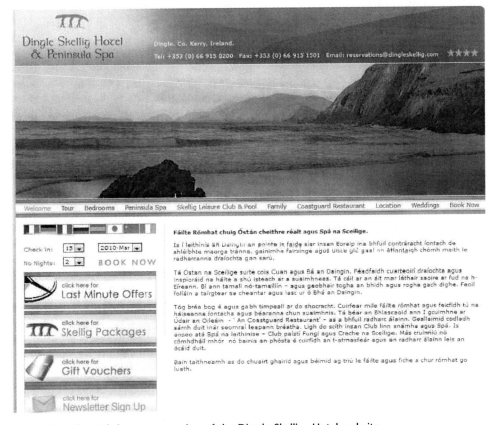

Figure 19.1 The Irish-language version of the Dingle Skelligs Hotel website.

For these reasons, new media contexts could be a potentially positive development for minority languages and linguistic diversity, in general, in terms of making documents and text available in those languages (cf. for example, Nicholls *et al.* 2005) A further claim made for the Web and digital technology goes beyond simply the provision of content in a variety of languages (which could be seen to support maintenance or even status aspirations) to predict an active role for new media in promoting revitalization. The potential of this role is highlighted by Kalish (2005: 182), who claims that 'questions asked by Tribal people who are engaged in revitalizing language and culture, and those that are asked by people who build various language technologies define the revitalization landscape'. However, Cunliffe and Herring (2005b) caution against an assumption that the mere presence of a minority language on the Web will automatically guarantee maintenance and revitalization (something that was previously claimed for traditional media, not only in terms of status (Fishman 1991) but also in terms of creating a media speech community to replace or supplement a 'face-to-face' speech community). As they point out, 'the actual effects of the Internet, and of computer technologies in general, on minority languages vary from situation to situation' (Cunliffe and Herring 2005b: 131). Furthermore, where language provision on the Web is driven primarily by top-down agents who are complying with language policy, rather than having a normalizing effect, the provision can reinforce existing norms and hierarchies (Kelly-Holmes 2006a). An important step forward, therefore, is to move beyond a situation whereby minority language speakers are simply consuming content made available in a minority language and using applications such as email, to developing bottom-up content that reflects the needs of minority language speakers and communities (cf. Cunliffe and Herring 2005a), summed up by Nicholls *et al.* (2005) as 'empowerment rather than gifting'.

Cunliffe and Herring (2005b: 131–2) also propose rethinking the digital divide not just in terms of those who have access to the Internet and new technologies, but also in terms of the divide between languages that are 'information rich' and languages that are 'information poor' with regard to online content and services'. Despite growing multilingualism and the conviction that the Internet is increasingly a space for other language communities (Block 2004: 23; cf. also Androutsopoulos 2007, 2006a; Danet and Herring 2007; Wright 2006, 2004; Cunliffe and Herring 2005a, 2005b), English has established itself as the language of science and technology (cf. Carli and Ammon 2008), and much World Wide Web housekeeping language takes place through English despite localization of content into other languages. Thus, even where a website is predominantly in a minority language, the housekeeping and legal aspects of the site may well be in the relevant majority language or in English, reinforcing in visual and paralinguistic terms, the marginal status of the particular language and its lack of global capital. Therefore, although it is still possible for the English speaker – and arguably also speakers of languages such as French and Spanish – to use the Web exhaustively in a monolingual way, for the speaker of a smaller language or even a big language that has limited Internet resources (e.g. Arabic), Internet use is predicated on being multilingual.

From the user point of view, multilingual use means many things. For example, individuals may use different languages for different purposes on the Web. For instance, university students in Kenya used Kiswahili for email correspondence with friends; however, the same students use English exclusively for consulting Internet content for general information or for their studies (Kelly-Holmes 2004). This shows how the Internet can reinforce existing diglossic situations, as sociolinguistic norms and language ideologies get transferred to a new medium. An additional dimension to multilingual Internet use is not just the idea of the multilingual individual using different languages to access different types of content and use the Internet in different ways, but also the provision of multilingual content, not just in terms of content being made available in multiple languages (parallel monolingualism), but also in mixed languages (heteroglossia) (cf. Androutsopoulos 2006a, 2006b; Wright 2006; Cunliffe and Herring 2005a; Danet and Herring 2003, 2007). The publishing norms of hard copy, which dictate generally that a text be in one language or another, do not necessarily apply in Internet publishing, particularly in bottom-up type applications such as blogs, chat rooms and social networking sites, and we are witnessing a huge wave of innovative and emergent heteroglossic practices in such forums, which involve not just mixing between languages but also between a range of semiotic resources (cf. Pietikäinen 2008a). Such heteroglossic and multimodal practices not only challenge existing norms, but also create new norms in terms not just of mixed language practices, but also in terms of combining language, paralanguage, visualities and genres, etc., and this too poses a challenge to prevailing language ideologies and new ways of thinking about and defining language.

Multilingualism in a media text and a mediatized text

In this final section, I would like to look at two linked examples of multilingual practices in contemporary media. One is at the *media* end of the textual continuum (an advertisement on an 'old' medium, namely television), and the other at the *mediatized* end (a discussion of the advertisement in a new media environment, namely the youtube.com website). In the television advertisement for Carlsberg lager, three young Irish men arrive in a bar in Rio de Janeiro, and are encouraged – perhaps even harassed – by their hosts (who speak English to them) to 'do something Irish'. After a brief consultation among themselves, one of the group begins to recite stock phrases and random words associated with school Irish ('May I go out to the toilet'; 'I like cake'; 'And a fox'), his friend telling the gathering that this is 'a poem in our native Irish tongue'. He then goes on to relate more meaningless phrases and words: the name of an attractive Irish-speaking female television presenter (Sharon Ní Bheoláin); 'I'm wearing a jumper'; 'There's a cloud in the sky'. In response to his passionate rendering of 'Give me the cake', the transfixed crowd repeat 'cake'. At this point, the Carlsberg 'voice' interjects with the current slogan 'It's not A or B, there's probably C', and switches to an image of a glass of the lager. Finally, we return to the bar to see that 'doing something Irish', in this case speaking Irish in this context, has made the young Irish man the most popular man in the Brazilian bar, and in the final shot he is pictured dancing with an attractive woman, who demands that he 'speak more Irish'. Now in full stride, his original hesitancy forgotten, he responds with the meaningless string of words 'quiet, road, girl, milk'. The following is a transcript of the advertisement (Irish text is highlighted in bold with explanations in parentheses and italics underneath):

IRISH MAN 1: Three Carlsberg please.
BARMAN: Sure. Where are you from?
IRISH MAN 2: Ireland
BARMAN: Ireland? Do something Irish.
THREE IRISH MEN: Like what?
MALE CUSTOMER: Do some Irish singing.
BARMAN: Exactly. What about the Irish dancing?
FEMALE CUSTOMER: Dance, or sing!
IRISH MAN 1: **An bhfuil cead agam dul amach go dtí an leithreas?**
 [May I go out {{}of the classroom{}}} to the toilet?]
IRISH MAN 2: A poem in our native Irish tongue.

IRISH MAN 1: **Agus mádra rua. Is maith liom cáca milis.**

[And a fox. I like cake.]

IRISH MAN 2: **Cáca milis**

[Cake.]

IRISH MAN 1: **Agus Sharon Ní Bheoláin. Tá geansaí orm. Tá scammail sa spéir. Tabhair dom an cáca milis.**

[And Sharon Ní Bheoláin. I'm wearing a jumper. There's a cloud in the sky. Give me the cake!]

TRANSFIXED CROWD: **Cáca milis!**

[Cake!]

MALE IRISH VOICE: It's not just A or B, there's probably C.

FEMALE CUSTOMER: Speak more Irish!

IRISH MAN 1: **Ciúnas, bóthar, cailín, bainne**

[Quiet, road, girl, milk]

This media text represents a highly controlled and planned genre, which in turn reflects minute attention to language choices and combinations – dictated by the cost of prime time television advertising. In official terms, Irish is, of course, the first official language in Ireland, with English being recognized as an additional language for use. However, as has been well documented (for an overview of the issues and the current sociolinguistic situation of Irish, cf. Ó Laoire (2005, 1995) and Mac Giolla Chríost (2005)), the reality of everyday usage is rather different. Irish is privileged in certain official domains, in particular the educational domain, through the operationalizing of an acquisition policy, which had its roots in the attempt by the newly independent state to make Ireland monolingually Irish-speaking. The policy has changed and adjusted over the decades since independence from the UK in the 1920s, and a monolingual Ireland is no longer an objective of the policy, with bilingualism favoured instead. However, the low level of fluency achieved by the majority of second language (L2) learners in schools, which is the primary means of achieving this bilingualism (along with regionally targeted support for first language (L1) speakers in *Gaeltacht* communities), is frequently the source of public debate and discussion. This low level of fluency is reflected in the young men's use of school Irish in the advertisement. The ad is bilingual, bilingualism here being interpreted as mixing Irish and English rather than parallel or strict bilingualism, which represent parallel monolingualisms reinforcing the territoriality principle. The use of the protagonists' limited school Irish in the context of an ad for a global brand, can be seen perhaps to legitimize, within this domain at least, their particular type of 'less than perfect' bilingualism.

This multilingual media text in turn prompted the creation of a second mediatized text. The advertisement was posted on the youtube.com video site and has to date attracted 107,200 viewings and 387 comments (available online at www.youtube.com/watch?v=DTNBmFveq2U, accessed on 8 May 2009). Perhaps encouraged by the protagonists in the advertisement and by the flexibility and freedom afforded by new media writing practices, contributors to the discussion have also tried out their 'imperfect' bilingualism, creating a linguistically hybrid site consisting of creative and idiolectal linguistic play, involving Irish and English, as the following examples highlight (translations appear in italics in parentheses below the particular terms):

(1) **Tír gan teanga, tír gan anam!**

[a country without a language is a country without a soul!]

In example 1, the poster has posted an Irish phrase into an otherwise predominantly English-language discussion, in response to a comment in English. The poster does not offer a translation of the phrase, which s/he assumes to be well known to the other posters.

(2) **Tar éis an fógra sin bainneann níos mó daoine trial as a chuid Gaeilge a labhairt!**
[This ad encourages people to use their Irish more]
Using **cúpla focail** in every day speech keeps the language alive.
       [a few words]

The poster in example 2 starts his/her post with a sentence in Irish, for which s/he does not offer a translation, and then continues in English, with a borrowing from Irish 'cúpla focail' or 'couple of words' used in the otherwise English-language sentence. The posts in general are characterized by a large degree of 'fluidity' in terms of language choices, mixing and standardization – with many different spellings being used for both English and Irish words. Overall, it is hard to classify the language of the entire conversation – it is neither fully Irish, nor fully English, but a mixture of both.

The language of the comments posted in response to the youtube.com video exemplify the phenomenon of mediatized texts, whereby texts can be created by individuals using their own linguistic norms, and without the intervention of a top-down agent of language policy. The freedom that mediatized texts afford, as well as the technology that makes them possible, fundamentally alters the relationship between multilingualism and media – multilingualism becomes a bottom-up rather than top-down phenomenon. Any individual (within the significant economic, education and geographical limits of access to digital media) can now create their own multilingual media.

Conclusion

Although new media seem to challenge diglossic media practices of previous eras, by breaking down the dichotomy between producer and consumer in media, and by a flowering of heteroglossic and idolectal practices in new media forums, many global media products still either enforce a one-language policy, generally English, or provide parallel monolingual channels (cf. Kelly-Holmes 2006b). So, although bottom-up media practices are growing, top-down policies do still dominate in many domains, and although there is greater control over the self-representation of speakers of various languages, there is still representation of speakers by others through media texts and speech acts (cf. Jaffe 2007). Furthermore, in many parts of the world, even national media have had to rely heavily on imported media products, and media products leak easily across designated 'linguistic borders', thus making the creation of homogenous speech communities more an aspiration than a reality in many cases. As the chapter shows, mediatization clearly seems to impact on multilingualism, but this is a reflexive relationship, and increasingly so. Multilingualism too impacts on media contexts, actors and speech communities that are constituted by media, and multilingual practices inevitably challenge the way in which media are constituted and perceived (cf. Androutsopoulos 2006a; Busch 2004; Leitner 1997; Boyd-Barrett *et al.* 1996). Media are a key site of multilingualism: a place where national and regional policies in relation to multilingualism are enacted, where speech communities are constituted, represented, fragmented and reconstituted, where the speech community experiences and learns about its multilingualism, and, increasingly too, a place where individuals and groups can create their own multilingualism.

Related topics

Multilingual citizenship and minority languages; multilingualism on the Internet; multilingualism and popular culture; multilingualism and multimodality; codeswitching; heteroglossia.

Further reading

Androutsopoulos, J. (2007) 'Bilingualism in the mass media and on the Internet', in M. Heller (ed.) *Bilingualism: A Social Approach*, Basingstoke and New York: Palgrave Macmillan.
(Provides an overview of research in the area of multilingualism and media.)

Cormack, M. and Hourigan, N. (eds) (2007) *Minority Language Media*, Clevedon: Multilingual Matters.
(Brings together case studies in and overview of the development of minority language media.)

Danet, B. and Herring, S. (eds) (2007) *The Multilingual Internet: Language, Culture, and Communication Online*, Oxford: Oxford University Press.
(Brings together the latest thinking on the area of new media and multilingualism.)

Johnson, S. A. and Ensslin, A. (2007b) 'Language in the media: Theory and practice', in S. A. Johnson and A. Ensslin (eds) *Language in the Media: Representations, Identities, Ideologies*, London and New York: Continuum.
(Provides an overview of how multilingualism is treated in the media.)

Kelly-Holmes, H. (2005) *Advertising as Multilingual Communication*, Basingstoke and New York: Palgrave Macmillan.
(Provides an overview of commercial multilingualism in the media.

Bibliography

Anderson, B. (1983) *Imagined Communities*, London: Verso.
Androutsopoulos, J. (ed.) (2006a) 'Sociolinguistics and computer-mediated communication', *Journal of Sociolinguistics* (special issue) 10(4).
——(2006b) 'Multilingualism, diaspora and the Internet: Codes and identities on German-based diaspora websites', *Journal of Sociolinguistics* 10(4): 524–51.
——(2007) 'Bilingualism in the mass media and on the Internet', in M. Heller (ed.) *Bilingualism: A Social Approach*, Basingstoke and New York: Palgrave Macmillan.
Bakhtin, M. M. (1981) *The Dialogic Imagination: Four Essays*, M. Holquist (ed.) C. Emerson, and M. Holquist (trans.), Austin: University of Texas Press.
Baron, N. S. (2008) *Always on: Language in an Online and Mobile World*, Oxford and New York: Oxford University Press.
Bell, A. (1984) 'Language style as audience design', *Language in Society* 13: 145–204.
Billig, M. (1995) *Banal Nationalism*, London: Sage.
Blackledge, A. J. (2006) 'The racialization of language in British political discourse', *Critical Discourse Studies* 3(1): 61–79.
Bishop, H. Coupland, N. and Garrett, P. (2005) 'Globalisation, advertising and shifting values for Welsh and Welshness: The case of Y Drych', *Multilingua* 24(4): 343–78.
Block, D. (2004) 'Globalization, transnational communication and the internet', *International Journal on Multicultural Societies* 6(1): 22–37.
Boyd-Barrett, O., Nootens, J. and Pugh, A. (1996) 'Multlingualism and the mass media', in H. Goebl, P. H. Nelde, Z. Starý and W. Wölck (eds) *Kontaktlinguistik*, Berlin and New York: Mouton de Gruyter.
Busch, B. (2004) *Sprachen im Disput. Medien und Oeffentlichkeit in Multilingualen Gesellschaften*, Klagenfurt: Drava.
Carli, A. and Ammon, A. (eds) (2008) 'Linguistic inequality in scientific communication today. What can future applied linguistics do to mitigate disadvantages for non-anglophones?' *AILA Review*, 20.
Cormack, M. and Hourigan, N. (eds) (2007) *Minority Language Media*, Clevedon: Multilingual Matters.
Cotter, C. (2001) 'Raidió na Life: Innovations in the use of media for language revitalisation', *International Journal of the Sociology of Language* 140: 136–47.
Coulmas, F. (2005) *Sociolinguistics: The Study of Speakers' Choices*, Cambridge: Cambridge University Press.
Crystal, D. (2001) *Language and the Internet*, Cambridge: Cambridge University Press.
Cunliffe, D. and Herring, S. (eds) (2005a) 'Minority languages, multimedia and the web, *New Review of Hypermedia and Multimedia* (special issue) 11(2).

——(2005b) 'Introduction to minority languages, multimedia and the web', *New Review of Hypermedia and Multimedia* 11(2).

Danet, B. and Herring, S. (eds) (2003) 'The multilingual internet', *Journal of Computer Mediated Communication* (special issue) 9(1).

——(2007) *The Multilingual Internet: Language, Culture, and Communication Online*, Oxford: Oxford University Press.

de Swaan, A. (2001) *Words of the World: The Global Language System*, Cambridge: Polity Press.

European Broadcasting Union (2007) *European Broadcasting Union*: Membership conditions, available online at: www.ebu.ch/en/ebu_members/admission/index.php

Fishman, J. (1991) *Reversing Language Shift*, Clevedon: Multilingual Matters.

Gee, Q. (2005) 'Review of script displays of African languages by current software', *New Review of Hypermedia and Multimedia* 11(2): 247–55.

Haarmann, H. (1989) *Symbolic Values of Foreign Language Use, From the Japanese Case to a General Sociolinguistic Perspective*, Berlin and New York: Mouton de Gruyter.

Heller, M. (1999) *Linguistic Minorities and Modernity: A Sociolinguistic Ethnography*. London: Longman.

——(2007) *Linguistic Minorities and Modernity: A Sociolinguistic Ethnography*, London and New York: Continuum.

Horner, K. (2007) 'Global challenges to nationalist ideologies. Language and education in the Luxembourg Press', in S. A. Johnson and A. Ensslin (eds) *Language in the Media: Representations, Identities, Ideologies*, London and New York: Continuum.

Hourigan, N. (2003) *Escaping the Global Village: Media, Language and Protest*, Lanham, MA: Lexington Books.

Jaffe, A. M. (2007) 'Corsican on the airwaves: Media discourse in a context of minority language shift', in S. A. Johnson and A. Ensslin (eds) (2007) *Language in the Media: Representations, Identities, Ideologies*, London and New York: Continuum.

——(2008) 'Sociolinguistic diversity in mainstream media: The construction of authenticity, legitimacy and expertise', paper presented at AILA, Essen, August.

Johnson, S. A. and Ensslin, A. (eds) (2007a) *Language in the Media: Representations, Identities, Ideologies*, London and New York: Continuum.

——(2007b) 'Language in the media: Theory and practice', in S. A. Johnson and A. Ensslin (eds) (2007a) *Language in the Media: Representations, Identities, Ideologies*, London and New York: Continuum.

Johnson, S.A. and Turner, W. (2008) 'Whose languages? Whose publics? Media representations of multilingualism on the "BBC Voices" website', paper presented at AILA, Essen, August.

Kalish, M. (2005) 'Immersion multimedia for adult Chiricahua language learners', *New Review of Hypermedia and Multimedia* 11(2): 181–203.

Kelly-Holmes, H. (ed.) (2001) *Minority Language Broadcasting: Breton and Irish*, Clevedon: Multilingual Matters.

——(2004) 'An analysis of the languages in students' repertoires and the languages they use on the Internet', *International Journal on Multicultural Society*, (special issue in co-operation with the B@bel Initiative, edited by Sue Wright) 6(4): 29–52.

——(2005) *Advertising as Multilingual Communication*, Basingstoke and New York: Palgrave Macmillan.

——(2006a) 'Irish on the World Wide Web: Searches and sites', *Journal of Language and Politics* 5(2): 217–38.

——(2006b) 'Multilingualism and commercial language practices on the Internet', *Journal of Sociolinguistics* 10(4): 507–20.

Leitner, G. (1997) 'The sociolinguistics of communication media', in F. Coulmas (ed.) *The Handbook of Sociolinguistics*, Oxford: Blackwell.

Mac Giolla Chríost, D. (2005) *The Irish Language in Ireland: From Goidel to Globalisation*, London: Routledge.

Mahootian, S. (2005) 'Linguistic change and social meaning: Codeswitching in the media', *International Journal of Bilingualism* 9(3–4): 361–75.

Martin, E. (2006) *Marketing Identities through Language: English and Global Imagery in French Advertising*, Basingstoke and New York: Palgrave Macmillan.

Menezes, C. (ed.) (2006) 'Languages of the Internet', *Journal of Language and Politics* (special issue) 5(2).

Perhaps the first widely documented reference to multilingualism in a religion is the biblical account of the Tower of Babel (Genesis 11: 7–9) when God intervened and terminated the heathenish tower project:

> Go to, let us go down, and there confound their language, that they may not understand one another's speech.
>
> So the Lord scattered them abroad from thence upon the face of all the earth, and they left off to build the city.
>
> Therefore is the name of it called Babel; because the Lord did there confound the language of all the earth; and from thence did the LORD scatter them abroad upon the face of all the earth.

The next example is also a biblically derived one. It is the account of the events of the Day of Pentecost, a Jewish festival:

> And ye shall receive power after the Holy Spirit has come upon you and you shall be witnesses unto me in all Judea and to the uttermost parts of the earth.
>
> *(Acts 1 v. 8)*

Implicit in this account is knowledge of language beyond local communicative needs and the capacity of the apostles to disseminate the gospel 'to the uttermost parts of the earth'.

Although religious practices were originally specific to individual cultures, missionaries and rituals crossed ethnolinguistic and ethnocultural boundaries as exemplified by Christianity – Protestantism and Catholicism – and the many sects of Islam. During the colonial era, Christian priests and missionaries went in large numbers to European colonies in Africa, Asia, South and Central America, taking with them their languages and imposing them on local populations as the language of worship. We now see the reversal of this process, on a much smaller scale, in missionary work that locates African priests in Europe's churches. However, this process has not mobilized African languages in a similar way. Nevertheless, the contemporary mobility of the clergy has facilitated the globalization of Outer Circle English accents complementary to the sociolinguistic consequence of African diasporic formation.[2] Previously non-mobile accents have now been granted mobility in the religious domain. In other words, a consequence is that hitherto marginal accents have acquired symbolic capital. The current Archbishop of York, Bishop John Setamu is perhaps the most visible representative of this category of clergy in the UK. Similarly, the reception of Pope Benedict XVI on papal tours in the USA and the UK suggest that accent marginality or better still Outer Circle and Expanding Circle Englishes may not correlate to degrees of acceptability in matters of reverence and divinity. It must be added though that in most instances the rough edges of difference may be smoothed down by globally mobile clergy to approximate or converge towards English as an International Language or English as a Lingua Franca.

In the era of globalization, media and digital evangelism have introduced a new mode of negotiating and crossing boundaries. The Christ Embassy Ministry, also called Believers Love World Ministries, is allegedly one of the fastest growing Pentecostal Evangelical Christian ministries with chapters spread around the world and web-based global television outreach at www.loveworldtv.com. On the back cover of their *Rhapsody of Realities* daily devotional, a monthly publication of the Ministry, the blurb claims that:

Several millions of copies of *Rhapsody of Realities*, the best-selling daily devotional and Bible study guide have been distributed in over a hundred and sixty countries in 145 languages of the world including Afrikaans, Arabic, Cantonese, Croatian, Dutch, English, Finnish, French, German, Hindi, Icelandic, Italian, Mandarin, Myanmar, Portuguese, Russian, Spanish ... Swahili and we're still counting. New languages are added regularly, making the devotional accessible to many more in different parts of the globe, bringing the richness of God's Word into their lives.

(LoveWorld Publishing, November 2011)

It is worth mentioning that this kind of religious literacy had been preceded by the work of the Summer Institute of Linguistics (SIL), which is credited not only with transforming many oral languages into written languages but also producing descriptive grammars for them. From a sociolinguistic perspective. However, SIL's incursion into rural Africa and Asia and Latin America is undoubtedly also associated with multilingualism in the sense that they were missionaries through whom European native languages were introduced into these new linguistic ecologies. Lamberty (2009) presented a survey of the sociolinguistic situation of Malimba in the Littoral Province of Cameroon conducted by SIL, which focused on language vitality and language attitudes.

Defining and counting languages and religions: issues and controversies

There are ongoing controversies over the enumeration of languages and over what qualifies as a language (see, for example, Makoni and Pennycook 2007). For instance, with reference to African languages, different scholars and publishers have differently tagged some dialects as languages and vice versa (Omoniyi 2004, 2006). The same controversy surrounds the definitions of religion and its distinction from faiths and spirituality. Resolving such controversies is not part of the remit for this chapter but it is worth mentioning as an indication of the existence of parallels in cultural processes of boundary marking.

According to Ethnologue, there are 6,909 languages in the world (Lewis 2010). Table 20.1 presents the distribution of the world's languages by continents. This shows that Asia and Africa have more languages than any of the other continents.

According to Adherents.com, an online database on religious information, there are 4,300 'faith groups' in the world. Twenty-two of these are described as 'major' religions based on the population of their adherents. The estimates for numbers of adherents on this database, and the languages involved, are as follows: Christianity (2.1 billion), Islam (1.5 billion), Hinduism

Table 20.1 Distribution of languages by continent of origin

Area	No. of languages		No. of speakers	
	Count	*%*	*Count*	*%*
Africa	2,110	30.5	726,453,403	12.2
Americas	993	14.4	50,496,321	0.8
Asia	2,322	33.6	3,622,771,264	60.8
Europe	234	3.4	1,553,360,941	26.1
Pacific	1,250	18.1	6,429,788	0.1
Totals	6,909	100.0	5,959,511,717	100.0

Source: Adapted from Ethnologue, 16th edn, M. Paul Lewis (ed.) Copyright © 2009, SIL International.

(900 million), Chinese Traditional Religions (394 million), Buddhism (376 million), African Traditional Religions (100 million), Sikhism (23 million), Judaism (14 million), Baha'i (7 million), Jainism (4.2 million), Shinto (4 million), Cao Dai (4 million), Zoroastrianism (2.6 million) and Rastafarianism (600,000). Some of these religions have had a proselytizing mission and have achieved global reach (e.g. Christianity and Islam). They have been historically centred on the use of one sacred language, e.g. Latin in Catholicism and Classical Arabic in Islam. However, patterns of language use actually diversified over time and space, as these religions spread out from Rome and from Mecca. Other religions have remained traditional and language-specific and language use in religious observance has remained largely monolingual. Take, for example, the case of Traditional African and Chinese Religions, or Shinto in Japan or Cao Dai in Vietnam.

National discourses about religion, along with the procedures and rationales for religious census-taking vary considerably. For example, the Indonesian Constitution only allows for five official religions: Islam, Hinduism, Buddhism, Protestantism and Catholicism. No allowance is made for traditional, animist practices. Citizens have to declare adherence to one of the five religions listed above. In the UK, there have been two religious censuses: one in 1851 and the second in 2001. The latter coincided with the turning point in the global politicization of religion following the September 11 debacle. In 2001 religious affiliations were divided into six very broad categories as follows: No Religion, Christian, Muslim, Hindu, Buddhist and Jewish. To my knowledge, there has not yet been any research into multilingualism among faith-workers from different religions, their transnational movements nor into their use of language in the local communities within which they work.

The relationship between multilingualism and religion

One of my core arguments in this chapter is that, in some multilingual contexts, it is not easy to discern the nature of the relationship between multilingualism and religion. However, there appear to be five broad trends: three of these are macro-historical trends involving different populations and social groups in different parts of the world; the other two are trends that can be observed at a local level – they are the consequences of macro-level processes – and are best viewed and researched from a micro-level perspective.

First, the spread of some religions (e.g. Catholicism and Protestantism) was historically linked to colonization. These religions were associated, from the outset, with languages that had considerable symbolic power (Bourdieu 1991) and that were associated with speakers who wielded considerable political and economic power e.g. Spanish, Portuguese and Dutch speakers in the sixteenth and seventeenth centuries, English and French speakers in the eighteenth and nineteenth centuries. The spread of these particular religions has given rise to specific localized religious phenomena and particular configurations of multilingualism, such as difaithia (Omoniyi 2006) and diglossia (Ferguson 1972, 1982; Fishman 1967). In some contexts, different 'high' languages have been imposed, leading to the creation of successive diglossic orders.

Second, those religions that have spread around the world have brought multilingualism in their wake. The spread of religion and the spread of multilingualism are interconnected cultural flows. Third, the creation of empires through colonization was accompanied by population movements, ranging from the forced movement of slaves and indentured labourers to the movement of people involved in commerce and trade. Linguistic, cultural and religious diversity became commonplace, particularly in key trading posts along global trade routes.

Fourth, because of the diverse nature of religious groupings in multilingual urban contexts, ritual practices in local sites of religious observance became increasingly multilingual in nature. The multilingual nature of religious practices continued into the post-colonial era and, with the increasing diversity of contemporary population flows, it has become even more evident. And, fifth, a close look at local ritual practices in particular sites of religious obser-vance reveals that language alternation across the different genres and activity types is quite commonplace, particularly in Christian congregations.

I will discuss each of these five trends in the sections below and I will draw on examples of research in different parts of the world.

Macro-historical and societal perspectives

Colonization, power asymmetries, 'endowed languages' and the spread of religions

Those religions that are associated with 'endowed languages' have had greater potential to assume transnational status than those associated with relatively weaker languages. By endowed languages, I am referring to those languages, which, in Bourdieuan discourse (Bourdieu 1991), have symbolic capital. Elsewhere, I have re-theorized this as language capital within the fra-mework of multilingualism and development in post-colonial societies (see Omoniyi 2003). Endowed languages, which are associated with the world's major religions, are unlikely to undergo language shift and death (Fishman 1991).

In many parts of the world, European colonialism was imposed 'through the Bible and the sword'. Take, for example, the close links between military conquest in South America, the spread of Catholicism and the imposition of Spanish in Peru and Portuguese in Brazil; or, the dissemination of Protestantism and the English language under British colonial rule in Africa; or the extension of Catholicism as part of the 'mission civilisatrice' under French colonial rule in Indo-China. The ideology underpinning the 'mission civilisatrice' was clearly articulated in the late nineteenth century by Bishop Depierre, the French bishop of Cochinchina in 1898, in the following terms:

> The precise honour of our country is to place intellectual, cultural and moral progress above any other preoccupations. Instead of exploiting its subjects and pressuring them to death as is still done in the Indies and to some extent throughout the Anglo-Saxon world, Frenchmen have always made it a point of honour to bring to the nations in which they establish themselves their ideas, their civilization and their faith.
>
> *(Osborne 1997: 42)*

Evangelism and missionary work reinforced the spread of particular religions within local colonial orders, particularly when there was an ideological commitment to translation of reli-gious texts into local languages. New writing systems were also introduced by priests and missionaries. The Roman alphabet was, for example, adapted to the writing of Vietnamese by Alexandre de Rhodes, a French missionary working in Vietnam in the early seventeenth century (Wright 2002: 22). In the same broad period in Brazil, the Jesuits were involved in developing a standardized written form of Tupi, the main contact language of the Amazonian region (Drumond Mendes Barros 2004). The twentieth century saw the intensification of missionary involvement in the development of writing systems and grammars for local languages, through the work of the Summer Institute for Linguistics.

A further element in the mix was the role of missionary schooling in colonial regimes e.g. in Africa and Asia. These schools generally served the needs of local elites, such as civil servants, working within the colonial system. The spread of Catholic and Protestant mission schools contributed to the creation of local situations of diglossia (Fishman 1967; Ferguson 1972). According to Ferguson (ibid.), diglossia means the delineation of low and high functions to languages based on association with religion and secular objectives. By extension, difaithia is the privileging of one religious faith or tradition over another in contexts where multiple faiths exist (Omoniyi 2006). One of the faiths is identified as the faith of the state and is thus accorded privileges over and above other faiths. Elsewhere, I have described the interaction between politico-religious change on the one hand and sociolinguistic change, on the other, as a movement from difaithia to diglossia (ibid.). In the relationship between Western European languages and the languages of those parts of the world with a colonial history, difaithia arguably preceded or actually occasioned diglossia.

During the period of European colonial rule in Africa and the ongoing missionary work, diglossic and difaithic orders sometimes shifted as a consequence of conflicts between European nation states. This is shown very clearly in this account below by Neba relating to the reconstruction of difaithia in the Cameroons and the introduction of a new diglossic order when French colonialism displaced German colonialism:

> First, the Catholic Church came to Cameroon in 1884 when the country became a German colony. The earliest German Catholic missionaries, the Pallotines, began their evangelisation work in the coastal region in 1890. They were followed by the German Sacred Heart Fathers, who entered the Grassfields in 1912 (Trudell, 2002: 9). German annexation of new land within Cameroon was halted by the First World War. In 1916, as Germany lost the war, its possessions were divided between France and Britain, with France taking some 4/5 of the territory. French Cameroon, which was governed directly from Paris, prescribed French as the only language to be used in all sectors of public life, including religion. German Catholic missionaries, who established missions such as the Marienberg Mission near Edea and the Shishong mission near Kumbo, had to leave the country. Their evangelising mission was to be continued by French priests, who came to replace them. In 1922, Monseigneur Francois-Xavier Vogt was appointed to be the first Catholic Bishop of Cameroon and, a few years later, the first local priests were ordained.
>
> *(1987: 141)*

Today, a contemporary difaithic order is in place in nations such as the UK where the Queen is both the head of the Church as well as the Head of State. Thus Islam, Sikhism, Hinduism and any other religions practised in England occupy a hierarchically lower rung on the status ladder. The status of Judaism in Israel and Islam in Saudi Arabia vis-à-vis other religions is the same as that portrayed above for Protestantism. Difaithia arose out of the colonial experience in Africa in which African Traditional Religions were constructed as 'paganism', serving idols rather than God.

The spread of multilingualism through religion

Here I shall deliberate on the capacity of religion to give rise to multilingualism. Take, for example, the case of Catholicism. This religion spread Latin through the liturgy and through devotional hymns. Both the spoken and written Latin formerly used in services around the world were modelled on the services organized in the Holy See in Rome. When Latin appeared in school books in Europe, it had liturgical literacy as a precursor. The point I want to make here is that some form of reduced multilingualism is an indication of the capacity that religion has to

Multilingualism in local religious practice.

Religion as a site of multilingual ritual practice

One of the hallmarks of Christian religious practice in post-colonial multilingual urban contexts is the provision for 'instantaneous translation'. There are three models: Model One has one dominant ethnic population with small numbers of other ethnic groups and as a result the primary language of liturgy is the language of the majority group with translation into the former colonial language. In Model Two, the cosmopolitan composition of the congregation is more obvious and acknowledged, with the former colonial language as the language of the liturgy and translation into the languages of the immediate community (Bamgbose 1991). In Model Three, churches run two or three language-specific services. Prime Time, whatever that may be, is occupied by the language service in the former colonial language. The other language services are scheduled before or after the main service.

Kouega (2008) reports on a study of the languages used during the Catholic mass. This study was carried out in the region of Cameroon where French is widely spoken, in one of the most multilingual countries in Africa. The study documented patterns of language use across different parts of the services in 60 churches: during the reading of the missal and the gospel and during sermons. This study shows Model Two in action:

> The analysis showed that while French and English, the country's joint official languages and Beti and Bassa two minority languages spoken in the Centre province of Cameroon are liturgical languages i.e. used for the Gospel, sermons etc, the other minority languages spoken by the inhabitants of the capital city are used mainly for singing and occasionally for epistle reading. Interestingly, the choice of these minority languages is determined by various nonsociolinguistic factors including the degree of their speakers' involvement in church issues.
>
> *(Kouega 2008: 140)*

Micro-perspectives on ritual practice: language alternation across different genres and activity types

Religion and religious practice is not monolithic in nature. In fact, what seems to be common is that there are several discernible aspects of religious practice. They may be observed and patterns of language use can be documented. Woods (2004: 148) identified liturgy, music, prayer, the Bible, and sermons as aspects of ritual practice. Based on her Melbourne study of ethnic churches, she posits that liturgies in such churches are often, although not exclusively, in the local community languages. Liturgies are modelled on or influenced by those used in the home countries, in the form of official or home-made translations. Decisions about language use are made either on the basis of principles such as 'that which is most easily understood by the congregation' or 'that which upholds the continuity of church tradition' irrespective of whether the congregation understands it or not.

Woods (2004) did record several instances of services being conducted predominantly in English with praise and worship choruses including songs from a variety of languages. The songs were not necessarily religious in origin. The practice of appropriating popular songs for religious worship by changing the lyrics to reflect Christian themes is a global phenomenon. Woods reported similar appropriation of popular Persian love songs (2004: 149). Appropriation in the opposite direction, i.e. from the sacred to the secular also takes place and this kind of appropriation occurs across languages.

In the 'Praise and Worship' component of services in evangelical churches it is not uncommon to observe the use of choruses from a variety of languages especially in urban multilingual environments. For instance, the chorus below, which is regularly sung in Evangelical church services and in Christian social gatherings like weddings and christenings in Nigeria has been released on commercial tapes and CD:

A ga m aja ya mma
Si n'ebiyebi, ebiyebi rue n'ebiyebi
A ga m aja ya mma
Si n'ebiyebi, ebiyebi rue n'ebiyebi

Ma yin Oluwa fun titi lailai,
Titi lailai, fun titi lailai
Ma yin Oluwa o fun titi lailai
Titi lailai fun titi lailai

We shall praise him from everlasting
Everlasting to everlasting
We shall praise him from everlasting
Everlasting to everlasting

Here, we have a trilingual rendering verse by verse in Igbo, Yoruba and English. Choruses may be perceived as an area of the ritual that facilitates the inclusion of local languages. Among diasporic congregations, the switch may be between transnational songs, that is, songs deriving from an ethnic group in one nation being co-sung by congregants who have a different homeland from that of the song source.

The illustrations (a) to (c) below, drawn from a variety of regions in Nigeria present an overview on how multilingualism actually works in religious practice. Following Bell (1984), I am presuming that, in the production of religious texts, the producers have particular audiences in mind and will therefore tailor the text bearing in mind the communicative characteristics and capacities of their audience.

(a) Redeem Christian Church of God, Obadore, Lagos
   - English sermons
   - Yoruba/Hausa/Igbo/Ijaw for prayer points and choruses
(b) Daystar Christian Centre, Ikosi Road, Ikeja
   - English sermons
   - Yoruba and Igbo for praise and worship
(c) Chapel of the Resurrection, University of Ibadan
   - Morning services entirely in English; [two services] except for songs and praise worship which are largely in Yoruba, Igbo and English.
   - Yoruba service in the evening
   - Igbo and Yoruba Bible classes in the evening – one hour sessions.

As I have shown thus far, the practice of multiple language use in the enactment of a religious ritual extends across religions. However, there are settings where there is a mismatch between the linguistic repertoires of religious leaders and different generations within a congregation. Writing on liturgical literacy among British Muslim communities of South Asian extraction in the West Midlands, Rosowsky notes that the 'language of the liturgy is often different from that spoken by the congregation' (2008: 78). In this Midlands setting, it is Classical Arabic that is being used for religious observance and Urdu, the national language of Pakistan, is being used in Quranic classes. Parents from the British Midlands community where Rosowsky carried out his study were concerned about 'the lack of use of English' (ibid.). The Imams have limited English and the children have limited Urdu but the Imams conduct their teaching of the Quran in Urdu. There is a disjuncture between the older generation clerics who are competent in Urdu and the younger generation pupils who are competent in English. Transmission of Urdu, Classical Arabic and the Islamic faith are seen as being under threat and are therefore a cause for concern, as shown in the excerpts below:

Discussion with British Muslim parents in the West Midlands

One of the parents, Aktar, responds to the prompt: 'So the speech is in Urdu not Punjabi?'

AKHTAR: The biggest gripe I have with them is that they won't preach in English …
RESEARCHER: Is it because of the language?
WAJIB: Yes, because of the language as well. Because most of the kids, they are very fluent in English and were born here and most of the kids speak English and some of them have difficulty understanding Mirpuri[3] or Urdu. Even Urdu. Mainly Urdu they have difficulty understanding it. I mean if they don't understand it how are they going to learn? So what I have been suggesting is that the teachers can't communicate well with kids and they can't get the message across. This is why we're falling behind.
MUNIR: I think myself, if children go to the mosque, they should read in Arabic and also in English as well. They should understand what the meaning of this word is. I mean, if they are reading that, and they don't understand, don't know what is the meaning of this, they are just wasting time. We want proper teachers. Qualified teachers, who can teach these children born in this country.

(2008: 79)

The last piece of research that I draw on here was based in Finland, in a Russian Orthodox cathedral. American anthropologist, Jim Wilce, whose current scholarship is focused on 'lament' as a ritual practice in Helsinki, Finland, shared with me an experience he had when attending a multidenominational service on the eve of Easter Day at the Uspenski Cathedral.[4] He recorded in his field diary the incidence of multilingualism in the religious rituals he observed. These rituals involved the use of up to ten different languages and language varieties, including Finnish, Swedish, Russian, Karelian and English, reflecting the diverse nature of the congregation.

There were perhaps a dozen priests moving in and out of the inner sanctum, together with altar boys (no girls as I remember). The boys circulated through the church late in the service taking up an offering. The choir was beautiful—and what endurance, singing for almost the whole four hours of the service. There was beautiful musical dialogue between solo priests and the choir. Noteworthy too is that the choir sung almost no contrapuntal music at all, i.e. only block chords. A youngish priest seemed to relish calling out *'Kristus nousi [kuolleista]*!' (Christ rose from the dead) and evoking responses of *'Totisesti nousi!'* (Verily he rose!). This was striking during the minutes we were outside, circumambulating the church in the not-too-cold (perhaps just above freezing) early spring temperature that is apparently very unusual for Easter here. The choirmaster was there too. In some inside as well as outside moments he turned from the choir to conduct the congregation singing *'Kristus nousi kuolleista, kuolemallaan kuoleman voitti ja haudoissa oleville elämän antoi'* (Christ rose from the dead, by his dying defeated death and gave life to those in the grave). I first noticed English outdoors. Ensio told me the singing indoors [he was not able to walk outside because of his legs] was in Finnish, Swedish, Russian … but at times far more languages than those. Very late in the service, with much devotional attention to a huge 'book' representing John's gospel, passages about the incarnation of the Christ were read by the priests in about ten languages, one of which was Karelian, said Ensio (I had thought it an odd mix of Russian and Finnish).

(Jim Wilce, field diary entry, 30 May, 2010)

The Uspenski is the largest Orthodox Cathedral in Western Europe with a congregation that runs into the thousands. Figures 20.2 and 20.3 are images of the Cathedral and a copy of the schedule of serices, respecitvely rendered in Swedish, English and Russian. Linguistic landscapes enthusiasts might read into the order of presentation of the languages on the list a reflection of ongoing linguistic reconfiguration and rehierarchization in Europe, especially those areas that had been previously under Russian influence, including in the domain of religion.

Because of the cosmopolitan nature of the congregation in this Russian Orthodox Church in Finland, language practice in religious rituals has become remarkably multilingual in nature. This led me to wonder about developments in Orthodox churches in areas of the former Soviet Union, particularly in the Baltic States. To what extent has the Russian Ortho-dox Church been able to sustain the use of Russian both inside and outside the Church in the newly independent states? Can new national and official languages in those countries, such as Estonian, Latvian and Lithuanian, which feed a sense of pride among their diaspora populations, also threaten Russian internally within the Church?

Future research directions

Future work in multilingualism and religion as a theme of scholarship may be approached from two perspectives, theoretical and methodological. First, different languages and religions have been treated in these discussions as neat categories but there are varying degrees of mixing or hybridity (Bhabha 1994) in actual language use and in religious or faith practices. Zuckermann (2009: 41) discusses hybridity in the context of the language he calls 'Israeli'. He notes that, 'whereas most forms of Israeli are Semitic, many of its patterns are European'.[5] How widespread hybridization is as a phenomenon and which languages and religions are involved are yet to be systematically studied. Thus they constitute a possible focus for researchers in the future.

Second, syncretism is represented as a recently developing world phenomenon (see Omoniyi 2006; Haynes 1996) but the biblical details of the Israelites' 40 years in the wilderness contains several exemplifications of this, albeit without information on the language dimen-sions of those wanderings. It would be interesting to explore the potential for syncretism to be globalized through the same valves through which transcultural flows occur. Is the formation or expansion of diasporas of populations associated with faith mixing a natural context for the spread of syncretism? The term has also been associated with Creole studies in linguistics in the description of contact phenomena of various forms of language mixing.

Finally, let us consider possible directions in the methodology of multilingualism and reli-gion scholarship. The investigation of hybridity can be carried out by looking at corpora within the framework of corpus linguistics or historical sociolinguistics. When a dialect or accent acquires symbolic capital like those of non-native English-speaking immigrant clergy, they become prime subjects for ethnographic exploration. For instance, some African pastors

Alexandre Duchêne and Ingrid Piller) on multilingual practices in the Swiss tourism industry, and on research funded by the Social Science and Humanities Research Council of Canada, conducted by Monica Heller and collaborators.

Language choice and the targeted market

Examining language choice in relation to globalization of the market requires locating the language used to sell a product, a place or a service. Language choice does not occur in a vacuum; it is a highly strategic choice that is contingent upon the desire to target a specific market. Our aim in this chapter is to examine the way language choice is part of the implicit and explicit internationalization process of businesses in the new economy. Within the Swiss project mentioned above, the research team has concluded conducting an ethnography of an institution in charge of marketing Switzerland nationally and internationally. During fieldwork we encountered the key issue of which languages tourism brochures should be translated into. Various considerations came into play when the organization had to make these decisions.

Because marketing materials should be useful for Swiss tourists, translation into German, French and Italian (the three major national languages) was a must, and, as these three languages are also languages of foreign countries (Belgium, Canada and France for French; Germany and Austria for German; Italy for Italian), these translations also served to internationalize the product. English was chosen as a de facto language for all English-speaking countries, as well as for all other language groups for which no translation into local languages was undertaken.

Beside the four languages mentioned, the agency considered further translation in relation to two central criteria. Statistics were examined to determine both the number of tourists coming to Switzerland and their national origin. In addition, the number of Internet hits from various countries was counted. Both criteria were decisive with respect to translating the website and with respect to the amount of money and time that would be invested in providing information in other languages. This was, for instance, the case with regard to Spanish: the translation of a city tourist brochure was decided on due to the dramatic increase of Spanish (from Spain) tourists to Switzerland as a result of low-cost air transport. Similarly, the number of Russians travelling to Switzerland increased, but not by as much as in the case of Spanish tourists. As a consequence, it was decided to only partially translate the aforementioned brochure into Russian (see Duchêne and Piller 2011).

Numbers were, however, not the only criteria. The National Tourism Board was very much interested in diversifying its targeted countries and in actively stimulating the growth of potential markets. This was particularly the case with Poland, and developing the Polish market formed the general strategy for a year in the National Tourism Board. As a result, many products were translated into Polish and a local office was created. A final criterion taken into consideration for language was the product itself. City brochures, for instance, were not translated into Dutch because Dutch tourists have been found to be less interested in city tourism. However, the hiking brochure was translated into Dutch because the residents of this country were considered to have an active interest in these particular areas.

If multilingualism and language choices increasingly become an object of attention in the marketing process in the new economy, locating the appropriate varieties of language will also be carefully considered. In the case of the brochure mentioned earlier, our fieldwork illustrated the particular concern with the correct language variety. This was particularly the case for French (Swiss-French variety or France-French variety) and Spanish (Spain-Spanish variety or

Latin-American variety). A representative of the Swiss National Tourism Board located in Barcelona but who had previously been posted in Paris mentions this struggle:

DIR: nous on a par exemple le problème que certains traducteurs en Suisse seront plutôt de souche erm sud américaine et l'espagnol le castillan en Espagne n'est pas tout à fait pareil, donc il y des nuances, c'est comme entre un français et un suisse
AD: uhmhu
DIR: à la limite, même si ces nuances sont faibles, on a le même problème. donc y faut vraiment quelqu'un ici qui qui est ici quoi, qui fasse ces textes ouais

Translation

DIR: We have, for example, the problem that some translators in Switzerland would be more of a Latin American background and Castilian Spanish in Spain is not really the same, so there is a nuance, it's like between a French and a Swiss
AD: mmm …
DIR: at the end of the day, even if these nuances are weak, we have the same problem, so we have to have someone here who does these texts, yes

DIR (the interviewee) presents a well-known discourse that has existed for decades on the relationship between language and culture. It also highlights the struggle over the legitimacy of language varieties. The concern with the quality of language in localization and internationalization processes also collides with concerns about efficiency. Indeed, multiple translations of the same brochure in multiple varieties of the same language were not an issue. This would clearly have gone too far. Therefore, the identification of the appropriate varieties was mainly made on the basis of the perceived market. For French, all translations were sent to France and were corrected by the Paris office. For Spanish, the translations were done in Spain. Implicitly, this language choice recreates and reproduces language hierarchies, and it was the market that defined the correct varieties. This was particularly true for written documents and for some languages. German or English were, however, not the object of this specific concern – and in a Swiss-based tourism call centre a local Swiss German accent was seen as an asset (Duchêne 2009a).

These various examples show how the market becomes multilingual due to strategic decisions based on 'rational' economic choices. Language contributes to successfully entering a market. However, besides the instrumental role language plays in internationalization, it also acquires a symbolic importance in providing products and goods to be sold with an added value in terms of authenticity, exoticism or 'uniqueness'. This aspect of the multilingual market is the focus of the next section.

Niche marketing: multilingualism, authenticity and commodity

Nowadays products, goods, ideas and services compete in the globalized market. The competition concerns the prices of products and services as well as product uniqueness and its local character. With regard to the second aspect, authenticity becomes one of the main selling points in the global network in that it creates a niche market. And language plays a central role in creating an air of authenticity. Discourse is one medium with which authenticity is produced and created (Coupland *et al.* 2005). In many tourist areas, an air of authenticity is achieved by quoting historical 'facts'. Artefacts, for example, are discursively marketed as authentic goods. Yet, there is also the fact that languages (usually local varieties) intervene as a central selling tool in light of a specific product. In their analysis of Chinatown's linguistic landscape in Washington DC, Leemann and Modan (2009) highlight the role the use of Chinese plays in displaying commercial ethnic identity as a commodity.

This is particularly true with regard to promoting and marketing local products. In the Canadian research project mentioned earlier, particular attention was paid to the circulation of Canadian artefacts and products between Canada and Europe. In 2006, a city located in the east of France nominated Canada as the guest country at their Marché de Noël (Christmas Fair). The market was 'decorated' in a presumably Canadian fashion – including penguins! Various stands proffered so-called typical Canadian products, such as maple syrup and buffalo meat. One of the stands sold Canadian soap made of goats' milk. The interview conducted[1] with one of the employees at this stand offers an insight into the role language plays as a means of authenticating a commodity and – very pragmatically – as a way of attracting clients:

MD: les magasins comme les grandes surfaces ont déjà ça c'est on n'aurait pas envie déjà de faire ça dedans parce qu'une grande surface c'est une grande surface c'est impersonnel c'est un c'est pas l'étagère qui va vous expliquer en quoi ils font les savons et nous on cherche quand même le contact euh le contact humain et euh surtout en France parce que les Français adorent le Québec et adorent nous entendre parler québécois et euh la plupart des gens qui qui viennent à mon stand ils viennent d'abord pour écouter mon accent pis moi j'arrive doucement à les diriger vers euh vers mes savons et à leur parler de ça et euh ils voient bien que je suis quelqu'un de de passionnée [...]

Translation

MD: shops like supermarkets have already it is we wouldn't like to do it inside it because a supermarket is a supermarket, it is impersonal, it is a it isn't the shelf that will explain what the soaps are made of and we are still looking for the contact, er, the human contact and, er, in France because the French adore Quebec and adore to hear us speak Québecois and, er, most of the people who who come to our stand, they come first to listen to my accent and I slowly succeed in directing them to my soaps and to talk about that and, er, they see that I'm passionate [...]

Interestingly enough, MD only lived in Quebec at an early age. She moved to France with her mother at the age of 3. However, during the whole interview she spoke with some kind of French-Canadian accent, as she did – in a more accentuated way – at her stand. How MD thinks of her accent is definitely linked to a marketing strategy associated with the idea that a product is 'special' because it is made in Canada. The geographic origin of a product is a competitive factor, but, at the same time, its authenticity and exoticism need to be accentuated. Thus, the seller's accent takes on new significance. It serves as an attraction (people first come to the stand because of her accent!) and confers a special touch to the product, and – with it – an added value.

In this specific case, local language varieties function as an instrument for selling products, but in some cases it is the multilingualism of a place itself that confers its uniqueness. This is what we have observed when considering marketing tools in Swiss tourism. The official multilingualism of Switzerland is often an object of attention and an object of discourse when Swiss tourism providers develop their marketing strategy. Indeed, in our data, Swiss multilingualism has emerged recurrently as a selling point in promotional tourism campaigns for Switzerland. To be exact, multilingualism is regarded as a Swiss particularity that enables and enhances the construction of Switzerland as a 'special' place. A representative of the National Tourism Board located in Toronto mentioned this aspect during an interview with Alexandre

A. Duchêne and M. Heller

Duchêne (AD). In the following excerpt she enumerates the various characteristics that make Switzerland attractive to Canadians:

RTO: yeah, it's erm Switzerland is attractive, it's erm a lot of different experience on a very small area you know compared to Canada
AD: mmm ...
RTO: then ah the four languages, the different food, the accessibility of our mountains like the Canadians have a lot of nature but you really have to walk to access it, in Switzerland even an elderly person or somebody who's handicapped can go up to the Jungfraujoch or something like that so I believe as the population is even aging, like Switzerland is actually even more attractive down the road. Ah ... they like the history ah they find us very friendly unlike the Swiss who always feel you know

This inventory underlines prototypical marketing arguments that can widely be found in promotional materials (the diversity, the four languages, the food, the nature, the history, the organization, etc.). Multilingualism is part of the uniqueness of Switzerland and constitutes part of its attractiveness. However, RTO points to another element regarding multilingualism that well illustrates some of the tensions regarding this marketing argument.

RTO: because it's-you can experience so much diversity in a very small ah area
AD: mmm ...
RTO: you know and then everybody speaks English so I mean they say oh I've been to the French speaking the Italian speaking part but everybody spoke English anyway, but they still see and feel that it's something different. It's always compared with the gro-with this big country where you have to go very far to see something very different you know

As RTO states, national multilingualism, on the one hand, is considered as an element of exoticism, making Switzerland attractive. On the other hand, multilingualism can be seen as problematic if English is not among the national languages. In order to gauge the risks of the negative component of multilingualism, RTO points out the fact that tourists are amazed that Swiss people have mastered the English language, thus allowing tourists to experience exoticism without getting lost. For RTO, although people in every region of Switzerland speak English, the cultural distinctions are not erased. Cultural exoticism is maintained. Of course this example cannot be generalized to all multilingual countries. Analyses of national marketing materials show a rather contrastive picture of the use of multilingualism as a strategic argument. Gaelic in Scotland, languages of the Incas in Peru or Singlish in Singapore, for instance, are similar examples of some kind of exotic features that serves the construction of place as unique. In other cases, like India for instance, languages are practically absent from the general narratives in tourism brochures. On the other hand, the linguistic diversity argument might also be associated with a particular group of tourists and might be considered as irrelevant to other groups. Further research on these issues definitely needs to be done. However, what seems to be clear is that linguistic diversity – if it appears as marketing arguments – is constantly linked to cultural diversity and constructed as a harmonious and conflict-free phenomenon.

We have argued that the new economy offers us a window through which we can better understand the role languages play in a global market. We have demonstrated that the linguistic market is not homogeneous in terms of language. The market is in fact multilingual. Language choice operates on the ground of strategic decisions based on the audiences that a business group in the new economy wishes to reach. Furthermore, we have shown that local language varieties as well as national multilingualism can serve as a distinctive marketing tool to construct the authenticity and uniqueness of a product or a place. We believe these findings encourage a sustained examination of the role multilingualism plays in transnational processes relevant to the new economy, processes that promote understanding and explaining language hierarchies and values associated with a particular language. Interestingly enough, despite the increase of multilingual practices, we still find ideologies that arose in the modern age. Languages – as well as products and goods – are still very much linked to nations and territories. However, their values are more dependent on local and global economic interests that are not stable, but rather constantly changing in deference to strategic market expansion.

These considerations lead us to another central issue. All the processes described earlier are predicated upon labour processes. Be it the translation and the drafting of texts (see also Pym 2004), the interaction with the client in his/her language, or the sale of authentic products, all are mainly linguistic activities. In our view, when examining the role of the new economy we must grasp how multilingualism becomes a particular instrument of work and how business in the new economy manages this intrinsic linguistic diversity. In doing so we would like to pay specific attention to the agents who make multilingualism possible, to those who produce these linguistic resources.

The 'new' management of multilingual resources

The inter-relationship between labour structure and language practices was the centre of interest for a group of researchers in France in the late 1980s. The Réseau Langage et Travail was a pioneer in this area in that they interrogated the role of language in traditional industrial workplaces from a critical perspective, but also in that they examined the shifting character of labour guidelines with regard to economic and social transformations at the workplace within the new economy. In the following we would like to highlight some of the central arguments produced by this group of researchers and add further considerations on the same issue from the standpoint of the English-language tradition.

Boutet (2008) analyses documents on work regulations from various factories, shops and mills at the end of the nineteenth century. She observes that many workplaces formulated various kinds of legal injunctions in written form and directed them at the worker who was to be regulated and controlled. Within these regulations, language appears systematically in the sense of an injunction to keep quiet.

Article 6, L'ordre et le plus grand silence doivent toujours régner dans les ateliers. Il est strictement défendu, sous peine d'amende, de chanter, lire, coudre et de s'occuper de tout autre chose que du travail qui a été confié à l'ouvrier (Filature de Lille 1866).

Translation
Order and complete silence should always reign in the workshops. It is strictly forbidden to sing, read, sew or otherwise attend to anything other than the work assigned.

(Boutet 2008: 29)

ART.15 Il est défendu aux ouvriers d'abandonner leur travail pour causer avec leurs camarades, ainsi que de chanter ou de siffler sous peine d'une amende de 50 centimes (Ateliers Charles Fiechter, Mulhouse 1866).

Translation
ART.15 Workers are forbidden to leave their work to talk with others, or to sing or whistle, subject to a fine of 50 centimes.

(ibid.)

Through these two examples we can see that language becomes at times part of the regulations of the workplace. In addition, language is clearly considered to be an obstacle to productivity as well as to the welfare of the employees. This view of work is derived directly from the highly influential work of Taylor, published in 1911, in which the key principles of work management were expounded on and largely adopted in the industrial sector. According to Taylor, the main goal was to achieve maximal efficiency in the production chain by means of segmentation, constantly controlling time needed for work, as well as strict and 'objective' (based on scientific calculation) management of the activities of the worker. In this theory of work, speaking was seen as a waste of time, a loss of productivity and, as a consequence, as Boutet states in the following excerpt, an illegitimate practice:

Taylor s'inscrit ainsi dans la conception que la Révolution industrielle a instaurée d'une parole ouvrière inutile et dénuée de pertinence: il a généralisé, rationalisé cette conception et lui a donné un support scientifique et non plus strictement disciplinaire, moral et coercitif. La parole ouvrière, ou salariée plus généralement, voit son illégitimité et son improductivité, clairement raisonnées.

Translation
Taylor subscribes to the idea originating in the Industrial Revolution that speaking among the workers is fruitless and without relevance: he generalized, rationalized this idea and gave it a scientific basis and not only a strictly disciplinary, moral and coercive one. Speaking among workers or among employees in general, sees its illegitimacy and unproductivity scientifically demonstrated.

(Boutet 2008: 69)

The general history of industrialization and its link to the emergence of capitalism is mirrored by regulatory measures for work processes in which language is clearly identified as both an object of regulation and an unprofitable resource at the workplace.

Within the new economy, the role of language has changed. In predominant sectors of the new economy (like the service industry), speaking is no longer forbidden at the workplace; on the contrary, it has become one of the most important tools. The new economy embraces language in the sense that language is informational and technological, and that commercial components are contingent on language (Gee *et al.* 1996). The previous section demonstrated that the globalized market employs multilingual practices involving language work. As a matter of fact, in various sectors of the economy the prohibition of speech has transformed into an invitation to speak. This represents a clear discrepancy between the old and the new economy. However, we do agree with Cameron (2000a), Boutet (2001, 2008) and Heller (2003, 2005) that this disparity in terms of what counts as a production resource (hand vs speech) also represents a continuity. In fact, within the new economy, the Taylorist approach, in terms of rationalization of labour and worker management, seems to be maintained.

This is particularly the case with regard to what we shall call the globalized industrialization of services, in such forms as call centres, localization and translation companies or domestic work. In these three exemplary sectors of the new economy, language is subject to heavy regulatory processes. Scripts, language and communication training, as well as regular control of the quality and time of commercial interactions, characterize work regulations at call centres

(Cameron 2000a, 2000b; Boutet 2008; Cowie 2007; Duchêne 2009a). The speed of translation and its automation emerge as a key issue in localization companies (Cronin 2003; Venuti 1992). Teaching appropriate communication and cultural skills, and testing language skills – as part of what Lorente (2010) calls the 'script of servitude' – is legion in the domestic worker industry. Productivity here is the number of phone calls answered, the number of successful transactions fulfilled, the number of words translated or the number of seconds needed to understand instructions. Taylorization looms and control over (linguistic) production operates within the strict dictates of rationalization and profitability.

These three areas also involve major economic issues in terms of managing multilingualism and, more precisely, the workforce: where can cost-efficient workers be found? In call centres, different answers were given: outsourcing to India (Sonntag 2006) or the Philippines (Friginal 2007) for English; to Senegal and Morocco for French, where workers have English or French language skills as part of their inheritance from colonialism and where labour is cheap; the location of call centres in poor bi- or multilingual areas such as in the Maritimes in Canada (Dubois *et al.* 2006) where the call centres provide services for Canada, including franco-phone Quebec, and the US, or in Biel/Bienne, a bilingual industrial city in Switzerland for the Swiss national market; the 'importation' of specific migrant workers for specific languages, for example, call centres in Ireland that advertise positions for call centres jobs at immigration facilities; finally, the positioning of multilingual call centres in big cities where a pool of multilingual yet low-qualified employees is available, for instance, in Zurich (Duchêne 2009a) or in Montreal (Roy 2003).

Similar questions arise in the case of localization companies: should a translation be outsourced to workers living in the country where the product will be used or should native speakers located in the country where the product is produced perform the translation? Both choices are contingent on cost-efficiency issues – it might be cheaper to employ workers in the target country, depending on the cost of local labour; however, they might have less training. The decision also hinges on the importance given to cultural adaptation – translators in the country where the product originates might be more familiar with the product, whereas local translators might be more aware of local 'culture' and thus more able to use appropriate language to describe the product.

In the case of domestic workers, the labour pool is also an issue (Lan 2003). Importing nannies from the Philippines, Latin America or from Africa as cheap labour is a booming business. Their language skills (English, Spanish and French) lend them an added value. Either the employers choose to hire someone who speaks the family language, or they decide to hire a nanny who can 'teach' their children another language, preferably a highly valorized one. Language skills and cheap labour accentuate the benefits on the part of the customer (Piller and Pavlenko 2009; Piller and Takahashi 2010).

This strategic decision making clearly indicates the status multilingual workers have in the organization of work itself. In these examples, language practices are highly standardized and controlled. Workers' multilingualism also contributes to managerial decisions in terms of geographic location, that is in turn linked to the cost of the workforce and their linguistic skills. Managing language and workers explicitly places attention and action on the language of workers and can be considered as a neo-liberal institutionalization of multilingual practices.

This is actually feasible if the market is predictable and can be clearly targeted. However, this is not always the case. Not all languages of the world can be industrialized in the manner described earlier; however, with an increased circulation of people, an increased number of languages circulate as well, thus inducing situations in which a wide range of languages might become important to fulfil work duties. In the travel industry, for instance, it is not unusual that passengers or hotel clients do not possess the language skills that were identified by businesses as the central ones. Problematic situations can occur involving language, for instance, a Mandarin-speaking passenger with no language skills in either French, English and German holding an invalid ticket at the airport in Zurich. In this case, the explicit management and regulation of target languages is of no help; for employees of the transit area in Zurich, English, German and French are the target languages regulated by evaluation processes at the recruitment stage.

However – and this is another way of managing multilingual resources – this problem could be solved by exploiting the existing multilingual repertoire of the workers, who are generally migrants working in marginalized places at the institutions, for instance the baggage worker or the cleaning woman. In this case, the management relies on a reduced inventory of people who happen to speak some kind of 'exotic' languages. At the airport, a long list is available online with all languages spoken by employees, who can then be called in to help. This list constitutes the key tool for managing unpredictable multilingual needs. There is no real concern on the part of the company for the quality of their language skills – a significant difference from institutionalized multilingualism – and this task is regarded as a natural service that workers provide to both the company and the customers. (The worker is often portrayed by the managers as a 'colleague' of the workers who serves as a translator.) For employees, the language service provided is often construed as rewarding, albeit in symbolic not financial terms – they are not paid. Becoming visible for a couple of minutes is regarded as a temporary promotion. For a brief instance their language competence is important for the company (see Duchêne 2011 for a detailed analysis of these issues).

In this example, Taylorization does not seem to be at issue. Multilingualism is not the object of control and standardization but rather the subject of soft management processes, such as a list. At the same time, these differences can be explained in the context of the value they hold for various tasks. Languages that are considered to be central for production and that pertain to a predictable market tend to be the object of specific attention of business and as such must be trained, controlled and managed in order to meet the Taylorist expectations. They are regarded as a commodity, and thus have to be carefully scrutinized. Languages outside an identified multilingual market, but that might serve the interest of the institution in a more unpredictable way, are constructed as natural and evident. Turning to workers who possess the unpredictable language skills actually constitutes a cost-efficient method of dealing with the diverse multilingual situations that emerge in businesses within the new economy.

These examples of the global internationalization of services highlight the role the management of workers plays with regard to multilingualism and how economic considerations and strategic decisions intersect with the resources available, the value of the services and the principle of cost-efficiency.

However different these movements are, they all indicate that multilingualism constitutes a commodity, a resource that has a specific value for business and that it wants to be managed in the most efficient way. However, if the 'new' management is new with regard to importance of language, it is not radically 'new' with regard to the work ideology behind it. The logic of cost-efficient productivity is in fact very similar to Taylorism. The methods of organization presented here obey the same logic as those of the classical industry (chain of production, accountability, flexibility, job insecurity). What is also not new is the reproduction of social inequalities with regard to social class, gender and ethnicity. The workers of the new economy – those who are exposed and who are the most vulnerable in terms of work stability – experience very much the same inequalities as did the factory workers of old. *Work* force is now *word* force (Heller 2010), *main d'oeuvre* is becoming *parole d'oeuvre* (Duchêne 2009a, 2009b); this

Multilingualism on the Internet is not a straightforward notion either. In principle it can refer to two phenomena (see Androutsopoulos 2006a, 2007). On the one hand, it can mean the choice and diversity of languages as a means of communication on the Internet, and analyses of their visibility, accessibility and status (Wright 2004; Danet and Herring 2007). Such analyses are typically motivated by the language-political concern that a globally powerful language, particularly English, can become the dominant language in Internet communication. Motivations for such studies range from protectionism to active attempts at language revitalization by political or practical measures in and via the Internet spaces in which endangered or minority languages are used (e.g. Warschauer and Donaghy 1997). On the other hand, multilingualism on the Internet can refer to the practices of multilingual Internet users and the ways in which they draw on and use resources provided by more languages than one in their CMC. As indicated in recent research, a case in point is the way in which non-Anglophone writers – particularly in informal, popular and youth cultural contexts on the Internet – draw on both their first language (L1) and English (e.g. Leppänen 2007a). In research on this type of multilingualism the focus has often been on the investigation of strategies of codeswitching and the ways in which they serve as a discursive, social and cultural resource in Internet communication (see e.g. Androutsopoulos 2007).

Early developments in the field – the dream of a genuinely multilingual Internet

The study of multilingualism on the Internet is a relatively new field. One of the reasons for this is the simple fact that in the early days the dominant language of the Internet was English. This was due to a number of factors. First, in the 1990s the great majority of websites and Internet users were English-speaking (Alis Technologies 1997; Androutsopoulos 2006a: 420). Second, English was often selected as the vehicular language for Internet users who did not have any other shared language (see e.g. Durham 2007). Third, the early computer scientists who designed personal computers and the Internet worked on the basis of the 'American Standard Code for Information Interchange' (ASCII), which made computing in other alphabets or character sets difficult or impossible (Warschauer and De Florio-Hansen 2003). However, Internet users who chose to use their own languages or language in other than Roman alphabets soon learnt to adapt them to the character sets available – such as US-ASCII, Extended ASCII and Unicode (see e.g. Danet and Herring 2007: 8–11; Palfreyman and al Khalil 2007; Peel 2004; Gerrard and Nakamura 2004). Although such innovations often initially arise from technical difficulties, they sometimes also end up having other meaning potential, for instance as resources for humour and group solidarity, especially in settings of transnational and diasporic contact (Androutsopoulos 2006b; Tseliga 2007). Besides the technological factors, certain social factors, such as the participation structure favouring the use of majority languages in Internet Relay Chat (IRC), may have made it difficult for small language groups to use their own language in communication: in many cases an easier option for them was to choose larger languages, such as English or Arabic, instead (Paolillo 2005).

All of this meant that at this stage, in the overwhelmingly monolingual Internet there simply was not much for scholars of multilingualism to investigate. In the early 2000s, in contrast, the picture was quite different. According to some estimates (www.Internetworldstats.com/stats7. htm), by this time English was quickly losing its privileged status, with only a third of Internet users being English-speaking, with Chinese speakers occupying second place (22.1 per cent) and Spanish speakers third (7.9 per cent). The linguistic diversification of the Internet was soon noticed by language scholars; for instance, in 2001 it was already apparent to such researchers as David Crystal.

Crystal (2001), whose work in the late 1990s did much to identify what were then often seen as the specific characteristics of Internet language use ('netlingo' or 'webspeak'), was also one of the first to point out the drawbacks of a genuinely multilingual Internet. In principle, for him the fact that English was losing its dominance on the Internet was a positive thing, but its potential dethronement also meant a new kind of global communicational challenge. This was because no Internet user could understand all the languages that the multilingual Internet spoke, and thus s/he still could not freely roam online. In Crystal's view (2001: 236), this kind of problematic multilingualism of the Internet posed a particular challenge to linguistics: in his opinion, it was the duty of linguists to provide the baseline information that would enable the development of programs with which Internet users could translate the other languages they encountered online into their own language. To ensure this, a great deal of linguistic, semantic, syntactic and pragmatic research was thus called for (ibid.). Although Crystal was aware that these kinds of translation technologies were too costly and commercially unviable to cater for all the world's (small, minority) languages, in principle he saw in machine translation a means through which the Internet could thrive as a truly multilingual space without sacrificing mutual comprehensibility or having to resort to a vehicular language (Crystal 2001; see also Climent et al. 2007: 215; Thurlow et al. 2004). Linguistics, combined with the right kind of technological solutions, could basically solve the problem of non-communication in the emergent multilingual Internet.

Technological advances have indeed been made towards developing translation services on the Internet. For example, the Google translator – one of the most developed of the translator applications on the Internet – claims in principle to be able to cross-translate 57 languages. Other examples of serious interest in translation as a key to creating a multilingual Internet include the BabelFish translation system (by Systran), and initiatives to develop machine translation systems between specific language pairs, such as Catalan and Spanish (Climent et al. 2007). In principle, Crystal has thus not been alone in his hope that linguistics can help to create a truly accessible multilingual Internet. In a way, this hope could even be seen as an echo of the techno-optimism of the early developers and advocates of the Internet as a democratic channel for the dissemination of information and knowledge, and a new kind of social force promoting international understanding and interaction (e.g. Hafner and Lyon 1996). In practice, however, translation systems on the Internet still need further development in order to work satisfactorily, in particular with languages that are typologically and structurally distant from one another.

Key issues of theory and method

As was mentioned above, research on multilingualism on the Internet can be divided into two broad categories – on the one hand, research into the choice and diversity of languages on the Internet and, on the other, research into the multilingual practices of Internet users (see e.g. Androutsopoulos 2006a: 428). Within these two general paradigmatic orientations, studies have drawn on a range of different theoretical and methodological orientations – these will be the focus of this section.

Measuring language choice and diversity on the Internet

One typical approach to investigating multilingualism on the Internet has been to attempt to *measure* how visible and accessible particular languages are. As suggested above, these studies have often been triggered by language-political motives, particularly by the concern that

English, as a particular side effect of increasing economic and media globalization, may become the dominant language on the Internet (Warschauer and De Florio-Hansen 2003; Wright 2004; Block 2004; Paolillo 2007). Studies like these often emphasize that the Internet needs better to reflect the actual linguistic diversity in the world (see also papers in Cunliffe and Herring 2005; Paolillo 2007). They insist that measures need to be taken online for language maintenance and revitalization, and that the Internet can be used effectively for this task, especially in situations of language shift (e.g. Buszard-Welcher 2001). The Internet can even have a language-ideological function in that it can be a means for lesser used and smaller languages to strengthen their identity as independent languages and it can provide them with more prestige (Eisenlohr 2004; cf. Warschauer 2002). The online quantity, visibility and accessibility of a language have thus been regarded as important safeguards of its vitality and importance.

In this type of research, languages have often been approached from a macro-sociological perspective and regarded as entities with a measurable presence on the Internet, whereas less attention has been paid to the particular ways in which language resources have actually been used. One approach to measuring linguistic diversity online has been to *survey* what Internet users report on their language choices. For instance, this particular method was used by the research team commissioned by UNESCO (see Wright 2004), who administered the same survey to students of English in ten countries (Tanzania, Indonesia, the United Arab Emirates, Oman, France, Italy, Poland, Macedonia, Japan and Ukraine). Motivated by a wish to develop viable Internet language policies, the specific aim of this comparative project was to investigate whether the Internet is leading to greater contact across language boundaries and whether or not English is the preferred medium for such exchanges (2004: 5). More specifically, the survey questionnaire asked students (c. 3000) to self-report the language and purpose of ten consecutive Internet sessions (2004: 8).

The survey's findings indicated that there is a digital and linguistic divide between Internet users in richer and poorer countries, manifesting itself not only in the different degrees of accessibility of the Internet (see e.g. Mafu 2004), but also in the amount of resources available to provide services in local languages. For example, in poorer countries Internet users tend to rely on English-medium sources, whereas users in richer countries are able to access information in their own language (Kelly-Holmes 2004). Thus, it was shown how, as Internet resources become increasingly available in the users' own languages, English language use decreases. However, on the basis of the findings it is not clear how, or whether, this disadvantages or advantages either group (2004: 74).

Because the survey method is based on Internet users' self-reports, it has been criticized by some for producing biased evidence on linguistic diversity on the Internet. In another set of studies commissioned by UNESCO (2005), an attempt was made to solve this problem by suggesting the use of *quantitative measures* to study linguistic diversity online. However, the report also emphasized that much of the work done on measuring the situation on the Internet has been seriously flawed (Paolillo 2005: 50). One of the reasons for this was argued that for a long time the measurements were carried out by marketing companies whose intentions were quite different from those of the scientific community, and who were not very concerned to document their methods (Pimienta 2005: 27). As a consequence, it was suggested, the figures that are frequently used to depict for example the proportion of English-language Internet users continue to be far too high. Another problem in many studies was alleged to be that they basically collect their evidence from unreliable or limited sources, for example by extrapolating figures from search engines by language, or from samples of several thousand websites through a random selection of Internet Protocol (IP) addresses (Pimienta 2005: 29–30). In their stead, it was argued (2005: 33), measurements should be based on more advanced methods, such as programs basically operating in the same way as spyware, which can measure the languages used in a number of contexts relevant as indicators of language diversity.

Other suggestions made in the report recommend yet other methods of measurement: for instance, Paolillo (2005: 51) recommended the use of a linguistic diversity index, a statistical measure, which, as part of the measurement of the languages used online, can take into account the variety of languages and the proportion of a particular language group in relation to other language groups of any one country. With the help of this measure, he was able to establish for example that, despite the fact that the countries of Africa and Oceania show the highest and the USA and China show the lowest linguistic diversity offline, the USA and China nevertheless seem to dominate the Internet. Furthermore, on the basis of previous studies on the distribution of languages on the Internet (e.g. Lavoie and O'Neill 2001), Paolillo came to the conclusion that the Internet favours large languages (particularly English) and technical standards associated with these (Paolillo 2005: 54–5, 79; see also Danet and Herring 2007: 22–3). As a result, Paolillo (2005: 55) argued that the linguistic diversity of the world is not represented on the Internet. However, he also suggested that the Internet can have two quite different kinds of impact on the fragile presence of many small and minority languages online: in some cases, these languages may weaken as the status of larger languages is consolidated also on the Internet, whereas in other cases the online presence of smaller languages can actually strengthen them.

What the attempts to measure linguistic diversity online make clear is the immensity of the challenge involved in attempting to provide incontrovertible numerical evidence on the basis of which clear conclusions could be drawn on not only the status and proportion of different languages on the Internet, but also the implications of this and the appropriate language-political measures that should follow from them. The question is, then, whether it is possible to measure the massively rhizomatic Internet in a reliable way. It seems that the use of a single method – such as the use of the survey or quantification – is simply not enough if we want more reliable data about how, why and for what purposes individuals and groups make use of particular languages in their Internet practices (see also Paolillo 2005: 62–4).

Evidence provided by measurements of the linguistic situation on the Internet have often led to specific attempts to document and advocate the use of the Internet to archive (Bennett 2003; Hinton 2001; Kroskrity 2002; Kroskrity and Reynolds 2001; Parks et al. 1999), promote and teach small, minority and endangered languages (Warschauer and Donaghy 1997; Warschauer 1998; Benton 1996; Haag and Coston 2002). Although these initiatives can be very important in raising awareness and increasing the appreciation of small or endangered languages, their success often critically depends on whether or not speakers of the lesser used languages themselves have access to the Internet and, if they do, are committed to actually using its resources to maintain and revitalize their language (Androutsopoulos 2006a: 429; Mafu 2004; Ouakrim 2001; Sperlich 2005).

Describing and explaining language choice and multilingual practices on the Internet

The available statistics, which often represent English as the largest language on the Internet, can be somewhat misleading, in that they suggest that the majority of Internet users are people for whom English is their primary linguistic code. In reality, however, most are non-native speakers of English, for whom English is a resource on which they draw in different ways, for example, by using it for some specific purpose – instead of their first language, mixing it with their L1 or other languages, or alternating between the use of English and their L1/other languages (see e.g. Warschauer and De Florio-Hansen 2003; Danet and Herring 2007: 5).

Besides the fact that most Internet users are non-native users of English, another increasingly crucial aspect of their Internet uses in the early 2000s is that for them the Internet is turning into a translocal affinity space. What this means is that, despite the different social, ethnic and linguistic backgrounds these individuals and groups may have, they have found on the Internet a place in which they can come together with other like-minded people to share their interests, concerns or causes (Danet and Herring 2007; Leppänen 2007a, 2007b, 2009; Leppänen and Piirainen-Marsh 2009; Leppänen et al. 2009). Thus, the translocal Internet has also become a linguistic contact zone in which multilingual resources and repertoires can turn out to be crucial capital for successful communication, action and interaction (Leppänen forthcoming). For researchers, this emergence of the translocal Internet in the early 2000s has meant a shift from globalization – measuring the global language and languages of the globe on the Internet, for example – to relocalization, to the investigation of local and situated language practices on the Internet (Warschauer and De Florio-Hansen 2003; Androutsopoulos 2007; Leppänen forthcoming). In this kind of research the focus is no longer on the measuring and surveying of the use of particular languages on the Internet, but on the specific multilingual practices of Internet users, the motivations behind their language choices and the functions and meanings these have for them in the specific Internet contexts in which they operate. What such language practices thus call for is research that can help us understand and explain them as situated and meaningful action: such as can be provided by qualitative discourse analytic, ethnographic, pragmatic and sociolinguistic investigations.

In research on language choice and multilingual practices by Internet users, important preliminary steps are to identify the language setting of the participants (Leppänen and Nikula 2007) and to specify whether or not they have a shared language(s), and to assess the functions the additional linguistic resources serve and the meaning potential they have in their particular setting.

Language choice in a setting with no shared language

In a language setting in which participants in an Internet space do not have a shared language, they must choose a vehicular language that will enable mutual communication, interaction and comprehension. In other words, in such a setting the participants need to find and use a language that they can relatively safely assume the other participants also know and are able to use in communication. This kind of setting is described by, for example, Durham's study (2007) on professional communication in multilingual Internet networks. In these networks the participants favoured English as their shared language because it ensured the widest possible understanding among the subscribers to the list. A similar case is also discussed by Wodak and Wright (2006): their study investigated the languages used in a European Union discussion forum, Futurum. Again, in a setting like this, where the participants' linguistic backgrounds vary a great deal, English was selected as the vehicular language that ensured mutual comprehensibility. Other languages were also used to some extent, representing the diversity of all the languages of the participants, but this trend was clearly a minor one compared with the use of English.

Language choice in a setting with a shared language

Another typical language setting in which participants in CMC can operate is one in which, despite the fact that they have a shared language, they nevertheless choose another language as either the primary communicative code or as an additional resource alternating and mixing with their primary language. In such a setting, the motivations for language choice can vary a great deal. Sometimes the choice can be an extension of the participants' multilingual language practices offline, but it can also be an outcome of an official or group-specific language policy or politics, specific to online communication. This is the case discussed in a study by Warschauer *et al.* (2002), for example, which showed how Egyptian professionals who have a shared first language prefer to use English in professional online communication and colloquial Arabic in informal emails and chats in almost a diglossic way. For this professional group their language choices online thus index the different goals, identities and discourses relevant in each communicative situation. These findings foreground, in fact, a recurrent strategy of language choice in Internet environments. There is evidence from different countries (see e.g. Warschauer 2002; Siebenhaar 2006; Androutsopoulos 2006a) that in the more spoken-like and dialogic Internet environments – in web discussion forums and different types of chat applications, for example – there is often a tendency for vernacular varieties to be used instead of more standard or formal varieties of the language.

Language choice as a semiotic strategy

At other times language choice can be a semiotic strategy through which participants seek to distinguish themselves and to create voices of their own in a multilingual online setting. Language choice can thus serve as a particular resource for the creation of stylistic and cultural effects, and for the negotiation of identity and communality. This kind of language situation is exemplified by Leppänen's study (2007b) in which she discusses a number of Internet and gaming settings where the participants draw not only on their L1, which they share with their anticipated audience, but also on English – which they can assume their anticipated audience will also understand. However, in each mediated setting the participants mobilize their language resources in somewhat different ways, for different purposes and different effects.

Example (1), a weblog entry from a young Finnish traveller in Mexico, can serve here as an illustration of how language choice can convey a range of meanings. In this blog entry the writer uses four languages to report on his travels to his obviously linguistically diverse audience. He begins his entry in English, but switches to Finnish in the second paragraph, and to French in the final paragraph. In each of these paragraphs he gives some of the same information about his itinerary, but he also reports on quite different things. In addition to the three languages mentioned, the writer also uses some Spanish. The English translations by Saija Peuronen of the Finnish and French sections are given in square brackets after the blogger's original Finnish text. (To protect the identity of the blogger, the link to his blog site is not included here.)

> Example (1)
> Greetings from Puerto Escondido, southern Mexico. We're spending our last latin days, 8 or so to go. At the moment I've caught a little cold, got some sun burn in the back and am tired of this same food everyday :) rice and beans, chicken, papa fritas, ice cream (either chocolate or strawberry), coffee tastes water.but hey! People are nice and this is pura vida. Tomorrow we are heading to Acapulco, which we have been warned about being way too touristic, oh well. Only reason to get there is the fact that we needed a compromising spot where everyone can find easily; to party. We're 30 altogether ... Finnish invasion, happy new year dudes and dudettes!!!
> Acapulco. Ei ihan viela mutta 10 tunnin paasta. Kuulin ekan kerran Acapulcosta jo vuonna 1988 kun Milli Vanilli esitti kyseisella nimella kulkevan kesahittinsa. Milli Vanillin kavi hassusti (musa-visa-knoppikysymys: Miten kavi?) mutta niin varmaan meidankin, onhan meita siella 30.

[Acapulco. Not just yet but in 10 hours. The first time I heard about Acapulco was back in 1988 when Milli Vanilli performed their summer hit with the same title. Things didn't turn out too well for Milli Vanilli (a quiz question: What happened?) and they probably won't for us either, after all there are going to be 30 of us.]

[...]

C'est jolie quoi! Au Mexique, au pays des ahoritas et margaritas. Je m'amuse ici jusqu'au janvier 6. Je voulais vous dire bonne nouvelle année 06! Bis.

[Isn't this great! In Mexico, in the land of ahoritas and margaritas. I enjoy my stay here until January 6. I would like to wish you happy new year 06! with love.]

A traveller meets people from different countries, and for this one addressing these friends and acquaintances in their own languages is not only a means of staying in touch with them and telling them about his journey, but also of reinforcing the close relationship he has with them. The use of Finnish, for its part, serves as a way of keeping his Finnish family and friends up to date. The Spanish insertions in the blog have a somewhat different meaning compared to all the other languages: they function metonymically and referentially to emphasize the fact that he is really visiting Mexico – using the local language communicates his experience of actually being there and enjoying it (e.g. 'People are nice and this is pura vida'). Interestingly, in all of the four languages, the writer uses an informal, spoken-like variety, which is generally typical of personal weblogs (Leppänen 2007b). At the same time the extract illustrates how the blogger's multiple language choices also represent him as a cosmopolitan globetrotter who can elegantly and skilfully travel not only from one country and continent to another, but also from one language to another. Thus, the language choices he makes in his blog are also functional and meaningful as means of constructing identity.

Approaches to linguistically mixed CMD

As outlined above, one particular variant of a multilingual setting on the Internet may be one where, besides using their primary language code, the participants draw on resources provided by other languages, and thus produce linguistically mixed discourse. In the analysis of such language practices, scholars have typically drawn on two general methodological orientations: one is the close and detailed analysis of discourse, and the other the ethnographic investigation of online practices, participants and settings. To some extent, mixed methodologies have also been used to gain a wider view of specific data (Androutsopoulos and Beißwenger 2008: 2). For example, studies by Androutsopoulos (2007) and Siebenhaar (2006) combined *quantitative* and *qualitative approaches* to study language choice and codeswitching in CMD.

However, in quite a few studies that have focused on spoken-like, interactive CMD, linguistically mixed CMD has been approached through *methods originally developed for the analysis of spoken interaction*. This is largely because theories and methods designed specifically for studying language mixing in CMC where users most often communicate through written language, have not yet been developed (but see e.g. Hinrichs 2006: 29–30; Sebba 2012; Leppänen 2012). Instead, scholars have drawn on, for example, interactional sociolinguistics (e.g. Gumperz 1982), discourse analysis and conversation analysis (e.g. Auer 1995) to explain the mixed-language features of Internet discourse. What this means is that so far there has not been enough consideration of the particular effects that computer-mediated environments might have on language use and frameworks of interaction (Androutsopoulos and Beißwenger 2008: 1–2; Beißwenger 2008: 1).

Perhaps not unsurprisingly, then, many of the findings concerning the types and functions of linguistically mixed CMD – especially in online discussions – are similar to those described in relation to conversational data (see Lam 2004; Androutsopoulos 2006b; Peuronen 2011). Participants in various modes of CMD have been shown to draw creatively on multiple languages and to appropriate them to their communicative purposes (Georgakopoulou 2006: 553). For example, drawing on interactional sociolinguistics, Lam (2004: 56, 58) has shown how Chinese students living in the USA used codeswitching between English and romanized Cantonese in their Internet chat and how their codeswitching had a number of functions, ranging from expressing modality to creating humour, selecting addressees and shifting their social alignments. The students were thus able to create a communicative style of their own, which helped them to identify themselves as bilingual Chinese emigrants. In a similar vein, Androutsopoulos (2006b) has shown how patterns of codeswitching in German-based diasporic Internet discussion forums conformed to findings in previous studies on offline codeswitching. Using conversation analysis, he investigated the sequential development of the online interaction and showed how codeswitching between German and the users' home languages was both interactionally and socially meaningful to the participants and was associated with performance-related activities, such as singing or joke-telling (Androutsopoulos 2006b: 532–3).

Whereas approaches to linguistically mixed Internet discussion formats that have drawn on models of conversational codeswitching have revealed similarities in the patterns and functions of codeswitching between off- and online discussions, other types of mixed-language genres on the Internet have called for quite different descriptive and explanatory frameworks. More written-like Internet genres such as blogs or fan fiction (alternative versions of such cultural products as TV series or films by fans) call for an analytic approach that makes use of concepts and methods developed in the context of *narrative analysis*.

For instance, the mixed-language features of a text such as the one illustrated in example (2), a snippet from a bilingual fan fiction story based on an American TV series, *Roswell*, by a young Finnish female writer, can be captured with the help of such stylistic and narrative concepts as point of view and narration. Example (2) describes a situation in which a young Finnish girl – not unlike the writer herself – wakes up one morning in the bed of one of the male protagonists of the TV series and realizes that the young man is, miraculously, her husband. (The sections originally in Finnish have been translated into English by Sirpa Leppänen and they are presented in square brackets after the Finnish sections. Again, to protect the identity of the writer, no link to the original site is included here.)

Example (2)
Mä makasin sängylläni ja ajattelin vanhoja tapahtumia. Mun poikaystävä jätti mut just kaks tuntia aikasemmin.
[I was lying on my bed thinking about what had happened. My boyfriend had left me two hours earlier.]
[...]
Aamulla mä herään taas. Mä huokasen.
[In the morning I wake up again. I sigh.]
'Good morning honey ... ' mä kuulen tutun äänen. Ennekun mä ehin reakoida mä tunsin lämpimät huulet mun huulilla. Ja kun suudelma loppui mä huomasin tuijottavani suor-aan Kyle Valentin silmiin.
[I hear a familiar voice. Before I have time to react I feel a pair of warm lips on my lips. And when the kiss is over I realised that I was looking straight into Kyle Valentin's eyes.]
[...]

'Are you okay, Milla?'

Milla?! Mitä nyt tapahtu?

[Milla?! What's happening now?]

'Um … yeah.' 'Good … 'cause breakfast is ready.'

'Good, I will go to the shower first.'

'I can see that English isn't your language … '

'What do you mean?'

'Don't worry. It's hard because you're from Finland.'

Mä hymyilin Kylelle ja menin suihkuun. Mä laitoin hanan päälle ja aloin miettimään asioita. Kun mä nostin käteni ylös mun naaman kohalle, mä näin sen. Mun vasemmassa sormessa oli sormus. Mä meinasin pyörtyy.

[I smiled at Kyle and went to have a shower. I turned on the tap and started thinking things over. When I raised my hand towards my face, I saw it. I had a ring on my left hand. I almost fainted.]

'Noniin … nyt mä käsitän. Mä nään unta. Ja ihanaa sellasta … mä oon naimisissa Kylen kanssa.'

[Well … now I understand. I'm having a dream. And it's a wonderful dream … I'm married to Kyle.]

This example illustrates how language alternation can be used as a narrative strategy: in this text, it functions as a resource with which the writer is able to depict both the fantastical situation and the identity of the protagonist in a believable way. More specifically, the systematic alternation between Finnish and English emphasizes the juxtaposition and coming together of two realms – the 'real' Finnish one of the young woman and the English-speaking fictional realm that the characters of the TV series inhabit. English is the language of the characters in the TV series, and by using it the writer can emphasize the fact that the young Finnish girl has really entered another reality – the fictional world of Roswell, where everyone speaks English. At the same time, the writer uses Finnish to represent the young female protagonist as Finnish and to underline her essential difference from the characters in the TV series. Furthermore, Finnish also serves to represent the young girl's thoughts and to narrate the story from her point of view, whereas English is used to report on the dialogue between the Finnish girl and the protagonist of the TV series. Both languages thus have distinct but complementary functions.

In this story, then, the two languages constitute a double identity for the Finnish girl: she is simultaneously an outsider, a Finnish fan, and an accidental insider in the TV series. The alternation of the two languages thus also contributes to the creation of a story in which the real and the fantastic intertwine. The alternation of Finnish and English is here one of the 'literary' devices with which the writer can create an appropriate and interesting fan fiction text. Importantly, however, it has been suggested (Leppänen 2012) that in many genres of CMD this kind of linguistic mixing is only one particular facet of their overall, heteroglossic character – of the mixing, alternation and combination of resources not only of different languages, but also of different registers, styles, genres and other texts. What this implies, then, is that, along with other semiotic resources, multilingualism is only one particular discursive resource for meaning-making for writers of this type of computer-mediated text.

What example (2) also illustrates is that in discursive analyses of CMD, *identity and social practice* have been central foci for researchers. In this kind of research identity is typically viewed as constructed and negotiated with the help of multilingual resources in which languages can both index identity and be sites for resistance, empowerment, solidarity or discrimination (cf. Pavlenko and Blackledge 2004: 4, 14). However, as Auer (2005: 407, 409) has argued, bilingual language varieties seldom directly express multilingual or multicultural identities; in order to be able to make claims about the relationship between language and identity, analysis is needed to find out what people actually do when alternating between two or more languages, also in the context of the multilingual Internet.

For instance, approaching the investigation of identity construction on the Internet from such a perspective, Georgakopoulou (1997: 148) found that participants in bilingual email discussions signalled 'their interpersonal relations and alignments' through codeswitching between Greek and English and style shifting between social varieties of Greek. She discovered that whereas codeswitches functioned as contextualization cues to negotiate personal footing, style shifting was used for evoking particular sociocultural frameworks in the context of this community. In this way the participants were able to position themselves in appropriate social roles according to each communicative situation as it rose, and create solidarity (mainly by means of humour) and consolidate their in-group membership.

Similarly, Hinrichs (2006: 89) explored social meanings connected to a certain language variety, Jamaican Creole, and the ways in which these meanings became activated when the variety was used in online interaction, in email and discussion forum interaction in particular. He (2006: 86, 137) argued that in CMD, which is more planned than speech, there were conscious switches to a vernacular variety (Jamaican Creole), which tended to have an 'added communicative value' in identity work. Codeswitching between two varieties was also used for creating a certain style, for example when performing 'the identity of a typical Jamaican in conversation' (2006: 110). On the other hand, patois was used as a resource for creating humour and irony, good-naturedly making fun of ordinary Jamaicans (2006: 113–14).

The particular nature of Internet practices as anonymous and yet public (Benwell and Stokoe 2006) naturally has an impact on language use and lays greater emphasis on the role of language in constructing identities, because such 'visible' identity markers as race, gender or social class are less evident there (Warschauer and de Florio-Hansen 2003: 5). At the same time, participants may index something of their real-life or desired identities by, for example, following certain specific interactional and cultural norms, by accommodating their language use to what is considered acceptable or appropriate in the particular online context to which they contribute and by using a variety of other highly indexical language features, such as the use of a group-specific register, or a socioculturally symbolic nickname, signature and slogan (Benwell and Stokoe 2006: 264–6; de Oliveira 2007; Panyametheekul and Herring 2007; Leppänen et al. 2009; Kytölä 2012).

Example (3) (see Table 22.1) illustrates how particular ways of mobilizing linguistic resources, including multilingual resources, are crucial in the negotiation of identity and the sense of belonging in CMD. This example is an extract from a discussion about football from a football forum based in Finland (for more details, see Kytölä 2012) in which a Finnish Swedish-speaking football fan uses three languages in his turn to both emphasize and comment on the forum's norms for language choice and linguistic mixing. The original (but visually modified) text by the fan is presented in the left-hand column, and its English translation by Sirpa Leppänen in the right-hand column. The middle column indicates the language choices made by the writer. Once more, for research ethical reasons, no link to the original site is included here.

In this example, the writer's alternation between Swedish, his first language, English, a foreign language, and Finnish, his second language, is an indirect, but very evocative way for him to comment on the constant language policing going on in this discussion forum. More particularly, his commentary is a reaction to the frequent outbursts of hate discourse in the forum about the use of other languages besides its default language, Finnish, (focused

Table 22.1 Example (3)

	Swedish		English
1 Ja ja ni kan tjata på hur mycket ni			yes yes you can go on as much as you
2 vill om att RoPs, Jaro och TP har			like about how RoPs, Jaro and TP have
3 minst lika långa resor, men ni lär	Swedish		at least as long journeys, but you must
4 väl bli medvetna om våra			know our ferry timetables when it is time
5 färjturlistor när det är dags för ett			to visit Åland.
6 ålandsbesök. Välkomna.			Welcome.
7 Och ni som inte orkar läsa allt som	Swedish		And those of you who don't have the
8 står på svenska,			patience to read everything that is said in Swedish,
9 I don't give a fuck.	English		I don't give a fuck.
10 Minä puhun ruotsia, ja en ymmärrä	Finnish		I speak Swedish, and I don't understand
11 paljon suomea.			much Finnish.
12 That's why I write in Swedish.	English		That's why I write in Swedish. Simple as
13 Simple as that.			that.
14 Tänk på all finsk text vi måste	Swedish		Think about all the Finnish text we have
15 traggla oss igenom för at ens fatta			to try and read to at least understand, and
16 om, och hur ni jävlas med oss.			how you make fun of us.

particularly on Swedish, the second official language in Finland, but also for example on native-like uses of English), as well as about 'wrong' or socially undesirable dialects or registers. Such hate discourse can range from explicit direct criticism of the use of specific languages or varieties to implicit criticism by humour, mimicking, repetition and parody, for example.

This kind of hate discourse is tackled here by the Swedish-speaking fan: he does this, on the one hand by explaining (lines 10–11) in Finnish to his mainly Finnish-speaking audience that his use of Swedish has an explanation – he does not know much Finnish. Immediately after this he switches to English as a vehicular language (lines 12–13) to make his point even clearer. Interestingly, he himself states his opinions most clearly in the Swedish parts of his entry (which the Finnish-speaking participants cannot understand that well). In them, he says for instance 'tänk på all finsk text vi måste traggla oss igenom for at ens fatta om, or hur ni jävlas med oss' ('think about all the Finnish text we have to try and read to at least understand, and how you make fun of us'). This particular entry thus crystallizes key language ideological and identity issues in this forum: the use of Swedish is often criticized in the forum and its users are frequently attacked by Finnish-speaking fans. Finnish, in contrast, is the norm to which participants are usually expected to orient, and whose users are treated by other participants as authentic fans of Finnish football. Acceptance of this normative order is thus a prerequisite for full membership in the football fan community: if, for some reason, conforming to this is not possible for certain fans, they may very quickly find themselves ridiculed or attacked, or totally excluded from the community (Kytölä 2012).

Besides discursive analyses of CMD, *online ethnography* is also a popular approach to observing how Internet users' language practices contribute to the establishment and negotiation of affinity spaces or even communities with shared cultural and social conventions. Research making use of an online ethnographic approach can be divided into two main categories (Androutsopoulos 2008: 4): studies that concentrate entirely on investigating online activities, with very little or no contact with the participants (see e.g. Paolillo 1999), and studies in which the observation of online activities in the selected sites is accompanied by fieldwork in offline settings in which the participants' Internet uses are examined by means of, for example, surveys, interviews and observations (Androutsopoulos 2008; see also Kytölä and Androutsopoulos forthcoming).

A multidimensional ethnographic investigation of Internet users' practices can indeed be a useful way of elucidating and understanding the ways in which Internet users themselves make sense of and account for their engagement with the Internet and the affordances it offers them for meaningful social and cultural action. A good illustration of this is a study by Nikula and Pitkänen-Huhta (2008; see also Leppänen *et al.* 2009), which looked at a group of Finnish teenagers' activities with various electronic and digital media, with the goal of exploring the presence of English in their everyday lives. During the research process the researchers aimed at an understanding of their social reality and how they make sense of their uses of English. This was done by using multiple methods including group and individual discussions with the participants, a number of visual tasks (e.g. photographs, drawings and collages) and literacy diaries. Using such methods Nikula and Pitkänen-Huhta were able to give a detailed account of how the everyday activities of young people in Finland increasingly revolve around electronic and digital media, and how these media uses by them are accompanied by a constant flow of English, which further shapes their media practices and opens up a new world of international contacts and translocal activity spaces beyond the local networks with which they can connect. At the same time, the different kinds of data used in this study demonstrated a great deal of variation within the teenagers' actual practices. An ethnographic approach thus made it possible for the researchers to show how young people engage with the media in highly personalized and self-regulated ways in order to meet their individual needs and aspirations.

Policy issues

It is not uncommon to find in research on language diversity of the Internet (UNESCO Institute for Statistics 2005; Wright 2004; Crystal 2001), strong pleas for action to ensure that digital access and digital literacy are upheld especially on behalf of the many linguistically diverse and developing countries of the world. For example, UNESCO (see e.g. UNESCO Institute for Statistics) recommends that the national, regional and international levels need to work together

> to provide the necessary resources and take the necessary measures to alleviate language barriers and promote human interaction on the Internet by encouraging the creation and processing of, and access to, educational, cultural and scientific content in digital form, so as to ensure that all cultures can express themselves and have access to cyberspace in all languages, including indigenous ones.
>
> *(2005: 11)*

At the same time, researchers are aware of the fact that no top-down, globally applicable Internet language policy is possible, because of the differences between the cultural, sociolinguistic and technical contexts of Internet use. Therefore, a more bottom-up approach to policy is usually recommended. For example, the UNESCO report (ibid.) recommends that it may be preferable that language policies are formulated by regional bodies whose studies could then be combined into an overall global perspective. A further factor complicating the formulation of a universal Internet language policy is the differences between different national language policies, which regulate language choice and use on official state and municipal websites. For instance, in officially bilingual Finland, citizens need to be given information on the Internet in both Finnish and Swedish, as well as in English. Thus, regional language policies may often be too general for regulating language choice and use in the varied local contexts in which people actually communicate on the Internet.

However, many Internet sites, although they seldom spell out an explicit language policy of their own, often in fact develop some kind of regulatory mechanisms that can also affect language choice and use. These might take the form of a collectively established and monitored etiquette, but also moderator and participant comments can effectively police the ways language or languages can and should be used in the Internet setting in question (Leppänen 2009; Leppänen and Piirainen-Marsh 2009). Thus, despite the fact that these kinds of regulatory mechanisms are not always spelled out, they are often a key factor in shaping language choice and use on the Internet, and thus something that a researcher on Internet language policy needs to find out about by means of surveys, interviews or participant observation, for example.

New research directions

The kind of research on multilingualism on the Internet outlined in this chapter suggests some possibilities and questions for future research. On a programmatic note, it could be argued that the diversity of the Internet as a linguistic, discursive and communicative space necessitates studies that can provide answers to such questions as

- What language(s), and forms and patterns of language are used on the Internet?
- In what ways and how frequently are these different languages actually used by Internet users?
- When, where, by whom, in what kinds of technological, social, cultural and generic contexts, and for what purposes are specific language(s) used on the Internet?
- Why are specific language(s) used, and how do Internet users themselves assess their language choice and use?
- What is the use of vehicular languages and linguistically mixed discourse like?
- What effects do language choice and use have, and what (discursive, semiotic, social, cultural, aesthetic, etc.) meanings do the language choices and uses have for the participants, and more generally?
- How does multilingualism on the Internet relate to offline realities, to e.g. societal, group, institutional and individual mono-multilingualism?

In other words, the multidimensionality of Internet multilingualism calls for studies that can approach it from a wide variety of perspectives and with various methodologies that can shed light, incrementally and complementarily, on both the specificities of and differences between the languages used, and the functions and meanings of these languages in the varied linguistic, communicative and discursive spaces of the Internet. In so doing, research on Internet multilingualism could benefit considerably from multi- and cross-disciplinarity: from approaches and insights provided by other types of Internet research (e.g. cybercultural studies, cybersociology, usability research, gaming research). Innovative interfaces between language-based research, and different strands within it, and with other forms of enquiry can also enrich our picture of the role and significance of language in communication, social interaction and cultural production on the Internet. For instance, bringing different methodologies into a dialogue – ethnography with discourse study, corpus analysis with close analysis of discourse data, survey research with the study of perceptions and assumptions by actual language users, ideologies of mono-multilingualism and actual language uses by individuals and groups – can help us understand and explain how complex the choice and use of languages on the Internet is. To account for this complexity, research on Internet multilingualism has a lot of ground to cover: it needs to find out not only about the types, dynamics, characteristics and meanings of specific language uses, types of communication and discourse on the Internet, but also about what Internet users themselves think about what they do – both as situated practices and as more general tendencies and frequencies – as well as about what structural (technological, social, political, cultural, economic) constraints and affordances there are for their activities.

Other, and more specific, future challenges in research on Internet multilingualism derive from the ongoing evolution of the Internet, or, more generally, of electronic and digital social media, as well as the ways in which these media are used. For example, it is argued by Androutsopoulos and Beißwenger (2008: 5) that it would be particularly useful for language-focused researchers 'to examine methodological differences between synchronous and asynchronous communication modes, and to consider whether different social uses of the same technology can be examined with the same methodology'. For them, this kind of a mission statement translates into research tasks that centre on the uses of CMC technology in different social situations, different platforms for social networking (e.g. Facebook, MySpace), content sharing (e.g. Flickr, YouTube), collaborative authoring (e.g. Wikipedia, Wictionary), the commonalities and differences among different types of online communities, and the use of multiple digital communication tools.

At the same time, in view of the variety of modes of communication and discourse on the Internet, an additional challenge for researchers into Internet multilingualism is to develop a more nuanced understanding of the specific characteristics of the different modes and genres on the Internet and the kinds of methodological tools their investigation necessitates. For example, textual genres such as blogs, websites, webzines and fan fiction clearly require different methods of analysis from dialogic and interactive CMD modes and genres. Another issue here is the central role that visual, video and audio material increasingly has on the Internet, which, in turn, underlines the importance of analytic approaches that have not traditionally been part of language scholars' repertoire. In other words, to capture the kind of Internet multilingualism that is conveyed in modalities other than the written language, scholars need to go beyond linguistic analysis and draw on methods suggested by other fields of research, such as multimodality, cinema and TV.

Finally, language scholars should also begin to pay more attention to the fact that the Internet is no longer a medium that is used on its own, and separately from other media. In at least the more affluent and ICT-saturated countries of the world, people lead increasingly mediated lives, surrounded by, operating and interacting actively with different types of media, in inter- and crossmedial spaces. What this means in terms of Internet multilingualism is that the kinds of language uses, types of communication and discourse that researchers have traditionally associated with the Internet only, may, in fact, be typical of other electronic and digital media contexts as well. A good example of this is the way in which chat shares many features with texting. Furthermore, the Internet is often used in relation to, or embedded in and embedding other media. An illustration of this could be the use of an Internet application to make a phone call in an environment that also offers other communicative modes and modalities (e.g. chat, webcam, file sharing). In an environment like this, communication and language use can take a range of different forms, spoken, written, telephonic, or face-to-face, for example. Analogously, in such a setting, multilingualism can be manifested in various ways, which poses yet another new challenge for its research.

Conclusion

In this chapter we have attempted to discuss the study of multilingualism on the Internet, looking at key concepts, approaches, developments and future challenges. Because this is a relatively new field of research, and because the technologies as well as the social and cultural spaces of the Internet keep changing constantly, anyone hoping to provide a definitive account of multilingualism on the Internet can only hope to offer partial, and partially out-dated accounts. Nevertheless, it is also true that the constant and dynamic change of the Internet also makes this research all the more timely, and the research-based evidence provided by language scholars can help us to understand, relate to, and act in and on the increasingly meaningful and powerful linguistic and sociocultural reality that the Internet is for many of the world's people, communities, institutions and societies.

Related topics

Multilingualism and popular culture; multilingualism and the media; codeswitching; heteroglossia.

Further reading

Androutsopoulos, J. (2006) 'Special issue on sociolinguistics and computer-mediated communication', *Journal of Sociolinguistics* 10(4).
(This collection of articles includes empirical studies on language use, online communities and social identities in CMD, paying attention to diverse multilingual contexts on the Internet.)

Danet, B. and Herring, S. C. (eds) (2007) *The Multilingual Internet: Language, Culture, and Communication Online*, New York: Oxford University Press.
(A collection of studies that focuses on the ways in which different languages are used in different forms of CMD. The themes of the book include creative use of writing systems, language choice and codeswitching.)

Hinrichs, L. (2006) *Codeswitching on the Web: English and Jamaican Creole in E-mail Communication*, Amsterdam: John Benjamins.
(Hinrichs uses email and online discussion forum data to analyse discourse functions between Jamaican Creole and Jamaican English. He describes situational, metaphorical and identity-related codeswitching and also considers the differences between spoken language and CMC in terms of the functions of Jamaican Creole.)

UNESCO Institute for Statistics (ed.) (2005) *Measuring Linguistic Diversity on the Internet*, Paris: UNESCO.
(This collection of papers presents analyses of measuring the use of languages on the Internet, discussing also the dominance of English and the future of other languages on the Internet.)

Wright, S. (guest ed.) (2004) 'A special issue on linguistic diversity, linguistic rights, and language policies', *International Journal on Multicultural Societies*, UNESCO 6(1).
(Based on a survey carried out among university and high school students in ten different countries, the chapters of the special issue address linguistic diversity by using the students' self-reports to examine their language choices and practices on the Internet.)

Bibliography

Alis Technologies (1997) 'Web languages hit parade', available online at http://alis.isoc.org/palmares. en.html

Androutsopoulos, J. (2006a) 'Introduction: Sociolinguistics and computer-mediated communication', *Journal of Sociolinguistics* 10(4): 419–38.

——(2006b) 'Multilingualism, diaspora, and the internet: Codes and identities on German-based diaspora websites', *Journal of Sociolinguistics* 10(4): 520–47.

——(2007) 'Language choice and code switching in German-based diasporic web forums', in B. Danet and S. C. Herring (eds) *The Multilingual Internet: Language, Culture, and Communication Online*, New York: Oxford University Press.

——(2008) 'Potentials and limitations of discourse-centred online ethnography', *Language@internet* 5, article 8, available online at www.languageatinternet.de/articles/2008/1610

Androutsopoulos, J. and Beißwenger, M. (2008) 'Introduction: Data and methods in computer-mediated discourse analysis', *Language@internet* 5, article 2, available online at www.languageatinternet.org/articles/2008/1609

Auer, P. (1995) 'The pragmatics of code-switching: A sequential approach', in L. Milroy and P. Muysken (eds) *One Speaker, Two Languages*, Cambridge: Cambridge University Press.

——(2005) 'A postscript: Code-switching and social identity', *Journal of Pragmatics* 37: 403–10.

Beißwenger, M. (2008) 'Situated chat analysis as a window to the user's perspective: Aspects of temporal and sequential organization', *Language@internet* 5, article 6, available online at www.languageatinternet.org/articles/2008/1532

Bennett, R. (2003) 'Saving a language with computers, tape recorders, and radio', in J. Reyhner, O. Trujillo, R. L. Carrasco and L. Lockard (eds) *Nurturing Native Languages*, Flagstaff: Northern Arizona University.

Benton, R. (1996) 'Making the medium the message: Using an electronic bulletin board system for promoting and revitalizing Maori', in M. Warschauer (ed.) *Telecollaboration in Foreign Language Learning*, Honolulu: University of Hawai'i Press.

Benwell, B. and Stokoe, E. (2006) *Discourse and Identity*, Edinburgh: Edinburgh University Press.

Block, D. (2004) 'Globalization, transnational communication and the internet', *International Journal on Multicultural Societies* 6(1): 22–37.

Buszard-Welcher, L. (2001) 'Can the Web save my language?' in L. Hinton and K. Hale (eds) *The Green Book of Language Revitalization in Practice*, San Diego: Academic Press.

Climent, S., Moré, J., Oliver, A., Salvatierra, M., Sànchez, I. and Taulé, M. (2007) 'Enhancing the status of Catalan versus Spanish in online academic forums: Obstacles to machine translation', in B. Danet and S. C. Herring (eds) *The Multilingual Internet: Language, Culture, and Communication Online*, New York: Oxford University Press.

Crystal, D. (2001) *Language and the Internet*, Cambridge: Cambridge University Press.

Cunliffe, D. and Herring, S. C. (eds) (2005) 'Introduction to minority languages, multimedia and the Web', *New Review of Hypermedia and Multimedia* 11(2): 131–7.

Danet, B. and Herring, S. C. (eds) (2007) *The Multilingual Internet: Language, Culture, and Communication Online*, New York: Oxford University Press.

de Oliveira, S.M. (2007) 'Breaking conversational norms on a Portuguese users' network: Men as adjudicators of politeness?' in B. Danet and S. C. Herring (eds) *The Multilingual Internet: Language, Culture, and Communication Online*, New York: Oxford University Press.

Durham, M. (2007) 'Language choice on a Swiss mailing list', in B. Danet and S. C. Herring (eds) *The Multilingual Internet: Language, Culture, and Communication Online*, New York: Oxford University Press.

Eisenlohr, P. (2004) 'Language revitalization and new technologies: Cultures of electronic mediation and the refiguring of communities', *Annual Review of Anthropology* 33: 21–35.

Georgakopoulou, A. (1997) 'Self-presentation and interactional alliances in e-mail discourse: The style- and code-switches of Greek messages', *International Journal of Applied Linguistics* 7(2): 141–64.

——(2006) 'Postscript: Computer-mediated communication in sociolinguistics', *Journal of Sociolinguistics* 10(4): 548–57.

Gerrard, H. and Nakamura, S. (2004) 'Japanese speakers and the internet', *International Journal on Multicultural Societies* 6(1): 173–83.

Gumperz, J. J. (1982) *Discourse Strategies*, Cambridge: Cambridge University Press.

Haag, M. and Coston, F. W. (2002) 'Early effects of technology on the Oklahoma Choctaw language community', *Language Learning & Technology* 6(2): 70–82.

Hafner, K. and Lyon, M. (1996) *Where Wizards Stay Up Late: The Origins of the Internet*, New York: Simon and Schuster.

Herring, S. C. (2003) 'Computer-mediated discourse', in D. Schiffrin, D. Tannen and H. E. Hamilton (eds) *The Handbook of Discourse Analysis*, Malden: Blackwell.

——(2004) 'Computer-mediated discourse analysis: An approach to researching online behaviour', in S. A. Barab, R. Kling and J. H. Gray (eds) *Designing for Virtual Communities in the Service of Learning*, New York: Cambridge University Press.

Hinrichs, L. (2006) *Codeswitching on the Web: English and Jamaican Creole in E-mail Communication*, Amsterdam: John Benjamins.

Hinton, L. (2001) 'Audio-video documentation', in L. Hinton and K. Hale (eds) *The Green Book of Language Revitalization in Practice*, San Diego: Academic Press.

Kelly-Holmes, H. (2004) 'An analysis of the language repertoires of students in higher education and their language choices on the internet (Ukraine, Poland, Macedonia, Italy, France, Tanzania, Oman and Indonesia)', *International Journal on Multicultural Societies* 6(1): 52–75.

Kroskrity, P. V. (2002) 'Language renewal and the technologies of literacy and postliteracy: Reflections from Western Mono', in W. Frawley, K. C. Hill and P. Munro (eds) *Making Dictionaries: Preserving Indigenous Languages in the Americas*, Berkeley: University of California Press.

Kroskrity, P. V. and Reynolds, J. F. (2001) 'Using multimedia in language renewal: Observations from making the CD-ROM Taitaduhaan (Western Mono ways of speaking)', in L. Hinton and K. Hale (eds) *The Green Book of Language Revitalization in Practice*, San Diego: Academic Press.

Kytölä, S. (2012) 'Ideology-laden peer normativity of linguistic resources-in-use: Two cases of nonstandard Englishes in Finnish online football forums', in J. Blommaert, S. Leppänen, P. Pahta and T. Räisänen (eds) *Dangerous Multilingualism*, London: Palgrave Macmillan.

Kytölä, S. and Androutsopoulos, J. (forthcoming) 'Ethnographic perspectives on multilingual computer-mediated discourse: Insights from Finnish football forums on the Web', in S. Gardner and M. Martin-Jones (eds) *Multilingualism, Discourse and Ethnography*, New York: Routledge.

Lam, W. S. E. (2004) 'Second language socialization in a bilingual chat room: Global and local considerations', *Language Learning & Technology* 8(3): 44–65.

Lavoie, B. F. and O'Neill, E. T. (2001) 'How "World Wide" is the Web?: Trends in the internationalization of web sites', *Journal of Library Administration* 34(3&4): 407–19.

Leppänen, S. (2007a) 'Cybergirls in trouble: Fan fiction as a discursive space for interrogating gender and sexuality', in C.-R. Caldas-Coulthard and R. Iedema (eds) *Identity in Trouble: Discursive Constructions*, London: Palgrave Macmillan.

——(2007b) 'Youth language in media contexts: Some insights into the spread of English in Finland', *World Englishes* 2(26): 149–69.

——(2009) 'Playing with and policing language use and textuality in fan fiction', in I. Hotz-Davies, A. Kirchhofer and S. Leppänen (eds) *Internet Fictions*, Newcastle upon Tyne: Cambridge Scholars Publishing.

——(2012) 'Linguistic and discursive heteroglossia on the translocal internet: The case of web writing', in M. Sebba, S. Mahootian and C. Jonsson (eds) *Language Mixing and Code-switching in Writing: Approaches to Mixed-Language Written Discourse*, Routledge.

Leppänen, S. and Nikula, T. (2007) 'Diverse uses of English in Finnish society: Discourse-pragmatic insights into media, educational and business contexts', *Multilingua* 26(4): 333–80.

Leppänen, S. and Piirainen-Marsh, A. (2009) 'Language policy in the making: An analysis of bilingual gaming activities', *Language Policy* 8(3): 261–84.

Leppänen, S., Pitkänen-Huhta, A., Piirainen-Marsh, A., Nikula, T. and Peuronen, S. (2009) 'Young people's translocal new media uses: A multiperspective analysis of language choice and heteroglossia', *Journal of Computer-Mediated Communication* 14(4): 1080–1107.

Mafu, S. (2004) 'From the oral tradition to the information era: The case of Tanzania', *International Journal on Multicultural Societies* 6(1): 99–124.

Nikula, T. and Pitkänen-Huhta, A. (2008) 'Using photographs to access stories of learning English', in A. M. F. Barcelos, P. Kalaja and V. Menezes (eds) *Narratives of Learning and Teaching EFL*, Basingstoke: Palgrave Macmillan.

Ouakrim, M. (2001) 'Promoting the maintenance of endangered languages through the internet: The case of Tamazight', in C. Moseley, N. Ostler and H. Ouzzate (eds) *Endangered Languages and the Media Proceedings of the Fifth FEL Conference, Agadir, Morocco 20–23 September 2001*, Bath: Foundation for Endangered Languages.

Palfreyman, D. and al Khalil, M. (2007) 'A funky language for teenz to use: Representing Gulf Arabic in instant messaging', in B. Danet and S. C. Herring (eds) *The Multilingual Internet: Language, Culture, and Communication Online*, New York: Oxford University Press.

Panyametheekul, S. and Herring, S. C. (2007) 'Gender and turn allocation in a Thai chat room', in B. Danet and S. C. Herring (eds) *The Multilingual Internet: Language, Culture, and Communication Online*, New York: Oxford University Press.

Paolillo, J. (1999) 'The virtual speech community: Social network and language variation on IRC', *Journal of Computer-Mediated Communication* 4(4), available online at http://jcmc.indiana.edu/vol4/issue4/paolillo.html

——(2005) 'Language diversity on the internet: Examining linguistic bias', in UNESCO Institute for Statistics (ed.) *Measuring Linguistic Diversity on the Internet*, Paris: UNESCO.

——(2007) 'How much multilingualism? Language diversity on the internet', in B. Danet and S. C. Herring (eds) *The Multilingual Internet: Language, Culture, and Communication Online*, New York: Oxford University Press.

Parks, D. R., Kushner, J., Hooper, W., Francis, F., Yellow Bird, D. and Ditmar, S. (1999) 'Documenting and maintaining native American languages for the 21st century: The Indiana University model', in J. Reyhner, G. Cantoni, R. St. Clair and E. Yazzie (eds) *Revitalizing Indigenous Languages*, Flagstaff: Northern Arizona University.

Pavlenko, A. and Blackledge, A. (eds) (2004) *Negotiation of Identities in Multilingual Contexts*, Clevedon: Multilingual Matters.

Peel, R. (2004) 'The internet and language use: A case study in the United Arab Emirates', *International Journal on Multicultural Societies* 6(1): 146–58.

Peuronen, S. (2011) '"Ride Hard, Live Forever": Translocal identities in an online community of extreme sports Christians', in C. Thurlow and K. Mroczek (eds) *Digital Discourse: Language in the New Media*, New York: Oxford University Press.

Pimienta, D. (2005) 'Linguistic diversity in cyberspace: Models for development and measurement', in UNESCO Institute for Statistics (ed.) *Measuring Linguistic Diversity on the Internet*, Paris: UNESCO.

Sebba, M. (2012) 'Researching and theorising mixed-language texts', in M. Sebba, S. Mahootian, and C. Jonsson (eds) *Language Mixing and Code-switching in Writing: Approaches to Mixed-language Written Discourse*, New York: Routledge.

Siebenhaar, B. (2006) 'Code choice and code-switching in Swiss-German internet Relay Chat rooms', *Journal of Sociolinguistics* 10(4): 481–506.

Sperlich, W. B. (2005) 'Will cyberforums save endangered languages? A Niuean case study', *International Journal of the Sociology of Language* 172: 51–77.

Thurlow, C., Lengel, L. and Tomic, A. (2004) *Computer-Mediated Communication: Social Interaction and the Internet*, London: Sage.

Tseliga, T. (2007) '"It's all Greeklish to me!" Linguistic and sociocultural perspectives on roman-alphabeted Greek in asynchronous computer-mediated communication', in B. Danet and S. C. Herring (eds) *The Multilingual Internet: Language, Culture, and Communication Online*, New York: Oxford University Press.

UNESCO Institute for Statistics (ed.) (2005) *Measuring Linguistic Diversity on the Internet*, Paris: UNESCO.

Warschauer, M. (1998) 'Technology and indigenous language revitalization: Analyzing the experience of Hawai'i', *Canadian Modern Language Review* 55(1): 140–61.

——(2002) 'Languages.com: the internet and linguistic pluralism', in I. Snyder (ed.) *Silicon Literacies: Communication, Innovation and Education in the Electronic Age*, London: Routledge.

Warschauer, M. and De Florio-Hansen, I. (2003) 'Multilingualism, identity, and the internet', in A. Hu and I. De Florio-Hansen (eds) *Multiple Identity and Multilingualism*, Tübingen: Stauffenburg.

Warschauer, M. and Donaghy, K. (1997) 'Leoki: A powerful voice of Hawaiian language revitalization', *Computer Assisted Language Learning* 10(4): 349–62.

Warschauer, M., Said, G. R. E. and Zohry, A. (2002) 'Language choice online: Globalization and identity in Egypt', *Journal of Computer-Mediated Communication* 7(4), available online at http://jcmc.indiana.edu/vol7/issue4/warschauer.html

Wodak, R. and Wright, S. (2006) 'The European Union in cyberspace: Multilingual democratic participation in a virtual public sphere?' *Journal of Language and Politics* 5(2): 251–75.

Wright, S. (2004) 'Introduction', *International Journal on Multicultural Societies* 6(1): 5–13.

23

Multilingualism and popular culture

Mela Sarkar and Bronwen Low

Multilingualism and popular culture: what's the link?

A research area in search of itself

From our current standpoint, it may appear normal and inevitable that peoples and cultures have been mixing and mingling as they have for well over half a century. To many people in the English-speaking world, being multilingual no longer seems rare and exotic; to many people elsewhere, it never did. University-age readers of a comprehensive handbook on multilingualism published around 2011 will not remember an era when most people stayed in the place where they were born, and when languages seemed tied down to specific nations and locations. Indeed, their *parents* are almost certainly too young to themselves remember the pre-Second World War (1939–45) years when the boundaries of Europe seemed indissoluble, and the colonized non-white peoples of Africa and Asia had not yet moved to take their political futures back into their own hands (see Canagarajah and Liyanage this volume; Ramanathan this volume; May 2001). Around this time – during the decades just before and after the Second World War years – British and European thinkers began to explore the idea that 'mass' or 'popular' culture, as distinct from either the 'High Culture' of the educated elite or the 'Folk Culture' collected by nineteenth-century scholars such as the Brothers Grimm, might actually be theoretically interesting, rather than deplorable (Strinati 2000). The idea that popular culture is a phenomenon deserving of study in its own right is therefore no longer new, as we shall see in more detail below.

In the past ten years or so, the field of multilingualism as a separate area within language studies generally has also started to come into its own. This is in contrast to the field of *bilingualism*, under which multilingualism has, until recently, been subsumed (typically, through the offhand use of the phrase 'bi- and/or multilingualism'). The publication of a handbook dedicated specifically to a broad spectrum of issues around multilingualism is itself evidence that the field has achieved a certain level of maturity and recognition.

It seems natural, therefore, to ask 'What about the study of multilingualism and popular culture together? What do we know about how multilingual popular culture is – or since when, where, why, and to what effect is it multilingual? How might looking at popular culture open up new ways to understand multilingually mixed populations?' Surprisingly, though, there is very little real research on this seemingly obvious topic. From the 1930s onwards, the study of popular culture and its importance in modern life has developed within a complex set of intersecting theoretical frameworks. Depending on the scholarly 'lens', for instance, it gets examined as semiotic 'text', as lived experience, and, alternately, as a site of 'mass culture' oppression or of resistance by 'the people'. As is the pattern in academia, its study has produced specialized conferences, journals, books, university syllabi and programmes. Popular culture has even been admitted to the classroom, considered a legitimate route to pedagogical innovation by progressive educators (Buckingham and Sefton-Green 1994; Giroux and Simon 1989). Until very recently, however, none of this work has taken much notice of the prevalence of different languages in popular culture, and of even *bi*lingual – let alone multilingual – language mixing. Work such as that of Ofelia García on multiple discursive or 'translanguaging' practices in multilingual classrooms (García 2009; this volume) offers one potentially very fruitful way forward. Educators who are progressive enough to bring popular culture into the classroom will, it is to be hoped, soon take the additional step of considering specifically multilingual forms of popular culture as interesting in their own right, in the same way that García proposes for other multilingual practices in classrooms.

Change is therefore fast arriving, having already won recognition for one form of popular culture – hip-hop – a phenomenon so important to late twentieth-century and early twenty-first century youth that it is fair to call it a cultural movement in its own right (Kitwana 2002; KRS-One 2000; Rose 1994). Perhaps because hip-hop's rise as an international youth movement is so recent and coincides with a scholarly awareness of the significance of the movement and mixing of people and languages across borders, there has been a groundswell of academic interest in language mixing by hip-hop-identified youth. Since roughly the year 2000, a number of published studies of mixed language in hip-hop lyrics have appeared (Androutsopoulos 2007, 2009; Higgins 2009; Lin 2009).

This body of work was jump-started, as it were, by an edited volume on international forms of hip-hop by Australian/New Zealand ethnomusicologist and popular studies scholar Tony Mitchell (Mitchell 2001), which did not focus specifically on language. Mitchell's *Global Noise* appeared a few years after a groundbreaking American study of hip-hop, Tricia Rose's *Black Noise* (1994), and 'sampled' or signified on the title of the earlier work in classic hip-hop style. In the field of language studies, special sessions at international conferences, themed journal issues and edited volumes devoted solely to mixed-language in hip-hop (Alim *et al.* 2009; Terkourati, 2010) have begun to appear. The work of Alastair Pennycook (Pennycook 2003, 2004, 2007) has been particularly important in this context, as his pioneering research on the ways in which the global spread of English has interacted with the global spread of hip-hop has provided theoretical underpinnings for scholars in other linguistic contexts.

The authors of this chapter situate themselves within the current of this new stream of study (Low *et al.* 2009; Sarkar 2009; Sarkar *et al.* 2007). We devote the central section of this chapter to a discussion of recent work on multilingualism in hip-hop culture as the area of study that most extensively combines scholarship on multilingualism with popular culture. We focus on mixed-language use in rap lyrics, using our work on Montreal hip-hop as our main example. To set the stage, however, we first map out some concepts and debates in popular culture studies, a specialized field readers of this *Handbook* may be less familiar with than applied and educational linguistics. This includes making some brief connections to the related field of cultural studies. We also speculate on reasons why research on multilingualism within the field of popular culture has, with the exception of hip-hop research, been so conspicuous by its absence. After an extended look at multilingual hip-hop research, we conclude the chapter by discussing what we consider to be some key issues in this emerging field, and outlining directions for future research.

A working definition of popular culture

Any principled definition of 'popular culture' must of necessity have packaged up in it an implicit or explicit definition of 'culture' itself. But 'culture', one of the two or three most complicated words in the English language (Williams 1976), is notoriously difficult to define. The *Oxford Online Dictionary* lists seven meanings of culture, of which the one closest to what we want here, 'the distinctive ideas, customs, social behaviour, products, or way of life of a particular society, people, or period', is the seventh (the first has to do with the original Latin meaning of 'cultivating, tilling the soil'). Nearly 60 years ago, two influential American anthropologists, in a then-state-of-the-art review of concepts and definitions related to 'culture', came up with 164 definitions of the word (Kroeber and Kluckhohn 1952). Since then, in sheer number, academic viewpoints on 'culture' have continued to proliferate, and to become, if anything, far more nuanced than post-war theorists could have imagined.

In this chapter, we work with an anthropological definition of culture as a whole way of life. This includes everything about the way a particular group of people live, except things pre-determined by biology (genetically encoded, so impossible to change). But with humans, so few things are genetically encoded in any kind of unchangeable way that for all practical purposes culture encompasses most things. (For instance, the ways we eat, reproduce the species – and speak – are all considered part of our genetic endowment, yet vary so much across human groups that they can be studied as part of 'culture'.) Why such a broad definition of culture in this introduction to popular culture from the standpoint of studies on multilingualism (and vice versa)? Because it helps to explain the ways that multilingual language use can enter into every aspect of the way people live.

When 'popular culture' began to be defined as an area of study within literary, sociological or anthropological studies more generally, it had first – as we saw briefly above – to be set off from 'High Culture' in the sense famously defined by British cultural critic Matthew Arnold (1822–88) as 'the best that has been thought and said' (Arnold 1869). By this Arnold most emphatically did *not* mean, for example, popular songs or literature of his own, Victorian era, nor British broadsheet advertising of the previous (eighteenth) century in working-class London. But scholars of popular culture study all those and many other such historical phenomena (Hoggart 1957), providing a wealth of information on how people have made and continue to make meaning. Arnold had in mind, for example, the plays of Shakespeare; the poetry of Milton (but not necessarily the novels of Dickens, extremely *popular* at that time); the music of Mozart or Beethoven (but not of Gilbert and Sullivan). From a twenty-first-century perspective the differences often seem negligible. For instance, is the 1996 Hollywood movie version of Shakespeare's *Romeo and Juliet* by film-maker Baz Luhrmann 'High Culture', popular culture or both?

In the other, 'low' direction, popular culture was formerly often distinguished from *folk* culture. The 'household tales' of a peasant society, such as those collected by the Brothers Grimm, the songs and sayings of such societies – agrarian, conservative, slow to change – from this perspective are of a piece with folk art forms such as quilting, basket weaving or country dancing. Many of these forms of culture, including, unfortunately, many formerly flourishing manifestations of traditional Indigenous cultures, are now known to be endangered. 'Folk culture' can in fact gain new life by teaming up with popular culture, and is constantly doing so, as in, for example, dance hall and bhangra cultures and music, both connected with 'folk' traditions in Jamaica and the Punjab where they originated.

405

Popular culture studies vs 'cultural studies'

One of the most influential academic movements to take popular culture seriously as an object of study is Cultural Studies, established as a field and method of inquiry with the founding of the Birmingham Centre for Cultural Studies in 1964 in Britain. Its founding figures include teachers working in adult education such as Raymond Williams and Richard Hoggart who recognized that the official curriculum, with its static and elitist notions of culture, was largely disconnected from the lives of their mostly working-class students. They began exploring culture as lived experience, linking everyday life to questions of power, ideology and social difference, particularly class, drawing on and reconstructing Marxist theories of historical materialism.

The methods and purposes for studying popular culture are varied and contested. Those working in the traditions of Cultural Studies (which in turn can be broken down into sub-categories such as British, American and 'Black') contrast their project with the less critical, less theoretically informed and largely celebratory work of some pop culture scholars, often associated with the Popular Culture Association (see, for instance, the critiques of Kellner 1995 and Fiske 1990). Cultural Studies scholars also distinguish their work from that of Frankfurt School scholars who drew rigid distinctions between 'high' and 'low' culture, and could see no possible value in the standardized and homogenous 'mass culture' produced by the 'culture industries'. Also debated is the use of the term 'popular', often used to describe the art and culture created by working-class and other marginalized peoples, or culture 'of, by, and for the people' (Kellner 1995: 33), but which now also gets used to reference mass-media culture. In response, Kellner (1995) rejects the 'popular' in favour of the term 'media culture', which signals the primacy of the media (including communications technologies and industries) in the production, distribution and dissemination of culture, and which does not collapse more grass-roots cultural forms with those primarily produced by the mass media. These distinctions between the critical and the celebratory (Dolby 2003) and the mass and the popular are by no means fixed, but may serve as useful heuristics for thinking about popular culture and multilingualism.

It is fair to say that the internationally based work on multilingual language use in hip-hop communities referred to above tends to align itself with critical (rather than purely celebratory) approaches to the analysis of language in society. As scholars, they (and we) tend to identify as critical theorists of language and/or ethnicity and/or education (across a spread of disciplines). That is to say, we assume an underlying concern with exposing and redressing imbalances of power at any and all levels of people's lives as they interact with, are influenced by, and/or help to create, debate and indeed often celebrate, popular/media culture.

Why bring in multilingualism? Why was it not brought in before?

Because popular culture crosses political and cultural borders with such ease, it lends itself to multilingual language mixing particularly well. The most obvious example is the globalizing force of American culture, which in the minds of many readers may be more or less equated with popular culture. Where Hollywood, pop music and hamburgers have gone, American (including African American) English has followed. What this has meant in many places is a *bi*lingual layer of popular culture, if only at the level of lexical borrowing. The international prestige of knowing English, which in symbolic-capital terms (Bourdieu and Passeron 1990) is 'like the [American] dollar' (Niño-Murcia 2003), has meant that English words and slang expressions may be liberally scattered over any number of discourse domains that would once have been monolingual in another language (see, for example, a Japanese version of this phenomenon at www.engrish.com).

This bilingual burgeoning has received a certain amount of scholarly attention for its own sake. What has hitherto not received special attention is the underlying complexity in places that are already bilingual or multilingual. The taxi driver in Lima, Peru, who asserted to the researcher that English was 'like the dollar' was in a place where by far the most common form of bilingualism is Quechua/Spanish, not Spanish/English. In Mexico, many rural speakers of another widespread Indigenous language, Nahuatl, are trying to graft English onto their Nahuatl/Spanish bilingualism as fast as they can. There are numerous other examples of places where Indigenous peoples and their languages are confronted with not one but two or more colonial languages (see Patrick this volume, for an Inuktitut/English/French example from Canada). And in very densely populated parts of the world, such as the South Asian subcontinent, the Southeast Asian/Oceania archipelagoes, or many countries in Africa, local bilingualism or multilingualism long predated the arrival of white European (or other) colonizers. In Mumbai, Kuala Lumpur or Nairobi, popular culture has long expressed itself through a mixture of local languages and English (or other colonizing languages) without attracting any particular notice; multilingualism in such places is a way of life.

We will take the position here that everywhere outside a restricted but influential cultural zone – roughly, the 'Anglo-American' part of the world that has had such a disproportionate share of the global economic, political and cultural markets up to now – popular culture is likely to have a strong multilingual flavour. If this has not hitherto been noticed or studied, it is because multilingualism as a field of study separate from bilingualism has only recently begun to attract scholarly attention. In fact, the notion of multilingualism as something unusual is badly in need of deconstruction (see Makoni and Pennycook this volume). It should probably be taken as the norm, with *mono*lingualism as an unfortunate and handicapping aberration for a (disproportionately influential) few. From that perspective, giving multilingualism and popular culture a chapter all its own is just a post hoc recognition of (and belated scholarly decision to start investigating) something that has been there all along.

Theorizing around multilingualism and popular culture: multilingual hip-hop studies

An international hip-hop Cypha of theory and hiphopography

If we have chosen to focus on studies of multilingual hip-hop as our only extended example of a currently active area of research on multilingualism and popular culture, it is because to the best of our knowledge, at the moment there *is* no other active area we can use as an example. Scholars of culture in places where popular culture is very actively studied (the USA is the best example) tend to be less aware of multilingualism, and are often monolingual. Although there are exceptions (Manuelito 2006; Soto 2006), the focus in such work, theoretically complex as it may be, is not on language diversity. It would typically be, rather, on issues of identity and belonging in a complex cultural matrix where language, if it is mentioned at all, is seen as an adjunct to culture.

On the flip side, scholars of language in places where multilingualism is the norm and scholarship on multilingual issues is active (India is the best example) tend to be less aware of popular culture as a possible object of investigation (Pattanayak 1990); their research energy has often, and understandably, been directed more at issues of access to education and language planning for a linguistically diverse, largely disenfranchised population. Popular films and songs in such places are being scrutinized intensively, and cultural studies territory is being seriously and critically mapped out (Mukhopadhyay 2006) but not from the standpoint of multilingual language use.

One of the reasons that hip-hop has lent itself so well to investigation by language scholars is that rap lyrics *demand* wordiness. Although in pop music, rhythm and lyrics often play second fiddle to melody, in rap, melody all but disappears and the lyrics and the beats take centre stage. Rap's lyrics are foregrounded over an underlying musical soundscape. The average rap's lyrics consists of several rapid-fire, language-packed verses, often by a number of different rap artists (MCs), separated by repetitions of a refrain. Rap is text-heavy and requires great verbal skill and unceasing inventiveness on the part of its creators. There is a built-in requirement for rap lyrics (like other forms of poetry – rap unquestionably qualifies as poetry) to contain a lot of near-cognate rhymes in highly constrained metric patterns (Costello and Foster Wallace 1990). This poetic device acts as a productive constraint on rap's language, forcing 'the extra linguistic creativity', including 'stretches' and 'improbable vocab', that 'makes a good rap a great rap' (ibid.). As we have affirmed above, there are many contexts in the world where the use of several languages in ordinary speech is common and unremarkable – for example, the Montreal youth communities where our sociolinguistic work is situated, or similarly multi-ethnic youth communities in other Western urban contexts such as London (Rampton this volume), not to mention examples from Africa (Higgins 2009; Omoniyi 2009) or Asia (Lin this volume; Pennycook 2003). It is natural and inevitable that rap artists in those contexts will draw on all the linguistic resources available to them in order to increase the pool of potential rhymes. And they do. Multilingual mixing in rap lyrics thus becomes a stylistic device, quite apart from the many uses it may have for creating new kinds of meaning with critical, analytical and sociopolitical purposes. Our team has remarked on this 'poetic' function of multilingual codeswitching in Montreal hip-hop (Sarkar and Winer 2006); Omoniyi (2009) and Lin (2009) discuss similar poetic uses in rap lyrics in Nigeria and Hong Kong, respectively.

Current scholarship in this field includes examinations of hip-hop multilingualism from the perspective of performativity theory in language, within which one produces, rather than reflects, identity through language work (Pennycook 2004). In contexts such as francophone Ontario schools, for example, African immigrant students, who speak French but have other first languages, quickly gravitate to BESL, or 'Black English as a second language' (Ibrahim 2003) as a tool of belonging. Our own work speaks to the phenomenon of multilingual codeswitching in Montreal hip-hop lyrics as a way of performing multilingual identity (see below, next section). In Alim *et al.* (2009), rap lyrics in a wide range of hip-hop communities across the globe are examined, including those found in Europe (Androutsopoulos 2009), Tanzania (Higgins 2009), Hong Kong (Lin 2009), Nigeria (Omoniyi 2009) and Australia (Pennycook and Mitchell 2009), drawing upon and developing theories of discourse, styling, crossing, codeswitching and post-colonial performance (see Lin, Omoniyi, Makoni and Pennycook this volume, for other examples of some current work). For the most part, this scholarship documents multilingual hip-hop practices in places where multilingualism is the norm (see also Auzanneau 2001; Auzanneau *et al.* 2003); this work may or may not be explicitly linked to popular culture studies, as the focus is often more purely sociolinguistic or sociological. What it is safe to say is that this is territory that has barely begun to be explored. The study of multilingual hip-hop practices alone, in itself a tiny fraction of what popular culture studies could potentially offer to scholars of multilingualism, is a subfield of applied linguistics that has already caused such dynamic cross-fertilization and innovative theorizing that no one can say which disciplines within language and/or culture studies (and the once inviolable disciplinary boundaries between them) may not eventually be affected.

We turn now to a discussion of multilingual mixing in Montreal hip-hop lyrics, using examples from ongoing work by our research team at McGill University.

Applying theory to a specific example: Montreal hip-hop

We began looking at Montreal hip-hop in 2002, gradually expanding the focus of analysis from the sociolinguistic to the sociological and cultural. To analyses of a corpus of about 30 songs released between 1999 and 2004, we added subsequent interviews with MCs and youth informants. All this material has borne out our initial hypothesis about the importance of multilingualism to much of the Montreal rap scene.

Why is it so important? It happened that the generation of young Québécois that has grown up with French as their common public language came to maturity in the 1990s at the same time as the Quebec hip-hop scene. A constant flow of family back and forth between the large Anglo-Caribbean (Jamaican, Trinidadian) and Franco-Caribbean (Haitian) expatriate communities of New York City and their Montreal contacts and counterparts meant that New York-based hip-hop cultural products became known in Montreal from the 1970s onwards (N. Indongo, personal communication, May 2008). However, the location of Quebec at a cultural crossroads between America and Europe also ensured the popularity of European French rappers such as MC Solaar and the Marseilles group IAM. The French that is the base language of Quebec rap, and of talk about rap and hip-hop, is a distinct and rapidly evolving French. Because of hip-hop's strong ties to African American culture, forms of AAVE (African American Vernacular English) shape Quebec hip-hop vernaculars. Standard and non-standard Quebec and European varieties of French, standard North American English, AAVE and hip-hop slang, Haitian French Creole, Jamaican English Creole, Spanish and Arabic are mixed creatively in the lyrics and speech of hip-hop performers and many audience members (Sarkar *et al.* 2005). This is a new way of using language that subtly undermines the original intentions of the Quebec language planners responsible for the legislation that created this multi-ethnic French-speaking youth population (through obligatory schooling in French) in the first place. Although by no means all Quebec rap lyrics are linguistically mixed, in lyrics and in the street it is taken for granted that mixing is acceptable on a wide scale. Multilingualism is positioned 'as a natural and desirable condition, whether or not everything is then comprehensible to everyone' (Sarkar and Winer 2006: 189).

When Montreal MCs first came out with raps in which several languages were freely mixed over a Quebec French base, the language of the lyrics reflected the language of the multi-ethnic Montreal neighbourhoods in which the lyrics were grounded:

> J'*check* Rob: '*What up dog?*'
> —'*What up yo!* **Shit**, les rues sont *fucked up!*'
> *Enough talk.* **Check** le reste du *squad.*
> On *set* un *get* ce soir. *Peace. Hang up the phone.*
> J'*step* dehors. Dès que j'sors, des nègs *blast* des *teck*, percent mon corps.
> J'saigne, *fuck up*, à l'hôpital, presque mort.
> *Help me y'all!*
>
> (Impossible of Muzion, *666 thème, Mentalité moune morne,* 1999)

This lyric, representing a stylized telephone conversation between Imposs and his interlocutor Rob, is a typical example of the language this generation of young Montrealers has evolved.

When we started analysing lyrics, certain coding decisions imposed themselves on the data. In order to indicate the origin of lexical items, we wound up using a coding scheme with nine categories under four superordinate-level headings, as follows:

FRENCH
Standard Quebec French (unmarked)
Non-standard Quebec French (bolded)
European French (bolded and underlined)

ENGLISH
Standard North American English (underlined)
African American Vernacular English (AAVE) (italicized)
Hip-Hop Keywords (italicized and underlined)

CARIBBEAN CREOLES
Haitian Creole (bolded and italicized)
Jamaican Creole (bolded, italicized and underlined)

OTHER LANGUAGES
Spanish (outlined)

Of these nine categories, five are relevant for the 'J'check Rob' lyric, which lasts 16 seconds. Quebec youth who participate in the hip-hop community would have no difficulty in understanding it; it is typical of the way many of them talk themselves.

Imposs introduces the simulated phone conversation with the non-standard Quebec French verb **checker**, from English 'to check', used by Quebec Francophones to mean 'to observe'. Here it means 'I call up Rob'. Imposs continues with the standard AAVE greeting *'What up dog?'* Rob's voice on the line answers with the equally conventional *'What up yo!'* then continues with **Shit** [non-standard Quebec French], les rues sont *fucked up*! [standard English]. The entire exchange is taking place in a Quebec French context; our decision to code 'shit' as French and 'fucked up' as English was subjective, based on our understanding that older monolingual French speakers normally have the first, but not the second, integrated into their French.

In the next two lines Imposs first answers Rob, then speaks as narrator: *'Enough talk* [English]. **Check** le reste du [the rest of the] *squad* [hip-hop word, coded as such because Imposs is speaking in the context of his crew meeting later on]. On [we] *set* [AAVE, 'set up'] un *get* [AAVE, 'get-together'] ce soir [this evening]. *Peace* [coded here as a hip-hop keyword because it is Imposs's conventional farewell to Rob]. Hang up the phone [straight English].

Imposs then '*step* dehors [outside]. Dès que je sors [as soon as I go out], des nègs ['niggas'; the French version has the same negative force as the English in normal language (Low 2007) and has been reclaimed in a similar way for French by young Black members of the hip-hop community] *blast* des *teck* ['Tech-1' semi-automatic weapons]. Gunshots 'percent mon corps [put holes in my body]. J'saigne [I bleed], *fuck up*, à l'hôpital, presque mort [at the hospital, almost dead]'. An ambulance siren sounds. The verse ends *'Help me y'all!'* The rapid-fire codeswitching we observe here can be further analysed in terms of the functions it serves in the composition of raps, which are highly scripted forms of language that differ in important ways from normal conversational speech.

It is likely that language like this can only be understood by young Quebec French speakers who are also very familiar with English, both standard North American and AAVE, particularly as it is used by Black American rap artists. Furthermore, speakers of this generation, whatever their ethnic background, have also integrated a number of words from both Haitian (French-based) and Jamaican (English-based) Creole into their everyday language and their raps. Some examples of these are *popo* ['police'], *patnai* ['good friend' (from English 'partner')], *kob* ['cash'], *ti-moun* ['little kid, kid' (from French 'petit monde'), *kget* (a swearword), all Haitian Creole; *ganja* ['marijuana', one of a long series of words with this meaning], *spliff* ['marijuana cigarette', also represented by a long series of words], *skettel* ['girl, loose woman'], *rude bwoy* ['aggressive youth'], all Jamaican Creole.

Recent sociological and sociolinguistic work on Montreal's new *francophonie* makes clear that the dynamic codeshifting we have been chronicling is part of a larger generational shift in attitudes towards multilingualism (Meintel 1992). Lamarre *et al.* (2002) describe the 'appreciable linguistic adaptability of many young Montrealers and their extremely varied language practices', which include, for instance, 'trilingual codeswitching, not so much for negotiating language use, but rather to express plural identities and ties to many social networks', as well as 'changing attitudes toward the maintenance of a minority language among young Allophones related to transnationalism and globalization'. The language of Montreal hip-hop's rap lyrics thus reflects the linguistic and cultural diversity found in schools and the young adult community as well as local rappers' sense that they are part of a self-defined, border-crossing 'Hip-Hop Nation' (Alim 2002; Mitchell 2001; Krims 2000).

Our interviews with six rappers active in the Montreal hip-hop community in 2004 (through commercially available CDs and live shows) made it clear that their multilingual codeswitching reflects some of the ways in which language is lived in contemporary Montreal. As rap group Muzion member J-Kyll puts it, 'en général, on chante, on rap comme on parle' ('in general, we sing, we rap like we speak'). SolValdez and 2Sai, of Dominican descent, born and brought up in Montreal, identify strongly with Dominican culture, especially its musical traditions, and with Spanish, but also with multilingual, multicultural Montreal. Of their codeswitching SolValdez commented, 'we might wind up saying a whole sentence in three languages ... And the sad part of it is that we don't even notice that we switched the languages, we just yo, and blah, blah, blah in Spanish and then switch to French'. Rapper Sans Pression, whose family has roots in the Congo but who has lived his whole life in North America, first in New York state and then in Montreal, describes the way his raps switch between French and English as 'that's how we talk' and 'putting both musics, both languages, is like, it just comes naturally'. As with Sol's not noticing the switching, Sans Pression says of lyrical codeshifting, 'I don't even think about it when I write it. It's crazy'. The idea that this language blending comes naturally and is somehow instinctive, not requiring reflection, suggests that it might indeed be a community norm as in the work of Lamarre *et al.* (2002). That said, Muzion member Dramatik describes the hybrid language of Montreal rap as a more conscious political choice from 'des artistes qui se décident à mettre la langue du peuple dans les textes' ('artists who decide to put the people's language into their texts'). Through their multilingual lyrics, the rappers work to create what they describe as the distinct Montreal style that deliberately draws on and so reflects available local cultural and linguistic resources. The rappers identify the codeswitching that happens in multilingual Montreal as, in Sans Pression's words, 'what's good about here'. What's good about here can be a source of surprise to others, as 2Sai remarks about the Puerto Rican artists who come to Montreal and see 'Latinos speaking French, English and Spanish'.

Codeswitching in the Montreal hip-hop scene enacts a model of multicultural community that is both local and international. Always shaped to a certain extent by one's audience, it may sometimes be intended for an in-group only, in which case learning to understand the codeswitching is an essential part of becoming a fully fledged member of that speech community. Examples of this phenomenon can of course be found elsewhere, in hip-hop communities in Africa (Higgins 2009) and Asia (Lin 2009; this volume; Pennycook 2003, 2007) as well as in other kinds of youth communities worldwide – for example, the online communities described for young Finns in the work of Leppänen (2007; this volume) and her colleagues (Leppänen *et al.* 2009), in which multilingualism is so clearly part of the overall message, and hip-hop only one of the forms of popular culture explored. The rappers we spoke to describe the multilingual hybridity of their rap as an *asset,* as an opening up to the world. As Sol says of the codeshifting, 'Some people might see it as a limitation, you know, that's one side of it. But if you look at it on the other side, it's more of an expansion'. The practitioners of Montreal hip-hop examined here celebrate multilingualism, in part because 'it's the way we talk' in a culturally diverse community and in part because it honours the diversity of this community.

Indeed, the public and performative use of wider linguistic codes – 'translanguaging', in García's (2009) sense – is implicitly rebellious, as multilingualism, like multiculturalism, is expressly *not* an official government policy. At the same time, most Montreal rappers draw on French as a powerful resource that connects them to hip-hop and other expressive traditions of the *Francophonie,* including France and countries like Senegal, Haiti and Algeria.

Preliminary analyses of the current phase of our research, which compares multilingual rap in Montreal and Toronto, suggest that although there is codeswitching in the work of some rappers in English Canada – e.g. the presence of bits of various Caribbean Creoles, particularly Jamaican Patwa, and hip-hop English along with Standard Canadian English in the work of Toronto rappers like Kardinall Offishall (Low 2001) – it does not compare to the much greater integration of such multilingualism in a good deal of the independent Montreal rap scene. To date it seems that the multilingual mixing in Montreal rap lyrics is the most extravagant in North America.

Popular culture in the [applied linguistics] academy

Asked to sum up the main issues related to the study of multilingualism and popular culture at this point, our answer is twofold. The first issue is: why isn't there more research on this? With the groundswell of academic interest in popular culture over the past few decades, combined with intense new research interest in multilingualism as opposed to bilingualism, how did this seemingly obvious area of overlap get overlooked? Our quick look at the recent, tightly delimited, but theoretically and empirically rich body of work on multilingual hip-hop culture makes it clear that complex and interesting scholarship is certainly possible in this field.

The second issue is to do with the challenge of making multilingually oriented research on popular culture (or popular culture-oriented research on multilingualism) into an 'unmarked' domain of study. Because of the monolingual mindset that has tended to characterize Anglo-American research on language issues, *bi*lingualism, not to mention multilingualism, may seem exotic to 'Western' researchers. We maintain, however, that there is nothing exotic or unusual about being multilingual, either for an individual or a community. There is, therefore, nothing exotic about creating culture, including popular culture, multilingually. At this point, the hybrid, multilingually mixed nature of much popular culture just *is,* even if it has not been much remarked on for its multilingual features. It is a fact neither to celebrate nor to deplore, but something to observe and examine with interest like anything else. This 'ordinariness' has been brought out by Pennycook in his discussion of 'socioblinguistics':[1]

To work socioblinguistically, then, I intend to take seriously the politics of language and the ordinariness of diversity. ... Difference and diversity, multilingualism and hybridity are not rare and exotic conditions to be sought out and celebrated but the quotidian ordinariness of everyday life.

(2007: 95)

There is a good case for arguing, furthermore, that the ordinariness we have been underlining for multilingualism in popular culture could be extended to different ways of looking at kinds of popular culture that have not usually been thought of as being bi- or multilingual. The extensive American literature on popular culture does not typically forefront the presence of diverse dialect use as an interesting phenomenon in itself (for example, the frequent juxtaposing of Standard American English with AAVE or other non-Standard varieties), taking it rather for granted as part of the sociocultural backdrop for theorizing. If more attention were paid to the presence in expressions of American (and other) popular culture of many different kinds of English alone, a significant step would be made in consciousness-raising about the role of language in this area. The coding decisions we made in our own hip-hop research work show one way in which this could be done; under each separate larger language category ('Kinds of English; Kinds of French; Kinds of Caribbean Creole'), we found that in order to do the data justice, we needed to subcategorize two or three different ways. If this were more commonly done in Anglo-American popular culture research, we anticipate that the field would open up considerably, in a way that would make connections to international language research not just likely, but inevitable. Making research links across sociopolitical and disciplinary borders in this way is long overdue.

The newness of looking at popular culture research this way supplies part of the answer to our first question above: why isn't this out there yet? It may just be too soon. Another part of the answer is perhaps that the subfield of multilingualism within applied linguistics is also very young. Looking at multilingualism as ordinary – deconstructing the exoticness of it all (Makoni and Pennycook this volume) is even younger.

We consider that in everything we have said thus far about multilingualism and popular culture as an independent area of study, we have been referring to one coin with two sides that are not usually looked at as being part of an integrated whole. What we have at this point are not answers, but questions about how best to proceed. From the perspective of work in language studies, how can we understand multilingualism better by including a focus on popular culture as one of many ways people express themselves multilingually? Conversely, how can incorporating the insights from work on multilingualism into the study of popular culture enrich popular culture/cultural studies as a field? Is the object of scrutiny multilingualism, with theorizing about popular culture as the 'lens'? Or is popular culture/cultural studies the object of study, with multilingual approaches to studying human language forming the interpretive frame?

The answer, of course, is that there is no need for the answer to be either/or. By agreeing that it is in the interests of scholars both of language and of popular culture to start thinking in multilingual terms about how to combine both, we can start to move several fields forward simultaneously. We anticipate that doing this will require one or more paradigm shifts on the part of those of us who have been accustomed to thinking of non-monolingual language use as in any way unusual. But, as one well-known scholar working in a multilingual context has said, it is rather the opposite point of view we should be taking as the norm: 'Any restriction on language use is intolerable. Two or three languages are barely tolerable and one language is absurd' (Pattanayak 2000).

Carrying popular culture forward multilingually: new research directions

As we have said, the study of multilingualism and popular culture as a single, multifaceted area of inquiry is in its infancy. The task of making this an 'ordinary', non-exotic field is a new research direction in itself, one that can be linked to ongoing work by Makoni and Pennycook (this volume; Makoni and Pennycook 2007) on the 'deconstructing' of the idea of separate, rigidly demarcated languages. Such a notion is rooted in a long tradition of Eurocentric scholarship that is showing signs of a few cracks in the foundations (Harris 2002). The need to fence oneself off from the Other may not be one we can afford to indulge much longer, in linguistics and language study any more than in other fields of human endeavour.

A related direction that could profitably be taken by workers in this area is a similar breaking away from Anglo-American conceptions of popular culture, which tend all too often to be monolingual. In Europe, popular culture has become more and more multilingual as European borders have become more porous (Androutsopoulos and Scholz 2003). In the countries of Africa and the South Asian subcontinent, it has been multilingual for decades. A Western visitor to any large city in India cannot fail to be impressed by the sheer multi-plicity of languages and cultures that jostle for place on Bollywood billboards, TV screens and radio stations. As in so many other places, the post-colonial mixing of English with the local language(s) is only one example. Local languages have long mixed with each other.

Indigenous contexts are another site where the study of multilingual language use and popular culture at the local level would, we believe, repay careful investigation. A start has been made in this direction, such as Pennycook and Mitchell's (2009) work with Australian 'Abo-digital' rapper Wire MC, or Mitchell's many other publications (which do not, however, focus specifically on language) in which he discusses Indigenous popular music produced by Samoan, Fijian and Maori artists. In the Canadian context, we are aware of several Indigenous rappers who use their traditional languages mixed in with the local colonial language (the mixed-language work of Algonkian/Québécois rappers Samian and Shauit can be heard online at, for example, www.samian.ca/ and www.myspace.com/shauit). Indigenous communities worldwide are obliged somehow to come to terms with the pressures that are being put on them by surrounding White society. Not all of them manage to retain their Indigenous language as the main medium of community use, but the possibilities of incorporating tradi-tional words, phrases and concepts into forms of culture that are likely to become widely known, i.e. local forms of popular culture, may be one way of keeping awareness levels high and youth interested in pursuing linguistic leads back to older identities.

This brings us to a more general point about the word-work of youth cultures as part of the study of multilingualism and its effects. Marginalized youth everywhere have seized on the possibilities of hip-hop as a text-loaded way of delivering their messages about their experi-ence of oppression; as we have seen, in places where youth communities are multi-ethnic, those messages are often multilingual. In some instances, the active mixing of languages can produce new languages, as in Blommaert's (2005) research on the *Wahuni* hip-hop community in Dar es Salaam, Tanzania, which revealed that they were actively creating a new 'antilanguage', *Kihuni*, which they were committed to formalizing and codifying through practices such as transcription. In contrast, the language practices of the Montreal hip-hop scene are less about inventing a new language and more about celebrating an attitude towards language, which is also an attitude toward community and diversity.

But popular culture takes many forms other than hip-hop, as we see in the work of Higgins (2004, 2007, 2009), who applies Blommaert's (2005; Blommaert *et al.* 2005) work on orders of indexicality in language to the study of several linked manifestations of popular culture in

Dar es Salaam. Higgins shows that youth communities in Dar es Salaam are using language mixing to actively create new relationships between varieties and levels of English, Swahili and other local languages in domains from rap lyrics to bus advertisements to popular anti-AIDS campaigns. Popular culture delivers powerful messages; multilingualism as the medium of those messages makes multilingualism itself a large part of the message.

This multilingual experimentation has some important implications for education; if schools are to remain relevant to the youth they serve, educational policy makers must acknowledge and engage multilingual and multivarietal popular formulations of language. This might mean, for instance, in Quebec, the need for a multidialectical approach to the teaching of French in school. Also promising are critical language awareness (Fairclough 1992) pedagogies, which teach young people about sociolinguistics and critical literacy and help them become ethnographers of the language practices, and their politics, of their own multilingual communities (see, for instance, Alim's (2004) *Hiphopographical* work in Black American contexts, which could and should be paralleled internationally and multilingually). Popular culture, often thought of as somehow belonging more to the young, is in any case a logical, inevitable and wholly fascinating place for up-and-coming scholars to concentrate their multilingual research energies. Together with established researchers in the field – such as Alim (2002, 2004), Androutsopoulos (2007, 2009), Higgins (2009), Lin (2009), Omoniyi (2009) and Pennycook (2003, 2007), who have produced outstanding scholarship across five continents – it is to be hoped that younger scholars will not hesitate to mark, by *un*marking, new multilingual territory across a wide range of popular culture forms.

Related topics

Crossing; codeswitching; heteroglossia; multilingualism on the Internet.

Note

1 Pennycook (2007) coined this term along with H. S. Alim and Awad Ibrahim (the co-edited book that gave rise to the discussion is Alim *et al.* 2009). 'Bling' is a term well known in the hip-hop community, as well as being on record in online urban dictionaries and elsewhere. It refers to 'expensive, ostentatious clothing and jewelry, or the wearing of them'. Socioblinguistics would thus be the sociolinguistics of urban 'linguistic bling' (extravagant multilingual display as NORMAL, in this context).

Further reading

Alim, S. H., Ibrahim, A. and Pennycook, A. (2009) *Global Linguistic Flows: Hip-hop Cultures, Youth Identities, and the Politics of Language*, London: Routledge
(A landmark edited collection, bringing together work on language and hip-hop from around the world by 14 scholars, many working in multilingual contexts.)

Androutsopolos, J. and Scholz, A. (2003) 'Spaghetti funk: Appropriations of hip-hop culture and rap music in Europe', *Popular Music and Society* 26: 463–79.
(European hip-hop, including multilingual examples from France, Germany, Italy, Spain and Greece, analysed from a media studies/cultural studies perspective.)

Low, B. (2001) 'Bakardi slang and the poetics of T-dot hip-hop', in G. Dimitriadis, T. Daspit, and J. Weaver (eds) *Hip-hop Pedagogies and Youth Cultures (special issue), Taboo: The Journal of Culture and Education* 5: 15–31.
(An in-depth treatment of one Toronto (Canada) rap number demonstrating how to analyse dialect diversity in a literary studies/cultural studies framework.)

Pennycook, A. (2007) *Global Englishes and Transcultural Flows*, London: Routledge.

(The classic critical applied linguistics treatment of hip-hop and language, with good coverage of the relevance of performativity theory.)

Sardar, Z. and Van Loon, B. (2004) *Introducing Cultural Studies*. London: Icon Books.
(Accessible, humourous introduction using sophisticated cartoon format.)

Bibliography

Alim, H. S. (2002) 'Street-conscious copula variation in the Hip-Hop Nation', *American Speech* 77: 288–304.

——(2004) *You Know my Steez: An Ethnographic and Sociolinguistic Study of Styleshifting in a Black American Speech Community*, Publication of the American Dialect Society No. 89, Annual Supplement to *American Speech*, Duke University Press.

Alim, H. S., Ibrahim, A., and Pennycook, A. (2009) *Global Linguistic Flows: Hip Hop Cultures, Youth Identities, and the Politics of Language*, London: Routledge.

Androutsopoulos, J. (2007) 'Style online: doing hip hop on the German-speaking web', in P. Auer (ed.) *Style and Social Identities: Alternative Approaches to Linguistic Heterogeneity*, Berlin: de Gruyter.

——(2009) 'Language and the three spheres of hip hop', in H. S. Alim, A. Ibrahim and A. Pennycook (eds) *Global Linguistic Flows: Hip Hop Cultures, Youth Identities, and the Politics of Language*, London: Routledge.

Androutsopoulos, J. and Scholz, A. (2003) 'Spaghetti funk: Appropriations of Hip-Hop culture and rap music in Europe', *Popular Music and Society* 26: 463–79.

Arnold, M. (1869) *Culture and Anarchy: An Essay in Political and Social Criticism*, Oxford: Project Gutenberg.

Auzanneau, M. (2001) 'Identités africaines: Le rap comme lieu d'expression', *Cahiers d'études Africaines*, 163–74, available online at http://etudesafricaines.revues.org/document117.html

Auzanneau, M., Bento, M., Fayolle, V., Lambert, P., Trimaille, C., Amar, L. and Fernandes, A. (2003) 'Le rap en France et ailleurs: Intérêt d'une démarche pluridisciplinaire', *CILL* 29(1–2): 109–30.

Blommaert, J. (2005) 'Situating language rights: English and Swahili in Tanzania revisited', *Journal of Sociolinguistics* 9: 390–417.

Blommaert, J., Collins, J. and Slembrouck, S. (2005) 'Spaces of multilingualism', *Language and Communication* 25: 197–216.

Bourdieu, P. and Passeron, J.-C. (1990) *Reproduction in Education, Society and Culture*, London: Sage.

Buckingham, D. and Sefton-Green, J. (1994) *Cultural Studies Goes to School: Reading and Teaching Popular Media*, London: Taylor & Francis.

Costello, M. and Foster Wallace, D. (1990) *Signifying Rappers: Rap and Race in the Urban Present*, Hopewell, NJ: The Ecco Press.

Dolby, N. (2003) 'Popular culture and democratic practice', *Harvard Educational Review* 73: 258–84.

Fairclough, N. (ed.) (1992) *Critical Language Awareness*, New York: Longmann.

Fiske, J. (1990) *Understanding Popular Culture*, London: Routledge.

García, O. (2009) 'Education, multilingualism and translanguaging in the 21st century', in T. Skutnabb-Kangas, R. Phillipson, A. K. Mohanty and M. Panda (eds) *Social Justice Through Multilingual Education*, Clevedon: Multilingual Matters.

Giroux, H. and Simon, R. (1989) *Popular Culture, Schooling, and Everyday Life*, Granby, MA: Bergin & Garvey.

Harris, R. (2002) 'The role of the language myth in the Western cultural tradition', in R. Harris (ed.) *The Language Myth in Western Culture*, Richmond: Curzon Press.

Higgins, C. (2004) 'AAVE returns to Africa: "Black English" among Tanzanian youth', poster presented at the American Association of Applied Linguistics Annual Meeting, Portland, Oregon.

——(2007) 'Battling HIV in Bongo Flava: Advocating for Tanzanian sexual morality in multiple codes', paper presented at ISB6 (Sixth International Symposium on Bilingualism), Hamburg, Germany.

——(2009) 'From Da Bomb to *Bomba*: Global Hip Hop Nation language in Tanzania', in H. S. Alim, A. Ibrahim and A. Pennycook (eds) *Global Linguistic Flows: Hip Hop Cultures, Youth Identities, and the Politics of Language'*, London: Routledge.

Hoggart, R. (1957) *The Uses of Literacy: Aspects of Working-class Life, with Special Reference to Publications and Entertainments*, London: Chatto & Windus.

Ibrahim, A. (2003) '"Whassup, homeboy?" Joining the African diaspora: Black English as a symbolic site of identification and language learning', in S. Makoni, G. Smitherman, A. F. Ball and A. K. Spears (eds) *Black Linguistics: Language, Society and Politics in Africa and the Americas*, London: Routledge.

Kellner, D. (1995) *Media Culture: Cultural Studies, Identity and Politics between the Modern and the Postmodern*, New York: Routledge.

Kitwana, B. (2002) *The Hip-Hop Generation: Young Blacks and the Crisis in African-American Culture*, New York: Perseus Books Group.

Krims, A. (2000) *Rap Music and the Poetics of Identity*, Cambridge: Cambridge University Press.

Kroeber, A. L. and Kluckhohn, C. (1952) *Culture: A Critical Review of Concepts and Definitions*, New York: Random House.

KRS-One. (2000) *KRS-One: A Retrospective*, BMG Canada: Zombia Recording Corporation.

Lamarre, P., Paquette, J., Kahn, E. and Ambrosi, S. (2002) 'Multilingual Montreal: Listening in on the language practices of young Montrealers', *Canadian Ethnic Studies* 34(1), available online at http://web.ebscohost.com/ehost/results

Leppänen, S. (2007) 'Youth language in media contexts: Insights into the functions of English in Finland', *World Englishes* 26(2): 149–69.

Leppänen, S., Pitkänen-Huhta, A., Piirainen-Marsh, A., Nikula, T. and Peuronen, S. (2009) 'Young people's translocal new media uses: A multiperspective analysis of language choice and heteroglossia', *Journal of Computer-Mediated Communication* 14: 1080–107.

Lin, A. (2009) '"Respect for Da Chopstick Hip Hop": The politics, poetics, and pedagogy of Cantonese verbal art in Hong Kong', in H. S. Alim, A. Ibrahim and A. Pennycook (eds) *Global Linguistic Flows: Hip Hop cultures, Youth Identities, and the Politics of Language*, London: Routledge.

Low, B. (2001) '"Bakardi Slang" and the language and poetics of T Dot Hip-Hop', *Taboo, Journal of Culture and Education* 5: 15–31.

——(2007) 'Hip-hop, language, and difference: The N-word as a pedagogical limit-case', *Journal of Language, Identity and Education* 6(1): 147–60.

Low, B., Sarkar, M. and Winer, L. (2009) '"Chus mon propre Bescherelle": Challenges from the Hip-Hop nation to the Quebec nation', *Journal of Sociolinguistics* 13(1): 59–82.

Makoni, S. and Pennycook, A. (2007) *Disinventing and Reconstituting Languages*, Clevedon: Multilingual Matters.

Manuelito, K. D. (2006) 'A Dine (Navajo) perspective on self-determination: An exposition of an egalitarian place,' *Taboo, Journal of Culture and Education* 10(1): 7–28.

May, S. (2001) *Language and Minority Rights: Ethnicity, Nationalism and the Politics of Language*, Harlow, U.K.: Pearson Education/Longman.

Meintel, D. (1992) 'L'identité ethnique chez les jeunes Montréalais d'origine immigrée', *Sociologie et Sociétés* 24: 73–89.

Mitchell, T. (ed.) (2001) *Global Noise: Rap and Hip-Hop Outside the USA'*, Middletown, CT: Wesleyan University Press.

Mukhopadhyay, B. (2006) 'Cultural studies and politics in India today', *Theory, Culture and Society* 23(7–8): 279–92.

Niño-Murcia, M. (2003) '"English is like the dollar": Hard currency ideology and the status of English in Peru', *World Englishes* 22: 121–42.

Omoniyi, T. (2009) '"So I choose to do Am Naija Style": Hip hop, language, and postcolonial identities', in H. S. Alim, A. Ibrahim and A. Pennycook (eds) *Global Linguistic Flows: Hip Hop Cultures, Youth Identities, and the Politics of Language*, New York: Routledge.

Oxford Online Dictionary http://oxforddictionaries.com

Pattanayak, D. P. (2000) 'Linguistic pluralism: a point of departure', in R. Phillipson (ed.) *Rights to Language: Equity, Power, and Education*, Mahwah, NJ: Lawrence Erlbaum.

——(ed.) (1990) *Multilingualism in India*, Hyderabad: Orient Longman.

Pennycook, A. (2003) 'Global Englishes, Rip Slyme, and performativity', *Journal of Sociolinguistics* 7 (4): 513–33.

——(2004) 'Performativity and language studies', *Critical Inquiry in Language Studies* 1: 1–19.

——(2007) *Global Englishes and Transcultural Flows*, London: Routledge.

Pennycook, A. and Mitchell, T. (2009) 'Hip hop as dusty foot philosophy: Engaging locality', in H. S. Alim, A. Ibrahim and A. Pennycook (eds) *Global Linguistic Flows: Hip Hop Cultures, Youth Identities, and the Politics of Language*, New York: Routledge.

Rose, T. (1994) *Black Noise: Rap Music and Black Culture in Contemporary America*, Hanover, NH: University Press of New England.

Sarkar, M. (2009) '"Still reppin' por mi gente": The transformative power of language mixing in Quebec Hip-Hop', in H. S. Alim, A. Ibrahim and A. Pennycook (eds) *Global Linguistic Flows: Hip Hop Cultures, Youth Identities, and the Politics of Language*, New York: Routledge.

Sarkar, M. and Winer, L. (2006) 'Multilingual code-switching in Quebec rap: Poetry, pragmatics, and performativity', *International Journal of Multilingualism* 3(3): 173–92.

Sarkar, M., Low, B. and Winer, L. (2007) '"Pour connecter avec le Peeps": Québéquicité and the Quebec Hip-Hop community', in M. Mantero (ed.) *Identity and Second Language Learning: Culture, Inquiry and Dialogic Activity in Educational Contexts*, Greenwich, CT: Information Age Publishing.

Sarkar, M., Winer, L. and Sarkar, K. (2005) 'Multilingual code-switching in Montreal Hip-Hop: Mayhem meets method, or, "Tout moune qui talk trash kiss mon black ass du nord"', in J. Cohen K. T. McAlister, K. Rolstad and J. MacSwan (eds) *ISB4: Proceedings of the 4th International Symposium on Bilingualism*, Somerville, MA: Cascadilla Press.

Soto, L. D. (2006) 'Border crossing identities: Critical multicultural ways of knowing', *Taboo: Journal of Culture and Education* 10(1): 111–20.

Strinati, D. (2000) *An Introduction to Studying Popular Culture*, London: Routledge.

Terkourati, M. (2010) *Languages of Global Hip Hop*. London: Continuum.

Williams, R. (1976) *Keywords: A Vocabulary of Culture and Society*, London: Fontana Press.

24

Multilingualism and gender[1]

Kimie Takahashi

Introduction

In recent decades, questions regarding multilingualism and gender have taken on increasing importance from both scholarly points of view and society at large. Globalization has opened up greater opportunities for people to come into contact, whether face-to-face or via electronic media, and with this has come new linguistic challenges that often intersect gender inequalities. The global economy offers an ever-expanding array of services and products in which women in particular bear the brunt of international labour market disparities. Against this backdrop, scholars from a variety of fields are increasingly situating their inquiries within multilingual and second language contexts as a way to examine the complex and diverse experiences of gendered ideologies. This chapter offers an account of these developments.

I begin by reviewing the expansion of the field of language and gender into multilingual and second language contexts, particularly focusing on the paradigm shift towards a post-structuralist approach. I then examine the intersection of multilingualism and gender in two key transnational contexts: the global politics of reproductive labour and cross-linguistic intimate relations. My inquiries in these two sites are inspired by the recent work by Piller and Pavlenko (2009); I explore the ways in which gendered identities are (re)produced in multilingual contexts, and how ideologies of language and gender embody social order and inequalities across the terrain of globalization.

Tracing the development

What we know today about multilingualism, gender and their inter-relationship has been learned through vibrant debate and research that has taken place over the last four decades. The study of language and gender initially emerged as a field of inquiry in the 1970s amid the rising feminist political movement concerning gender inequalities in the West. In the early period, Lakoff (1975) and Thorne and Henley (1975) laid the groundwork for gender research on linguistic practices; the role of gender in multilingual and second language learning contexts was also considered 'a promising area of inquiry' in the same period (Pavlenko and Piller 2001: 18). Pavlenko and Piller (2001) note, however, that the study of multilingualism, second language learning and gender did not gain a strong currency until Burton, Dyson and Ardener's *Bilingual Women* (1994) sparked a renewed interest. Since then the field has grown significantly, as shown by the increasing volume of research that takes multilingual and second language learning contexts as sites of inquiry. Today, the study of gender, multilingualism and second language learning is a lively field, with an ever-expanding body of monographs (Goldstein 1996; Norton 2000; Piller 2002; Takahashi forthcoming; Lan 2006; Okita 2002), edited volumes (Burton 1994; McElhinny 2007; Norton and Pavlenko 2004; Pavlenko *et al.* 2001; Okita 2002; Piller 2002; Takahashi forthcoming) and review articles (Pavlenko and Piller 2001, 2008; Piller and Pavlenko 2001, 2007, 2009; Piller and Takahashi 2010a; Besnier 2007; Davis and Skilton-Silvester 2004; Ehrlich 1997; Gordon 2008; Nelson 2006; Takahashi 2009). The continuing growth of the field has also entailed the 'post-modern turn' of the 1990s, or the theoretical shift towards the *diversity* framework (Pavlenko 2008; Cameron 1985; Eckert and McConnell-Ginet 1992), marking a move away from the earlier *deficiency, dominance* and *difference* frameworks.

Both the *deficiency* and *dominance* frameworks sought to explore unequal power relations between men and women by taking their linguistic differences as the starting point of investigations. Based on Lakoff's (1975) work on language and women's place, the *deficiency* framework considered women as 'inferior language users' (Piller and Pavlenko 2004), linking their subordinate position in society with the negative aspects of women's language use, such as hedges, hyper-correct grammar and pronunciation, tag questions and (super) polite forms. In the mid-1970s, the *dominance* framework suggested that gender inequalities resulted from male domination and female oppression in social interaction: men exerted power over women by interrupting and overlapping women's speech, for example. In the study of bilingualism and language learning, both approaches proposed that as an oppressed group of 'inferior language users', women were less bi-multilingual than men (e.g. Stevens 1986). In the 1980s the *difference* framework emerged as a popular alternative to the earlier models, due largely to Tannen's (1990) *You Just Don't Understand*. The *difference* framework suggested that men and women communicate differently because they follow gender-specific and gender-appropriate interactional styles acquired through socialization since childhood. A communication breakdown between men and women was thus considered the result of 'misunderstanding' the intention of the other sex. Unlike the former approaches, the *difference* approach produced a number of studies, particularly in the field of Second Language Acquisition, suggesting that women were superior language learners (e.g. Oxford 1993; Ellis 1994).

In the 1990s, feminist linguists began challenging these frameworks. The earlier models were criticized as inadequate and in many cases, 'damaging to emancipatory practices' (Davis and Skilton-Silvester 2004: 383). According to Piller and Pavlenko (2004: 58), the main critiques of the earlier approaches centred on:

> their essentialist assumptions about 'men' and 'women' as homogeneous categories, ... lack of attention to the role of context and power relations, and ... insensitivity to ethnic, racial, social, and cultural diversity that mediates gendered behaviours, performance, and outcomes.

Although scholars acknowledge the contributions of earlier models, they have increasingly adopted a new framework that focuses on diversity of gendered identities and linguistic practices (Eckert and McConnell-Ginet 1992; Pavlenko 2008; Cameron 1985), and have reconceptualized 'language' and 'gender' as well as the inter-relationship between them.

The *diversity* framework, advocated by Cameron (1985), largely draws on feminist post-structuralist approaches to language and gender. Rejecting the notion of language as a set of disembodied structures, the framework considers language as a site of identity construction and negotiation, a source of power (Weedon 1997), and a form of symbolic capital (Bourdieu 1991). As Heller (2007a: 2) articulates, language is increasingly approached as 'a set of resources which circulate in unequal ways in social networks and discursive spaces, and whose meaning and value are socially constructed within the constraints of social organisational processes, under specific historical conditions'. One important implication of this view is the acknowledgement that not all forms of bi-multilingualism are equally valued (Piller and Pavlenko 2007); the processes by which certain languages or accents, hence the combination of them, become valorized or devalued has social, historical, political and gendered underpinnings. Access to linguistic resources as well as the ability to transform linguistic capital into other forms of capital are considered as mediated by a host of social and economic factors, and most importantly for this chapter, gender.

In the *diversity* framework, gender is no longer seen as something that men and women 'are' or 'have'. Instead, feminist linguists consider gender as a product of social doing – something people 'do' and 'perform' in and through talk or other discursive means (Butler 1990) as a process of constructing their consciousness and negotiating their being in everyday life in and across various communities of practice (Eckert and McConnell-Ginet 1992). Gender thus becomes 'a system of social relations and discursive practices' (Pavlenko and Piller 2001: 23). This view considers performing gender as mediated by situated ideologies of gender and language, or circulating ideas and beliefs about the normative practice of being men or masculine and women or feminine, which vary across time and the social, cultural and political landscape. The locus of inquiry is thus no longer on women and men as two separate groups and how they differ linguistically; it has shifted to the *diversity* of gendered identities and discursive practices in context, ideologies that inform beliefs about what is normative (e.g. heterosexuality, monolingualism) and the discursive processes through which people take up, resist, blend or reshape these ideologies (Piller and Pavlenko 2004).

This line of inquiry is consistent with the notion of intersectionality (Yuval-Davis 2007; Valentine 2007; Christensen 2009), which considers it 'impossible to separate out gender from the political and cultural intersections in which it is invariably produced and maintained' (Butler 1990: 3). Thus, in order to understand the (re)production of power, social order and change, the *diversity* framework pays close attention to the ways in which gender intersects with other discursive categorizations, such as race, ethnicity, age, nationality, sexuality, religion and socio-economic status (Eckert and McConnell-Ginet 1992; Heller 2007b). In addition, the unit of analysis within the framework focuses not on men and women's language per se, but on activity – what, how and why individuals desire or are (un)able to do with language in a specific context and time (Pavlenko 2008). Researchers associated with the *diversity* framework thus tend to adopt a context-specific approach to data collection (e.g. ethnographic approaches, including participant-observation and interviews) and analytic techniques (e.g. discourse analysis, critical discourse analysis) (see Pavlenko 2008 for issues in research design within the *diversity* framework).

Another important aspect of the *diversity* framework that has expanded the field over the last decade is its increasing concern with global processes, broadly termed as globalization and transnationalism (Piller and Pavlenko 2007, 2009; Heller 2003; Besnier 2007; Piller and Takahashi 2010a; McElhinny 2007; Block and Cameron 2002; Han 2007). Globalization has generally been conceived as consisting of 'flows' (Appadurai 1990) or movements of people, capital, goods, communication, images and desires in an increasingly 'borderless' world. Transnationalism emphasizes, however, that nation-states continue to exercise their power over these flows, dynamically controlling the accumulation and transfer of various forms of capital across, between and beyond national boundaries (Ong 1999; Constable 2003). Recent literature has increasingly addressed the ways in which transnational processes and ideologies of language and gender intersect with gendered identities and practices, including the commodification of multilingual language work in the new global economy (Heller 2003, 2007b), the global care chain of migrant reproductive workers (Piller and Pavlenko 2007, 2009), the language education market (Kinginger 2008b; Piller and Takahashi 2006), and bilingual couplehood and family (Piller 2002; Okita 2002).

Adopting the *diversity* framework, the rest of the chapter examines the ways in which multilingualism and gender intersect in transnational spaces. Piller and Pavlenko (2007: 16) have highlighted that economic production and social reproduction are 'the key areas where gender is produced and reproduced' and that they have undergone tremendous changes in conjunction with recent global processes. In keeping with their argument and following Piller and Takahashi (2010a), I focus on two transnational spaces in which the political economy of language and transnational identity serve to produce gendered opportunities and challenges: the global politics of reproductive labour and cross-linguistic intimate relations.

The global politics of reproductive labour

This section examines linguistic challenges and gender inequalities that are embodied in the feminization of international migration. Traditional research on migration often assumed men to be economic migrants and women to be 'associational', following their male spouse and reproducing the family, and hence irrelevant to the labour market (Hondagneu-Sotelo 2003: 5; see also Kofman and Raghuram 2006). As Lan (2008) points out, this approach no longer captures the complex reality of contemporary international migration and the globalized labour market. An increasing number of women move in search of work abroad, often as a sole migrant either with or without legal documents (De Regt 2010; Anderson 1997; Ehrenreich and Hochschild 2003a). These women on the move are often united under the rhetoric that heralds globalization as a marker of women's increased social and economic mobility. However, recent feminist scholarship has highlighted that migrant women's trajectories are profoundly shaped by 'a structural relationship of inequality based on class, race, gender and (nation-based) citizenship' (Parreñas 2001: 73). At the same time it is only recently that language has received systematic attention as a key factor that intersects this relationship of inequality (Heller 2003; McElhinny 2007; Piller and Takahashi 2010a; Piller and Pavlenko 2009, 2007). This section foregrounds language as an overarching issue in the global politics of reproductive labour and the everyday experience of reproductive migrant workers.

Reproductive migrant workers

Reproductive work (work and care necessary to sustain and reproduce the family) has traditionally been the responsibility of female family members. As many women in the first-world have begun pursuing paid work outside the home, men have not picked up their share of domestic work; thus reproductive work has increasingly been outsourced or become the domain of migrant women's work, in particular the work of migrant women of colour (Yuval-Davis 2009; Piller and Takahashi 2010a). Furthermore, the expansion of tourism, leisure and aesthetic industries has also enlarged the demand for women migrant workers in low wage, low status occupations such as cleaners, nail beauticians, masseuses and sex workers. As Hondagneu-Sotelo (2007: 3) rightly points out, without migrant women's labour in many affluent global cities, an array of products and services that are widely available today at an affordable price would simply disappear. The lifestyle many citizens of the First World enjoy today relies on the low wage and physically and emotionally intensive labour provided by migrant women from the Third World (Ehrenreich and Hochschild 2003b; Anderson 1997).

A growing body of literature on migrant reproductive workers suggest that their experiences are profoundly embedded in linguistic and communicative inequalities. For instance, in her ethnography of Latino nannies and house cleaners in the USA, Hondagneu-Sotelo (2007: 3) reports that the ability to speak English, and the attributes of race and cultural background are especially important criteria for determining the prestige and amount of labour entailed by the jobs available to migrant women. The researcher notes that in the USA, where the 'English Only' campaign and racial discrimination continue to intensify, many employers believe that they could acquire more status or employees who speak better English 'if they employ a white, fair-haired nanny, who may hail from Iowa or Australia' (2007: 100–1). In fact, English-speaking white nannies from Australia and the UK dominate the high-end jobs, serving wealthy families as nannies without house-cleaning duties. Mid-range jobs that combine the work of nannies *and* house cleaners, often in well-to-do families, are dominated by young, documented Latino women who speak English relatively well. The low-end jobs, which often involve the most strenuous, exploitative form of employment, namely live-in jobs (with salaries as low as $100 a week), tend to employ Latino women who lack English fluency, experience and authorized documents.

Yet, some employers prefer non-English-speaking Latino women for a number of reasons (see also Piller and Pavlenko 2007, 2009). First, these women cost significantly less than English-speaking white nannies, a commodity value that in itself reproduces their inferiority. Second, their lack of English proficiency and limited social access outside the Latino community assure employers that these women will not be able to reveal the intimate details of the employers' private lives to other English speakers of the same class. And third, their linguistic deficiency and racial inferiority allow the employers to exclude them, treat them as inferior *Others* and humiliate them as illiterate during 'blowups' (Hondagneu-Sotelo 2007: 114). According to Hondagneu-Sotelo (2007: 3), employment agencies feel that employers who 'switch' from a Latino woman to an English-speaking white nanny need to be 're-educated' and 'monitored' – they cannot treat the white nanny with the same disregard they had shown their Latina employee. The researcher observes that '[I]n this racial hierarchy, only employers of white nannies require any monitoring' (2007: 103).

As Piller and Pavlenko (2009) point out, lack of proficiency in the majority language per se does not always disadvantage migrant women. Rather, the issue pertains to the political economy of languages in the host country that these women can or cannot speak or are seen to be able or unable to speak. In some cases, limited proficiency may not be a disadvantage, particularly if they speak a language of significant symbolic status, i.e. English. For example, Filipina reproductive workers are highly sought after because of their fluency in English and relatively high education compared to migrant women from other South East Asian countries (ibid.). Their ability to speak English not only renders them more competitive in the global market, but also operates as symbolic capital with which they can negotiate identity and power relations with their employers, as demonstrated in Lan's (2003, 2006) study on Filipina maids in Taiwan.

Lan (2003, 2006) found that in Taiwan, where the boom for English language learning has intensified, English-speaking Filipina maids have become a status marker for newly rich Taiwanese. Many of Lan's participants, college-educated women with professional work experience in the Philippines, faced relentless subordination by their employers. But they engaged in resistance in a number of ways that drew on their superior English-speaking identity. For instance, they ridiculed the way their employers gave directions in limited English, as in this example: 'divorce [divide] the chicken and pry [fry] it when oil is dancing [boiling]' (2006: 173). They also deliberately followed 'wrong' instructions: when one employer ordered her maid to '*throw* some letters (put letters in the mailbox), the maid dutifully dumped them in the garbage' (ibid., italic in the original). They regularly joked about the employers' poor English or 'funny' accents with their fellow Filipina friends on their rare days off (see also Constable 1997). The sense of empowerment that Lan's participants felt is well-captured in one maid's comment: 'They have more money, but we can speak better English than most of them' (2003: 13).

Jokes and ridicule may momentarily empower them, but Lan (2006) notes that these exchanges were conducted 'backstage' among their trusted fellow countrywomen. To avoid the risk of losing their jobs, these maids mostly interacted with their employers on the basis of 'the script of deferential performance, while cautiously exercising linguistic resistance in disguise' (2006: 173). The researcher also observed that the popularity of Indonesian maids was on the rise. They are perceived as more 'docile', due in large part to their limited linguistic means (both in English and Chinese) of negotiating their subordinate position. As Lan (2003: 156) notes, the backstage exchanges of jokes and the ascent of Indonesian maids demonstrate how 'language becomes a means of symbolic domination to consolidate the employer's authority and silence the migrant workers'.

It is misleading to suggest that all domestic migrant workers are simply victims. Many take pride, for instance, in making much needed economic contributions to their families back home (Ehrenreich and Hochschild 2003b). The fact remains, however, that work that takes place behind closed doors in a stranger's home in a foreign country renders domestic migrant women highly vulnerable. Many thus opt out of a domestic setting and choose instead institutional sites such as cleaning companies and hotels. The expanding service industry, however, also thrives on migrant women's linguistic and social disadvantages, as illustrated by Alcorso (2003).

In her study on migrant workers in two four-star hotels in Australia, Alcorso (2003) found that 'back-of-the-house' work, namely the housekeeping work, was dominated by middle-aged migrant women from non-English-speaking countries (NESC). Within the hotels, housekeeping was widely acknowledged as 'the hardest place to work' (2003: 25) with low wages, an elevated risk of occupational injuries and job cuts in times of economic downturn. The housekeeping women were considered to be 'loyal' (2003: 24) by the managers because most had been working at the hotels for a long time, even without being promoted to a less strenuous or higher paying position. As Masterman-Smith and Pocock (2008) point out, opportunities for such promotion are really rare in hotel housekeeping – it is a 'dead-end' low-paid job/industry. Hotel managers justified the concentration and entrapment of NESC migrant women in housekeeping by insisting that their accented English would be difficult to understand and thus inconvenience hotel guests who are 'not expected to perform labour of active listening' (2008: 29).

However, Alcorso found this puzzling because some of the 'front-of-house' jobs (e.g. banquets in a hotel) did not necessitate fluent English, many housekeepers were English-speaking Filipino women and, and although expressing a lack of confidence, most of her housekeeping participants did possess effective communication skills in English. There was also no staff assistance in improving their English; in contrast to the availability of other forms of job training. As Piller and Takahashi (Piller and Takahashi 2010a, 2010b) suggest, discrimination based on language proficiency and accent can often substitute for racial, ethnic and gender discrimination, particularly in societies that see themselves as non-racist or post racist (Hill 2008). The housekeeping migrant women's ability to transform their linguistic capital into economic and social gains is largely limited by employers' desire that NESC migrant women remain linguistically unconfident, lest they disrupt traditional ethnic and gendered divisions of work that serve the service industry well (see also Adib and Guerrier 2003).

De-skilling of skilled migrant women

It is by no means only unskilled reproductive workers who face linguistic challenges. Despite their professional qualifications and expertise, skilled migrant women are also subject to de-skilling and discrimination in host countries (see Piller this volume). Literature on the most recent wave of skilled migrant women, overseas-qualified nurses, increasingly highlights that language proficiency and race are both public and hidden sites where control and discrimination are exercised (Lan 2008; Kingma 2007; Yeates 2009; Kofman and Raghuram 2006).

In her study on the career paths of migrant nurses in Australia, Hawthorne (2001) found that linguistic and racial discrimination were undisputable. She reports the 'doubt and penury' experienced by migrant nurses from non-English-speaking backgrounds (NESB), as opposed to the 'instancy of professional acceptance' for those from English-speaking backgrounds (ESB), particularly from the UK (2001: 219). Although both NESB and ESB migrant nurses found professional employment after obtaining recognition of their qualifications, there was significant labour market segmentation over time: NESB nurses were much less likely than ESB nurses to have advanced beyond the baseline registered nursing employment and gained access to managerial or supervisory positions. The employment of NESB nurses, particularly from Eastern Europe and non-Commonwealth Asia, was most concentrated in public hospitals and nursing homes – the latter a sector uniformly stigmatized as well as increasingly redefined as for 'foreign labour'. Many NESB nurses reported 'hidden and clear discrimination as well as outright racism by Anglo-Saxon nurses' (2001: 225); one Filipino nurse explained that the discrimination was targeted at 'only my colour and the way I pronounced words [so] that you are always laughed at, degraded' (ibid.), whereas an Indonesian nurse considered her nursing skills to be compromised by exclusion from teams. Comments such as those above starkly contrasted 'NESB nurses' pride in their skills, and their intense sense of advantage in terms of linguistic and cross-cultural experience' (ibid.).

Discrimination based on linguistic proficiency is a means of control over the flow of foreign nurses and care workers employed by many receiving countries, as the case of Japan further demonstrates (Takahashi 2010a). Japan's ageing population and the growing number of young Japanese shunning '3D' jobs (dirty, dangerous and demanding) has created an increasing demand for foreign nurses and eldercare workers. In response, the Japanese government has recently started to recruit nurses and caregivers from Indonesia and the Philippines. The conditions imposed by Japanese officials include the requirement that Indonesian and Filipino nurses attend six months of language training as well as pass the Japanese national exam within two to four years of their arrival. They face repatriation if they fail the exam. This scheme is considered as fraught with inequality and the language requirement is seen as 'insurmountable' (The Japan Times 2009). Many of these women will face immediate downward occupation mobility from qualified nurses to nurse assistants. They also must prepare for the difficult exam while engaged in on-the-job training. This unrealistic language requirement is part and parcel of the mounting opposition from the Japanese Nursing Association and their nurse members who see foreign nurses as 'substandard' and a threat to their own job security (The Japan Times 2009).

I end this section with a story of Kurdish nurse Fatima Ansari from Kingma's (2007) study on migrant nurses. Fatima was born to her Kurdish parents in the Middle East. She pursued a nursing career, but once qualified, her ethnic background made it difficult to secure employment and she experienced discrimination from her colleagues once she found a job. Disillusioned with career prospects there, Fatima moved to Sweden where her sister was already working. The employment agency she consulted assured her that she would have no problem finding a job; her 'only' obstacle was language. She enrolled in an intensive course to learn a totally unfamiliar language, Swedish. Before becoming a fully qualified nurse, Fatima faced more challenges, of course, as she had to pass an exam on health regulations in Sweden, and had to work as a nursing assistant. Although she often feels lonely and understands that she is a 'foreigner' in Sweden, she considers herself 'very lucky' and feels safe among her new colleagues. Her next aspiration is to move to Africa and work in humanitarian aid.

Multilingualism is profoundly embodied in Fatima's labour migration trajectory in that the hard-earned proficiency in the new language allowed her to finally build her career as a nurse. Unlike the foreign nurses in Australia discussed above, Fatima feels included by her colleagues, even with her new identity as a 'second language user' of Swedish and as a 'foreign' nurse. The contrast between Fatima's story in Sweden and the cases of Australia and Japan reminds us that only by examining the situated practices and ideologies of language, gender, race and class in both sending and receiving countries, can we fully understand the intersection of the global politics of reproductive labour and the concerns, inequalities, aspirations and successes that embody the everyday experience of migrant women (and that obviously it is not only national categories that explain those differences).

Multilingualism and intimate relations

In addition to reproductive labour as discussed in the last section, another key site where gendered identities and multilingualism powerfully intersect and where ideologies of gender and language are produced and reproduced is cross-linguistic intimacy. Following Constable (2009: 50), I consider intimate relations as 'social relationships that are physically and emotionally close, personal, sexually intimate, private, caring, or loving'. Intimate gendered encounters that take place across linguistic or national borders are not at all a new phenomenon (Piller 2002). At the same time, the recent globalization has opened up greater spaces in which people from different backgrounds are able or bound to encounter romantic and sexual experiences – whether wanted or unwanted (Piller 2007). As Willies and Murphy-Shigematsu (2008) point out, this can happen to individuals even if they are not themselves on the move; there are countless stories of romantic or sexual encounters between 'mobile' individuals and 'locals', whether in the context of migration, tourism, study overseas or online communication. Although Gal's (1978) pioneering work on young women's conflated desire for the German language and German-speaking romantic partners in the bilingual Austrian–Hungarian peasant community of Oberwart was not taken up in the following decades (Pavlenko and Piller 2001), the link between the political economy of language, gender and intimate encounters has recently received increasing research attention from researchers from a variety of fields (Takahashi forthcoming; Piller 2002, 2008; Kinginger 2008b; Bailey 2002; Takahashi 2010b). This section reviews recent studies that illuminate this link and its multifaceted implications. I will focus on language education as a site of inquiry, particularly language study overseas and language learning materials.

Language desire

'誰だって何者かになれる！' [*Anybody can be somebody!*]; 'なぜニューヨークは夢にきくのか か　なりたい自分になるための留学' [*Why is New York good for dreams? Study overseas to become who you want to be*]. Headlines on study overseas programmes such as these commonly appear in women's magazines and other media texts in Japan (Piller and Takahashi 2006). English study overseas and language tourism – two key services in the multimillion-dollar language education and tourism industries – are constantly pitched as a glamorous means of reinventing one's womanhood. English language learning (ELL) is presented as a 'weapon' for Japanese women to cope with or move away from chauvinistic Japan, towards a more modern Western world of gender equality *and* 'white Prince Charmings' (Kelsky 2001). That the discourse of language study overseas in Japan is clearly gendered is neither unique to this country, nor a new phenomenon (Gore 2005; Kelsky 2001). As Kinginger (2008b) reports, the study overseas programmes are also a gendered enterprise in the USA and elsewhere. Since the 1990s, empirical studies unanimously point to the complex, gendered nature of desire for such activities and its impact on participants' experience in destination countries (Kinginger 2009, 2008a, 2004; Kobayashi 2007; Kelsky 2001; Freed 1995).

One notion of gendered desire associated with language study overseas that has recently been offered is *language desire*. Originated in Piller (2002) and expanded in Piller and Takahashi's (2006; Takahashi forthcoming) research, language desire refers to a bundle of desires – desire for identity transformation, for a mastery of a desired language, and/or for friendship/romance with a speaker of the desired language – all of which intersect with each other. The notion seeks to explore the dialectic relationship between public discourses and subjective agency in shaping individuals' private desires and how these desires mediate approaches to learning and using the desired language. Central to this understanding of desire is the conception of power on two fronts. Following Foucault (1980), Piller and Takahashi (2006: 61) argue that 'the workings of power include the inculcation of desires that lead individuals to modify their own bodies and personalities'. As the studies below demonstrate, language desire may thus work against the individuals, particularly if the expected outcomes are not met (Lukes 1974). Second, adopting the intersectional approach (Butler 1990), power is approached as multidirectional, (re)produced at the intersection of gender, language, race, sexuality and other discursively constituted identities.

One of the early inquiries that demonstrated the inter-relationship of gender and multilingualism in producing intimate encounters in a study abroad context comes from Polanyi (1995). In her study of American students on a study abroad programme in Russia, Polanyi found that gender powerfully mediated the students' interactional opportunities in a way that advantaged American men over women. The men achieved linguistic gains from socializing with and romancing Russian women, whereas American women were often subjected to unwanted sexual attention or harassment by Russian men, resulting in reluctance to interact with Russians and little linguistic gain when tested on return. Along with others (Brecht *et al.* 1995), Polanyi's (1995) work sparked widespread attention to the gender bias in foreign language education and language testing in the USA, which often disadvantaged women and inspired subsequent research into the relationship between gender and qualities of learning experience in the study abroad contexts (Talburt and Stewart 1999; Ehrlich 2001; Kinginger 2004).

In a series of recent publications, Kinginger (2004, 2006, 2008b, 2009) has significantly extended this area of inquiry by illuminating the intersection of public discourses and private desires in shaping American sojourners' gendered experience in France. Noting that study abroad has long been a gendered tradition in the USA (Gore 2005), Kinginger (2008b: 91) reports that the enduring popularity of France as a destination among American young women embodies the perpetual media image of French women as the ultimate models of 'playfully anachronistic femininity' and the 'promised' effect of French femininity as an enhanced magnetism to men, which Kinginger (2006) calls the 'Sabrina Syndrome'. Similar to

Polanyi's (1995) findings above, American male participants benefited from numerous interactional opportunities in French, due largely to their ability to position themselves as deserving of others' attention and as men of gender equity and heroism. In contrast, whereas some women, who managed to adopt the French discourse of fashion and femininity, gained access to a local community of French speakers (Kinginger 2004), others developed aversion, particularly towards the representation of sexuality and the performance of gender relations in public space. One participant, Deirdre, concluded that French women were 'snotty' (Kinginger 2008b: 96) and that the French people in general had no respect for women, resulting in feelings of national superiority (of American over French women), little contact with French native speakers and diminished interest in learning or keeping up French beyond this study abroad programme.

An ethnography of Japanese sojourners in Australia conducted by Piller and Takahashi (2006; Takahashi forthcoming) adds an important dimension of race to the intersection of multilingualism and gender in the study abroad contexts (see also Talburt and Stewart 1999; Norrie 2007). Growing up in a country where media often glorify all things Western (Kelsky 2001), Japanese women in this study developed *akogare* or desire for the West, particularly for celebrities such as Tom Cruise and Brad Pitt, in their youth (for the author's personal experience, see Takahashi 2010b). Following their adolescent dreams, they all arrived in Australia with the desire to find 'a new self', and under the assumption that they would achieve an instant mastery of English through unlimited access to native speakers. However, they soon found their assumption unfounded – they often felt rejected by native speakers of English, who, in their view, had little patience for Asians, seen as 'second class citizens'. One participant became disenchanted with her Asian identity: Yoko felt depressed every time she saw herself in the mirror and found that she had not transformed into a white woman.

It was in this context where an English-speaking romantic partner emerged as the most promising access point to the English-speaking world. The women first and foremost pursued white native English-speaking men as romantic partners, the ultimate object of Japanese women's desire, perpetually linking and reproducing the symbolic ownership of English and race (Takahashi 2010b). However, in Sydney's romantic market, which partly sees Japanese women as desired oriental *Other*, some could construct themselves as deserving of men's time and attention, to the extent that often allowed them to accept, control or reject certain types of romantically charged encounters on their own terms. Unlike the American men in Russia or France, however, Japanese men in their study had little access to local, Australian white women as romantic partners or linguistic resources. Located within the widely circulating international image of Japanese men as sexist, ugly and narrow-minded (Kelsky 2001), they are often excluded and remain invisible in one interactional space; the romantic inter-racial market.

Gendering and sexualizing language education

As the studies above demonstrate, sojourners bring with them pre-arrival expectations and assumptions, which, if they are not met, can lead to confusion, depression and/or loss of investment in learning and using the desired language. This makes it urgent to address the question of how such expectations are formed, and for that matter, why they are so remote from the reality many sojourners frequently face. One approach that has produced useful insights is the investigation into the images of study abroad and cross-cultural communication that language learners have access to, i.e. language learning materials. These are often saturated with the representation of language learners as warmly welcomed by accommodating native speakers of the target language. It rarely engages with how learners' gender, sexual or racial backgrounds may intersect with those of their interlocutors to structure interactional opportunities or create social and linguistic challenges, as reported by Shardakova and Pavlenko (2004).

Analysing identity options of 'imagined' learners and interlocutors in two Russian textbooks, the above researchers report that the main characters in both textbooks were white heterosexual middle-class college-educated men, with a professional interest in Russian. Jim, the main character in *Nachalo*, is represented as a confident speaker of Russian, who experiences no miscommunication or limit to social interactional opportunities throughout his stay in Russia. His value as an American man is hailed by his friends, who admire his cooking skills, and by the mother of his girlfriend, who considers American husbands an 'achievement' for Russian women. The researchers argue that by the choice of 'a typical American man', i.e. a hetero-sexual white man, as the main character, the textbook authors fail to address difficult encounters faced by women from diverse backgrounds and students from minority groups, leaving them with insufficient linguistic resources to defend themselves in unwanted sexual encounters. In terms of the construction of gendered identities for Russian interlocutors, Russian women are constantly portrayed as dependent on men, who are in turn depicted as disrespectful to women, treating them as sexual objects. The researchers argue that this depiction of female interlocutors draws on and perpetuates the cultural stereotypes of Russian women produced by American media that portrays them as sexually available to foreign men and as pursuers of, and ideal for, American men seeking traditional wives (Pavlenko 2002).

The textbooks analysed by Shardakova and Pavlenko (2004) first and foremost serve educational purposes in an institutional context. When we turn to learning aids that adopt a more specific or commercial purpose, i.e. to establish and conduct a romantic relationship in a foreign/second language, we find ideologies of gender and race and the political economy of language and sexuality even more profoundly at play (Takahashi 2010c). According to Piller and Pavlenko (2009), English for Relationship Purposes (ERP) is the latest addition to the ever-expanding spectrum of English of Specific Purposes (ESP). ERP materials include vocabulary, phrases and communicative routines deemed useful for the purpose of conducting romantic and sexual relationships with foreigners. Some may find such materials necessary, and beneficial for all parties involved (Webb 2007). However, on closer inspection, the com-mercial discourse of ERP emerges as a site where cultural, racial and sexual stereotypes are (re)produced, propagating existing unequal gender relations. These materials largely target non-English-speaking women as consumers, and construct English-speaking Western men as the object of desire, as reported in the contexts of Germany (Piller and Pavlenko 2007; Piller 2008), Russia (Kubota 2008) and Japan (Piller and Takahashi 2006, 2010a). Across these different geographical locations, the notion that the ERP discourse relies on, and reproduces, remains the same: 'romance and sex with foreign men are a key to success in English language learning and vice versa' (Piller and Takahashi 2010a). This point has been demonstrated in the critical discourse analysis of an ERP textbook, *Roppongi English*, by Piller and Takahashi (2010a; Takahashi forthcoming).

Set in the transnational space of Roppongi in Tokyo, *Roppongi English* (Johnson 2006) is a comic-style ERP textbook about two heterosexual couples, Tomoko and Kevin, and Naomi and Tony. Tomoko is a shy Japanese university student, whose English improves through romance with Kevin, a university-educated white American man who teaches English in Japan. Naomi is a cool bilingual woman, who grew up in California and pairs off with Tony, a divorced, African-American ex-navy DJ. The two women's sexual identities are dichotomized with Tomoko being feminine (e.g. 'Be gentle with me', 2006: 65), and Naomi being sexually aggressive (e.g. 'Harder, faster, deeper!' 2006: 87). Kevin is depicted as a handsome, caring gentleman who is attentive to Tomoko's emotional and sexual needs. In contrast, Tony is presented as an 'asshole' (2006: 124), who is a culturally unsophisticated sexual pervert. In the section on 'Fighting', for instance, both men are caught cheating. Whereas Kevin sweetly apologies ('I can't live without you', 2006: 115), Tony loses his temper, calling Naomi 'You bitch' (2006: 125). As a nice girl, Tomoko eventually forgives Kevin and resurrects their relationship, but Naomi threatens to call the police when Tony tries to smooth things over through the blunt offer of sex. Piller and Takahashi (2010a) argue that despite the prevailing hypermodern image of Roppongi, *Roppongi English* propagates a traditional discourse of inter-racial relationships: it valorizes traditional Japanese femininity and white masculinity as the norm, and assigns low levels of morality to hybrid/bilingual Japanese womanhood and black sexuality, respectively, and in combination.

Conclusion

This chapter has examined developments in research on multilingualism and gender and explored the role of gender in multilingual contexts within two key transnational spaces: the global politics of reproductive labour and cross-linguistic intimacy. The review of ethnographic findings reveals that the trajectories of reproductive migrant workers embody the global economy and its inequalities, in both the sending and receiving countries. For migrant women who depart from their impoverished homes to work in the First World, whereas multilingualism may afford them access to mobility and employment, it often becomes a discursive means of control for employers and nation-states to govern their workers as inferior *Other*. In addition, I have highlighted language education as a key site where ideologies of language, gender and intercultural intimacy are (re)produced. Unlike the traditional view of motivation as an individual attribute, the notion of language desire captures the dialectic relationship between powerful market interests and private desire, and explains how hegemonic notions of masculinity and femininity are produced. Language desire thus becomes a discursive site where hierarchies of identities and languages as well as normative conceptions of intimate relations are established and played out in context.

These inquiries make it clear that gender inequalities are profoundly embedded in the hierarchy of other aspects of identity, particularly race, ethnicity and class, as seen in the case of reproductive migrant women and Japanese language sojourners in Australia. As Pavlenko (2008: 172) has argued, in many contexts gender inequalities are 'exacerbated and sometimes even eclipsed by disparities created by class and race'. At the same time, discrimination based on language has increasingly become a convenient substitute for racial and gender discrimination on the terrain of transnationalism (Piller and Takahashi 2010a). Future research needs to explore how ideologies of multilingualism and gender operate as such in a variety of contexts by asking whose interests are served and disserved, and how people exert agency to negotiate these challenges and opportunities opened up by global processes. The study of multilingualism and gender can then make more explicit the role of the intersection between structural forces and agency in shaping people's everyday lives.

Related topics

Multilingual workplaces; multilingualism and social exclusion; multilingualism in the new economy.

Note

1 Acknowledgement: I am indebted to Dr Emily Farrell for her support and valuable comments throughout the writing process. I would also like to express my utmost 感謝 to Professor Ingrid

Piller for her thorough review of the earlier drafts. In addition, I have benefited from discussions on the topic of the chapter with Vera Tetteh, Jie Zhang, Emi Otsuji, Huamei Han and Ryuko Kubota, as well as editing support from Louisa O'Kelly and Brie Willoughby-Knox. All mistakes are my own.

Further reading

Kinginger, C. (2008) 'Language learning in study abroad: Case studies of Americans in France', *The Modern Language Journal*, 1–124.
(An example of the gendered experience of American sojourners in France and their consequences.)

Lan, P. C. (2006) *Global Cinderellas: Migrant Domestics and Newly Rich Employers in Taiwan*, Durham: Duke University Press.
(An account of the negotiation of power between Filipino migrant women and their Taiwanese employers on the basis of English language proficiency.)

Pavlenko, A., Blackledge, A., Piller, I. and Teutsch-Dwyer, M. (2001) *Multilingualism, Second Language Learning, and Gender*, Berlin, New York: Mouton de Gruyter.
(A collection of work on multilingualism, second language learning and gender with a must-read introduction by Piller and Pavlenko.)

Piller, I. and Pavlenko, A. (2009) 'Globalization, multilingualism, and gender: Looking into the future', in W. Li and V. Cook (eds) *Continuum Contemporary Applied Linguistics*, vol. 2 *Linguistics for the Real World*, London: Continuum.
(A review of multilingualism and gender in the context of globalization.)

Takahashi, K. (forthcoming) *Language Desire: Gender, Sexuality and Second Language Learning*, Multilingual Matters.
(A discussion of Japanese women's desire for English and the West.)

Bibliography

Adib, A. and Guerrier, Y. (2003) 'The interlocking of gender with nationality, race, ethnicity and class: The narratives of women in hotel work', *Gender, Work and Organization* 413–32.
Alcorso, C. (2003) 'Immigrant employees in hotels', *Labour and Industry* 17–40.
Anderson, B. (1997) 'Servants and slaves: Europe's domestic workers', *Race and Class* 37–49.
Appadurai, A. (1990) 'Disjuncture and difference in the global cultural economy', in M. Featherston (ed.) *Global Culture: Nationalism, Globalization and Modernity*, London: Sage.
Bailey, K. D. (2002) *Living in the Eikaiwa Wonderland: English Language Learning, Socioeconomic Transformation and Gender Alterities in Modern Japan*, unpublished doctoral dissertation, Lexington: University of Kentucky.
Besnier, N. (2007) 'Language and gender research at the intersection of the global and the local', *Gender and Language* 67–78.
Block, D. and Cameron, D. (eds) (2002) *Globalization and Language Teaching*, London: Routledge.
Bourdieu, P. (1991) *Language and Symbolic Power*, Cambridge: Polity Press.
Brecht, R., Davidson, D. and Ginsburg, R. (1995) 'Predictors of foreign language gain during study abroad', in B. Freed (ed.) *Second Language Acquisition in a Study Abroad Context*, Philadelphia: John Benjamins.
Burton, P. (1994) 'Women and second-language use: An introduction', in P. Burton, K. K. Dyson and Ardener (eds) *Bilingual Women*, Oxford: Berg.
Burton, P., Dyson, K. K. and Ardener, S. (1994) *Bilingual Women*, Oxford: Berg.
Butler, J. (1990) *Gender Trouble: Feminism and the Subversion of Identity*, New York: Routledge.
Cameron, D. (1985) *Feminism and Linguistic Theory*, London: Macmillan.
Christensen, A.-D. (2009) 'Belonging and unbelonging from an intersectional perspective', *Gender, Technology and Development* 21–41.
Constable, N. (1997) *Maid to Order in Hong Kong: Stories of Filipina Workers*, Ithaca, NY: Cornell University Press.
——(2003) *Romance on a Global Stage: Pen Pals, Virtual Ethnography, and 'Mail Order' Marriages*, Berkeley, CA: University of California Press.

——(2009) 'The commodification of intimacy: Marriage, sex, and reproductive labor', *Annual Review of Anthropology* 49–64.

Davis, K. A. and Skilton-Silvester, E. (2004) 'Looking back, taking stock, moving forward: Investigating gender in TESOL', *TESOL Quarterly* 381–404.

De Regt, M. (2010) 'Ways to come, ways to leave: Gender, mobility, and il/legality among Ethiopian domestic workers in Yemen', *Gender Society* 237–60.

Eckert, P. and McConnell-Ginet, S. (1992) 'Think practically and look locally: Language and gender as community-based practice', *Annual Review of Anthropology* 461–90.

Ehrenreich, B. and Hochschild, A. R. (2003a) *Global Woman: Nannies, Maids, and Sex Workers in the New Economy*, New York: Metropolitan Press.

——(2003b) 'Introduction', in B. Ehrenreich and A. R. Hochschild (eds) *Global Woman: Nannies, Maids, and Sex Workers in the New Economy*, New York: Metropolitan Press.

Ehrlich, S. (1997) 'Gender as social practice: Implications for second language acquisition', *Studies in Second Language Acquisition* 421–46.

——(2001) 'Gendering the "learner": Sexual harassment and second language acquisition', in A. Pavlenko, A. Blackledge, I. Piller and M. Teutsch-Dwyer (eds) *Multilingualism, Second Language Learning, and Gender*, Berlin, Germany: Mouton de Gruyter.

Ellis, R. (1994) *The Study of Second Language Acquisition*, Oxford: Oxford University Press.

Foucault, M. (1980) *Power/knowledge: Selected Interviews and Other Writings 1972–1977*, New York: Pantheon Books.

Freed, B. F. (ed.) (1995) *Second Language Acquisition in a Study Abroad Context*, Amsterdam, John Benjamins.

Gal, S. (1978) 'Peasant men don't get wives: Language and sex roles in a bilingual community', *Language in Society* 1–17.

Goldstein, T. (1996) *Two Languages at Work: Bilingual Life on the Production Floor*, Berlin: Mouton de Gruyter.

Gordon, D. (2008) 'Gendered second language socialization', in N. H. Hornberger and S. May (eds) *Encyclopedia of Language and Education*, 2nd edn, New York: Springer.

Gore, J. E. (2005) *Dominant Beliefs and Alternative Voices: Discourse, Belief, and Gender in American Study Abroad*, New York, London: Routledge.

Han, H. (2007) 'Calm and humble in and through evangelical Christianity: A Chinese immigrant couple in Toronto', in J. Allyson (ed.) *Language and Religious Identity: Women in Discourse*, Basingstoke and New York: Palgrave Macmillan.

Hawthorne, L. (2001) 'The globalisation of the nursing workforce: Barriers confronting overseas qualified nurses in Australia', *Nursing Inquiry* 213–29.

Heller, M. (2003) 'Globalization, the new economy, and the commodification of language and identity', *Journal of Sociolinguistics* 473–92.

——(2007a) 'Bilingualism as ideology and practice', in M. Heller (ed.) *Bilingualism: A Social Approach*, Basingstoke and New York: Palgrave Macmillan.

——(2007b) 'Gender and bilingualism in the new economy', in B. McElhinny (ed.) *Words, Worlds, and Material Girls: Language, Gender, Globalization*, Berlin and New York: Mouton de Gruyter.

Hill, J. H. (2008) *The Everyday Language of White Racism*, Malden, MA: Wiley-Blackwell.

Hondagneu-Sotelo, P. (2003) 'Gender and immigration: A retrospective and introduction', in P. Hondagneu-Sotelo (ed.) *Gender and U.S. Immigration: Contemporary Trends*, Berkeley: University of California Press.

——(2007) *Doméstica: Immigrant Workers Cleaning and Caring in the Shadows of Affluence*, Berkeley: University of California Press.

Johnson, B. G. (2006) *Roppongi English*, Tokyo: Aoba.

Kelsky, K. (2001) *Women on the Verge: Japanese Women, Western Dreams*, Durham: Duke University Press.

Kinginger, C. (2004) 'Alice doesn't live here anymore: Foreign language learning and identity reconstruction', in A. Pavlenko and A. Blackledge (eds) *Negotiation of Identities in Multilingual Contexts*, Hawthorne, NY: Mouton de Gruyter.

——(2006) *The Sabrina Syndrome: Intertexuality and Performance of Identity in American Students' Narratives of Learning French'*, Montreal: American Association of Applied Linguistics and the Canadian Association for Applied Linguistics.

——(2008a) *Language Learning in Study Abroad: Case Histories of Americans in France*, Oxford: Blackwell.

——(2008b) 'Language learning in study abroad: Case studies of Americans in France', *The Modern Language Journal* 1–124.

——(ed.) (2009) *Language Learning and Study Abroad: A Critical Reading of Research?* Palgrave Macmillan.

Kingma, M. (2007) *Nurses on the Move: Migration and the Global Health Care Economy*, Ithaca: Cornell University Press

Kobayashi, Y. (2007) 'Japanese working women and English study abroad', *World Englishes* 62–71.

Kofman, E. and Raghuram, P. (2006) 'Gender and global labour migrations: Incorporating skilled workers', *Antipode* 282–303.

Kubota, R. (2008) 'A critical glance at romance, gender, and language teaching', *Essential Teacher.*

Lakoff, R. (1975) *Language and Woman's Place*, New York: Harper and Row.

Lan, P. C. (2003) '"They have more money but I speak better English!": Transnational encounters between Filipina domestics and Taiwanese employers', *Identities: Global Studies in Culture and Power* 133–61.

——(2006) *Global Cinderellas: Migrant Domestics and Newly Rich Employers in Taiwan*, Durham: Duke University Press

——(2008) 'New global politics of reproductive labor: Gendered labor and marriage migration', *Sociology Compass* 1801–15.

Lukes, S. (1974) *Power: A Radical View*, London: Macmillan.

Masterman-Smith, H. and Pocock, B. (2008) *Living Low Paid: The Dark Side of Prosperous Australia*, Sydney: Allen & Unwin.

McElhinny, B. (2007) 'Introduction: language, gender and economies in global transitions: Provocative and provoking questions about how gender is articulated', in B. McElhinny (ed.) *Words, Worlds, and Material Girls: Language, Gender, Globalization*, Berlin and New York: Mouton de Gruyter.

Nelson, C. D. (2006) 'Queer Inquiry in Language Education', *Journal of Language, Identity and Education* 1–9.

Norrie, J. (2007) *On a Lovestruck Mission to Learn English, The Sydney Morning Herald*, available online at www.smh.com.au/news/world/on-a-lovestruck-mission-to-learn-english/2007/11/30/1196394619042.html

Norton, B. (2000) *Identity and Language Learning: Gender, Ethnicity and Educational Change*, Harlow: Longman.

Norton, B. and Pavlenko, A. (2004) 'Addressing gender in the ESL/EFL classroom', *TESOL Quarterly* 504–14.

Okita, T. (2002) *Invisible Work: Bilingualism, Language Choice and Childrearing in Intermarried Families*, Amsterdam and Philadelphia: John Benjamins.

Ong, A. (1999) *Flexible Citizenship: The Cultural Logics of Transnationality*, Durham: Duke University Press.

Oxford, R. (1993) 'Gender differences in styles and strategies for language learning: What do they mean? Should we pay attention?' in J. Alatis (ed.) *Strategic Interaction and Language Acquisition: Theory, Practice, and Research*, Washington, DC: Georgetown University Press.

Parreñas, R. S. (2001) *Servants of Globalization: Women, Migration and Domestic Work*, Stanford: Stanford University Press.

Pavlenko, A. (2002) 'Socioeconomic conditions and discursive construction of women's identities in post-Soviet countries', in M. Kelemen and M. Kostera (eds) *Critical Management Research in Eastern Europe: Managing the Transition*, London: Palgrave Macmillan.

——(2008) 'Research methods in the study of gender in second/foreign language education', in N. H. Hornberger and S. May (eds) *Encyclopedia of Language and Education: Research Methods in Language and Education*, New York: Springer.

Pavlenko, A., Blackledge, A., Piller, I. and Teutsch-Dwyer, M. (2001) *Multilingualism, Second Language Learning, and Gender*, Berlin and New York: Mouton de Gruyter.

Pavlenko, A. and Piller, I. (2001) 'New directions in the study of multilingualism, second language learning, and gender', in A. Pavlenko, A. Blackledge, I. Piller and M. Teutsch-Dwyer (eds) *Multilingualism, Second Language Learning, and Gender*, Berlin: Mouton de Gruyter.

——(2008) 'Language education and gender', in S. May (ed.) *The Encyclopedia of Language and Education*, 2nd edn, New York: Springer.

Piller, I. (2002) *Bilingual Couples Talk: The Discursive Construction of Hybridity*, Amsterdam: John Benjamins.

——(2007) 'Linguistics and intercultural communication', *Language and Linguistic Compass* 208–26.

——(2008) '"I always wanted to marry a cowboy:" Bilingual couples, language and desire', in T. A. Karis and D. K. Killian (eds) *Intercultural Couples: Exploring Diversity in Intimate Relationships*, London: Routledge.

Piller, I. and Pavlenko, A. (2001) 'Introduction: Multilingualism, second language learning, and gender', in A. Pavlenko, A. Blackledge, I. Piller and M. Teutsch-Dwyer (eds) *Multilingualism, Second Language Learning, and Gender*, Berlin and New York: Mouton de Gruyter.

——(2004) 'Bilingualism and gender', in T. K. Bhatia and C. W. Ritchie (eds) *The Handbook of Bilingualism*, Oxford: Blackwell.

——(2007) 'Globalization, gender, and multilingualism', in H. Decke-Cornill and L. Volkmann (eds) *Gender Studies and Foreign Language Teaching*, Tübingen: Narr.

——(2009) 'Globalization, multilingualism, and gender: Looking into the future', in W. Li and V. Cook (eds) *Continuum Contemporary Applied Linguistics,* vol. 2. *Linguistics for the Real World*, London: Continuum.

Piller, I. and Takahashi, K. (2006) 'A passion for English: Desire and the language market', in A. Pavlenko (ed.) *Bilingual Minds: Emotional Experience, Expression and Representation*, Clevedon: Multilingual Matters.

——(2010a) 'At the intersection of gender, language and transnationalism', in N. Coupland (ed.) *The Handbook of Language and Globalization*, Oxford: Blackwell.

——(2010b) 'Language, migration and human rights', in R. Wodak, B. Johnstone and P. Kerswill (eds) *Sage Handbook of Sociolinguistics,* London: Sage.

Polanyi, L. (1995) 'Language learning and living abroad: Stories from the field', in B. F. Freed (ed.) *Second Language Acquisition in a Study Abroad Context*, Amsterdam: John Benjamins.

Shardakova, M. and Pavlenko, A. (2004) 'Identity options in Russian textbooks', *Journal of Language, Identity, and Education* 25–46.

Stevens, G. (1986) 'Sex differences in language shift in the United States', *Sociology and Social Research* 31–4.

Takahashi, K. (2009) 'Migration, gender and second language learning [Gender to dainigengo gakushuu: Iminjyosei no shigoto]', in C. Kawamura, A. Kondoh and H. Nakamoto (eds) *Living Together in a Multicultural Society: Approaches to Immigration Policy [Iminseisaku eno approach: Raifusaikuru to tabunkakyousei]*, Tokyo: Akashi Shoten Publishing.

——(2010a) 'Foreign nurses face the Kanji hurdle', *Language on the Move*, available online at www.languageonthemove.com/blog/2010/02/17/foreign-nurses-face-the-kanji-hurdle/

——(2010b) 'Multilingual couplehood: romance, identity and the political economy of language', in D. Nunan and J. Choi (eds) *Language and Culture: Reflective Narratives and the Emergence of Identity*, New York: Routledge.

——(2010c) 'What has western masculinity got to do with English language learning for Japanese women? *Language on the Move*, available online at www.languageonthemove.com/blog/2009/11/05/what-has-western-masculinity-got-to-do-with-english-language-learning-for-japanese-women/.

——(forthcoming) *Language Desire: Gender, Sexuality and Second Language Learning*, Bristol: Multilingual Matters.

Talburt, S. and Stewart, M. (1999) 'What's the object of study abroad? race, gender, and "living culture"', *The Modern Language Journal* 163–75.

Tannen, D. (1990) *You Just Don't Understand: Women and Men in Conversation*, New York: Morrow.

The Japan Times (2009) *Filipino Caregivers Coming This Year*, available online at http://search.japantimes.co.jp/cgi-bin/nn20090113a3.html

Thorne, B. and Henley, N. (1975) *Language and Sex: Difference and Dominance*, Rowley, MA: Newbury House.

Valentine, G. (2007) 'Theorizing and researching intersectionality: A challenge for feminist geography', *The Professional Geographer* 10–21.

Webb, E. (2007) 'A foreign language for a foreign affair', *Essential Teacher* 14–16.

Weedon, C. (1997) *Feminist Practice and Poststructuralist Theory*, Oxford: Blackwell.

Willies, D. B. and Murphy-Shigematsu, S. (2008) 'Transcultural Japan: Metamorphosis in the cultural borderlands and beyond', in D. B. Willies and S. Murphy-Shigematsu (eds) *Transcultural Japan: At the Borderlands of Race, Gender, and Identity*, London and New York: Routledge.

Yeates, N. (2009) 'Production for export: The role of the state in the development and operation of global care chains', *Population, Space and Place* 175–87.

Yuval-Davis, N. (2007) 'Intersectionality, citizenship and contemporary politics of belonging', *Critical Review of International Social and Political Philosophy* 561–74.

——(2009) 'Women, globalization and contemporary politics of belonging', *Gender Technology and Development* 1–19.

Part V
Situated practices, lived realities

25

Disinventing multilingualism

From monological multilingualism to multilingua francas

Sinfree Makoni and Alastair Pennycook

Introduction

Assumptions about the existence of languages and, *ipso facto*, multilingualism, are so deeply embedded in predominant paradigms of language studies that they are rarely questioned. Multilingualism, furthermore, viewed from this perspective, is an indomitably good thing; the task of linguists, sociolinguists, applied linguists and educational linguists is to enhance our understanding of multilingualism, to overcome the monolingual blinkers of Anglo- or Eurocentric thought, to encourage both the understanding of and the practices of multi-lingualism. The relevance of such models to diverse contexts, however, is often taken for granted. As Haugen once observed

> [t]he concept of language as a rigid, monolithic structure is false, even if it has proved to be a useful fiction in the development of linguistics. It is the kind of simplification that is necessary at a certain stage of a science, but which can now be replaced by more sophisticated models.
>
> *(1972: 25)*

In this chapter we argue that it is indeed time for more sophisticated models, not models that replace monolingualism with multilingualism, as both concepts emerge from the same intellectual context, but rather models that question the very foundations that underpin such linguistic simplifications.

Drawing on different intellectual traditions, from philosophy to anthropology (Davidson 1986; Whorf 1988), that have dealt with the existence of languages with some skepticism, we therefore make an unequivocal case that "not all people have 'a language/languages' in the sense in which the term is currently used in English" (Heryanto 1990: 41). To this end we will first turn to the sociohistorical contexts in which notions of languages as "hermetically sealed units" (Makoni 1998) emerged, and how particular understandings of multilingualism emerged as plural monolingualisms. This will be followed by a broader discussion of contexts of diverse language use, where the notion of multilingualism is eschewed in favor of a more comprehensive understanding of the mobilization of diverse language resources. Once we go beyond a framing of languages as discrete entities, it may be plausible to write productively about multilingualism. In order to do so we therefore pose the following three questions:

- If languages are not "primordial," the question is under what sociohistorical contexts did they emerge, what are the philosophical strategies used in their construction and how does invention impact the linguistic practices of the users, and our own understanding of multilingualism?
- What are the metadiscursive regimes (Bauman and Briggs 2003) used in the construction of "languages"? Drawing on examples from different parts of the world, but with a particular focus on Africa, we further ask how diverse communities talk about their languages and what light these metalinguistic framings shed on the "world views," and "orientations" of these communities. What is the impact of particular metalanguages on our understanding of multilingualism?
- If languages do not exist as discrete entities, and language is not universal in the sense of unified systems, how does communication occur in the absence of languages as things?

Framing invention/disinvention: language myths and ideologies

A number of theoretical positions coalesce around a critique of language as discrete, unified systems. Prominent among these is Integrational Linguistics (Harris 2009), and the key claim that the idea of language is a "myth" (see Harris 1980, 1981, 1998, 2009; Harris and Taylor 1997; Pennycook 2007b). In Integrational Linguistics "people use signs in order to communicate," but the signs are not pre-assembled and there is a sharp dissonance between form and meaning. Language from this point of view is so deeply embedded in context that it cannot be separated from it. Communication occurs through a process of mutual adjustment: "when we speak or write, we take those imperfectly remembered prior (a priori) texts and reshape them into new contexts" (Becker 1995:15). Communication may be understood as "multidirectional, interactive, (and) participatory" (Khubchandani 2003), a position quite at odds with a sender/receiver model or "fixed-telementation" in which the thoughts of one person are transported to another through the use of a particular code (Toolan 2009). As Harris (1990: 45) remarks, "linguistics does not need to postulate the existence of languages as part of its theoretical apparatus." Once we make communication central to our thinking, languages may be a "variable extra" (Harris 2009: 44).

A related orientation that also undermines the idea of language as a preformed object is Hopper's (1998) *emergent grammar*, a term borrowed from anthropology (Clifford and Marcus 1986). For Hopper the apparent structure or regularity of grammar is an emergent property that "is shaped by discourse in an ongoing process. Grammar is, in this view, simply the name for certain categories of observed repetitions in discourse" (1998: 156). This is not merely an observation that languages are always changing and that grammar is always therefore, in the longer term, temporary, but rather that the notion of systematicity embedded in the concept of grammar is itself a product of repeated social activity. Language use draws on "lingual memory" shaped in part by each individual's life experiences (Becker 1995; Johnstone 1996). Hence

> there is no natural fixed structure to language. Rather, speakers borrow heavily from their previous experiences of communication in similar circumstances, on similar topics, and with similar interlocutors. Systematicity, in this view, is an illusion produced by the partial settling or *sedimentation* of frequently used forms into temporary subsystems.
>
> *(Hopper 1998: 157–8)*

From this point of view, then, linguistic structure is seen not as an independent set of pre-given laws but rather "as a response to discourse needs" (Bybee and Hopper 2001: 2). "The notion of language as a monolythic system," Bybee and Hopper (2001: 3) go on to argue, "has had to give way to that of a language as a massive collection of heterogeneous *constructions*, each with affinities to different contexts and in constant structural adaptation to usage."

Whereas linguists such as Harris, Hopper and Bybee have thus shown good cause to understand language as integrated and emergent (rather than independent or preordained), Yngve's (1996; Yngve and Wasik 2004) critique of linguistics from the point of view of the philosophy of science suggests that unlike other scientific enterprises, linguistics creates its objects anew and shapes the nature of the object of its analysis. According to Yngve, the irony is that language research can make substantial progress when it frames itself not as a science, but situates itself as part of a long tradition of philosophy and grammatical analysis, a tradition that does not claim the existence of language as an object of analysis in advance of its metalanguage. Once we situate linguistics within specific rhetorical or grammatical traditions, rather than a putative science that invents the objects of its descriptions, the culture-specific nature of linguistic inquiry becomes more evident. The immediate relevance of sociolinguistic concepts such as multilingualism thus becomes suspect in diverse contexts (Love 2009). Multilingualism from such a perspective is therefore not a universal category; indeed the very idea that multilingualism could refer to the same thing in diverse contexts of communication is revealed as an absurdity.

Linguistic anthropologists and others studying Creole languages have also cast suspicion on the ways in which languages have been described and mapped onto communities. Le Page and Tabouret-Keller (1985), for example, argue that in extremely complex heterogeneous contexts not every speech event or language will necessarily belong to a nameable language system. Furthermore, speakers may not necessarily have a clearly defined idea of what language they are speaking, and what does or does not constitute "a language." As a result, rather than focusing on languages and their users, we would be better off focusing on the "acts of identity" involved in different interactions. In a related vein, Schiefflien's (1990) research on Kaluli demonstrates that children are not taught language or verbal behavior as such, but rather are taught appropriate social behavior during interactional movements. This perspective echoes research into other post-colonial contexts (see Makoni and Makoni 2010; Pennycook 2010) that suggests that to study language, we always need to incorporate social activity, location, movement, interaction and history, as well as, wherever possible, users' perspectives. The focus of such work is therefore on a human-centered multilingualism as opposed to a language-centered multilingualism. The latter makes a multiplicity of language systems central to its analysis; the former takes the social grounding of human interaction as central.

From the perspective of linguistic anthropology, with a particular interest in the notion of language ideologies, or regimes of language (Kroskrity 2000), the question becomes one of asking how it is that languages are understood locally. As Woolard (2004: 58) notes, such work has shown that "linguistic ideologies are never just about language, but rather also concern such fundamental social notions as community, nation, and humanity itself." For linguistic anthropologists, the problem was that the "surgical removal of language from context produced an amputated 'language' that was the preferred object of the language sciences for most of the twentieth century" (Kroskrity 2000: 5). By studying language ideologies as contextual sets of belief about languages, or as Irvine (1989: 255) puts it, "the cultural system of ideas about social and linguistic relationships, together with their loading of moral and political interests," this line of work has shown the significance of local knowledge about language. At the very least, this sheds light on Mühlhäusler's (2000) point that the notion of a "language" "is a recent culture-specific notion associated with the rise of European nation-states and the Enlightenment. The notion of 'a language' makes little sense in most traditional societies" (Mühlhäusler 2000: 358). Because of the centrality of Eurocentric concepts of language, mother tongues and other monoglot perspectives and related notions "what has passed for a science of language (*including multilingualism*) over the past 150 years has been nothing but an exercise in culture maintenance" (Love 2009: 31, emphasis ours).

Although starting from different theoretical vantage points, these and many other approaches to language study are highly skeptical of the idea of languages as discrete, preformed and independent objects. In order to construct itself as a respectable discipline, linguistics had to make an extensive series of exclusions, relegating people, history, society, culture and politics to a role external to languages: "If the history of a language and its users is not factored into the theory as a primary standpoint" argues Nakata (2007: 37), "then any knowledge generated about that language is flawed." This is not, as Nakata points out, to reject the whole body or work carried out by linguists—this would be foolish in the extreme—but it is to point to the problem that a linguistic focus on formal aspects of a language "fundamentally separates the language from the people; it falsely separates the act of speaking from what is being spoken." For Nakata, at the heart of the problem is the linguistic assumption that languages are "floating in a vacuum, 'ready-made' within a system of phonetic, grammatical and lexical forms and divorced from the social context in which the speech is being uttered."

Such studies assume that language is a "solved problem, a stable and determined entity" (Harpham 2002: ix). As Harpham argues, attempts to pin down languages are hampered because there is both too much and too little information:

> Somewhere in the vast domain of linguistics can be found tokens of virtually anything at all, including order, arbitrariness, social cohesion, individual creativity, freedom, the unconscious, excess, nature, culture—anything. That is why all characterizations of the essence or true nature of language are tendentious.
>
> *(2002: x)*

This critique of the notion of separable languages, or the idea that there are "language-free communities" (Heryanto 2007) does not of course in any way suggest that some people do not use language, or because they do not have a view of "a language" that they do not communicate in language. There is very good reason to question common assumptions about the existence of separate, namcable and numerable languages. And thus there is also good reason to question the assumptions that underlie the notion of multilingualism to the extent that the term refers to little more than a plurality of languages. If the status of languages as objects is questionable, so too is their pluralization.

The development of languages: language invention

The construct of "language itself as an all or nothing affair" (Rajagopolan 2007: 194), as well as many of the ideas that are part of this metalinguistic package—standard language, dialect, acrolect, mesolect and basilect, language varieties and so forth—need to be understood as an invention. They are excellent examples of nineteenth-century social and scholarly invention in Europe and colonial contexts (Mudimbe 1988; Spear 2003; Errington 2008). Language invention happens at several levels: the very notion of languages as entities linked to nations, ethnicities, peoples, territories is first of all transported into unfamiliar territory. The local linguistic chaos is then sorted out to fit languages onto categorizations of people, and, where extra work is needed, languages are specifically created and renamed in order to fit preferred linguistic conditions. Shona in Zimbabwe, for example, was created on the basis of a two-stage process: first, a codification of dialects associated with different missionary stations. Second, the unification of the dialects by colonial linguists (Makoni *et al.* 2007). Similarly, Mannheim describes the emergence of Quecha in Latin America as a product of Spanish invasion. Prior to the Spanish invasion, the Quecha did not need a construct of language, indeed like many other communities they did not have any specific names to refer to what they spoke (Mannheim 1991). Once this sorting out has been achieved, this invented world of languages and ethnicities is reported as if it were an objective reality that has always been in place (Harris 2009).

Similarly, in Indonesia Heryanto (2007) demonstrates how the notion of "language" did not exist in pre-colonial Indonesia leading him to claim that "language is not a universal category." Of course this does not mean there was no communication prior to the emergence of Bahasa Indonesia as a language, but rather that the idea of language brought in with its introduction, and the appropriation of the notion of *Bahasa* in the process, was a major shift in how language was understood in the region. If language was relevant at all, it was something that was the possession of each individual and not necessarily shared by social groups. From such an individual perspective languages cannot be construed as a collection of objects (Love 2009).

Looking at language descriptions in the same region, van der Tuuk (1971) condemns the pointless attempts to "find a strict system in such language ruins as Javanese and Malay." It is impossible, he suggests, to "represent a language well" unless we disabuse ourselves of the attempt to describe

> a complete system, for every language is more or less a ruin, in which the plan of the architect cannot be discovered, until one has learned to supply from other works by the same hand what is missing in order to grasp the original design.
>
> *(ibid.)*

If van der Tuuk's view of languages as "ruins" perhaps seems unduly negative, and suggests a possible progression from language to decay, it nevertheless highlights well the fruitless search for order amid a much more chaotic linguistic reality. We also have to appreciate in these and other contexts that many languages, such as Igbo or Yoruba in the nineteenth century had different meanings prior to colonial encounters (Irvine 2009), and that what was understood by many people as their language was simply their description for how they spoke (Crowley 1999).

The process of invention is a complicated one consisting of transforming dialogical and "heteroglossic" material into monological texts (Blommaert 2008). The invented linguistic artifacts were textualized in a wide range of genres: grammatical outlines, grammatical sketches, word lists, orthographies, and so on (Blommaert 2008; Errington 2001, 2008). In this codification process, the serious complexities of different sociolinguistic contexts were reduced through the technical apparatus of monological sociolinguistics into "equally serious simplicities" (Dasgupta 1997: 21). In most colonial contexts, local languages were standardized by outsiders without the direct involvement of the local population, except as informants based on a series of texts, folklore, narratives, and so on (Blommaert 2008). The objective was to produce European bilingual speakers "competent" in the varieties of African languages, which they had created in conjunction with European languages (Fabian 1986; Jeater 2007). The overall effects of this intervention were a European appropriation of and creation of African standardized languages by non-native speakers.

In a bid to regain control of their languages from colonial dictionary makers, local language users increasingly produced monolingual dictionaries, grammars, and so on. Monolingualism became salient as a consequence of an imposed multilingualism when local speakers felt they had lost control of how they were to represent their languages. Such resistance to outsider multilingualism, however, was more random than systematic. The attempts to regain the representation of sociolinguistic situations were limited by the fact that resistance to multilingual grammars and dictionaries by the use of largely monolingual ones was nevertheless conducted by linguistic elites along the lines already laid down for the description of languages. Thus

> the modern language elite, in his role as a liaison between western language values and indigenous language patterns, has appropriated for himself the gatekeeper's privilege of approving or disapproving various shifts being introduced in verbal repertoire. Mostly the elite cartels manage interactions among themselves, very little realizing the indifference of the masses to such endeavors in their everyday speech activity.
>
> *(Khubchandani 2003)*

This process then becomes naturalized so that, for example, the sociolinguistic truism that multilingualism is the natural and common condition for the majority world obscures the implicit language categorizations that lurk behind such apparently descriptive categorizations. What is often overlooked is that multilingualism is a way of thinking, a world view, an intellectual orientation that forces us to look backwards under the burden of a backward-looking metalanguage, which was never designed "for our modern priorities" (Harris 2009: 33). The sociolinguistics of multilingualism is thus all too often akin to driving a car on a highway while looking only at the rear view mirror, an activity with the potential to see only what has gone before (which may be catching us up) while risking the dangers of crashing into the diversity of what lies ahead.

Multilingualism or monolingualism of humanity

A central argument in many contemporary accounts of multilingualism is that language research has tended to work with monolingualism as a norm, and that such a construct is inappropriate because a majority, if not most of the people, are multilingual. This line of argumentation, which celebrates the shift or break from monolingualism to multilingualism, does not, from the point of view of disinvention, do enough to question the underlying premises of its own position. It underestimates the social impact and intellectual resilience of monolingual philosophy. Although we share many of the concerns over the monolingual bias at the heart of much research on language, therefore, we are also concerned that the resultant ideas of enumerable languages have the effect of promoting a form of plural monolingualism (Heller 2007; Makoni 1998). The case we wish to make here, then, is that although the critique of monolingualism has taken us some distance, the focus on multilingualism does not take us far enough. One way forward here, in fact, may be described as a return to monolingualism, but a very different monolingualism from the narrow vision that was developed as part of the alliance between linguistics, colonialism, and the nation-state. Rather, a new sense of monolingualism might be envisaged that has at its heart an understanding of diversity that goes beyond the pluralism of multilingualism.

Even if we accept that there has been a conceptual and administrative shift from a focus on monolingualism to multilingualism as reflected in the discourses of much established scholarship (see many contributions to this volume), there is, however, another strand of research that is relatively less well known in colonial and post-colonial contexts, the current impulse of which consists of running by contrast not from monolingualism to multilingualism, but the reverse. The idea of "a language" creates a philosophical bind for sociolinguistics. If we accept the construct of "a language" (albeit a product of complex interplay between sociohistorical factors and politics), then multilingualism may be made up of different autonomous objects, a plural or multiple monolingualism. If, however, we grasp the full implication of the impossibility of the central construct of "a language," it becomes clear that we cannot in fact critique monolingualism as there can be no such thing.

The irrelevance of the monolingual/multilingual dichotomy has also anecdotally been reported in some European contexts. Harris (2009) reports the following anecdote told by Nabokov. He tells us that, when he was a boy, for a number of years he did not grasp that French and Russian were different. "Without realizing it, he was equally fluent in both" (Harris 2009: 29). Most students in early years of schooling attend school without knowing that they are multilingual. Being multilingual is something they discover at school through a radical process that alters their self-perception and identity when pedagogy forces them to discover languages as separate entities. Pedagogy entails teaching a specific view and understanding of language. In such cases pedagogy creates objects: language reinforced by the presence of "subjects" like English, Shona, Yoruba on the timetable alongside mathematics, biology, health science, etc. The idea of "a language" as an educational construct is also reflected in debates as to whether Caribbean Creole (CC) is a variety of English or a separate language. Nero (2006) cites examples of some Jamaican speakers of CC who thought they spoke English until they were assigned to ESL classes, thus challenging their sense of being native speakers of English.

Although sociolinguists have long had to acknowledge the messiness of the category "language," and have used, for example, notions such as continua to account for the impossibility of imposing borders between creoles and related languages, the Caribbean Creole (CC) example illustrates further how languages are constructs of the frameworks that make them. Clearly, for Jamaicans, Caribbean Creole (CC) was English, whereas their experience when assigned to an ESL class undermines that very same belief. So CC gets caught between speakers' beliefs about what they speak (English), institutional language ascriptions (ESL classes as English is a second language for CC speakers), a fully fledged creole language from the point of view of creole studies, and a subvariety of English that cannot be counted as a world English on a par with Indian or Singaporean English from the point of view of the world Englishes framework. As Mufwene (2001: 107) has noted, "the naming practices of new Englishes has to do more with the racial identity of those who speak them than with how these varieties developed and the extent of their structural deviations." In Liberia, speakers of what some linguistics might call Liberian Pidgin are adamant that what they speak is a variety of English. In Ghana, educated Ghanaian speakers find the reference to what they speak as Ghanaian English as offensive since they perceive their English to be indistinguishable from standard English.

These examples point to several concerns about the linguistic analyses on which many accounts of language in the contemporary world rely. Although the serious study of creoles by linguists and the concomitant acceptance of creoles as languages like any other has been a great advance from earlier views of Creole languages as somehow deficient, the incorporation of these languages into a standard linguistic framework has also caused what Grace (n.d.) calls "collateral damage." By turning them into languages like any other, the very distinctiveness, diversity, and creativity of creoles is reduced to questions of uniformity, origins, and substrata. A similar point is made by Branson and Miller (2007) with respect to sign languages. Although much was gained initially by finally treating sign languages as languages like any other, rather than as mere gesture or the gestural representation of pre-existing languages, much has also been lost by the inability to see their uniqueness as gestural languages that operate spatially and temporally in ways quite different from other languages. The example of Ghanaian English also draws our attention to the need to incorporate local perspective and the locus of enunciation into any analysis of language use: When Ghanaians and indeed other Third World-educated individuals insist that what they speak is English, this does not suggest that they are unaware of linguistic differences between them and other users, but rather that at times the differences are insignificant to them (Rajagopolan 2007).

Lurking behind many of the arguments made in this chapter is the perennial controversial notion of the native speaker. If Indigenous languages were invented and are a fiction, then the languages created cannot have native speakers. They will, however, have people who may claim to be experts in them, and others who resist their formation as part of a prolonged process of disinventing them. The constructed languages may be legitimate in the eyes of political administrators and those who are experts in them, but the notion of a native speaker may be unnecessary. The myth, however, of the native speaker is reinforced by plural monolingual models. The idea of autonomous languages may correspond with that of native speakers but when multilingualism is viewed differently in terms of a lingua franca in which diverse features are blended together, reflecting each individual's personal experiences, which are inevitably different from one another, then the only reasonable conclusion is to say that each person is a native speaker of what they speak, no more no less.

Plural monolingualism is a powerful ideological position because it is supported by powerful discourses. Plural monolingual discourses are mutually reinforced and complemented by discourses of language rights, which assign rights to individual and autonomous languages (May 2005). The individuality and autonomous nature of language is further consolidated by discourses of language rights in which it is individual languages that have rights assigned to them, which then creates an impression of a language-centered universe where human concerns are of secondary significance (see Blommaert 2008). If the idea of independent languages is not readily applicable to some global contexts, advocates of language rights find themselves in an invidious position of supporting very specific and culturally grounded views of both language and rights as if they were universal.

By promoting "alien" concepts without accommodating the specificities of local interpretation of variants of those concepts, advocates of language rights undermine interests of the communities they seek to serve (May 2005). To some extent human rights discourses are imperialistic insofar as they tend to override other world views and discourses. The language rights discourses sidestep the languages they are seeking to promote by not examining how language rights are interpreted by the vernaculars whose rights they are seeking to advance. As Heller and Duchêne suggest, we need to

> rethink the reasons why we hold onto the ideas about language and identity which emerged from modernity. Rather than assuming we must save languages, perhaps we should be asking instead who benefits and who loses from understanding languages the way we do, what is at stake for whom, and how and why language serves as a terrain for competition.
> *(2007: 11)*

Lingua franca, grassroots and urban multilingualism

Although, as we have suggested, the burden of current research tends towards a pluralization of monolingualism, there are also a number of different ways in which we can move towards a more productive understanding of language use. Fardon and Furniss (1984), for example, propose that multilingualism is "Africa's lingua franca." The view that multilingualism is a lingua franca is in sharp contrast to concepts such as plural/multiple monolingualism. In plural monolingualism languages are distinct, and autonomous, whereas in lingua franca multilingualism languages are so deeply intertwined and fused into each other that the level of fluidity renders it difficult to determine any boundaries that may indicate that there are different languages involved. Hence plural monolingualism is consistent with a model that renders it possible to choose between languages; multilingualism as a lingua franca, by contrast, militates against this trend and conjures a very different notion of "language." In lingua franca multilingualism language is viewed as a multilayered chain that is constantly combined and recombined and in which "secondary" language learning takes place more or less simultaneously with language use. In describing lingua franca multilingualism, Fardon and Furniss point out that language is conceptualized as

> a multilayered and partially connected. ... chain that offers a choice of varieties and registers in the speaker's immediate environment, and a steadily diminishing set of options to be employed in more distant interactions, albeit a set that is always liable to be reconnected more densely to a new environment by rapid secondary learning, or by the development of new languages.
>
> *(1984: 4)*

This makes the notion of language that forms the basis of all analyses in linguistic theorizing of dubious validity. It is worth observing too that this idea is very different from the current thinking about English as a lingua franca (ELF) (Jenkins 2006; Seidlhofer 2001). Although this understanding of flexible, multiple English may provide a more dynamic model of English than some of the current analyses of varieties of English along national lines, it still keeps in place a notion of English as a language with core and variant properties. As Pennycook (2007b) has argued, there are good reasons to do away with these myths about English (or any other language): to speak of English (as international language, a lingua franca, a second/ foreign language and so forth) is not so much an act of description of linguistic reality as it is a discursive act that brings ideologies of English into being. Canagarajah (2007: 91), by contrast, offers a version of lingua franca English (LFE) that is closer to the position we are arguing for here, suggesting that "LFE does not exist as a system out there. It is constantly brought into being in each context of communication." From this point of view, "there is no meaning for form, grammar or language ability outside the realm of practice. LFE is not a product located in the mind of the speaker; it is a social process constantly reconstructed in sensitivity to environmental factors" (Canagarajah 2007: 94).

Grassroots multilingualism is evident in popular culture, the study of which creates opportunities to advance an analysis of multilingualism that links music, language, paintings, and at times public transport in taxis driven largely by young males in Africa with low levels of formal education. An analysis that combines these diverse modalities has to be transmodal (Pennycook 2007a; Makoni and Makoni 2009) rather than multimodal (Kress 2003; Kress and van Leeuwen 2001). It has to be transmodal because meanings or communication in such situations are borne out by a complex reading of different modalities, at times reading them against each other, and not separately, which would echo a plural monolingualism. A transmodal analysis should capture the dynamic and evolving relationships between languages and other modalities. The meaning is an evolving art and drama of communication because the semiotic systems are constructed in context and are always in a state of being, inchoate, fragmented, and historically contingent.

From this point of view, an understanding of multilingua francas incorporates not only the linguistic resources speakers draw on but also elements of the accompanying soundtracks. Language use in parts of South Africa may be interwoven with *kwaito* (a version of South African hip-hop) and its various associations. In such contexts, sampling of sounds, genres, languages, and cultures is the norm (Pennycook 2007a; Alim *et al.* 2009; Makoni *et al.* 2010). This view of language is human-centered insofar as it stresses agency (albeit with constraints) and explores how individuals and communities express "voice" (Blommaert 2005), "playing" around with semiotics with fragmented and open designs, which can be manipulated to clarify, obfuscate or make meanings ambiguous (Khubchandani 1997: 70, Makoni and Makoni 2010). This ambiguity or meaning obfuscation contrasts sharply with the type of multilingual school language practices "which puts premium on the explicit, unambiguous, overt manifestation through language by laying undue stress on its rationale and overt use" (Khubchandani 1997: 226). This dynamic and fluidity calls for a need to reimagine new metaphors to describe multilingual density. One way of describing them is to borrow from Illich and Sander's description of vernacular grammars in the late fifteenth century, "lingua or tongue was less like one drawer in a bureau than one color in a spectrum. The comprehensibility of speech was comparable to the intensity of a color" (1989: 62–3).

Bosire argues that the

> hybrid languages of Africa are contact outcomes that have evolved at a time when African communities are coming to terms with the colonial and postcolonial situation that included rapid urbanization and a bringing together of different ethnic communities and cultures with a concomitant exposure to different ways of being.
>
> *(2006: 192)*

At the same time, "young people are caught up in this transition; they are children of two worlds and want a way to express this duality, this new 'ethnicity'." Out of this mix emerge new language varieties, such as "Sheng," a Swahili/ English hybrid, which provides urban youth with "a way to break away from the old fraternities that put particular ethnic communities in particular neighborhoods/estates and give them a global urban ethnicity, the urbanite: sophisticated, street smart, new generation, tough" (ibid.). Higgins' (2009) work on English as a local and multivocal language in East Africa destabilizes some of the dominant conceptualizations of English as a distinct code, as a global language, as an entity bounded by particular domains of use. Instead, she suggests, we need to grasp the implications of the hybridity and linguistic bricolage in which English so often participates.

The next step, therefore, is to move towards an understanding of the relationships among language resources as used by certain communities (the linguistic resources users draw on), local language practices (the use of these language resources in specific contexts), and language users' relationship to language varieties (the social, economic, and cultural positioning of the speakers). From this point of view, therefore, we can start to move away from both mono- and multilingual orientations to language, and take on board recent understandings of translingual practices (Jacquemet 2005; Pennycook 2010) across communities other than those defined along national, ethnic, geographic, or cultural criteria. The interest here is in "the communicative practices of transnational groups that interact using different languages and communicative codes simultaneously present in a range of communicative channels, both local and distant" (Jacquemet 2005: 265). These transidiomatic practices, Jacquemet explains, "are the results of the co-presence of multilingual talk (exercised by de/reterritorialized speakers) and electronic media, in contexts heavily structured by social indexicalities and semiotic codes." For Jacquemet, such practices are dependent on "transnational environments," the mediation of "deterritorialized technologies," and interaction "with both present and distant people" (ibid.).

Such language use can also be usefully be described in terms of *metrolingualism* (Otsuji and Pennycook 2010), a product typically of modern and mainly urban interaction. Drawing on the notion of metroethnicity that seeks ethnic reconstitution by challenging ethnic and language orthodoxies through the possibilities of a new ethnic *cool* (Maher 2005), metrolingualism describes the ways in which people of different and mixed backgrounds use, play with and negotiate identities through language; it does not assume connections between language, culture, ethnicity, nationality, or geography, but rather seeks to explore how such relations are produced, resisted, defied, or rearranged. Although Jørgensen (2008) and Møller (2008) have posed similar questions about language reifications and proposed the notion of *polylingualism* in place of multilingualism, the notion of metrolingualism, like the idea of a multilingua franca, has the advantage of avoiding the pluralization strategies of parallel terminology (multilingualism, plurilingualism, polylingualism) and instead posits mixed language as the singular norm where the notion of language in time and space (metro), rather than countability, becomes the language modifier.

The rise of new forms of urban multiple language use has a long history. These new *urbi- or metro-lingualisms* pose challenges to the study of multiple language and render it necessary to construct new metaphors to capture the unfolding social, political, and linguistic complexity. They draw on and use a wide range of local and non-local languages, and create new and fragmented semiotic systems; they are constantly in flux; they are predominantly oral; they are street languages, and as such are often linked to popular culture, crime, and urban unrest. To speak these languages, it is necessary to draw on multilingual resources, and yet these urban languages are also multilanguages in themselves, diverse, shifting, constantly evolving, and unpredictable in their usage. They may vary according to who is using them to whom, while at the same time each speaker may retain a form of multilingualism peculiar to them: a form of idiolectal multilingualism. The variability in the use of and facility in the use of multilingualism as play compels us to reintroduce the idea of individual creativity within multilingualism.

Conclusions and new research directions

Recent research has started to question whether these old categorizations of language—varieties, codeswitching, bilingualism, mother tongue, multilingualism, and borrowing—as well as the identities that are assumed along lines of language, location, ethnicity, culture really work any more. Developed in contexts very different to those in which language analysis is now being carried out (urban, grassroots, popular culture), many of these concepts simply do not seem to address the forms of hybrid urbilingualism that are common across the world. Indeed, there are strong reasons to question the very notion of language as a discrete entity that is describable in terms of core and variation. On the one hand, then, there are the changing realities of urban life, with enhanced mobility, shifting populations, social upheaval, health and climate crises, and increased access to diverse media, particularly forms of popular culture. On the other hand, is the growing concern that we need to rethink the ways in which language has been conceptualized.

The assumption that monolingualism and multilingualism are two important pillars which might be used to frame sociolinguistic analysis, and that studies of multilingualism are attempting to move beyond the blinkered monolingualism that has constricted a lot of thought about language use, takes us a certain way but then stops short. For many people—whether the Quecha in Latin America (Mannheim 1991) or different people across Africa and Asia—the critical issue is not whether one is monolingual or multilingual but that one uses language. This is why the ultimate move here may not only be from monolingualism to multilingualism but also back to monolingualism, where the latter is understood in very different ways from the monological, one-variety concept that linguistics has been trying to escape. This is the mono-lingualism of humanity, which can be better captured not by pluri-poly- or multilingualism but by non-pluralized ideas such as urbilingualism, metrolingualism, or a multilingua franca.

Treating languages as socially and historically constructed provides space and latitude for social and political change, and takes cognizance of individuals' social and adaptive strategies and their resistance to some of the constructed languages. If Indigenous languages are socially constructed through a complex interplay of philosophy and politics, they are more akin to other artificial constructs such as customary law, which is a form of codified traditional law rather than any naturally occurring tradition. Joseph's (2006) reminder that languages are "political from top to bottom" is useful here as it draws attention yet again to the point that both the invention of languages and their disinvention are steeped in relations of power and politics.

In conclusion, we now return to the questions we posed at the beginning of the chapter. If languages are not "primordial," under what conditions did they emerge, and what are the implications of the processes of invention that brought them into being? Although research discussed above has started to document the histories of language invention, particularly in colonial contexts (Errington 2008), there is clearly a great deal more work that could be done here. In order to understand the metadiscursive regimes used in the construction of "languages," we need both a critical history of linguistics in its many contexts, as well as a great deal more work in linguistic anthropology in order to understand the ways in which languages are locally used and understood, and the effects of particular metadiscursive regimes on the workings of local languages. And finally, if we can do away with our language enumerations that sit so often at the heart of multilingualism, a great deal of productive research could start to open up the real complexities of grassroots metro- or urbilingualism.

Related topics

Lessons from pre-colonial multilingualism; discourses about linguistic diversity; language rights; heteroglossia.

Further reading

Errington, J. (2008) *Linguistics in a Colonial World: A Story of Language, Meaning and Power*, Oxford: Blackwell.
(*Linguistics in a Colonial World* gives a significant account of the role of linguists within colonialism, showing how the political and epistemological orientations of empire worked together to produce particular ways of thinking about language(s).)
Heller, M. (2007) *Bilingualism: A Social Approach*, Basingstoke: Palgrave Macmillan.
(Monica Heller's collection opens with an illuminating chapter in which she does a powerful critique of bilingualism, proposing a strong social approach. Her critique is similar to the one laid out in this book on issues about the limitations of constructs such as codes and boundedness as bases for the analysis of language. In addition to her introduction, there are a number of other chapters dealing with a wide range of topics from minority language movements to language rights and bilingualism in the mass media.)
Khubchandani, L. (2004) *Balance of the Current Sociolinguistic Research: New Trends and New Paradigms*, Linguapax Congress, Linguistic Diversity, Sustainability and Peace, Congress Report (19–23), Barcelona, April 2002, www.linguapax.org/congres/plenaries/khubchandani.html

(Khubchandani provides an excellent example of post-colonial Indian interpretation of multilingualism.)

Ranger, T. (1983) 'The invention of tradition in colonial Africa', in E. Hobsbawm and T. Ranger (eds) *The Invention of Tradition*, Cambridge: Cambridge University Press.
(Ranger's work on the invention of tradition in Africa is an early key text for thinking about invention. Although he subsequently had concerns that it downplays the agency and significance of local traditions, preferring instead Andersen's (1983) *Imagined Communities*, invention is preferable because the construct of invention neatly encapsulates the constructed nature of major African social formations. The social formation takes place over a long period of time, and indeed at times there is controversy about which features are relevant and how they should be represented, and interpreted.)

Williams, G. (1992) *Sociolinguistics: A Sociological Critique*, London and New York: Routledge.
(Williams provides a particularly incisive critique of some of the central concepts in sociolinguistics of multilingualism, corpus and state planning, and the limitations of language planning as an instrument of social change.)

Bibliography

Alim, S, Ibrahim, A. and Pennycook, A. (eds) (2009) *Global Linguistic Flows: Hip Hop Cultures, Youth Identities and the Politics of Language*, New York: Routledge.
Bauman, R. and Briggs, C. (2003) *Voices of Modernity Language Ideologies and the Politics of Inequality*, Cambridge: Cambridge University Press.
Becker, A. L. (1995) *Beyond Translation: Essays in Modern Philology*, Ann Arbor: The University of Michigan Press.
Blommaert, J. (2005) *Discourse*, Cambridge: Cambridge University Press.
——(2008) 'Artefactual ideologies and the textual production of African languages', *Language and Communication*, 28(4): 291–307.
Bosire, M. (2006) 'Hybrid languages: the case of Sheng', in O. F. Arasanyin and M. A. Pemberton (eds) *Selected Proceedings of the 36th Annual Conference on African Linguistics*, Somerville, MA: Cascadilla Proceedings Project.
Branson, J and Miller, D. (2007) 'Beyond "language": linguistic imperialism, sign languages and linguistic anthropology', in S. Makoni and A. Pennycook (eds) *Disinventing and Reconstituting Languages*, Clevedon: Multilingual Matters.
Bybee, J. and Hopper, P. (2001) 'Introduction to frequency and the emergence of linguistic structure', in J. Bybee and P. Hopper (eds) *Frequency and the Emergence of Linguistic Structure*, Amsterdam: John Benjamins.
Canagarajah, S. (2007) 'The ecology of global English', *International Multilingual Research Journal* 1(2): 89–100.
Clifford, J. and Marcus, G. (1986) *Writing Culture: The Poetics of Ethnography*, Berkeley: University of California Press.
Crowley, T. (1999) 'Linguistic diversity in the Pacific', *Journal of Sociolinguistics* 3(1): 81–103.
Dasgupta, P. (1997) 'Foreword', *Revisualizing Boundaries: A Plurilingual Ethos*, New Delhi/Thousand Oaks, London: Sage.
Davidson, D. (1986) 'A nice derangement of epitaphs', in E. Lepore (ed.) *Truth and Interpretation Perspectives on the Philosophy of Donald Davidson*, Oxford: Blackwell.
Errington, J. (2001) 'Colonial linguistics', *Annual Review of Anthropology* 30: 19–39.
——(2008) *Linguistics in a Colonial World: A Story of Language, Meaning and Power*, Oxford: Blackwell.
Fabian, J. (1986) *Language and Colonial Power*, Cambridge: Cambridge University Press.
Fardon, G. and Furniss, R. (1984) *African Languages, Development and the State*, London: Routledge.
Grace, G. (n.d.) available online at http://www2.hawaii.edu~grace.
Harpham, G. (2002) *Language Alone: The Critical Fetish of Modernity*, London: Routledge.
Harris, R. (1980) *The Language-Makers*, Ithaca, NY: Cornell University Press.
——(1981) *The Language Myth in Western Culture*, London: Duckworth.
——(1990) 'On redefining linguistics', in H. Davis and T. Taylor (eds) *Redefining Linguistics*, London: Routledge.
——(1998) *Introduction to Integrational Linguistics*, Oxford: Pergamon.

——(2009) 'Implicit and explicit language teaching', in M. Toolan (ed.) *Language Teaching, Integrational Linguistic Approaches*, London: Routledge.

Harris, R. and Taylor, T. (1997) (eds) *Landmarks in Linguistic Thought*, vol. 1. *The Western Tradition from Socrates to Saussure*, 2nd edn, London: Routledge.

Haugen, E (1972) *The Ecology of Language*. California: Stanford University Press.

Heller, M. (2007) 'Bilingualism as ideology and practice', in M. Heller (ed.) *Bilingualism: A Social Approach*, London: Macmillan.

Heller, M. and Duchêne, A. (2007) 'Discourses of endangerment: Sociolinguistics, globalization and social order', in A. Duchêne and M. Heller (eds) *Discourses of Endangerment: Ideology and Interest in the Defense of Languages*, London: Continuum.

Heryanto, A. (1990) 'The making of language: developmentalism in Indonesia', *Prisma* 50: 40–53.

——(2007) 'Then there were languages: Bahasa Indonesia was one among many', in S. Makoni and A. Pennycook (eds) *Disinventing and Reconstituting Languages*, Clevedon: Multilingual Matters.

Higgins, C. (2009) *English as a Local Language: Post-colonial Identities and Multilingual Practices*, Clevedon: Multilingual Matters.

Hopper, P. (1998) 'Emergent grammar', in M. Tomasello (ed.) *The New Psychology of Language*, Mahwah, NJ: Lawrence Erlbaum.

Illich, I. and Sander, B. (1989) *ABC: The Alphabetization of the Popular Mind*, London: Penguin.

Irvine, J. (1989) 'When talk isn't cheap: language and political economy', *American Ethnologist* 16: 248–67.

——(2009) 'Subjected words: African linguistics and the colonial encounter', *Language and Communication* 28(4): 291–408.

Jacquemet, M. (2005) 'Transidiomatic practices: Language and power in the age of globalization', *Language and Communication* 25: 257–77.

Jeater, D. (2007) *Language and Sciences: The Invention of the 'Native Mind' in Southern Rhodesia*, Portsmouth, USA: Heinemann/Greenwood.

Jenkins, J. (2006) 'Current perspectives on teaching world Englishes and English as a lingua franca', *TESOL Quarterly* 40(1): 157–81.

Johnstone, B. (1996) *The Linguistic Individual: Self-expression in Language and Linguistics*, New York and Oxford: Oxford University Press.

Jørgensen, J. N. (2008) 'Polylingual languaging around and among children and adolescents', *International Journal of Multilingualism* 5(3): 161–76.

Joseph, J. (2006) *Language and Politic*, Edinburgh: Edinburgh University Press.

Khubchandani, L. M. (1983) *Demographic Imperatives in Language Planning*, www.linguapax.org/congres/plenaries/Khubchandani.html

——(1997) Bilingual Education for Indigenous groups in India, in J. Cummins and D. Corson (eds) *Encylopaedia and Language Education*, vol. 5. *Bilingual Education* (67–76) Dordrecht, Netherlands: Kluwer.

——(2003) 'Defining mother tongue education in plurilingual contexts', *Language Policy* 2: 239–54.

Kress, G. (2003) *Literacy in the New Media*, London: Routledge.

Kress, G. and van Leeuwen, T. (2001) *Reading Images the Grammar of Visual Design*, London: Routledge.

Kroskrity (2000) 'Regimenting languages: Language ideological perspectives', in P. V. Kroskrity (ed.) *Regimes of Language: Ideologies, Politics and Identities*, Santa Fe, NM: School of American Research Press.

Le Page, R. and Tabouret-Keller, A. (1985) *Acts of Identity*, Cambridge: Cambridge University Press.

Love, N. (2009) 'Science, language and linguistic culture', *Language and Communication* 29: 26–46.

Maher, J. (2005) 'Metroethnicity, language, and the principle of cool', *International Journal of the Sociology of Language* 175/176: 83–102.

Makoni, S. (1998) 'African languages as European scripts the shaping of communal memory', in S. Nuttall and C. Cotzee (eds) *Negotiating the Past: The Making of Memory in South Africa*, Oxford: Oxford University Press.

Makoni, S. and Makoni, B. (2010) 'Multilingual discourses on wheels and public English in Africa: A case for "vague linguistique"', in J. Maybin and J. Swann (eds) *The Routledge Companion to English Language Studies*, Abingdon, Oxford: Routledge.

——(2009) English and education in Anglophone Africa: Historical and current realities', in M. Shepard Wong and S. Canagarajah (eds) *Christian and Critical English Language Education Educators in Dialogue: Pedagogical and Ethical Dilemmas*, New York and London: Routledge.

Makoni, S., Brutt-Griffler, J. and Mashiri, P. (2007) 'The use of "indigenous" and urban vernaculars in Zimbabwe', *Language in Society* 36: 25–49.

Makoni, S., Makoni, B. and Rosenberg, A. (2010) 'Wordy worlds of music: Implications for language in education', *Language, Identity, and Education* 9 (1): 1–10.

Makoni, S. and Pennycook, A. (2007) (eds) *Disinventing and Reconstituting Languages*, Clevedon: Multilingual Matters.

Mannheim, B. (1991) *The Language of the Inkha: Since the European Invasion*, Austin: University of Texas.

May, S. (2005) 'Moving the language debates forward', *Journal of Sociolinguistics* 9(3): 319–47.

Møller, J. S. (2008) 'Polylingual performance among Turkish-Danes in late-modern Copenhagen', *International Journal of Multilingualism* 5(3): 217–36.

Mudimbe, V. (1988) *The Invention of Africa: Gnosis, Philosophy, and the Order of Knowledge*, Bloomington: Indiana University Press.

Mufwene, S. (2001) *The Ecology of Language Evolution*, Cambridge: Cambridge University Press.

Mühlhäusler, P. (2000) 'Language planning and language ecology', *Current Issues in Language Planning* 1(3): 306–67.

Nakata, M. (2007) *Disciplining the Savages: Savaging the Disciplines*, Canberra: Aboriginal Studies Press.

Nero, S. (2006) 'Language, identity and education of Caribbean English speakers', *World Englishes* 25(3/4): 501–11.

Otsuji, E. and Pennycook, A. (2010) 'Metrolingualism: Fixity, fluidity and language in flux', *International Journal of Multilingualism* 7 (3): 240–54.

Pennycook, A. (2007a) *Global Englishes and Transcultural Flows*, London and New York: Routledge.

——(2007b) 'The myth of English as an international language', in S. Makoni and A. Pennycook (eds) *Disinventing and Reconstituting Languages*, Clevedon: Multilingual Matters.

——(2010) *Language as a Local Practice*, London: Routledge.

Rajagopalan, K. (2007) 'Revisiting the nativity scene', *Studies in Language* 31(1): 193–205.

Ranger, T. (1983) 'The invention of tradition in colonial Africa', in E. Hobsbawm and T. Ranger (eds) *The Invention of Tradition*, Cambridge: Cambridge University Press.

Schiefflien, B. (1990) *The Give and Take of Everyday Life: Language Socialization of the Kaluli Children*, New York and Cambridge: Cambridge University Press.

Seidlhofer, B. (2001) 'Closing a conceptual gap: The case for a description of English as a lingua franca', *International Review of Applied Linguistics* 11(2): 133–58.

Spear, T. (2003) 'Neo-traditionalism and the limits of invention in British Colonial Africa', *Journal of African History* 44: 3–27.

Toolan, M. (2009) (ed.) *Language Teaching and Integrational Linguistics*, London: Routledge.

van der Tuuk, N. H. (1971) *A Grammar of Toba Batak*, Voor De Trope, available online at www2.hawaii.edu/langue.html

Whorf, B. (1988) *Language, Thought, and Reality: Selected Writings of Benjamin Lee Whorf*, John Carroll (ed.), Cambridge, MA: MIT Press.

Woolard, K. (2004) 'Is the past a foreign country?: Time, language origins, and the nation in early modern Spain', *Journal of Linguistic Anthropology* 14(1): 57–80.

Yngve, V. (1996) *From Grammar to Science. New Foundations for General Linguistics*, Philadelphia: John Benjamins.

Yngve, V. and Wasik, Z. (eds) (2004) *Hard-Science Linguistics*, New York: Continuum.

26

Multilingualism and emotions

Aneta Pavlenko

Emotions constitute an intrinsic part of our language attitudes and linguistic interaction and yet they have remained under-researched and undertheorized in the field of multilingualism. The key reason for this is a narrow understanding of the relationship between multilingualism and emotions that until recently dominated the field and limited the inquiry to the influence of affective factors on second language (L2) learning. A recent surge of scholarship opened up other venues for inquiry, such as emotionality of multilinguals' languages or acquisition and use of emotion lexicons, revealing that the inter-relationship between multilingualism and emotions is much more complex than imagined earlier. The purpose of this chapter is to outline the limitations of traditional inquiry into affective factors, to summarize recent research on multilingualism and emotions, and to point to fruitful directions for future inquiry.

Affective factors in L2 learning

There is no doubt that throughout their existence the fields of Second Language Acquisition (SLA) and multilingualism have acknowledged the role of emotions in the language learning process, yet the conceptions of emotions and of their contribution have been extremely narrow. Emotions have been reduced to a laundry list of decontextualized and poorly defined socio-psychological constructs, such as affective factors, anxiety, attitudes, motivation, self-esteem, empathy, and risk taking (e.g. Arnold 1999; Ortega 2009; Oxford 2002). Their interaction with language has been reduced to the influence on the L2 learning process, leaving out the interplay between emotions and the rest of multilingual phenomena.

Within this narrow frame, two main claims have been put forth in SLA research. The first claim is that positive attitudes toward the L2 and its speakers and an integrative motivation, or identification with the L2 group, facilitate L2 acquisition and lead to better outcomes (Gardner and Lambert 1972). The second claim is that language learning anxiety is the best single correlate of foreign language achievement, whereby higher levels of anxiety lead to lower levels of achievement (Horwitz 2001; MacIntyre and Gardner 1994).

At first glance, both statements appear to be self-evident. A closer scrutiny, however, reduces their validity. Critics of the causal relationship between attitudes and achievement argue that attitudes and motivation are socially constructed and dynamic phenomena, which cannot be captured through questionnaires, and that the relationship between the two is reciprocal rather than unidirectional (e.g. Baker 1992; Dörnyei and Ushioda 2011). Similar arguments have been put forth with regard to the causal relationship between anxiety and achievement. Critics argue that anxiety is a complex phenomenon, which in some cases may facilitate, rather than con-strain, L2 learning, and that the relationship between the two is reciprocal, with anxiety often the outcome and not the cause of difficulties in the learning process (e.g. Dewaele 2010; Sparks and Ganshow 2001). One can further add that the key factors in language achievement—people's actions—are shaped by more than just language attitudes or feelings of anxiety. Consequently, positive attitudes and integrative motivation (as elicited by questionnaires) do not guarantee speedy learning (for empirical support see e.g. Piller and Takahashi 2006). In turn, high levels of anxiety, negative attitudes toward the L2 group or lack of identification with L2 Speakers do not necessarily prevent L2 learning, as seen, for instance, in the case of Israeli Arabs learning Hebrew.

There is, however, a deeper problem with the affective factors perspective. These constructs are of limited use in the study of multilingualism because they have emerged from one of the world's last monolingual preserves, North America, in an attempt to capture the experi-ence of monolingual English-speaking students learning foreign languages in the classroom. Generations of these students grew up with a deep conviction that foreign language learning is a challenging process in which they cannot succeed unless they have "language learning apti-tude." More importantly, they also saw it as a process in which native speakers of English do not have to succeed in a globalized world that accommodates their linguistic needs. The experiences of these privileged learners are distinct from those of immigrants and guest workers who strive to join the global marketplace and whose fears are fueled not by test-taking anxiety but by gatekeeping practices and power relations that constrain access to target language communities (Bremer *et al.* 1996; Norton 2000). They are equally distinct from experiences of those who live in multilingual societies and continue to learn and use different languages throughout their lives without ever stopping to think about "the fear of failure." Ironically, these experiences are not even representative of the whole population of English-speaking L2 learners—recent studies show that the language learning experiences of North American women, racial, ethnic, and sexual minorities, and working-class individuals differ from those of heterosexual white middle-class males (e.g. Kinginger 2004a; Talburt and Stewart 1999).

Having said this, I do not deny that L2 learners and users experience anxiety in and outside of the classroom. Undoubtedly they do, but the causes of this anxiety, as well as the causes of other multiple and contradictory emotions associated with language learning and use, cannot be studied through questionnaires, rather they need to be examined in their social contexts, where L2 speakers struggle to establish their legitimacy in the face of indifference, disinterest, and sometimes linguistic, ethnic, racial, or gender discrimination.

Languages and emotions, languages of emotions

To understand the behavior of multilinguals as social beings, multilingualism scholars had to depart from the sociopsychological approaches toward a more comprehensive understanding of emotions and their relationship to languages. To do so, they drew on research on language and emotions in linguistics, anthropology, psychology, and neurobiology. Below, I will define the key terms used in the present chapter and then outline two key insights into multilingualism and emotions that guide the current inquiry.

Emotions and emotion concepts

Emotions are notoriously hard to pin down—it appears that any definition of emotions in strictly mental, behavioral, or physiological terms will be hopelessly oversimplified and easily met with counterexamples (Fehr and Russell 1984). For the purposes of the present overview, I will adopt a process view of *emotions*, seeing them not only as inner somatic states (e.g. anger, love) but also as relational phenomena (e.g. anger at X, love for Y), interpreted through linguistic categories available to individual speakers, or *emotion words*. The usage of these words is guided by *emotion concepts* or *categories*, seen here as prototypical scripts that are embedded within larger systems of beliefs and formed as a result of repeated experiences; these scripts involve causal antecedents, appraisals, physiological reactions, consequences, and means of regulation and display (ibid.; Pavlenko 2005, 2008a; Russell 1991).

Appropriation of emotion concepts allows speakers to categorize events and phenomena in language- and culture-appropriate ways, to evaluate them, and to respond to them in ways comprehensible to other members of the speech community in question.

Languages and emotions

The first insight that had transformed the study of multilingualism and emotions comes from more than a century of research on psychoanalysis and from recent investigations in neurobiology and neuropsychology of language and emotions. Psychoanalysts, beginning with Freud, have repeatedly noticed that multilingual patients often display different selves in their respective languages with mother tongues being at the root of deep-seated anxieties and later learned languages functioning as a means of distancing from traumatic experiences (Amati-Mehler *et al.* 1993; Buxbaum 1949; Ferenczi 1916; Freud 1893; Greenson 1950; Krapf 1955). Current advances in the study of neuroscience of emotion (Damasio 1994, 2003; Ochsner and Feldman Barrett 2001) and classical conditioning (LeDoux 2002; Mathews *et al.* 1989) suggest that this perception is not unwarranted. Based on their findings and on the work of Harris and associates (Harris 2004; Harris *et al.* 2003, 2006) discussed later in the chapter, Pavlenko (2005) put forth a theory of language embodiment that differentiates between primary and secondary language acquisition processes.

In this view two inter-related processes take place during primary language acquisition. The first is *conceptual development*, where children form emotion categories that include information from all modalities—visual, auditory, olfactory, tactile, kinesthetic, and visceral—and are subject to ongoing modification that takes place in the language socialization process. The parallel process involves *affective linguistic conditioning*, where words and phrases acquire affective connotations and personal meanings through association and integration with emotionally charged memories and experiences. Some words become linked to positive memories (e.g. ice cream) or personal fears (e.g. spider), whereas taboo and swear words (e.g. shit) become associated with prohibition, punishment and social stigmatization. Together, the two processes contribute to the perception of *language embodiment*, whereby first language (L1) words invoke sensory images, physiological reactions, and sometimes also feelings of anxiety, shame, or guilt. Foreign language words, on the other hand, do not elicit emotional reactions, because language learning in the classroom takes place without significant involvement of the limbic system or the majority of the sensory modalities (for an in-depth discussion, see Pavlenko 2005).

Importantly, the theory does not make a dichotomous distinction, where the L1 is always the language of emotions and an L2 the language of detachment. Rather, it posits a language learning continuum, where on the one end we have primary language acquisition, always an emotional and contextualized process that may take place in more than one language, and, on the other, foreign language learning, a process that is usually fairly decontextualized. In the middle of the continuum is additional language learning in naturalistic contexts that may lead to additional affective linguistic conditioning and conceptual development, thus creating the perception of embodiment of later learned languages and opening the path for new "languages of emotions."

Languages of emotions

The second insight derived from the previous scholarship shifts the focus of attention to cross-linguistic differences in languages of emotions. Cross-linguistic studies show that languages differ in the size of emotion lexicons, in morphosyntactic categories favored for emotion encoding (e.g. verbs vs adjectives), and in conceptual organization of the emotion domain, reflecting distinct cultural norms governing the domain in different societies (for overviews see Pavlenko 2005; Russell 1991; Wilce 2009). In some languages, the emotion domain may be more salient, differentiated, and codable than in others: as a result, some emotion words may have no translation equivalents in other languages, whereas others may have two or three partial equivalents (e.g. Lutz 1988; Panayiotou 2004a, 2004b, 2006; Pavlenko 2005, 2008a; Wierzbicka 2004). As a result of these differences, speakers of different languages may differ in their perceptions and evaluation of different events and phenomena and possibly even inner states.

Importantly, the functions of emotion words are not limited to conveying speaker's feelings or making suppositions about others' feelings, they also perform a variety of interactional functions, from assigning causes and motives to actions to explaining the intricacies of social relationships. In turn, affect is conveyed not only through emotion words, but also through non-verbal means, vocal cues, emotion-laden words, such as swear words or endearments, and a variety of other linguistic means, from honorifics and diminutives to intensifiers and figurative language. These linguistic resources, as well as values placed on levels of emotional engagement and expressivity, vary across speech communities, even though within each community there is always a range of variation in individual affective styles.

Taken together, the two insights suggest that multilinguals' languages may offer them distinct affective repertoires and, depending on the age and context of acquisition, may have different levels of emotionality. These two perspectives opened up new possibilities for research on multilingualism and emotions. In what follows, I will offer an overview of this research and its implications for multilinguals' behaviors and experiences across all areas of life.

Multilingualism and emotions

Multilingual lexicon and autobiographic memory

Studies of the multilingual lexicon reveal the impact of both cross-linguistic differences and differential emotionality. Cross-linguistic differences have been shown to influence the conceptual organization in the mental lexicon. Beginning and intermediate L2 learners and proficient learners with low degrees of acculturation may rely on L1 emotion concepts when using the L2 (Pavlenko and Driagina 2007; Toya and Kodis 1996). People socialized in the L2 community may internalize new emotion categories that are not encoded in their native language (Panayiotou 2004a, 2004b). In the presence of partial equivalents, L2 users may experience conceptual restructuring, whereby the previously existing L1 concept has been modified but does not fully approximate the target (Panayiotou 2006; Stepanova Sachs and Coley 2006). Another possible outcome of partial equivalence is conceptual convergence, whereby the two concepts merge into a unitary category. Alternatively, bilinguals may be able to preserve two sets of concepts and in that case perform according to the constraints of their respective languages (Pavlenko 2002b; Stepanova Sachs and Coley 2006). Under the influence of the L2, some may also experience conceptual shift and display L2 influence on L1 emotion categories and even attrition of particular concepts and distinctions (Drennan *et al.* 1991; Pavlenko 2002b).

Depending on the age and context of acquisition, words in the multilingual lexicon may also differ in emotionality. Harris and associates (Harris 2004; Harris *et al.* 2003, 2006) revealed these differences through the study of skin conductance response (SCR) to different categories of words, where higher levels of SCR indicate greater levels of autonomic arousal and thus emotionality. Harris and associates (2003) found that in late Turkish–English bilinguals, L1 taboo words and reprimands elicited greater levels of SCR than L2 taboo words and reprimands. At the same time, in both Turkish–English and Spanish–English bilinguals, L2 taboo words elicited higher SCRs than other L2 word categories (Harris 2004; Harris *et al.* 2003, 2006). These results provide direct evidence for childhood affective linguistic conditioning and for L2 socialization effects and show that words of languages learned in naturalistic contexts are processed through both cognitive and affective channels.

Words in the multilingual lexicon also differ in the strength of the links to autobiographic memory: these links appear to be stronger between the memories and the words of the language in which the events took place. Two findings in the study of bilingual autobiographic memory give rise to this argument: a *language specificity effect*, whereby memories are more likely to be activated by the language in which the original events took place (e.g. Marian and Neisser 2000; Schrauf and Rubin 1998, 2004), and a *language congruity effect*, whereby memories elicited in the language in which they were encoded are more detailed and higher in emotional intensity (e.g. Javier *et al.* 1993; Marian and Kaushanskaya 2004).

Second language learning

The research on L2 learning has also benefited from the new perspectives. Instead of seeing emotions as beliefs (motivation) or as individual somatic states (anxiety), recent scholarship views *language-related emotions* as social and relational phenomena, embedded within identity narratives and experienced from particular subject positions. In this view, L2 learners make investments into desired identities and memberships in imagined communities, be it professional communities or the L2 community as a whole (Dörnyei and Ushioda 2011; Kinginger 2004a; Norton 2000; Piller and Takahashi 2006). When these investments, and with them the imagined future, are questioned or threatened—in other words, at junctures, where there are changes in goals, plans, or likely outcomes of plans—emotions help individuals to evaluate the changes, to continue, relinquish, or modify their plans and goals and to take action (for expanded accounts of the process, see Damasio 1994; Oatley 1992; Pavlenko 2005).

Several studies show that L2 learning—sometimes coupled with L1 rejection—is powerfully motivated by emotions linked to desired identities. In the 1960s young Hungarian women in Austrian villages began shifting to German because this language opened doors to the industrial workplaces and urban lifestyles they desired (Gal 1978). Similarly, peasant Breton mothers in France refused to transmit Breton to their children, behaving as if the language itself smelled of cow-shit, whereas French offered affinity and sophistication, moving them up the social ladder all the way to the middle class (McDonald 1994). Importantly, it is not only the shift from a minority to a majority language that can be powered by the new desired identities. Kinginger's (2004a, 2004b) work documents instances in which native speakers of English opted to fashion new identities for themselves through French. For a working-class American woman, Alice, just as for peasant women in Austria (Gal 1978) and France (McDonald 1994) or immigrant women in Canada (Norton 2000), the emotional investment in French became a bid for transcending class lines and engaging in a better life, a life of civilization and cultural refinement.

Piller and Takahashi (2006) argue that the focus on economic and social advantages offered by particular languages has obscured other appeals. Following Piller (2002), they put forth the notion of *language desire*, a desire to become a legitimate speaker of a particular language, to construct a new social identity in this language, and to form a romantic relationship with the speaker of that language (possibly to get the coveted legitimacy). Drawing on Foucault (1980), the researchers argue that the workings of power include the inculcation of desires that drive individuals to modify their bodies, personalities, life trajectories, or, for that matter, linguistic repertoires. As a result, language desire, too, may be a hegemonic instrument through which individuals conspire in their own oppression. To illustrate their ideas, Piller and Takahashi (2006) show how the English teaching industry in Japan draws on the discourse of *akogare*, a desire for West and Western men, and has become a powerful intermediary between female consumers and an English-speaking identity. The authors then follow the trajectories of five Japanese women who moved to Australia in search of better futures, English proficiency and English-speaking boyfriends, who are seen by them as optimal vehicles for instruction. They show that at the end pursuing *akogare* turned out to be a self-defeating proposition for the study participants—although it did turn on their agency, their dreams of becoming White and Western were impossible to achieve, and this failure turned them to depression and silence. Ironically, but not surprisingly, the participant who ended up with the highest fluency had the least amount of *akogare*.

One of the attractions of new languages involves new affective repertoires. These repertoires are not, however, easy to acquire and the task goes far beyond the learning of new emotion vocabulary. To master the intricacies of conventionalized indexing of affect in the new language, L2 learners have to: (1) restructure the vocal space to accommodate conventionalized meanings of particular vocal cues; (2) restructure the conceptual space, adopting new emotion categories and modifying existing ones; and (3) adjust patterns of structural selection (e.g. switch from verbs to adjectives). This task is extremely challenging and L2 learners with lower levels of proficiency may experience difficulties both in comprehension of emotional expression and in conveying their own feelings (Ho 2009; Rintell 1984, 1990). The lack of appropriate means of affective expression may leave individuals feeling frustrated, powerless, vulnerable, and ashamed of themselves and their inability to express their feelings.

Let us now consider each aspect of the learning process in turn, starting with vocal cues. Vocal cues are often believed to be the key indicator of emotional meanings in everyday interaction. Even though the matches between particular vocal cues and meanings are never absolute, either within or across languages, in each speech community there are prosodic patterns that signal conventionalized affective meanings (e.g. Holden and Hogan 1993; Ohara 2001). Studies of emotional expression show that, in the beginning and intermediate stages, L2 learners tend to rely on L1 prosodic patterns, which may lead to misinterpretation of the affective content of their utterances (e.g. Holden and Hogan 1993; Ohara 2001). Studies of emotion identification reveal that native speakers are usually more accurate than non-native speakers in identifying emotions based exclusively on vocal cues (e.g. Graham *et al.* 2001; Rintell 1984; Scherer *et al.* 2001; for an overview of this research see Pavlenko 2005). These studies also show that L2 users improve their performance over time and become as good as native speakers at emotion identification (Graham *et al.* 2001; Rintell 1984; Scherer *et al.* 2001).

Conceptual space is even more challenging for the L2 learners. Studies to date show that speakers with lower levels of proficiency often experience difficulties in understanding and appropriating the meanings of language-specific emotion words and in developing conceptual representations for these words (Panayiotou 2004a; Pavlenko and Driagina 2007). The success of this development is mediated by the relationship between translation equivalents in their respective languages: (1) conceptual equivalence facilitates internalization of new emotion vocabulary; (2) partial equivalence facilitates initial acquisition but also leads to L1 transfer, where L2 learners select and use L2 words in accordance with L1 constraints; (3) the lack of conceptual equivalents in the L1 complicates acquisition (Pavlenko 2008b; Pavlenko and Driagina 2007). In the process of L2 socialization, however, L2 users do develop new emotion concepts, down to somatic states associated with them, and sometimes even experience L2 influence on L1 emotion concepts (Panayiotou 2004a; Pavlenko 2002b).

In addition to words, concepts, and prosody, researchers have also begun to examine ways in which L2 learners adjust patterns of structural selection, that is preferences for emotion verbs, adjectives, or nouns. Pavlenko and associates (Pavlenko 2002a, 2002b, 2008b; Pavlenko and Driagina 2007) have examined these patterns in English–Russian and Russian–English bilinguals. Studies with monolingual participants demonstrated that, in narratives elicited by the same stimuli, English speakers favor adjectival constructions combining state and change-of-state verbs with emotion adjectives or pseudo-participles, whereas Russian speakers favor intransitive emotion verbs or adverbial constructions (Pavlenko 2002a, 2008b; Pavlenko and Driagina 2007). Studies of L1 English learners of L2 Russian and L1 Russian learners of L2 English demonstrated that learners do internalize new patterns of structural preference, although some L1 transfer was evident in the transfer of the adjectival pattern from L1 English into L2 Russian (Pavlenko 2008b; Pavlenko and Driagina 2007). Russian–English bilinguals residing in the USA displayed L2 influence on L1 in favoring adjectival constructions in Russian, sometimes in violation of Russian morphosyntactic constraints (Pavlenko 2002b).

Together, these findings suggest that the process of L2 learning may be guided by emotional investments in new identities and by language-related emotions, such as language desire. In the process, affective repertoires, from vocal cues to linguistic categories and patterns of structural selection, may be expanded and restructured. Structural and conceptual equivalence will facilitate the learning of L2 emotion vocabulary, whereas partial or complete conceptual non-equivalence will complicate target-like acquisition and lead to instances of negative transfer, lexical borrowing, and avoidance. Structural non-equivalence may lead to some instances of L1 transfer but will not preclude internalization of L2 patterns of structural selection.

Multilingual interaction: language choice, codeswitching, and performance of affect

Cross-linguistic differences and differences in language emotionality also have implications for multilingual interaction, and in particular for language choice and codeswitching. Language emotionality emerges as an important factor that influences language choice in both speaking and writing. Multilingual writers, like Czeslaw Milosz or Isaac Bashevis Singer, often cite the superior emotionality of the L1 as a reason for which they cannot imagine writing in any other language (Kellman 2000; Pavlenko 2005). Multilingual parents state that they can create an emotional connection only in the L1, the language of their own childhood, and to do it in another language would feel "fake" and "unnatural" (Pavlenko 2004). However, a lower level of emotionality associated with the L2 may also have an appeal. In psychoanalytic sessions with multilingual therapists, a later learned language is often used to discuss taboo topics, such as sex, or traumatic childhood events (Amati-Mehler et al. 1993; Buxbaum 1949; Greenson 1950;

Krapf 1955; Movahedi 1996). Similarly, some bilingual writers—including a Polish–English bilingual Jerzy Kosinski, an Israeli Arab Anton Shammas and an English–French bilingual Nancy Huston—have admitted selecting a "stepmother tongue" in order to distance themselves from the memories, taboos, anxieties, and a visceral emotionality of the L1 and to gain control over their words, stories, and plots (Kellman 2000; Kinginger 2004b; Pavlenko 2005).

Codeswitching is also affected by the perceived emotionality of the languages in question. L1, for instance, is a common choice for expression of positive affect and the use of endearments among parents who are raising their children in L2 (Pavlenko 2004). Individuals who remain dominant in their L1 and perceive it as most emotional may also spontaneously revert to L1 to argue with spouses and partners, to scold and discipline their children, and to use taboo and swearwords to maximum effect and satisfaction (Dewaele 2004a, 2004b, 2006; Pavlenko 2004, 2005, 2008a). These switches are particularly interesting because some speakers choose the L1 even though their partners have little or no proficiency in the language (Pavlenko 2005). In doing so, they go against the grain of linguistic theories such as the Gricean maxims and the Cooperative Principle (Grice 1975) that frame argument as a cooperative activity (e.g. Walton 1998) and language choice as determined by the interlocutor's competence. Their behavior suggests that internal satisfaction may be an additional factor guiding affective codeswitching.

Codeswitching may also take place in the direction of the language perceived as less emotional. Some multilinguals prefer to use taboo and swear words in later learned languages, because this choice allows them to avoid the guilt and discomfort associated with the L1 words (Dewaele 2010; Ferenczi 1916; Koven 2006; Krapf 1955; Movahedi 1996; Pavlenko 2005). Others, whose native languages have constraints on direct expression of positive affect, prefer to do so in the L2, with the easy-going English "I love you" emerging as a particularly popular choice among speakers of different languages (Pavlenko 2005; Wilkins and Gareis 2006). Yet others may favor L2 endearments for their sparkle, novelty, and emotional force, and perceive the L1 words as overused, tired, and "worn out" (Pavlenko 2004; Piller and Takahashi 2006). Japanese participants in Piller and Takahashi's (2006: 72) study revealed a distinct preference for L2 English endearments, with Ichi stating: "Westerners often say 'darling', 'sweetie' and 'babe' [...] I have a soft spot for these words" and Eika admitting: "what made me happy about it [her relationship with a native speaker of English] was the sound ... the sound of 'honey, darling'."

Cross-linguistic differences in emotion lexicons also influence codeswitching and language choice. Some respondents to Dewaele and Pavlenko's (2001–3) Web questionnaire stated that they have distinct linguistic preferences for expression of particular emotions. English, for instance, was favored by some Japanese–English and German–English bilinguals for expression of negative affect because it allows for direct expression of anger and offers a rich array of swearwords, and Spanish was favored for expression of positive affect because of the large array of diminutives and the terms of endearment (Pavlenko 2005). Some also stated that they like multilingual wordplay, Frenchifying Spanish terms of endearment or adding English endings to Russian diminutives (Pavlenko 2004).

Multilingual speakers may also find themselves in a situation where the base language of the conversation does not encode the affective meanings they would like to express and to convey their message precisely they have to appeal to codeswitching (Panayiotou 2004a, 2004b; Pavlenko 2005; Wierzbicka 2004). Interestingly, there may be constraints on which terms can be borrowed in which contexts. Panayiotou (2004a, 2004b) found that Greek–English and English–Greek bilinguals in her study used the Greek terms *stenahoria* (discomfort/sadness/suffocation) and *ypohreosi* (deep sense of cultural and social obligation) only in discussions of

Greek contexts, because these feelings, in their view, "could never arise in the US" (Panayiotou 2004b: 133). In contrast, terms specific to English, such as *frustration*, were used in both languages regardless of the context, suggesting that concepts coming from a global language may be more pervasive and appear more applicable across situations and contexts.

Studies conducted with Portuguese–French (Koven, 2006, 2007), Greek–English and English–Greek (Panayiotou 2004a, 2004b, 2006), and Russian–English bilinguals (Pavlenko 2002b) also reveal that bicultural bilinguals, socialized in different contexts, may display somewhat different affective styles due to different affective repertoires internalized in respective speech communities. These affective repertoires are not, however, switched "on" and "off," rather, as seen in instances of codeswitching or multilingual wordplay, multilingual speakers draw on the full range of their repertoires and "do emotions" in more than one language.

Language attrition

Language emotionality and cross-linguistic differences are also important factors in understanding language attrition. Cross-linguistic differences help us understand what may be lost or at least inhibited in the attrition process. The studies to date show that attrition may result in the diminishment or loss of emotional expressivity (Ben-Rafael 2004; Pavlenko 2004; Tomiyama 1999; Waas 1996), in the loss of particular conceptual distinctions (Drennan *et al.* 1991), in the inhibition of particular emotion words and concepts (Pavlenko 2002b), and in the lowered perception of language emotionality (Dewaele 2004c). Bi- and multilinguals who experience L1 attrition and are dominant in another language are also less likely to appeal to L1 for emotional expression (ibid.).

Language-related emotions, linked to identity narratives and subject positions, may underlie language rejection and resulting attrition. Thus, peasant women in Austria and France rejected their native minority languages, Hungarian and Breton, in favor of majority German and French that promised new economic and social opportunities (Gal 1978; McDonald 1994). An even more convincing example of emotionally motivated L1 rejection is offered in Schmid's (2002, 2004) study of L1 attrition in German Jews who immigrated to English-speaking countries prior to the Second World War. The analysis of 35 autobiographic interviews collected from these speakers demonstrated that participants who experienced the highest degree of attrition were not those who left Germany earliest, not those who came to the USA youngest, and not even those who used German least. The only significant predictor of attrition was the time of emigration: attrition was highest among those who left Germany last, after the Kristallnacht of 1938, when the persecution of Jews turned into genocide. The emotional trauma had led these speakers to distance themselves from the past and the language associated with it.

Language conflicts and policies

The discussion above demonstrates that the relationship between multilingualism and emotions is not exclusively an individual phenomenon—it also plays out on the societal level in multilingual contexts, where groups of individuals and sometimes whole communities are often engaged in heated conflicts about which language or languages should have rights, visibility, and legitimacy. As linguistic human beings, we get emotional about when and how particular languages should be used, what values should be assigned to them, and what constitutes proper usage and linguistic purity. It is not surprising then that language policy decisions may elicit very emotional reactions, sometimes dividing societies and pitting individuals against each other.

The associations between languages, identities, and emotions are commonly formed through two processes, simultaneously social and cognitive: identification and misrecognition (Bourdieu 1991; Irvine and Gal 2000). In the process of *identification*, languages become symbolically linked to particular groups of people and emblematic of particular identities. In the process of *misrecognition*, languages and linguistic varieties become linked with character types and cultural traits, so that linguistic behaviors of others are seen as deriving from speakers' political agendas, intellectual abilities, and social and moral character, rather than from historical accident. I will add to these processes a third, *dissociation*, where the links between languages and their symbolic values are dissolved in the process of historic and sociopolitical change.

The effects of identification are visible in the case of language loyalty, where ideologies and discourses of language and identity position mother tongue as the language of the self, of the heart, of one's ethnic, national, and cultural identity, and argue that losing one's language is tantamount to losing one's self. In some groups these discourses gain a lot of currency, and in the context of ethnic strife, members of these groups may be willing to fight, go to jail, and even die, rather than to give up their mother tongue. A vivid example is seen in the Tamil language movement in South India, where from the 1930s and into the 1960s, young men fasted, died under police fire, and burned themselves alive to protest the compulsory study of Hindi and to promote their native Tamil (Amritavalli and Jayaseelan 2007; Ramaswamy 1997). In 1968 the movement succeeded in removing Hindi from the school curriculum.

The oppositional nature of the Tamil language movement, which was in effect an anti-Hindi movement, also illustrates how languages become imbued with negative values in the process of misrecognition. For speakers of Tamil, Hindi became linked with race and caste and implicated in oppression and domination, just as for speakers of Hindi, English was the symbol of exploitation and oppression. Decades later, in the post-Soviet context, a similar status was assigned to Russian, positioned as the language of the oppressor and the Big Brother. In most newly formed post-Soviet countries, ethno-nationalist elites adopted one nation one language policies, oftentimes with the support of local language scholars, such as Ukrainian linguist Masenko (2004) who passionately argued that just as a child can have only one biological mother, a country can have only one language. The proponents of these policies began shaming Belarussians, Ukrainians, Kazakhs, and Kyrgyzs who used Russian as their everyday language, calling them "memoryless Ivans" and urging them to shift to their "true" languages, i.e. the languages of their ethnicity. For many individuals, this situation created a conflict between their actual mother tongue, that is the language of their childhood (Russian), and the language they "ought to speak," given their ethnic belonging.

Both contexts, India and post-Soviet countries, also illustrate the effects of dissociation. In South India, English ceased to be the symbol of oppression and emerged as a viable alternative to Hindi, leading to the 1967 amendment that proclaimed English an associate official language, allowing for creation of a bilingual English–Tamil school system (Amritavalli and Jayaseelan 2007). Belarus, Kazakhstan, and Kyrgyzstan similarly upheld the status of Russian, which eventually became the second state language in Belarus and the official language in Kazakhstan and Kyrgyzstan; it is also continuously used through the east and south of officially monolingual Ukraine (Pavlenko 2008c).

Importantly, even mother tongue loyalty is not necessarily a given in multilingual contexts. As already discussed earlier, in the process of dissociation, people may willingly give up their native languages, either because alternative subject positions carry more emotional appeal (Gal 1978; McDonald 1994) or because experiences linked to the native language make its maintenance untenable (Schmid 2002, 2004). A prime example of this dissociation is seen in the case of Zionist socialists, who had arrived in Palestine in the first half of the twentieth century—these new arrivals willingly left their mother tongues behind, together with the history of oppression they symbolized, and enthusiastically adopted Hebrew that promised liberation and authenticity.

Together, these cases of identification, misrecognition, and dissociation challenge an essentialist meta-narrative of the self as permanently bounded to the first learned language and show that debates about language are rarely about language alone—in reality these disputes are about moral superiority, citizenship, belonging, and political and social status quo.

Summary

To sum up, research to date reveals a two-way interaction between languages and emotions in multilingual speakers. On the one hand, emotions—which run a gamut from language attachment and desire to language anxiety and rejection—shape speakers' language choices, investments, and learning trajectories. On the other hand, cross-linguistic differences in emotion lexicons and affective repertoires influence ways in which multilingual speakers perceive themselves, ways in which they relate to the world, and ways in which they use their linguistic resources in oral interaction and in writing.

Directions for future research

The overview above makes apparent both the achievements and the gaps in the research on multilingualism and emotions to date. The first such gap is the lack of studies of affective socialization of multilingual children. Available evidence indicates that bi- and multilingual parents may assign somewhat distinct affective roles to their languages, with some languages judged best for everyday interaction, and others for scolding or praise and terms of endearment (Luykx 2003; Pavlenko 2004, 2005). In other contexts, children may be exposed to different repertoires because they are learning one language in the family and the other one through peer interaction. Consequently, even when two or more languages are learned from infancy or early childhood, children may be socialized into different affective repertoires in their respective languages and thus different ways of relating to others. The consequences of such differential socialization have been explored by Koven (2006, 2007) with Portuguese–French bilinguals, but the process of affective socialization still awaits further inquiry. The field also lacks studies of affective (re-)socialization of children and adults in a new linguistic environment.

Another gap involves information about the performance of simultaneous bilinguals and of multilinguals. The majority of the studies to date have focused on late bilinguals who learned their respective languages in distinct contexts. Although informative, the findings of these studies cannot be generalized to the whole bi- and multilingual population and more information is necessary about the processes taking place in simultaneous acquisition of two or more languages and in interaction between three or more languages.

Many questions also remain unanswered regarding reconstruction of emotion categories in the process of additional language learning. Do speakers whose languages encode emotions as inner states begin seeing them as interpersonal processes—and vice versa—when learning a new language? Do they begin associating distinct physical experiences with the new concepts? Does learning new conceptual distinctions in emotion categories lead to new ways of reasoning? Answers to these questions have potential to transform our understanding of emotions and their relationship with language, yet the inquiry needs to proceed very carefully, as the learning process may be influenced by the differences in language status, power, and prestige, so that concepts encoded in more powerful global languages would appear more applicable and universal than those encoded in languages of limited spread.

This notion brings us to another intriguing venue for future research, namely the increasing domination of the Anglo discourses of emotion, spread through Hollywood films and the media, and the resulting *globalization of the semantic space*, that is adoption and spread of English-language categories, such as *frustration* or *depression*. The social, political, and economic prestige of English makes its emotion terms look desirable (Piller and Takahashi 2006) and universally applicable (Panayiotou 2004a, 2004b, 2006), yet it is still unclear how these lexical borrowings may influence self-perception of speakers of other languages.

The innovative studies discussed here also offer useful templates for future inquiry. Koven's (2006, 2007) nuanced analysis of bilinguals' affective displays provides an excellent framework for future studies of how multilinguals "do emotions." The work by Piller and Takahashi (2006) offers an intriguing direction for research on the relationship between desire, agency, and achievement. Theoretical and methodological sophistication of Schmid's (2002, 2004) work provides solid ground for future studies of the impact of language-related emotions on language choice, maintenance, and attrition. It is my sincere hope that future studies will reflect the complex relationship between the multilingualism and emotions superbly captured by a bilingual writer and scholar Pérez Firmat (2003: 3) who reminds us that "languages not only inspire loyalty, they also provoke fear, hatred, resentment, jealousy, love, euphoria—the entire gamut of human emotion."

Related topics

Multilingualism and gender; multilingualism and social exclusion; multilingualism and the media; codeswitching.

Further reading

Dewaele, J.-M. (2010) *Emotions in Multiple Languages*, Palgrave Macmillan
(A monograph dedicated to quantitative results of the Dewaele–Pavlenko (2001–3) questionnaire study.)

Lutz, C. (1988) *Unnatural Emotions: Everyday Sentiments on a Micronesian Atoll and Their Challenge to Western Theory*, Chicago, IL: University of Chicago Press.
(A groundbreaking study of non-Western emotion concepts.)

Pavlenko, A. (2005) *Emotions and Multilingualism*, Cambridge University Press.
(A comprehensive synthesis of the research.)

Pavlenko, A. (ed.) (2006) *Bilingual Minds: Emotional Experience, Expression, and Representation*, Clevedon: Multilingual Matters.
(A collection of empirical studies of multilingualism and emotions.)

Pavlenko, A. and J.-M. Dewaele (2004) 'Languages and emotions: A cross-linguistic perspective (guest-edited special issue)', *Journal of Multilingual and Multicultural Development*, 25: 2–3.
(A collection of empirical studies of multilingualism and emotions.)

Wilce, J. (2009) *Language and Emotion*, Cambridge: Cambridge University Press.
(An overview of nearly 100 ethnographic studies of language and emotions around the world.)

Bibliography

Amati-Mehler, J., Argentieri, S. and J. Canestri (1993) *The Babel of the Unconscious: Mother Tongue and Foreign Languages in the Psychoanalytic Dimension,* J. Whitelaw-Cucco, (trans.) Madison, CT: International Universities Press.

Amritavalli, R. and Jayaseelan, K. A. (2007) 'India', in A. Simpson, (ed.) *Language and National Identity in Asia,* Oxford: Oxford University Press.

Arnold, J. (ed.) (1999) *Affect in Language Learning,* Cambridge: Cambridge University Press.

Baker, C. (1992) *Attitudes and Language,* Clevedon: Multilingual Matters.

Ben-Rafael, M. (2004) 'Language contact and attrition: The spoken French of Israeli Francophones', in M. Schmid, B. Köpke, M. Keijzer and L. Weilemar (eds) *First Language Attrition: Interdisciplinary Perspectives on Methodological Issues,* Amsterdam and Philadelphia: John Benjamins.

Bourdieu, P. (1991) *Language and Symbolic Power,* Cambridge: Polity Press.

Bremer, K., Roberts, C., Vasseur, M.-T., Simonot, M. and Broeder (1996) *Achieving Understanding: Discourse in Intercultural Encounters,* Harlow: Longman.

Buxbaum, E. (1949) 'The role of a second language in the formation of ego and superego', *Psychoanalytic Quarterly* 18: 279–89.

Damasio, A. (1994) *Descartes' Error: Emotion, Reason, and the Human Brain,* New York: Putnam.

——(2003) *Looking for Spinoza: Joy, Sorrow, and the Feeling Brain,* New York: Harcourt Brace.

Dewaele, J.-M. (2004a) 'Blistering barnacles! What language do multilinguals swear in?!' *Estudios de Sociolingüística* 5(1): 83–105.

——(2004b) 'The emotional force of swearwords and taboo words in the speech of Multilinguals', *Journal of Multilingual and Multicultural Development* 25(2–3): 204–22.

——(2004c) 'Perceived language dominance and language preference for emotional speech: The implications for attrition research', in M. Schmid, B. Köpke, M. Keijzer and L. Weilemar (eds) *First Language Attrition: Interdisciplinary Perspectives on Methodological Issues,* Amsterdam and Philadelphia: John Benjamins.

——(2006) 'Expressing anger in multiple languages', in A. Pavlenko (ed.) *Bilingual Minds: Emotional Experience, Expression, and Representation,* Clevedon: Multilingual Matters.

——(2010) *Emotions in Multiple Languages,* Basingstoke: Palgrave Macmillan.

Dörnyei, Z. and Ushioda, E. (2011) *Teaching and Researching Motivation,* 2nd edn, Harlow: Pearson.

Drennan, G., Levett, A. and Swartz, L. (1991) 'Hidden dimensions of power and resistance in the translation process: A South African study', *Culture, Medicine, and Psychiatry* 15: 361–81.

Fehr, B. and Russell, J. (1984) 'Concept of emotion viewed from a prototype perspective', *Journal of Experimental Psychology: General* 11(3): 464–86.

Ferenczi, S. (1916) *Contributions to Psychoanalysis,* Boston, MA: Badger.

Foucault, M. (1980) *Power/Knowledge: Selected Interviews and Other Writings, 1972–1977,* New York: Pantheon.

Freud, S. (1893) *The Psychical Mechanisms of Hysterical Phenomena,* London: Hogarth Press.

Gal, S. (1978) 'Peasant men can't get wives: Language and sex roles in a bilingual community', *Language in Society* 7(1): 1–17.

Gardner, R. and W. Lambert (1972) *Attitudes and Motivation in Second Language Learning,* Rowley, MA: Newbury House.

Graham, R., Hamblin, A. and S. Feldstein (2001) 'Recognition of emotion in English voice by speakers of Japanese, Spanish, and English', *International Review of Applied Linguistics* 39: 19–37.

Greenson, R. (1950) 'The mother tongue and the mother', *International Journal of Psycho-Analysis* 31: 18–23.

Grice, P. (1975) 'Logic and conversation', in P. Cole and J. Morgan (eds) *Syntax and Semantics, Vol. 9: Pragmatics,* New York: Academic Press.

Harris, C. (2004) 'Bilingual speakers in the lab: Psychophysical measures of emotional reactivity', *Journal of Multilingual and Multicultural Development* 25(2–3): 223–47.

Harris, C., Ayçiçegi, A. and Gleason, J. (2003) 'Taboo words and reprimands elicit greater autonomic reactivity in a first language than in a second language', *Applied Psycholinguistics* 24(4): 561–71.

Harris, C., Berko Gleason, J. and Ayçiçegi, A. (2006) 'When is a first language more emotional? Psychophysiological evidence from bilingual speakers', in A. Pavlenko (ed.) *Bilingual Minds: Emotional Experience, Expression, and Representation,* Clevedon: Multilingual Matters.

Ho, J. W. Y. (2009) 'The language of anger in Chinese and English narratives', *International Journal of Bilingualism* 13(4): 481–500.

Holden, K. and Hogan, J. (1993) 'The emotive impact of foreign intonation: An experiment in switching English and Russian intonation', *Language and Speech* 36(1): 67–88.

Horwitz, E. (2001) 'Language anxiety and achievement', *Annual Review of Applied Linguistics* 21: 112–26.

Irvine, J. and Gal, S. (2000) 'Language ideology and linguistic differentiation', in P. Kroskrity (ed.) *Regimes of Language: Ideologies, Politics, and Identities*, Santa Fe, NM: School of American Research Press.

Javier, R., Barroso, F. and Muñoz, M. (1993) 'Autobiographical memory in bilinguals', *Journal of Psycholinguistic Research* 22(3): 319–38.

Kellman, S. (2000) *The Translingual Imagination*, Lincoln: University of Nebraska Press.

Kinginger, C. (2004a) 'Alice doesn't live here anymore: Foreign language learning and identity reconstruction', in A. Pavlenko and A. Blackledge (eds) *Negotiation of Identities in Multilingual Contexts*, Clevedon: Multilingual Matters.

——(2004b) 'Bilingualism and emotions in the autobiographical works of Nancy Huston', *Journal of Multilingual and Multicultural Development*, 25(2–3): 159–78.

Koven, M. (2006) 'Feeling in two languages: A comparative analysis of a bilingual's affective displays in French and Portuguese', in A. Pavlenko (ed.) *Bilingual Minds: Emotional Experience, Expression, and Representation*, Clevedon: Multilingual Matters.

——(2007) *Selves in Two Languages: Bilinguals' Verbal Enactments of Identity in French and Portuguese*, Amsterdam and Philadelphia: John Benjamins.

Krapf, E. (1955) 'The choice of language in polyglot psychoanalysis', *Psychoanalytic Quarterly* 24: 343–57.

LeDoux, J. (2002) 'Emotion, memory, and the brain', *Scientific American* 12(1): 62–71.

Lutz, C. (1988) *Unnatural Emotions: Everyday Sentiments on a Micronesian Atoll and their Challenge to Western Theory*, Chicago, IL: University of Chicago Press.

Luykx, A. (2003) 'Weaving languages together: Family language policy and gender socialization in bilingual Aymara households', in R. Bayley and S. Schecter (eds) *Language Socialization in Bilingual and Multilingual Societies*, Clevedon: Multilingual Matters.

MacIntyre, P. and Gardner, R. (1994) 'The subtle effects of language anxiety on cognitive processing in the second language', *Language Learning* 44: 283–305.

McDonald, M. (1994) 'Women and linguistic innovation in Brittany', in P. Burton, K. Dyson and Sh. Ardener (eds) *Bilingual Women: Anthropological Approaches to Second Language Use*, Oxford and Providence: Berg.

Marian, V. and Kaushanskaya, M. (2004) 'Self-construal and emotion in bicultural bilinguals', *Journal of Memory and Language* 51: 190–201.

Marian, V. and Neisser, U. (2000) 'Language-dependent recall of autobiographical memories', *Journal of Experimental Psychology: General* 129(3): 361–8.

Masenko, L. (2004) *Mova i Suspilstvo: Postkolonialnyi Vymir* [Language and Society: A Postcolonial Dimension], Kyiv: Kyiv-Mohyla Academy.

Mathews, A., Richards, A. and Eysenck, M. (1989) 'Interpretation of homophones related to threat in anxiety states', *Journal of Abnormal Psychology* 98: 31–4.

Movahedi, S. (1996) 'Metalinguistic analysis of therapeutic discourse: Flight into a second language when the analyst and the analysand are multilingual', *Journal of the American Psychoanalytic Association* 44(3): 837–62.

Norton, B. (2000) *Identity and Language Learning: Gender, Ethnicity, and Educational Change*, London: Longman.

Oatley, K. (1992) *Best Laid Schemes: The Psychology of Emotions*, Cambridge: Cambridge University Press.

Ochsner, K. and Feldman Barrett, L. (2001) 'A multiprocess perspective on the neuroscience of emotion', in T. Mayne and G. Bonanno (eds) *Emotions: Current Issues and Future Directions*, New York: Guilford Press.

Ohara, Y. (2001) 'Finding one's voice in Japanese: A study of the pitch levels of L2 users', in A. Pavlenko, A. Blackledge, I. Piller and M. Teutsch Dwyer (eds) *Multilingualism, Second Language Learning, and Gender*, Berlin and New York: Mouton De Gruyter.

Ortega, L. (2009) *Understanding Second Language Acquisition*, London: Hodder Education.

Oxford, R. (2002) 'Sources of variation in language learning', in R. Kaplan (ed.) *The Oxford Handbook of Applied Linguistics*, Oxford: Oxford University Press.

Panayiotou, A. (2004a) 'Bilingual emotions: The untranslatable self', *Estudios de Sociolingüística* 5(1): 1–19.

——(2004b) 'Switching codes, switching code: Bilinguals' emotional responses in English and Greek, *Journal of Multilingual and Multicultural Development* 25(2–3): 124–39.

——(2006) 'Translating guilt: an endeavour of shame in the Mediterranean?' in A. Pavlenko (ed.) *Bilingual Minds: Emotional Experience, Expression, and Representation*, Clevedon: Multilingual Matters.

Pavlenko, A. (2002a) 'Emotions and the body in Russian and English', *Pragmatics and Cognition* 10(1–2): 201–36.

——(2002b) 'Bilingualism and emotions', *Multilingua* 21(1): 45–78.

——(2004) '"Stop doing that, *ia komu skazala!*": Language choice and emotions in parent-child communication', *Journal of Multilingual and Multicultural Development* 25(2–3): 179–203.

——(2005) *Emotions and Multilingualism*, Cambridge: Cambridge University Press.

——(2008a) 'Emotion and emotion-laden words in the bilingual lexicon', *Bilingualism: Language and Cognition* 11(2): 147–64.

——(2008b) 'Structural and conceptual equivalence in the acquisition and use of emotion words in a second language', *Mental Lexicon* 3(1): 91–120.

——(2008c) 'Multilingualism in post-Soviet countries: Language revival, language removal, and sociolinguistic theory', *International Journal of Bilingual Education and Bilingualism* 11(3–4): 275–314.

Pavlenko, A. and Driagina, V. (2007) 'Russian emotion vocabulary in American learners' narratives', *Modern Language Journal* 91(2) 213–34.

Pérez Firmat, G. (2003) *Tongue Ties: Logo-eroticism in Anglo-Hispanic Literature*, New York: Palgrave Macmillan.

Piller, I. (2002) *Bilingual Couples Talk: The Discursive Construction of Hybridity*, Amsterdam and Philadelphia: John Benjamins.

Piller, I. and Takahashi, K. (2006) 'A passion for English: desire and the language market', in A. Pavlenko (ed.) *Bilingual Minds: Emotional Experience, Expression, and Representation*, Clevedon: Multilingual Matters.

Ramaswamy, S. (1997) *Passions of the Tongue: Language Devotion in Tamil India*, Berkeley: University of California Press.

Rintell, E. (1984) 'But how did you FEEL about that? The learners' perception of emotion in speech', *Applied Linguistics* 5(3): 255–64.

——(1990) 'That's incredible: Stories of emotion told by second language learners and native speakers', in R. Scarcella, E. Andersen and S. Krashen (eds) *Developing Communicative Competence in a Second Language*, Boston: Heinle & Heinle.

Russell, J. (1991) 'Culture and the categorization of emotions', *Psychological Bulletin* 110(3): 426–50.

Scherer, K., Banse, R. and Wallbott, H. (2001) 'Emotion inferences from vocal expression correlate across languages and cultures', *Journal of Cross-Cultural Psychology* 32(1): 76–92.

Schmid, M. (2002) *First Language Attrition, Use, and Maintenance: The Case of German Jews in Anglophone Countries*, Amsterdam and Philadelphia: John Benjamins.

——(2004) 'Identity and first language attrition: A historical approach', *Estudios de Sociolingüística* 5(1): 41–58.

Schrauf, R. and Rubin, D. (1998) 'Bilingual autobiographical memory in older adult immigrants: test of cognitive explanations of the reminiscence bump and the linguistic encoding of memories', *Journal of Memory and Language* 39: 437–57.

——(2004) 'The 'language' and 'feel' of bilingual memory: mnemonic traces', *Estudios de Sociolingüística* 5(1): 21–39.

Sparks, R. and Ganshow, L. (2001) 'Aptitude for learning a foreign language', *Annual Review of Applied Linguistics* 21: 90–111.

Stepanova Sachs, O. and Coley, J. (2006) 'Envy and jealousy in Russian and English: Labelling and conceptualization of emotions by monolinguals and bilinguals', in A. Pavlenko (ed.) *Bilingual Minds: Emotional Experience, Expression, and Representation*, Clevedon: Multilingual Matters.

Talburt, S. and Stewart, M. (1999) 'What's the subject of study abroad?: Race, gender, and "living culture"', *Modern Language Journal* 83(2): 163–75.

Tomiyama, M. (1999) 'The first stage of second language attrition: A case study of a Japanese returnee', in L. Hansen. (ed.) *Second Language Attrition in Japanese Contexts,* Oxford: Oxford University Press.

Toya, M. and Kodis, M. (1996) 'But I don't want to be rude: On learning how to express anger in the L2', *JALT Journal* 18(2): 279–95.

Waas, M. (1996) *Language Attrition Downunder: German Speakers in Australia,* Frankfurt and New York: Peter Lang.

Walton, D. (1998) *The New Dialectic: Conversational Contexts of Argument,* Toronto: University of Toronto Press.

Wierzbicka, A. (2004) 'Preface: Bilingual lives, bilingual experience', *Journal of Multilingual and Multicultural Development,* 25(2–3): 94–104.

Wilce, J. (2009) *Language and Emotion,* Cambridge: Cambridge University Press.

Wilkins, R. and Gareis, E. (2006) 'Emotion expression and the locution "I love you": A cross-cultural study', *International Journal of Intercultural Relations* 30: 51–75.

27

Codeswitching

Angel Y. M. Lin and David C. S. Li

Introduction

Codeswitching (CS) is one of the best-known and most widely researched language-contact phenomena. Languages do not come into contact; people do. When speakers of one language are exposed to another language over a sustained period of time, they will become bilingual, albeit to differing extents. CS refers to 'the alternating use of two languages in the same stretch of discourse by a bilingual speaker' (Bullock and Toribio 2009: xii). CS is analogous to style shifting, which takes place within one and the same language. For example, in Hong Kong, newscasters may be using formal Cantonese when reporting 'on air', but they may use collo-quial Cantonese with each other during the commercial break. When similar shifts occur across language boundaries, this will result in CS. CS may occur in writing as well as in speech, but by far the bulk of CS research to date is based on the analysis of naturally occurring bilingual speech data. For convenience of exposition, the term 'bilingual' is used synonymously here with 'multilingual', making reference to 'two or more languages'.

Although naturalistic CS has been researched using datasets from various language pairs, including typologically unrelated languages (Chan 2009), there continues to be a widespread, popular belief in multilingual societies that CS is linguistically anomalous, or simply 'bad', as it reflects the speaker-writers' inability to express themselves properly in one 'pure' lan-guage or another. One interesting consequence is that where CS is common, pejorative labels tend to be ascribed, e.g. *Spanglish, Tex-Mex* (Spanish–English), *Chinglish* (Chinese–English), *Japlish* (Japanese–English), *Franglais* (French–English) and *Bahasa Rojak* (Malay–English), reflecting the bilingual community's disapproval of CS as a form of 'random', and 'disorderly' mixing of languages.

Terms in the research literature

Different terms have been used to refer to similar phenomena in bilingual speech. The term 'codeswitching' is by far the most commonly used. Some scholars reserve the term CS for 'inter-sentential CS', i.e. switches at clause boundaries, and use the term codemixing (CM) to designate switches that take place within a clause, i.e. 'intra-sentential CS'. Muysken (2000), for example, uses 'codemixing' in his book-length account of 'bilingual speech', on the grounds that the book deals primarily with intra- rather than inter-sentential CS. Other scholars prefer to use CS as a generic term to cover both inter- and intra-sentential CS, but they normally make it clear which type of switch is more prevalent in the dataset(s) being analysed (e.g. Clyne 2003; Myers-Scotton 2002). In addition, the term 'code-alternation' is often used by those scholars who want to maintain a systematic distinction between inter- and intra-sentential CS (e.g. Auer 1995). For our purpose in this chapter, we will follow the general trend of using CS as the umbrella term for switching between clauses as well as switching within a clause.

In the next section of the chapter, we give a brief overview of the development of socio-linguistic approaches to CS, taking account of research in different domains of social life: in local lifeworlds and in institutional worlds. We will then turn to one specific domain in which there has been a particularly robust tradition of research on CS and that is classroom-based research.

Researching the social meanings of CS

The investigation of the social meanings of CS in bilingual interactions represented an important part of research in 'interactional sociolinguistics' (e.g. Gumperz 1982, 1984, 1986). Early research on CS motivations identified an important distinction between 'metaphorical CS' and 'situational CS' (Blom and Gumperz 1972). Sometimes a switch redefines a situation, as when Flemish–French bilingual employees in a Belgian bank greet and chat with one another before office hours in Flemish, their shared vernacular, but conduct formal banking business in French. This CS pattern is so common in diglossic communities that a switch triggered by a change in situation is almost predictable, hence 'situational CS'. Where there is no perceptible change in situation, bilingual speakers may sometimes switch to another language due to a change in topic or because special social meanings are being evoked. Holmes (1992: 48) cites an example in Papua New Guinea where a bilingual codeswitches between Tok Pisin and Buang to demonstrate his double identity: being a businessman (Tok Pisin) and a member of the Buang community. Such instances of CS are known as 'metaphorical CS'.

In terms of theory-building, there are two main interactional approaches to the investigation of social aspects of CS: the markedness model (Myers-Scotton 1993a, 1993b, 1998) and conversation analysis (CA) (Auer 1995; Li 1994, 2002). On the basis of extensive data gathered in East Africa, Myers-Scotton (1998) argues that in any bilingual speech community, code choice is rational based on three inter-related postulates: (1) bilingual speakers are rational actors who are eager to 'optimize' their own interactional outcomes; (2) a speaker's linguistic repertoire constitutes an 'opportunity set' from which code choices are made through 'interaction-specific cognitive calculations'; and (3) communication is goal-directed and guided cognitively and rationally by a cost–benefit analysis of different 'readings of markedness' indexed by discrete 'rights and obligations sets', which explains why to a bilingual speaker, 'making marked choices has different consequences from making unmarked choices' (Myers-Scotton 1998: 16–22; see also Li and Tse 2002: 148). As a key construct, 'markedness' is based on the opposition between unmarked versus marked code choices, and functions as a heuristic for explaining a bilingual's social and psychological motivations for code choice in context-specific interactions with others.

Myers-Scotton's approach may be characterized as analysing CS motivations using socio-psychological factors external to specific contexts in which CS take place. Advocates of the conversation analysis (CA) approach (e.g. Auer 1995, 1998; Gafaranga 2007), however, insist that all attributions of CS motivations should be dynamic, constructivist, and grounded in fine-grained turn-by-turn analysis, taking into account all pertinent contextualization cues such as prosodic features and the duration of pauses, which contribute significantly to meaning-making in bilingual interactions. According to this view, the main research question is as follows: 'What does the codeswitcher want to do or accomplish with CS?' This question cannot be adequately addressed without examining all relevant contextualization cues in bilingual interactions, which helps explain CA analysts' insistence that rigorous protocols must be met when recording and transcribing naturally occurring CS data.

Regardless of how language-contact phenomena, such as CS, are analysed by researchers, they constitute part of the linguistic resources available to the bilingual, whose main concern in bilingual interaction is typically the moment-by-moment meaning-making when conversing with someone with a similar linguistic background or repertoire. As the research literature on CS is vast, we will focus here on one domain of research, namely research on classroom CS (including second language classrooms, foreign language classrooms and bilingual pro-grammes). As we will show, the research trends and paradigms in this research tradition echo wider developments in the field of CS. Classroom CS is complex and often controversial, especially in those contexts where there is a tension between using the mother tongue as the medium of instruction (MOI) to facilitate students' understanding, and using the target language (TL) as MOI to give students more exposure to the TL.

Classroom CS

Although classroom CS studies have been conducted in diverse contexts, the often-quoted early studies were chiefly conducted in North American settings. They were based in classrooms in two main kinds of contexts: second language contexts (e.g. ESL classrooms) and bilingual education classrooms. The research methods largely included quantitative and functional coding analysis (see below for details of these methods). Research interest has mainly been directed at two aspects of bilingual education: the relative quantities of first language (L1) and second language (L2) use in different activity settings, and the functional distribution of L1 and L2. Below is a review of the research methods used in some early studies.

Early studies on relative amounts of L1/L2 use across activity types and settings

This type of research was largely conducted with children in bilingual education programmes in the USA (e.g. Wong-Fillmore 1980). The main emphasis of such work is to investigate whether linguistic minority children's L1 (e.g. Spanish, Chinese) and the wider, societal language (English) were given equal emphasis by calculating the degree to which they were each used in the classroom (in terms of the number of utterances in each code or the time spent on it). Data for such studies was typically collected through class visits and observations with subsequent analysis of field notes and audio/videotapes. It was found that a greater amount of L1 tended to be used in less formal, more intimate participant structures.

In another study (Frohlich *et al.* 1985), this time in Canada, on the communicative orientation of L2 classrooms in four different programmes (e.g. core French, French immersion, extended French with subject matter courses, ESL classrooms), teacher talk in all four programmes was found to reflect very high L2 use (96 per cent). However, the researchers noted that students generally used the target language only while the teacher exercised control over classroom activities. During seatwork most interaction occurred in the students' L1.

These early studies relied on the notion of activity type or setting (e.g. individual seatwork, group work, whole-class instruction) as an important factor affecting the relative amounts of

L1/L2 use in both studies above. In contrast, other work used functional coding systems in their analysis to develop categories of functions for which L1 is used.

Early studies on functional distribution of L1/L2 use

Many of the functional studies were also conducted in bilingual content classrooms in the USA and only a few on second and foreign language classrooms. In these studies classroom utterances were usually coded by the observer with a functional system (e.g. Flanders 1970) yielding frequency counts of distribution of L1 and L2 over different functional categories (i.e. communicative and/or pragmatic functions identified by the researcher). For instance, in a study based on observations of five kindergartens in Spanish bilingual programmes and using an adaptation of Flanders' Multiple Coding System, Legarreta (1977) reported on the functional distribution of Spanish (L1) and English (L2) in two different models of bilingual education: the Concurrent Translation (CT) and Alternative Days (AD). She found that the AD model generated an equal distribution of Spanish and English by teachers and children overall, with more Spanish used for 'encouraging' (referred to as 'warming' by Legarreta) and 'directing' functions and English as the primary choice for disciplining children. However, in the CT model, instead of using the L1 (Spanish) of the majority of the pupils to express solidarity (warming, accepting, amplifying), the teachers and aides predominantly used English for these functions.

In another study, Milk (1981) coded teacher talk in a twelfth-grade bilingual civics lesson according to eight basic pedagogical functions (e.g. informative, directive, humour-expressive) based on Sinclair and Coulthard (1975). English (L2) was found to dominate the teacher's directives (92 per cent) and meta-statements (63 per cent), whereas there was a greater balance between L1 and L2 in other functions (e.g. elicitation, expressive, reply, informative). In addition, Milk described the skilful manner in which the bilingual teacher employed extensive switching between Spanish and English to create humour, both as a means of social control (via the creation of a sense of solidarity) and as a way to arouse students' interest.

Guthrie (1984) used similar research methods in a study of an ESL lesson attended by 11 first-grade Cantonese–American students (ranging from limited English proficiency to fluent). Two types of lessons were analysed: reading in English with a Cantonese–English bilingual teacher, and oral language with an English monolingual teacher. Field notes and audio-recording of six hours of lessons were gathered and were accompanied by coding by two bilingual observers. The functions of the bilingual teacher's L1 use reported by Guthrie can be summarized as: (1) to act as a 'we-code' for solidarity; (2) to clarify or check for understanding; (3) to contrast variable meanings in L1 and L2; and (4) to anticipate likely sources of confusion for students.

So, although the functional coding approach dominated early work in some studies (e.g. Milk 1981; Guthrie 1984), there was also some preliminary use of ethnographic interviews and interactional sociolinguistic methods, a trend that continued in later works.

The interpretive and critical turns in classroom CS research

Many early studies seemed to have worked with the assumption that functional categories were stable, valid categories of classroom speech and that analysts could reliably assign utterances to each category. Yet the functional coding approach in early studies actually involved a lot of sociolinguistic interpretive work on the part of the coder. This interpretive work was, however, not made explicit but taken for granted in the form of final frequency counts of L1 and L2 distributed across different functional categories.

Later studies (e.g. Adendorff 1993; Cincotta-Segi 2009; Creese 2005; Heller 1999, 2001; Lin 1990, 1996, 1999; Li and Martin 2009; Martin 1996, 1999, 2003; Martin-Jones and Saxena 1996, 2003; Polio and Duff 1994) have, to varying degrees, dispensed with a priori lists of functional categories and drawn on research approaches from interactional sociolinguistics and ethnography of communication (e.g. Goffman 1974; Gumperz 1982, 1986); conversation analysis (Sacks [1965]1992); interpretive research paradigms; critical social theory (Bourdieu and Passeron 1977); and critical research paradigms to study classroom CS.

As interactional sociolinguistics (IS) and ethnography of communication (EC) provide the most useful analytic tools for researching and understanding CS in different settings in society, their concepts and methods have been drawn from classroom studies on CS. The concepts that have been most frequently and fruitfully used are CS as a contextualization cue (Gumperz 1984) to signal a shift in the frame or footing (Goffman 1974) of the current interaction (e.g. see Adendorff 1993). Frame or footing is the definition of what is happening and it is constantly being negotiated, proposed (signalled) and re-defined by the speakers engaged in interaction. The different frames or footings that are being evoked (or signalled and proposed by a speaker) involve the simultaneous negotiation of different role-relationships and the associated sets of rights/obligations. Lin's studies (1990, 1996), for instance, drew on these interactional sociolinguistic concepts to analyse CS in Hong Kong classrooms. Below is an example from Lin's (1996) reanalysis of Johnson's (1985) data in Hong Kong secondary schools, using IS analytic concepts. The data presentation format is as in Johnson's: tape-recorder counter numbers precede utterances; bold italics indicate originally Cantonese utterances, and only teacher's utterances have been transcribed.

Example (1)

A junior secondary math teacher in Hong Kong begins his lesson in English and then breaks off and switches to Cantonese to deal with late-comers; once they are settled, he switches back to English to continue with the lesson work:

008 Close all your text books and class work books.
012 *There are some classmates not back yet. Be quick!*
Now, any problem about the class work?

(Johnson 1985: 47)

Johnson (ibid.) analyses the Cantonese utterance as an example of an informal aside done in Cantonese. Although agreeing partially with this analysis, we note, however, that if it is to mark out a mere topical digression, the teacher could well have done this by other means than codeswitches, e.g. intonational changes, hand-claps or pauses to bracket the aside (see example in Lin 1990: 32–6). The use of these contextualization cues (Gumperz 1984) does not involve a violation of the institutional 'use-English-only' constraint, which teachers in Anglo-Chinese secondary schools in Hong Kong were well aware of. It can, therefore, be argued that what is being signalled here is not only a topical aside, but also a radical break in the English pedagogic frame and an urgent change in the teacher's concerns. This break in the English pedagogic frame to highlight a different, urgent set of concerns cannot have been achieved without the teacher's switch from English (L2) to Cantonese (L1).

The key to understanding the implicit meanings signalled by codeswitches, therefore, lies in a recognition of the sociolinguistic fact that whenever Hong Kong Cantonese have something urgent and earnest to relay to one another, they do so in their shared native language; whenever Hong Kong Cantonese speak to one another in English despite their having a common native language, it is usually because of institutionally given reasons, for instance, to teach and learn the English language in an English immersion classroom. When teachers want to establish a less distanced and non-institutionally defined relationship with their students, they will also find it necessary to switch to their shared native language, Cantonese.

In studies along this line, IS and EC analytical concepts and methods are drawn from in order to analyse instances of classroom CS. The findings look remarkably similar across different sociocultural contexts. CS is seen as an additional resource in the bilingual teacher's communicative repertoire, enabling her/him to signal and negotiate different frames and footings, role-relationships, cultural values, identities and so on in the classroom (e.g. Li and Martin 2009). These studies have the effect of uncovering the good sense or the local rationality (or functions) of classroom CS. To summarize by drawing on the functional framework of language from Halliday (1994), CS can be seen as a communicative resource readily drawn on by classroom participants (usually the teacher but sometimes also students) to achieve three kinds of purposes as follows:

Ideational functions: Providing limited-L2-proficiency students with access to the L2-mediated curriculum by switching to the students' L1 (or stronger language) to translate or annotate (e.g. key L2 terms), explain, elaborate or exemplify L2 academic content (e.g. drawing on students' familiar lifeworld experiences as examples to explain a science concept in the L2 textbook/curriculum). This is very important in mediating the meaning of academic texts, which are written in a poorly understood language – the L2 of the students.

Textual functions: Highlighting (signalling) topic shifts, marking out transitions between different activity types or different focuses (e.g. focusing on technical definitions of terms vs exemplifications of the terms in students' everyday life).

Interpersonal functions: Signalling and negotiating shifts in frames and footings, role-relationships and identities, change in social distance/closeness (e.g. negotiating for in-group solidarity), and appealing to shared cultural values or institutional norms.

Apart from the above studies, which draw on interpretive research paradigms, there is also a major trend of studies led by Monica Heller and Marilyn Martin-Jones (e.g. in their edited 2001 book *Voices of Authority: Education and Linguistic Difference*), which draws on both interpretive and critical research paradigms, and they relate micro interactional functions of classroom CS to larger societal issues, such as the reproduction or sometimes contestation of linguistic ideologies in the larger society (e.g. which/whose language counts as standard and valued language; which/whose language counts as inferior or not-valued language).

Heller and Martin-Jones (2001) provide some examples on how micro ethnographic studies of classroom CS are not actually 'micro' in their implications if we see the classroom as a discursive site for reproduction or contestation of linguistic ideologies and hierarchies. The discursive construction/negotiation of what counts as front stage and back stage (e.g. Arthur 1996, drawing on Goffman 1974) and the legitimation of what goes on in the front stage (largely controlled and set up by the teacher) as legitimate, standard, valued language vs what gets marginalized, reproduced as inferior, non/substandard language in the back stage. Usually the societal dominant L2 occupies the former position and students' L1 occupies the latter position. For instance, in Ndayipfukamiye's (2001) study of Kirundi–French CS in Burundi classrooms, the bilingual teacher is seen to be using Kirundi (students' familiar language) to annotate, explain and exemplify French (L2) terms and academic content. Although the linguistic brokering function of CS is affirmed (i.e. the value of providing students with access to the educationally dominant language, French), the linguistic hierarchy as institutionalized in the French immersion education policy in Burundi is largely reproduced in these CS practices.

However, not all studies are about reproduction of linguistic ideologies and practices. For instance, Canagarajah (2001) shows how ESL teachers and students in Jaffna (the northern peninsula of Sri Lanka that has been the political centre of the Tamils) negotiated hybrid identities through CS between Tamil and English, defying both the Tamil-only ideology in the public domains and institutions, and the English-only ideology from the ESL/TESOL peda-gogical prescriptions from the West. Canagarajah argued that both teachers and students, by switching comfortably between these two languages were also constructing their bilingual identities, refusing to be pigeonholed by essentializing political ideologies (of Tamil nationalism) or English-only pedagogical ideologies.

Lin (1999) also showed that by skilfully intertwining the use of L1 (Cantonese) for a story focus with the use of L2 (English) for a language focus, a bilingual teacher in a Hong Kong English-language classroom successfully got her students interested in learning English and gaining confidence in reading English storybooks, and thus transforming the habitus of these working-class students for whom English had been an alien language irrelevant to their daily life. Drawing on the discourse-analytical methods of conversation analysis applied to educa-tional settings (Heap 1985), Lin (1999) offered a fine-grained analysis of how L1–L2 CS was built into two kinds of Initiation–Response–Feedback (IRF) discourse formats to enable the teacher (Teacher D) to engage students in both enjoying the story and in learning English through this process ('L1/L2' denotes 'L1 or L2'):

> Teacher D uses two different IRF formats in the following cycle in the reading lesson:
>
> (1) Story-Focus-IRF:
> Teacher-Initiation [L1]
> Student-Response [L1]
> Teacher-Feedback [L1]
>
> (2) Language-Focus-IRF:
> Teacher-Initiation [L1/L2]
> Student-Response [L1/L2]
> Teacher-Feedback [L2], or use (2) again until Student-Response is in L2
>
> (3) Start (2) again to focus on another linguistic aspect of the L2 response elicited in (2); or return to (1) to focus on the story again.
>
> *(Lin 1999)*

This kind of discourse practice allows the teacher to interlock a story focus with a language focus in the reading lesson. There can be enjoyment of the story, via the use of the story-focus IRF, intertwined with a language-learning focus, via the use of the language-focus IRF. We have noted above that the teacher never starts an initiation in L2. She always starts in L1. This stands in sharp contrast with the discourse practices of Teacher C (another teacher in the study) who always starts with L2 texts or questions in her initiations. It appears that by always starting in L1, Teacher D always starts from where the student is – from what the student can fully understand and is familiar with. On the other hand, by using the language-focus IRF format immediately after the story-focus IRF format, she can also push the students to move from what they are familiar with (e.g. L1 expressions) to what they need to become more familiar with (e.g. L2 counterparts of the L1 expressions) (see Lin 1999).

The current 'state of the art' in researching classroom CS

In the early studies, researching CS in the classroom, unlike researching other kinds of related classroom phenomena (e.g. classroom discourse, classroom interactions), was often associated, consciously or unconsciously, with corrective motives. In the interactional studies, researchers have investigated classroom CS practices either to seek out their 'good sense' and local rationality or to document their pitfalls or pedagogical inefficacy. These studies have been common in contexts where there has been an official pedagogical principle of prescribing the use of only one language in the classroom (Lin and Martin 2005; Haroon 2005). These two (implicit) aims have often shaped the research questions and research approaches used in classroom CS studies.

Because of these (implicit) 'legitimating' concerns of researchers, the studies in the interactional literature tend to stop short of pointing to ways forward for analysing how CS practices can be better understood to achieve better pedagogical and social critical purposes. They tend to be descriptive rather than interventionist; i.e. they describe existing practices (neither approving of nor condemning them) rather than engaging with practitioners to identify innovative CS practices that provide access to L2, while at the same time critiquing linguistic ideologies and hierarchies in the larger society and institutions. Because of the lack of critical, interventionist research questions, the majority of studies in the classroom CS literature tend to offer few new insights into how existing classroom CS can be further changed to achieve more: e.g. more of the transformation (as hinted at by Lin 1999 and Canagarajah 2001), and avoid the reproduction consequences (e.g. reproducing societal ideologies about linguistic hierarchies, marginalizing the students' familiar languages while privileging the dominant societal languages). The findings of the existing research literature thus seem to be variations on similar themes (as summarized above) without providing new research questions and research approaches. In our concluding section, we therefore sketch out what we see as possible future lines of enquiry in studies of classroom CS.

Future directions for research on classroom CS

To our knowledge, there have been no published studies of a longitudinal, interventionist type. Moreover, most studies have been conducted by a sociolinguist or a discourse analyst, usually an outsider coming into the classroom studying the interactional practices of classroom participants. As we have shown above, many studies draw mainly on the interpretive research paradigms (IS, EC and CA research approaches). This makes it difficult for us to know what would happen if classroom participants (e.g. teachers, students) themselves become researchers of their own classroom practices, and what would happen if they embarked on systematic studies of their own, getting a deeper understanding of their own practices through their own research and then, perhaps, modifying their own practices with systematic action plans and studying the consequences. This type of interventionist approach would be broadly akin to the kind of action-research carried out by teacher-researchers. Below, we outline what kind of studies might be designed in the future with a view to gleaning new insights into classroom CS.

First, such studies would involve longitudinal research. Instead of one-shot classroom video/audio-taping studies, we need to have studies that follow the same classroom for a longer period of time; e.g. a whole course or a whole semester.

Second, following our comments above, the studies would need to take on an interventionist research agenda: we would need to integrate sociolinguistic interpretive and conversation analytic approaches with action-research approaches so that teachers become conscious of trying out specific bilingual classroom strategies with respect to achieving specific sets of goals. We also need to build into the research design ways of ascertaining the degree to which these goals are achieved. This is similar to the design of teacher action-research. Close collaboration between teacher and researcher is also needed, or the teacher can also be the researcher. Likewise, depending on the readiness of the students, they can also be encouraged to become researchers in the study of their own bilingual classroom practices.

Third, teachers and researchers need to identify specific goals and design-specific bilingual classroom strategies to achieve those goals: this would require the teacher and researcher to understand the specific situated needs and goals of the educational context in which they find themselves. These educational goals need to be set up with reference to the needs and choices of participants in those contexts. It is not possible to identify a universal set of goals for bilingual or multilingual classroom communication.

Fourth, future studies also need to draw on research methods such as genre analysis of domain-specific academic discourses and literacies: for instance, we need to know what the specific genre features, discourse structures and registers of a biology course are in order to design bilingual strategies to provide students with access to biology discourses through familiar everyday discourses. There will be frequent interweaving between academic discourses (mostly mediated in a less familiar language to the students such as the L2 or the 'standard' dialect) and students' familiar discourses (e.g. everyday life examples and experiences mediated in students' familiar languages such as their L1 or a community dialect; e.g. as described in McGlynn and Martin 2009). The key research question would be: how does the teacher provide access to the formal, academic (often L2) discourses through the informal, everyday, familiar (often L1) discourses of the students?

Fifth, in order to carry out systematic studies of the effectiveness of different bilingual class-room strategies, there needs to be carefully planned integration of different research paradigms (including interventionist action-research, interpretive, critical) and research approaches (including those from sociolinguistics, academic genre analysis, pedagogical analysis, analysis of students' spoken and written samples of academic work, plus assessment of students' mastery of genre-specific features and skills in performing academic tasks, using the appropriate registers).

And, finally, the approaches need to be holistic and contextualized. We need to situate the classroom in its larger socio-economic and political contexts and examine the pedagogic goals of the classroom to see if they are really serving the interests of the students. We then need to explore possible ways to redefine these goals, including bilingual classroom strategies and other communicative strategies. The research also needs to compare and contrast traditional (e.g. teacher whole-class instruction) and progressive pedagogies (student-inquiry groups) and consider which CS patterns can be intertwined with which pedagogical patterns and participant structures. All these require an approach that allows for a healthy cycle: try-and-see and then document; re-try another pattern and see what happens and re-design future action plans that will progressively better achieve the new goals through both bilingual and other pedagogical practices.

The recommendations above might sound like an 'unholy' eclectic approach to the research methodological purist. However, to have breakthroughs in our current state of affairs in researching classroom CS, we need to be both pragmatic and flexible in our research paradigms and approaches and we need to ensure that our studies have an impact. As CS in the classroom is still seen as a negative practice in many mainstream educational contexts, we need concrete designs of bilingual classroom strategies and research studies that can systematically develop these designs, show their effectiveness (with respect to the situated goals of the classroom) and demonstrate the good, rational sense and the communicative potential of bilingual/multilingual classroom communication.

Concluding comment

People engage in language practices that fulfil their communicative needs and very often they draw on multiple resources in their communicative repertoires, both in the classroom and beyond. Future research might embark on a theoretical re-visioning of the usefulness of conceptualizing CS as switching between codes with solid boundaries, or as language practice that is inherently realized in diverse ways, both drawing on and renewing diverse linguistic resources that are not bounded by solid linguistic code boundaries (Pennycook 2010).

Related topics

Discourses about linguistic diversity; multilingualism in education in post-colonial contexts; multilingual pedagogies; heteroglossia; disinventing multilingualism.

Further reading

Creese, A. (2005) *Teacher Collaboration and Talk in Multilingual Classrooms*, Clevedon: Multilingual Matters.
(Provides a good account of teacher collaboration and talk in multilingual classrooms.)
Heller, M. and Martin-Jones, M. (eds) (2001) *Voices of Authority: Education and Linguistic Difference*, Westport, CT and London: Ablex.
(Remains a classic volume of studies that sets out the major approaches and problematics in this area.)
Li, W. and Martin, P. (eds) (2009) 'Conflicts and tensions in classroom codeswitching', *International Journal of Bilingual Education and Bilingualism* (special issue) 12(2).
(A collection of recent studies on classroom codeswitching.)
Luk, J. C. M. and Lin, A. M. Y. (2006) *Classroom Interactions as Cross-Cultural Encounters: Native Speakers in EFL lessons*, Mahwah, NJ: Lawrence Erlbaum.
(Provides some good analysis of classroom verbal play by students who engage in codeswitching creatively as a resource to have fun.)
Martin-Jones, M. (2000) 'Bilingual classroom interaction: a review of recent research', *Language Teaching* 33(1): 1–9.
(Provides good reviews of classroom codeswitching research from 1970s to the late 1990s.)
——(2007) 'Bilingualism, education and the regulation of access to language resources', in M. Heller (ed.) *Bilingualism: A Social Approach*, Basingstoke: Palgrave Macmillan.
(Provides good reviews of classroom CS research, and discourses about bilingual education, from the 1970s to the first decade of the twenty-first century.)

Bibliography

Adendorff, R. (1993) 'Codeswitching amongst Zulu-speaking teachers and their pupils: Its functions and implications for teacher education', *Language and Education* 7(3): 41–162.
Arthur, J. (1996) 'Codeswitching and collusion: classroom interaction in Botswana classrooms', *Linguistics and Education* 8(1): 17–34.
Auer, P. (1995) 'The pragmatics of codeswitching: A sequential approach', in L. Milroy and P. Muysken (eds) *One Speaker, Two Languages: Cross-Disciplinary Perspectives on Codeswitching*, Cambridge: Cambridge University Press.
——(ed.) (1998) *Codeswitching in Conversation: Language, Interaction and Identity*, London and New York: Routledge.

Blom, J.-P. and Gumperz, J. (1972) 'Social meaning in linguistic structures: Code switching in northern Norway', in: J. Gumperz and D. Hymes (eds) *Directions in Sociolinguistics: The Ethnography of Communication*, New York: Holt, Rinehart, and Winston.

Bourdieu, P. and Passeron, J. C. (1977) *Reproduction in Education, Society and Culture*, London: Sage.

Bullock, B. E. and Toribio, A. J. (eds) (2009) *The Cambridge Handbook of Linguistic Codeswitching*, Cambridge: Cambridge University Press.

Canagarajah, S. (2001) 'Constructing hybrid postcolonial subjects: Codeswitching in Jaffna classrooms', in M. Heller and M. M. Jones (eds), *Voices of Authority: Education and Linguistic Difference*, Westport, CT and London: Ablex.

Chan, B. H. S. (2009) 'Codeswitching between typologically distinct languages', in B. E. Bullock and A. J. Toribio (eds) *The Cambridge Handbook of Linguistic Codeswitching*, Cambridge: Cambridge University Press.

Cincotta-Segi, A. (2009) 'The big ones swallow the small ones. Or do they? The language policy and practice of ethnic minority education in the Lao PDR: a case study from Nalae', unpublished PhD thesis, Australian National University.

Clyne, M. (2003) *Dynamics of Language Contact*, Cambridge: Cambridge University Press.

Creese, A. (2005) *Teacher Collaboration and Talk in Multilingual Classrooms*, Clevedon: Multilingual Matters.

Flanders, N. A. (1970) *Analyzing Teaching Behavior*, Reading, MA: Addison-Wesley.

Frohlich, M., Spada, N. and Allen, P. (1985) 'Differences in the communicative orientation of L2 Classrooms', *TESOL Quarterly* 19(1): 27–57.

Gafaranga, J. (2007) 'Codeswitching as a conversational strategy', in P. Auer and W. Li (eds) *Handbook of Multilingualism and Multilingual Communication*, Berlin: Mouton de Gruyter.

Goffman, E. (1974) *Frame Analysis*, New York: Harper and Row.

Gumperz, J. J. (1982) *Discourse Strategies*, London: Cambridge University Press.

——(1984) 'Ethnography in urban communication', in J. C. P. Auer and A. Luzio (eds) *Interpretive Sociolinguistics: Migrants, Children, Migrant Children*, Tubingen: Narr.

——(1986) 'Interactional sociolinguistics in the study of schooling', in J. J. Gumperz (ed.) *The Social Construction of Literacy*, Cambridge: Cambridge University Press.

Guthrie, L. F. (1984) 'Contrasts in teachers' language use in a Chinese-English bilingual classroom', in J. Handscombe, R. A. Orem and B. P. Taylor (eds) *TESOL, 83: 'The Question of Control'*, 39–52.

Halliday, M. A. K. (1994) *An Introduction to Functional Grammar*, 2nd edn, London: Edward Arnold.

Haroon, H. A. (2005) 'Teacher codeswitching and its functions in mathematics and science lessons', *Asia Pacific Journal of Language in Education* 7(1): 1–25.

Heap, J. L. (1985) 'Discourse in the production of classroom knowledge: Reading lessons', *Curriculum Inquiry* 15(3): 345–79.

Heller, M. (1999) *Linguistic Minorities and Modernity*, London: Longman.

——(2001) 'Legitimate language in a multilingual school', in M. Heller and M. M. Jones (eds), *Voices of Authority: Education and Linguistic Difference*, Westport, CT and London: Ablex.

Heller, M. and Martin-Jones, M. (eds) (2001) *Voices of Authority: Education and Linguistic Difference*, Westport, CT and London: Ablex.

Holmes, J. (1992) *An Introduction to Sociolinguistics*, London and New York: Longman.

Johnson, R. K. (1985) *Report of the ELTU Study of the Oral Medium of Instruction in Anglo-Chinese Secondary School Classroom*, Hong Kong: Faculty of Education, University of Hong Kong.

Legarreta, D. (1977) 'Language choice in bilingual classrooms', *Journal of Social Issues* 23: 9–16.

Li, D. C. S. and Tse, E. C. Y. (2002) 'One day in the life of a "purist"', *International Journal of Bilingualism* 6(2): 147–202.

Li, W. (1994) *Three Generations, Two Languages, One Family: Language Choice and Language Shift in a Chinese Community in Britain*, Clevedon and Philadelphia: Multilingual Matters.

——(2002) '"What do you want me to say?" On the conversation analysis approach to bilingual interaction', *Language in Society* 31: 159–80.

Li, W. and Martin, P. (eds) (2009) 'Conflicts and tensions in classroom codeswitching', *International Journal of Bilingual Education and Bilingualism* (special issue) 12(2).

Lin, A. (1990) *Teaching in Two Tongues: Language Alternation in Foreign Language Classrooms, Research Report No. 3*, Hong Kong: City Polytechnic of Hong Kong.

——(1996) 'Bilingualism or linguistic segregation? symbolic domination, resistance and codeswitching in Hong Kong schools', *Linguistics and Education* 8(1): 49–84.

——(1999) 'Doing-English-lessons in the reproduction or transformation of social worlds?' *TESOL Quarterly* 33(3): 393–412.

Lin, A. and Martin, P. (eds) (2005) *Decolonisation, Globalisation: Language-in-Education Policy and Practice*, Clevedon: Multilingual Matters.

Martin, P. W. (1996) 'Codeswitching in the primary classroom: One response to the planned and unplanned language environment in Brunei', *Journal of Multilingual and Multicultural Development* 17(2–4): 128–44.

——(1999) 'Bilingual unpacking of monolingual texts in two primary classrooms in Brunei Darussalam', *Language and Education* 13(1): 38–58.

——(2003) 'Bilingual encounters in the classroom', in J.-M. Dewaele, A. Housen and W. Li (eds), *Bilingualism: Beyond Basic Principles*, Clevedon: Multilingual Matters.

Martin-Jones, M. and Saxena, M. (1996) 'Turn-taking and the positioning of bilingual participants in classroom discourse', in M. Martin-Jones and M. Heller (eds) *Linguistics and Education* 8(1): 105–23.

——(2003) 'Bilingual resources and "funds of knowledge" for teaching and learning in multiethnic classes in Britain,' *International Journal of Bilingual Education and Bilingualism* 6(3–4) (special issue on 'Multilingual classroom ecologies'): 267–82.

McGlynn, C. and Martin, P. (2009) '"No vernacular": Tensions in language choice in a sexual health lesson in The Gambia', *International Journal of Bilingual Education and Bilingualism* 12(2): 137–55.

Milk, R. (1981) 'An analysis of the functional allocation of Spanish and English in a bilingual classrooms', *C. A. B. E. Research Journal* 2(2): 11–26.

Muysken, P. (2000) *Bilingual Speech. A Typology of Code-Mixing*, Cambridge: Cambridge University Press.

Myers-Scotton, C. (1993a) *Duelling Languages: Grammatical Structure in Codeswitching*, Oxford: Oxford University Press.

——(1993b) *Social Motivations for Codeswitching: Evidence from Africa*, Oxford: Oxford University Press.

——(ed.) (1998) *Codes and Consequences*, New York and Oxford: Oxford University Press.

——(2002) *Contact Linguistics. Bilingual Encounters and Grammatical Outcomes*, Oxford: Oxford University Press.

Ndayipfukamiye, L. (2001) 'The contradictions of teaching bilingually in postcolonial Burundi: from Nyakatsi to Maisons en Etages', in M. Heller and M. M. Jones (eds) *Voices of Authority: Education and Linguistic Difference*, Westport, CT and London: Ablex.

Pennycook, A. (2010). *Language as local practice*. New York: Routledge.

Polio, C. G. and Duff, P. A. (1994) 'Teachers' language use in university foreign language classrooms: A qualitative analysis of English and target language alternation', *The Modern Language Journal* 78(3): 313–26.

Sacks, H. ([1965]1992) 'Lectures on conversation', in G. Jefferson (ed.) *Lectures on Conversation*, Oxford and Cambridge: Blackwell.

Sinclair, J. and Coulthard, R. M. (1975) *Towards an Analysis of Discourse*, London: Oxford University Press.

Wong-Fillmore, L. (1980) 'Learning a second language: Chinese children in the American classroom', in J. E. Alatis (ed.) *Current Issues in Bilingual Education: Georgetown University Round Table on Languages and Linguistics*, Washington, DC: Georgetown University Press.

28

Crossing

Ben Rampton and Constadina Charalambous

This chapter discusses 'language crossing', the use of a language or variety that feels anomalously 'other' for the participants in an activity, involving movement across quite sharply sensed social or ethnic boundaries, in ways that can raise questions of legitimacy. The chapter begins by linking research on crossing to a more general shift in the assumptions governing linguistics and the study of multilingualism, and it then differentiates 'crossing' from other kinds of mixed speech. Our third section identifies several major themes emerging in recent empirical work, and in the fourth, our focus shifts from sites of urban migration and popular culture to educationally sponsored crossing in a conflict-ridden context (Cyprus). Our final section points to areas for further work. Other overviews of crossing can be found in Auer (2006), Coupland (2007), Quist and Jørgensen (2009) and Rampton (2001, 2003).

Crossing and the regrounding of linguistics

For much of the twentieth century, linguistics was dominated by two assumptions: (1) language study should be centrally concerned with regularity in grammar and coherence in discourse; and (2) these properties derive from community membership – people learn to talk grammatically and coherently from extensive early experience of living in families and fairly stable local social networks. Mary Louise Pratt characterizes this approach as 'the linguistics of community', sees it in a good deal of sociolinguistics in the 1970s and 1980s, and argues that it is built on an idealization of the nation-state, obscuring its social hierarchies and divisions (1987). Instead, she calls for a 'linguistics of contact', which (1) extends the focus of language study beyond convention and cooperation to improvisation, conflict and resistance; (2) investigates the impact of media culture and not just home socialization; (3) attends to the unevenness in a person's abilities to produce, recognize and understand language; and (4) looks beyond intra-group language to the use of language *across* social boundaries. Pratt's programme for a 'linguistics of contact' has a great deal in common with Bakhtin's pragmatics (1981, 1984), as well as with post-structuralism much more generally (Rampton 2006: Part 1, 1.2).

Crossing involves white Londoners using quasi-Jamaican, or youngsters of Caribbean descent using Punjabi, or majority ethnic Germans using Turkish in peer group interaction, and as such, it is a salient interactional practice that contests preconceived ideas about family rootedness, makes extensive use of (non-family) material from public and popular media, and involves elements of unexpected improvisation, which are highly problematic for any linguistics that takes structural regularity and tacit systematicity as its governing preoccupations. In this way, crossing provides a vivid *empirical* illustration of the relevance of Pratt's 'linguistics of contact', and it refutes any accusation that in linguistics, post-structuralism (or post-modernism) is necessarily theory-obsessed and unable to connect with language in the real world (Davies 1999: 131, 142). In crossing, people foreground the sociosymbolic connotations/indexical values of particular linguistic forms, implying that they have special relevance to some aspect of interaction in the here-and-now, and for researchers, crossing requires multilayered, case-by-case analysis to understand the significance of this, running the range of descriptive levels and concepts, from linguistic structures and conversational sequences through stances, genres and participant constellations, to personal and group relations, social networks, institutions and historical junctures (Rampton 1999a; Alim 2009: 10).

So crossing provides an empirical warrant for the philosophical reorientation associated with Pratt's 'linguistics of contact'. This need not lead to a rejection of every description of bilingualism and codeswitching influenced by the 'linguistics of community', but it does encourage a reassessment of the assumptions underlying a good deal of the research on multilingualism. Urla, for example, notes that the promotion of minority language bilingualism is often based on monolingual models of literacy, schooling and language codification – 'the nation or linguistic community is imagined in the singular and envisioned primarily as a reading and writing public' (1995: 246) – and Auer argues that

> research on code-switching ... tends to start from the assumption that the languages used in a bilingual encounter are ... equally accessible and available to all participants, and the participants belong to one bilingual community in which a common repertoire of resources is shared. Often, the languages of this repertoire are organized along such dimensions as we-code/they-code, minority/majority language or standard/non-standard.
>
> *(2006: 490)*

'This assumption', he says, 'is justified in many cases, [but] it amounts to a considerable idealization of the facts in others' (ibid.). In cases where the facts *do* fit the conventional model, it is just as important to attend to the historical and ideological processes that produced this relatively 'focused' pattern as it is with situations where speech forms and relations are more diffuse (as LePage argued from the 1970s onwards, motivated by his research on Creole in the Caribbean (e.g. LePage 1980; LePage and Tabouret-Keller 1985)). And to challenge the default status often given to the idealization of bi- and multilingualism as the shared command of two or more languages-as-bounded-systems, Jørgensen introduces the notion of polylingualism, which he uses to characterize situations of social change where people use fragments from differently valued languages that they do not speak proficiently or share with their interlocutors, where linguistic forms can be hard to link to designated source languages, where we-code/they-code (or minority/majority language) interpretations oversimplify, and where the linguistic combinations often stand out to participants as non-routine, not just to analysts (Jørgensen 2008: 169).

Crossing displays a range of characteristics typical of polylingualism, and we will elaborate on this in the section on empirical trends. But before that, it is important to differentiate crossing from other types of plurilingual practice.

Distinguishing crossing from other language practices

The difficulties involved in classifying language mixing have long been recognized (Romaine 1988: 114). In addition, in the situations where crossing occurs, sensitivity to the form and significance of social or ethnic boundaries can be locally variable and partially open to negotiation, with the result that ambiguity is often intrinsic to boundary-crossing practices themselves – an issue we will return to at the end of the section. Nevertheless, it is worth using the terms 'crossing', 'stylization', 'codeswitching', 'codemixing' and 'multi-ethnic vernacular' to differentiate a number of important ways in which language use can vary in plurilingual situations (see also Auer 2003).

Multi-ethnic vernaculars can be defined as local versions of dominant/majority languages – English, Danish, German, etc. – that emerge over time among mixed populations in mainly working-class urban areas where there has been substantial immigration from abroad. In such settings, habitual everyday speech often carries small phonological, lexical and/or grammatical traces which reflect the influence of migrant speech and language varieties that are either more distinct in older generations, and/or are still used in intra-ethnic contexts (cf. Hewitt 1986; Rampton 1995). Linguists and outsiders (as well as locals when they step back) may be able to identify influences from, for example, Jamaican Creole in the English of young Londoners of different ethnic backgrounds, or Turkish in the Danish around Copenhagen. But participants treat these elements as routine and unremarkable in their interactions. With codemixing, the combination of words, phrases and longer sequences from different lexico-grammatical codes is more conspicuous, making it easier for linguists to classify the speech involved as more than just a subvariety of the national language, but the changes from one code to another do not reframe the ongoing interaction or impact on its unfolding (Auer 2003: 76–7). As in multi-ethnic vernacular speech, the combination of linguistic elements with objectively different histories is treated as unmarked.

In contrast, with 'codeswitching', 'stylization' and 'crossing', the move from one variety or style to another has significance in the moment-to-moment development of the talk itself. Auer (1988) suggests that in codeswitching there are two broad ways in which people make sense of the switch as it occurs. They may either interpret it as a sign of a participant's linguistic preference or proficiency, or they may see it as relevant to a shift in the discourse – for example, the move from shared to new information, from a story-preface to the story itself, from one addressee to another. Codeswitching does not necessarily require high levels of proficiency in the languages involved (Auer 2003: 84), but the speaker's use of these languages is not normally treated by recipients as noteworthy or unusual in itself, and they are able to continue the interaction as normal. This is not the case with stylization. In stylization, speakers shift into varieties or exaggerated styles that are seen as lying beyond their normal range, beyond what participants ordinarily expect of them, and this disjunction of speaker and voice draws attention to the speaker herself/himself, temporarily positioning the recipient(s) as spectator(s), and at least momentarily reframing the talk as non-routine – a joke, for example, or some kind of artful performance. Much the same occurs in crossing, *except* that in crossing the speaker's use of another voice raises wider issues of entitlement. To illustrate the difference: when the young Londoners in Rampton (2006) did stylized posh, Cockney or German in the school corridors, or when vernacular English speakers with Punjabi backgrounds stylized Indian English (Rampton 1995), they spoke in exaggerated voices and codes that they would never use in ordinary talk with friends. But nobody accused them of expropriating linguistic resources that did not belong to them, or of using language to which they had no right. In contrast, the use of Indian English could be very risky for white and black kids, as could white and Asian uses of Caribbean Creole. The circumambient politics of race made ethnolinguistic boundaries very sensitive. When crossing recipients encountered the gap between the voice and the speaker's ethnic background, the interactional question 'why that now?' was supplemented with a more political 'by what right?', and it often took special circumstances to circumvent this – close friendship, a game or some opposition to authority (see below).

Of course the range, subtleties and ambiguities of interactional practice exceed a classification scheme like this. So, for example, where close social ties allow a white person to make use of their friends' minority ethnic variety without any challenge, it can be hard to class this as 'crossing' rather than codemixing, switching or stylization (Sweetland 2002). Equally, there may be situations (such as advanced language shift) where the notional inheritors of a minority language use the code in ways that closely resemble the 'crossing' of their other-ethnic friends (cf. Auer 2003: 84; Hewitt 1986: 114, 153). In both these – and indeed most other – cases, it is important to study the reception of alternative forms very closely, and to probe at sociolinguistic perceptions with playback and other kinds of metalinguistic interview. Nevertheless, first, it makes intuitive sense to use 'stylization' vs 'crossing' to distinguish, for example, someone's impersonation of older members of their own group from their use of a language saliently associated with an ethnic outgroup. Second, the distinctions outlined above can be helpful in the study of change over time, as when once-stylized language forms cease to be seen as specially marked and simply become features of style (Bakhtin 1984: 190), or when uses of language that once counted as 'crossing' lose their ethnolinguistic specificity, blending into local multi-ethnic vernaculars. And third, the differences can matter to informants. Hewitt found, for example, that if 'a white youngster wishes to use a certain [Creole] word ... he or she may have to make it appear 'natural' to their speech if they are to avoid the possibility of being challenged' (1986: 151). This can be done either by claiming family ties to the ethnic group with which the forms are associated (Trosset 1986: 187–8; Hewitt 1986: 165, 195), or much less dramatically, by delivering the word in such a way that it seems like a routine element in the multi-ethnic vernacular.

Equipped with understanding of the kinds of interpretive leeway required in the use of notions like crossing and stylization, we can now turn to a description of some of the main trends in the empirical descriptions of these practices.

Some empirical trends

Crossing and stylization are probably as old as speech itself. In the USA, for example, Hill dates the 'appropriation of African American cultural and linguistic materials' by whites back at least 150 years (1999: 544), whereas white appropriations from Native American languages began in the seventeenth century (2008. Chapter 6). But in spite of some exceptional studies (e.g. Basso 1979; Hill and Coombs 1982), polylingual practices were largely peripheral to the 'linguistics of community'. This changed with the post-structuralist 'linguistics of contact'. Also impelled by a sense that these were paradigmatic practices in contemporary globalization, crossing and stylization became a major focus in sociolinguistics from the mid-/late 1990s onwards, so that in one form or another, they have now been described in, *inter alia*, the UK, mainland Europe, North and South America, South Africa, Hong Kong, Japan, Australia, New Zealand (see e.g. Rampton 1999b; Auer 2007; Alim *et al.* 2009; Reyes and Lo 2009).

It is difficult to summarize this work, and general definitions of crossing that declare, for example, that it is ludic or 'expresses identification with the outgroup' are impossible to sustain when it is studied in close-up. In any given site, there are likely to be different types of crossing, produced and construed on different kinds of occasion by people with different commitments and positions. Crossing can be mocking, admiring, an end in itself or the first step in a longer journey, and it may strengthen boundaries, undermine them or assert their irrelevance. And of course researchers themselves may have different inclinations, seeming to others either unduly cynical or romantic in their interpretations. That said, there are at least three related themes that recur in the research: (1) race or ethnic difference in sociolinguistically differentiated class societies governed by standard language ideologies; (2) public discourses, media representations and their interplay with local practices; and (3) non-routine, 'keyed' interactional moments and activities as sites for crossing and stylization.

(1) Race/ethnic difference in class-stratified societies governed by standard language ideologies

A substantial number of European studies have focused on crossing among youth in multi-ethnic urban working-class locations where there have been substantial post-war histories of labour immigration from abroad (e.g. Auer and Dirim 2003; Doran 2004; Hewitt 1986; Jaspers 2005; Lytra 2007; Quist and Jørgensen 2009; Rampton 1995). As well as disrupting the normal relationship between speaker and voice, the crossing practices described here often depart from the forms and decorums of educated national standard languages, so there are good reasons for seeing this polylingualism as itself a 'low', 'slang', vernacular style counterposed to 'posh', whether 'posh' is mono- or multilingual (Rampton 2009b, 2010; on multilingual posh, see e.g. Heller 2007: 151; Pujolar 2007: 77). At the same time, the languages, registers and styles in a given environment generally differ in their histories, status, social purchase and symbolic connotations, and as such, they constitute a differentiated 'sociolinguistic economy' that provides very significant resources for the positioning of selves and others.

So, in a study of two classrooms in Antwerp, Belgium, Jaspers found that '[m]ultilingualism … consisted of varieties of Arabic … varieties of Berber … varieties of Turkish, and Dutch varieties. I could also regularly hear phrases in English and French, often in combination with the rap or hip hop in these boys' cassette-, CD- or minidisk-players' (Jaspers 2005: 286). In some cases, the sociolinguistic stratification among these varieties was long-standing (e.g. Dutch above Flemish, Arabic above Berber), whereas with others, it was more recent, and Jaspers focuses on the perceptions and performances of teenage boys of Moroccan descent, particularly in and around Dutch. These boys accepted that standard Dutch would be an asset in the longer term, and even though they themselves spoke a non-standard variety, they rated this much higher than the Antwerp dialect of their white peers or the learner Dutch of migrant newcomers. Their self- and other-positioning practices included derogatory impersonations of Antwerp dialect; foreigner talk addressed to Turkish boys; and parodically ultra-standard Dutch in situations where they themselves felt targeted by the potentially critical gaze of better-positioned white observers.

Jaspers describes a situation where among things, the extremist nationalist Vlaams Blok party had a strong and adverse influence on ethnolinguistic relations, but elsewhere, the local urban sociolinguistic economy may be much more open. In some German studies, crossing into Turkish and the stylization of Turkish–German are associated with racism and intergroup hostility (Hinnenkamp 1987; Depperman 2007), but in research on Hamburg neighbourhoods with a high density of people of Turkish background, Auer and Dirim (2003) reveal a much more differentiated picture. Auer and Dirim provide case studies of the Turkish of 25 young people of different ethnicities (German, Afghan, Greek, Moroccan, etc.), and they describe how the language is variously seen as valuable for getting by in localities and networks; as salient in youth cultural style; as congruent with a commitment to mainstream success; as linked to subcultural delinquency; as principally associated with Turkish neighbours, and/or Turkish cultural practices, and/or Turkish media and/or Turkey itself. In a similar vein, the practical use of Turkish itself extends well beyond crossing and stylization to 'include code-switching and code-mixing, almost monolingual Turkish as well as German conversations in which an occasional word of Turkish is inserted' (2003: 224).

In spite of the presence of a lot of other languages, the speech of second and third generation Turkish Germans is widely regarded as the most significant local ethnic influence on urban youth culture in Germany (Auer and Dirim 2003). Turkish has similar status in multiethnic urban youth vernaculars in Denmark, and, in the UK, Jamaican Creole often plays a lead role reinvigorating non-standard English among young people (Hewitt 1986; Harris 2006). But in the USA, race and class have been equated for far longer, and in spite of considerable ethnic diversity, African American Vernacular English (AAVE) stands out as the principal polar contrast to middle-class standard American English. In North America, there are a number of studies of mixing and crossing among people with Asian Pacific and Spanish–American backgrounds (e.g. Reyes and Lo 2009; Zentella 1997; Bailey 2000), and some of this operates more or less independently of the black–white binary, with young people engaging with ethnically specific stereotypes (Lo 1999; Reyes 2009), or negotiating a relationship with ethnic ingroup newcomers to the USA ('FOBs'/'fresh off the boat' – e.g. Talmy 2009). But Bucholtz proposes that for Asian Americans, the 'identity project is complicated by the need to navigate the hegemonic US model of race as a dichotomy between blackness and whiteness' (2009: 21), and she illustrates this with a study of how two Laotian American girls display contrasting orientations to school through different uses of AAVE. Elsewhere, the hegemonic black–white binary is invoked when white youth appropriate AAVE to differentiate themselves from their families (Cutler 1999), or when black students stylize white to parody their (black) teacher (Clark 2003), and it also infiltrates the efforts of Dominican American adolescents to differentiate themselves from immigrant peers (Bailey 2007).

So far, we have described crossing and stylization invoking different codes in plurilingual landscapes that are dominated by monoglot standard languages and where, in some cases, there is also a very strong influence from particular non-standard ethnic varieties conspicuously counterposed to this. Of course, public discourses and mediated popular culture also play a crucial part in all this, introducing dynamics of their own.

(2) Public discourses, mediated popular culture and their interplay with local practices

The institutions, policies and official discourses in the nation-state have a major influence on the evaluation and use of different language varieties, promoting the national standard, facilitating or discouraging schooled bilingualism, shaping the image of second language learning. So do the representations of migrant neighbourhoods and ethnic populations that circulate through the mainstream press and media. Analyses of the impact of these discourses focus on, among other things the manner and extent to which commercial representations of ethnic speech entail mocking derogation (Hill 1995; Lippi-Green 1997; Chun 2009); the way in which groups with no links to migrant or minority neighbourhoods learn to cross and stylize from the screen and other sources (Androutsopoulos 2001; Cutler 1999); how crossing and stylization variously align or distance speakers from dominant representations (e.g. Rampton 1995: Chapter 3; Reyes and Lo 2009; Jaspers 2005); and how opposition to state representatives, such as teachers, can provide specially licensed sites for crossing (e.g. Quist and Jørgensen 2009: 376–7).

Directly counterposed to educated mainstream standards, mediated musical cultures have had a massive influence on crossing and stylization, and in recent years, AAVE has gained global currency through hip-hop (e.g. in Brazil, Greece, Germany, Tanzania, Nigeria, Hong Kong and Japan – see Alim *et al.* 2009). As well as displaying affiliation to a larger transnational community, these appropriations are also sometimes redirected towards local political struggles, articulating opposition to, for example, racialized exclusion in Brazil (Roth-Gordon 2009) or the unspoken idealization of white Frenchness in Montreal (Sarkar 2009: 153; see also Urla 1995), although the engagement can also be lighter, more aesthetics and fashion than politics (Maher 2005). Other kinds of media product that circulate through diasporic networks can also influence stylization and crossing – Shankar shows how Hindi films provide Californian youngsters with resources they transpose to real interactions (2009: 328), and Auer (2003: 85–90) shows a Turkish and a Jordanian girl stylizing a Turkish TV and video genre. At the same time, certain youngsters may be deterred by the higher popular cultural profile of a given language – whereas white and black boys in Rampton (1995: Chapter 10) made ample use of Punjabi in playground interaction, they generally stepped back in the context of *bhangra* music, and instead it was the white girls who were enthusiastic.

More work is still needed on the local interactional processes involved in the appropriation and assessment of widely circulating popular cultural materials (Alim 2009: 17; Rampton 2006: Chapter 3), but in a wide-ranging review of 'Bilingualism in the mass media and on the Internet', Androutsopoulos (2007) suggests that there is a prominent and enduring place for polylingualism, crossing and stylization in media communication.

Although he says it 'thrives at the "periphery" rather than the [monoglot] "core"' (2007: 226), Androutsopoulos argues that 'linguistic diversity is gaining an unprecedented visibility in the mediascapes of the late twentieth and early twenty first century' (2007: 207), and he identifies at least three processes we can call polylingual. First, diaspora media often have to reckon with the fact that much of their audience has limited competence in the language of the homeland, and so producers position 'tiny amounts of [the] language ... at the margins of text and talk units ... thereby ... exploit[ing] the symbolic, rather than the referential, function ... evok[ing] social identities and relationships associated with the minimally used language' (2007: 214). Second, starting in advertising but extending now beyond nation-wide media to niche, commercial and non-profit media for various contemporary youth-cultural communities and audiences (2007: 223–4), Androutsopoulos notes the widespread stylization of non-national language forms: '[w]hen media makers devise an advertisement, plan a lifestyle magazine or set up a website, they may select linguistic codes (a second language, a mixed code) just for specific portions of their product, based on anticipations of their aesthetic value, their indexical or symbolic force, and, ultimately, their effects on the audience' (2007: 215; see e.g. Bell 1999). Third, as producers design ethnically marked materials to carry beyond local audiences to wider publics, a sense of crossing – in reception if not production – may be built into the audiences' experience. Androutsopoulos gives the example of Algerian *rai* music lyrics:

> early *rai* recordings capitalize on an 'insertion style' with frequent incorporation of French nouns and clauses in an Arabic matrix, which bears close resemblance to code mixing in urban Algerian communities. But in later production the languages are more separated, their distribution bearing a 'more systematic relationship to the structure of the song' (Bentahila and Davies 2002: 202). Rather than reflecting societal language change, this shift from mixing to a generic separation of languages is motivated by a shift in target audiences: As *rai* music became more popular in France, its artists and producers turn to

a more prominent use of French for key phrases, refrains and titles in order to increase its chances of exposure to a French audience.

(2007: 214; see also Woolard 1988)

In addition, of course

[i]n the era of digital technologies, the sampling and recontextualisation of media content is a basic practice in popular media culture: rap artists sample foreign voices in their song; entertainment shows feature snatches of other-language broadcasts for humour; internet users engage in linguistic *bricolage* on their homepages.

(2007: 208)

We said earlier that crossing and stylization were generally treated as noteworthy or unusual, and that recipients needed to engage in extra inferential work to answer ever-pressing inter-actional questions like 'why that now?' and 'what next?'. This is quite easy to see in mediated contexts like the ones discussed above, where crossing and stylization are often specially framed as artful performance, with speakers and producers assuming 'responsibility for a display of communicative competence', designing language for 'enhancement of [the] experience' of their audience (Bauman [1975]2001: 178). But these practices are also framed as non-routine in more everyday environments.

(3) Crossing and stylization in 'keyed' interactional moments and activities

Interactional analysis reveals that crossing and stylization often occurs in moments and activities when the ordinary commonsense world is problematized or partially suspended (Rampton 1995, 1999a). Artful performance – stories, songs, jokes, etc. – is one type of environment where the special framing of the activity licenses the use of styles and forms that would otherwise seem unaccountable, and games, where there is an agreed relaxation of routine interaction's rules and constraints (Rampton 1995: Chapters 6.7, 7.2), are another. Interpersonal verbal rituals are a third. These occur at moments of heightened interactional uncertainty – on meeting new people, at the start of an encounter, close to a breach of etiquette, etc. – and the uncertainty on hand temporarily jeopardizes the reassuring, orderly flow of interaction, intensifying the need to show respect for social relations to compensate. To do this, people generally increase the symbolic dimensions of their conduct (Goffman 1967, 1971, 1981: 20–1), shifting briefly away from the (appropriately modulated) production of propositional utterances geared to truth and falsity. Instead, they turn up the ritual aspects through a range of inherited symbolic formulae – farewell and greeting routines, apologies, thanks, expletives, expressions of sympathy, disapproval, dismay or surprise – and by invoking well-established material authored by tradition, they display an orientation to wider social collectivities capable of overriding the temporary disturbance immediately on hand. Very often, these ritual actions are convergent, providing the participants with some common ground on which to (re)establish synchronized, affiliative action, affirming dominant social orders, drawing on shared cultural inheritance, and one way of doing this is to codeswitch into a shared language that is either more intimate or more elevated. But these showcased moments for the symbolic display of social allegiance can also be used more divergently, and they are a prime site for all sorts of creativity – one often hears people putting on 'funny voices' at junctures like these.

In Goffman's terms, artful performance, games and verbal rituals in which participants amplify their non-normality by the use of unexpected voices, are all examples of 'keying' – interaction framed in a way that shows it is somehow special and not to be taken 'straight' or treated naively (1974: Chapter 3). Goffman identifies several very basic keys, and some of these fit with the activities identified immediately above – artful performance falls into his category 'make-believe', games fit with his 'contests' and interpersonal verbal rituals can be classed as one of his 'ceremonials'. The centrality of 'keying' to crossing and stylization has two general implications.

First, crossing's occurrence in interactional moments that are specially marked as unusual and non-routine carries the implication that the speaker is not really claiming unqualified open access to the identity associated with the language they are crossing into – their speech does not finally imply that he or she can move unproblematically in and out of their associates' heritage language in any new kind of open bicultural codeswitching. At the same time, however, the intensity of keying can vary a great deal, from events that are very conspicuously staged to acts in which there is merely the lightest suggestion that things are not quite what they seem. This range is important for understanding how, over time, routine vernacular practice can gradually come to absorb forms that were once clearly marked as 'other' (see 'Distinguishing crossing from other language practices', above). Whereas games and artful performance provide rather well-demarcated frames for often quite spectacular crossing and stylization, interpersonal verbal rituals are more closely woven into everyday activity, and can provide a safer and more ordinary environment in which a speaker can try to slip into their speech an other-ethnic form as if it was their own (Rampton 2009a).

So far, most of this overview of recent work on crossing and stylization has focused on young people and the kinds of urban polylingualism associated with migration, globalization and mediated popular cultures. But these are far from being the only scenes for language crossing, and in the next section, we turn to a post-conflict environment with recent memories of war, where there is some official institutional support for crossing, where adults engage in it as much as youth, where crossing is challenged by ingroup rather than the outgroup members and where it is keyed in hitherto undocumented ways.

Teaching and learning Turkish in Greek–Cypriot classes in Cyprus – a case study

In Cyprus, the Greek-Cypriot and Turkish-Cypriot communities have a long history of violent conflict. Since the 1974 war, Cyprus has been de facto divided into north and south, with substantial displacement in both populations, and until 2003 communication between the two parts was almost impossible.

Historically, education has been very closely linked with the formation and 'imagining' of these two Cypriot communities, seeing them as parts of two different and already rival 'Motherlands' – Greece and Turkey. Even after the establishment of the Cyprus Republic (1960), education was 'strictly communal' and monolingual (Karyolemou 2003), and in both communities, schools were responsible for creating what Bryant (2004) calls 'true Greeks' or 'true Turks'. Most educational researchers agree that Greek-Cypriot education has been dominated by Hellenocentric discourses, which emphasize 'Greekness' and construct the 'Turks' as the perennial enemy and 'primary Other' (cf. Spyrou 2006), and within this context, speaking the language of the opposite community seemed not only undesirable but also a betrayal of one's own nation and ethnic group (Ozerk 2001). Up until 2003, although it was an official language of the Cyprus Republic, the Turkish language had never existed in any Greek-Cypriot formal school curricula.

In April 2003, however, the Turkish language was introduced in Greek-Cypriot formal education as part of a package of measures 'of support to the Turkish-Cypriots' and 'for building trust'. At the same time, the Cypriot government set up free Greek and Turkish afternoon language-classes for Turkish-Cypriot and Greek-Cypriot adults, respectively, and this coincided with the Turkish-Cypriot authorities' partial lifting of the restrictions of movement across the buffer zone. Interviewing Greek-Cypriot Ministry of Education Officials, C. Charalambous (2009) found a lack of emphasis on issues of linguistic achievement and proficiency, and instead, Turkish-language classes were seen as an 'offer' of tangible recognition for Turkish-Cypriots, as a token of 'goodwill' and as a first step towards the two communities' rapprochement. Rather than seeking to establish functional bilingualism, the language classes were designed as a symbolic reconciliatory gesture. As such, set within the historical hostility between these two communities and the education system's traditionally very strong ethno-linguistic boundary maintenance, there are grounds for seeing these classes as a type of institutionally sponsored crossing. Charalambous studied the effects of this both in the adult afternoon classes and in secondary schools (ibid.).

The rapprochement rhetoric was certainly congruent with what Charalambous observed in the Turkish-language classes for adults. All the adult learners appeared to be at least sympathetic towards the other community. Some stated that it was their ideological opposition to nationalism and their desire to demonstrate this to their Turkish-Cypriot compatriots that had prompted them to learn the language, whereas there were also others whose initial motivation was, for example, promotion at work, where Turkish language counted as an extra qualification. But all of these adults had sustained contacts with Turkish-Cypriots and the structure of the lessons took this for granted – there were dialogues based on experiences of real encounters, students posed specific questions on how to say certain things that they wanted, etc. In addition, the teacher organized informal visits to the northern part of Cyprus and students contributed to the organization of these events by suggesting specific people or organizations to visit (e.g. the editor of a Turkish-Cypriot newspaper with whom someone in the class was acquainted). Finally, as Greek and Turkish language learning was organized at the same governmental institution, students had the opportunity to meet people from the other community in the corridors before or after lessons, and on several occasions, if Turkish-Cypriot students had arrived early, they would go and sit in a Turkish-language teaching class and vice versa.

So teachers and students in the adult classes sought opportunities for intercommunal communication, and crossing was a standard everyday practice on which teachers also drew for language teaching purposes. For example, in brief corridor encounters outside class, learners from both communities would greet one another in the opposite language even if they did not know each other. Those who had formed friendships with learners from the opposite community would try to produce the other language as much as possible when chatting before or after class with their friends and acquaintances, and rather than responding in the language in which they had been addressed, they would cross back into their interlocutor's first language, filling in the gaps in English. English would form the bulk of the talk for people who were not advanced in the other language, but the opening and closing of the encounters were always in the other language, and in interviews, both Greek- and Turkish-language learners explained this by saying that just a couple of words in the other language were enough to 'break the ice'. The two teachers in the more advanced-level classes took advantage of these practices, and at the end of one term, they joined the Greek and Turkish language classes together to 'roleplay' a famous market in Cyprus back in the 1960s, before the intercommunal troubles. Students acted as retailers, customers, strollers and even when the task was for everyone to speak their own language, they did not stick to it, and instead, they constantly alternated between Greek and Turkish.

Activities like these were greatly enjoyed, but crossing into Turkish (or Greek for Turkish-Cypriots) also involved a very strong sense of ethnolinguistic boundary transgression, accompanied by a feeling of risk. However, it was not the owners of the language who presented any threat, and in and around the lessons, their crossing was partly sheltered by the institutional arrangements. Instead, learners faced criticism and disapproval from members of their own ethnic group, and some reported having to hide their Turkish books at home because their partners could not stand seeing anything in the Turkish language.

Although some learners were very keen and sometimes anxious to achieve high levels of proficiency either for personal or for what they called 'ideological reasons', proficiency and the communicative dimensions of other language learning seemed secondary to 'breaking the ice', and overall, the ritual dimension of other language learning was very pronounced. Ritual, suggests Rampton,

> can be defined as formulaic conduct that displays an orientation to issues of respect for social order and that emerges from some sense of the (actual or potential) problematicity of social relations. Typically, ritual gives a more prominent role to symbols than to propositional expression, it elicits a marked emotional response, it creates an increased feeling of collectivity between at least some of the participants and it is itself subject to comment and sanctions (2005: 82). Ritual is a form of action that is typically (though not invariably) intended to help people get past such difficulties and on with normal life, albeit often in a new state.
>
> *(2006: 174)*

A history of conflict and some still very powerful nationalist discourses have made Greek- and Turkish-Cypriot relations potentially very problematic, but the ritual learning and use of the other's language sought to generate and/or re-establish new solidarities, displaying the participants' commitment to reconciliation and their acceptance of the 'Others'. So in the adult classes, crossing seemed to be an *enacted* (rather than simply a stated) denial of nationalism and rigid ethnic boundaries.

The situation in the secondary school language lessons was very different. As already mentioned, formal Greek-Cypriot education constructs a particularly hostile image of the Turks, in textbooks, literature and history lessons, as well as through national celebrations (cf. Christou 2007; Papadakis 2008; P. Charalambous 2009; Hadjipavlou-Trigeorgis 2000). A recent attempt by the Minister of Education to introduce 'reconciliation' as an educational goal met with immense resistance from teachers, parents and media (see Zembylas *et al.* 2011), and there is currently a great deal of controversy in Greek-Cypriot society about changing history textbooks. Although the introduction of the Turkish language into the Greek-Cypriot Modern Foreign Languages curriculum had reconciliatory intentions, it came into conflict with formal schooling's strong traditional Hellenocentrism, and even though Turkish-language classes were an official part of the curriculum, both the teacher and the students faced criticism from their associates. 'What world do you live in? They have occupied half of our country and you are teaching their language?' was one example of the type of reaction that Mr A., the Turkish-language teacher, had to face when he told his staffroom colleagues what he taught and all students reported that their peers called them 'traitors' for learning Turkish.

Mr A.'s strategy for dealing with this was radically different from the processes encountered in the adult classes. Throughout his regular Turkish-language lessons, he consistently tried to erase any political or ideological resonance that the Turkish language could have, and to suppress the emblematic character of Turkish-language learning as an 'offer' to the Turkish-Cypriots.

In the 32 hours during which Charalambous observed his classes, Mr A. constantly avoided talking or even naming the Turks and Turkish-Cypriots – in all, he used these labels only four times. Instead, he focused exclusively on grammar and vocabulary. He explicitly avoided any 'political' discussions in the classroom, and even when he dedicated two sessions to 'teaching culture', he still managed to re-direct the focus of his lesson away from the Turks or Turkish-Cypriots. In the first, he taught a Turkish adaptation of a *Greek* song, limiting the 'Turkish-ness' of the lesson's content to just the language, and in the second session, he talked about Muslims, constructing an ambivalent category from which he excluded the Turks ('children (.) all the Turks are Muslims (.) almost ... But when we say Muslims we do not mean the Turks we mean *all* the *Muslims* who are almost all the Arabic-the ... Arabian countries').

In the sensitive political boundary situations where crossing emerges, one can often find quite conspicuous patterns of avoidance, in which individuals and groups take care *not* to use the other language in particular contexts, with particular others (cf. Hewitt 1986; Rampton 1995; also Kamwangamalu 2001 on post-apartheid South Africa). These secondary school language lessons present an interesting variation on this. The teacher and the students did use the Turkish language, but they persistently tried to cut out the social indexicality/cultural associations that the Turkish language carries in Greek-Cypriot society. Returning to Goffman, this practice fits with a fourth very basic type of 'keying' – 'technical redoings' (1974: 58ff). 'Technical redoings' refer to activities that are 'performed out of their usual context, for utilitarian purposes openly different from those of the original performance, the understanding being that the original outcome of the activity will not occur' (1974: 59). Goffman also points out 'these run-throughs are an important part of modern life' – demonstrations, exhibitions and rehearsals are typical examples – and their purpose is usually 'to give the neophyte experience in performing under conditions in which (it is felt) no actual engagement with the world is allowed' (ibid.). In the Greek-Cypriot classroom, the indexical associations of the Turkish language appeared to be so powerful that Mr A. had little room to renegotiate or redefine them, and because of this, the only strategy he could find was to extract the language from its original setting, and to reconstruct Turkish as a neutral and ideology-free linguistic system. Crossing into Turkish in these classrooms seemed so politically transgressive that it was only possible when keyed as a 'technical redoing'.

Areas for further work

(1) Crossing is very much a linguistic anthropological/ethnographic topic, and it provides a window on major social and cultural changes that starts very close to lived experience and practical activity. Both in social sciences and public institutions, there is growing recognition that traditional social and ethnic classification can no longer account for the splits and alignments emerging in contemporary urban environments (Vertovec 2007; Platt 2008), and the significance of informal processes, local 'conviviality' and low-key 'civility' is increasingly stressed (Gilroy 2006; Vertovec 2007). These informal processes can be hard to access with the interview and survey tools that dominate British social sciences (Savage and Burrows 2007), but they are central in research on polylingualism, and in future work, it is essential to make the kinds of linguistic ethnographic analysis associated with the study of crossing and stylization more widely available to social research, increasing its ability to deal with practices that are indirect, implicit, grounded in activity and background understanding, weakening its dependence for evidence on explicit claims and propositions. So in the first instance, it is important to continue to treat crossing as a point of entry into the understanding of social process rather than as an

autonomous topic in its own right. That said, we can identify a number of areas for further development.

(2) In the metropolitan contexts that have so far featured most centrally in the research on crossing and stylization, there are several directions worth pursuing. First, it is important to extend the focus well beyond ethnicity and youth. Of course, even though the linguistic forms used in crossing may be identified first and foremost with a particular ethnic group, the personae or images that they are used to project are often multidimensional, displaying classed, gendered, generational and local characteristics as well, and in addition, the political and cultural issues thematized in crossing acts may also be treated by analysts more as matters of gender or class (e.g. Bucholtz 1999a; Rampton 2009b). Nevertheless, crossing and stylization with other kinds of voice deserve more attention (for gender, see e.g. Hall 1995; Barrett 1997; Georgakopoulou 2007; for class (and gender), Bucholtz 1999b; Rampton 2006), and with so much research focusing on working-class schools, there is an urgent need for studies of crossing and stylization in independent and elite institutions. Following Hewitt 1986, it is quite often assumed that crossing declines post-adolescence, but this needs empirical investigation, particularly in countries like the UK, where, for example, 48 per cent of Caribbean men in couples and 34 per cent of Caribbean women live in interethnic partnerships (Platt 2008: 7), or even in the USA, where 30 per cent of married US-born Asians and Latinos have an other-ethnic spouse, and one-tenth of young blacks marry someone of a different racial background (Lee and Bean 2004: 228). In addition, in as much new work as possible, it is important to examine the inter-relationship between the different registers and varieties used in crossing and stylization, as much of their ideological meaning derives from the contrasts and complementarities between them (Irvine 2001; Rampton 2010).

(3) As a concept, crossing is tightly linked to boundaries and the renegotiation of traditional interethnic relations, and as such, it may be particularly useful in peace education projects researching contexts of intractable conflict. We have discussed 'Other-language' teaching and learning in Cyprus as a reconciliatory gesture, and similar classes have been established in Israel, teaching Hebrew to Arabs and Arabic to Jewish students (see e.g. Bekerman 2004; Bekerman and Horenczyk 2004; Bekerman and Shhadi 2003). These are important contexts for studying crossing as an institutionally sponsored practice designed to change hostile intergroup relations (Charalambous and Rampton forthcoming).

(4) Lastly, there is a need for detailed longitudinal studies of how language forms become variously routinized or denaturalized, occurring at one time/place only in crossing and stylization, forming part of habitual speech at another. This is a significant issue for variationist studies of long-term language change (see e.g. Johnstone and Andrus 2006), and for research on the language development of individuals.

Related topics

Codeswitching; heteroglossia; discourses about linguistic diversity; multilingualism and the media; multilingualism and popular culture; linguistic diversity and education.

Further reading

Alim, S., Ibrahim, A. and Pennycook, A. (eds) (2009) *Global Linguistic Flows: Hip Hop Cultures, Youth Identities and the Politics of Language*, London: Routledge.
(An important collection on hip-hop language practices.)

Coupland, N. (2007) *Style*, Cambridge: Cambridge University Press.
(An authoritative overview of stylization and crossing in the wider context of sociolinguistic research on style.)

Hewitt, R. (1986) *White Talk Black Talk*, Cambridge: Cambridge University Press.
(A ground-breaking ethnography of local speech and social relations among black and white youth in London.)

Jaspers, J. (2005) 'Linguistic sabotage in a context of monolingualism and standardization', *Language and Communication* 25(3): 279–98.
(A short but very vivid description of polylingual practices.)

Rampton, B. ([1995]2005) *Crossing: Language and Ethnicity among Adolescents*, 2nd edn., London: Longman, Manchester: St Jerome Publishing.
(Detailed ethnographic and interactional examination of stylization and crossing between three varieties: Creole, Punjabi and Asian English.)

Bibliography

Alim, S. (2009) 'Straight outta Compton, straight *aus München:* Global linguistic flows, identities, and the politics of language in a Global Hip Hop Nation', in S. Alim, A. Ibrahim and A. Pennycook (eds) *Global Linguistic Flows: Hip Hop Cultures, Youth Identities and the Politics of Language,* London: Routledge.

Alim, S., Ibrahim, A. and Pennycook, A. (eds) (2009) *Global Linguistic Flows: Hip Hop Cultures, Youth Identities and the Politics of Language,* London: Routledge.

Anderson, B. (1983) *Imagined Communities*, London: Verso.

Androutsopoulos, J. (2001) 'From the streets to the screens and back again: on the mediated diffusion of ethnolectal patterns in contemporary German', in *Essen: LAUD 2001,* Paper 522, Essen: Linguistic Agency, University of Essen.

——(2007) 'Bilingualism in the mass media and on the internet', in M. Heller (ed.) *Bilingualism: A Social Approach,* Basingstoke: Palgrave Macmillan.

Auer, P. (1988) 'A conversation analytic approach to code-switching and transfer', in M. Heller (ed.) *Codeswitching: Anthropological and Sociolinguistic Perspectives,* Berlin: Mouton de Gruyter.

——(1995) 'The pragmatics of code-switching: A sequential approach', in L. Milroy and P. Muysken (eds) *One Speaker, Two Languages,* Cambridge: Cambridge University Press.

——(1998) *Code-Switching in Conversation: Language, Interaction and Identity,* London: Routledge.

——(2003) 'Crossing' the language border into Turkish? Uses of Turkish by non-Turks in Germany', in L. Mondada and S. Pekarek-Doehler (eds) *Plurilinguisme – Mehrsprachigkeit – Plurilingualism: Festschrift for Georges Lüdi,* Tübingen: Francke.

——(2006) 'Sociolinguistic crossing', in K. Brown (ed.) *Encyclopedia of Language and Linguistics,* 2nd edn, vol. 11, Amsterdam: Elsevier.

——(ed.) (2007). *Style and Social Identities.* Berlin: Mouton de Gruyter.

Auer, P. and I. Dirim (2003) 'Socio-cultural orientation, urban youth styles and the spontaneous acquisition of Turkish by non-Turkish adolescents in Germany', in J. Androutsopoulos and A. Georgakopoulou (eds) *Discourse Constructions of Youth Identities,* Amsterdam: John Benjamins.

Bailey, B. (2000) 'Language and negotiation of ethnic/racial identity among Dominican Americans', *Language in Society* 29(4): 555–82.

——(2007) 'Language alternation as a resource for identity negotiations among Dominican American bilinguals', in P. Auer (ed.) *Style and Social Identities,* Berlin: Mouton de Gruyter.

Bakhtin, M. M. (1981) *The Dialogic Imagination: Four Essays*, M. Holquist (ed.), C. Emerson and M. Holquist (trans.), Austin: University of Texas Press.

——(1984) *Problems in Dostoevsky's Poetics*, Minneapolis: University of Minnesota Press.

Barrett, R. (1997) 'The 'homo-genius' speech community', in A. Livia and K. Hall (eds) *Queerly Phrased,* Oxford: Oxford University Press.

Basso, K. (1979) *Portraits of 'the White Man': Linguistic Play and Cultural Symbols among the Western Apache,* Cambridge: Cambridge University Press.

Bauman, R. ([1975] 2001) 'Verbal art as performance', *American Anthropologist* 77: 290–311. (Also in A. Duranti (ed.) 2001 *Linguistic Anthropology: A Reader*, Oxford: Blackwell.)

Bekerman, Z. (2004) 'Potential and limitations of multicultural education in conflict-ridden areas: Bilingual Palestinian-Jewish schools in Israel', *The Teachers College Record* 106(3): 574–610.

Bekerman, Z. and Horenczyk, G. (2004) 'Arab-Jewish bilingual coeducation in Israel: A long-term approach to intergroup conflict resolution', *Journal of Social Issues* 60(2): 389–404.

Bekerman, Z. and Shhadi, N. (2003) 'Palestinian-Jewish bilingual education in Israel: Its influence on cultural identities and its impact on intergroup conflict', *Journal of Multilingual and Multicultural Development* 24(6): 473–84.

Bell, A. (1999) 'Styling the other to define the self: A study in New Zealand identity-making', *Journal of Sociolinguistics* 3(4): 523–41.

Bentahila, A. and Davies, E. (2002) 'Language mixing in rai music: Localisation or globalization?' *Language and Communication* 22: 187–207.

Bryant, R. (2004) *Imagining the Modern: The Cultures of Nationalism in Cyprus*, London: I. B. Tauris.

Bucholtz, M. (1999a) 'You da man: Narrating the racial other in the production of white masculinity', *Journal of Sociolinguistics* 3(4): 443–60.

——(1999b) 'Why be normal?': Language and identity practices in a community of nerd girls', *Language in Society* 28(2): 203–23.

——(2009) 'Styles and stereotypes: Laotian American girls' linguistic negotiation of identity', in A. Reyes and A. Lo (eds) *Beyond Yellow English: Towards a Linguistic Anthropology of Asian Pacific America*, Oxford: Oxford University Press.

Charalambous, C. (2009) 'Learning the Language of 'The Other': A Linguistic Ethnography of Turkish-Language Classes in a Greek-Cypriot School,' unpublished PhD thesis, King's College, London.

Charalambous. C.and Rampton, B. (forthcoming) 'Learning the language of 'The Other': Identity, conflict and intercultural communication', in J. Jackson, *Handbook in Intercultural Communication*, London: Routledge.

Charalambous, P. (2009) 'Classroom constructions of 'militant ethos': Social representations and ideologies of text in Greek-Cypriot literature education practices', *Cyprus Colloquium: Discourse and Education in the Process of Reconciliation*, May, London Metropolitan.

Christou, M. (2007) 'The language of patriotism: Sacred history and dangerous memories', *British Journal of Sociology of Education* 28(6): 709–22.

Chun, E. (2009) 'Ideologies of legitimate mockery: Margaret Cho's revoicings of mock Asian', in A. Reyes and A. Lo (eds) *Beyond Yellow English: Towards a Linguistic Anthropology of Asian Pacific America*, Oxford: Oxford University Press.

Clark, J. T. (2003) 'Abstract inquiry and the patrolling of black/white borders through linguistic stylization', in R. Harris and B. Rampton (eds) *The Language, Ethnicity and Race Reader*, London: Routledge.

Coupland, N. (2007) *Style*, Cambridge: Cambridge University Press.

Cutler, A. ([1999]2003) 'Yorkville crossing. White teens, hip hop, and African American English', *Journal of Sociolinguistics* 3(4): 428–42, reprinted in R. Harris and B. Rampton (eds) *The Language, Ethnicity and Race Reader*, London: Routledge.

Davies, A. (1999) *An Introduction to Applied Linguistics*, Edinburgh: Edinburgh University Press.

Depperman, A. (2007) 'Playing with the voice of the other: Stylised *Kanaksprak* in conversations among German adolescents', in P. Auer (ed.) *Style and Social Identities*, Berlin: Mouton de Gruyter.

Doran, M. (2004) 'Negotiating between "Bourge" and "Racaille": Verlan as youth identity practice in suburban Paris', in A. Pavlenko and A. Blackledge (eds) *Negotiating Identity in Multilingual Contexts*, Clevedon: Multilingual Matters.

Georgakopoulou, A. (2007) 'Positioning in style: Men in women's jointly produced stories', in P. Auer (ed.) *Style and Social Identities*, Berlin: Mouton de Gruyter.

Gilroy, P. (2006) 'Multiculture in times of war: An inaugural lecture given at the London School of Economics', *Critical Quarterly* 48(4): 27–45.

Goffman, E. (1967) *Interaction Ritual*, Harmondsworth: Penguin.

——(1971) *Relations in Public*, London: Allen Lane.

——(1974) *Frame Analysis: An Essay on the Organization of Experience*, Harmondsworth: Penguin.

——(1981) *Forms of Talk*, Oxford: Blackwell.

Gumperz, J. J. (1982) *Discourse Strategies*, Cambridge: Cambridge University Press.

Hadjipavlou-Trigeorgis, M. (2000) 'A partnership between peace education and conflict resolution: The case of Cyprus', in G. Salomon and B. Nevo (eds) *Peace Education,* Mahwah, NJ and London: Lawrence Erlbaum.

Hall, K. (1995) 'Lip service on the fantasy lines', in K. Hall and M. Bucholtz (eds) *Gender Articulated,* London: Routledge.

Harris, R. (2006) *New Ethnicities and Language Use,* Basingstoke: Palgrave Macmillan.

Heller, M. (2007) 'Bilingualism as ideology and practice', in M. Heller (ed.) *Bilingualism: A Social Approach,* Basingstoke: Palgrave Macmillan.

Hewitt, R. (1986) *White Talk Black Talk,* Cambridge: Cambridge University Press.

Hill, J. ([1995]2003) 'Junk Spanish, covert racism, and the (leaky) boundary between public and private spheres', *Pragmatics* 5(2): 197–212, reprinted in R. Harris and B. Rampton (eds) *The Language, Ethnicity and Race Reader,* London: Routledge.

——(1999) 'Styling locally, styling globally: What does it mean?' *Journal of Sociolinguistics* 3(4): 542–56.

——(2008) *The Everyday Language of White Racism.* Oxford: Wiley Blackwell.

Hill, J. and Coombs, D. (1982) 'The vernacular remodelling of national and international languages', *Applied Linguistics* 3: 224–34.

Hinnenkamp V. (1987) 'Foreigner talk, code-switching and the concept of trouble', in K. Knapp, W. Enninger, and A. Knapp-Potthof (eds) *Analyzing Intercultural Communication,* Amsterdam: Mouton de Gruyter.

Irvine, J. (2001) '"Style" as distinctiveness: the culture and ideology of linguistic differentiation', in P. Eckert and J. Rickford (eds) *Style and Sociolinguistic Variation,* Cambridge: Cambridge University Press.

Jaspers, J. (2005) 'Linguistic sabotage in a context of monolingualism and standardization', *Language and Communication* 25(3): 279–98.

Johnstone, B. and Andrus, J. (2006) 'Mobility, indexicality and the enregisterment of "Pittsburghese"', *Journal of English Linguistics* 34(2): 77–104.

Jørgensen, N. (2008) 'Polylingual languaging around and among children and adolescents', *International Journal of Multilingualism* 5(3): 161–76.

Kamwangamalu, N. M. (2001) 'Ethnicity and language crossing in post-apartheid South Africa', *International Journal of the Sociology of Language* 2001(152): 75–95.

Karyolemou, M. (2003) '"Keep your language and I will keep mine": Politics, language, and the construction of identities in Cyprus', in D. Nelson and M. Dedaic-Nelson (eds) *At War with Words,* Berlin and New York: Mouton de Gruyter.

Lee, J. and Bean, F. (2004) 'America's changing color lines: Immigration, race/ethnicity, and multiracial identification', *Annual Review of Sociology* 30: 221–42.

LePage, R. (1980) 'Projection, Focusing and Diffusion', *York Papers in Linguistics* 9.

LePage, R. and Tabouret-Keller, A. (1985) *Acts of Identity,* Cambridge: Cambridge University Press.

Lippi-Green, R. (1997) *English with an Accent,* London: Routledge.

Lo, A. (1999) 'Codeswitching, speech community, and the construction of ethnic identity', *Journal of Sociolinguistics* 3(4): 461–79.

Lytra, V. (2007) *Play Frames and Social Identities,* Amsterdam: John Benjamins.

Maher, J. (2005) 'Metroethnicity, language and the principle of Cool', *International Journal of the Sociology of Language* 175(6): 83–102.

Ozerk, K. Z. (2001) 'Reciprocal bilingualism as a challenge and opportunity: The case of Cyprus', *International Review of Education* 47(3–4): 253–65.

Papadakis, Y. (2008) 'Narrative, memory and history education in divided Cyprus: a comparison of schoolbooks on the "History of Cyprus"', *History & Memory* 20(2): 128–48.

Platt, L. (2008) *Ethnicity and Family: Relationships within and between Ethnic Groups: An Analysis Using the Labour Force Survey,* Equality and Human Rights Commission.

Pratt, M. L. (1987) 'Linguistic Utopias', in N. Fabb, D. Attridge, A. Durant and C. MacCabe (eds) *The Linguistics of Writing,* Manchester: Manchester University Press.

Pujolar, J. (2007) 'Bilingualism and the nation-state in the post-national era', in M. Heller (ed.) *Bilingualism: A Social Approach,* Basingstoke: Palgrave Macmillan.

Quist, P. and Jørgensen, N. (2009) 'Crossing – negotiating social boundaries', in P. Auer and W. Li (eds) *Handbook of Multilingualism and Multilingual Communication,* Berlin: Mouton de Gruyter.

Rampton, B. ([1995]2005) *Crossing: Language and Ethnicity among Adolescents*, 2nd edn, London: Longman Manchester: St Jerome Publishing.
——(1999a) 'Sociolinguistics and cultural studies: New ethnicities, liminality and interaction', *Social Semiotics* 9(3): 355–76.
——(ed.) (1999b) '*Styling the Other*', *Journal of Sociolinguistics* (special issue) 3(4): 421–556.
——(2001) 'Crossing', in A. Duranti (ed.) *Key Concepts in Language & Culture*, pp. 49–51, Oxford: Blackwell.
——(2003) 'Ethnicity and the crossing of boundaries', in R. Mesthrie (ed.) *Concise Encyclopedia of Sociolinguistics*, Oxford: Elsevier Science.
——(2006) *Language in Late Modernity: Interaction in an Urban School'*, Cambridge: Cambridge University.
——(2009a) Interaction ritual and not just artful performance in crossing and stylization, *Language in Society* 38(02): 149–76.
——(2009b) 'Crossing into class', in D. Watts and C. Llamas (eds) *Language and Identity*, Edinburgh: Edinburgh University Press
——(2010) 'Style contrasts, migration and social class', *Journal of Pragmatics* 43: 1236–50.
Reyes, A. (2009) 'Asian American stereotypes as circulating resource', in A. Reyes and A. Lo (eds) *Beyond Yellow English: Towards a Linguistic Anthropology of Asian Pacific America*, Oxford: Oxford University Press.
Reyes, A. and Lo, A. (eds) (2009) *Beyond Yellow English: Towards a Linguistic Anthropology of Asian Pacific America*, Oxford: Oxford University Press.
Romaine, S. (1988) *Bilingualism*, Oxford: Blackwell
Roth-Gordon, J. (2009) 'Conversational sampling, race trafficking and the invocation of the *Gueto* in Brazilian Hip Hop', in S. Alim, A. Ibrahim and A. Pennycook (eds) *Global Linguistic Flows: Hip Hop Cultures, Youth Identities and the Politics of Language*, London: Routledge.
Sarkar, M. (2009) '"Still reppin por mi gente": The transformative power of language mixing in Quebec Hip Hop', in S. Alim, A. Ibrahim and A. Pennycook (eds) *Global Linguistic Flows: Hip Hop Cultures, Youth Identities and the Politics of Language*, London: Routledge.
Savage, M. (2007) 'The coming crisis of empirical sociology', *Sociology* 41(5): 885–99.
Shankar, S. (2009) 'Reel to real: Desi teens' linguistic engagements with Bollywood', in A. Reyes and A. Lo (eds) *Beyond Yellow English: Towards a Linguistic Anthropology of Asian Pacific America*, Oxford: Oxford University Press.
Spyrou, S. (2006) 'Constructing "the Turk" as an enemy: The complexity of stereotypes in children's everyday worlds', *South European Society & Politics* 11(1): 95–110.
Sweetland, J. (2002) 'Unexpected authentic use of an ethnically-marked dialect', *Journal of Sociolinguistics* 6(4): 514–37.
Talmy, S. (2009) 'Forever FOB? Resisting and reproducing the other in high school ESL', in A. Reyes and A. Lo (eds) *Beyond Yellow English: Towards a Linguistic Anthropology of Asian Pacific America*, Oxford: Oxford University Press.
Trosset C. (1986) 'The social identity of Welsh learners', *Language in Society* 15(2): 165–92.
Urla, J. ([1995]2003) 'Outlaw language: Creating an alternative public sphere in Basque radio', *Pragmatics* 5: 245–62; reprinted 2003 in R. Harris and B. Rampton (eds) *The Language, Ethnicity and Race Reader*, London: Routledge.
Vertovec, S. (2007) *New Complexities of Cohesion in Britain: Superdiversity, Transnationalism and Civil-Integration*, University of Oxford: COMPAS.
Woolard K (1988) 'Codeswitching and comedy in Catalonia', in M. Heller (ed.) *Codeswitching: Anthropological and Sociolinguistic Perspectives*, Berlin: Mouton de Gruyter.
Zembylas, M., Charalambous, C., Charalambous, P. and Kendeou, P. (2011) 'Promoting peaceful coexistence in conflict-ridden Cyprus: Teachers' difficulties and emotions towards a new policy initiative', *Teaching and Teacher Education* 27(2): 332–441.
Zentella, A. (1997) *Growing Up Bilingual*, Oxford: Blackwell.

29

Heteroglossia

Benjamin Bailey

Introduction

Heteroglossia is a translation of the Russian term *raznorechie*, which was coined by Russian literary analyst and language philosopher Mikhail Bakhtin. The term refers to (1) the simultaneous use of different kinds of forms or signs; and (2) the tensions and conflicts among those signs, based on the sociohistorical associations they carry with them (Ivanov 2001: 259). The first part of this definition subsumes multilingualism, but includes a broader range of linguistic phenomena. Although multilingualism typically refers to situations and practices that involve "distinct languages," the different kinds of forms or signs of heteroglossia include intra-language social variation, e.g. regional dialects and registers related to profession or age. Bakhtin coined the Russian term *raznorechie* specifically to refer to such intra-language variety within Russian, varieties with competing social and political implications, and the term is sometimes translated as "the social diversity of speech types" rather than "heteroglossia."

What is distinctive about heteroglossia is not its reference to different kinds of linguistic signs and forms, however, but rather its focus on social tensions inherent in language. Social and political tensions and struggles that exist in society inhabit language, making it alive with social meanings. A primary tension in language is between pulls toward a (national) standard form of language—Bakhtin referred to these forces as "centripetal" forces—and forces that push toward various local, non-standard, or demotic forms, which he called "centrifugal" forces. Words are not neutral instruments, and these social tensions are at work even if the speaker does not intend them and is not conscious of them: "Every concrete utterance of a speaking subject serves as a point where centrifugal as well as centripetal forces are brought to bear. The processes of centralization and decentralization, of unification and disunification, intersect in the utterance" (Bakhtin 1981: 272). To speak then, is to participate in these ongoing processes, regardless of one's intentions to participate in them or not. Our words have already been used by others, accruing social associations, and our use of these words continues the process of accruing and shedding meanings.

The emphasis of heteroglossia on the social and political nature of language contrasts with the relatively formal and synchronic emphases of most linguistics. From the perspective of heteroglossia, language is not a neutral, abstract system of reference but a medium through which one participates in a historical flow of social relationships, struggles, and meanings. Linguistic signs come with social and historical associations, and they gain new ones in their situated use. This focus on the social dimension of language use makes heteroglossia distinct from both popular and formal linguistic notions of "multilingualism," which conceptualize it as the coexistence of multiple linguistic systems that are discrete, ahistorical, and relatively self-contained.

The fact that heteroglossia takes social and political dimensions of speech as its starting point puts it superficially at odds with the more formal, organizing trope and title of this *Handbook*, "Multilingualism." The contributions to this *Handbook*, however, emphasize the social contexts and functioning of multilingualism, whether at the level of polities, education, or other institutions. Heteroglossia represents a philosophical perspective on language and communicative practices from which to approach contexts, practices, and meanings of multilingualism.

Heteroglossia versus formal linguistic approaches

Bakhtin coined the term heteroglossia (*raznorechie*) in his 1930s essay *Discourse in the Novel*. He used the term and perspective to analyze how meanings in novels were generated and the ways in which language and processes of signification in novels were distinct from those of other literary genres such as epic poetry. This work remained unpublished under various Soviet regimes until 1975, and his notion of heteroglossia did not receive significant attention in the English-speaking world until the publication of a translation by Emerson and Holquist (Bakhtin 1981). Since that time, the term has been extremely popular in literary studies and the work of scholars interested in social and political meanings in language.

Although the ostensible focus of Bakhtin's essay is ways in which meanings are generated in novels, the essay presents a distinctive philosophy of language and meaning. This philosophy of language—which emphasizes the social and historical nature of language—directly countered the dominant linguistic paradigm of his time, the structuralism of Saussure, a paradigm that championed the formalism that has remained central in most linguistics. Briefly reviewing Saussure's notions of language and meaning can serve to highlight the distinctiveness of Bakhtin's perspective of heteroglossia and its ongoing relevance.

Saussure's 1916 *Course in General Linguistics* (Saussure 1983) distinguished between *parole*—the messy phenomenon of actual acts of speaking—and *langue*—the underlying, abstract principles of language that allow for referential meaning to be generated. It is this second dimension of language, the abstract, formal system of principles that Saussure found to be the proper focus of linguistics. Within this approach, he conceptualized meaning in terms of "signs." Signs, according to Saussure, have two components: a "signifier" (*significant*) and a "signified" (*signifie*). The *signifier* is the form of the word or sign, whereas the *signified* is the idea or concept connected to that sign. The relationship between signifier and signified is arbitrary, i.e. there is no inherent or natural relationship between a signifier and its meanings. This type of meaning is sometimes called denotation or referential meaning.

The Saussurean privileging of the formal and referential characteristics of language informs contemporary popular and academic language ideologies. From a popular, Western folk perspective, language is a system of denotation, in which words stand for, or represent, things or ideas. The function of language is popularly seen as the communication of propositional information, as in a conduit metaphor (Reddy 1979). Non-referential dimensions of meaning are seen as secondary or epiphenomenal in this folk model. This folk understanding is layered with hegemonic ideologies that favor language varieties that are associated with powerful and privileged groups in society. These prestigious varieties are seen as being "standard" or correct forms of the language and ideal for "good," i.e. propositionally efficient, communication.

Formal linguistics also treats the social and political functioning of language as marginal, approaching language as a semiotic system in and of itself. The primary interest is in relationships among elements of this system, abstracted from any actual instances of language, for example Chomsky's privileging of linguistic competence over linguistic performance as the proper object of study. The boundaries of the system are implicitly taken to be the boundaries of the language-as-idealized, rather than of actual speech, which may or may not be mono-lingual. Formal linguists focus on meanings and relationships that remain stable across time, speakers, and contexts, and pay relatively little attention to actual use of language. In taking a formal, synchronic approach to language, formal linguists thus neglect relationships between linguistic forms and the social and political worlds that inhabit speech.

Bakhtin approached language entirely differently, conceptualizing it not as an abstract, synchronic system but rather as a medium through which one participates in a historical flow of social relationships, struggles, and meanings. His focus is the relationships between language and social and historical worlds, rather than relationships among elements in an idealized system. Bakhtin opens the essay in which he introduces the concept of heteroglossia with the claim that language is essentially a social phenomenon, and that issues of form and ideology are not separable:

> The principal idea of this essay is that the study of verbal art can and must overcome the divorce between an abstract "formal" approach and an equally abstract "ideological" approach. Form and content in discourse are one, once we understand that verbal dis-course is a social phenomenon—social throughout its entire range and in each and every of its factors, from the sound image to the furthest reaches of abstract meaning.
>
> *(1981: 259)*

Bakhtin argues that language cannot be studied as a system in-and-of-itself. Abstractions from language, such as *langue*, are not the phenomenon itself, but only idealizations of one dimension of language: "It [language] is unitary only as an abstract grammatical system of normative forms, taken in isolation from the concrete, ideological conceptualizations that fill it, and in isolation from the uninterrupted process of historical becoming that is a characteristic of all living language" (1981: 288). For Bakhtin, language is a medium that is alive and moving with the consciousness and practices of people. Language as a self-contained system is always an idealization, "a theoretical expression of the historical processes of linguistic unification and centralization, an express of the centripetal forces of language" (1981: 270). Formal, abstract approaches to language capture the tendencies toward standardization in language, but they ignore the equally present centrifugal forces that fragment language and move it away from unitary standards. He argues that such theoretical idealizations are opposed to the reality of actual language: "A unitary language is not something given but is always in essence posited—and at every moment of its linguistic life it is opposed to the realities of heteroglossia" (ibid.). The closest that language gets to being an abstract, formal system is when the force toward standardization ("centripetal force") is conceptualized as an idealized, static state rather than an analytical construct created from one moment in an ongoing process.

This conceptualization of language as a medium of participation in social life embraces a distinctively social and political notion of *meaning*. For Bakhtin, "no living word relates to its object in a *singular* way" (1981: 276). The signifier–signified relationship (referential meaning) posited by Saussure represents only one dimension of meaning. For Bakhtin, social and

501

pragmatic meanings are the *actual* meanings of language. He argues that linguists and language philosophers do not pay sufficient attention to actual discourse, which leads them to focus on referential meaning: "Linguistics and the philosophy of language acknowledge only a passive understanding of discourse ... it is an understanding of an utterance's *neutral signification* and not its *actual meaning*" (1981: 281).

The perspective of heteroglossia recognizes that meanings are not stable across people, activities, or contexts. Utterances occur in contexts that are not neutral, and the relationship between a word and its object is shaped by this context, including prior uses and associations of that word:

> The living utterance, having taken meaning and shape at a particular historical moment in a socially specific environment, cannot fail to brush up against thousands of living dialogic threads, woven by socio-ideological consciousness around the given object of an utterance; it cannot fail to become an active participant in social dialogue. After all, the utterance arises out of this dialogue as a continuation of it and as a rejoinder to it—it does not approach the object from the sidelines.
>
> *(Bakhtin 1981: 276–7)*

The relationships between utterances and meanings are not drawn from a neutral, external reservoir of signifier–signified relationships. Utterances come with social and historical associations from prior usage, and they gain and shed meanings in their situated use.

The Bakhtinian notion of heteroglossia overlaps in significant ways with the semiotic and linguistic anthropological notion of non-referential indexicality as developed by Peirce (1955) and Silverstein (1976). Both heteroglossia and indexicality rely on notions of intertextuality, in which meanings of forms depend on past usages and associations of those forms rather than on arbitrary referential meaning inherent in the form. A regional accent is an example of an index. The relationship between that accent and that region is established through the historical fact of speakers from that region speaking in a particular way. There is no inherent relationship between the indexical form and meaning, simply one of historical association. The relationship is not arbitrary, as with denotation, but rather historically specific. Like heteroglossia, approaches to language that center on indexicality recognize the referential function of language, but conceptualize reference as merely one pragmatic function among many in a system that is intrinsically pragmatic (Silverstein 1976: 20).

Heteroglossia in a multilingual segment of talk

Heteroglossia represents a general philosophy of language and meaning, but the examples Bakhtin gives of its workings are limited to textual examples from novels and literary texts. In this section, I use the perspective to analyze a brief transcript of multilingual interaction between two teenagers to illustrate how it can shed light on social and communicative worlds. This segment of talk includes both Spanish and English, but it also includes other kinds of social variation. I describe the variety of forms in this interaction and the tensions and conflicts among those forms, based on the sociohistorical associations they carry with them. Addressing both of these levels in this segment—the variation in forms and the sociohistorical associations of such forms—provides a window onto some of the ways that these two teenagers position themselves in the world and negotiate a historical moment.

The participants in the following exchange, Isabella and Janelle, are two high school friends whose parents emigrated from the Dominican Republic to the USA. Isabella came to the USA during first grade, at about the age of seven. Janelle was US-born and raised. They speak Spanish with their parents and newly arrived relatives, but they generally speak English with each other, occasionally including Spanish phrases or words. They are academically successful students at an urban, low-income school in Providence, Rhode Island. In the interaction represented in the transcript below, they are sitting on steps outside of their school building at the end of their lunch period. Isabella has returned from eating lunch at a diner near the school, and she has been describing the turkey club sandwich and cheeseburger she had just eaten.

JANELLE: Okay, a turkey club is *pan to(s)ta(d)o* ['toasted white bread']

ISABELLA: *pan to(s)ta(d)o*. Like regular *pan-* ['bread']

JANELLE: yeah

ISABELLA: *to(s)ta(d)o* ['toasted']. With ... um ... tomatoes and lettuce. And it has mayonnaise.

JANELLE: And turkey.

ISABELLA: Then ... No, that's the ...

JANELLE: the top

ISABELLA: first part. And then it has another *pan* ['slice of bread'] in the middle, and the bottom has more mayonnaise and turkey. Oh it has bacon on it too.

ISABELLA: Just slamming ['great']!

JANELLE: How do you eat that?

ISABELLA: Then they- she cut it in half for me and I ate that, gluk gluk. And I was like, 'Yo, let me get a cheeseburger'. A cheeseburger has lettuce, tomatoes, whatever you want to put on it, like a Whopper you can make out of a cheeseburger.

[TWO BRIEF TURNS OMITTED]

JANELLE: Damn /de' əm/. I can't //eat all that.

ISABELLA: //Then I drank the lemonade.

JANELLE: Only with that turkey thingee //*ya yo estoy llena*. ['I'm already full'].

Meanings of multilingualism

A traditional way of approaching such interactions in literature on multilingual interaction is to describe the forms and various possible functions of such language switching. Following this approach may be of limited value here. Although Janelle and Isabella codeswitch into Spanish several times in this segment, it is not clear what distinctive functions the switches serve in this segment. The uses of Spanish in the first half of this segment may help achieve reference tracking of the sandwich components, but this could also be achieved monolingually. Seeking functions of codeswitching can be analytically productive in terms of revealing some of the social and linguistic functions that can be achieved through language alternation, but this approach can also reproduce the ideology that it is natural to speak only one language in a speech exchange. The fact that social and cultural linguists have focused so much attention on the meanings and functions of codeswitching, for example—while paying relatively less attention to corresponding monolingual speech—reflects the monolingual ideology that codeswitching is not an entirely natural form, but something that is in need of explanation (Woolard 2004).

A growing body of literature since the early 1980s has challenged the assumption that the languages used in codeswitching are essentially distinct and that codeswitching necessarily generates local meanings that are distinct from ones communicated through monolingual talk (Heller 2007; Meeuwis and Blommaert 1998; Woolard 2004). The multilingual practice that most directly undermines assumed distinctions among languages is the relatively frequent, intra-sentential codeswitching that has been widely documented both in intra-group peer interaction among the children of international labor migrants to Western societies and in many urban, African contexts (e.g. Myers-Scotton 1993; Swigart 1992). In such cases, the search for a function of a particular switch may be akin to trying to explain why a monolingual speaker selects one synonym or phrasing over another (Zentella 1997: 101). When language alternation functions as a discourse mode in its own right (Poplack 1980), it undermines the assumption of meaningful opposition between languages.

At the same time that multilingual speakers themselves do *not* treat different languages as distinct in some contexts, dominant groups in Western societies regularly *do* see languages in multilingual contexts as distinct. For example, Janelle and Isabella treat these codeswitches as unmarked in the segment above, but in the wider US context, language alternation is nearly always socially marked. Being a monolingual English speaker is an ideological default against which difference or distinctiveness is constructed in the USA (Urciuoli 1996). Various, nativist, English-only groups, for example, have sponsored legislation to criminalize the use of languages other than English in many contexts, including school, government, and workplace. They portray such language alternation as undermining American unity, citizenship, and decency.

Many academics since the 1970s, in contrast, have celebrated the linguistic sophistication displayed in codeswitching and the social strategies that some forms of it imply (Gumperz 1982; cf. Myers-Scotton 1993: 74; cf. Woolard 2004). For more politically oriented analysts, such codeswitching can be seen as a form of resistance to dominant discourses of unquestioning assimilation (Gal 1988: 259) and a means to constructing a positive self in a political and economic context that disparages immigrant phenotypes, language, class status, and ethnic origins (Zentella 1997). The meanings and implications of particular forms are a function of the interpreter's subject position in a larger sociopolitical field. The notion of heteroglossia embraces such competing social and political meanings of multilingual talk.

Multilingualism versus language-internal variation

Focus on constellations of linguistic features that are officially authorized as codes or languages, for example "English" or "Spanish," can contribute to neglect of the diversity of socially indexical linguistic resources *within* languages. From the perspective of heteroglossia, multilingual speech is simply one way of negotiating social and communicative worlds. If one's starting point is social meanings, it is not central whether a speaker is switching languages, alternating between a dialect and a national standard, register shifting, or speaking monolingually in a variety that highlights language contact. This relieves the analyst of formal questions of what exactly constitutes multiple languages versus multiple dialects (Alvarez-Caccamo 1998, 2001), what is a codeswitch versus a loanword or borrowing, and what constitutes the competence level in a second or third language that allows one's speech to count as multilingual (Meeuwis and Blommaert 1998). The focus can thus shift to individuals as social actors using heteroglossic (Bakhtin 1981) sets of linguistic resources to negotiate the social world.

Both the English and the Spanish that Isabella and Janelle use contain diverse forms that index aspects of their social experiences and perspectives. The English that they use in the exchange above, for example, includes forms with widely varying social associations. They use "standard" American English forms ("Oh, it has bacon on it too"), which are prestigious in institutional contexts such as education, government, and the professions. They use vernacular forms associated with youth ("I was like, 'Yo, let me get a cheeseburger'"), which serve to mark an adolescent identity that is distinct from those of children and adults. Some of these youth expressions are associated with African American English ("Just slamming" and "Damn" dé əm/), which further distinguishes their speech from the mainstream adult world.

Their brief uses of Spanish similarly index particular linguistic histories. Both Janelle and Isabella elide syllable final /s/ (*to(s)tado, e(s)toy*) and intervocalic /d/ (tosta(d)o), and both pronounce /n/ as a nasal velar /ŋ/ (*pan*). Additionally, Janelle pronounces word-initial *y* and *ll* as an affricate /ĵ/ (*ya, yo, llena*). All of these pronunciations are characteristic of Caribbean Spanish, particularly Dominican and lower-class varieties, and are widely perceived as such by Spanish speakers (Lipski 1994).

Finally, the word order used by Isabella—"like a Whopper you can make out of a cheeseburger"—suggests the influence of Spanish discourse patterns on her English, reflecting her bilingual socialization. She preposes the direct object ("Whopper") of the verb in this segment in what has been called fronting, focal object construction (Silva-Corvalán 1983: 135), or focus-movement (Prince 1981).

Language, whether monolingual or multilingual, carries social meanings through phonological, lexical, grammatical, and discourse level forms. These forms index various aspects of individuals' and communities' social histories, circumstances, and identities. The wide range of monolingual forms that can carry indexical meanings and the wide variation in indexical objects of such forms (e.g. education, bilingual heritage, regional origins) suggest the limitations of formal approaches to multilingualism. Attending to a wider range of form-meaning relationships, whether in monolingual or multilingual speech, can better shed light on social and communicative worlds.

Heteroglossia as perspective on social history and power

A distinctive characteristic of heteroglossia is that it conceptualizes language meaning as a function of both linguistic forms and historical social relations. This inclusion of historical social tensions and inequality helps to explain the relative salience and meanings of the linguistic features noted in Isabella and Janelle's conversation, above. Meaningful oppositions or distinctions among these features arise not on the basis of formal distance among forms, but on the basis of historical power differentials and struggles with which particular forms are associated. Their codeswitching, or multilingualism, has no *inherent* meaning, for example, but becomes meaningful in the context of political projects and interests, both historical and contemporary. In nineteenth-century Europe, nation-building projects explicitly linked language, identity, and nation, naturalizing monolingualism and monolingual speech. Currently, US nativism and ideologies of assimilation make Isabella and Janelle's codeswitching not only a marked form, but also a disparaged one in the larger society.

Similarly, their Caribbean Spanish phonology is socially meaningful because of historical power relations. Their phonology contrasts, in particular, with Castilian, the prestigious variety spoken around Madrid, Spain. Caribbean varieties of Spanish are descendants of varieties spoken in the southern Spanish province of Andalusia. The fact that Castile, rather than Andalusia, has been the center of executive power in Spain over the last 500 years has made Castilian the most prestigious variety of Spanish. Through processes of hegemony, historical power differentials are translated into present-day judgments of value, correctness, and prestige, leading many Spanish speakers to see Dominican Spanish as bad, or wrong, Spanish.

Finally, the meanings of their use of African American English expressions are a direct function of historical social inequality. The coercive history of African slavery in the USA has resulted in the maintenance of distinctively African American ways of speaking and ongoing stigmatization of African American English in the larger society. The very existence of this way of speaking, as well as its social evaluation in the larger society, is a direct result of this social history. In each of these cases, the meaningful opposition is between forms associated with groups historically or currently in power—monolingual Americans, speakers of Castilian varieties of Spanish, and White Americans—and forms associated with speakers in lower positions in social hierarchies.

Joining the linguistic utterance with social history

The perspective of heteroglossia explicitly joins the linguistic utterance in the present and the sociohistorical relationships that give meanings to those utterances. Patterns and meanings of multilingual talk at the local level can thus be linked to larger sociohistorical questions in ways that are not possible with a more formal approach. Poplack (1988), for example, shows that contrasting patterns of codeswitching in two bilingual communities—a New York Puerto Rican one and a Ottawa-Hull French Canadian one—correlate to contrasting social histories of the two groups. Even though the genetic relationship between French and English is virtually identical to the genetic relationship between Spanish and English, both the use and interpretation of codeswitching are very different in the two communities.

Bilingual New York Puerto Rican switches tend to be smooth and seamless, that is unmarked, whereas French–English switches tend to be highlighted, or marked, through repetition, hesitation, intonational highlighting, and even explicit metalinguistic commentary. Whereas bilingualism is seen to be emblematic of New York Puerto Rican identity—differentiating members from island Puerto Ricans and non-Puerto Rican Anglophones—Ottawa-Hull French Canadian bilingualism is not associated with a social identity distinct from that of local monolingual French Canadians. For New York Puerto Ricans, the use of two languages is both an emblem of a distinctive identity and a practice that draws in immigrant newcomers. In the French Canadian situation, there is no stream of newcomers to incorporate and no distinctive identity bridging disparate communities that needs to be enacted or maintained through language.

Gal (1988: 247) argues that particular multilingual ideologies and practices can be linked to even broader political economic and historical contexts. Thus, groups with similar structural positions in the world system—for example second-generation labor migrants to Western, industrialized states—will display similarities in codeswitching meanings and practices. Thus, Italian–German switching among the children of Italian labor migrants to German will be similar to that of Spanish–English codeswitching among second-generation Puerto Ricans in the USA, both in terms of patterns and local functions.

Studying multilingualism can be a route to understanding social worlds not because of formal linguistic distinctions among languages, but because of the inherent social and political nature of language. In contexts such as Western societies, where multilingual talk has been made to count as marked and socially meaningful, insights into communicative worlds can come from attention to the social and political processes that have made monolingual versus multilingual speech a meaningful opposition. The processual and socially infused concept of heteroglossia captures the irreducibly sociohistorical and ideological bases of language meaning and use. Heteroglossia encourages us to interpret the meanings of talk in terms of the social worlds, past and present, of which words are part and parcel, rather than in terms of formal systems, such as "languages," that can veil actual speakers, uses, and contexts.

Related topics

Codeswitching; discourses about linguistic diversity.

Further reading

Heller, M. (ed.) (2007) *Bilingualism: A Social Approach*, New York: Palgrave Macmillan.
(In this edited volume, 20 contributors present perspectives that emphasize the social and political embeddedness of multilingualism, countering commonsense assumptions about and notions of multilingualism.)

Holquist, M. (ed.) (1981) *The Dialogic Imagination: Four Essays by M.M. Bakhtin*, C. Emerson and M. Holquist (trans.), Austin: University of Texas Press.
(This volume contains the essay *Discourse in the Novel* in which Bakhtin coins the term "heteroglossia" and lays out his philosophy of language as social.)

Bibliography

Alvarez-Caccamo, C. (1998) 'From "switching code" to "code-switching": Towards a reconceptualisation of communicative codes', in P. Auer (ed.) *Code-Switching in Conversation: Language, Interaction, and Identity*, London and New York: Routledge.
——(2001) 'Codes', in A. Duranti (ed.) *Key Terms in Language and Culture*, Malden, MA: Blackwell.
Bakhtin, M. M. (1981) *The Dialogic Imagination: Four Essays*, M. Holquist (ed.), C. Emerson and M. Holquist (trans.) Austin: University of Texas Press.
Gal, S. (1988) 'The political economy of code choice', in M. Heller (ed.) *Codeswitching: Anthropological and Sociolinguistic Perspectives*, Berlin, New York and Amsterdam: Mouton de Gruyter.
Gumperz, J. J. (1982) *Discourse Strategies*, Cambridge and New York: Cambridge University Press.
Heller, M. (ed.) (2007) *Bilingualism: A Social Approach*, Basingstoke: Palgrave Macmillan.
Ivanov, V. (2001) 'Heteroglossia', in A. Duranti (ed.) *Key Terms in Language and Culture*, Oxford and Malden, MA: Blackwell.
Lipski, J. M. (1994) *Latin American Spanish*, London and New York: Longman.
Meeuwis, M. and Blommaert, J. (1998) 'A monolectal view of code-switching: Layered code-switching among Zairians in Belgium', in P. Auer (ed.) *Code-Switching in Conversation: Language, Interaction and Identity*, London and New York: Routledge.
Myers-Scotton, C. (1993) *Social Motivations for Codeswitching: Evidence from Africa*, Oxford: Clarendon Press.
Peirce, C. S. (1955) 'Logic as semiotic: The theory of signs', in J. Buchler (ed.) *Philosophical Writings of Peirce*, New York: Dover Publications.
Poplack, S. (1980) 'Sometimes I'll start a sentence in Spanish y termino en Espanol: Toward a typology of code-switching', *Linguistics* 18(7–8): 581–618.
——(1988) 'Contrasting patterns of codeswitching in two communities', in M. Heller (ed.) *Codeswitching: Anthropological and Sociolinguistic Perspectives*, Berlin, New York and Amsterdam: Mouton de Gruyter.
Prince, E. (1981) 'Topicalization, focus-movement and Yiddish-movement: A pragmatic differentiation', *Proceedings of the Seventh Annual Meeting of the Berkeley Linguistics Society*: 249–64.
Reddy, M. (1979) 'The conduit metaphor: A case of frame conflict in our language about language', in A. Ortony (ed.) *Metaphor and Thought*, Cambridge: Cambridge University Press.
Saussure, F. de. (1983) *Course in General Linguistics*, London: Duckworth.
Silva-Corvalán, C. (1983) 'On the interaction of word order and intonation: Some OV constructions in Spanish', in F. Klein-Andreu (ed.) *Discourse Perspectives on Syntax*, New York: Academic Press, Inc.
Silverstein, M. (1976) 'Shifters, linguistic categories, and cultural description', in K. Basso and H. A. Selby (eds) *Meaning in Anthropology*, Albuquerque: University of New Mexico Press.
Swigart, L. (1992) 'Two codes or one? The insiders's view and the description of codeswitching in Dakar', *Journal of Multilingual and Multicultural Development* 13: 83–102.
Urciuoli, B. (1996) *Exposing Prejudice: Puerto Rican Experiences of Language, Race, and Class*, Boulder, CO: Westview Press.
Woolard, K. A. (2004) 'Codeswitching', in A. Duranti (ed.) *A Companion to Linguistic Anthropology*, Malden, MA: Blackwell.
Zentella, A. C. (1997) *Growing up Bilingual: Puerto Rican Children in New York*, Malden, MA: Blackwell.

30

Multilingual literacies

Doris S. Warriner

Introduction

Although multilingualism is a centuries-old phenomenon, debates about the value of multi-lingualism and multilingual literacies in social, educational, and workplace contexts continue to attract great interest in scholarly and public conversations worldwide (Hornberger 2009). This is especially true in geographic contexts where the constant movement of people, goods, ideas, and practices has become increasingly commonplace, and this is clearly demonstrated by the sig-nificant body of research conducted on literacy and biliteracy among (emergent, partial, and fluent) bilinguals from a range of linguistic, cultural, and national backgrounds. Over the past three decades, the research conducted on bi-multilingual literacies has provided nuanced accounts of the non-linear dimensions of literacy development, including how multiple literacies interact, and the socially situated ways in which bi-multiliteracy might facilitate language revitalization efforts, intergroup connections, and academic achievement. In addition, research on multilingual literacies has added to our understanding of the relationship between trans-national processes, social practices, and the social identities of multilingual learners themselves. At the same time, the field remains relatively new, and so we are still actively trying to identify the actual processes by which the transnational movement of people and ideas contributes to language contact and change, influences the relative prestige and power of local languages and literacies, or impacts the interactional dynamics and educational opportunities of multilingual peoples. Of particular interest is the influence of literacy in and through two or more languages on the locally specific ways that multilingual peoples might live, work, and learn together. The field also continues to wrestle with the many logistical and pedagogical challenges that arise when attempts are made to enact educational policies that would support, foster, or curtail multilingual literacies, especially in a time of increased standardization and accountability worldwide.

This chapter aims to provide an overview of research on multilingual literacies in order to historicize and contextualize such developments and challenges, to highlight foundational theories and key developments in the field, to synthesize recent work, and to indicate promis-ing directions for future research. I begin with early developments in the study of multilingual literacies, move to a discussion of theory and method, outline the policy implications of recent research, and provide an overview on new research directions. The chapter not only addresses the large amount of research conducted since the 1980s on the topic of multilingual literacies, it illustrates how theoretical advances might inform both methodological approaches and pedagogical practices. By highlighting representative work on multilingual literacies, I demonstrate how influential theories and advances in methodological approaches have informed the investigation of social practices and situated processes that are highly consequential for bi-multilingual individuals and communities worldwide. I also highlight conceptual advances that have been made in recent work, while identifying some of the central tensions/questions that remain under-theorized or unexplored. In addition to providing an overview and update on representative work in the field, the chapter will inform the ongoing work of educational researchers, educational anthropologists, and/or applied linguists who seek to examine the actual practices and processes by which multilingual literacies are promoted or sustained in an increasingly interconnected world. Drawing on exemplary work in applied linguistics, sociolinguistics, educational anthropology, and language planning/policy, this chapter will be of interest to educational researchers, policy makers, and practitioners (teachers and administrators) who are committed to providing more equitable learning opportunities for the large and growing number of students from multicultural, transnational, and multilingual backgrounds.

Before embarking on this journey, however, I wish to provide a few definitions and clarifications. First, it is important to note that I draw on Hornberger's (1990: 213) definition of biliteracy/multiliteracy as "any and all instances in which communication occurs in two (or more) languages in or around writing." Further, I understand multilingual literacies to be instances of social practice that are situated in specific local contexts but also influenced by a range of social, cultural, political, institutional, ideological, and interactional factors. Multilingual literacies are therefore uniquely realized in specific situational contexts *and* subject to influences (material, discursive, and ideological) that are broadly defined and widely circulating (Warriner 2009). For this reason, the topic of multilingual literacies provides an ideal basis for examining the complex relationships, tensions, and contradictions that exist in the spaces between locally situated practices and historical influences (Warriner 2004a, 2007a, 2009; see also Holland and Lave 2001).

In addition, I would like to clarify the intended scope and focus of this chapter. Although some might include mention of any work about multilingualism (without a focus on literacy per se) and/or the work on literacy as a socially situated practice (without explicit reference to biliteracy or multiliteracy) in a chapter such as this, I have decided to narrow the scope and focus on work that explicitly addresses questions about literacy development, literacy practices, and the consequences of literacy as experienced by bi-multilingual individuals and in communities.

Early developments in the field

Starting in the mid-1980s, Edelsky (1986) and Hornberger (1988, 1989) produced groundbreaking research on the reading and writing practices of bilingual or multilingual students living in the American Southwest and Peru. Although coming out of different research contexts, both researchers identified similar kinds of phenomenon in each of their respective settings. For instance, both recognized that something distinct and noteworthy was occurring among the students they interviewed and observed, particularly with regard to their efforts to read and write in two languages within contexts heavily influenced by ideologies of language that devalued minoritized languages and their speakers. With a focus on the role of reading and writing in two languages in fostering emergent or existing bilingualism, their work provided powerful examples of the crucial role of biliteracy in both maintaining and strengthening the languages, the identities, and the communities of immigrant and Indigenous students. With regard to "the experimental bilingual education project of Puno [Peru]," Hornberger (1988, 1989) found that the active promotion of a minority language such as Quechua in local classrooms served as a critical mechanism by which community members might strengthen the language's value and prestige in other community domains. At the same time, she also found that the ideologies of language held by teachers, students, and parents were very resistant to change. Edelsky (1986) also found that myths about language proficiency, biliteracy, and bilingual education were difficult to dismantle, even though her first-hand participant observation and analysis of documents from the site demonstrated powerfully the positive educational consequences associated with actively fostering biliteracy among students in the first-, second- and third-grade classrooms that she observed.

Hornberger would soon develop the *continua of biliteracy* framework in an effort to identify a methodological approach that would allow researchers to explore the nature (and educational consequences) of bi- and multiliteracy among immigrant and refugee learners. This framework was informed by her work in Peru and her subsequent research with Puerto Rican and Cambodian students living in Philadelphia. First proposed in 1989, the framework has developed and expanded over the years to become what Hornberger (2003a: xii) now describes as a "comprehensive yet flexible model to guide educators, researchers, and policy-makers in designing, carrying out, and evaluating educational programs for the development of multilingual learners, each program adapted to its own specific context, media, and contexts."

Also during the 1980s, and taking a more anthropological perspective, language socialization work examined the processes by which bilinguals (emergent, partial and fluent) learned to read and write in two languages. Through rich ethnographic detail, such work demonstrated how language learning and identity construction go hand in hand, as well as the social processes that influence how speakers learn to be a member of a group in and through using the language of that group (see Schieffelin and Gilmore, 1986; Ada's 1988 work with Spanish-speaking parents in the Pájaro Valley, California; Au's 1993 description of literacy instruction in multicultural settings; Hudelson's 1994 account of the literacy development of second language learners; and a study by Jiménez *et al.* 1995 about three children reading strategically in two languages).

The work that was conducted in the late 1980s and throughout the 1990s on processes and practices of biliteracy helped to move the study of second language acquisition, bilingualism, and language socialization forward in significant ways. Researchers understood that although first language learning/literacy and second language learning/literacy were distinct processes, there was also a relationship between them and this relationship had a significant influence on the educational experiences of many second language learners whether they were emergent, partial, or fluent bilinguals. The volume edited by Martin-Jones and Jones (2000) illustrated the influence of multilingualism on literacy, and the influence of literacy on multilingualism. The collection included chapters that laid definitional or conceptual groundwork (e.g. Barton 2000; Martin-Jones and Jones 2000; Street 2000), as well as reports of ethnographic work on multilingualism in urban communities in Britain. For instance, Gregory and Williams (2000) described "unofficial" literacies in the lives of two East London communities; Blackledge (2000) explored issues of power in the socially constructed notion of literacy and illiteracy by focusing on the experiences of Bangladeshi women in Birmingham, and Ran (2000) examined the experiences of Chinese children who lived in Britain learning to read and write at home. By examining the locally situated nature of language and literacy practices in relation to questions and observations about global processes (e.g. immigration, transnationalism, globalization), this kind of work highlighted the value of theorizing the language–literacy–culture–power intersections from an ethnographic perspective. Such work also demonstrated the range and variation of practices that might be considered literacy and, in doing so, inspired later research on the locally specific (sometimes contested) manifestations of multilingual literacies in complex linguistic ecologies.

Key issues of theory and method

Since the early days of research on literacy/biliteracy in multilingual settings, key work in the field has viewed the language and literacy practices that second language learners bring with them to school as a resource. Building on Schieffelin and Gilmore's (1986) language socialization work, this work identified and documented the abilities and resources that multilingual families and communities had, rather than the abilities, resources, or proficiencies it did not have (e.g. Bayley and Schecter 2003; Zentella 2005). Whether highlighting a community's "funds of knowledge" (González et al. 2005; Moll et al. 1992; Velez-Ibanez and Greenberg 1992) or documenting the Spanish-language resources of a minoritized group in California (e.g. Valdes et al. 2006), this kind of approach has had at least two significant implications for teacher education and qualitative research alike. As a result of this research, teachers and teacher educators now appreciate the need to understand and build on the capacities of the students they teach, and this awareness has inspired curricular innovations and pedagogical practices that have improved the educational achievement and biliteracy development of many bilingual students. Unfortunately, however, the "funds of knowledge" work has also been used less productively, by some practitioners, to over-generalize the characteristics and potential contributions of groups or learners that are internally quite diverse.

Recent research has drawn on these various perspectives (language socialization, ecology of language, and funds of knowledge) in examining teaching and learning processes in multi-ethnic and multilingual classrooms in the UK (Martin-Jones and Saxena 2003); in reconceptualizing the literacies of Latina/o youth (Martinez-Roldan and Franquiz 2009); and in documenting biliteracy development among Latina/o and especially Puerto Rican youth in New York City (Mercado 2003, 2005). Additionally, there has been research conducted with Latino families to identify and build an understanding of the multiple kinds of resources, proficiencies, and knowledges that are present in family literacy practices (e.g. Orellana et al. 2003; Reyes and Moll 2008; Reyes et al. 2009; Zentella 2005). Importantly, recent work on multilingual literacies has explored the complicated dimensions of the language and literacy brokering/translation work performed by immigrant youth and re-positioned such youth as capable, resourceful, achieving, and contributing members of classrooms and communities (e.g. Orellana et al. 2003; Orellana and Reynolds 2008; Sánchez 2007).

Another approach to the study of multilingual literacies is captured by the continua of biliteracy framework (Hornberger 1989, 2003a, 2003b), a model that has been used to identify a range of individual-level, institutional-level and societal-level phenomena that influence (bi) literacy practices for bi-multilingual speakers across a range of contexts, in response to diverse audiences, with various purposes, and through different media. The continua of biliteracy framework has clarified the many dimensions of language learning and identified the processes that influence educational achievement (and assessment) and the socially situated nature of such processes. It has also revealed where intersections and tensions exist between and within languages, speakers, locations, and contexts. Although many assume that there is a relationship between the languages and literacies that multilingual learners access and use (e.g. Gort 2006; Reyes 2006; Reyes and Azuara 2008; Reyes and Moll 2008), more work needs to be done to better understand the actual processes and practices involved in bi-multilingual literacies. In particular, the complicated relationship between first language literacy and second language learning/literacy promises to become an important future direction for the field, in large part because the exact nature of that relationship is still little understood (August and Shanahan 2006; Berríz 2000; Caldas 2006; Lanauze and Snow 1989; Martínez-Roldán 2006; Pérez and Torres-Guzmán 2002). An important focus of this future work will be on whether two sets of literacies might interact during literacy/biliteracy development, the nature of this interaction, and the potential implications for language policies, pedagogical practices, and theories of learning and language learning (e.g. Dworin 2003; Jiménez et al. 1995, 1996; Moll and Dworin 1996; Valdés 2004).

Other approaches to the study of multilingual literacies involve the exploration of the connections and relationships between individuals, groups, institutions, systems, or ideologies (e.g. de La Piedra 2006; Ernst-Slavit 1997; Garcia et al. 2006; Garcia and Bartlett 2007; Hornberger 2003b; 2006b; 2009; Martínez-Roldán 2006, 2004; Watahomigie and McCarty 1996). The examination of such relationships has often relied on an explicitly or implicitly ecological perspective. For some, the goal has been to recognize and value certain interactional dynamics between speakers as representatives of particular communities of practice. In such research, there has been an increased and demonstrated commitment to understanding how processes—individual, social, ideological, material—are intimately connected, mutually influential, and yet also sometimes internally contradictory. The assumption is that multilingual literacies are influenced by individual actions, interactional dynamics, educational policies, societal norms, language ideologies, institutional constraints, and material realities.

At the same time, and in spite of the emergence of new directions, there continues to be great interest in questions that have challenged the field of literacy studies for some time. These are questions such as what counts as literacy, under what circumstances, and according to whose definition, whose literacy counts, and how we should conceptualize the relationship between literacy and social, economic, and political change (Bartlett 2008; Robinson-Pant 2004; Rubenstein-Avila 2007; Street 1984, 2000). Increasingly, recent work on multilingualism and multiliteracies has taken up these and a range of other questions about the processes involved in the transnational movement of people, goods, ideas, and practices (e.g. Bartlett 2007; Rubenstein-Avila 2007; Sánchez 2007; Warriner 2007a, 2007b, 2009). For instance, Rubenstein-Avila (2007: 571) explores "how living in a transnational space affects immigrant students' literacy practices and their values, perspectives, beliefs, and actions in relation to literacy." Also, Bartlett (2007: 215) paints a detailed portrait of one transnational student from the Dominican Republic and how she "drew upon the locally defined model of school success to position herself—and be positioned—as a successful student through bilingual literacy practices."

The work on multilingual literacies described here shares an orientation to literacy and biliteracy as situated, contested, social practices—where languages (and linguistic competencies) are more related than distinct, where orality and literacy are viewed as related points on a continuum rather than polar opposites, where context is defined not only situationally but also interactionally, and where the analysis of contemporary linguistic ecologies takes into account questions of discourse, ideology, and power. As a result, it is clear that any effort to investigate how bilinguals become biliterate, and with what consequence, takes place within an exceedingly complicated terrain. Moreover, newer questions have arisen from more theoretically grounded approaches and newer, more robust methodological approaches are being developed.

Policy issues

Within this context, researchers, policy makers, teachers, and parents face increasingly urgent and controversial questions about whether and how educational policies might be used to promote the linguistic resources of (im)migrant or Indigenous learners in order to facilitate their educational, social, and economic inclusion and opportunity. A number of scholars have pursued such research agendas and made a variety of valuable contributions to our collective understanding of how multilingual literacies are fostered and maintained across a variety of contexts. In Tollefson and Tsui's (2004) edited book, contributors explore how the "medium of instruction policies" in various national contexts has managed to promote language learning and literacy development in ways that foster language revitalization, bilingualism and biliteracy, or ethnolinguistic nationalism. Zakharia (2008, 2009) too describes the language policy implications of medium of instruction debates in contemporary Lebanon in relation to questions of nationalism and identity. In the USA there has been a focus on the influence of national initiatives such as Reading First and No Child Left Behind (NCLB) on multilingual learners' language learning and literacy development. For instance, Caldas (2006) explores how bilingual–biliterate children are being raised in monolingual cultures; Rivera and Collum (2006) examine state assessment policy for English language learners; Menken (2008) examines the ways that the standardized testing craze operates as a de facto language policy that dramatically influences the educational and language learning opportunities available to English-language learners in US schools; and McCarty (2009) examines the impact of high-stakes testing practices (e.g. those found in NCLB) on Native American learners.

Hornberger (2003b) has described multilingual language policies from an ecology of language perspective with a focus on the ways that biliteracy development is context-dependent and therefore subject to the influences of local power relations. In recent work she has used this framework to explore a number of language policy issues such as the roles of voice and biliteracy in indigenous language revitalization efforts in Quechua, Guarani, and Maori contexts (Hornberger 2006a); multilingual language policy and school linguistic practices in India, Singapore, and South Africa (Hornberger and Vaish 2009); and ten "certainties" about multilingual education policy based on ethnographic work done with Indigenous teachers and learners across multiple continents over the past three decades (Hornberger 2009). Hornberger (ibid.) argues that "multilingual education is in its essence an instance of biliteracy" (2009: 198) and describes the very central role that literacy plays in Indigenous language revitalization to support this claim.

García et al. (2006) have proposed that we should reimagine bilingualism and biliteracy as critical components of multilingual schools in an age of "glocalization." Their edited volume showcases recent work by prominent scholars in the field and focuses on issues such as the creative construction of identity through multiliteracies pedagogy (Cummins 2006); the process of "reimagining multilingual America" by examining the lived experiences of Native American youth (McCarty et al. 2006a, 2006b; McCarty and Zepeda 2010); "monolingual assessment and emerging bilinguals" (Escamilla 2006); US language education policy from Lau v. Nichols (1974) to the present, including No Child Left Behind (Hornberger 2006b); multilingualism and Indigenous education in Latin America (López 2006); and questions of class in relation to mother tongue education in India (Mohanty 2006).

New research directions

One exciting development in the study of multilingual literacies has been a demonstrated interest in exploring different kinds of movement (of people, ideas, goods, and practices) in relation to literacy practices, identity issues, and educational opportunities. Drawing on insights from semiotics, the anthropology of space and place, sociology, sociology of language, and cultural studies, literacy scholars have recently examined the local manifestations of intersections and contestations inherent in, and constitutive of, far-reaching global processes. Contributions to a special issue of *Linguistics and Education* on "Transnational Literacies: Immigration, Language Learning and Identity" examined the specific ways that literacy and identity trajectories might be traced across time and space; how multiple literacies—and identities—could be created, narrated, and transformed by individual actors living in particular contexts; and the importance of thinking and writing in "spatial terms" while investigating such processes. In the "Introduction" to that special issue, I wrote: "By examining the literacy practices of different immigrant learners across contexts of home, school and community through a transnational lens, the authors make visible the specific ways that literacy practices, as one type of 'situated cultural practice', influence and mediate situated learning, social identity formation and transformation, and historically structured processes" (Warriner 2007a: 213).

A rapidly growing body of work has explored questions of transnationalism and transnationality in relation to migrants' use of digital technologies and their digital literacies (e.g. Black 2007, 2009; Jacquemet 2005; Lam 2000, 2006, 2009, Lam and Rosario-Ramos 2009; Lee 2007; McGinnis *et al.* 2007; Yi 2009). The focus in such work is on literacy practices that are used to create transnational social and information networks by immigrant youth (Lam and Rosario-Ramos 2009); the "development of multiliteracies in the context of transnational migration and new media of communication" (Lam 2009); and the attendant identities that are often negotiated through participation on online processes (Yi 2009). In addition, some of this work has examined the specific ways that English-language learners design digital futures and identities through participation in online fan fiction (Black 2007); how new media and technologies might influence "modern configurations of imagination, identity, communication, and writing" (Black 2009); and the "text-making practices" that are evident in instant messaging (IM) (Lee 2007). Collectively, this growing body of research on information communication technologies has enhanced our understanding of multilingual literacies by illuminating the various ways that transnationalism and globalization might be investigated through the lens (empirical and theoretical) of digital literacy practices. This work has also highlighted the complicated relationship between movement (of people, ideas, practices), digital literacy practices, and the situated identities of immigrant youth living in increasingly interconnected and globalized contexts. Finally, it raises questions about certain definitions and methodological approaches used to examine such practices. Jacquemet (2005: 257), for instance, calls for a "reconceptualization of what we consider the communicative environment" in order to better understand "communicative practices based on multilingual talk (most of the times exercised by de/reterritorialized speakers) channeled through both local and electronic media."

On other fronts, important work is being done on the complex linguistic ecologies that contribute to, or stand in the way of, language shift. A recent special issue of the *International Journal of the Sociology of Language* (vol. 195) was devoted to the sociolinguistic and subjective aspects of Welsh in Wales and its diaspora, aiming to understand some of the factors contributing to its relative strength and ethnolinguistic vitality. Of particular interest here is the article by Martin-Jones *et al.* (2009: 39) that describes "how the young people's language choices and literacy practices were shaped by the nature of the land-based enterprises they were involved in."

Reporting on circumstances with a more worrisome outcome, contributions to a special issue of the *Journal of Language, Identity and Education* report on ethnographic work in communities undergoing rapid language shift (Lee 2009; McCarty and Wyman 2009; McCarty 2009; Messing 2009; Nicholas 2009). Although the context is North America, where language shift to the dominant/colonizing language has been both recent and rapid, this work highlights new directions in research on Indigenous youth and bilingualism, and the implications of this research for understanding the survival and vitality of Indigenous languages and communities worldwide are vast. Calling their work "explicitly praxis-oriented," the contributors to this volume provide a useful "three-pronged look at contemporary Indigenous youth language practices, communicative repertoires, and language attitudes and ideologies" (McCarty and Wyman 2009: 279).

Concluding comments

Limitations of space have allowed only a brief mention of the vast amount of scholarship on multilingual literacies that has been conducted over the past three decades. My hope is that the reader will find at least some of their interests represented in what I have discussed here and will decide to pursue those interests independently by consulting some of the many references included in the bibliography at the end of the chapter. Although the study of multilingual literacies began decades ago, it remains an exciting and active area of study with far-reaching implications for educational policy and practice as well as theories of second language learning, bilingualism, and literacy development. Drawing on a variety of disciplinary perspectives and methodological approaches, and rejecting deficit views of multilingualism and multiliteracy, recent scholarship has contributed important insights into the social, educational, and economic benefits and advantages of multilingual literacy practices. I expect that the study of multilingual literacies will continue to address issues of curriculum, pedagogy, policy, and opportunity by drawing on relevant insights and contributions from the many fields that inform and expand the study of literacy in two or more languages, including anthropology, sociology, literacy studies, applied linguistics, and education. The study of multilingual literacies, in all its complicated and contradictory manifestations, remains an exciting and promising area of research, and many years of fruitful discovery lie ahead.

Related topics

Indigenous contexts; Indigenous education; linguistic diversity and education; regional minorities, education and language revitalization; multilingual pedagogies; multilingualism and social exclusion; multilingualism on the Internet.

Further reading

Baynham, M. and Prinsloo, M. (eds) (2009) *The Future of Literacy Studies*, Basingstoke: Palgrave Macmillan.
(Introduces what the editors say is "the current third generation empirical work which is pushing the boundaries of literacy research in a number of key directions" (2009: 2). Viewing literacy as social practice that is situated locally and globally, textual, and aesthetic, the authors of this edited volume raise questions about and assert new directions for the future of the field, where mobility, digital literacies, and new modes of meaning-making influence language learning and literacy practices in important ways across a range of geographic contexts.)

González, N., Moll, L. C. and Amanti, C. (eds) (2005) *Funds of Knowledge: Theorizing Practices in Households and Classroom*, Mahwah, NJ: Lawrence Erlbaum.
(Provides a theoretical and methodological overview/guide to conducting research in local communities in order to identify, document and build on the knowledge and life experiences students from such communities bring with them to schools and classrooms. Attempts to alter the perceptions of working-class or poor communities by viewing their households primarily in terms of their strengths and resources, rather than their deficits.)

Hornberger, N. H. (ed.) (2003) *Continua of Biliteracy: An Ecological Framework for Educational Policy, Research, and Practice in Multilingual Settings*, Clevedon: Multilingual Matters.
(Includes a comprehensive history of the development of the continua of biliteracy and explains how the model might guide the design, execution, and evaluation of educational programs for the development of bilingual and multilingual learners. Scholarship draws on the continua framework to analyze instances of biliteracy, programmatic concerns, or policy implications of biliteracy across a range of contexts.)

Martin-Jones, M. and Jones, K. (eds) (2000) *Multilingual Literacies: Reading and Writing Different Worlds*, Amsterdam: John Benjamins.
(Draws on the theories and methodologies from literacy studies and the study of bilingualism to provide compelling portraits of how speakers from a range of contexts read and write in two or more languages. Focusing on the language and literacy experiences of adults and youth, the chapters illuminate the complicated relationship between language, literacy, culture, and identity in multi-ethnic contexts.)

Zentella, A. C. (ed.) (2005) *Building on Strength: Language and Literacy in Latino Families and Communities*, New York and London: Teachers College Press and CABE.
(Examines the role and nature of language socialization in Latino families and communities from a historical, political, and cultural perspective. Demonstrates the diversity within Latino communities while contributing to an enhanced understanding of the conflicting cultural processes that influence language socialization practices.)

Bibliography

Ada, A. F. (1988) 'Experience: Working with Spanish-speaking parents to develop children's reading and writing skills in the home through the use of children's literature', in T. Skutnabb-Kangas and J. Cummins (eds) *Minority Education: From Shame to Struggle,* Clevedon: Multilingual Matters.

Au, K. H. (1993) *Literacy instruction in multicultural settings*, Fort Worth, TX: Harcourt Brace Jovanovich.

August, D. and Shanahan, T. (eds) (2006) *Developing Literacy in Second-Language Learners: Report of the National Literacy Panel on Language-Minority Children and Youth*, Mahwah, NJ: Lawrence Erlbaum.

Bartlett, L. (2008) 'Literacy's verb: Exploring what literacy is and what literacy does', *International Journal of Educational Development* 28(6): 737–53.

——(2007) 'Bilingual literacies, social identification, and educational trajectories', *Linguistics and Education* 18: 215–31.

Barton, D. (2000) 'Foreword', in M. Martin-Jones and K. Jones (eds) *Multilingual Literacies: Reading and Writing Different Worlds*, Amsterdam: John Benjamins.

Bayley, R. and Schecter, S. (eds) (2003) *Language Socialization in Bilingual and Multilingual Societies*, Clevedon: Multilingual Matters.

Berriz, B. (2000) 'Raising children's cultural voices: Strategies for developing literacy in two languages', in Z. Beykont (ed.) *Lifting Every Voice: Pedagogy and Politics of Bilingualism,* Cambridge, MA: Harvard Education Publishing Group.

Black, R. (2007) 'Digital design: English language learners and reader reviews in online fiction', in M. Knobel and C. Lankshear (eds) *A New Literacies Sampler,* New York: Peter Lang.

——(2009) 'Online fan fiction, global identities, and imagination', *Research in the Teaching of English* 43(4): 397–425.

Blackledge, A. (2000) 'Power relations and the social construction of 'literacy' and 'illiteracy': The experience of Bangladeshi women in Birmingham', in M. Martin-Jones and K. Jones (eds) *Multilingual Literacies*, Philadelphia: John Benjamins.

Caldas, S. J. (2006) *Raising Bilingual-Biliterate Children in Monolingual Cultures*, Clevedon: Multilingual Matters.

Cummins, J. (2006) 'Identity texts: The imaginative construction of self through multiliteracies pedagogy', in O. García, T. Skutnabb-Kangas, and M. Torres-Guzmán (eds) *Imagining Multilingual Schools: Languages in Education and Glocalization*, Clevedon: Multilingual Matters.

de La Piedra, T. (2006) 'Literacies and Quechua oral language: Connecting sociocultural worlds and linguistic resources for biliteracy development', *Journal of Early Childhood Literacy* 6(3): 383–406.

Dworin, J. E. (2003) 'Insights into biliteracy development: Toward a bidirectional theory of bilingual pedagogy', *Journal of Hispanic Higher Education* 2: 171–86.

Edelsky (1986) *Writing in a Bilingual Program: Había Una Vez*, Norwood, NJ: Ablex.

Escamilla, K. (2006) 'Monolingual assessment and emerging bilinguals: a case study in the US', in O. García, T. Skutnabb-Kangas, and M. Torres-Guzmán (eds) *Imagining Multilingual Schools: Languages in Education and Glocalization*, Clevedon: Multilingual Matters.

Ernst-Slavit, G. (1997) 'Different words, different worlds: Language use, power and authorized language in a bilingual classroom', *Linguistics and Education* 9: 25–47.

García, O. and Bartlett, L. (2007) 'A speech community model of bilingual education: Educating Latino newcomers in the USA', *International Journal of Bilingual Education and Bilingualism* 10(1): 1–25.

García, O., Skutnabb-Kangas, T. and Torres-Guzmán, M. E. (eds) (2006) *Imagining Multilingual Schools: Languages in Education and Globalization*, Clevedon: Multilingual Matters.

González, N., Moll, L., Floyd Tenery, M., Rivera, A., Rendón, P., Gonzales, R. and Amanti, C. (2005) 'Funds of knowledge for teaching in Latino households', in N. González, L. C. Moll and C. Amanti (eds) *Funds of Knowledge: Theorizing Practices in Households and Classroom*, Mahwah, NJ: Lawrence Erlbaum.

Gort, M. (2006) 'Strategic codeswitching, interliteracy, and other phenomena of emergent bilingual writing: Lessons from first grade dual language classrooms', *Journal of Early Childhood Literacy* 6(3): 323–54.

Gregory, E. and Williams, A. (2000) 'Work or play? 'Unofficial' literacies in the lives of two East London communities', in M. Martin-Jones and K. Jones (eds) *Multilingual Literacies*, Philadelphia: John Benjamins.

Holland, D. and Lave, J. (2001) 'History in person: an introduction', in D. Holland and J. Lave (eds) *History in Person: Enduring Struggles, Contentious Practice, Intimate Identities*, Santa Fe: School of American Research Press.

Hornberger, N. H. (1988) *Bilingual Education and Language Maintenance: A Southern Peruvian Quechua Case*, Providence, RI: Foris Publications.

——(1989) 'Continua of biliteracy', *Review of Educational Research* 59(3): 271–96.

——(1990) 'Creating successful learning contexts for bilingual literacy', *Teachers College Record* 92: 212–29.

——(2003a) 'Introduction', in N. H. Hornberger (ed.) *Continua of Biliteracy: An Ecological Framework for Educational Policy, Research, and Practice in Multilingual Settings*, Clevedon: Multilingual Matters.

——(2003b) 'Multilingual language policies and the continua of biliteracy: An ecological approach', in N. H. Hornberger (ed.) *Continua of Biliteracy: An Ecological Framework for Educational Policy, Research, and Practice in Multilingual Settings*, Clevedon: Multilingual Matters.

——(2006a) 'Voice and biliteracy in Indigenous language revitalization: Contentious educational practices in Quechua, Guarani, and Maori contexts', *Journal of Language, Identity, and Education* 5(4): 277–92.

——(2006b) 'From Nichols to NCLB: Local and global perspectives on US language education policy', in O. García, T. Skutnabb-Kangas and M. Torres-Guzmán (eds) *Imagining Multilingual Schools: Languages in Education and Glocalization*, Clevedon: Multilingual Matters.

——(2009) 'Multilingual education policy and practice: Ten certainties (grounded in Indigenous experience)', *Language Teaching* 42(2): 197–211.

Hornberger, N. H. and Vaish, V. (2009) 'Multilingual language policy and school linguistic practice: Globalization and English-language teaching in India, Singapore, and South Africa', *Compare: A Journal of Comparative Education* 39(3): 305–20.

Hudelson, S. (1994) 'Literacy development of second language children', in F. Genesee (ed.) *Educating Second Language Children*, New York: Cambridge University Press.

——(1999) 'Evaluating reading, valuing the reader', in E. Franklin (ed.) *Reading and Writing in More than One Language: Lessons for Teachers*, Alexandria, VA: Teachers of English to Speakers of Other Languages.

Jacquemet, M. (2005) 'Transidiomatic practices: Language and power in an age of globalization', *Language and Communication* 25: 257–77.

Jiménez, R. T., García, G. E. and Pearson, P. D. (1995) 'Three children, two languages, and strategic reading: Case studies in bilingual/monolingual reading', *American Educational Research Journal* 32(1): 67–97.
——(1996) 'The reading strategies of bilingual Latina/o students who are successful English readers: Opportunities and obstacles', *Reading Research Quarterly* 31: 90–112.
Lam, W. S. E. (2000) 'Literacy and the design of the self: A case study of a teenager writing on the internet', *TESOL Quarterly* 34: 457–82.
——(2006) 'Re-envisioning language, literacy, and the immigrant subject in new mediascapes', *Pedagogies: An International Journal* 1(3): 171–95.
——(2009) 'Multiliteracies on instant messaging in negotiating local, translocal, and transnational affiliations: A case of an adolescent immigrant', *Reading Research Quarterly* 44(4).
Lam, W. S. E. and Rosario-Ramos, E. (2009) 'Multilingual literacies in transnational digitally-mediated contexts: An exploratory study of immigrant teens in the U.S', *Language and Education* 23(2): 171–90.
Lanauze, M. and Snow, C. (1989) 'The relation between first- and second-language writing skills: Evidence from Puerto Rican elementary school children in bilingual programs', *Linguistics and Education* 1: 323–39.
Lee, Carmen K. M. (2007) 'Affordances and text-making practices in online instant messaging', *Written Communication* 24(3): 223–49.
Lee, T. S. (2009) 'Language, identity, and power: Navajo and pueblo young adults' perspectives and experiences with competing language ideologies', *Journal of Language, Identity and Education* 8(4): 307–20.
López, L. E. (2006) 'Cultural diversity, multilingualism and indigenous education in Latin America', in O. García, T. Skutnabb-Kangas and M. Torres-Guzmán (eds) *Imagining Multilingual Schools: Languages in Education and Glocalization,* pp. 238–61, Clevedon, UK: Multilingual Matters.
McCarty, T. L. (2009) 'The impact of high-stakes accountability policies on Native American learners: Evidence from research', *Teaching Education* 20(1): 7–29.
McCarty, T. L., Romero-Little, M. E. and Zepeda, O. (2006a) 'Reimagining multilingual America: lessons from Native American youth', in O. García, T. Skutnabb-Kangas and M. Torres-Guzmán (eds) *Imagining Multilingual Schools: Languages in Education and Glocalization,* Clevedon: Multilingual Matters.
——(2006b) 'Native American youth discourses on language shift and retention: Ideological cross-currents and their implications for language planning', *International Journal of Bilingual Education and Bilingualism* 9(5): 659–77.
McCarty, T. L., Romero-Little, M. E., Warhol., L. and Zepeda, O. (2009) '"I'm speaking English instead of my culture": Portraits of language use and change among Native American youth', in M. Farr, L. Seloni and J. Song (eds) *Ethnolinguistic Diversity and Education,* New York: Routledge.
McCarty, T. L. and Wyman, L. (2009) 'Introduction: Indigenous youth and bilingualism: Theory, research, praxis', *Journal of Language, Identity and Education* 8(4): 279–90.
McCarty, T. L. and Zepeda, O. (2010) 'Native Americans', in J. A. Fishman and O. García (eds) *Language and Ethnic Identity,* vol. 1: *Disciplinary and Regional Perspectives,* 2nd edn, Oxford: Oxford University Press.
McGinnis, T., Goodstein-Stolzenberg, A. and Costa Saliani, E. (2007) '"indnpride": Online spaces of transnational youth as sites of creative and sophisticated literacy and identity work', *Linguistics and Education* 18(3): 283–304.
Martin-Jones, M., Hughes, B. and Williams, A. (2009) 'Bilingual literacy in and on working lives on the land: Case studies of young Welsh speakers in North Wales', *International Journal of the Sociology of Language* 195(1): 39–62.
Martin-Jones, M. and Jones, K. (2000) 'Introduction: Multilingual literacies', in M. Martin-Jones and K. Jones (eds) *Multilingual Literacies,* Philadelphia: John Benjamins.
Martin-Jones, M. and Saxena, M. (2003) 'Bilingual resources and "funds of knowledge" for teaching and learning in multi-ethnic classrooms in Britain', *International Journal of Bilingual Education and Bilingualism* 6(3/4): 267–82.
Martínez-Roldán, C. M. (2006) 'Linguistic borderlands: Latino students' transactions with narrative texts', *Journal of Early Childhood Literacy* 6(3): 293–322
Mardínez Roldán, C. M. and Malavé, G. (2004) 'Language ideologies mediating literacy and identity in bilingual contexts,' *Journal of Early Childhood Literacy* 4(2), 155–180.

Martínez-Roldán, C. M. and Franquiz, M. (2009) 'Latino/a youth literacies: Hidden funds of knowledge', in *Handbook of Adolescent Literacy*, New York: Guilford Press.

Menken, K. (2008) *English Learners Left Behind: Standardized Testing as Language Policy*, Clevedon: Multilingual Matters.

Mercado, C. (2003) 'Biliteracy development among Latino youth in New York City communities: An unexploited potential', in N. H. Hornberger (ed.) *Continua of Biliteracy: An Ecological Framework for Educational Policy, Research, and Practice in Multilingual Settings*, Clevedon: Multilingual Matters.

——(2005) 'Seeing what's there: Language and literacy funds of knowledge in New York Puerto Rican homes', in A. C. Zentella (ed.) *Building on Strength: Language and Literacy in Latino Families and Communities*, New York and London: Teachers College Press.

Messing, J. (2009) '"I didn't know you knew Mexicano!" Shifting ideologies, identities, and ambivalence among youth in Tlaxcala, Mexico', *Journal of Language, Identity and Education* 8(4): 350–64.

Mohanty, A. K. (2006) 'Multilingualism of the unequals and predicaments of education in India: Mother tongue or other tongue?' in O. García, T. Skutnabb-Kangas and M. E. Torres-Guzmán (eds) (2006) *Imagining Multilingual Schools: Languages in Education and Globalization*, Clevedon: Multilingual Matters.

Moll, L., Amanti, C., Neff, D. and González, N. (1992) 'Funds of knowledge for teaching: Using a qualitative approach to connect homes and classrooms', *Theory into Practice* 31(2): 132–41.

Moll, L. C. and Dworin, J. E. (1996) 'Biliteracy development in classrooms: Social dynamics and cultural possibilities', in D. Hicks (ed.) *Discourse, Learning and Schooling: An Interdisciplinary Perspective*, Cambridge: Cambridge University Press.

Nicholas, S. E. (2009) '"I live Hopi; I just don't speak it": The critical intersection of language, culture, and identity in the contemporary lives of Hopi youth', *Journal of Language, Identity and Education* 8(4): 321–34.

Orellana, M. F. and Reynolds, J. F. (2008) 'Cultural modeling: Leveraging bilingual skills for school paraphrasing tasks'. *Reading Research Quarterly*, 43(1): 48–65.

Orellana, M. F., Reynolds, J., Dorner, L. and Meza, M. (2003) 'In other words: Translating or "para-phrasing" as a family literacy practice in immigrant households', *Reading Research Quarterly* 38(1): 12–34.

Pérez, B. and Torres-Guzmán, M. (2002) *Learning in Two Worlds: An Integrated Spanish/English Biliteracy Approach*, 3rd edn, Boston, MA: Allyn & Bacon.

Ran, A. (2000) 'Learning to read and write at home: The experience of Chinese families in Britain', in M. Martin-Jones and K. Jones (eds) *Multilingual Literacies: Reading and Writing Different Worlds*, Amsterdam: John Benjamins.

Reyes, I. (2006) 'Exploring connections between emergent biliteracy and bilingualism', *Journal of Early Childhood Literacy* 6(3): 267–92.

Reyes, I. and Azuara, P. (2008) 'Emergent biliteracy in Young Mexican immigrant children', *Reading Research Quarterly* 43(4): 374–98.

Reyes, I. and Moll, L. (2008) 'Bilingual and biliterate practices at home and school', in B. Spolsky and F. Hult (eds) *The Handbook of Educational Linguistics*, Malden, MA: Blackwell.

Reyes, I., Wyman, L., González, N., Rubenstein Avila, E., Spear-Ellinwood, L., Gilmore, P. and Moll, L. C. (2009). 'What do we know about the discourse patterns of diverse students in multiple settings?', in L. Morrow, R. Rueda, and D. Lapp (eds) *Handbook of Research of Literacy Instruction: Issues of Diversity, Policy, and Equity*, New York: Guilford Press.

Rivera, C. and Collum, E. (eds) (2006) *State Assessment Policy and Practice for English Language Learners*, Mahwah, NJ: Lawrence Erlbaum.

Robinson-Pant, A. (2004) *Women, Literacy, and Development: Alternative Perspectives*, New York: Routledge.

Rubenstein-Avila, E. (2007) 'From the Dominican Republic to Drew High: What counts as literacy for Yanira Lara?' *Reading Research Quarterly* 42(4): 568–89.

Sánchez, P. (2007) 'Cultural authenticity and transnational Latina youth: Constructing a meta-narrative across borders', *Linguistics and Education* 18(3&4): 258–82.

Schieffelin, B. and Gilmore, P. (1986) *The Acquisition of Literacy: Ethnographic Perspectives*, Norwood, NJ: Ablex.

Street, B. (1984) *Literacy in Theory and Practice*, New York: Cambridge University Press.

——(2000) 'Literacy events and literacy practices: Theory and practice in the New Literacy Studies', in M. Martin-Jones and K. Jones (eds) *Multilingual Literacies: Reading and Writing Different Worlds,* Amsterdam: John Benjamins.

——(2000) 'Literacy events and literacy practices: theory and practice in the New Literacy Studies', in M. Martin-Jones and K. Jones (eds) *Multilingual Literacies,* Philadelphia: John Benjamins.

Tollefson, J. W. and Tsui, A. B. M. (2004) *Medium of Instruction Policies: Which Agenda? Whose Agenda?* Mahwah, NJ: Lawrence Erlbaum.

Valdés, G. (2004) 'Between support and marginalization: The development of academic language in linguistic minority children', *Bilingual Education and Bilingualism* 7(2–3): 102–30.

Valdés, G., Fishman, J. A., Chavez, R. and Perez, W. (2006) *Developing Minority Language Resources: The Case of Spanish in California,* Clevedon: Multilingual Matters.

Velez-Ibanez, C. and Greenberg, J. (1992) 'Formation and transformation of funds of knowledge among U.S. Mexican households', *Anthropology and Education Quarterly* 23(4): 313–35.

Warriner, D. S. (2004a) '"The days now is very hard for my family": The negotiation and construction of gendered work identities among newly arrived women refugees', *Journal of Language, Identity, and Education* 3(4): 279–94.

——(2004b) 'Multiple literacies and identities: The experiences of two women refugees', *Women's Studies Quarterly* 32(1–2): 179–95.

——(2007a) 'Introduction: Transnational literacies: Immigration, language learning and identity', *Linguistics and Education* 18(3–4): 201–14.

——(2007b) '"It's just the nature of the beast": Re-imagining the literacies of schooling', *Linguistics and Education* 18(3–4): 305–24.

——(2009) 'Transnational literacies: Examining global flows through the lens of social practice', in M. Baynham and M. Prinsloo (eds) *The Future of Literacy Studies,* New York: Palgrave Macmillan.

Watahomigie, J. and McCarty, T. (1996) 'Literacy for what? Hualapai literacy and language maintenance', in N. H. Hornberger (ed.) *Indigenous Literacies in the Americas: Language Planning from the Bottom Up,* Berlin: Mouton de Gruyter.

Yi, Y. (2009) 'Adolescent literacy and identity construction among 1.5 generation students: From a transnational perspective', *Journal of Asian Pacific Communication* 19(1): 100–29.

Zakharia, Z. (2008) 'Heteroglossic bilingual education policy: The Arab Middle East and North Africa', in O. García (ed.) *Bilingual Education in the 21st Century: A Global Perspective,* Oxford: Blackwell.

——(2009) 'Language-in-education policies in contemporary Lebanon: youth perspectives', in O. Abi-Mershed (ed.) *Trajectories of Education in the Arab World: Legacies and Challenges,* New York: Routledge.

Zentella, A. C. (2005) 'Premises, promises, and pitfalls of language socialization research in Latino families and communities', in A. C. Zentella (ed.) *Building on Strength: Language and Literacy in Latino Families and Communities,* New York and London: Teachers College Press and CABE.

31

Multilingualism and multimodality

Vally Lytra

Introduction

Recent studies of multilingualism in different societies have questioned the notion of languages as whole, bounded systems and have argued for a view of language 'as a set of resources which circulate in unequal ways in social networks and discursive spaces, and whose meaning and values are socially constructed within the constraints of social organizational processes, under specific historical conditions' (Heller 2007: 2). This understanding of language foregrounds the political and sociohistorical associations of linguistic forms and characterizes language users as social actors. It stresses the different ways language users are constantly employing, creating, and interpreting sets of linguistic resources to communicate across contexts and participants and perform their different subjectivities. This means that 'participants' awareness of "language" or "code" is backgrounded and "signs" are combined and put to work in the message being negotiated at hand' (Creese and Blackledge 2010a: 2; also Creese and Blackledge 2010b; Blackledge and Creese 2010). This conceptualization of language captures the heteroglossic nature of communication, or what Bailey describes as '(a) the simultaneous use of different kinds of forms or signs and (b) the tensions and conflicts among those signs, based on the sociohistorical associations they carry with them' (2007: 257). The focus on signs and sets of linguistic resources affords new analytical insights into our understanding of language and human interaction more generally as essentially social. Although acknowledging that linguistic signs are the primary semiotic tools for representing and negotiating meaning and social relations, this focus can account for the increasing recognition in current research on multilingualism of the highly multimodal nature of communication. Following Pahl and Rowsell, in this chapter multimodality refers to 'communication in the widest sense, including gesture, oral performance, artistic, linguistic, digital, electronic, graphic and artefact-related' (2006: 6).

In the ensuing sections, I present key issues of theory and method and review some of the relevant literature that merges multilingualism with a multimodal perspective in an attempt to map key areas of the research space. I go on to explore the intersection of multilingualism and multimodality by drawing on my own research of classroom talk and action in Turkish complementary (community) schools in London. I conclude this chapter with a brief discussion of directions for future research.

Key issues of theory and method

There are a number of disciplines and theoretical approaches that have sought to explore aspects of the multimodal communicational landscape. Jewitt traces the theoretical underpinnings of multimodality to linguistics, in particular Halliday's social semiotic theory of communication (Halliday 1978) but also to cognitive and sociocultural research (e.g. Arnheim 1969) as well as anthropological and social approaches (e.g. Goffman 1979) (Jewitt 2008: 357–58).

One influential approach that has contributed to theory-building in multimodality is social semiotics. Multimodal social semiotics, as it is widely referred to, focuses on signs of all kinds, in all forms, the sign makers and the social environments in which these signs are produced (Kress et al. 2005: 22). Bezemer and Kress usefully define a 'mode' as 'a socially and culturally shaped resource for making meaning' (e.g. image, writing, speech, moving image, action, artefacts) (2008: 6; also Kress and van Leeuwen 2001). They go on to argue that meaning makers or 'sign makers' can make meaning drawing on a variety of modes that do not occur in isolation but always with others in ensembles. Moreover, different modes may share similar and/ or different 'modal resources' [italics in the original] (e.g. writing has syntactic, grammatical, graphic resources whereas image has resources that include the position of elements in a frame, size, colour, shape). These differences in resources, they further argue, have important implications for the ways modes can be used to accomplish different kinds of semiotic work, which means that 'modes have different affordances [italics in the original] – potentials and constraints for making meaning' (ibid.). Bezemer and Kress point out that a discussion of different modes for meaning making and their affordances needs to be considered together with the medium of distribution involved (e.g. print, electronic, digital) (2008: 7).

Multimodal social semiotics views linguistic signs (both monolingual and multilingual) as part of a wider repertoire of modal resources that sign makers have at their disposal and that carry particular sociohistorical and political associations. As Kress et al. elaborate in their description of English as core subject in urban multilingual classrooms,

> signs are always multimodal and each modality brings the possibility of expressing and shaping meanings. A poster, part of a display on a wall for example, is a complex of signs: it may be a student's handwritten text, left with spelling and grammatical slips rather than the word-processed writing of an official document, carefully edited, mounted on board rather than pinned up, laminated maybe, displayed in a prominent position or perhaps somewhere barely noticeable. When we look at such a post-sign the many meanings made as signs in the various modes are there in one complex multimodal sign.
>
> *(2005: 22)*

In this approach, language is seen as a central mode of communication but at the same time it is examined in relation to the other modes that sign makers can choose from for meaning making and social identification. In this sense, a multimodal semiotic approach to meaning making can provide 'a fuller, richer and more accurate sense of what language is, and what it is not' (2005: 2). Kress et al. further argue that

> where before there was a common sense about the capacities of language, which left the potentials of what language can do in many ways implicit and unexamined, now, looking at language in the context of other means of making meaning gives the possibility of a much sharper, more precise, and more nuanced understanding both of the (different) potentials of speech and of writing, and of their limitations.
>
> *(ibid.)*

The multimodal social semiotic approach is thus congruous with recent perspectives on multilingualism that view language as essentially social instead of neutral or ahistorical (cf. Heller 2007; Creese and Blackledge 2010a; Blackledge and Creese 2010).

Recent research on multilingualism has been inspired by the multimodal social semiotics approach and has stretched our understanding of the ways children combine different modes and media across social contexts and negotiate social identities. Kenner reports on how bilingual/ biliterate young children learn different writing systems (English, Chinese, Arabic and Spanish) at home, in the complementary and in the mainstream primary school in the UK. Her work illustrates how a focus on different modes, including the children's sets of linguistic resources, can foreground the different culture-specific ways multilingual children mesh the visual and actional modes (i.e. make use of shape, size and location of symbols on the page, directionality, type of stroke) in the process of learning how to write in two languages (2004: 75). Moreover, such a focus shows the different ways multilingual children combine and juxtapose scripts as well as explore connections and differences between their available writing systems in their text making. By drawing on more than one set of linguistic and other modal resources to construct bilingual texts in settings where multilingual communication was encouraged, Kenner argued, children could 'express their sense of living in multiple social and cultural worlds' (2004: 118).

One important line of research that has developed from the increasing recognition of the need to situate language within a much broader communication landscape combines the theoretical perspectives of multimodality and literacy, in particular the New Literacy Studies approach, offering as Jewitt argues 'a distinct theoretical accent to multimodality' (2008: 359). The New Literacy Studies radically reconceptualized the nature of literacy from a neutral set of skills that are acquired across different contexts to 'a set of social practices' that are 'embedded in relations of culture and power in specific contexts' (Prinsloo and Baynham 2008: 2). The theoretical insights afforded by combining multimodality and the New Literacy Studies perspectives have been usefully extended to research on multilingualism, in the study of multilingual texts, talk and practices. This line of research provides a unique point of entry into approaching multilingual texts as material objects and understanding how multilingual practices are situated within a web of multimodal practices (cf. Pahl and Rowsell 2006).

In her own research, Pahl has fruitfully combined these theoretical approaches to study children's multimodal/multilingual text production (e.g. drawings, oral and written narratives). Pahl shows how 'visual and verbal resources were interwoven to construct a richly patterned narrative' within homes (2004: 339). These narratives, she maintains, link together stories with visual displays (e.g. drawings, material artefacts) and photographs spanning time frames and geographical spaces. They illustrate how meaning is made by the combination of different modes and how it links with processes of (bi-)cultural identity construction. These findings resonate with work by Sánchez focusing on how immigrant students draw on different language and literacy practices for the presentation of self as they co-author a bilingual (Spanish–English) children's picture book documenting their cross-border (USA–Mexico) experience in the context of an out-of-school literacy project (2007: 259). She concurs with Pahl about the centrality of artefacts in the triggering of family narratives from or about Mexico and shows how the authors/illustrators make use of pictorial artefacts in the bilingual book scenes with the view of generating similar family bilingual/bicultural narratives of transnational experiences among their young readers (2007: 277).

The conceptual link between multilingualism, multimodality and the New Literacy Studies has provided a wealth of insights into the ways participants mesh different modes and media across contexts and cultural worlds highlighting the ideological nature of both literacy practices and multimodal/multilingual practices in shaping social relations and forms of identity (cf. Street 2008). Stein and Slonimsky's study of literacy practices in three socio-economically, educationally and linguistically diverse Johannesburg homes (in South Africa), shows how adult family members socialize their young children into what counts as 'good reading practices' in their household and how the identities of the children as 'readers' and 'subjects' are constituted (2006: 118). The authors demonstrate how the literacy practices shifted radically from one family to the next as children and adults drew on a range of representational resources (including different sets of linguistic resources) to decode, interpret and transform multimodal texts. During this process, they observed that children were not only socialized into becoming literate in particular ways shaped by culturally established conventions but also into developing particular future orientations and aspirations in the 'real' world (2006: 143).

Drawing on their research on transnational youth and their out-of-school digital practices, McGinnis et al. (2007) illustrate how three young people create their own online texts in the form of blogs and personal webpages to express multiple loyalties. Making use of Kress' (2003) notion of 'design' that is the ways multimodal forms are combined to convey meaning, the authors scrutinize the different layers of the webpages' 'design' to show how the young people mix and juxtapose different sets of linguistic resources, images, streamed video and music to enact their multiple identifications (McGinnis et al. 2007: 299–300). Their online textual practices reveal their ability to communicate across multiple modes, media, languages and geographical spaces in order to create their own spaces where they can engage in local, national and global issues that are of interest to them (2007: 300–1).

By situating participants' multilingual resources and practices within a wider communicational landscape, researchers have been able to provide more detailed and nuanced connections between local and broader institutional and social practices, discourses and processes. Both Stein and Slonimsky (2007) and McGinnis et al. (2007) highlight the need to consider ways to build bridges between the young people's rich multilingual and multimodal experiences outside school with their academic worlds. In Lytra et al. (2010), the authors' investigation of multilingual/multimodal pedagogic practices sheds light on some of the tensions and contradictions about what counts as legitimate modes in Turkish and Gujarati complementary school classrooms in the UK and how these are linked to broader social contexts, such as language hierarchies and language and literacy practices in the countries of origin, the diasporas as well as within and across complementary school settings. Moyer (2010) examines the institutionally supported multilingual/multimodal practices (e.g. translation of written texts, telephone translation services, videos to instruct mothers about how to take care of their children) in a Barcelona health clinic servicing a large migrant clientele. She traces the tensions and conflicts that arise between social actors (e.g. health staff, patients) with asymmetries of social roles, levels of language competence and specialized knowledge as they seek to bridge communication difficulties.

The focus on the use of multiple modes as a point of entry into the investigation of language and human action has also been a concern of studies drawing on sociolinguistics and linguistic anthropology. The work by Goodwin (2000) in particular sets out a theoretical framework to consider how different sets of linguistic resources interact with visual, kinaesthetic and artefact-related resources as well as participation frameworks, larger sequential structures and encompassing activities through which participants display their embodied orientation in the context of, for instance, a dispute over playing hopscotch. Taking as a point of departure that 'in the human sciences in general, language and the material world are treated as entirely separate domains of inquiry' (2000: 1491), Goodwin postulates that a theory of action must come to terms with both the details of language use and the way in which the social, cultural, material and sequential structure of the environment where action occurs, figures into its organization.

(ibid.)

Goodwin develops the concept of 'semiotic fields' to capture the process by which various sign systems (e.g. talk, gesture, posture, graphics) instantiated in different media are juxtaposed and mutually elaborate each other. A cluster of 'semiotic fields', he elaborates, to which participants orient at a given moment is called a 'contextual configuration' (2000: 1490). Both 'semiotic fields' and their 'contextual configurations' are in a continuous process of change as action unfolds: new semiotic fields become relevant whereas others are no longer attended to. The focus on 'semiotic fields' and 'contextual configurations' assumes an understanding of language as grounded in its sociohistorical and political context, which goes against 'the usual analytic and disciplinary boundaries that isolate language from its environment and create a dichotomy between text and context' (ibid.). Like multimodal social semiotics, Goodwin's theory of action within human interaction is thus congruous with recent perspectives on multilingualism, which view language as essentially a social phenomenon.

Theoretical insights from Goodwin's theory of action have inspired research on multilingualism in order to explore how multilingual talk is juxtaposed with other kinds of modes and how 'the human body is made publicly visible as the site for a range of structurally different kinds of displays implicated in the constitution of the actions of the moment' (2000: 1492). In his own research exploring a dispute between three young girls of Mexican and Central American heritage in a playground in California, Goodwin shows how the girls perform the dispute not only via different streams of multilingual talk but also through the simultaneous deployment of different clusters of signs, for example gestures, gaze and bodily displays, which change over time as the interaction unfolds (2000: 1499). Equally importantly, he illustrates how the hopscotch grid on the playground, which is seen as a semiotic structure in the built environment, provides the organizational framework for building the girls' action, which could not exist without it; it is the medium used to determine successful jumps, outs, etc. (2000: 1505; see also Goodwin *et al.* 2002). Inspired by Goodwin's work, Piirainen-Marsh and Tainio (2009) explore collaborative game-play, namely a Japanese fantasy role play game translated and localized into English, among Finnish adolescents. They focus on the juxtaposition and meshing of two boys' sets of linguistic resources (Finnish, English and its varieties) with other modes and media, including the material resources of technology. Like the hopscotch grid in Goodwin's (2000) study, the authors attend to the ways in which the video game provides the material and semiotic structure that shapes interaction between the two game players 'to participate in and constitute the social activity of playing, construct their interpretations of the game and organise their experience of game-play as a meaningful social and situated learning activity' (Piirainen-Marsh and Tainio 2009: 179).

A common methodological focus of research combining theoretical insights from multilingualism and multimodality is ethnography as a methodology. The focus of ethnography of immersing in the field and of uncovering patterns of meanings over time are central to making sense of how local knowledge is built, how 'emic' and 'etic' categories emerge and how the construction of knowledge is linked with broader social, historical and political contexts. Ethnography allows us to view how multilingualism and multimodality intersect and sit in the broader communicational landscape, enabled by rapid technological advances, which in turn have triggered new modes of textual practices and new communities of practice. Green and Bloome make a useful distinction among three approaches to ethnography: 'doing ethnography', 'adopting an ethnographic perspective' and 'using ethnographic tools'. 'Doing ethnography', they argue, involves 'a broad, in-depth, and long-term study of a social or cultural group' (1997: 183), whereas 'adopting an ethnographic perspective' implies taking a 'more focused approach (i.e. doing less than a comprehensive ethnography) to study particular aspects of everyday life and cultural practices of a social group' (ibid.). Finally, 'using ethnographic tools' means making 'use of the methods and techniques usually associated with fieldwork' (1997: 184). From a methodological standpoint, research at the intersection of multilingualism and multimodality is diverse. It includes traditional full-blown ethnographies, as well as more limited studies employing an ethnographic perspective or making use of ethnographic methods. Besides the use of staple ethnographic methods such as participant observation, interview and documentary data and in keeping with the multimodal approach, a number of studies make extensive use of photography, participant diaries and diary interviews, audio and video data as well as different texts, including digital texts, such as weblogs and personal webpages (e.g. Goodwin 2000; Kenner 2004; Lytra *et al.* 2010; Martin-Jones 2009; Martin-Jones *et al.* 2009; McGinnis *et al.* 2007; Sánchez 2007).

Adopting a multimodal lens: insights from recent ethnographic research

This section draws on research from an Economic and Social Research Council funded project that explored multilingualism and identities in complementary schools.[1] The purpose of this section is to investigate the participants' use of different sets of linguistic resources during Turkish literacy teaching and to view these practices through the lens of multimodality. Although a focus on multimodality was not part of the project's research aims, the following data analysis has been inspired by the increasing recognition within educational research that multilingual interaction is more than simply the juxtaposition of sets of linguistic resources (e.g. the collection of papers in Warriner 2007; Martin-Jones 2009). This recognition goes hand in hand with an increasing acceptance that adopting a multimodal lens on classroom interaction more generally is necessary to make sense of the participants' (teachers and pupils) linguistic resources and practices, ways of talking and doing across different classroom settings (e.g. Bezemer 2008; Flewitt 2005; Kenner 2004; Kress *et al.* 2005; Lytra *et al.* 2010; Pahl 2009).

More specifically, the aim of this section is to explore how a group of ten-year-old boys of mainland Turkish and Cypriot-Turkish heritage combined and juxtaposed the use of different sets of linguistic resources with other semiotic resources to engage in music sharing and to evaluate shared songs mediated through mobile phones in a London Turkish literacy class.[2] I examine how the participants drew on strips of talk, their bodies, the material structure in the surround, in particular their mobile phones, the sequential organization of their talk and action, participation frameworks and the encompassing Turkish literacy activities to negotiate their media engagement, construct their interpersonal relationships and display different forms of knowledge and expertise in the complementary school setting. The exploration of the ways the boys combined sets of linguistic resources with other semiotic resources in sharing music and evaluating shared songs provides a point of entry to the investigation of how out-of-school practices and linguistic and cultural resources are transported into the classroom. I argue that the boys' media engagement emerged in parallel with rather than in opposition to their engagement with Turkish literacy learning providing them with an interactional space to negotiate and share linguistic and cultural resources that were sanctioned in the official classroom space. The data were collected over a ten-week data collection period adopting an 'ethnographic perspective' (cf. Green and Bloome 1997). For this section, I draw on participant observations, digital recordings of informal peer talk during literacy teaching and still photography collected in one Turkish literacy class (for a fully fledged description of the project methodology and data collection, see Creese *et al.* 2008).

As I discussed in the introduction to this chapter, the framework of analysis was informed by recent research on multilingualism that views language as social practice and language users as social actors who draw on their linguistic and other semiotic resources in more or less strategic ways to suit their interactional goals (e.g. Creese and Blackledge 2010; Heller 2007). The analysis also draws on studies that have sought to include a multimodal perspective on the investigation of multilingualism and situated interaction. The work by Goodwin (2000) focusing on the here-and-now and the local organization of situated interaction provides useful analytical tools to explore the boys' media engagement, the deployment of their different semiotic resources and the ways these resources shape and are shaped by the affordances of the mobile phone during Turkish literacy teaching. Following Goodwin, the mobile phone is seen as a key 'semiotic artefact' providing 'a crucial framework for the building of action that could not exist without it' (2000: 1505): the boys connect remotely to each other's mobile phones, they share, collect, store, delete, 'hack into', listen to music on their mobile phones, they discuss the different types of features on their mobile phones and evaluate the content of their shared music.

Like the hopscotch grid in Goodwin's (2000) and the video game in Piirainen-Marsh and Tainio's (2009) study, the mobile phone not only provides a semiotic system for the organization of talk and the posturing and orientation of the bodies of the actors but also brings into sharp focus the significance of the mobile phone as a material artefact, built of (more or less) durable material, which has been transported by the boys into the unofficial classroom space.

The analytical focus on the mobile phone as a key 'semiotic and material artefact' calls for the need to situate the data analysis in recent developments in mobile communication studies. The mobile phone has developed into one of the key portable objects young people use to navigate their way in the present-day information-rich era (Ito *et al.* 2005; see also the collection of papers in Katz 2008). Like online spaces (e.g. social network sites, online games, video-sharing sites), mobile phones enable young people to be 'always on'. This allows them to maintain a continuous presence in different contexts, even in settings such as school class-rooms where using mobile phones is explicitly sanctioned. In these settings young people often develop 'work-arounds' or ways to bypass the institutional constraints placed upon them and continue their ongoing media engagement (Ito *et al.* 2008). Most research on mobile commu-nication up to the present has looked at how mobile phones have redefined time, space and social interaction focusing on their multiple uses in interpersonal communication and on the different ways they have been employed to negotiate interpersonal relationships and social identities (e.g. Baron 2008; Ito *et al.* 2005; Spilioti 2007 to mention a few). However, as mobile phones become increasingly multifunctional devices to include features such as web applica-tions, music players, photo and video applications, there is a need to expand the research focus to document an emergent range of digital practices such as using camera phones, mobile gaming and music sharing (cf. Ito *et al.* 2008). This analytical section seeks to contribute to this direction by focusing on two interconnected activities, music sharing and evaluating shared songs.

The boys' engagement with music sharing and evaluating shared songs while the lesson is in full swing raises the question of what happens when such informal out-of-school practices travel into the classroom setting. In this analytical section, I draw on insights from New Literacies Studies, in particular Moje's (2000) research that has sought to explore this question. Moje points out that 'we know little about how adolescents … weave their unsanctioned or alternative literacies together with academic literacies' (2000: 653). She argues that research into the ways that young people, especially marginalized youth, transport their informal literacy practices into the classroom setting has tended to put forth resistance-oriented explanations that advance the view that young people make use of their informal literacy practices during the lesson only in reactive and oppositional ways (2000: 634). She cautions against this approach and suggests examining the proactive ways in which young people draw on their informal literacies during the lesson to explore linkages between their out-of-school and school contexts for meaning making and identity work (ibid.). Besides providing important linkages between contexts, a focus on how out-of-school practices travel into the Turkish heritage language classroom draws our attention to the ways participants intertwine their linguistic resources with other semiotic resources and artefacts in the built environment, highlighting their materiality and multimodal features. Moreover, it draws our attention to the ways this media engagement sits in the pedagogic practices and routines and pervasive language ideologies of Turkish complementary school classrooms.

The following ethnographic vignette documents the pedagogic practices prevalent in the Turkish literacy classroom against which the boys' engagement with their mobile phones emerged. Like other classroom contexts, the use of mobile phones during the lesson was explicitly sanctioned under the watchful eye of the teacher. Nevertheless, this did not stop the boys from transporting their media engagement into the classroom.

Turkish literacy class

Hasan Bey[3] starts off the lesson by handing out a photocopied text titled *Aslan Payı* [The Lion's Share]. The text reminds me of one of Aesop's fables. He asks the children the meaning of the title in (standard) Turkish and a couple of children shout out their answers also in (standard) Turkish. From the onset of the lesson I notice that Metin and Baran seem to be constantly chatting in English (but I'm too far to hear what they are talking about). Another boy seems to be texting on his mobile while chatting with the boy sitting next to him. The teacher asks the children to read the text silently. He walks around reminding them to stay focused on the reading task. He notices that Metin has his mobile phone prominently displayed on his desk and asks him to put it away. Metin begrudgingly complies and puts the mobile phone in this bag. After a while, the teacher tells the children to stop reading and asks them to answer in writing the reading comprehension questions he has written on the back of the sheet. He comes up to Metin and Baran and asks the latter to do the first question which he does effortlessly. The teacher goes around asking a couple of the other boys the answers to the next two questions. They all seem to be able to answer them fluently by reproducing verbatim parts of the text in (standard) Turkish.

(from field notes VL06/05/06)

The vignette shows that Turkish literacy teaching was characterized by whole-class teacher-fronted instruction heavily relying on the traditional Initiation–Response–Feedback (IRF) sequence, substitution drills and the reading of texts on worksheets followed by sets of reading comprehension questions. Classroom discourse tended to encourage decontextualized knowledge, modelling and chorus-style responses to teacher prompts (Lytra and Baraç 2008, 2009). As the vignette illustrates, the default mode of classroom interaction with the teacher during Turkish literacy teaching tended to be (standard) Turkish, whereas off-task talk among peers tended to be English. Generally, the use of English and vernacular forms of Turkish during Turkish literacy teaching was frowned upon, although occasionally deemed necessary for communication purposes (ibid.).

The boys' media engagement was low-key. It was triggered and sustained by their mobile phones usually stowed away in a school bag casually lying on the desk next to school work sheets but within easy reach or kept in their hand or pockets throughout the duration of the lesson. The mobile phones allowed them to 'stay connected' across space, both inside and outside the classroom. Boys usually sat along the back rows, sometimes sitting on their own or in pairs, whereas girls sat in close proximity to each other, in two long rows, occupying the front right of the classroom. In this context, mobile phones radically transformed the classroom environment both physically and socially: they provided opportunities for communication across classroom space and for different forms of peer interaction (e.g. sharing and listening to music during the lesson, evaluating shared songs, comparing features of mobile phones).

Figure 31.1 reveals a typical scene during this Turkish literacy class: boys in twos or threes comparing features of their mobile phones. On this occasion the lesson has been put on hold while Hasan Bey, the teacher, is going from desk to desk checking and marking work sheets. A little earlier, he had distributed a set of reading comprehension questions to do in class. Metin and Cem seem to have finished the assigned task and have turned their attention to their mobile phones. In fact, if we look closely we see that Metin has turned his work sheet upside down (facing the teacher) perhaps signalling to Hasan Bey that he has finished the assigned task and that the teacher could now check and mark his work.

The still photo reveals Metin and Cem's intense engagement with the former's mobile. This is not only manifested through their talk (e.g. they appear to be talking about some feature on Metin's mobile) but also through their 'embodied mutual orientation' to the activity they are

Figure 31.1 Metin showing Cem a particular feature on his mobile phone during Turkish literacy teaching.

engaged in (Goodwin 2000: 1497): Metin has turned his body sideways away from his desk towards Cem and Cem is leaning forwards towards Metin. They are both looking intently at some text on the screen of Metin's mobile. Through their talk, body and gestural displays, the two boys are co-constructing their shared orientation towards the activity in the context of a two-party participation framework, illustrating how 'human action is built through the simultaneous deployment of a range of quite different kinds of semiotic resources' (Goodwin 2000: 1489).

The digitally recorded episode below captures a music sharing activity between Metin whom we can see in the photo above and Baran, another child who is not in the photo. It was recorded on a different day from when the photo above was taken. Metin and Baran are sitting next to each other, sharing the same desk. Metin, who is the sender, has selected a song he wants to send to Baran urging him to accept the connection that allows for the music file to be copied across mobiles. Baran seems to be refusing to accept the connection, first seeking to clarify the content of the music files and second accusing Metin of trying to 'hack into' his mobile phone before he finally accedes. This episode is part of an intermittent exchange of songs and talk about mobiles phones mainly between Metin and Baran over the past 50 minutes prior to this episode. The boys dip in and out of sharing songs and talking about their mobile phones as they read silently an assigned text and complete a series of reading comprehension questions on their work sheets.

Episode 1: Music sharing

BARAN: ((humming, alternating between high and low pitch)) I feel like PLAYING FOOTBALL NOW OH MY GOD

METIN: ((to Baran)) accept

BARAN: wha are you sending?

METIN: accept ... right 1,2,3,4. OK

BARAN: why you hacking me?

METIN: ((laughs)) why I wanna see wha you got. I'm not hacking you don WORRY.ACCEPT LET'S SAY ACCEPT ((IN WINNING VOICE)) ARE YOU DUN MAN ... ACCEPT IT. I'M NOT HACKING YOU. I'M GONNA ... I'M JUST GONNA GET ... SEND BUT.AA MAN ACCEPT IT. HEY BRO SEND ME THE ACCEPT!

BARAN: stop man

METIN: alright alright just send me oh man send it send it. I've done wrong. SEND IT. HEY MAN WHY DON YOU SAY ACCEPT? [...]

BARAN: It's done.

(Digital recording, Baran 10/06/06)

As the music sharing episode above reveals, these activities occurred as a backdrop to pedagogic routines and practices occupying the official classroom space (e.g. doing an assigned task, reading silently, writing the answers to a set of reading comprehension questions on the whiteboard). They also emerged during 'liminal' moments seen as transition points outside normal social structures during which the boys passed from one social status to another (Turner 1974: 58) (e.g. when the lesson has been put on hold and the teacher is going around checking coursework as in the case of the boys' talk about mobile phones in the still photography). Thus, music sharing commonly took place in the periphery of the main classroom talk and activity resembling what Maybin has aptly called literacies 'under the desk' to capture 'a range of unofficial literacy activities which appeared to be clearly "off-task" in terms of institutional norms' (2007: 519).

The boys drew on different sets of verbal and non-verbal linguistic resources (i.e. standard and vernacular forms of English and Turkish as well as singing, humming and prosody) to frame the music sharing activities mediated via their mobile phones. Some of these English linguistic resources documented in the music sharing episode above include the dropping of the copula (line 6), the dropping of word-final dental [t] (lines 4, 7, 13), slang terms ('bro', 'man'), medium-specific vocabulary ('accept', 'hacking') as well as singing and humming of tunes (line 1), repetition (lines 7–10) and manipulation of prosodic cues (line 8). The frequent use of vernacular forms of English and Turkish in peer talk more generally was in contrast with the use of more or less standard forms of Turkish and occasionally English in official teacher–pupil talk (Lytra and Baraç 2008; Baraç 2009). The boys' different sets of linguistic resources were intertwined with the manipulation of their mobile phones (e.g. sending, accepting or rejecting music files, 'hacking into' each other's mobile phones) as well as actively listening to, singing and humming raps in English and Turkish (see the next episode). Their media engagement occurred in parallel with their ongoing engagement with the assigned task (e.g. reading a text silently and completing the reading comprehension questions) and the manipulation of artefacts associated with Turkish language learning (e.g. work sheets, notebooks, pens and pencils).

The next episode took place about 40 minutes after the first episode. Baran and Metin continued sharing songs on and off and listening to them on their mobiles. Cem occasionally joined in too. The last song Metin had sent Baran was a rap song by the Turkish rapper *Ceza* [Punishment]. The boys considered *Ceza* to be one of the most influential Turkish rappers. Perhaps what added to his appeal were their shared diasporic experiences: he was originally from Turkey but had been living and working in Germany where he had become known throughout the Turkish-speaking diaspora. As Baran is listening to *Ceza's* rap he challenges Metin about his comprehension of the Turkish rap song before he goes on to positively evaluate it. Shortly after, while another rap song can be heard in the background, Baran resumes his evaluation of Turkish rap this time comparing the lyrics of *Ceza* and other Turkish rappers to the African American rapper 50Cent, arguing that they all swear the same way.

Episode 2: Evaluating shared songs

METIN: ((to Baran)) accept it ((the Turkish rap song he is listening to))
BARAN: wha?
METIN: accept it
BARAN: I did … ((rap song can be heard in the background)) bu swear if you
UNDERSTAND TURKISH BU SWEAR ,,, IT'S QUITE GOOD YEAH
[…]
METIN: send it to me
BARAN: alright man
((TURKISH RAP SONG CAN BE HEARD IN THE BACKGROUND))
BARAN: you listen to your rap like 50Cent when he swears yeah
IT'S EXACTLY LIKE IN TURKISH ((LOUDLY)) ANYWAYS
METIN: so send me and I'll accept it
BARAN: sennnddd
CEM: what song do you want?
BARAN: I'm sending man

(Digital recording, Baran 10/06/06)

As the two episodes have illustrated, attending to the ways Baran and Metin combined different sets of linguistic resources (standard and vernacular forms of English) with other semiotic resources and artefacts (e.g. listening to, singing and humming raps, manipulating features and applications on their mobile phones) revealed their different forms of media engagement as these intersected with their participation in the lesson and their negotiation of a sense of self vis-à-vis their peers. In their work on young people's digital practices, Ito *et al.* discuss different 'genres of participation' available to young people to 'describe different degrees of commitment and sophistication to media engagement' (2008: 10). Baran and Metin's engagement with music sharing and evaluating shared songs mediated via their mobile phones resonates with what the authors refer to as 'hanging out' practices, 'the desire to maintain social connections to friends' (2008: 20). Baran and Metin attempted to overcome the institutional and spatio-temporal constraints of the community language classroom by finding ways to be 'always on' and to engage with each other and their peers with whom they shared similar music and technology interests. As Ito *et al.* argue, this ongoing media engagement is central to becoming socialized into youth culture and to identity formation among young people (2008: 14). The mobile phone, thus, became the vehicle through which the boys could discuss and debate their tastes in music and popular culture and display their linguistic sophistication not only by passing aesthetic judgements but also by comparing raps across languages and cultures. At the same time, the boys' media engagement reveals 'the beginning of a more media-centric form of engagement' or 'messing around' (2008: 20). The authors suggest that

> when messing around, young people begin to take an interest in and focus on the workings and content of technology and media themselves, tinkering, exploring, and extending their understanding.
>
> *(ibid.)*

The boys' media engagement seemed to suggest that besides building and maintaining social relations and managing peer hierarchies in the complementary school setting, they also sought to enhance their knowledge of mobile technology and develop their expertise in manipulating different mobile phone features and applications. For instance, the boys experimented with the possibilities and limitations of mobile technology, by 'hacking into' each other's phone or by rejecting a song file. These forms of experimentation and exploration mediated via mobile phones were important steps to becoming 'experts' and potentially 'brokers' for peers, siblings or parents who lacked the requisite media and technology knowledge and to enhancing their reputation and status among peers.

Following resistance-oriented approaches to interpreting the boys' media engagement during Turkish literacy teaching, one would be inclined to argue that the boys were reacting to an often mundane and repetitive curriculum saturated by endless substitution drills and the reading of texts followed by sets of reading comprehension questions that made very few connections to their lived youth and diasporic realities. The boys were simply bored, and sharing and evaluating music was fun and provided an outlet to their boredom. Without disregarding this interpretation, the intensity and sophistication of the boys' media engagement also calls for the need to examine the proactive ways they drew on their media engagement during Turkish literacy teaching. Rather than being disengaged from the learning process, the boys actively contributed to the lesson: they successfully completed the assigned tasks, they volunteered to read aloud a text or go to the whiteboard to do a grammar substitution drill (see Lytra and Baraç 2009; Lytra *et al.* 2010). Rather than being marginalized in the community language classroom, they were active participants in the ongoing accomplishment of the lesson. In this context, their media engagement emerged in parallel with, instead of in opposition to, their participation in pedagogic routines and practices (cf. Maybin 2007). When seen in this light, the boys' fluent movement between their media engagement and engagement with the lesson can be viewed as ways of making linkages between out-of-school and school worlds, practices and linguistic and cultural resources. The fluid movement between these two forms of engagement required that the boys' drew on different sets of linguistic resources: mainly forms of standard Turkish and occasionally English for Turkish literacy teaching and mainly forms of vernacular English and sometimes Turkish in music sharing and evaluating shared songs. Their media engagement provided them with an interactional space to display, negotiate and share aspects of their linguistic and cultural fluency that were sanctioned in the official classroom space of the community language classroom. At the same time, this interactional space was linked with spaces outside the classroom, both online and offline, such as the global African American and diasporic Turkish rap scenes and the local London Turkish communities where different linguistic ecologies and language hierarchies other from those of the Turkish literacy classroom were in operation.

Adopting a multimodal lens on the study of the boys' different sets of linguistic resources in a Turkish complementary school class alerted us to the ways these resources were combined with other semiotic resources and artefacts in the built environment, in particular their mobile phones, foregrounding the materiality and multimodal features of classroom interaction. As the still photo of Metin and Baran's media engagement revealed, the mobile phone emerged as an important 'semiotic and material artefact' that organized both the strips of talk and the body and gestural displays of the boys providing a framework for a range of mediated practices, including sharing songs and evaluating shared songs. Both the classroom vignette and the two digitally recorded episodes strongly suggested that these mediated practices emerged in parallel rather than in opposition to the boys' engagement with pedagogic practices and routines in the Turkish heritage classroom. Notwithstanding its entertainment value against an often repetitive and mundane curriculum, by transporting their media engagement inside the classroom the boys sought to create an interactional space that allowed them to always 'stay connected' among like-minded peers, share their knowledge and develop their expertise in popular culture and new technologies across languages and cultures and experiment with the affordances of the medium.

Directions for future research

This chapter has sought to illustrate the possibilities for multilingualism research of adopting a multimodal lens on the study of participants' sets of linguistic resources. Adopting a multimodal perspective implies a theoretical and analytical shift for studies on multilingualism from focusing exclusively on language as the primary site for meaning making to recognizing the role that other modes (e.g. visual, aural, oral, kinaesthetic, artefact-related) and media play in the communicational landscape (Street 2008). As Kress and Street put it, the multimodal perspective provides '"a language of description" for these modes, that enable us to see their characteristic forms, their affordances and the distinctive ways they interact with each other' (2006: vii). In this sense, including a multimodal perspective on studies of multilingualism provides a powerful lens for 'stretch[ing] out meaning' by 'extending the *affordances* of meaning making' (Pahl and Rowsell 2006: 6–7, italics in the original).

However, much of multilingualism research to date focuses exclusively on language as the primary site for meaning making. There is, therefore, a need for more work at the intersection of multilingualism and multimodality. Taking as a point of departure the analysis of the boys' media engagement during Turkish literacy teaching, one promising area for further future research is new media and new technologies. Video-sharing sites, online games, video games, social network sites and gadgets such as webcams, mobile phones and iPods permeate our daily lives opening up new possibilities for communication, friendship and self-expression. Adopting a multimodal lens can shed light on how the users' sets of linguistic resources are intertwined with other semiotic resources and how they shape and are shaped by the possibilities and limitations of the built environment. Moreover, it can enhance our understanding of the relevant temporal and spatial dimensions of mediated practices and offer connections between micro-interactional processes and macro social-historical conditions. Teasing out the spatio-temporal and sociohistorical anchoring of the users' semiotic resources is a key theoretical and analytical focus for further future research given the increasing recognition of the ways new media and new technologies have transformed space and time constraints. At the same time, exploring the users' sets of linguistic resources through a multimodal lens can open up methodological challenges and opportunities in the collection and analysis of new media and new technologies data and in developing ethnographic approaches.

Another area for further future research is classroom interaction. Although a significant body of research has explored the interconnections and intersections of multilingualism, multimodality and literacy (e.g. Kress *et al.* 2005; Kenner 2004; Pahl 2004 to mention a few), there has been less of an uptake in adopting a multimodal lens in studies of multilingual classrooms. A multimodal perspective can bring to the fore the materiality and multimodal features of pedagogic routines and practices in the negotiation of literacy, learning and authoritative knowledge: official teacher–pupil talk is combined with visual images and writing to convey meaning and much of that talk is centred around texts. It can also highlight some of the unofficial 'off-task' practices and activities that occur outside the teacher's gaze (e.g. sharing music and evaluating shared songs mediated via mobile phones) and how these interpenetrate official school sanctioned practices and procedures. This line of research can enhance our understanding of the heterogeneity of classroom talk and the hybrid mixture of official and unofficial practices and activities in classroom interaction.

Related topics

Multilingual literacies; multilingualism and popular culture; multilingualism on the Internet; linguistic diversity and education; multilingual pedagogies.

Notes

1 'Investigating Multilingualism in Complementary Schools in Four Communities' (ESRC 00231180) with Angela Creese, Taşın Baraç, Arvind Bhatt, Adrian Blackledge, Shahela Hamid, Li Wei, Vally Lytra, Peter Martin, Chao-Jung Wu and Dilek Yağcıoğlu-Ali (Creese *et al.* 2008).
2 Earlier versions of this data section were presented in Sociolinguistics Symposium 17 (Amsterdam, 3–5 April 2008) and the AILA Migration and Language Research Network seminar (Southampton, June 2–3 2008). I am indebted to Alexandra Georgakopoulou, Kate Pahl, Gabi Budach, James Collins, Tağkın Baraç, Villy Tsakona and other participants for their useful comments. All shortcomings are, of course, mine.
3 All names are pseudonyms.

Further reading

Goodwin, C. (2000) 'Action and embodiment within situated human interaction', *Journal of Pragmatics* 32: 1489–1522.

(The author discusses some of the key concepts of the theory of action and embodiment within situated human interaction and provides illustrative examples.)

Kenner, C. (2004) *Becoming Biliterate. Young Children Learning Different Writing Systems*, Stoke on Trent: Trentham.
(The author explores how bilingual children learn to read and write in mainstream and complementary schools and at home. Her research incorporates a multimodal social semiotics approach.)

Kress, G., Jewitt, C., Bourne, J., Franks, A., Hardcastle, J., Jones, K. and Reid, E. (2005) *English in Urban Classrooms: A Multimodal Perspective on Teaching and Learning*, London: Routledge Falmer.
(The authors explore the centrality of multimodal communication in the teaching of the subject of English in linguistically and culturally diverse inner London secondary schools.)

Pahl, K. and Rowsell, J. (eds) (2006) *Travel Notes from the New Literacy Studies. Instances of Practice*, Clevedon: Multilingual Matters.
(This edited book contains a number of chapters combining insights from multilingualism, multimodality and literacy.)

Warriner, D. S. (ed.) (2007) Transnational Literacies: Immigration, Language Learning, and Identity *Linguistics and Education* (special issue) 18: 201–14.
(This special issue contains five articles and two commentaries drawing on connections between multilingualism, multimodality and literacy.)

Bibliography

Arnheim, R. (1969) *Visual Thinking*, Berkeley: University of California Press.

Bailey, B. (2007) 'Heteroglossia and boundaries', in M. Heller (ed.) *Bilingualism: A Social Approach*, Basingstoke: Palgrave Macmillan.

Baraç, T. (2009) 'Language Use and Emerging Ethnicities among London Born Youth of Turkish Descent', unpublished MA thesis, King's College London.

Baron, N. S. (2008) *Always On: Language in an Online and Mobile World*, Oxford: Oxford University Press.

Blackledge, A. and Creese, A. (2010) *Multilingualism. A Critical Perspective*, London: Continuum.

Bezemer, J. (2008) '"Displaying orientation in the classroom": Students 'multimodal responses to teacher instructions', *Linguistics and Education* 19: 166–78.

Bezemer, J. and Kress, G. (2008) 'Writing in multimodal texts: a social semiotic account of designs for learning', *Written Communication* 25(2): 166–95.

Creese, A., Baraç, T., Blackledge, A., Bhatt, A., Hamid, S., Li, W., Lytra, V., Martin, P., Wu, C.-J. and Yağcıoğlu-Ali, D. (2008) *Investigating Multilingualism in Complementary Schools in Four Communities*, End-of-project report, available online at www.esrcsocietytoday.ac.uk/esrcinfocentre/viewawardpage.aspx?awardnumber=RES-000–023-1180

Creese, A. and Blackledge, A. (with Baraç, T., Bhatt, A., Hamid, S., Li, W., Lytra, V., Martin, P., Wu, C.-J. and Yağcıoğlu-Ali, D.) (2010a) 'Separate and flexible bilingualism in complementary schools', *Journal of Pragmatics* 43(5): 1196–208.

Creese, A. and Blackledge, A. (2010b) 'Translanguaging in the bilingual classroom: A pedagogy for learning and teaching?' *The Modern Language Journal* 94(1): 103–15.

Goffman, E. (1979) *Gender Advertisements*, New York: Harper.

Goodwin, C. (2000) 'Action and embodiment within situated human interaction', *Journal of Pragmatics* 32: 1489–522.

Goodwin, M. H., Goodwin, C. and Yaeger-Dor, M. (2002) 'Multi-modality in girls' game disputes', *Journal of Pragmatics* 34: 1621–49.

Green, J. and Bloome, D. (1997) 'Ethnography and ethnographers of and in education: A situated perspective', in J. Flood, S. Heath and D. Lapp (eds) *A Handbook of Research on Teaching Literacy through the Communicative and Visual Arts*, New York: Simon & Shuster Macmillan.

Flewitt, R. S. (2005) 'Using multimodal analysis to unravel a silent child's learning', *Early Childhood Practice: The Journal for Multi-Professional Partnerships* 7(2): 5–16.

Heller, M. (2007) 'Bilingualism as ideology and practice', in M. Heller (ed.) *Bilingualism: A Social Approach*, Basingstoke: Palgrave Macmillan.

Halliday, M. A. K. (1978) *Language as Social Semiotic: The Social Interpretation of Language and Meaning*, Baltimore: University Park Press.

Ito, M., Okabe, D. and Matsuda, M. (eds) (2005) *Personal, Portable, Pedestrian: Mobile Phones in Japanese Life*, Cambridge: MIT Press.

Ito, M., Horst, H., Bittani, M., Boyd, D., Herr-Stephenson, B., Lange, P. G., Pascoe, C. J. and Robinson, L. (2008) *Living and Learning with New Media: Summary Findings from the Digital Youth Project*, The John D. and Catherine T. MacArthur Foundation, available online at http://digitalyouth.ischool.berkeley.edu/report

Jewitt, C. (2008) 'Multimodal discourses across the curriculum', in M. Martin-Jones, A.-M. de Mejía and N. H. Hornberger (eds) *Encyclopedia of Language and Education,* vol. 3: *Discourse and Education,* New York: Springer.

Katz, J. E. (ed.) (2008) *Handbook of Mobile Communication Studies*, Cambridge: MIT Press.

Kenner, C. (2004) *Becoming Biliterate: Young Children Learning Different Writing Systems*, Stoke on Trent: Trentham.

Kress, G. (2003) *Literacy in the New Media Age*, London: Routledge.

Kress, G. and van Leeuwen, T. (2001) *Multimodal Discourse: The Modes and Media of Contemporary Communication*, London: Arnold.

Kress, G., Jewitt, C., Bourne, J., Franks, A., Hardcastle, J., Jones, K. and Reid, E. (2005) *English in Urban Classrooms: Multimodal Perspectives on Teaching and Learning*, London: Routledge Falmer.

Kress, G. and Street, B. (2006) 'Foreword', in K. Pahl and J. Rowsell (eds) *Travel Notes from the New Literacy Studies. Instances of Practice,* Clevedon: Multilingual Matters.

Lytra. V. and Baraç, T. (Creese, A., Baraç, T., Blackledge, A., Bhatt, A., Hamid, S., Li, W., Lytra, V., Martin, P., Wu, C.-J. and Yağcıoğlu-Ali, D.) (2008) 'Language practices, language ideologies and identity construction in London Turkish complementary schools', in V. Lytra and N. Jørgensen (eds) *Multilingualism and Identities across Contexts: Cross-Disciplinary Perspectives on Turkish Speaking Young People in Europe. Copenhagen Studies in Bilingualism* 45: 15–43.

Lytra, V. and Baraç, T. (2009) 'Meaning making and identity negotiations among Turkish-speaking young people in a diasporic context', in A.-B. Stenstrom and A. Jorgensen (eds) *Youngspeak in a Multilingual Perspective,* Amsterdam and Philadelphia: John Benjamins.

Lytra, V., Martin, P., Baraç, T. And Bhatt, A. (2010) 'Investigating the intersection of multi-lingualism and multimodality in Turkish and Gujarati literacy classes', in V. Lytra and P. Martin (eds) *Sites of Multilingualism. Complementary Schools in Britain Today,* Stoke on Trent: Trentham.

Martin-Jones, M. (2009) 'From life worlds and work worlds to college: The bilingual literacy practices of young Welsh speakers', *Welsh Journal of Education* 14(2): 45–62.

Martin-Jones, M., Hughes B. and Williams, A. (2009) 'Bilingual literacy in and for working lives on the land: Case studies of young Welsh speakers in North Wales', *International Journal of the Sociology of Language* 195: 39–62.

Maybin, J. (2007) 'Literacy under and over the desk: Oppositions and heterogeneity', *Language and Education* 21(6): 515–30.

McGinnis, T., Goodstein-Stolzenberg, A. and Costa Saliani, E. (2007) '"Indipride": Online spaces of transnational youth as sites of creative and sophisticated literacy and identity work', in D. S. Warriner (ed.) 'Transnational literacies: Immigration, language learning, and identity' *Linguistics and Education* (special issue) 18: 283–304.

Moje, E. B. (2000) '"To be part of the story": The literacy practices of gangsta adolescents', *Teachers College Record* 102: 651–90.

Moyer, M. (2010) 'What multilingualism? Agency and unintended consequences of multilingual practices in a Barcelona health clinic', *Journal of Pragmatics* 43(5): 1209–221.

Pahl, K. (2004) 'Narratives, artifacts and cultural identities: An ethnographic study of communicative practices in homes', *Linguistics and Education* 15: 339–58.

——(2009) 'Interactions, intersections and improvisations: Studying multimodal texts and classroom talk of six and seven year olds', *Journal of Early Childhood Studies* 9(2): 188–210.

Pahl, K. and Rowsell, J. (2006) 'Introduction', in K. Pahl and J. Rowsell (eds) *Travel Notes from the New Literacy Studies. Instances of Practice,* Clevedon: Multilingual Matters.

Piirainen-Marsh, A. and Tainio, L. (2009) 'Collaborative game-play as a site for participation and situated learning of second language', *Scandinavian Journal of Educational Research* 53(2): 167–83.

Prinsloo, M. and Baynham, M. (2008) 'Introduction. Renewing literacy studies', in M. Prinsloo and M. Baynham (eds) *Literacies Global and Local*, Amsterdam and Philadelphia: John Benjamins.

Sánchez, P. (2007) 'Cultural authenticity and transnational Latina youth', in D. S. Warriner (ed.) 'Transnational literacies: Immigration, language learning, and identity', *Linguistics and Education* (special issue) 18: 258–82.

Spilioti, T. (2007) *Text Messages and Social Interaction: Genre, Norms and Sociability in Greek SMS*, unpublished PhD thesis, King's College London.

Stein, P. and Slonimsky, L. (2006) 'An eye on the text and an eye on the future: Multimodal literacy in three Johannesburg families', in K. Pahl and J. Rowsell (2006) (eds) *Travel Notes from the New Literacy Studies. Instances of Practice*, Clevedon: Multilingual Matters.

Street, B. (2008) 'New literacies, new times: Developments in literacy studies', in B. V. Street and N. H. Hornberger (eds) *Encyclopedia of Language and Education*, 2nd edn, New York: Springer.

Turner, V. (1974) 'Liminal to liminoid in play, flow and ritual', *Rice University Studies* 60: 53–92.

Warriner, D. S. (ed.) (2007) 'Transnational literacies: Immigration, language learning, and identity', *Linguistics and Education* (special issue) 18: 201–14.

32

Linguistic landscapes and multilingualism

Elana Shohamy

Language in public places

The study of Linguistic Landscape (LL), referring to research about the presence, representation, meanings and interpretation of language displayed in public places, has become a dynamic area of research in the past decade. Languages are spoken and heard, they are also represented and displayed, at times for functional reasons, at other times for symbolic purposes. These items offer rich and stimulating texts on multiple levels: single words with deep meanings and shared knowledge, colourful images, sounds and moving objects, billboards, graffiti as well as a variety of text types displayed in cyber space, open without being physically present. All these items shape the ecology in local, global and transnational contexts and in multiple languages. Most studies of LL build on a definition offered by Landry and Bourhis:

> The language of public road signs, advertising billboards, street names, place names, commercial shop signs, and public signs on government buildings combines to form the linguistic landscape of a given territory, region, or urban agglomeration.
>
> *(1997: 25)*

Yet these displayed languages of the public space are closely related to people as people are the ones who hang the signs, display posters, design advertisements and create websites. It is also people who read, attend to, decipher and interpret these language displays, or at times choose to overlook, ignore or erase them. Indeed work on LL not only focuses on signs per se, but on how people interact with them.

The main goal of LL studies is to describe and identify systematic patterns of the presence and absence of languages in public spaces and to understand the motives, pressures, ideologies, reactions and decision making of people regarding the creation of public signage. In other words, for LL researchers, language in public spaces is not arbitrary and random. Rather, they attempt to explore systematic patterns in the relationship between LL and society, people, politics, ideology, economics, policy, class, identities, multilingualism, multimodalities and to describe and analyse various forms of representation. Research on LL is grounded therefore in multiple theories and varied disciplines, such as applied linguistics, sociolinguistics, language policy, literacy studies, sociology, political science, education, art, semiotics, architecture, critical geography, urban planning and economics. The very research in the field therefore employed methodology grounded in these disciplines using qualitative, quantitative and mixed methods approaches. In the past few years, there has been growing interest in broader definitions of the notion of LL. It has been argued that LL research should go beyond the varied text types displayed in public spaces of written languages on signs, and it should include images, sounds, drawings and movement, in line with current theories about multimodality.

Research on LL has been very dynamic as can be witnessed by the large number of publications and presentations on the topic in the past few years in the form of journal articles, conference symposia and colloquia, books and edited collections. There have also been three international conferences focusing on the topic (Tel Aviv 2008; Sienna 2009; Strasbourg 2010). Although attention to language in public space is not new, as studies on the topic were carried out in the past, the current attention paid to the field of LL can be explained by the growing attention to multilingualism, the increased focus on ecology and on the environment in understanding linguistic and social phenomena and the emergence of the fields of eco- and geolinguistics. In addition, the advances in documenting technologies have played a role, particularly the advent of digital cameras and access to cyber space, with its multimodal forms of representation. We now have a heightened awareness of the significance of languages in public places and spaces.

Relationship with multilingualism

Although there has been interest, for some time, in the ways in which written languages are displayed in public places (Coulmas 2009), one of the main characteristics of this new strand of research on LL lies in its special focus on multilingualism and researchers have been spurred on by the realization that the study of language in public spaces offers a unique lens on multilingualism. Thus, a large number of LL studies focus on the presence or absence of *multiple* languages and of hybridized language forms in public spaces. A substantial body of work also investigates forms of representation, motives for and reactions to the display of different languages. The focus of such studies varies enormously and ranges from the impact of English as a global language to public display of national, official, heritage and transnational languages in various types of spaces. This research into language displayed in public places can provide additional indices and criteria for building an understanding of multilingualism in local communities beyond the study of everyday spoken language. The language forms displayed in local public spaces do not always reflect the actual spoken uses of languages by local people. This is the reason why the phenomenon of LL is referred to as the '*symbolic* construction' of the public space (Ben Rafael *et al.* 2006; Ben Rafael 2009).

Early developments in the field

Coulmas (2009) writes that 'linguistic landscaping' is as old as writing and that the beginning of writing coincided with urbanization and the creation of the public sphere. Several early studies documented language use in public spaces in urban settings and tried to understand the phenomenon by drawing on the sociolinguistics theories of the time. One such study is that by Spolsky and Cooper (1991), who documented multilingualism in the public spaces of the Old City of Jerusalem. They placed the LL they observed in the early 1990s in Jerusalem within a wider sociolinguistic and historical context, sketching out key dimensions to bear in mind when studying communities and neighbourhoods. A study by Landry and Bourhis (1997) in French

Canada triggered the current interest in LL. They drew attention to the significance of language in public spaces and showed how LL provided major indicators of language attitudes and of relevant information about societies, about the vitality of particular languages and the inter-relationship of linguistic and ethnic groups, especially in areas of language contestation. The focus of the work of these researchers was on attitudes and perceptions and these were investigated by means of sociolinguistic surveys and questionnaires.

Current research: different themes and foci

In current studies, there has been a methodological shift towards actual documentation of LL in public spaces. The earliest set of publications using this approach appeared in the 2006 thematic issue of the *International Journal of Multilingualism*. They were later published as a thematic book (Gorter 2006). Whereas Landry and Bourhis examined reactions to LL, the current studies focus mostly on documentation and analysis of actual LL practices, on what actors who produce and interpret LL actually *do*. They also take account of different semiotic modes: written language, images, colour and so on. As to the specific methods of analysis, once the languages in the public space are documented using different sampling methods, the frequency of the occurrence of signs in different languages is calculated and analysed using a variety of criteria and statistical methods. This makes it possible to make general statements about the degree to which different languages are represented in various locations. Also, comparisons are made between different kinds of signs, for example 'top-down' versus 'bottom-up' flows. 'Top-down' refers to signs posted by government offices and other central authorities, whereas 'bottom-up' refers to signs posted by individual actors such as shopkeepers or organizers of local events. This work is increasingly interdisciplinary and draws on different orienting theories.

Research on LL in multilingual settings has different foci, and different themes have emerged. I discuss some of these below, with reference to particular studies. A number of these articles have been published in a recent edited collection (Shohamy and Gorter 2009).

Research focusing on particular cities and neighbourhoods

Some recent studies have taken one urban neighbourhood as the main research site. Take, for example, a study by Bogatto and Hélot (2010) in the Quartier gare (railway station district) of Strasbourg, in France. These researchers found that the commercial signage in the area reflected the multilingual composition of the neighbourhood. They also showed that the regional language (Alsatien) intermingled with the other languages displayed in the local LL.

There is also research that documents the emergence of new diasporic spaces within cities. For instance, Miriam Ben Rafael and Eliezer Ben Rafael (2010) report on changes in local LLs in the city of Netanya in Israel, which reflect the presence of French-speaking Jews who have recently settled in the country and who continue to define themselves as a distinct group.

Comparisons across multilingual settings

Some recent studies of LLs in multilingual urban settings have had a comparative design: there have been comparisons across cities within the same country and also cross-national studies. I will focus here on two studies that provide particularly good illustrations of the value of comparative work.

A study by Ben Rafael *et al.* (2006) focused on the uses of Arabic and Hebrew in LL in different cities in Israel. These researchers documented top-down and bottom-up signs in a range of settings. The top-down signs were in settings that included religious, governmental, municipal-cultural, educational and medical institutions. They also took into account public signs, such as announcements and street names. The bottom-up signs included those of shops, private businesses, private announcements (e.g. 'want ads', sale or rentals of flats or cars). The data collection method was the systematic documentation of each and every sign in the downtown areas of several cities and the use of still photography to capture the detail of a sample of signs in the top-down flow. The study focused on the representation of each of the two official languages of Israel, Hebrew and Arabic, and on the presence of English.

The main findings were that there were significant differences in the representation of the three languages depending on the patterns of residence in the different neighbourhoods. Thus, in the Jewish areas, there were mostly Hebrew and English signs; in Arab areas the signs were mostly in Arabic and Hebrew and in East Jerusalem (an area that is considered by some as occupied by Israel), it was mostly Arabic and English and hardly any Hebrew, except in top-down signs. The results were analysed per city, per neighbourhood, per direction of flow (top-down vs bottom-up) and per area of social life.

Figure 32.1 shows how one can learn about language hierarchies in certain neighbourhoods from the study of LL, based on actual documentation of this kind. The findings of the study by Ben Rafael *et al.* (2006) were explained as follows: the top-down flows in the different urban areas reflected the official status of Hebrew and Arabic, the official languages of Israel. In contrast, the bottom-up flow reflected two key aspects of social life: *either* the demands of commerce and the everyday business of buying and selling, *or* local ideological or political concerns. The use of English was explained with reference to broader commercial and market principles, to the presence of English speakers and to its potential as a status symbol. This study provides us with a deeper understanding of the ways in which LLs are given shape by specific economic, ideological and political forces and conjunctures. However, it is also important to note that the public display of languages did not reflect the actual linguistic diversity in the different neighbourhoods in the study. A wide range of languages are spoken

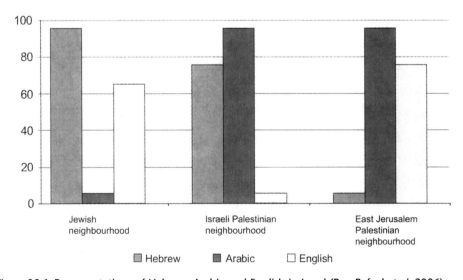

Figure 32.1 Representations of Hebrew, Arabic and English in Israel (Ben Rafael *et al.* 2006).

among different groups in multilingual Israel. So the public signage documented in this study favoured only the official languages and English.

Whereas Ben Rafael *et al.* (2006) compared different urban settings in one country, Cenoz and Gorter (2006) conducted a comparative study of minority language use in urban LLs, in two different areas in Europe. Their study was carried out in two cities where minority languages are widely spoken: San Sebastian (in the Basque country, in the north-west of Spain) and Leewarden (in Friesland, in the North of the Netherlands). Their data was collected in the two main streets of the two cities and the main focus of the study was on examining the presence and/or absence of the minority languages (Basque and Frisian, respectively) in relation to national languages and English. Cenoz and Gorter documented and analysed the different constellations of multilingualism in the LLs of the main thoroughfares of these cities.

Another recent study, comparing the presence and absence of a minority language in regional urban LLs was carried out by Blackwood (2010). In this study, two cities in France – Rennes and Perpignan – were compared. Breton is the minority language spoken in Rennes and Catalan is spoken in Perpignan. The role of these two languages in local LL was found to be very different.

The impact of globalization

There is also a growing tradition of research on the impact of globalization and the global spread of English on LL in cities. Several studies of this kind have been done in East Asia and in South East Asia.

One study was carried out by Heubner (2006). He demonstrated how language hybridization between English and Thai is becoming an increasingly salient phenomenon in Bangkok. The linguistic hybridization of local LL in this context includes both codemixing and the creative use of different writing systems. This hybridization is clearly a consequence of globalization and, especially, the global movement of people (e.g. through tourism). A similar study of the presence of different languages, including English, in the landscape of Tokyo was conducted by Backhaus (2006) and published as a book (Backhaus 2007).

Signs, scripts and identities

Some studies of LL have addressed issues of identity as manifested via LL. These studies have investigated the ways in which individual, collective and national identities are represented and/or contested. Curtin (2009) has explored the ways in which collective national identity is constructed in and through the indexical properties of the scripts used for different languages in the LLs in public spaces in Taipei, Taiwan. She describes the competing systems for the Romanization of Chinese in official signage and demonstrates how these systems evoke intense public discussions regarding ethnic, cultural, linguistic, political and (trans)national identities. Former group identities are being challenged and new ones, associated with social and political change in Taiwan, are unfolding. Throughout this process, notions of 'Chinese-ness' versus 'Taiwanese-ness' are being interrogated as debates unfold about their political, historical, cultural, ethnic, linguistic, socio-economic and even geographic import. Curtin argues that LLs are being *experienced* as an important part of the fluid processes of identification at work in contemporary Taiwan.

The construction of national and ethnic identities in LLs has also been described by Trumper-Hecht (2009) in the politically charged context of towns in Israel with both Jewish and Arab residents. She has focused on the mixed Arab–Jewish city of Upper Nazareth and has analysed the legal battles for the representation of Arabic on public signs and on private signs in the city's mall. In this context, the use of LL in the public space is hotly contested as Arabic-speaking groups see the presence of their language in the local LL as recognition of their collective presence in this city.

Kallen (2009) focuses on issues related to LLs in Ireland where Irish is used, alongside English, in LLs in urban spaces that are regularly visited by tourists. The purpose of this use of Irish is symbolic: it is designed to evoke a distinct Irish identity and it is one of the ways in which the Irish language is commodified for the tourist gaze. Kallen shows that this Irish signage is placed in anticipation of the arrival of tourists, so as to fulfil their need for an 'authentic' experience of Irishness. He applies this approach to the bilingual signage in 'an Irish walkabout', focusing on the LLs of four urban areas in the Irish Republic and Northern Ireland.

The discursive construction of urban spaces

Some current work (e.g. Shohamy *et al.* 2010) focuses on LLs in rapidly changing urban spaces, examining particular dimensions and themes associated with such urban spaces. Du Plessis (2010) has, for example, focused on cities in South Africa in the post-apartheid era and has documented the transformation of linguistic landscapes: this transformation is occurring as part of a wider process involving the standardization of orthographic conventions for writing place names. A study by Leeman and Modan (2010) was based in Washington DC where LLs are being constructed as part of official city policy to commodify them and to drive the symbolic economy. Another study by Jaworski and Yeung (2010), based on different neighbourhoods in Hong Kong, focuses on the ways in which the nature and form of LLs is shaped by economic factors. Another study by Lou (2010), also about Washington DC, shows how the values accorded to various forms and varieties of the Chinese language in Chinatown are contingent not only on spatial scales but also on the discursive reconstruction of Chinatown, which involves conjuring up contemporary China and simultaneously disconnecting Chinatown from its original history as an immigrant enclave. Lastly, there is a study by Waksman and Shohamy (2010) on how the municipality of Tel Aviv is using various types of LL in public spaces to deliver a redefinition of the city as part of preparations for its centennial.

In addition to these studies of changing urban LLs, there are a number of studies about the reactions of passers-by to the LLs in public spaces in cities. These include the following: research by Aiestaran *et al.* (2010) into the perceptions of the value of multilingual signs; an investigation by Trumper-Hecht (2010) into reactions to signs in mixed Arab–Jewish cities; and a study by Garvin (2010) into the reactions of pedestrians to urban LLs using a method called 'the postmodern walking tour interview'. In this study, participants provided self-reports of their emotional responses to and visual perceptions of the LLs in their city of Memphis.

Linguistic landscapes and official language policies

A number of LL researchers have explored the connections between LLs and official language policies, that is, between top-down and bottom-up flows. One example of studies in this area is that by Pavlenko (2010), which describes LL in Kiev, Ukraine. Pavlenko shows that, despite the government's efforts to relegate Russian as a 'foreign language' and to promote the Ukrainian language, top-down imposition of linguistic policies in LLs are not all-powerful.

Ideologues and politicians tend to see the public space as an arena over which to exercise influence and to deliver messages. This often results in the dominance of certain languages over others within this sphere (Shohamy 2008). In addition to the study by Pavlenko, mentioned briefly above, studies of the role of LL in language policy have been conducted in places as diverse as Canada, Japan, Belarus, Czech Republic, Israel, Slovakia, Ethiopia and Italy. For example, it has been shown that people constructing LLs often defy formal and explicit policies. New words and new orthographic conventions are created and displayed in public spaces and we see the emergence of hybridized language forms and fusion of local and global varieties. Thus, in some LLs in public spaces, we see the creation of language policy from below. This is especially noticeable when examining language in cyber space. There, mixing of languages is commonplace, and new linguistic rules of syntax and spelling are applied, often combined with other semiotic modes such as sounds and images.

Backhaus (2007) conducted a comparative study of LL policy in Canada and Japan. He analysed and compared rules and regulations imposed by the government of the province of Quebec, Canada regarding the use of French, with the laissez-faire approach regarding the use of English and other foreign languages in Tokyo, Japan. He argued that Quebec and Tokyo can be placed on two opposite poles in the broad spectrum of LL policies worldwide. He also noted that linguistic landscaping in Quebec was highly regulated with respect to both status and corpus planning issues.

I will make brief mention here of three other studies of LLs and language policy in multilingual settings. My aim is to show how widely this approach has been applied. The first study was conducted by Sloboda (2009). He carried out comparative research into the dialectical relationship between LL and state ideology in three countries in Eastern Europe: Belarus, the Czech Republic and Slovakia. These are all countries that have recently undergone substantial social and political transformation since the end of the Cold War. Nevertheless, Sloboda found that state ideology is still manifested in LLs. In particular, the state still takes on the role of a mediator between the local and the global.

The second study is one based in sub-Saharan Africa: in Ethiopia. Lanza and Woldemariam (2009) carried out extended research of the LL in the regional capital of Mekele, where three languages are used: Tigrinya, the official regional language; Amharic, the national working language; and English. In their research, these researchers showed how Tigrinya, Amharic and English compete in the public space in this urban setting. They focused on how language choices for signage were made. In some cases, the choice of language was strategic and conscious and in other cases this was guided by force of habit and uncritical acceptance of language hierarchies.

The third LL study is one done by Dal Negro (2009) in a rural context, in three small mountain villages in the North of Italy. The sociolinguistic context was multilingual and reflected the history of the region: Italian, German and local varieties of German were in everyday use in these villages. Dal Negro showed that local language policies had an influence on the ways in which these different language varieties were used in the LL. In the province of South Tyrol, language policy dictated the use of (standard) German and this accounted for the preponderance of bilingual German–Italian signs. However, in the German speech enclaves outside South Tyrol, where local varieties of German were spoken, local language varieties were used more often in LL to reflect local traditions and 'uniqueness'.

The studies that I have reviewed in this section are only a few examples of a much larger repertoire of studies that examine the relationship of LL to language policy. This is a key area of empirical work on LL in multilingual settings, urban and rural, in different parts of the world.

Diverse theories and interdisciplinary perspectives

As I noted in the introduction to this chapter, LL studies have been grounded in the traditions of research associated with different disciplines and have been guided by different orienting theories. For example, Cenoz and Gorter (2009) have introduced an economic perspective on LL research in multilingual settings. They have adopted the 'Contingent Valuation Method', which has been applied in studies of environmental economics. They argue that the economic values of signs can be determined by focusing on non-market values. In their most recent work (Aiestaran, Cenoz and Gorter 2010), they demonstrate how this method can be used to approximate values of LLs as well as aspects of multilingualism and language diversity.

Spolsky (2009) argues that there is still scope for theory-building in the LL field. He claims that LLs need to be understood with reference to the state of literacy in the multilingual population where the various languages are spoken. Otherwise it would not be possible to explain why a language is or is not written. Drawing on the data collected for the Spolsky and Cooper (1991) study in Jerusalem, he also focuses on the problem of conceptualizing agency in LL research and the processes by which signs are produced. The theory he offers is anchored in a sociolinguistics of language choice, which is in line with his own theory of language policy. He calls this approach 'language management'.

Heubner (2009) contextualizes his LL research within the tradition of linguistic anthropology. He proposes the use of the 'SPEAKING' model offered by Hymes (1972) as a means of determining appropriate units of analysis and argues that analyses of LL need to take account of the setting, the participants, the ends, act sequences, the key, instrumentalities, norms and genres. In order to illustrate this approach, he draws on his own research in Thailand and on other LL studies. He highlights the importance of the immediate context of a sign, the authors of the sign, the passers-by and the 'place' in which the sign appears.

Hult (2009) contextualizes LL research within an 'ecology of language' approach, specifically addressing aspects of multilingualism that are mapped through individual language choices in their social environment. He argues for grounding LL research in the combined theories of both 'ecology of language' and nexus analysis (Scollon and Scollon 2003, 2004). He claims that these theories can be used in conjunction to foreground the ecological dimension of LL research in multilingual settings.

Ben Rafael (2009) proposes that LL can be accounted for by drawing on sociological theories that represent LL as a mass of symbols that structure public space. He argues that LL is like a text into which one may read power, specific areas of influence and the traces of processes like globalization, the assertion of national identities or ideological and political agendas. He also argues that, in such texts, the peculiarities of the various scenes of the public space are also manifested in LLs, with all their incoherence and contradictions

Methodological developments

A significant number of LL studies have incorporated mixed method approaches, combining qualitative with quantitative analysis. However, qualitative, interpretive research predominates. Some qualitative studies have focused on classifying, documenting and characterizing the signs observed in particular locations. Others have combined description and analysis with interviews with sign producers and/or passers-by. Now, we are beginning to see the development of more advanced and specialized methods of analysis being employed.

One such advanced method of data collection and analysis is used by Barni and Bagna (2009), consisting of documentation and mapping using advanced computer programs taken from the field of geography. The research tool developed is entitled 'MapGeoLing' and it has been used in a study of LL in different cities and regions of Italy. The focus of the study has been on documenting LLs in immigrant neighbourhoods in Rome and in other urban areas. They have also utilized this method to document 'Italianisms' in different neighbourhoods and in different urban settings in 21 different countries. The software has the built-in possibility of adding different codes for the signs documented, for example, codes relating to the text genre, the domain of use and the context, as well as the linguistic features of the texts in the signs.

In a study in northern California, Malinowski (2009) has explored the potential of the interview in LL research. He is especially interested in the 'authorship' of LL signs and has conducted in-depth interviews with Korean-American business owners in Oakland, in the San Francisco Bay Area. The interviews focused in particular on their motivations for writing and displaying signs in specific languages and on the symbolic and political significance of the adoption of Korean or English on their bilingual signs. Malinowski's study is also anchored within the recent strand of research on the multimodality of LL.

Expanding definitions: the multimodality of LL

A broader perspective on LLs has been emerging in the past few years. It is now widely agreed that definitions of the concept of LL need to go beyond the verbal, written texts of signs, whether monolingual or multilingual, so as to include other semiotic modes such as images, objects, sounds, designs, maps, diagrams, spectacles, poems, memories, gestures, and placements in time and space (Shohamy and Waksman 2009). This approach follows the seminal writing of Lefebvre (1991, 1996), who argued that the public space is a dynamic, flowing, non-linear and interactive arena that allows for the production of varied and diverse text types. Lefebvre also views the public space not as a neutral arena but rather as negotiated and contested, and as embedded in history, culture, ideology and geography. This approach to LL research enables us to provide deeper insights into the meanings associated with LLs in particular public spaces. As Canagarajah (2007) has reminded us, meanings are socially situated, contextualized and sensitive to ecological resources.

This newer approach to LL research stretches back to early, interdisciplinary work in semiotics (Barthes 1985; Mitchell 1986, 2002) and, at the same time, builds on recent advances in the study of multimodality. In particular, it builds on the seminal work on multimodality by Auge (1995), members of the New London Group (1996), Kress and van Leeuwen (2001) and Scollon and Scollon (2003, 2004). Scollon and Scollon, in particular, have demonstrated the importance of understanding the ways in which objects are placed and presented in the physical world and how this contributes to meaning making.

The study of graffiti illustrates particularly well the need for an expanded view of LLs as it involves the creation of hybrid forms of text and pictures. Moreover, it is now clear that the multimodal resources that graffiti artists draw on have both global and local meanings. Pennycook (2009) shows that local instances of graffiti need to be interpreted as part of a transgressive semiotics, within a global flow of practices. He raises questions about why some signs have more importance than others, how and why signs are made, how they are read and interpreted and how different linguistic resources are used. Graffiti is not only illegal (in most cases), it also is about production, about learning skills, about style and identity, as well as about different ways of claiming space by interacting with it. Various other studies have also examined LL from this expanded perspective (see Jaworski and Thurlow 2010).

The implications for language education

Growing attention has been given recently to the role of displayed languages in language learning. Immigrants and tourists coming to new places are often drawn to signs in their primary encounters with new cultural practices. They also use public signage as they try to make sense of new environments and the messages they convey. Thus, a LL can serve as a powerful tool for learning second and foreign languages and for language awareness. For example, Dagenais *et al.* (2009) are engaged in a large study in Quebec and Vancouver where elementary school students are documenting their contacts with a variety of languages in their local communities. They are describing how children co-construct representations of languages, language speakers and language learning through these language awareness activities. These researchers recommend the use of LL as a tool for increasing language awareness. They show how children engaging in multilingual awareness activities can develop a critical perspective on language diversity and literacy practices, especially in socially and politically contested areas.

Other studies also show how LLs can serve as resources for teaching languages and for raising cultural and linguistic awareness. Thus, Sayer (2009) showed how a LL can be used for pedagogical purposes via a study in Mexico. He involved students as language investigators employing multiple research methods to analyse the social meanings of public signs where English was used. He presents a framework distinguishing between intercultural and intracultural uses, and between iconic and innovative uses of English on signs. He argues that the project is useful both for thinking about the innovative ways in which people use the language in local contexts and as a template for a classroom-based project that teachers can implement. This is a means of engaging EFL students in investigating and talking about social aspects of language use.

Hanauer (2009) focused on the LLs of educational institutions. He presented a study of the different genres incorporated in the wall display of a microbiology laboratory. This laboratory was part of a project where high school and undergraduate students were brought together to engage in joint microbiological inquiry. Wall space was used to facilitate the flow of knowledge throughout the laboratory and to illustrate the procedural aspects of conducting scientific inquiry. Hanauer used genre analysis and multimodal analysis to show how an understanding of this type of LL can promote the scientific and educational aims of learning and knowledge exchange.

Linguistic landscapes as contested spaces

LLs provide rich contexts for learning about the ways in which meanings are constructed and manipulated using a variety of signs. The study of linguistic landscapes reveals the tip of the iceberg of meaningful phenomena in society and the ways in which signs are embedded in history and culture. LLs not only reflect social structure and the dynamics of social relations but they are also arenas through which various agendas are dictated, battled over or negotiated. Moreover, space and geography are not separate and passive dimensions, but rather are actively drawn on in the theatre of the social life. LLs are constructed by different discourse communities with multiple and often contradictory ideologies regarding the role of the *shared* public space. Texts in public spaces are displayed and created within a larger ecology, which is not neutral. Kramsch's account of language ecology is particularly apt here. She defines it as follows:

> A nonlinear, relational human activity, co-constructed between humans and their environment, contingent upon their position in space and history, and a site of struggle for the control of social power and cultural memory.
>
> *(Kramsch 2002: 5)*

The contestation and claiming of public space often originate from underlying assumptions about its ownership. Public space is sometimes referred to as a free zone that belongs to and is shared by all. However, questions need to be raised about the extent to which it does indeed belong to all and about what ownership really means and implies. Does it mean that munici-palities and corporations can shape the space according to their own interests? Or does the crafting of a public space need to be addressed and negotiated with local people (e.g. displaying an advertisement of a nude man/woman in public)? To what extent is contestation possible? As I see it, struggles, negotiations and contestation over LLs originate from underlying assumptions about ownership of public space. The LL issues that now need to be addressed relate to the social and political levels of public space. They include questions such as: are certain groups included/excluded by displaying different LL texts? How do those processes of inclusion/exclusion take place through the use of multimodal, multilingual resources? Policy makers (that is, politicians and economic czars) mark public space with specific languages in order to exercise influence and disseminate propaganda, so the study of LLs allows us to throw light on these social and ideological processes.

Future research issues

Various issues in relation to LLs are still left unanswered: on the conceptual level, Landry and Bourhis (1997) set us a compelling challenge: that of providing a visual record of the identities, values and relationships within a given territory, region or urban area. However, a number of issues have emerged in devising research projects aimed at addressing this challenge. I outline some of these issues below and I point to areas of LL research that need to be addressed in the future.

There are still different views in the field about what constitutes a LL: does it refer to language only or to additional signs and modes of communication, such as images, sounds, buildings, clothes or even people? Can these even be separated from one another? What is public and what is private, in this day and age? How are signs, and people, and languages connected in LL? What role does a LL play in policy making and what effects does it have on de facto language practices? What kind of reality does a LL create and shape? What motivates people to display different languages? With regard to this question, we need a special research focus on the author. How do people value LL? What messages are being delivered to passers-by? How do they interpret these messages? What types of language resources and what hybrid forms are being created in the public space? How do images and all other representations interact? How different is the spoken/heard language from the represented variety? What are the applications of LL to education and to language learning? Can contemporary LLs be accounted for within existing theories or should we perhaps create theories of linguistic ecology and space? What does the study of LL in its many perspectives add to our understanding of language, society and people?

Now that the Pandora's box of language in public spaces has been opened, endless opportun-ities for its exploration are available and researchers across different disciplines are articulating different ways of seeing LLs. Within the field of applied linguistics, the notion of ecology is getting to be seen as an increasingly important lens on language in social life. I would argue that it is a key analytic tool in applied linguistic research in the multilingual and multimodal world in which we now live. Moreover, our research methods are becoming more refined: the technology for collecting and analysing LL data is becoming much more accessible, so this area of research is gaining more attention. Interest is likely to increase in the years to come and many of the questions listed above are still open. We need further data, from different cultural and historical contexts, and more interdisciplinary theory-building. The task ahead is that of achieving a deeper understanding of the use of different languages, in different forms, in the increasingly diverse urban spaces of the late modern era.

Related topics

Multilingualism and the media; multilingual literacies; multilingualism and multimodality; multilingual pedagogies.

Further reading

Cenoz, J, and Gorter, D. (2006) 'Linguistic landscape and minority languages', *International Journal of Multilingualism* 3(1): 67–80.

Gorter, D. (ed.) (2006) *Linguistic Landscape: A New Approach to Multilingualism*, Clevedon: Multilingual Matters.

Scollon, R. and Scollon, S. W. (2003) *Discourses in Place: Language in the Material World*, London: Routledge.

Shohamy, E. and Gorter, D. (eds) (2009) *Linguistic Landscape: Expanding the Scenery*, London: Routledge.

Bibliography

Aiestaran, J., Cenoz, J. and Gorter, D. (2010) 'Multilingual cityscapes: Perceptions and preferences of the inhabitants of the city of Donostia-San Sebastian', in E. Shohamy, E. Ben Rafael, and C. Barni (eds) *Linguistic Landscape in the City*, Clevedon: Multilingual Matters.

Auge, M. (1995) *Non-Places: Introduction to an Anthropology in Supermodernity*, translated by J. Howe (trans.), London: Verso.

Backhaus, P. (2006) 'Multilingualism in Tokyo: A look into the linguistic landscape', in D. Gorter (ed.) *Linguistic Landscape: A New Approach to Multilingualism*, Clevedon: Multilingual Matters.

——(2007) *Linguistic Landscapes: A Comparative Study of Urban Multilingualism in Tokyo*, Clevedon: Multilingual Matters.

Barni, M. and Bagna, C. (2009) 'A mapping technique and the linguistic landscape', in E. Shohamy and D. Gorter (eds) *Linguistic Landscape: Expanding the Scenery*, London: Routledge.

Barthes, R. (1985) 'Rhetoric of the image', in R. Barthes (ed.) *The Responsibility of Forms*, New York: Hill and Wang.

Ben Rafael, E. (2009) 'A sociological approach to the study of linguistic landscapes', in E. Shohamy and D. Gorter (eds) *Linguistic Landscape: Expanding the Scenery*, London: Routledge.

Ben Rafael, E. and Ben Rafael, M. (2010) 'Diaspora and returning diaspora: French-Hebrew and vice-versa', in E. Shohamy, E. Ben Rafael and C. Barni, (eds) *Linguistic Landscape in the City*, Clevedon: Multilingual Matters.

Ben Rafael, E., Shohamy, E., Amara, M. H. and Trumper-Hecht, N. (2006) 'Linguistic landscape as a symbolic construction of the public space: The case of Israel', *International Journal of Multilingualism* 3(1): 7–31.

Blackwood, R. (2010) 'Marking France's public space: Empirical surveys on regional heritage languages in Provincial cities', in E. Shohamy, E. Ben Rafael and C. Barni (eds) *Linguistic Landscape in the City*, Clevedon: Multilingual Matters.

Bogatto, F. and Hélot, C., (2010) What does the linguistic landscape tell us about language diversity in Strasbourg? in E. Shohamy, E. Ben Rafael and C. Barni (eds) *Linguistic Landscape in the City*, Clevedon: Multilingual Matters.

Canagarajah, S. (2007) 'The ecology of global English', *International Multilingualism Research Journal* 1(2): 89–100.

Cenoz, J, and Gorter, D. (2006) 'Linguistic landscape and minority languages', *International Journal of Multilingualism* 3(1): 67–80.

——(2009) 'Language economy and linguistic landscape', in E. Shohamy and D. Gorter (eds) *Linguistic Landscape: Expanding the Scenery*, London: Routledge.

Coulmas, F. (2009) 'Linguistic landscaping and the seed of the public sphere', in E. Shohamy and D. Gorter (ed.) *Linguistic Landscape: Expanding the Scenery*, London: Routledge.

Curtin, M. L. (2009) 'Languages on display: Indexical signs, identities and the linguistic landscape of Taipei', in E. Shohamy and D. Gorter (eds) *Linguistic Landscape: Expanding the Scenery*, London: Routledge.

Dagenais, D., Moore, D., Sabatier, C., Lamarre, P. and Armand, F. (2009) 'Linguistic landscape and language awareness', in E. Shohamy and D. Gorter (eds) *Linguistic Landscape: Expanding the Scenery*, London: Routledge.

Dal Negro, S. (2009) 'Language policy modelling the linguistic landscape', in E. Shohamy and D. Gorter (eds) *Linguistic Landscape: Expanding the Scenery*, London: Routledge.

du Plessis, T. (2010) 'Bloemfontein/Mangaung, a city on the move', in E. Shohamy, E. Ben Rafael and C. Barni (eds) *Linguistic Landscape in the City*, Clevedon: Multilingual Matters.

Garvin, R. (2010) 'Postmodern walking tour', in E. Shohamy, E. Ben Rafael and C. Barni (eds) *Linguistic Landscape in the City*, Clevedon: Multilingual Matters.

Gorter, D. (ed.) (2006) *Linguistic Landscape: A New Approach to Multilingualism*, Clevedon: Multilingual Matters.

Hanauer, D. (2009) 'Science and the linguistic landscape: A genre analysis of representational wall space in a micro-biology laboratory', in E. Shohamy and D. Gorter (eds) *Linguistic Landscape: Expanding the Scenery*, London: Routledge.

Heubner, T. (2006) 'Bangkok's linguistic landscape: Environmental print, codemixing and language change', *International Journal of Multilingualism* 3(1): 33–54.

——(2009) 'A framework for the linguistic analysis of linguistic landscapes', *International Journal of Multilingualism* 3(1): 70–87.

Hult, F. (2009) 'Language ecology and linguistic landscape analysis', *International Journal of Multilingualism* 3(1): 88–103.

Hymes, D. (1972) 'Models of the interaction of language and social life', in J. J. Gumperz and D. Hymes (eds) *Directions in Sociolinguistics, the Ethnography of Communication*, New York: Holt, Rinehard and Winston.

Jaworski, A. and Thurlow, C. (2010) (eds) *Semiotic Landscapes: Language, Space, Image*, London: Continuum.

Jaworski, A. and Yeung, S. (2010) 'Life in the garden of Eden: Naming in Hong Kong', in E. Shohamy, E. Ben Rafael and C. Barni (eds) *Linguistic Landscape in the City*, Clevedon: Multilingual Matters.

Kallen, J. (2009) 'Tourism and representation in the Irish linguistic landscape', in E. Shohamy and D. Gorter (eds) *Linguistic Landscape: Expanding the Scenery*, London: Routledge.

Kramsch, C. J. (2002) 'How can we tell the dancer from the dance?' in C. J. Kramsch (ed.) *Language Acquisition and Language Socialization: Ecological Perspectives*, New York: Continuum.

Kress, G. and van Leeuwen, T. (2001) *Multimodal Discourse*, London: Arnold.

Landry, R. and Bourhis, R. (1997) 'Linguistic landscape and ethnolinguistic vitality: An empirical study', *Journal of Language and Social Psychology* 16: 23–49.

Lanza, E. and Woldemariam, H. (2009) 'Language ideology and linguistic landscapes: Language policy and globalization in a regional capital of Ethiopia', in E. Shohamy and D. Gorter (eds) *Linguistic Landscape: Expanding the Scenery*, London: Routledge.

Laur, E. (2006) Review of D. Gorter (ed.) *Linguistic Landscape: A New Approach to Multilingualism*, Clevedon: Multilingual Matters, available online on the Linguists List at http://listserv.linguistlist.org

Leeman, J. and Modan, G. (2010) 'Selling the city: Language, ethnicity and commodified space', in E. Shohamy, E. Ben Rafael and C. Barni (eds) *Linguistic Landscape in the City*, Clevedon: Multilingual Matters.

Lefebvre, H. (1991) *The Production of Space*, Oxford: Blackwell.

——(1996) *Writings on Cities*, Oxford: Blackwell.

Lou, J. J. (2010) 'Chinese on the side: The marginalization of Chinese on the linguistic landscape of Chinatown in Washington, DC', in E. Shohamy, E. Ben Rafael and C. Barni (eds) *Linguistic Landscape in the City*, Clevedon: Multilingual Matters.

Malinowski, D. (2009) 'Authorship in the linguistic landscape: A multimodal, performative view', in E. Shohamy and D. Gorter (eds) *Linguistic Landscape: Expanding the Scenery*, London: Routledge.

Mitchell, W. J. T. (1986) *Iconology, Image, Text, Ideology*, Chicago: University of Chicago Press.

——(ed.) (2002) *Landscape and Power*, Chicago: University of Chicago Press.

New London Group (1996) 'A pedagogy of multiliteracies: Designing social futures', *Harvard Educational Review* 66(1): 60–92.

Pavlenko, A. (2010) 'Linguistic landscape of Kyiv, Ukraine: A diachronic study', in E. Shohamy, E. Ben Rafael and C. Barni (eds) *Linguistic Landscape in the City*, Clevedon: Multilingual Matters.

Pennycook, A. (2009) 'Linguistic landscapes and the transgressive semiotics of graffiti', in E. Shohamy and D. Gorter (eds) *Linguistic Landscape: Expanding the Scenery*, London: Routledge.

Sayer, P. (2009) 'Using the linguistic landscape as a pedagogical resource', *ELT Journal Advance Access* July (15): 2–12.

Scollon, R. and Scollon, S. W. (2003) *Discourses in Place: Language in the Material World*, London: Routledge.

——(2004) *Nexus Analysis: Discourse and the Emerging Internet*, London: Routledge.

Shohamy, E. (2008) 'At what cost? Methods of language revival and protection: Examples from Hebrew', in K. King, N. Shilling-Estes, L. Fogle, J. Lou and B. Soukup (eds) *Sustaining Linguistic Diversity: Endangered Languages and Language Varieties*, Washington, DC: Georgetown University Press.

Shohamy, E. and Gorter, D. (eds) (2009) *Linguistic Landscape: Expanding the Scenery*, London: Routledge.

Shohamy, E., Ben Rafael, E. and Barni, C. (eds) (2010) *Linguistic Landscape in the City*, Clevedon: Multilingual Matters.

Shohamy, E. and Waksman, S. (2009) 'Linguistic landscape as an ecological arena: Modalities, meanings, negotiations, education', in E. Shohamy and D. Gorter (eds) *Linguistic Landscape: Expanding the Scenery*, London: Routledge.

——(2010) 'Building the nation, writing the past: History and textuality at the Haapala memorial in Tel Aviv-Jaffa', in A. Jaworsky and C. Thurlow (eds) *Semiotic Landscapes: Language, Space, Image,* London: Continuum.

Sloboda, M. (2009) 'State ideology and linguistic landscape: A comparative analysis of (post) Communist Belarus, Czech Republic and Slovakia', in E. Shohamy and D. Gorter (eds) *Linguistic Landscape: Expanding the Scenery*, London: Routledge.

Spolsky, B. (2009) 'Prolegomena to a sociolinguistic theory of public signage', in E. Shohamy and D. Gorter (eds) *Linguistic Landscape: Expanding the Scenery*, London: Routledge.

Spolsky, B. and Cooper, R. L. (1991) *The Languages of Jerusalem*, Oxford: Clarendon Press.

Trumper-Hecht, N. (2009) 'Constructing national identity in mixed cities in Israel: Arabic on signs in the public space of upper Nazareth', in E. Shohamy and D. Gorter (eds) *Linguistic Landscape: Expanding the Scenery*, London: Routledge.

——(2010) 'The perspective of the walkers in an Israeli mixed city', in E. Shohamy, E. Ben Rafael and C. Barni (eds) *Linguistic Landscape in the City*, Clevedon: Multilingual Matters.

Waksman, S. and Shohamy, E. (2010) 'The competing narratives of Tel Aviv-Jaffa's approaching its centennial', in E. Shohamy, E. Ben Rafael and C. Barni (eds) *Linguistic Landscape in the City*, Clevedon: Multilingual Matters.

Index

Abdulaziz, M.H. 169, 171–72, 180
accent marginality 348
Adam, R. 14, 100–115
advertising 335–36, 342
affective linguistic conditioning 456–58
affective repertoires 19, 457, 460, 462, 464
Afrikaans 275–77, 349
Alcorso, C. 424, 431
Alexander, N. 170, 175–76, 181, 382
Alidou, H. 170, 172–76, 181–82
Alim, S. 404, 408, 411, 415–18, 448, 451, 483, 485, 488, 494–95, 498
Allen, P. 22, 41, 46–47, 100, 103, 114, 212, 229, 295, 433, 480, 496
Androutsopoulos, J. 334–36, 338, 340–41, 343–44, 385–86, 388–92, 396, 398–401, 408, 414–16, 487–88, 495
Angola 176, 354
approaches to language education: cognitive 238, 253; communicative 236–38, 241–42, 245, 250, 252–53, 256; grammatical 237; heteroglossic multilingual 236, 238
Arabic 222, 228, 250, 340, 349–50, 353, 356, 359, 385, 390, 409, 486, 488, 493–94, 523, 541, 543
Argentina 160, 209, 211, 252, 255, 261
Artic Quebec community 48
audism 102
Auer, P. 6, 21, 24, 81, 196, 246, 298, 312, 391, 393, 400, 416, 471, 479–80, 482–88, 495–97, 507
Australia 17, 44, 109, 146, 150–51, 199, 201–2, 204, 230, 249, 253, 269–70, 285, 288–95, 316–17, 354, 356, 408, 423–26, 428, 430, 459, 485
Austria 5, 189, 254, 256, 354, 373, 459
authenticity 8, 374–75, 377, 381

Backhaus, P. 542, 544, 549
Bahan, B. 105–6, 112–14
Bailey, B. 20, 487, 495, 499–507
Bakhtin, M.M. 8–9, 20–21, 50, 63, 120, 128, 335, 344, 482, 485, 495, 499–502, 504, 507
Bakker, P. 38, 47

Bamgbose, A. 170, 172–73, 178, 181, 357, 364
Baraç, T. 528, 531–32, 534–36
Bartlett, L. 246, 512, 516–17
Basque 25, 186–87, 189–91, 199, 203, 206–7, 216, 542
Basque Autonomous Community 191
Basque Country 191, 199, 203, 206–7, 216, 542
Bauman, R. 11–12, 21, 440, 451, 489, 495
Beacco, J. 83, 85–87, 98, 220–22, 229
Beißwenger, M. 391, 398, 400
Bekerman, Z. 494, 496
Belarus 463, 544
Belgian Assize Court 305
Belgian asylum procedure 130, 298
Belgium 17, 91, 119, 122, 170–71, 187, 193, 269, 298–99, 305, 354, 373, 486
Believers Love World Ministries 348–49
Ben Rafael, E. 539–42, 545, 549–51
Berber 189, 486
Bezemer, J. 522, 526, 535
Bhatia, T. 53–54, 63–64, 211–12, 335, 346, 434
bilingual education: bilingual education (with English) 16, 247–60; Corsican 89–90, 94; deaf 100, 103, 109; developmental 207, 235; dynamic bi/plurilingual 237; indigenous 150, 157, 162–65; multiple multilingual 58, 236; poly-directional 236; post-colonial 172–73, 175, 178–79, 181–83; transitional 158, 187, 202, 235, 241; weak and strong forms 187; *see also* Content and Language Integrated Learning (CLIL); *see also* immersion education
bilingualism: additive 50, 57, 155, 158–59, 221, 233–36, 239, 241, 244, 260; child bilingualism 90, 100, 178–79, 184, 187, 225, 227, 236–41, 244, 472, 523; dynamic 233, 236–39, 243–44; recursive 221, 233, 235; subtractive 50, 57, 149–51, 158–59, 233–35, 239–41, 244
biliteracy 47, 64, 154–55, 169, 180, 194, 227, 241–42, 246, 508–13; convergent biliterate 241; convergent monoliterate 241; flexible multiple 241–42; separation biliterate 241

552

Index

Billig, M. 120, 125, 128, 133, 141, 335, 337, 344
Birchardt, T. 281, 283, 293
Blackledge, A. 1–26, 66–68, 80–82, 114, 118–19, 123–24, 127–28, 169, 181, 195–97, 245, 247, 261, 297, 309, 312–13, 337, 344, 393, 402, 431–34, 467, 496, 510, 516, 521, 523, 527, 534–36
Blommaert, J. 2, 7–8, 12, 21–22, 25, 51, 62–63, 67, 81, 84, 97–98, 117–22, 126–29, 131, 138–39, 141, 169, 176, 181, 287, 293, 298, 303, 305, 311–13, 401, 414, 416, 443, 446, 448, 451, 503–4, 507
Bloomfield, J. 4, 22, 33–34
Botswana 21, 169, 172
Bourdieu, P. 5, 22, 31, 47, 117, 121, 128, 134, 141, 285, 293, 350–51, 364, 371–72, 382, 406, 416, 421, 431, 463, 466, 474, 480
Bourhis, R. 196, 538–40, 548, 550
Boutet, J. 88, 99, 377–79, 382
Brazil 6, 149, 250–51, 262, 351, 488
Britain 104, 110–11, 123–26, 135, 170–71, 217, 249, 253, 255, 259, 322, 352, 354, 406, 510
British Sign Language 17, 109, 113, 115, 314, 317
Bucholtz, M. 487, 494, 496–97
Bunyi, G. 178–79, 181
Burundi 175, 475–76
business(es) 249, 254, 257, 259, 273–76, 292, 315–16, 372–73, 376–77, 380, 471, 541, 546
Butler, Y. 251–52, 261, 321, 328, 421, 431
Bybee, J. 441, 451
Byram, M. 83, 85–86, 98, 219–22, 229

Cameron, D. 84, 98–99, 118, 128, 248, 251, 261–63, 378–79, 382, 420–21, 431
Cameroon 349, 352, 357
Campbell, L. 37, 47
Campbell-Makini, Z.M.R. 170–71, 175–77, 181
Canada 5–6, 32, 36, 38, 40–41, 44, 120, 146, 151, 155–56, 199–200, 202–4, 210, 234, 237, 269, 354, 373, 375–76, 379, 407, 412, 459, 472, 540, 544
Canagarajah, A.S. 6, 14, 22, 49–65, 66–67, 81, 138, 141, 160, 162, 180–81, 403, 447, 451–52, 476–77, 480, 546, 549
Cantonese 259, 274, 322, 349, 392, 470, 473–76
Carter, R. 71, 217, 229, 247, 261
Catalan 3, 186, 189–91, 194, 204–6, 254, 336, 339, 542
Catalonia 5, 136, 186, 189, 199, 203–6
Cenoz, J. 15, 184–98, 205–6, 208, 211–12, 215, 228–31, 256, 542, 545, 549
Charalambous, C. 20, 126, 482–98
Charter for Regional or Minority Languages 185, 192

Chimbutane, F.S. 3, 6, 22, 167–82
China 146, 250–52, 256–58, 269, 351, 356, 388, 543
Chiswick, B.R. 286, 294
cities 21, 540–43, 546
citizenship: acts of citizenship 84–85; linguistic citizenship 14, 84, 179; multilingual citizenship 83, 328, 343; participatory citizenship 84; plurilingual citizenship 86, 94, 96–97
civic engagement 66, 74, 76, 79
civic multilingualism 131–40
Clark, M. 36, 330, 487, 496
classroom practices 16, 97, 214, 477–78
classroom talk 209, 521, 530, 534
Clerc, L. 101–2, 114
code-alternation 471
codeswitching 10, 15, 19–24, 54, 93, 126, 199, 208, 227, 238–40, 244, 255, 276, 343, 362, 385, 391–92, 394, 408, 410–12, 449, 460–62, 470–71, 473, 475, 477, 483–84, 487, 490, 494, 503–6; classroom codeswitching 19, 209, 240, 472–80; codeswitching motivations 471–72; metaphorical code-switching 471; situational codeswitching 471; see also sociolinguistics and codeswitching
Cohn, C. 149–50, 165
Colic-Peisker, V. 289–90, 294
Colombia 106, 209–10
colonial languages 31, 35–36, 146, 150, 170–72, 174, 176, 179, 407
colonization 14, 18, 29, 31, 39, 43, 46, 49, 51, 57, 137, 273, 350–51, 353
communicative repertoire 51, 126, 305, 475
community: bilingual community 470; Chinese community 121; community classes 1; community domain 67; community interpreters 309–10; community interpreting 313, 315–16, 328–29, 331; community involvement 153; community language(s) 127, 532–33; community life 84; community membership 75, 145, 482; community participation 75; community relations 138; community service 72; community ties 273; community work 76–77; community-based education 147, 152; community-based learning 149; complementary (community) school class 21, 521; Corsican community 96; hip-hop community 410, 414–15; Inuit community 25, 43; Iranian community 356; L2 community 457–58; linguistics of community 2–4, 6, 482–83, 485; minority community 102–10, 383; notion of community 57, 85; on-line community 394–95; religious community 353; speech community 4, 50, 52, 57, 59, 334–35, 337–38, 340, 343, 361, 412, 416, 456–57, 459, 471,